邓嗣禹文集

李剑农／著

第六卷

中国近百年政治史

邓嗣禹　Jeremy Ingalls／编译

彭　靖／主编

華中師範大學出版社

新出图证（鄂）字 10 号

图书在版编目（CIP）数据

邓嗣禹文集. 第 6 卷 ：英文 / 李剑农著 ；（美）邓嗣禹，（美）杰里米·英格尔斯（Jeremy Ingalls）编译 ；彭靖主编. — 武汉 ：华中师范大学出版社，2021. 12

ISBN 978-7-5622-9592-1

Ⅰ. ①邓…　Ⅱ. ①李…　②邓…　③杰…　④彭…　Ⅲ. ①邓嗣禹—文集—英文②政治制度史—中国—近现代—英文　Ⅳ. ①K207-53 ②D69

中国版本图书馆 CIP 数据核字（2022）第 004120 号

邓嗣禹文集　第六卷

©李剑农著　（美）邓嗣禹，杰里米·英格尔斯（Jeremy Ingalls）编译

彭靖　主编

责任编辑： 廖国春　**责任校对：** 王　炜　**封面设计：** 罗明波

编辑室： 学术出版中心　**电话：** 027-67863220

出版发行： 华中师范大学出版社有限责任公司　**邮编：** 430079

社址： 湖北省武汉市洪山区珞喻路 152 号

销售电话： 027-67863426（发行部）　**传真：** 027-67863291

网址： http://press. ccnu. edu. cn　**电子信箱：** press@mail. ccnu. edu. cn

印刷： 湖北恒泰印务有限公司　**督印：** 刘　敏

开本： 710mm×1000mm　1/16　**印张：** 50. 25　**字数：** 793 千字

版次： 2023 年 3 月第 1 版　**印次：** 2023 年 3 月第 1 次印刷

定价： 251. 00 元

欢迎上网查询、购书

文集作者与主编简介

编译者简介：

邓嗣禹（1905—1988），当代著名历史学家、文献目录学家和汉学家，中国科举制度研究的奠基人。1935 年燕京大学硕士毕业后，留校任教。1938 年留学哈佛大学，师从著名汉学家费正清，1942 年获博士学位。历任芝加哥大学东方研究院院长、印第安纳大学历史系主任、东亚研究中心主任等职，著有《中国考试制度史》《张喜与南京条约》等 30 余部历史学著作，并将《中国近百年政治史》《颜氏家训》等中国学术名著译成英文版。他的论著曾被翻译成 10 多种语言。2020 年，俄文版《中国考试制度史》获批为“中华学术外译”资助项目，将由俄罗斯圣彼得堡大学出版社出版。

主编简介：

彭靖（1962— ），《邓嗣禹文集》主编，“中华学术外译”项目入选者。21 岁发表译作，38 岁获得教授职称。早年曾师从中国社会科学院近代史研究所所长步平，在《中国考试》《学术界》《教育与考试》等期刊上发表科举与历史学研究论文 100 余篇，译著有《重访中国》《张喜与南京条约》。历任北京大学、香港国际商学院 EMBA 总裁班特聘（客座）教授，在美国与中国出版《尘封的历史》等十余部著作。曾获得“鲁迅文学杯”全国文化精英大赛金奖、第十届“丁玲文学奖”提名奖等多种奖项。

再版序言
邓嗣禹与英文版《中国近百年政治史》

彭　靖

著名史学家李剑农（1880—1963）曾任武汉大学史学系主任，是中国近代史研究的重要开拓者，对中国近代史和中国古代经济史研究做出了许多开创性的贡献。他所著的《中国近百年政治史》一书被美国汉学泰斗费正清誉为“对中国近代史的最清晰、唯一全面的评述”。该书 1956 年由邓嗣禹及他的学生 Ingalls 首次编辑、翻译成英文版后，在美国、印度多次再版。1991 年，李剑农与陈寅恪、陈垣等 14 人被收录于美国纽约格林伍德公司出版的《近代国际大史学家辞典》中，成为国际知名的史学大师。

2013 年是李剑农逝世五十周年，由武汉大学出版社主持的“武汉大学百年名典”系列首次在国内将英文版《中国近百年政治史》再版。2019 年，国家出版基金项目《邓嗣禹文集》将这本学术名著列为第六卷，再次推荐给海内外读者。

多版本出版过程与译评

《中国近百年政治史》是目前国内外学者经常参阅和广泛引用的经典著作，该书在李剑农 1930 年所著《最近三十年中国政治史》基础上，因大学教学需要，增补了鸦片战争到中日甲午战争这段历史，更名为《中国近百年政治史》，1942 年由蓝田国立师范学院史地学会印刷出版。此书一出，市场上很快售空，而“各处尚有来函索者”，1943 年又交由蓝田书报合作社印刷发行，1946 年由蓝田启明书局改印成线装四册本出版，1947 年由商务印书馆制成平装本，分上下两册出版，1948 年再版。近年，复旦大学、武汉大学等国内著名大学和出版机构又多次再版。中国台湾商务印书馆也曾于 1963 年刊行该书，后又于 1992 年再版。

值得一提的是，1942 年书报合作社版在紧接李剑农所写卷头语后，曾有一小段再版补充语：

去岁由史地学会印行之本，字迹既甚模糊，讹误之字又多，谬蒙读者垂爱，甚感惭愧。兹以各处尚有来函索者，而史地学会已无存书，蓝田书报合作社愿意再承印，遂复付梓。讹误之字虽勉为校正，但恐尚不能免，乞读者垂谅。

民国三十二年二月　著者附识

而此后发行的各种版本《中国近百年政治史》均没有这段附识，看来都不是以蓝田书报合作社版本为原本的，而是以同样创立于当地的蓝田启明书局 1946 年发行的版本为基础。而启明书店似乎直接以史地学会版为原本，都跳过了书报合作社版。

该书英文版由留美学者邓嗣禹潜心数年，精心译介。中国另一部文学名著《颜氏家训》也是他在燕京大学时着手翻译，并于 1968 年在英国出版的。邓嗣禹早年毕业于燕京大学历史系，后留学美国哈佛大学，师从费正清，1942 年获得博士学位，先后在燕京大学、芝加哥大学、哈佛大学、北京大学、印地安纳大学任教。1950 年，邓嗣禹在印地安纳大学执教中国近代史时，由于缺乏教学资料，便将李剑农《中国近百年政治史》的部分内容译成英文，用作研究生参考教材。他于 1950 年 5 月在美国《远东季刊》上发表书评，认为“该书既不太详细也不太简短。它没有包含太多不必要的人名。作者的观点中肯客观，不偏不倚，是一本理想教材”。之后几年中，他以 1948 年商务印书馆的版本为基础，对全书进行翻译，并增补了若干内容，后经他在芝加哥任教时期的硕士生，时任 Rockford 学院讲师的英格尔斯（Ingalls）参与润色，1956 年首先在美国 D. Van Nostrand 出版社出版，书名为 *The Political History of China, 1840—1928*（《中国政治史，1840—1928》）。该出版社先后于 1962 年、1963 年、1964 年、1968 年再版该书；斯坦福大学出版社（Stanford Univ. Press）在 1956 年 6 月、1967 年、1969 年三次出版该书；1963 年，美国东西出版社（East-West Press）也曾出版过此书；1964 年印度版本在新德里出版。

该书在美国 20 世纪 50 至 70 年代期间是研究生教学中非常流行的参考书。这部著作不仅取材精准、叙事准确，对历史事件注意追根求源，并联系当时社会形势全面分析，还历史的原貌，评论时局无所忌讳，秉公伸张正义。2006 年，著名学者萧致治在武汉大学版《中国近百年政治史》再版前言中介绍："该书英文版前后共计发行了 5200 册，其数量之多，在美国同类著作中实属少见。"2011 年，美国 Literary Licensing（LLC）出版社在两个月（9—10 月）期间又曾两次再版（书面注明李剑农、邓嗣禹著）。2013 年 11 月，武汉大学出版社首次在国内出版英文精装版。

邓嗣禹在英文版《中国近百年政治史》出版之前，首先交给费正清审阅，并在此书第一页显著位置注明"献给费正清"（To John King Fairbank）。费正清回信认为《中国近百年政治史》是"中国近代政治史的最清晰的唯一全面的评述……对于西方的研究学者来说，作为一种可靠的纪实史和重要资料的简编具有重要价值"。

这本书被译成英文出版后，曾受到国际史学界广泛赞誉。耶鲁大学的汉学家沃尔克（Richard L. Walker）看到英译本，于 1957 年 4 月在《美国历史评论》上发书评指出"李剑农的著作具有很高的学术价值，它不仅是作为这一时期研究生的基本参考书目，而且也作为这一历史时期中国学术评价的观点，引入到西方。邓嗣禹和英格尔斯在编辑与翻译中克服了许多困难，将原始的中国资料转变成易懂的英文。通过删掉重复的内容和增加系统的注释、索引和文献目录，将李著的价值进一步凸显出来"。哥伦比亚大学的伟伯（C. Martin Wilbur）对此也强调指出"翻译者通过删除书中许多累赘的内容，缩短了书籍的篇幅，对原书内容重新进行了文献编辑，对许多来路不明的词句增加了引文，同时还增加了效果良好的书目提要和地图，各层面的学生都将受益于这些工作"（*Pacific Affairs*，第 2 期，1957 年 6 月）。华盛顿大学的斯坦利（Spector Stanley）也在 1958 年发表书评指出"对于一本学院层面的教科书而言，译者不仅提供了鲜活的评述内容，而且还提供了一种广泛了解中国历史著作的翻译标准。这本书将为一直备受困扰的美国教师与学生提供最大的实用价值"（*The Journal of Asian Studies*，第 4 期，1958 年 4 月）。

译本特色与翻译标准

为了帮助西方读者更好地理解《中国近百年政治史》的内容，体现原著学术价值，译者在准确理解和精心翻译的同时，在征得李剑农先生同意之后，对原著进行了调整和增删。首先是在正文之外增加了五个辅助部分：译者前言、参考书目、阅读背景与注释、人名与地名索引、每章均插入1—2张中国分区地图。在正文中主要增加的是背景知识，有些是直接加在书中，有些则是以尾注的方式，放在了书后增加的Notes部分之中。据笔者统计，英译本各章节中，仅增加的注释数目就有196条之多，涉及历史人物、革命事件、社会运动、官职名称、民族习俗等内容。这就意味着，译者不仅需要调动多方位、多学科、多视角的知识储备，还要倾注大量心血与研究心得，同时还要有宏观考量与微观分析、取舍的多重能力。

其一，历史人物注。此类注解主要涉及中国不同时代的历史和政治人物，能够拓展读者的历史知识背景，营造著作中的历史语境。在这部著作中，几乎涉及民国各个时期的重要人物。除了一少部分研究中国历史的汉学家之外，对于大多数西方读者来说，在阅读关于中国的历史文章或学术著作时，最大障碍就是难以把人名弄清楚，他们怎么能把众多的中国历史人物的名字记住呢？这主要是靠译者注释中的内容产生各种联想。如果读者在注释中得知某人是中国的大政治家或哲学家，就会对他肃然起敬；若再读过他的诗文，更会感到像遇到老朋友一样，数页之后再见到这个名字，必定知道是同一人。如在第十二章：护法运动中北洋军阀的分裂与军阀的离合，注释中简明介绍了主要人物的演变过程，可让读者在阅读本章节时有一个大概了解："1913年10月，袁世凯成为任期五年的法定总统。在袁死后，黎元洪接替他出任大总统。在黎辞职之后，副总统冯之继接替他，直到1918年10月。当五年期结束时，徐树铮在1918年9月被选举为总统。"

其二，官职名称注。太平天国时期的许多官职名称，对于今天中国的许多读者而言都是生僻的，更不用说西方读者了。书中如"两司马"的注释简洁明了，寥寥数语："两司马是古代军队中，最下层基本的官职，管理财政、教育、司法等一切政务，由25名士兵组成。"再如"四大将领"的注解简明扼要，一目了然："现代人们常说清朝时期湘军的'四大将领'指的是曾国藩、左宗棠、彭玉麟和胡林翼，他们是在太平天国时期都有卓越功绩的将领。"

总体来说，近二百条的注释内容大多采用音译加意译的方式，通过尾注内容阐明音译，扩展意译，整体格式简明扼要，分析明快，客观自然，符合史实。从读者阅读接受和跨文化传播的角度而言，这种注释是必要而且成功的。从李著英译本1956年在美国出版以来，许多读者发表的书评文章中，也得到了进一步的验证。

李著英译本的另一特色，是在书中每一章节几乎都增加了中国分区地图，既有黑白的，也有彩色的。这对于不熟悉中国地理知识的读者来说，从地图中的描述城市位置、行进方向等内容，就可很快地理解书中叙述的内容。但同时也大大增加了译者在翻译作品时的难度。

与增添的内容相比，删节的较少，主要是李剑农加在目录前的卷头语没有翻译，导论部分中“百年前的世界趋势”等一节也没有翻译。这些内容对于西方读者来说是常识的问题，也就没有必要再翻译了。再有就是如许多书评作者指出的，删掉了一些书中前后重复的内容。

从译本最后的参考文献中能够了解到，邓嗣禹在翻译时曾参考过多种英文文献。例如，就阅读背景而言，他曾参考过的书籍就有：顾立雅（H. G. Creel）的《从孔子到毛泽东的中国思想》，1953年版；费正清的《美国与中国》，1948年版；冯友兰的《中国哲学史》，卜德英译本，1953年版；李约瑟（Joseph Needham）的《中国科学技术史》，1954年版等书。

正是由于李著英译本具备了上述优点与特色，其著作出版之后在国外学术界大获好评，近年来也再版不断。长期以来，忠实原文被视为翻译实践的天条、翻译理论的当然假设。而忠实的文本大多未能实现走出去的目标。在漫长的历史过程中，众多的翻译文本，真正走出去的却屈指可数，大多数则淹没于漫漫历史长河中（吕世生：《18世纪以来“走出去”的中国翻译改写模式》，《中国翻译》2013年第5期）。正如美国汉学家在书评中指出的，李著英译本“提供了一种广泛了解中国历史著作的翻译标准”，“将李著的价值进一步强调出来”，可为读者“提供最大的实用价值”。

FOREWORD

During the past decade general readers as well as college students have given increasingly close attention to Far Eastern history. For either the formal or the informal student in this field, however, there are in English still too few books providing translations of the original sources, particularly in the area of Chinese domestic politics. To make accessible a work which, written by a Chinese, contains many directly cited source materials—letters, telegrams, diaries, memoirs—we have undertaken to translate Li Chien-nung's *Political History of China in the Past Century* (*Chung-kuo chin-pai-nien cheng-chih shih*) published by the Commercial Press, Shanghai, in 1948.

In addition to valuable materials either not available or not readily attainable in Western languages, Li Chien-nung's work has the further advantage of maximum lucidity and lively narration. For the pleasure of his style we are indebted to Li's original intention, to compose a study of Chinese political history for Chinese college students. Li's work is, moreover, free from both partisan propaganda and undocumented speculation. As a well-trained scholar, Li views events succinctly in their context as internal political problems and applies to their evaluation the techniques of the modern historian, further enlightened by his own broad and unparochial appreciation of his own society.

Li Chien-nung was born in Shaoyang, Hunan, a province which has produced an extraordinary number of politicians and political theorists, representing every variety of political persuasion during the past hundred years. Li's classical Chinese education was followed by further academic training in Japan. In 1917 he became an editor of the *Pacific Magazine* (*T'ai-p'ing-yang tsa-chih*) and commentator on political events and constitutional problems. For many years a professor of history at National

Wuhan University, Li prepared a number of commentaries on history and politics (see S-Y. Teng's "Chinese Historiography in the Last Fifty Years," *Far Eastern Quarterly*, Vol. 8 (1949) pp. 131 ff.) and compiled the papers of Ts'ai Sung-po (*Ts'ai Sung-po hsien-sheng i-chi*). Since 1950, when he was about seventy years old, his friends have had no further news of him. Letters of inquiry sent periodically since 1951 concerning him and his book have been neither answered nor returned.

Translated word for word into English, Li's *Political History* amounts to nearly two thousand typescript pages. With the necessary English expansion of many Chinese turns of phrase, the complete typescript, as we first produced it, created an impression of prolixity unjust to the Chinese style. Li's frequent repetitions for the purposes of classroom instruction, when fully rendered into English, also gave the English working script a heavily didactic tone. Familiar to Chinese students of the early years of this century, these repetitions seemed likely to oppress rather than to profit the present Western reader. Consequently, to conserve Li's basic facts and interpretations and still present a vigorous and agreeably readable translation, we have undertaken to edit the English version.

We have canceled such repetitions as had a solely pedagogic purpose and have excised a few names and terms which do not bear crucially on the sequence of facts or the tenor of Li's arguments. We have found it generally desirable to omit ellipses, parentheses, and square brackets. Nevertheless, as a service to those interested in consulting Li's original text, we have continued to indicate whatever ellipses occur in Li's cited source materials as here translated. We have supplied in square brackets brief information as to the meaning of particular terms, year dates, and other clarifying details. In making excisions in handling the body of the text we believe that we have in no case omitted any materials which affect matters of fact or, by their omission, alter the general tone or intention of the work. In deference to a public untrained in Chinese, and to our publishers, we have omitted all Chinese characters and in certain other respects departed from accepted Sinological conventions. In sum, we have sought to conserve and to make available to Western readers the essential form and content of Li's study.

Of the notes to each chapter, following the body of the text, only some twenty out of the more than two hundred annotations are notes from Li Chien-nung's own text. Consequently, reversing the usual procedure, we have omitted the notation "Ed." —since the editors' notes predominate — and have provided instead the notation "[L. Cn.]" in brackets to identify the few notes provided directly by Li Chien-nung. Like most Asian scholars, particularly of the older generation, in providing his occasional notes Li Chien-nung may name a text or an author but almost never details publication data. Where such data have now been supplied as a supplement within Li's own notes, we have set them in square brackets.

With regard to the information we have supplied as to Chinese sources for Li's cited texts it must be recognized that although such sources as we name now contain the same primary texts, these collections cited in our notes are not necessarily the collections which Li himself used. He was often either observer or participant in events he expounds and had at hand materials from sources more immediate than the compilations we have listed. For some citations the only currently accessible source is Li's own Chinese text, which has itself been cited by scholars as the source of information nowhere else now accessibly recorded.

Besides the notes on Chinese sources for some of the autograph data as well as recorded conversations, telegrams, and official documents, we have supplied references to a few Western texts containing translations of related materials and provided a few annotations on matters familiar to Li's Chinese students but less familiar to English readers.

Li's history ends summarily with the account of the final disruption of the Peiyang military cliques in 1928. Western readers will doubtless wish for equally detailed information about Chinese domestic politics after 1928, involving many of the same figures who play major roles in Li's account up to that date. A similarly adequate treatment of the convulsive period from 1928 to the present, however, would require a separate volume. For the reader interested in investigating the general context of the events detailed in Li's *Political History* or in consulting analyses of more recent events we have provided in the appendix a selected bibliography. To attempt any other approach to the more recent events would invite nearly annual correction and revision on matters still too close for adequate perspective. Therefore we are presenting the work with Li's own conclusion, his terse final paragraph marking the fall of the Peiyang warlords.

In reading Li's work as here presented we have the advantage of permanent primary information on Chinese politics up to 1928, on which the reader is at liberty to construct his own further speculations. Presenting Li's work without supplement, we believe, is to transmit in its basic form a classic of modern Chinese scholarship.

To Professor Ralph L. Powell we wish to express our deep gratitude for his cooperation in the initial labors of editing. We regret that, though his services as coeditor were sought, his heavy duties at the National War College have prevented him from continuing with us. We thank Professor Robert H. Ferrel for his kindness in reading Chapter 3 and for helpful suggestions. We wish to express our appreciation to Professors Earl H. Pritchard and Harold C. Hinton for their encouragement toward the early publication of this volume. We wish to express our thanks also to Patricia Gamber, Edwin Kapos, Nancy Adams, Ruth C. Heffner, and Dale S. Bailey for the preparation of the typescript and to Mrs. Heffner and Mr. Bailey for suggestions in matters of expression.

We owe further special debts of thanks to Professor Wu Hsiang-hsiang who, with his associate Chang Tsun-wu, gave generous time and assistance in locating from resources on Taiwan some of the sources of Li's citations. We also record our appreciation for the generous cooperation of Onogawa Hidemi of the Research Institute of Humanistic Sciences, Kyoto University, and of the Commission for Research on Modern China at Tokyo University. First and finally we are indebted to Margaret (Mrs. S-Y.) Teng and to Johanna M. Menzel for their unfailing assistance throughout the progress of the work—to Miss Menzel for the checking of the proofs and to Margaret Teng for the preparation of the index.

From our combined efforts we trust we have made available to Western students a definitive study of China's political struggles from 1840 to 1928. As Li Chien-nung's work in Chinese is of permanent value, we have tried by careful editing and supplementation to make this English edition of it both sound and trustworthy.

S-Y. TENG AND J. INGALLS

Indiana University
and
Rockford College
June 1956

CONTENTS

INTRODUCTION
CHINA—FROM EMPIRE TO NATION

Many of the great changes occurring in Chinese political history during the past hundred years are the traceable results of events which occurred during the period approximating the reigns of Ch'ien-lung [1736-1795] and Chia-ch'ing [1796-1820]. This heyday of the Manchu or Ch'ing dynasty marked also the beginning of general decline in China.

Adequate perspective on changing Chinese conditions during the eighteenth and early nineteenth centuries must include a survey of European technological and political developments during the same period. James Watt's steam engine [1765], Arkwright's spinning frames and cotton mill [1768], and Robert Fulton's steamship [1807] all accelerated the industrial revolution. Political and social change was also given impetus by the speculations and theories of such writers as Montesquieu, Voltaire, and Rousseau. Adam Smith's *Wealth of Nations*, earning its author the appellation of "father of modern economics," championed an economic policy of *laissez faire*. Quesnay's physiocratic views also included support for the theory of *laissez faire*. Changes in practice and theory, enormously altering the old structure of European society, also spread in a great tide over the rest of the world.

The European powers were competing among themselves in their attempts to found colonies in all parts of the globe. During the eighteenth century Spain's supremacy in sea power gradually passed to England. Parliamentary England competed with France, a strong centralized monarchy. The War of the Austrian Succession first extended the Anglo-French contest to India. The Seven Years' War [1756-1763] intensified the conflict over India. By the Treaty of Paris in 1763 India passed almost completely to Britain. A contest for the New World ran concurrently with the struggle in India. Taking Quebec in 1759 and in the next year occupying Canada, Britain gained predominance in North America.

After this bitter competition for colonies two major political changes occurred. One was the war for independence won by England's colonies in America. The other was the French Revolution. After the restoration of peace in 1815, however, the French government, which had been under Napoleon's control, was returned to the Bourbons.

The French July Revolution of 1830 brought into power the new industrial and commercial bourgeoisie. In England the Reform Act of 1832 confirmed the British industrial and commercial bourgeoisie in parliamentary strength and reinforced the drive toward overseas expansion. Despite the efforts of the Holy Alliance formed by the rulers of Russia, Austria, and Prussia in 1815 to suppress the revolutionary movement in Europe, concern for new opportunities in both politics and economics fed the surge toward democratic freedom.

CHINA'S INTERNAL CONDITIONS

In China during the eighteenth century the civil administration and military prowess of the Manchu government reached their zenith. The contest between England and France in India and North America, the founding of the United States of America, and the French Revolution all occurred during the reign of Ch'ien-lung; the rise and fall of Napoleon coincided with the reign of Emperor Chia-ch'ing.

While eighteenth-century Europe and America burgeoned with political change and technological developments, Chinese scholarship also flourished. The most outstanding classical scholars of the Ch'ing (Manchu) dynasty were Tai Chen [1724-1777], Tuan Yü-ts'ai [1735-1815], Wang Nien-sun [1744-1832], and his son Wang Yin-chih [1766-1834]. In the Ch'ien-lung period Tai received a *ch'ü-jen* [the second academic degree] and served as a compiler of the *Ssu-k'u ch'üan-shu*

[*Complete Collection of Books Classified into Four Divisions*]. These four comprehensive divisions were classics, history, philosophy, and belles-lettres. Also in the Ch'ien-lung period Tuan Yü-ts'ai, one of Tai's students, and Wang Nien-sun both received a *chinshih* [the highest academic degree]. In the Chia-ch'ing period Wang Yin-chih became a *chin-shih*.

Although these scholars used scientific methods in their research, their intellectual ability was, unfortunately for China, largely dissipated in the writing of classical commentaries. Their contributions can be justly compared with those of European scholarship during the European Renaissance; but the work of these Chinese scholars had little effect upon the Chinese social and political life of their time.

The most important scholar, Tai Chen, gave serious attention to practical affairs and mathematics, but the application of his thinking was confined by the conventional political theories of his time. Tai's philosophical ideas were similar to the utilitarian principles of Bentham in England, but the literati, taking note of his critical, classical studies, ignored his philosophical theories.

Moreover, Emperor Ch'ien-lung confined the wisdom and talent of brilliant scholars to the interpretation of old manuscripts rather than encouraging them to devote themselves to independent philosophical inquiry. By establishing a large bureau to compile the *Complete Collection of Books Classified into Four Divisions*, he dictated the people's thinking much as the first emperor of the Ming dynasty [1368-1643] had done when he made the "eight-legged essay" a required style for civil-service examinations. Emperor Ch'ien-lung also ordered many books dealing with his political regime and with the origin of the Manchu race to be destroyed *in toto* or in part. Such books were termed subversive. From 1774 to 1781 there were twenty-four occasions when the so-called subversive books were destroyed. A total of 538 titles in 13,862 volumes were demolished. Still afraid that the purge was not thorough, the emperor in 1788 commanded that the vigilant search for and banning of undesirable books be continued.

The special English envoy Lord Macartney made his eyewitness observations of the Chinese in 1793. He said that Chinese scientific knowledge was far inferior to that of other nations. For instance, a high Chinese dignitary had been greatly surprised at seeing the striking and lighting of a match. Macartney said that while he was in Jehol he had told some officials about several European scientific inventions and had advised them to buy a balloon or "light-air-ball." He also encouraged China to employ Western technicians to instruct the Chinese in scientific and technological subjects, but the Chinese officials were indifferent to his advice.

Macartney observed that in spite of the fact that Emperor Ch'ien-lung was spirited, ambitious for personal glory, and anxious that his country keep abreast of other nations, he actually was not so farsighted and enlightened as Emperor K'ang-hsi [1662-1722] had been. Emperor Ch'ien-lung knew how to prevent seditious activity among his subjects but did not know how to develop their power to learn.

THE MANCHU GOVERNMENT

The political organization of this period was an autocratic form of government which had been handed down since the Ch'in and Han dynasties [221 B. C. -A. D. 220]. During the Ch'ing dynasty [1664-1911] its organization became even more rigid. In order to make comprehensible the changes in the centers of political power during the final century of the Ch'ing dynasty, the central government's most important offices must be explained.

The Grand Secretariat and the Grand Council

The Grand Secretariat [*Nei-ko*] was the leading organization in the central government until 1729. Then secret military and important state affairs began to be handled by a new office called the Grand Council [*Chün-chi ch'u*, literally "Place for Military Strategy"].

The term *Nei-ko* before 1912 did not signify "cabinet," which is its modern meaning. Each member of the Grand Secretariat was called a grand secretary [*ta-hsüeh-shih*, literally "great scholar"]. There were sometimes two Manchu and two Chinese grand secretaries, but there could be six grand secretaries. In addition, there were assistant grand secretaries and subchancellors of the Grand Secretariat. At the beginning of the dynasty, it was the duty of the grand secretaries to forward to the emperor memorials, petitions, or suggestions received from officials. They also drafted endorsements for the throne and participated in the discussion of military strategy.

Subsequently, in order to obtain more efficient conduct of warfare, the Grand Council was created. Originally the Grand Council had special charge of secret military affairs. Later the members of the council were simultaneously grand secretaries of the Grand Secretariat. Thus the authority of the grand secretaries was absorbed by the Grand Council. After the middle of the Ch'ien-lung period, the term grand secretary became merely an honorary title conferred upon meritorious high officials. Their actual duties were limited to receiving and sending memorials and decrees.

There was no fixed number of grand councilors, and there was at first no definite rule for an equal representation of Manchus and Chinese in the Grand Council. Selection of councilors depended solely upon the wish of the emperor, who chose them either from among the members of his family, from the grand secretaries, or from the state ministers. The grand councilors participated in important political decisions, appointments, dismissals, and promotions or demotions of high officials. They also assisted in planning military operations.

In this governmental organization there was no cabinet leader such as a premier. The emperor was the sole source of authority. Neither grand secretaries nor grand councilors had the right to send orders to ministries, to provincial governors-general, or to governors. The emperor alone could issue decrees and instructions.

The Six Ministries

Prior to 1901 the central administrative organs of the Ch'ing government consisted of the Six Ministries or Boards, which had been inherited from the preceding dynasties. These agencies were the Ministries of Civil Appointments, Revenue, Ceremonies, War, Punishments, and Public Works. The principal posts within the ministries were equally divided between the Manchus and Chinese. At the head of each board were two ministers [*shang-shu*], while next in line were senior and junior vice-ministers.

Although these six ministries were the central administrative organs, ministers had no authority to send orders directly to the heads of provincial and other local governments. Commands had to come from the emperor in the form of imperial instructions and decrees. When two senior members of a ministry disagreed, it was customary for them to ask the emperor to be their arbiter. Thus no member of a ministry ever controlled the entire organization.

The Censorate

The Censorate [*Tu-ch'a Yüan*] was the general supervisory organ of the Ch'ing dynasty. Its chief members were the president, senior and junior vice -presidents, twenty supervising censors, and forty-four inspecting censors. The supervising censors supervised all offices within the capital; the inspecting censors divided the nation into various districts and inspected the offices of local governments. Although the censors had specific spheres of jurisdiction, they could exercise the authority of censorship anywhere at any time. Censors could impeach an official no matter how high his rank. They could pry into and object to any matter, regardless of its nature. It was their privilege to commend or refute the memorials or reports from officials of all ranks. Even the emperor's decrees and instructions could be opposed. They could submit a petition to the emperor on behalf of a minor official who was not entitled to do so himself. They could also redress grievances for the common people. In short, the entire state was subject to the censors.

Even so, the authority of censorship was not exercised by the body of the Censorate. An individual censor might impeach singlehandedly any high official except the emperor. Furthermore, selection and appointment of censors was not limited to those who had political and administrative experience, nor were censors privileged with tenure or special protection. They could be appointed or shifted to other posts at any time. Once a censor was demoted to some other official appointment, he was subject to the same censorship which he had imposed upon others. Finally, the duties and privileges of the censors were always ultimately determined by the emperor. Often an emperor did not hold a censor responsible for an inaccurate report or a false accusation. If, no matter how justifiably, an emperor's favorite were censored, however, the censor was usually punished.

The Governors-General and Governors

The Ch'ing dynasty employed a local government system which had already been established in the Ming period [1368-1644]. Governors-general and governors were appointed as the highest civil authorities in the provinces. A governor-general usually administered two provinces. Occasionally he managed three, as in the case of the Three Eastern Provinces [Manchuria], or only one, as in the case of Chihli. Since in most provinces there was also a governor, the governor-general might have no territory under his direct jurisdiction.

Originally the duties of a governor-general and of a governor were different. A governor-general usually had charge of two provinces, where he maintained peace and order and tried to work harmoniously with the governors and other officials. A governor attended to the administrative affairs of one province. His duties included supervision of civil servants, pacification of the people, transportation of grain, and collection of taxes. In the *Comprehensive Statutes of the Great Ch'ing* [*Ta-Ch'ing hui-tien*], compiled during the Ch'ien-lung period, the duties of the two officials were defined thus: "A governor-general takes general charge of civil and military affairs and vigilantly supervises soldiers and civilians, while a governor takes charge of educational, financial, judicial, and administrative matters." In the mid-nineteenth century the duties of governors-general and governors were gradually altered and soon became almost identical.

Governors-general and governors were the chief local administrators. Each had the right to report directly to the throne. Furthermore, they were not subject to direct orders from the Grand Secretariat, Grand Council, or the Six Ministries. A governor-general was ex officio invested as an associate of the Censorate, and a governor bore ex officio the title of vicepresident of that agency. Each could perform impeachments and submit reports to the throne without consulting the other. A governor-general could impeach a governor, while the latter could impeach a governor-general, supposedly his superior. When a governor-general and a governor had different opinions, they both reported the case to the emperor for His Majesty's decision or arbitration. Although a governor-general and a governor seemed to be superior and subordinate respectively, actually they were almost equal. Only the emperor was their superior.

Judging from the several key organizations explained above, we reach the following conclusions: (1) All power was in the hands of the emperor, and (2) within any one office all officials counterbalanced one another. The political theories "divide and rule" and "balance and check" were fully put into practice by the Manchu rulers. Thus we may say that the monarchial and autocratic organization of China down to the Ch'ing dynasty was very strict. But such a complete autocracy required a very capable emperor.

Manchu Rule Before the Opium War

Emperor Ch'ien-lung was an able man who could make use of such an organization. His government was a thorough despotism. After Emperor Chia-ch'ing the Manchu rulers were of much inferior caliber; then too, encroachments on China by foreign powers were accelerated. After this period even the most complete and strict governmental organization could not cope with new complexities for which the monarchial system had no precedent experience.

At the age of eighty-five, after sixty years on the throne, Emperor Ch'ien-lung abdicated in favor of his son, the Emperor Chia-ch'ing. The old ruler, however, made the final decisions concerning important political affairs. When Emperor Ch'ien-lung was more than eighty years old, he boasted that he was the most extraordinary emperor China had had since ancient times. He wrote an essay in 1792 entitled *Shih-ch'üan chi* in which he enumerated the ten major victories of his reign. He professed to have twice defeated the Sungars in Outer Mongolia and Sinkiang, once suppressed the rebellion of Moslems in Turkestan, twice put down insurrections in the Chin-ch'uan region in western Szechwan, once pacified a rebellion in Taiwan, subjugated Burma and Annam, and twice vanquished the Gurkhas.

But all Emperor Ch'ien-lung's military successes could not overshadow the weak points in his administration. For over twenty years he personally supported a very greedy Manchu, Ho-shen. Ho-shen recommended many self-seeking governors-general and governors who extracted millions of dollars from the people. Before Emperor Ch'ien-lung's abdication, numerous bribery cases were exposed, but not until the emperor's death could the full account of the situation be revealed. His censors dared not attack the fountainhead (Ho-shen) of the corruption until the emperor could do them no harm.

Finally his successor ordered Ho-shen to commit suicide and confiscated his properties. Altogether there were 109 lists of Ho-shen's possessions, which he had acquired by simultaneously holding many lucrative posts. The property was roughly estimated to be worth 800,000,000 taels. Thus the new emperor received a huge unexpected income totaling more than ten times the annual revenue of the national treasury.

Many rapacious officials followed Ho-shen's example in swindling the people in every possible way. A depression and a series of local uprisings resulted. Already in 1795 rebellions of the Miao tribesmen disturbed Kweichow and Hunan. Then in 1796, the first year of the Chia-ch'ing reign, the revolt of the secret White Lotus Society started in Hupeh and Szechwan. This spread to five provinces and lasted eight or nine years, consuming 200,000,000 taels of military funds before it was suppressed. At the same time pirates headed by Ts'ai Ch'ien and others, with their headquarters in Annam, raided the coast of Kwangtung, Kwangsi, Fukien, and Chekiang. They were not suppressed until 1810. Then members of a secret religious society called the *T'ien-li-chiao*, led by Li Wen-ch'eng, Lin Ch'ing, and others, raised disturbances in Shantung and Chihli. They even tried to attack the imperial palace in 1813. During the 1820's government forces required several years to curb a Moslem rebellion directed by Chang Ko-erh (Jehangir) in Turkestan.

All these uprisings had been gathering force during the later Ch'ien-lung period, but they burst out in the Chia-ch'ing era. The so-called great victories of Emperor Ch'ien-lung had been sowing the seeds of future rebellions.

During the rebellion of the White Lotus Society, one great defect in

Manchu power was disclosed. The standing army, consisting of the Eight Banners and the Army of the Green Standard, was already too corrupt to be of much use. Local militias were called out to suppress the rebellion. A contemporary account states that militiamen were used as a vanguard; the Green Standards, which were made up of Chinese, followed; the Eight Banners came last. The rebel army drove refugees to meet the vanguard; the real rebels stood behind them. While the militia and the refugees were fighting against each other, government troops and rebel soldiers had no direct contact. The casualties of the militia were usually not reported. However, when a victory was won by the militia, it was attributed to the government forces, even though the government men were often encamped at a spot where there were no rebels. Military costs were high because military funds were usually embezzled or consumed in elaborate banquets for generals and officers.

Military discipline was corrupted to such a degree that rebellions like that of the White Lotus Society often lasted a number of years. Moreover, the suppression of the White Lotus Rebellion was not carried out by the standing army, but by the local militia, who used a scorched-earth policy called "cleaning up the country," that is, leaving no food and shelter for the rebels. This method was first applied to Hupeh with considerable effect. It was then extended to Szechwan, Shensi, Honan, and other provinces.

The organization of militias to replace the impotent Eight Banners, who were frequently accused of doing the people more harm than bandits, was suggested by one magistrate, and money for maintaining a militia was raised from each locality where such a force was needed. Hence the national treasury bore no pecuniary burden and the local people could enjoy more efficient protection. This arrangement should have pleased the government as well as the people, but a Manchu governor-general of Shensi and Kansu objected, saying that it would be dangerous if the people were given weapons.

In spite of such objection the government had no alternative but to train militias. The number of such troops in Szechwan was reported to be as large as 300,000 men. Nevertheless, as soon as a rebellion was pacified, the militia's weapons were immediately taken away by the Manchu rulers. Because the government distrusted the militias and the government's standing army was itself inadequate even to check civil wars, it naturally could not resist foreign aggression. In the nineteenth century, when the Chinese army had to combat Western military power, it was always defeated.

SUMMARY: A HUNDRED YEARS OF POLITICAL CHANGE

The preceding review helps us to realize that China's defeat in the Opium War [1840-1842] was not accidental. After the war the door of China was open, and Western influence inevitably induced political adjustments.

The political history of China in the past hundred years may be divided into three major periods. The first begins with the Opium War and ends with the Sino-Japanese War of 1894. The second starts in 1895 and includes both the reform movement of 1898 and the revolution of 1911. The third covers the foundation of the Republic of China and the Northern Expedition launched by the Kuomintang from Canton in 1926. The first phase was a period of foreign invasion and of the formation of new ideas. The second was a time of progress in revolutionary strength and was marked by the overthrow of the Manchu dynasty. The third period presented a struggle of the various revolutionary groups against the remaining officials of the Manchu regime and against warlords. The important political events of these three long periods may be redivided into shorter spans.

The ardent efforts of the British to extend their commercial markets in China were frequently repulsed by the Manchu government. The British, using the opium problem as a fuse to start the Opium War in 1840, concluded in 1842 *the Treaty of Nanking*, which ceded the island of Hong Kong to England and opened five treaty ports for trade. China's defeat in the Opium War exposed the weakness of the Manchu regime to the Chinese people, who slowly began to see weaknesses of the Manchu court as well as to sense more directly the impact from the West.

In 1851 began the Taiping Rebellion, which was not suppressed until 1864, thirteen years later. During this time the Chinese people began to seize more political power from the Manchu government. At the time of the Taiping Rebellion the English and French allies fought their way to the Celestial Court and signed *the Treaty of Peking* in 1860.

Thereafter foreign pressure on China increased. During the years of combat against the Taipings, China employed a small number of foreign officers and used some foreign-made weapons. After the rebellion a few Chinese leaders recognized the superiority of Western military equipment and techniques. They became interested in foreign machines and international affairs, which were then referred to as "foreign matters." [*yang-wu*]

These progressives tried to imitate Western methods in building ships, manufacturing weapons, training soldiers, and raising funds. The last forty years of the nineteenth century may be considered an era when the Chinese slowly studied "foreign matters" and copied Western methods. Nevertheless, China's superficial imitation of the West could not produce an effect strong enough to resist foreign aggression. Symptomatically, in 1885 when China and France were at war over the Annam problem, the Foochow shipyard, which was the first naval construction base patterned after Western plans, was destroyed by a French force. As a consequence, China's tributary state Annam was lost. Nevertheless, the policy of superficial imitation of Western methods continued in spite of this defeat. Another great failure in the Sino-

Japanese War in 1894, however, completely uncovered China's weakness.

The stimulation from the defeat of China by Japan finally stirred many scholar-officials. These men, at last beginning to doubt the strength of China's political system, launched a reform movement. The movement gained the support of the young emperor and the Hundred Days' Reform reached a climax in the summer of 1898.

When with the suppression of the reformers the conservative Empress Dowager Tz'u-hsi again ruled the empire, a further period of reaction set in. Some members of the imperial clan who wished to make use of the Boxers to seize political power and repel the progressive party made a grave mistake by having China declare war against the great Western powers in 1900. This decision brought the invasion of the Chinese capital by an expeditionary force of foreign allies.

The humiliation of signing *the Boxer Protocol* (1901) made the Manchu government itself realize the necessity for change. A reform program was now sponsored by a few governors-general and governors. Japan's success in the Russo-Japanese War (1904-1905) made the Chinese scholars conclude that a constitutional monarchy was superior to autocracy. Consequently, five high officials were sent to foreign countries to investigate constitutional governments. This period marked the revival of the reform movement.

After the Boxer uprising, however, the resentment of the Chinese people against the Manchu government could not be pacified merely by promises of constitutional monarchy. While the five senior officials were investigating constitutional governments abroad in 1905, the Chinese Covenant Society [*Chung-kuo T'ung-meng Hui*] was formed in Tokyo by Sun Yat-sen. Thereafter, two factions, one preparing for a constitutional monarchy and one promoting revolution, operated simultaneously. The insincerity of the Manchu government's promises about constitutional monarchy became more obvious each day. At the same time the revolutionary movement was daily expanding. In the autumn of 1911 the revolution exploded at Wuchang.

From the outset of the 1911 revolution to the establishment of the Republic of China in the following March, Chinese political power gradually was transferred from the Manchu dynasty to Yüan Shih-k'ai, the leader of the Peiyang military clique. The initial stage of struggle between the Kuomintang and the Peiyang warlords took shape in the early part of 1912, when the provisional central government had moved from Nanking to Peking and the China Covenant Society was reorganized into the Kuomintang. A "second revolution" took place in 1913 when the Kiangsi revolutionist Li Lieh-chiin declared war against Yüan Shih-k'ai, and several other provinces announced independence of Yüan's central government. This revolution was preceded by the murder of Sung Chiao-jen, an influential Kuomintang leader. It was followed by the defeat of the Kuomintang and the dissolution of the parliament.

After the first dissolution of the parliament, Yüan Shih-k'ai attempted to become emperor. His first step was to revise the constitution. His second step was to organize in the winter of 1915 the Society for Assuring Peace [*Chou-an Hui*]. Its object was to make Yüan emperor. Yüan died, however, in the following June.

After Yüan Shih-k'ai's death the power of the Peiyang warlords was still formidable. They were opposed to the old constitution, which was somewhat more democratic than the newer document giving almost unlimited power to the president. In the struggle the older and more democratic constitution was briefly restored in 1917; but in the same year the problem of declaring war against Germany caused the dissolution of parliament for the second time in its history, and the militarists once again dominated the Peking government.

Prolonged warfare for the protection of the old constitution then ensued as the government in Southern China and that in the North fought against each other. During the war the Peiyang military clique was split into the Chihli and Anhwei factions. The minor warlords in South China were also divided. Down to the autumn of 1920 the Chihli and Anhwei factions openly fought one another. The government of South China at Canton was also dissolved. This was a time of a pro-constitution movement and the disintegration of the warlords' control in South and North China.

After the crumbling of the Chihli and Anhwei factions in the North and the discontinuation of the military government in the South in 1920, the war for protection of the constitution still continued. The political center of gravity, however, was lost to both South and North China. A movement for self-government developed in many provinces, its supporters hoping that China might have a federal government like the United States. However, the warlords merely used this movement as a pretext for occupying and usurping territory for the alleged purpose of establishing selfgovernment. Struggles were unavoidable among the militarists, all of whom were trying to expand their personal power. The years from 1920 to the winter of 1923, when Ts'ao K'un usurped the position of president of China, were filled with agitation for federalism and local autonomy. At the same time chaotic fighting among the warlords convulsed the country.

In the spring of 1924 the reorganized Kuomintang slowly gained power. Ts'ao K'un was defeated and a provisional executive government, which was later overthrown, was established in Peking. By 1926 the preparations for the Northern Expedition by the Kuomintang were completed, and the main power of the Peiyang warlords was destroyed. Thus begins the last stage of three major periods in recent Chinese political history. The details of all three periods will be elaborated in the following chapters.

CHAPTER ONE
THE OPIUM WAR

The Anglo-Chinese war, 1840-1842, is customarily called the Opium War because, from the Chinese point of view, the opium trade was the main cause. From the British standpoint the motive for the war was not opium prohibition but rather the repeated insults and humiliations the British had received from the Chinese government. The conflict had been brewing for many decades. Opium prohibition was merely its precipitating cause. To understand the real significance of the Opium War, we must first understand Sino-English relations before its occurrence, and in general, relations of China with foreign countries.

CHINA'S FOREIGN RELATIONS BEFORE THE OPIUM WAR

China's foreign relations prior to the war may be explained by her political isolation, her trade system, and her commercial relations with Great Britain.

China's Political Isolation

China as a nation was not a member of any international organization. Before the Opium War, although Western nations had established traditional trade relations with China and had undertaken evangelistic work there, none of them except Russia had signed any treaties with her.

Russia, as a result of a controversy concerning boundaries in the northwest of Manchuria, signed in 1689 the Treaty of Nerchinsk, the first treaty ever to be drawn up between China and a European power. The two nations agreed to the Treaty of Kiachta in 1727. Other governments had no treaty relations with China. Even the lease of Macao by Portugal was passed down from the Ming dynasty as a *fait accompli*. Portugal in actuality had no treaty agreement with the Manchu government, which theoretically still owned and controlled Macao.

China's Trade System

Before the Opium War three irregular practices existed in China's trade system. The first was the uncertain rate of custom duties. Traditionally, China was not so vigilant in collecting commercial duties as she was in collecting land taxes. Some extra charge by customs officers became a prevalent evil habit. When foreign businessmen, ignorant of her language and local conditions, came to China for the first time, the exactions imposed by customs officers were made even larger.

The second difficulty was the irregular process of limitations with regard to trading ports. In the early years of the Ch'ing dynasty, foreign merchants were concentrated in Canton. Officials of all levels in that province naturally had special opportunities to make fortunes. Sometimes a foreign merchant who found the exactions unbearable tried to develop his business at Amoy, Ningpo, or other ports of Fukien or Chekiang. However, there too, local officials who desired to become wealthy at the expense of foreigners treated the merchants unfairly and overcharged them.

The third difficulty was the Hong monopolies. The numerous foreign merchants in Canton frequently had trouble transacting business with the Chinese. Therefore one merchant was formally appointed by the emperor in 1702 as sole broker for foreign trade at Canton. All goods imported or exported had to be handled by him. Foreign merchants complained about this inconvenient restriction, and it was abolished. In 1720 Kwangtung merchants organized what was called the Co-hong [*Kung-hang*; loosely translated "official guild"] to take the place of the government-appointed merchant in dealing with foreigners.

The Co-hong was not organized by the government. But it met with informal approval, for it was covertly a means whereby officials could make a profit. Since the Co-hong monopolized foreign trade, extra charges for foreign merchants increased, although government revenue from customs duties was still small. A large part of the customs duties went into the pockets of officials and to the Hong merchants. Even though foreign traders repeatedly requested a decrease in duties, their requests were of no avail. Such was the general condition before 1736. During the second half of the reign of Ch'ien-lung, the irregular trading practices became even more reprehensible.

An imperial decree of 1757 limited trade with foreigners to Canton. Foreign ships were not permitted to enter any ports in Fukien and Chekiang. The attempt of English merchants to obtain permission from the government to open Amoy and Ningpo as trading ports was a failure. In 1760 the government formally recognized as a Co-hong a corporation of nine merchants who monopolized the foreign trade. By 1771 many Hong merchants were bankrupt because, being in arrears with the dues payable to their government, they also were indebted to foreigners. The Co-hong was officially dissolved for a time, but was very soon reorganized.

The Hong merchants unloaded commodities for foreigners, established their market prices, and also served as an agency for transacting official and business affairs involving the government and foreign merchants. Reporting and paying of customs duties was also handled by the Hong merchants. A petition or complaint from foreign merchants to the Chinese government could not be sent directly, but had to be submitted through the Hong merchants. Since personal activities of foreign merchants were also supervised by the Hong, acting under governmental directives, the Co-hong became an important liaison agency between the government and foreigners.

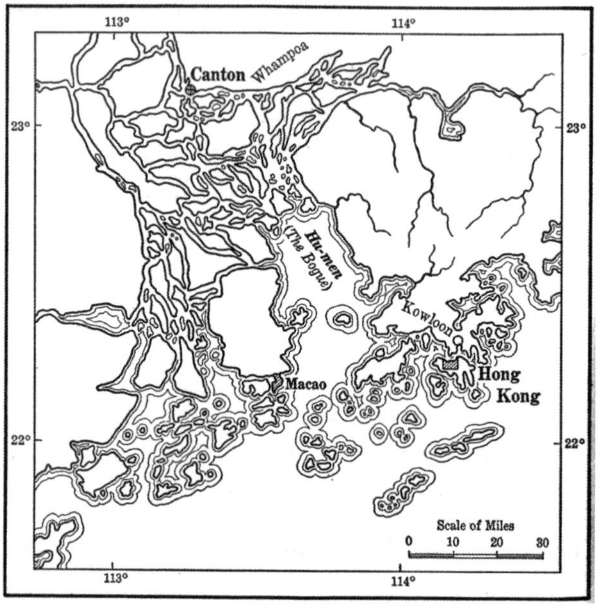

CANTON AND THE EARLY TRADING SETTLEMENTS

Regulations for Foreign Factories

In 1759 the governor-general of Kwangtung, Li Shih-yao, entreated the emperor to take measures to restrict the actions of foreigners, against whom he harbored personal suspicions. The attitude of Emperor Ch'ien-lung toward foreigners was not as lenient and magnanimous as that of Emperor K'ang-hsi had been. Ch'ien-lung required that restrictive measures be taken against barbarians, the measures outlined in Li Shih-yao's memorial issued in 1760. The Hong merchants were ordered by the emperor to announce the regulations to the foreign factories or trading stations in Canton, and from that time down to the 1830's the regulations were enforced with only occasional modifications. Finally, in 1835 Lu K'un, Ch'i-kung, and others drew up eight new regulations, the gist of which is as follows:

1. Foreign warships were not to enter Humen [the Bogue].
2. Neither women nor guns and other weapons could be brought to the factories or trading stations where commercial agents resided and transacted business.
3. All river pilots and ships' compradors employed by foreigners were to be registered at the office of the Chinese subprefect at Macao (which was still under Chinese jurisdiction). A license granted by that office to the employed person was to be carried at all times for examination.
4. The number of Chinese servants at each factory was restricted. (At first the employment of Chinese servants was forbidden, but this rule was later modified with limitation as to number.)
5. Foreigners who lived in the factories were not allowed to go out for boat excursions except on three specific days—the eighth, eighteenth, and twenty-eighth of each month. On these days foreigners might visit the flower gardens and monasteries of Honan Island, but they had to be accompanied by interpreters. If their conduct was improper, the interpreters would be held responsible.
6. Foreigners were not allowed to submit petitions to the local government. If they had a complaint, the document was to be transmitted through the Hong merchants.
7. The Hong merchants were not to owe debts to foreigners, but they had the responsibility of advising and protecting foreigners.
8. Every year there was a time limit for foreigners residing in their factories in Kwangtung to manage their business. They had then to return home or go to Macao.

These regulations obviously could not be strictly enforced, but they were obeyed to a large extent. Sending petitions directly to the local government was absolutely impossible. Because foreign merchants had also no right to send petitions directly to the imperial government, they were completely in the control of the Hong merchants. Nevertheless, the monopoly of these merchants was obtained from the government, and they were under official pressure to obey the government's commands. Unscrupulous officials and the Hong merchants jointly played havoc among the foreigners. To both officials and merchants, factories were sources for graft.

Britain's Share in the Chinese Trade

In the eighteenth century, Great Britain had the closest commercial relations with China, although the nations which had first developed the trade were Portugal, Spain, and Holland. At this time English sea power had surpassed that of other nations, and Britain's trade in China also jumped to the first position. Out of eighteen foreign commercial ships which docked at Canton in 1751, nine were British, four Dutch, two French, two Swedish, and one Danish. By 1789 the number of foreign ships at Canton had increased to eighty-six, of which sixty-one were English, fifteen American, five Dutch, one French, one Danish, and three Portuguese.

Although during the time of Napoleon I most European nations except England were under the control of France, France could not challenge the supremacy of British power on the sea. The United States was not affected because of her observance of neutrality. In this period the commercial influence of England in China continued to increase, and the United States ranked second. England had a base in India; the United States had none in the Orient; so England got the lion's share of Chinese trade.

SINO-BRITISH NEGOTIATIONS BEFORE THE OPIUM WAR

Before 1842 England and other sea powers had no treaties with

China. British merchants received the same treatment from the Chinese as the traders of other nations. But since England occupied the first commercial position and had more ships docking in China than other nations, she expected special consideration. From the closing decades of the eighteenth century to the beginning of the Opium War, England conducted three important negotiations with China.

The First British Embassy to China, 1792: Macartney

The special envoy, Lord Macartney, sailed from Portsmouth in September 1792 and arrived at Taku, near Tientsin, in August 1793. As was customary, he was treated by the Ch'ing government as a tributary envoy, and his suite on the ship was supplied by the Chinese government with good food and liquor. A flag inscribed with large Chinese characters signifying "Ambassador Bearing Tribute from the Country of England" was raised on Macartney's ship.

Similarly, in the early years of the Ch'ing dynasty when Portugal, Spain, and Holland had also repeatedly sent ambassadors to China requesting the conclusion of commercial treaties, the Ch'ing government always regarded them as tributary envoys and treated them as if they were on the same level as envoys from China's vassal states. They were ordered to perform the ceremony of three kneelings and nine bows. These the earlier envoys, though reluctantly, had performed.

When Ambassador Macartney arrived, Emperor Ch'ien-lung was in his Summer Palace at Jehol; he granted the British envoy an interview at the palace. Although Macartney was graciously entertained, he adamantly refused to perform the kotow ceremony before the emperor. After many negotiations he was permitted to use the same ceremony before the emperor which he was accustomed to use at an audience with the British king.

When Macartney returned to Peking to take up the problem of concluding a commercial treaty with the Manchu court, the grand councilors avoided discussing any of his suggestions by relying upon entertainment and polite conversation to kill time. They even hinted that he should return to England. Finally, Macartney presented a letter to the grand councilors containing the following requests:

1. That the English be permitted to trade at Chusan, Ningpo, Tientsin, and other ports.
2. That they be allowed a warehouse at Peking, following the example of the Russians who enjoyed this privilege.
3. That they be allowed some small unfortified depot near Chusan where their people might reside and their goods be stored.
4. That the same privilege be allowed near Canton.
5. That the transit duties between Macao and Canton be abolished or reduced.
6. That all charges at Canton except the imperial duties be abolished, and that a copy of the imperial duties be given to the English.
7. That the English be allowed to teach Christianity in China.

The Macartney embassy left Peking on October 7. By imperial reply, all seven requests were virtually refused. Thus Macartney achieved nothing beyond polite treatment from the Ch'ing government.

The Second British Embassy to China, 1816: Amherst

Lord Amherst, who arrived at Tientsin in July 1816, was also treated as a tributary envoy by the Chinese government. At a banquet given for him in Tientsin, Chinese high officials ordered him to perform the kotow ceremony before the table of the emperor so that he might express his gratitude. Lord Amherst refused, and trouble followed.

The envoy's program in Peking had been arranged by imperial decree. The seventh day was set aside for his interview with the emperor; the eighth for giving him a banquet and gifts; the ninth for his visit to the Summer Palace; the eleventh for another banquet to be given in his honor by the ministry of ceremonies; and the thirteenth for his departure from the capital. Afraid that the British envoy was ignorant of the required ceremonies, the emperor sent special officials to Tungchow to instruct him further about the kotow ceremony. If he performed it well, he was to be escorted to the capital. Lord Amherst flatly refused to accept such instruction, but the special officials, fearing punishment, avoided reporting to the emperor except in ambiguous terms.

On the sixth day the British envoy was urged to go to Peking so that he might have an interview with the emperor the following morning. On account of fatigue resulting from long, rugged traveling and because his baggage, in which his formal clothes and credentials were packed, had not yet arrived, the British envoy declined to have an immediate interview with the emperor as was scheduled. Although urged again and again, Lord Amherst refused to go to the palace.

The special commissioner and other high officials assigned to care for the British ambassador told the emperor a lie, saying that as the envoy was walking to the front of the palace, he had collapsed with a sudden illness. Since the emperor did not know the truth of the story, he ordered the ambassador to return to his residence to recuperate and honored him with an examination by the court physicians. He then commanded the vice-envoy to come to the interview on Lord Amherst's behalf. Soon after, the vice-envoy was also reported to have collapsed on account of illness. Learning from imperial physicians that both men were in normal health, the emperor was greatly angered. He condemned the British envoys for arrogance in that they despised "the ruler of all under heaven" [*t'ien-hsia kung-chu*]. He issued a mandate ordering them to leave the capital and to return to their country immediately.

As a matter of fact, the British envoys were not arrogant. But because the high commissioners and special officials who were assigned to entertain the ambassadors had no way to solve the kotow problem, they had to employ some means of compulsion and deceit to make the British envoys return home in order that, as Chinese officials, they might finish their own assignment without incurring blame. The emperor charged the envoys with despising "the ruler of all under heaven"; Lord Amherst complained that the Manchu court insulted the commissioners of England. Except for creating ill feeling on both sides, nothing was achieved.[1]

The Third British Negotiations, 1834: Napier

Six years before the outbreak of the Opium War, when relations between Britain and China were already greatly strained, England sent a superintendent of trade to China following the dissolution of the British East India Company in 1834. Before that time, while China's foreign trade was monopolized by the Hong merchants at Canton, British trade in China had been monopolized by the East India Company. There was no comparable monopoly organization of American merchants in China; the Americans were free and active in the Oriental market. Some British industrialists and merchants now also preferred the adoption of free trade as against the monopoly of the East India Company. This preference, supported by public opinion, resulted in the abolition of the East India Company.

Prior to the disintegration of the company, all problems of English merchants in connection with Chinese trade had been managed by the taipan [*ta-pan*] as the responsible head of the mercantile community. When the governor-general of Kwangtung and Kwangsi, Li Hung-pin, heard that the East India Company was about to be dissolved, he was afraid that after its liquidation there would be no chief for British merchants and no way to control them. Therefore, in 1830 he ordered the Hong merchants to suggest to the company that a general manager comparable with the taipan be appointed to take charge of commercial transactions. Learning the desire of the Chinese authorities, the British parliament passed the Act to Regulate the Trade to China and India by which the monopoly and control of the East India Company was abolished and a chief superintendent and second and third vice-superintendent were appointed as supervisors of British trade in China.

Lord Napier was appointed the first chief superintendent, William Plowden was the second superintendent, and John Davis the third. Napier was of noble parentage and had served as an admiral, a position of distinction in England. In selecting him the British government hoped to increase friendly relations between China and England. His title implied that he was merely an overseer of trade, but his position was actually tantamount to that of an ambassador. The original expectation of the governor-general of Kwangtung and Kwangsi, of course, was that England would appoint another merchant leader like the former taipan of the East India Company. He did not anticipate that the new man would have the powers of an ambassador. There was misunderstanding on both sides.

Lord Napier was given the following set of instructions by the king of England and the foreign secretary, Lord Palmerston:

1. The chief superintendent was to exercise judicial power over British subjects, but there must be an important case before he opened court.
2. The sphere of superintendency was limited to the harbors of Kwangtung.
3. A peaceful attitude should be maintained with regard to the Chinese government. The use of menacing language or the making of any appeal for protection by the British military or naval forces was to be avoided. No British ship of war was to sail into Hu-men. Chinese laws and customs were to be carefully observed by British subjects.

When Napier was about to start his journey, Lord Palmerston gave him other special instructions, directing him to be very careful in performing his duties. The gist of these instructions was as follows:

1. When he reached Canton, a letter should be sent directly to the governor-general of Kwangtung and Kwangsi announcing his

arrival.

2. His most important duty, apart from protecting the British trade in Kwangtung, was to study the possibility of extending British trade to other ports.

3. For achieving this aim every effort should be made to conform to Chinese regulations and to consider Chinese prejudices. Attempts should be made to establish direct communications with the Peking court.

4. Napier was to be extremely cautious and avoid any conduct or demeanor which would excite the Chinese government's fear or distrust. He was not to expect to achieve his aims too quickly, lest he endanger existent relations. In compliance with this cautious policy, he was not to hold negotiations or discussions with the Chinese government unless some extraordinary matter arose. If a chance for negotiations evolved, he was to report immediately to his government and wait for instruction. Before receiving a reply, he was not to take any action.

The British government was being cautious. But, as the text shows, the instructions are rather imprecise as to the official capacity of the chief superintendent. On one hand, the British government wished its superintendent to promote friendly relations between the two governments, to observe Chinese laws and customs, and to keep from arousing suspicion and antagonism. On the other hand, it ordered him to write a letter directly to the governor-general when he reached Canton. Such a unilateral action to alter well-established procedure was contrary to current Chinese law and usage. Consequently, as soon as Napier reached Canton, insoluble disputes occurred.

Napier reached Macao on July 15, 1834, and arrived at the British factory in the suburb of Canton on July 25. Before he reached Canton, the governor-general of Kwangtung, Lu K'un, had been told that a British *i-mu* [barbarian chief] had recently docked. He immediately ordered the

Hong merchants to find out whether the newly arrived person was comparable to the former taipan. Upon learning that the superintendent was very different from a taipan, he dispatched on July 21 two Hong merchants to take an order to Macao. The new barbarian chief was informed that if the purpose of his coming to China was to discuss methods of trade after the liquidation of the East India Company, he would not be allowed to go to Canton, since according to Chinese law no one was allowed to go there without first obtaining a passport from the Peking government. If he had other special functions, Napier was told, he should wait until the governor-general reported to the emperor and received the imperial instructions.

Although this order was sent on the twenty-first, time was consumed in forwarding it, and Napier arrived in Canton before receiving the letter. When the Hong merchants carrying the letter rushed back to Canton, Napier was just asking his translator to copy a letter of his own to the governor-general. After being informed of the contents of the governor-general's letter, he refused it politely, saying that he was the representative of the king of England and he could not receive a document in the form of a Chinese government command.

The general theme of Napier's letter to the Kwangtung governor-general was that he was a superintendent of trade appointed by the king of England and that he had two associates, the second and the third superintendents. These three superintendents had authority to protect and promote English trade; they also had judicial power over British subjects in China to be exercised when needed. And, said Napier, they hoped to have an interview with the governor-general to discuss these matters.

It was intended that the letter should be sent directly to the governor-general's yamen on July 26. A messenger took it to the Canton city guard, asking that it be forwarded to the governor-general. The city guard told the messenger that all barbarian petitions had to be submitted through the Hong merchants. Later a higher officer arrived and insisted that the direct delivery of a letter was against well-established precedent. Moreover, since the envelope was written in the form of a letter between equals, he refused to accept it. The Hong merchants advised Napier to present the letter in the form of a petition and to submit it through them, but Napier stubbornly rejected their advice. Consequently, there was no way for his letter to reach the office of the governor-general.

Governor-general Lu K'un considered the newly arrived barbarian chief ignorant of established regulations since he had not received a "red card" before coming to Canton. Lu issued another order on July 27, instructing the Hong merchants and interpreters to explain procedures clearly to Napier and to curb his actions, which were contrary to the Chinese legal system. If the Hong merchants failed to do so, they were to be punished.

A résumé of the order follows:

(1) Foreigners were allowed to stay only at Macao and if they came to Canton on a business trip, they must receive a "red card" from the customs office.

(2) Since Napier had come to China for the first time and was unfamiliar with Chinese regulations, his actions were excusable and he might still be allowed to investigate trade conditions at Canton, but he must return to Macao after the investigation.

(3) Chinese high officials traditionally had no authority to receive private letters from foreigners; messages from a barbarian chief could not be accepted by a local governor.

(4) Chinese authorities traditionally let the Hong merchants handle foreign-trade affairs; if a barbarian wished to change trade regulations, he should consult the Hong merchants first, and then send a petition through them to the provincial government, which would forward it to the emperor for His Majesty's decision before any change took place.

The Hong merchants were blamed by the government for dealing with Napier improperly. At the same time, they had no way to make

Napier leave Canton. They were in a dilemma. On August 10 they summoned the British merchants for a meeting to discuss methods for making a compromise. Napier did not permit British merchants to attend the meeting because he believed that the Hong merchants could not change the mind of the governor-general. The effect of his prohibition was that no Britisher participated in the scheduled meeting.

On August 16 the Hong merchants, in order to protect their own positions, decided to stop British trade. They did not unload any British commodities, and at the same time they petitioned the government to seal up British storehouses. On August 18, Lu K'un issued an instruction saying that the barbarian chief Napier, because of his own stupidity and ignorance, had disregarded the Chinese legal system and had broken down long-established friendly relations between China and England in spite of the wishes of the English king. Furthermore, he said that England depended on Chinese tea, rhubarb, and silk for its livelihood, while imported British woolen goods were insignificant to the Chinese, who would suffer no loss even if trade with England were discontinued. However, to stop trade on account of one barbarian chief who infringed on Chinese rights was not the wish of the Celestial Court, concerned for those coming from afar. "Therefore," said the governor-general, "let us treat him leniently for a few more days and await his repentance and awakening." The governor-general did not know that the Hong had already stopped trade with the British merchants.

On August 23 Lu K'un sent a subprefect and another officer to the British factory to ask Napier three things: Why had he come to Kwangtung? What were the duties entrusted to him by his government? When did he plan to return to Macao?

In reply to the first question, Napier said that his mission was based upon a suggestion made by the governor-general of Canton in 1830 that after the closing of the East India Company, England should send a representative with authority to regulate the trade. The reply to the second question, he said, was elucidated in his letter to the governor-general, and if the two officials opened it, they could read it. Having read it, they were to take the letter to the governor-general. To the last question he responded that he would return to Macao at his convenience. The two officers naturally did not dare to open the letter which was addressed to the governor-general. They returned without achieving answers agreeable to Lu K'un.

After the stoppage of trade, the British merchants organized a meeting which was held on August 25. Napier took this opportunity to make a speech charging that Governor-General Lu K'un was unreasonable. He said that the former governor-general requested England to dispatch an authorized representative to Canton to reorganize trade after the dissolution of the East India Company, and that he was the special representative of the king of England. He revealed that he had attempted to exchange correspondence with the governor-general, who had declined, and that then the Hong merchants had stopped the English trade which was mutually beneficial. However, he said that he would not give up trying to establish communications on an equal basis between the two nations.

On September 2 the governor-general formally announced the stoppage of trade with the British. After this announcement there were disturbances at Canton. The government police closely watched comings and goings at the British factory, thus causing the residents great anxiety. On September 5 Napier ordered the two ships which had escorted him to China to sail into Humen [the Bogue], but they were stopped from doing so by gunfire from the Chinese fort. The two ships returned the fire and forced their way to Whampoa.

Napier on September 8 also issued a public notice in the name of the British merchants. This declaration criticized the governor-general for his deceitful words and actions which had prodded the Chinese emperor into creating conditions which verged upon warfare between England and

China. The power of the king of England was strongly emphasized. In conclusion the declaration hinted that under no circumstances would the British king tolerate the present unjustified pressure.

On September 11 Lu K'un ordered the Co-hong to tell the British merchants that it was acceptable for England to replace the taipan by a superintendent, although Chinese high officials heretofore had had no direct communications with the barbarian chiefs except in receiving tribute bearers. With regard to Napier's mission, Lu K'un's message continued, England had not formally notified China beforehand, nor had Napier brought any credentials with him. How could China know that he was an official sent by his government? Furthermore, had he not suddenly intruded into Canton without allowing the governor-general any time to ask instructions from the emperor? Had he not used warships to force his way to Canton? Indeed, his audacity and unseemly behavior had been extreme. Therefore, if he did not return to Macao, China would use military power to curb his actions.

At this time war between the two countries seemed imminent. Napier's convoy fleet, however, was very small. In addition, the British envoy, tired from overwork and wrath, contracted a fever at the beginning of September. On the fourteenth, the British merchants received the information from the Co-hong that if Napier withdrew to Macao with the fleet, the order which had stopped British trade might be revoked. Napier was also strongly advised by his physician to take a rest at Macao. Hence, on September 21 he ordered the two British ships to sail out of Humen. He himself, five days later, boarded another small boat to retire to Macao. The Kwangtung governor-general ordered resumption of trade on the twenty-ninth. Napier died at Macao on October 11, and the great dispute fell temporarily into abeyance.

Although the dispute had been aggravated by the stubbornness of Lu K'un, who refused to accept Napier's letter, that stubbornness was not personal to Lu K'un but had its root in the scholar-official class which failed to recognize any other nation as the equal of China. Lu K'un was only fulfilling his duty as an official of the Manchu monarchy when he repudiated correspondence with the British envoy. This rule was based on a phrase in the *Spring and Autumn Annals* which said that a high official was to have no private correspondence. When Lu K'un reported to the throne his methods of dealing with the newly arrived barbarian chief, the emperor's endorsement of Lu's memorial read, "What he did was proper and his point of view was correct." When the British warships entered Hu-men, the emperor blamed Lu K'un for not having taken preventive measures, but did not dismiss him.

Napier's difficulties also had part of their cause in the policy of his own nation. Before Napier left England for Canton, he had requested that his government give him credentials and that it notify the Peking court or Kwangtung authorities in advance; the British foreign secretary, Palmerston, deemed these procedures unnecessary. Not knowing that it was very difficult for a foreigner to have correspondence with a Chinese official, Palmerston aggravated Napier's problem further by ordering him to inform the Kwangtung governor-general by letter when he reached Canton. Several Britishers subsequently supported the Chinese in their complaint that they had had no advance notice and that Napier had no credentials. They criticized Palmerston for his negligence and his lack of knowledge about the Orient.

Charles Elliot as Superintendent

After Napier returned to Macao, trade relations were resumed and for a time peace prevailed between the two nations. The problem, however, was not solved. After the death of Napier, Davis was promoted to be chief superintendent. Davis had been employed by the East India Company and had spent a long time in the Orient; hence he had a good knowledge of the Chinese language. He had predicted that Napier's action would bear no fruit. When he was promoted to the chief superintendency, he neither carried on correspondence with the Kwangtung governor-general nor went to Canton, but stayed at Macao, quietly reporting everything to the British government and waiting for instructions. In 1835 he resigned and returned to England.

Davis, in turn, was replaced by George Robinson, who had been the third superintendent under Lord Napier. When Robinson took over the superintendency, he followed the methods of Davis; he also installed a new branch office on Lintin Island. After two years Robinson also retired, and the position was taken by Captain Elliot. When Charles Elliot was made the chief superintendent, changes were made in the duties of his office and the Chinese began to call him consul.

The British merchants in China had not liked Davis' policy of acquiescence. They blamed Robinson for lack of ability and submitted a joint petition to the London government complaining that the authority of the superintendent was too insignificant. They urged that the superintendent be given special authority and adequate military support in order that he might negotiate directly with the Chinese central government. They also requested that the trading ports be extended outside of Canton. Furthermore, they stressed the point that it was unbearable to obey all the orders of Chinese authorities.

The British foreign secretary was apparently affected by the petition of His Majesty's merchants in China. He informed Superintendent Charles Elliot that his government had heretofore used peaceful means to maintain trade relations with China, but since the British merchants in Kwangtung objected to this policy, he was inclined to think that by normal means it was difficult to accomplish much toward trade extension. This instruction indicated that the government was about to adopt more active procedures.

After Elliot took over the superintendency, he essayed to exchange official documents with the Kwangtung governor-general. Elliot cleverly addressed the envelope of his letter in the form of a petition, lest it should be rejected. The governor-general, who was then Teng T'ing-chen, accepted it. Teng's reply, however, was still phrased as an official command and was delivered through the Hong merchants, who were instructed to tell Elliot that at present he should stay at Macao, until he received permission by an imperial decree to proceed to Canton. This permission soon arrived.

From Canton Elliot reported to the British foreign office that he had been successful in exchanging official dispatches with the Kwangtung governor-general by using a form similar to the report of Chinese officials to their superiors, though different from what is called a petition in English. Palmerston did not approve of this method. He sent instructions again and again to Elliot insisting that, in exchanging documents with the Chinese governor-general, he should not have the document delivered through the hands of the Hong merchants nor should he use a form like that of a petition. Palmerston's idea was that Elliot must fight for equal rights with the governor-general.

After Elliot received these instructions, he tried to test the attitude of the governor-general toward a revised procedure of communication, but as a result he was sent a stern reprimand. The governor-general's admonition to Elliot contained such phrases as: "It is really improper" for the taipan not to employ the courteous expression "the Celestial Court," but rather to use the equal term, "your honorable country"; "the dignity of the great Manchu empire should not be offended by the taipan"; "you should be careful to protect your position," etc. Elliot reported these expressions to his foreign secretary and concluded that equal rights with China could not be obtained except by military force.

At this time China was gradually taking serious measures to suppress the import and consumption of opium. For this reason Elliot reported to his government that sooner or later there would be a conflict concerning the opium problem, and that on this account he hoped that Britain would send a considerable military force to the East. In November 1837 the

British government ordered Rear Admiral Frederick Maitland, the commander of the East Indian squadron, to send a few warships to China. He was instructed to protect English interests by supporting, with the aid of the chief superintendent, the complaints of the British merchants against Chinese officials. The British merchants in Kwangtung were to obey his orders.

Chinese officials of all levels were still living in a dream. They frequently ordered the Hong merchants to control the barbarians and to forbid them to act lawlessly. They did not realize that war was near nor did they recognize that the opium problem provided an excellent fuse already lit and leading to a military explosion.

LIN TSE-HSÜ'S SEVERE POLICY OF OPIUM PROHIBITION

Already during the T'ang dynasty the Chinese knew a drug called opium poppy [*ying-su*] which was used exclusively as a medicine. The practice of making it into paste for smoking, however, seems to have commenced around the early part of the seventeenth century. At that time commerce in the Far East was in the hands of the Portuguese, who brought opium to China from India. The annual amount was then very small; in 1589, for instance, the customs report listed 10 catties [*ca.1 1/3* pounds] of opium as sold for 12 silver ingots. By 1729, because the people along the southeastern coast of China had now become addicted to opium smoking, the first imperial decree prohibiting this practice was issued. At that time the annual import was still only 200 chests [each chest was 133 1/3 pounds]. But the prohibition order was not strictly enforced and the number of addicts and the amount of opium imported were both increasing each year.

Since the prohibition of 1729 was limited to opium smoking and not to its purchase, opium was still in the inventory as a medicine on which customs duties were paid. The Canton customs record in 1753 listed one chest of opium, on which three taels were paid as duty. The annual rate of increase was about twenty chests, until 1767, when imports reached 1000 chests.

In 1773 the British East India Company obtained a monopoly of the opium trade in the Far East. By 1790 more than 4000 chests a year were purchased. England, which occupied the first place in commerce with China, encouraged this traffic. Once constituting only one-sixth of the British trade in China, at the end of the eighteenth century opium occupied more than one-half of British cargo to China from India. The remaining commodities were Indian cotton, which was about one-fourth of her trade, and British woolen goods, which provided only one-eighth. Among the exported goods, three-fifths was tea, one-fifth raw silk and silk fabrics, and the remainder cotton fabrics. During these years British trade in China formed a triangle with India; that is, British manufactured goods were transported to India, Indian products to China, and Chinese products to England. The profits were either sent back to England or invested in India.

The evil habit of smoking opium gradually spread over the whole Chinese Empire. In compliance with a request made by the governor-general at Canton, the Peking court in 1796 issued an imperial decree prohibiting the import of opium. Four years later another prohibiting decree was issued. Henceforth opium was a contraband article.

Nevertheless, opium imports continued to increase, in spite of interdiction, from 4000 or 5000 chests to larger figures. The exact volume traded is hard to ascertain because after its prohibition, Chinese opium records did not pass through the customs office. According to foreign records, the import was nearly 10,000 chests after 1810. From 1820 to 1830 the average annual figure was 16,000 chests, and in 1836 it totaled more than 20,000 chests.

Before 1800 the opium trade was handled mainly by the East India

Company and the Hong merchants in Canton. After the stringent interdicts of that year, the place of transaction was shifted from Canton to Macao and to Whampoa (Huang-pu). In 1821 officials of all levels in Canton had a great dispute over the unequal distribution of bribes and illegal charges from the smuggling of opium. This quarrel resulted in another interdiction against the poisonous goods, issued in 1821 by Emperor Tao-kuang at the request of Juan Yüan, who was then governor-general at Canton. Before 1821 the opium trade in Macao and Whampoa was half-open, half-secret. After the interdiction, the trading centers were moved to Lintin Island, Hong Kong, Chin-hsing-men, and other places; hence, the total traffic was even larger than before.

Why was it that the more severe the interdictions became, the larger the import of opium grew? Before its prohibition, customs officers had already demanded extra pay or bribes, but remitted the regular duties to the imperial treasury. After opium became a contraband commodity, senior and junior officials held the interdictions in one hand and reached for bribes with the other. After receiving their bribes, they cooperated with the merchants and gave protection to the illegal trade. Government officials not only exercised great authority over this illicit business, but even became shareholders in it. The obstacles to distributing the goods were reduced to a minimum. At times government ships were used for transporting opium for the foreign merchants. These corrupt practices were widely known, except to the emperor and to an occasional governor-general in Canton who did not wish to soil his hands.

The scandalous opium dealings created another problem: unbalanced imports and exports. At the beginning of China's foreign trade, her exports exceeded her imports. The increased import of smuggled opium, which had to be paid for by specie, reversed the balance of trade. Most seriously, the drainage of bullion caused an inflation in China.

In 1835-1836 the exorbitant price of silver stimulated two divergent opinions regarding the opium problem. One, supported by Hsü Nai-chi, favored legalization of the opium trade. Hsü, who had once served as the provincial judge of Kwangtung, was familiar with the underhand dealings in opium at Canton. The other, represented by Huang Chüeh-tzu, advocated absolute prohibition of the opium traffic by increasing punishment for offenders. Huang was the director of the court of state ceremonials.

In 1836 Hsü Nai-chi presented a memorial to the throne. In sum, Hsü rehearsed the history of opium as follows: that it was originally a drug which could be imported by paying a customs duty; that because opium addicts did society much harm, the smoking and selling of opium were banned; that evil customs officers and cunning merchants joined hands to make the prohibition ineffective and to bring in even more opium, and their great profits made them heedless of the death penalty. Continuing his memorial, Hsü goes on to say that formerly opium was imported on a barter basis; no silver was drained. But since the wily merchants began smuggling opium which was paid for by cash, drains upon the silver supply increased, the price of silver became exorbitantly high, and the nation became poorer and poorer. "It would be better," Hsü Nai-chi suggested, "to relax the prohibition on opium, and to permit its import as before upon payment of customs duties, so that it might again be exchanged for tea, rhubarb, and silk rather than silver." He also suggested that it should be permissible to plant opium in China in order to avoid the troubles caused by importing it; that officials, soldiers, and students should be severely forbidden to smoke it; but that other people should be free to do so without government restriction.

Emperor Tao-kuang was dubious of such proposals. Unable to make a decision about Hsü Nai-chi's requests, he transferred the memorial to the governor-general and other high officials in Kwangtung in order that they might discuss it thoroughly and report the results to him. After the governor-general, Teng T'ing-chen, received this decree, he ordered his subordinates and the Hong merchants to express their opinions. The result was unanimous support for repeal of the opium prohibition. This information was reported to the emperor. After obtaining news of the repeal of opium prohibition, the British merchants were more active, and within two years, approximately 50,000 chests were imported.

But in May 1838 Huang Chüeh-tzu submitted a memorial to the throne requesting an absolute stoppage of the exchange of silver for the baneful article which was undermining the foundations of the nation. Emperor Tao-kuang ordered the governors-general and governors of the whole empire to express opinions and to report to him promptly. The consensus of opinion was then in support of severe prohibition.

At that time Lin Tse-hsü, governor-general of Hunan and Hupeh, sent a memorial to the throne concerning his own plan for eradicating opium. Emperor Tao-kuang, now convinced by Lin's theories, was determined to execute strictly the policy of severe prohibition. He also degraded Hsü Nai-chi and ordered him to retire. In November 1838 Lin Tse-hsü was appointed imperial commissioner and ordered to Kwangtung to investigate, invested with full military and political power so that he could liquidate the opium business completely. The war cloud between China and England grew darker.

In March 1839 when Lin Tse-hsü went to Canton, Governor-General Teng, who had learned of Lin's appointment, suddenly urged his subordinates to enforce the opium interdictions very carefully. At this time some smuggled opium was discovered on a foreign ship, which was immediately ordered to sail from Kwangtung. Foreign merchants were warned that trade would be stopped. A few Chinese offenders were arrested and executed in front of the foreign factories. A multitude of people watched the executions. The foreigners lowered their flags as a sign of protest, but the governor-general paid no attention.

That the British government had not as yet a fixed intention to protect its merchants in their opium trade we can see from Captain Elliot's public notice to British merchants. He stressed the point that the British government did not wish its subjects to break the laws of the country with which they had trade relations. He said further that if they infringed upon the laws and incurred trouble, their government had no duty to protect them. So it seems clear that England did not wish to open hostilities with China on account of the infamous trade. If the Chinese had had some knowledge of international conditions, and had not considered the foreigners barbarians, their prohibition of opium need not have caused the war.

Among the high officials of the Tao-kuang period, Lin Tse-hsü was an outstandingly dutiful and efficient person. His straightforwardness and sincerity deserve respect and admiration, but his knowledge of foreign countries was necessarily restricted, and his methods were not free from error. His attention was concentrated on one thing—the perniciousness of opium. He wanted to destroy the opium which was currently in Kwangtung, and he wanted to cut off completely the sources of supply. Every means that could help him to achieve these two aims was fully tried.

On March 18, the eighth day after his arrival in Canton, Lin joined the governor-general and governor in assembling the members of the Co-hong at a meeting at which they were given two imperial decrees. One was an instruction to Chinese merchants; the other was addressed to foreign merchants, explaining to them candidly that the sale of opium was illegal and immoral. Foreign traders were informed that all opium on ships in Chinese waters must be surrendered to the government and none should be concealed; and that bonds in English and Chinese as a pledge of good conduct must be signed, declaring that "hereafter this ship will never smuggle any opium. If it does and is discovered, the goods will be entirely confiscated and the person responsible will be executed according to law."

The day after these instructions had been given, foreign merchants in

Canton were informed that until they had completely surrendered their opium, they would not be permitted to leave Canton. Before long the entrances to foreign factories were guarded by policing officials and soldiers, who examined the people coming in or going out of these business agencies. Navigation from the factories to Whampoa and Macao was prohibited, and private correspondence was banned. Shortly after, Chinese compradors and servants employed by foreigners were dismissed by the Chinese government and were not permitted to go to the factories. Foreigners were confined in the factories as if they were prisoners. It was difficult for them to secure provisions, though they were not entirely deprived of food. According to a memorial from Lin Tse-hsü, "Five days after the compradors were dismissed, the food of foreign factories began to run short, but our ministers immediately gave them meat supplies and other items." The foreigners' accusation that Lin completely cut off their food supply was not entirely true, but since they hated Lin, they exaggerated the food restrictions.

Why did Lin adopt such a harsh method? Because the British merchants upon learning that the imperial commissioner was about to arrive, had ordered their ships, loaded with opium, to sail to the far side of Lintin Island. Lin wished to destroy completely all opium in these ships, yet he had no way to recall them to Canton. Though the ships were anchored outside of Canton, he thought that treacherous opium dealers at work in the factories might be compelled, by an effective siege, to surrender their opium to him.

After several days of confinement, the British merchants yielded 1037 chests of opium. But Lin understood that each of their twenty storage ships carried more than 1000 chests; making an approximate total of over 20,000. The small number of chests given up was only one-twentieth of the total amount; he therefore refused to accept them.

When Lin ordered a siege of the factories, the British commercial superintendent, Charles Elliot, was at Macao. He came to Canton on

March 24, after the proclamation of the order. Elliot entered the factory without hindrance, even though it was besieged. But in the factory he could not see a single Chinese servant or comprador, nor was he allowed to go out again.

Thereupon, Elliot wrote a letter to Imperial Commissioner Lin applying for passports for all British people. Lin replied that until the opium was completely surrendered, the request would not be complied with. Elliot then ordered British merchants to give up all opium in their hands and notified Imperial Commissioner Lin that the total number of 20, 283 chests of opium owned by British merchants would be delivered at a designated place. Since the ships loaded with opium were scattered and the amount was so large, it took nearly two months (from March 27 to May 21) to have the ships concentrated and checked. After all opium was delivered, the emperor ordered its destruction.

During the progress of this surrender of opium, confinement of the British to their factories was not completely abolished. Compradors and servants did return to work, however, and inspection at the factory gates was not as vigilant as before. But foreign merchants still could not leave Canton. Elliot ordered the British merchants to yield to Lin's demand because of duress and to prove the Chinese authorities responsible for depriving British subjects by force of property, life, and freedom. Thus he sought to arouse his government to take military action against China.

Lin Tse-hsü had achieved his first objective by destroying the extant supply of the pernicious import. However his second problem, that of eliminating its sources, was still unsolved. The bonds, which he demanded that all merchants sign, were adamantly rejected by Elliot. Elliot feared that whenever opium was discovered, it would be confiscated and the smuggler executed without formal judicial procedure. Since such coercion could not be tolerated from the viewpoint of English law, he resolutely forbade English merchants to sign such a document. After the complete delivery of opium and the raising of the siege of the factories,

Elliot immediately ordered the whole body of English merchants to retire from Canton. Thereafter, only several dozen American merchants lived in the Canton factories.

After Lin Tse-hsü had forced the foreign merchants to deliver up their opium, he made it clear that if only the merchants signed the bonds, they would be permitted to do business as before. In spite of Elliot's objections, some British merchants were willing to obey the command. For a long time Elliot wished to take military action, but he had not yet received definite instructions to do so from the British government. Only two or three warships with a small military force were at his disposal, and the British government did not invest him with much authority. He was therefore not in a position to make an immediate break with China.

When Elliot retired from Canton to Macao, he planned to use Macao as his provisional headquarters to handle the problems of the British merchants. He asked the imperial commissioner Lin to send an official to Macao for a conference on the problems existing between China and England and to give permission to English merchants to unload commodities at Macao. Without hesitation Lin consented to send a subprefect to the Macao conference; but he denied the second request because he was afraid that the English merchant ships might use Macao as a storehouse for opium. He preferred that all ships come to the river and report for examination at Whampoa, where commodities were to be unloaded. When the Chinese official arrived at Macao, Elliot ignored him. Elliot felt that since the request to unload goods at Macao was not complied with there was nothing worth discussing at a conference. Then on July 7 a critical incident occurred: Lin Wei-hsi, a villager who lived near Hong Kong, was beaten to death by English sailors quarreling over a wine order.

Because Elliot knew that the death was brought about by English sailors, he organized a navy court martial and acted as the chief judge. During the court martial the principal murderer was not examined, but the other five sailors voluntarily pleaded guilty. Three of them were sentenced to pay a fine of twenty pounds and to serve six months' imprisonment; two of them were sentenced to pay a fine of fifty pounds and to serve three months' imprisonment. Imprisonment was to be in a jail in England. When Elliot organized the court martial, he notified the Chinese authorities to send high officials to be inspectors and guaranteed that they would be treated with due courtesy. Chinese authorities maintained that since the murder was committed in Chinese territory where English jurisdiction was not recognized, the murderers should be surrendered and examined by a Chinese court. Elliot put off the request under the pretext of being unable to determine the chief murderer.

After more than a month, no decision was reached. Accordingly, Lin Tse-hsü, following the precedent of boycotting British trade established in the Chia-ch'ing period, forbade the supply of fuel or food to Englishmen and banned the British from Macao. Lin's memorial to the throne stated that he had ordered Elliot to hand over the murderer to be examined according to usual procedure, but that Elliot had delayed for about two months, rejecting letters and instructions sent by Chinese authorities. Lin continues: "We reverently found that in 1807 when the chief of British soldiers and others violated our law at Macao, an imperial decree ordered the stoppage of their supply of provisions. We should follow the precedent of 1807 in cutting off supplies completely from the British barbarians and also removing their compradors and servants." During the ten days from August 17 to 27, Elliot and fifty-seven British families in Macao moved to adjacent territory.

The magistrate of Siangshan District was subsequently ordered to issue a notice to the effect that (1) ships which carried no opium would be permitted to enter the river, report to the customs office for examination of their goods, and open their cabins for trade, but ships which had no reason to enter the river should sail away at once and not be permitted to dally around the mouth of the river; (2) the culprit who caused the death of Lin Wei-hsi should be ostracized and those who were protecting him should receive the same treatment. After this public notice, the English restricted themselves to their ships, sailing about the islands near Hong Kong. Elliot filed a protest with the Chinese authorities at Kowloon and also ordered several armed ships to open fire on Chinese naval vessels in order to demonstrate their power. He intended to blockade the Pearl River, but because his military force was too small, he was unable to put the blockade into effect.

At this time some British merchants who had been unbearably oppressed by the Chinese government voluntarily signed the required bonds and entered the river to resume trade. Elliot did not approve of such individual action, but he could not stop it. Lin Tse-hsü began to think that, by and large, the British were yielding to his terms. But there were still a large number of English merchants unwilling to sign the pledges. Lin believed that their ships must be either directly controlled by Elliot or loaded with opium which was to be smuggled into China. He ordered his "naval" force and the forts along the Pearl River to keep a close watch on these ships. He also urged Elliot to turn over the murderer to China.

At the beginning of November, Elliot requested Captain Smith, commander of a newly arrived fleet, to lead several ships to Chuenpi [*ch'uan-pi*, the "nostrils" of the river] in order that the Chinese authorities might be intimidated. The Chinese admiral, Kuan T'ien-p'ei, upon seeing the approach of British warships, prepared for action. On November 3, 1839, the British fleet opened fire, and Kuan T'ien-p'ei responded to the attack. A gun duel ensued, resulting in the sinking of three Chinese gunboats. Lin Tse-hsü reported to the emperor the circumstances of the sea battle at Chuenpi as well as the events which during the last seven months had been leading to belligerency. At the beginning of January 1840 an imperial decree formally declared the stoppage of trade with England; military action followed.

THE PROGRESS AND RESULTS OF THE WAR

The battle at Chuenpi on November 3, 1839 and other preceding actions were all directed by Captain Charles Elliot, who acted according to the exigency of the circumstances. In England, because of the continued reports from Elliot and news of the recent fighting, people gradually became aroused. The government party charged that China had infringed upon the freedom of life and property of British subjects and had insulted the British race; it advocated war against China. The opposition party blamed its government for the opium traffic and held the government responsible for the Chuenpi incident; it objected to the use of force. However, various industrial and commercial elements in London desired to expand their markets and were in sympathy with the English merchants in China. They urged the government to take strong and prompt action. The forces which wanted war became stronger. Palmerston therefore approved Elliot's activities in China. In April 1840, after a debate in Parliament, a motion to wage war in China was passed by a narrow margin.

On the other side, Emperor Tao-kuang supported the actions taken by Lin Tse-hsü. In his endorsement to Lin's memorial he said, "I am not worrying about your prowess, but I warn you against timidity." And he added, "The barbarian chief intended to open hostilities. Since you have already given him a good lesson, what difficulty would there be in further demonstrating our military might?" Thereupon, Lin busily engaged in preparing for war. He worked on defensive measures to prevent the barbarian ships from intruding into the river again, even though there was no effective way to bar their entrance. The events from the first attack to the signing of the peace treaty at Nanking may be divided into three periods: (1) from 1840 to the first truce, (2) from the first to the second truce, and (3) from the resumption of the war to the Treaty of Nanking.

The War from 1840 to the Chuenpi Convention, January 1841

In early 1840 the English government appointed George Elliot, a cousin of Captain Charles Elliot, to be senior commissioner to China. A number of warships were sent, responsible to Sir J. G. Bremer as the commander of the marine forces, but George Elliot was commander in chief of both army and navy units of the British assigned to China. In June they reached the entrance of the Pearl River with 16 warships, 540 guns, 4 armed steamships, 28 army transports and supply ships, and 4000 well-equipped men to carry out the British government's order for a blockade of the Pearl River and of the harbors near Canton.

A public notice in Chinese, signed by Captain Charles Elliot, ran to the following effect: Chinese high commissioners Lin, Teng, and others had disobeyed the imperial decree, oppressed the British commercial superintendent and merchants, and beclouded the facts, in reporting to the Chinese emperor, by using deceitful words; therefore the king of Great Britain had especially commissioned high officials to China's seacoasts with the hope of reporting the real conditions to the Chinese emperor in order to seek peace and to promote commerce; if the inhabitants of all places were not hostile to the British troops and civilians, they would receive protection; if they brought food and other goods to supply the needs of the British forces, they would be well paid. Moreover, Elliot's notice went on, since Lin and Teng fabricated some reason to ask for an imperial order to stop trade with England, both Chinese and foreign merchants were suffering. The notice added that the generals and admirals of England could permit no Chinese to go in and out of Canton, but they had no objection to small boats coming to the anchorage of British ships to do business.

That the British intended to alienate Chinese merchants from their government and to encourage treachery by means of this notice is evident. In order also to make the Chinese court distrust Lin and Teng, it falsely charged them with disobeying imperial decrees and with deceiving the emperor. It also aimed at sowing dissension among the people.

Chinese records frequently boast that the careful defensive measures of Lin Tse-hsü left no weak spot for the British to attack and that for this reason the British gave up taking Kwangtung to advance northward. In reality it was a predetermined British plan not to attack Canton first. After placing Canton under blockade, the ships were to advance northward for the purpose of negotiating with the Peking government.

When George Elliot started his journey from England to China, Lord Palmerston gave him instructions and three letters supplied with Chinese translations which were addressed to Chinese high officials. One of the letters was to be sent to the authorities at Canton. Should this mission not be achieved, George Elliot was to go northward so that he might present the second letter to the officials stationed near the entrance of the Yangtze River. If he was still unsuccessful, he was to proceed farther north in order to present the third letter to the senior officials at Tientsin.

As soon as George Elliot reached Canton, he realized that Lin Tse-hsü was in an aggressive mood. He therefore adopted the policy of blockading Canton and proceeding to the north. [2]

George and Charles Elliot led a fleet northward from Canton on June 30. When they passed Amoy on July 2, they sent a fast boat ahead with a white flag to deliver the first letter to the Fukien authorities. The Amoy garrison officers, since they did not know that a white flag indicated cessation of fighting, opened fire on the boat. The British fleet fired back to meet the challenge, and the first letter could not be delivered.

On July 4 the fleet reached Tinghai on Chusan Island, where they met no resistance. The British force occupied it the next day. On the tenth the fleet advanced to Ningpo, where a small boat with a white flag was dispatched for the purpose of delivering the second letter to the senior authorities of Chekiang Province. Luckily for the British, the messenger boat was not fired upon. The authorities received the letter, made a copy, and returned the original. The Chekiang officials did not report the full contents of the letter to the emperor. They did say, however, that British barbarians had forced Chinese sailors to bring a letter addressed to the throne, requesting permission for the British to have a larger volume of trade with China. The letter, it was stated, was instantly given back to the British, lest it be part of a malicious plot.

Elliot blockaded the ports from Ningpo to the mouth of the Yangtze River. The British proceeded to the mouth of the Pei-ho near Tientsin on July 28, and the third letter was presented to Ch'i-shan (or Kishen), governor-general of Chihli, who accepted it.

Ch'i-shan had an interview with Charles Elliot. He also reported the general content of the original letter of the British foreign secretary to the imperial court, saying that England "sent a letter to state her grievances." In order to conclude hostilities as soon as possible, Ch'i-shan wished to use peaceful means to persuade the Elliot cousins and the British fleet to return to Kwangtung.

After Captain Charles Elliot proclaimed the public notice which contained charges against Lin and Teng, as previously mentioned, the coastal provinces were invaded by the British fleet. The provincial authorities blamed Lin Tse-hsü for his activities by which, they stated, he had provoked war in order to receive credit from the emperor. Such criticism against Lin was widespread. In the central government the chief grand councilor, Mu-chang-a, also disapproved of Lin's actions and incited criticism from behind the scenes. Gradually Emperor Tao-kuang's confidence in Lin was shaken. He came to suspect that the English might have some justified grievances and that Lin must have actually fabricated information to confuse the court.

Meanwhile the British fleet demonstrated its power outside the mouth of the Pei-ho, causing extreme uneasiness at Peking. Since Ch'i-shan was governor-general of Chihli, he was responsible for the safety of the capital. If the British fleet intruded into the Pei-ho and menaced the security of the capital, he would receive severe punishment. Therefore his great concern was to make the English fleet move southward. For this reason the imperial court appointed another high official whose duty was to make an investigation in Canton. Captain Charles Elliot was requested to lead his fleet southward to Canton for negotiations, so that local conditions could be thoroughly probed before any decision was made. Attracted by the possibility of negotiations, Elliot on September 15 left the Pei-ho for Tinghai on Chusan Island.

After Tinghai was lost, I-li-pu was appointed imperial commissioner and ordered to go to Chekiang province where he could study conditions with the hope of retaking Tinghai. Ch'i-shan was also appointed imperial commissioner and given a mission which was identical to I-li-pu's. Both Lin Tse-hsü and Teng T'ing-chen, dismissed from their offices, were awaiting sentence by the ministry of punishments. Lin had been dismissed in September 1840 but was ordered to remain in Canton for consultation. Then he was commanded to render service in Chekiang. In May 1841 he was sentenced to be exiled to Ili.

Captain Elliot, after some preliminary truce discussions with I-li-pu on the battlefield near Chusan, went southward to Macao. Ch'i-shan arrived at Canton on December 16, and shortly after opened negotiations with Elliot. Ch'i-shan thought that the primary desire of the English was trade and believed that as soon as trade relations were restored, everything could be peacefully settled. In Tientsin he used every means to persuade Elliot to leave northern China.

When Ch'i-shan came to Canton, he still wished to use peaceful methods to conclude the matter. He adopted a very conciliatory manner toward Elliot, in direct contrast to Lin Tse-hsü's policy of resistance. However, he refused Elliot's demand to cede Hong Kong to England, on the grounds that it would not be sanctioned by the emperor. After realizing that Ch'i-shan was unwilling to yield, Elliot attacked the forts at Chuenpi on January 7, 1841, and was on the point of taking Humen.

Ch'i-shan, frightened, signed the Chuenpi Convention with Elliot on January 20. The terms of this convention called for the Chinese:

1. To cede the entire island and harbor of Hong Kong to the British crown. (Regular customs duties were still to be paid to the Chinese government as if the trade were conducted at Whampoa.)
2. To pay as an indemnity six million dollars* to the English government, one million payable at once and the rest by installments before the end of 1846.
3. To provide direct official intercourse on equal terms between the two nations.
4. To reopen the port of Canton for trade before February 1.

The text of this convention presented to the throne by Ch'i-shan, some sections sent in before and some after the affixing of his signature, was different from that proclaimed by the English. According to Ch'i-shan's memorials, the first article granted the English permission to reside in a place called Hong Kong, with the provision that this residence might be granted to them on a permanent basis. It also stated that the British would never cause trouble, nor go to other provinces for trade. The second article was not reported. The third article was summarized ambiguously.[3]

After signing this convention, Elliot simultaneously returned to China the two forts near Humen and Tinghai on Chusan Island. Ch'i-shan hoped that the restitution of these places would alleviate the wrath of the emperor. In Canton Ch'i-shan announced that Hong Kong was under the control of the British, who had begun to administer the island shortly after the signing of the convention.

From the First to the Second Truce

The Chuenpi Convention, or the first truce, negotiated by Elliot and

---

* "Dollars" (or $) in this book refers to Chinese silver dollars.

Ch'i-shan, was repudiated by both the British and the Chinese governments. The British government criticized Elliot for not obeying its instructions. The government considered the indemnity too small and objected that the cession of Hong Kong should be contingent upon the payment of duties. It could not, as yet, be considered an English colony. Charles Elliot was recalled and Sir Henry Pottinger was appointed sole plenipotentiary.

The Chinese also objected to the convention, explaining that although Ch'i-shan was an imperial commissioner and the emperor's proxy, his main duty was to "investigate" whether Lin Tse-hsü's handling of the English was proper or not, as well as to correct Lin's actions.[4] Thus, they asked how could he have had the right to cede territory and pay an indemnity to England?

Ch'i-shan overstepped his duties, no doubt, because he was badly pressed by the emperor to settle the affair and greatly awed by the military might of England. At first he thought that the demands might be put off by indecisiveness, but the British took positive action. At length he reported to the throne that England was previously known as being strong on the sea, and now, unexpectedly, her army and weapons were both found to be frightful. Thus he solicited the emperor on behalf of the English for a lodging place (Hong Kong) near the shore of the ocean. He also touched upon the fact that Hong Kong had already been given to England.

The cession of Hong Kong was clearly reported to the emperor by I-li-pu on February 26. The emperor, in thundering wrath, immediately appointed his nephew, I-shan, to be General for Suppressing the Barbarians [*Ching-ni chiang-chün*] and concurrently made him the imperial commissioner. Lung-wen and Yang Fang were made assistant commissioners. A large force was sent to Canton to renew warfare. It was expected that this force could wipe out the British troops.

When Ch'i-shan received the news that troops had been sent to

Kwangtung, he was both embarrassed and horrified. Again he memorialized the throne saying, "England has now sent delegates to Chekiang and has promised to return to China both Tinghai and the forts near Hu-men, as well as the salt transportation ships. All have been received. Their war vessels have been entirely withdrawn to the open ocean. Your slave has inspected all conditions here and found the topography indefensible. We have neither good weapons, effective troops, nor high morale to depend upon. Thus it would be better for us to hold them under control by peaceful means."[5]

The endorsement of the emperor on the memorial read: "I absolutely cannot be a fool like you, happy to receive insults ... You even dare to disobey my instructions and to accept the requests set forth in barbarian letters ... Now you list several points to frighten me. I am not to be disheartened." Ch'i-shan was soon dismissed and escorted to Peking in chains. All his family properties were confiscated.

George Elliot, anticipating the advance of a large Chinese force, at once took the initiative by moving troops toward Hu-men on February 26 and occupying all its adjacent forts. The garrison commander, Admiral Kuan T'ien-p'ei, died on the battlefield. The defenses prepared by Lin Tse-hsü in the Pearl River were destroyed. At this time a large force, said to be 10,000 strong, commanded by General Yang Fang arrived at Canton. But since all strategic points in the Pearl River had been occupied by the British forces, Yang Fang could do nothing. Foreign merchants advised him to ask for a truce. Although Elliot consented to the negotiations, he did not remove his combat equipment. On April 14 a large Chinese force under the command of I-shan and Lung-wen reached Canton. Elliot dispatched a message to inquire about the reason; the reply was evasive and war was resumed. Hostilities continued until May 25, when all forts and strategic points surrounding Canton were entirely lost to the British. A siege was laid on the city in which several hundred thousand Chinese soldiers were trapped. Following this incident, I-shan had to entreat the British for peace. However, his entreaty was denied; later on, through the earnest solicitations of the Hong merchants and the Canton prefect, the British stopped the warfare.

On May 27, 1841, the second truce was signed, which contained these terms: (1) Six million dollars were to be paid to Britain within one week for the use of the Crown of England; one million was to be paid before sunset of the twenty-seventh. (2) The Chinese government troops were to be removed within six days to a zone sixty miles outside of Canton. (3) The British force was to withdraw from Hu-men. (4) The cession of Hong Kong was to be decided by a later agreement. (5) Prisoners were to be exchanged.

Thus Canton was "ransomed" for the sum of six million dollars to save its people and their property from devastation. When the emperor received Yang Fang's memorial asking permission for a truce, he severely reprimanded Yang Fang for his cowardice in accepting a truce instead of fighting to the bitter end. When Ch'i-shan had reported the previous convention to the emperor, he had said that it was the British who had requested a peace. The emperor still naively believed that the truce was really solicited by the English.

The endorsement on I-shan's memorial read: "I understand your predicament and allow you to let the British resume trade with us, but you should not permit them to smuggle in any contraband opium."[6]

The emperor was still not aware of the seriousness of the problem involved in the cession of Hong Kong. For more than a month after the second truce, I-shan procrastinated about Hong Kong, with no courage to whisper a single word concerning the situation to the emperor, who was still living in a dream world and ordering British barbarians not to smuggle opium. In October and November the emperor repeatedly asked I-shan why he did not recover Hong Kong. The latter reported that the foreigners would not stay long at Hong Kong.

Though the English knew that the Chinese emperor had not yet sanctioned the cession of Hong Kong, they organized an administrative office for the island and proclaimed regulations concerning the harbor. Then on August 10 Sir Henry Pottinger, England's newly appointed minister plenipotentiary, arrived at Macao. He initiated activities which resulted in the last phase of the war.

The Resumption of the War

Palmerston had instructed Pottinger that he should not carry on any negotiations with high Chinese officials in Canton except for the retention of Hong Kong as a base. He was informed that he should advance to the north to reoccupy Tinghai, which had been returned, and to seize other sites of military importance along the Yangtze Valley, or that he should go northward to the mouth of the Pei-ho before opening negotiations. During the conference he was to demand an indemnity and to investigate the terms of indemnity in detail in order to obtain satisfactory results; he was not to cease bargaining until he fulfilled the aims of protection for the British merchants in China, expansion of trade ports, and cession of Hong Kong.

When Pottinger came to Macao, Kwangtung was quiet. Leaving a few warships to guard Hong Kong, he commanded the remaining fleet to attack Amoy on August 26 and left some troops to guard the newly occupied city. Proceeding farther north, he reached the vicinity of Tinghai on September 5 and occupied it on October 1. The British force then recaptured Chinhai on the tenth and Ningpo on the thirteenth. The imperial commissioner, Yü-ch'ien, committed suicide. Eastern Chekiang was entirely under the control of the British forces.

Upon hearing this bad news, Emperor Tao-kuang was furious. He appointed I-ch'ing the General to Augment Prestige [*Yang-wei chiang-chün*], designated to mobilize troops from Szechwan, Shensi, and other provinces. In addition several hundred thousand patriotic militiamen were recruited from South China for the purpose of recovering all lost territories.

In September the English government summoned army and navy reinforcements from India to strengthen its position in China. Pottinger, after capturing various cities in eastern Chekiang and while awaiting reinforcements, gave his troops a chance to rest. He returned to Hong Kong to manage commercial affairs.

In Kwangtung, after the second convention was signed between I-shan and Elliot, trade relations were restored at once, although the provinces along the seacoast east of Kwangtung were still living under wartime conditions. Although I-shan repaired the forts to prevent another assault from the British force, in reality the latter did not pay much attention to Canton.

After English reinforcements, which included 20 ships of war carrying 68 guns, 14 armed ships carrying 56 guns, 9 hospital ships and other vessels, plus more than 10,000 troops, reached the arena, the military campaign resumed at Ningpo. I-ch'ing's plan for recovering eastern Chekiang was a complete failure. The British force captured Chapu on May 18, 1842, Woosung on June 16, and Shanghai on June 19. From Shanghai they advanced up the Yangtze River and took Chinkiang on July 21. Chinkiang, about forty miles below Nanking and at the junction of the Grand Canal with the Yangtze, was a pivotal city in transportation of food and other essential materials from southern to northern China. Its loss was a great blow both to the government and to private merchants. From Chinkiang the enemy went on to storm Nanking, which by August 10 was under the menace of British guns. The opportunity for peace negotiation was then ripe.

The important officials during the Chinkiang campaign were Ch'i-ying [Kiying], who was the imperial commissioner and acting provincial commander in chief at Hangchow; I-li-pu [Ilipu], who was formerly imperial commissioner, but who later was deprived of this rank on account of the loss of Tinghai; Liu Yün-k'o, governor of Chekiang; and

Niu Chien, governor-general of Liang-kiang.[7] After the failure to recover eastern Chekiang, these men, losing courage to resist, worked hard for peace negotiations. But their gestures for peace were not trusted by the British, nor was it easy for them to secure approval from the emperor.

Their peace tenders followed the movement of the British force from Chapu to Woosung and Shanghai, but the British, heedless of their requests, moved westward. The Chinese officials had an even more difficult time expressing their desire for peace in memorials, because the stubborn emperor insisted upon war. After the loss of Woosung and Shanghai, Niu Chien requested that he be allowed to discontinue hostilities. The response from the emperor read: "I cannot help but resort to arms ... I think that you must have been persuaded by I-li-pu. Your request aggravates my anxiety and anger."

After the loss of Chinkiang, the emperor began to realize that his own military knowledge was untrustworthy; he began to defer to the judgment of Ch'i-ying and other generals at the front.

The Treaty of Nanking

Upon receiving a hint of the emperor's permission to discuss peace, Ch'i-ying and others asked the English to do so. Pottinger at first thought that they had no authority to negotiate peace and rejected their request. On August 14 when they produced evidence of plenipotentiary authority, Pottinger listed the minimum articles for peace negotiations, which they had to accept unconditionally if they did not want to be bombarded. Helplessly Ch'i-ying and others agreed to all the articles without examining them Carefully.[8] On August 29, 1842, Ch'i-ying, Niu Chien, and I-li-pu went aboard the British warship *Cornwallis* to put their signatures with Pottinger's on the Treaty of Nanking, which consisted of thirteen articles. The main points of the treaty were:

1. The Chinese government agreed to pay the English government $21,000,000, of which $12,000,000 was for indemnity,

$3,000,000 for the settlement of debts due to British merchants from Hong merchants (the Hong monopoly had been permanently abolished), and $6,000,000 as reparations for the destroyed opium.

2. The Chinese government permanently ceded the whole island of Hong Kong to England.
3. The Chinese government opened Canton, Foochow, Amoy, Ningpo, and Shanghai as the five trade ports where England could establish factories and where British merchants and their families could come and go freely.
4. A uniform and moderate tariff on imports and exports was to be imposed. The customs duties for British commodities were to be established according to a fixed rate, after the payment of which a commodity could be transported to any spot in the interior without further tax.
5. Official correspondence between the two nations was to be in the form used among equals.

This treaty was a humiliating document signed under the enemy's artillery. The British wrote the articles; the Chinese were only permitted to polish the translations and to reword some small items. They were not permitted to revise or alter the content, nor were there many negotiations except exchanges of acrimonious expressions. This marks the beginning of unequal treaties. When the Treaty of Nanking was signed, Chinese authorities were overwhelmed by apprehension and anxiety lest Nanking be bombarded. Consequently, they agreed to the treaty in great haste. The opium problem, which was considered by China to be the main cause of the war, was mentioned only briefly in the treaty in connection with reparations for the value of the opium destroyed. There was no provision against its import and use.

English grievances were all fully adjusted; Hong Kong was obtained and the rate of customs duties fixed by mutual agreement. Loss of territory and payment of an indemnity may be humiliations which a defeated nation should suffer, but the undue restriction of tariff autonomy was really a fatal blow to China. Strangely, among Chinese governmental authorities, there was not a single one who foresaw its harm at this time. Instead they most feared the adoption of an equal form for official dispatches between the two nations. In their opinion, this disparaged the dignity of the Celestial Court. They said of this innovation, "Heaven and earth are upside down." But since they could not resist the barbarians' gunfire, they tolerated this loss of celestial dignity for the time being.

THE SIGNIFICANCE OF THE OPIUM WAR

The war between China and England, caused superficially by the problem of opium prohibition, may actually be viewed as a conflict of Western and Eastern cultures. In spite of the fact that trade relations had existed between them for many years, the East and West had entirely different conceptions in regard to their nations, governments, and all forms of social life.

Different Conceptions of International Society

The conception of an equal international society is fundamentally a product of modern history. In Europe it gradually developed after the Treaty of Westphalia in 1648. China, on the other hand, in ancient times had formed the conception that the entire world should be under the control of one emperor. During the periods called the Spring and Autumn [722-482 B. C.] and the Warring States [481-221 B. C.], the numerous feudal lords were independent under conditions resembling those of modern European international societies. However, above all the feudal lords was the figurehead of the emperor of the Chou dynasty [ca. 1100-221 B. C.]. Mencius quoted Confucius as saying, "In the sky there is no more than one sun, and above the people there is no more than one emperor." After Ch'in Shih-huang-ti unified China [221 B. C.] the conception of having a large, self-sufficient empire controlled by one royal family was even more firmly implanted, and the conception has been maintained ever since.

The ideal empire was demarcated by a line which separated the Chinese from the barbarians. The five kinds of domain were explicitly defined in the chapter *Yü-kung* [Tribute of Yü] in the *Book of History*. Within the first five hundred li [a li is one-third of a mile] from the capital was the imperial domain. Next came the domain of the nobles; beyond that was the so-called peace-securing domain. Next came the domain of restraint. The remotest five hundred li constituted the wild domain. Boundary lines between Chinese and barbarians were gradually expanded so as not to be confined by the ideal radius of 2500 li described in the *Yü-kung*. This was the world-nation conception of the Chinese as well as their conception of international society; the tradition was handed down for millennia and was reinforced by the Ch'in and Han dynasties.

Because this conception was deeply rooted in the minds of the Chinese people, they regarded all special envoys sent by Western nations as tributebearers. They flatly rejected the suggestion that they exchange ministers as well as maintain diplomatic intercourse on an equal footing with other nations. In the long history of China, foreigners have seldom been regarded as equals. The marriage of the women of the Han dynasty to the barbarian Hsiung-nu, for example, and the treaty which made the Sung rulers and the Khitan "brothers" were taken as great humiliations. How could the Chinese be expected to lower their pride and dignity before people with blue eyes and red beards, or easily break down the old boundaries between themselves and barbarians? On the other hand, in Europe after the Treaty of Westphalia, even a tiny state enjoyed its status of equality in international society. Hence, how could England, which had vast overseas possessions, be willing to take insults from the Chinese government?

Different Conceptions of Economic Life

In Europe after the feudal system broke down, mercantilism became the core of economic life until the nineteenth century, when industrial capitalism was developed and international trade became the ruling concept. Since China was blessed with a large territory and adequate natural resources, her people were accustomed to their own products, "not esteeming strange objects" and "not considering goods coming from afar to be precious." They were prejudiced against businessmen and in favor of farmers. Since they regarded domestic industry and commerce as trifles, they naturally disliked international trade, which involved a dangerous breakdown of the boundary between Chinese and barbarians.

But the scope of the economic activities of mankind has a natural tendency toward expansion. Even in China, commerce between the barbarians and Chinese had been increasing since the T'ang dynasty [618-907]. In the eyes of the Chinese scholar-officials, such commerce was used as a means to keep the barbarians under control and not as a necessity for the economic life of the people. If the barbarians did not obey restrictions, but infringed upon political rights and cultural prestige, the national door would be closed by suspending the traffic and boycotting their goods. Trade relations were considered to be to the advantage of the barbarians, not to China; the object of boycotting was to harm the barbarians alone. Such conceptions can be found throughout Chinese diplomatic documents from the middle of the Ch'ing dynasty. For instance, the imperial instructions of Emperor Ch'ien-lung to King George III of England say:

> The Celestial Court has abundant natural resources. It has everything and fundamentally does not rely on any foreign goods to make up deficiencies. Only because the production of tea, porcelain, and silk by the Celestial Kingdom is indispensable to European

nations and your nation, I, therefore, extend my grace and consideration to allow you to open commercial agencies at Macao so as to enable you to secure a source of supply for your daily needs, and also to let you make some profit. [9]

Again let us examine Emperor Tao-kuang's communication drafted by Lin Tse-hsü to Queen Victoria, in which he says:

> Take tea and rhubarb, for example: the foreign countries cannot get along for a single day without them. If China cuts off these benefits with no sympathy for those who are to suffer, then what can the barbarians rely upon to keep themselves alive? Moreover, the woolen, camlets, and longells [i. e., textiles] of foreign countries cannot be woven unless they obtain Chinese silk. If China again cuts off this beneficial export, what profit can the barbarians expect to make? ... On the other hand, articles coming from the outside to China can only be used as toys. We can accept them or get along without them. Since they are not needed by China, what difficulty would there be if we closed the frontier and stopped the trade?[10]

The Chinese usually thought of foreign merchants as wily barbarians and regarded their own people who secretly went abroad to do business in foreign countries as treacherous men who should be heavily punished.

Westerners considered international trade to be a matter beneficial to all parties concerned. They could not understand why Chinese authorities made so many restrictions to impede the development of the national economic life of their subjects.

Different Legal Conceptions

The direct causes of the Opium War were the seizure of foreign factories, the demand that foreign merchants sign a bond pledging not to sell opium, and the suspension of the supply of provisions to the British after the murder of Lin Wei-hsi. To the English there was a distinction between laws and orders. In their view, a government could not issue an order at random creating a new crime. The responsibility for a given action could be borne only by the person in question, and not by other persons related in some way to him. Facts which formed a legal charge had, furthermore, to be supported by sufficient evidence. In addition, before it had been clearly established that a person had violated a law, he could not be stripped of personal liberty nor could his life be endangered.

Hence the British thought that the actions of Lin Tse-hsü were violent and unlawful. They considered that the bond which stated that if opium were smuggled, "the goods would be entirely confiscated by the government and the person responsible immediately executed" would make it possible to incriminate and execute a man without sufficient evidence. The seizing of factories and the cutting off of provisions were actions which, in the eyes of the Englishmen, were taken before the facts of responsibility had been definitely established. They held that these actions, carelessly placing the blame on all foreigners, deprived them of personal freedom and endangered their lives without due cause.

In contrast, under the autocratic government of the Chinese empire, the emperor's words were sacred; an imperial decree or instruction could become a new law. Officials with the seal of imperial commissioners [*chin-ch'ai ta-ch'en*] could "perform duties according to the exigency of the circumstances [*p'ien-i hsing-shih*]." In other words, the emperor was almost the only source of law. A new crime could be defined at any time either by his imperial decree or by his overt sanction or silent consent.

As to the problem of responsibility before the law, although there was a proverb, "A person who violates the law should be faced by himself alone," joint liability [*lien-tso*] was a customary legal practice to which there was no limit. Sometimes one person was involved; sometimes even the members of an entire clan were annihilated if the culprit could not be arrested. The leader of a community was held responsible for the actions of its members, The imperial decree condemned opium as an illicit traffic and Lin Tse-hsü as the imperial commissioner could perform his duty in any way he saw fit and effective, including the required signing of a bond. To lay siege to the foreign factories was to apply the principle of group responsibility "in order to eradicate the contraband commodity." In the opinion of the Chinese, since Elliot was the barbarian chief of England, he could bear group responsibility.

Once when the Hong merchants who had borrowed money from foreigners were unable to pay their debts, the Chinese government had paid them from the official treasury. If Chinese authorities were responsible for the conduct of their merchants in China, why shouldn't the British barbarian chiefs be responsible for the activities of their subjects in China? In accord with this reasoning, Elliot was confined in the factories and was not permitted to leave until the British merchants surrendered their opium to the Chinese government. Since Lin Wei-hsi had been beaten to death by sailors from a British ship, the barbarian chief was blamed for not handing over the murderer to the Chinese authorities and for his failure to control the actions of his subordinates. To follow the precedent of 1808 by severing the supply of provisions to foreigners was, according to the reasoning of Chinese scholar-officials, a legitimate act.

These various concepts produced almost continuous conflicts until at last there was no alternative but war. The resultant Treaty of Nanking was a great shame and disgrace to China. Nevertheless, the roots of conflicts and conceptual differences still existed. At this time the Chinese still maintained that China was the source of civilization for the whole world, that the Western barbarians had no culture worth regarding, and that the power of Western guns was not a consequence of Western science. They took the recent defeat by the barbarians as merely an accident such as China had weathered many times in her long history. On the other hand, the Westerners recognized the inadequacies in this ancient Oriental nation. They assumed the knowledge and the techniques of Oriental peoples to be not much superior to those of African Negroes or South Pacific islanders. "Oriental civilization" seemed to them merely an empty phrase. Aware of China's weaknesses, they extended their aggression step by step. China could no longer slumber. The Taiping Rebellion burst out; then the Anglo-French allies invaded Peking; and the imperial court was subjected to further rounds of insults.

CHAPTER TWO
THE TAIPING REBELLION

The Taiping Rebellion broke out in 1850,[1] eight years after the Opium War. In the following year the name Heavenly Kingdom of Great Peace [*T'ai-p'ing t'ien-kuo*] was adopted by the Taipings as the title of their state. In 1853 Nanking was captured and used as the capital of this kingdom. The Heavenly Kingdom of Great Peace was finally destroyed by the imperial armies in 1864 after fourteen years of warfare. These long years of hostilities served as a trial period for the later struggle between the Chinese and the Manchus.

Although the Chinese Taiping Rebellion against the Manchu dynasty failed, the failure was brought about by Chinese loyalists, whose own position and power under the foreign Manchu regime had been greatly enhanced. During the period of the rebellion, Western powers penetrated more deeply into China than before and the Chinese thereafter had to shoulder heavier political responsibilities. The Taiping uprising was the largest internal upheaval of the nineteenth century and the forerunner of subsequent revolutions.

BACKGROUND OF THE TAIPING REBELLION

Although the Taiping Rebellion actually broke out in 1850, an analysis of its background should begin with a study of conditions which before the Opium War were already serving as a prelude to the revolution.

The Economic Background

Chinese history has had a kind of cyclic development, "a period of peace and a period of war" [*i-chih i-luan*]. After each two or three hundred years, similar events reoccurred. Since the Ch'in and Han dynasties these cyclic recurrences are clearly indicated. Though the causes were manifold, the most significant cause was China's dependence on an economy which was almost entirely agricultural. The welfare of her people depended on the productive power of the soil. When the population surpassed figures which this agricultural economy could support, large numbers of people lacked employment and were short of food and, led by a few courageous individuals, started a rebellion. Such rebellions resulted chiefly in a reduction of population; the land could once more maintain those who lived on it and another interval of peace and order ensued.

Population figures recorded during the Ch'ing dynasty[2] show an almost uninterrupted rise in population from the second half of the seventeenth century to the decade before the outbreak of the Taiping Rebellion [as shown in the accompanying table].

POPULATION OF CHINA, 1661–1841

Year	*Population*	*Year*	*Population*
1661	21,068,609	1792	307,467,279
1711	24,621,324	1801	297,501,548
1741	143,411,559	1821	355,540,258
1749	177,495,039	1841	413,457,311
1762	200,472,461		

In the span of a hundred years from 1741 to 1841 the population increased nearly three times. The temporary decrease between 1792 and 1801 shows the effects of the rebellion led by the White Lotus Society.

That the increase in arable land did not keep pace with the tremendous general increase in population can be seen by taking available recorded figures for *ch'ing* [*a ch'ing* =100 *mou* = 15.13 acres] of arable land from 1661 through the year 1833.

ARABLE LAND IN CHINA, 1661–1833

Year	*Ch'ing*
1661	5,265,028

1685	6,070,430
1724	6,837,914
1766	7,414,495
1812	7,915,251
1833	7,375,129

That in 1833 the amount of arable land [see the table] was 540,000 *ch'ing* smaller than in 1812 further emphasizes the fact that the proportion of farming land to people dependent on the land was inadequate. Whenever an area of arable land could no longer support an increasing family and there was no other way to make a living, farmers had to incur debts and sell land to affluent merchants and other rich men. Arable lands concentrated in the hands of a small number of landlords created sharp distinctions between the rich and the poor. In industrially developed nations landless laborers were absorbed by large factories but, before the middle of the nineteenth century, China possessed no such means to accommodate the poverty-stricken and unemployed.

Another factor aggravated the poverty of small farmers. The ever-increasing import of opium caused a great outflow of silver, a devaluation of copper coins, and an inflation of other commodities. Since the land tax was fixed on the basis of silver, the peasants, commuting their hard-earned coins into silver dollars, were actually paying higher taxes. Their lives became more difficult.

Worse still, near the end of the Tao-kuang period [1821-1850] floods and droughts occurred almost every year in many of the provinces along the valleys of the Yellow River and the Yangtze. All these combined events accelerated the miseries of the common people.

The Political Background

Political conditions under the reign of Tao-kuang, besides being corrupt, showed a further ruinous tendency—described by Tseng Kuo-fan as a tendency "to gloss over, to make up, and to steal days of ease." This habit was also discussed by Lung Ch'i-jui, a scholar of Kwangsi, who said that the reason the magistrates could not suppress secret societies was not that they were incapable or powerless, but that the governor-general and governor did not like to have magistrates take any responsibility for punishing lawbreakers. Instead, the high provincial authorities were happy to tolerate and to gloss over infringements of law so that there might appear to be no disturbances in the area under their jurisdiction. If no disclosures were made during their tenure of office, they saved themselves, even though their successors might incur the blame for the existence of secret societies. If they reported the actual situation to the court, they might also be rebuked by the chief minister.

The chief minister said that flood, drought, and bandits should not be reported to the throne because such news would cause His Majesty anxiety; the appropriation of revenue was predetermined and could not be shifted for such trifling matters as famine and bandits. Therefore officials kept silent with regard to national policy. The members of secret societies at Chint'ien, Kwangsi, began to be restless, in 1834. The governor, who was enjoying himself in making mountain excursions, composing poems, and drinking wine, did nothing about the situation. His successors imitated him in pursuing a nonactive policy.

Under the reign of Tao-kuang, two chief ministers were employed. One Was Ts'ao Chen-yung, who in 1834 at the age of eighty was still the dean of court officials. During his incumbency the central government became chiefly an agency for issuing stereotyped decrees, for glossing over errors, and for putting aside reforms. Ts'ao tried to keep officials silent and to discourage or frighten them by inflicting severe punishment upon any of them who made a suggestion to the throne.

The other chief minister was Mu-chang-a, who was even more addlebrained and incompetent than Ts'ao. It was he who undermined Lin

Tse-hsü's relations with the emperor. At this time a high official who spoke about government affairs was considered vulgar. The governors of Kwangsi, one after another, did not like to be bothered by administrative work, Governor Cheng Tsu-ch'en, for instance, was a devotee of Buddhism, praying to Buddha every day to dispel catastrophes. It was during this term that the Taiping Rebellion broke out in Kwangsi. Such was the immediate political background—general lethargy and irresponsibility—which paved the way for the Taipings' rapid development.

The Racial Background

Ever since the establishment of Manchu rule, those loyal to the Ming dynasty had been spreading the slogan "Rebel against the Ch'ing and restore the Ming." Even though strong pressure and clever means were employed by emperors K'ang-hsi, Yung-cheng, and Ch'ien-lung to nip the buds of nationalism, its seeds could not be eradicated. In 1786 Lin Shuangwen of the Heaven and Earth Society [*T'ien-ti-hui*] started a year-long revolt in Taiwan against the government. Although Lin failed, another uprising broke out in 1793 under the leadership of Liu Chih-hsieh, who was a member of the White Lotus Society. Liu tried to declare a small child emperor, claiming that he was a descendant of the imperial Chu family of the Ming dynasty. Liu failed also, but the members of the White Lotus Society were dispersed to Hupeh, Szechwan, Shensi, and the North China Plain. There they subsequently incited widespread outbreaks which developed into the famous rebellion of the White Lotus Society in the years of 1796-1804. Although the rebellion was suppressed, the idea "Rebel against the Ch'ing and restore the Ming" covertly persisted in the minds of the masses.

Two decades before the Opium War, riots occurred in many parts of the country. For example, in 1822 a secret-society bandit, Smallpox Chu, caused trouble in Hsin-ts'ai, Honan. In 1826 another disturbance was created in Taiwan. In 1831 the members of the Triads and the Yao tribe raised a great storm in Hunan, known as the rebellion of Chao Chin-lung. A secret society started an uprising in 1835 in the district of Ch'ao-ch'eng, Shansi, where the magistrate and all his family were killed.

These troublemaking organizations were called "The Sect" [*Chiao or Chiao-tang*] in North China, and "The Society" [*Hui or Hui-tang*] in South China. The *Chiao-tang* was headed by the White Lotus Society [*Pai-lien-chiao*], whose branches consisted of the *Pai-yang pa-kua* [Eight Diagrams], *Hung-yang*, and others. The *Hui-tang* was under the general leadership of the Heaven and Earth Society, whose branches included the Triads [*San-ho* or *San-tien*] and others. All these societies copied old religious ceremonies and were united under the slogan "Rebel against the Ch'ing, restore the Ming."

The court at Peking repeatedly ordered provincial authorities to arrest these secret-society bandits. A strict law was enacted in 1832 to the effect that "the leaders of the *Chiao* bandits will not be pardoned when there is a general amnesty." However, old seeds of nationalism could not be destroyed. Moreover, Western religion was spreading new seeds of nationalism in China. And during the Opium War there were several incidents which had direct bearing on the Taiping Rebellion.

(1) The corrupt troops gave much trouble to the local people. When I-shan was sent to Kwangtung, he transferred to the front approximately 30,000 men from Honan, Kiangsi, Hunan, Kweichow, Kwangsi, and other provinces. These soldiers, though useless in fighting against the foreigners, very efficiently disturbed the areas through which they passed or at which they were stationed. According to the *Yang-ch'eng fih-pao*, a daily news report published at Canton, these troops after their mobilization robbed along the way and, when they reached Kwangtung, created riots and disturbances. They accused Chinese refugees of being

traitors in order to take away their belongings. They fought each other even on the drill ground. The same source adds that Hunan soldiers broke into the thirteen factories and carried off valuable property. They also went to the countryside in groups, staying there for days without returning to the barracks.

(2) The militia and "patriotic volunteers" [*i-yung*] caused trouble. In Kwangtung after the murder of Lin Wei-hsi by a British sailor, Lin Tse-hsü issued public notices to all places along the coast ordering the people to purchase weapons and to train a militia for self-protection. After the opening of hostilities, since the standing army could not resist the enemy, it was necessary to recruit some 20,000 or 30,000 militiamen. After the war the militia and the "patriotic volunteers" were disbanded simultaneously; their weapons, dispersed among the people, served as a temptation and aid to rebellion.

(3) A growing national awareness goaded the people to revolt. During the war sentiment was diverted temporarily from hating the Manchu to "driving out the foreign devils." Characteristically, an anti-British corps was formed with its headquarters at the village of San-yüan-li, near Canton. There some 10,000 people were said to have been mustered in a short time. But the incompetence and lawlessness of the Ch'ing troops caused the people's sentiments to shift again from hating "the foreign devils" to despising the Manchus. When the British laid siege to Canton, their force was composed of no more than 2000 men, while the Chinese troops within the city walls were no fewer than 20,000. Even so, the defenders did not dare to go out from the walls to challenge the enemy. Instead, they accepted a surrender treaty and asked the people for a huge amount of money to pay a ransom for Canton. The people were angry at soldiers who not only failed to fight against the enemy but even hindered the action of the anti-British corps of San-yüan-li. A Chekiang scholar, Ch'ien Chiang, was then the intellectual leader of the anti-British

corps. This same Ch'ien Chiang later on tried to advise the Taiping leader, Hung Hsiu-ch'füan, to take Peking.

Disorders After the Opium War

In general, after the Opium War the prestige of the Manchu government was destroyed and the invitation to rebellion was ever-present. From 1841 to 1850 there was not a single year free from local uprisings. A glance over the memorials in the *Tung-hua-lu* will reveal many examples.

A native of Ch'ung-yang, Hupeh, established a military government with the aid of followers in 1841, proclaimed himself king, and attacked the two neighboring districts in the same province. He was not defeated until the next year.

The people of Wu-kiang, Hunan, tried to stop the transportation of rice from their province. They killed the local officer and occupied a mountain base in 1843. Though they attempted to start a major revolt, they were soon brought under control.

Hung Hsieh and others aroused about two thousand people who disturbed the peace in Taiwan in 1844. They were soon arrested. In the same year, two clans of Lei-yang in Hunan persuaded more than a thousand persons to reject the collection of taxes. They openly attacked the city of Lei-yang. This rebellion lasted for more than a month before it was suppressed.

The Nien-fei in Anhwei, Honan, and Shantung had assembled a huge multitude to fight against the government troops ever since the 1840's. Later on they overran several provinces in northern China. They were not wiped out until 1868.

In regard to Kwangtung, where local bandits were also active in many districts, an imperial instruction to the Grand Council reads:

> It has been reported that the bandits in the area around Canton make a living from pillage. They continue to form societies and gather several hundred thousand members .... The arrest of members of the Sleeping Dragon, the Triads, and other societies last year was incomplete. Bandits have again appeared in Hsin-an and other districts, who persuaded the people to join their-societies .... They do everything without any restriction .... The local military and civil officials are unwilling to arrest them. [3]

On account of the prevalence of bandits in Kwangtung, an imperial decree ordered that the population be vigilantly checked and that the practice of group responsibility be enforced.

In 1847 a member of the Yao tribe, Lei Tsai-hao, in Hsing-ning, Hunan, fostered an insurrection which was silenced after long warfare only by the combined forces of the two provinces of Hunan and Kwangsi. Because the governor of Hunan was incompetent, the governor-general of Hunan and Hupeh was ordered by the emperor in 1850 to lead troops to suppress the bandits in cooperation with the Kwangsi forces.

These are but a few examples of uprisings mentioned in imperial decrees and official compilations. Actually disturbances existed in nearly all provinces, but especially in Kwangtung, Kwangsi, and the southern part of Hunan. Along the boundary lines of these three provinces, the bandits were described as being "numerous as hairs." The bandit chiefs were also leaders of secret societies and thus had hundreds of thousands of followers.

The leaders in Kwangtung, such as Ta Li-yü [Great Carp] and Ta-t'ou Yang [Big-headed Ram], claimed to have 8000 staunch supporters who were in communication with the "bandits" in Kwangsi. The chiefs in Hunan, though less famous than others, also had a large number of followers. Shortly after the beginning of the Taiping Rebellion, Tseng

Kuo-fan memorialized the throne, saying that after the Kwangsi bandits entered Hunan, a majority of the local secret-society members joined them.

Tseng Kuo-fan went on to say that such secret societies as the Red and Black, the Coins, and the Incense-burning Society were trying to enlarge their forces in mountainous areas in the southeast and southwest of the province. He reported that the provincial officials understood thoroughly that these forces were formidable, yet they did not want to take the initiative to suppress the societies during their tenure of office. The officials were trying their best to "gloss over, to make up," and "to steal days of ease."[4] The Kwangsi governor, Cheng Tsu-ch'en, was a prime example of a man who took it easy day after day. It was in his province that the Taiping Rebellion gathered force like a mountain torrent.

THE HEAVENLY KINGDOM OF GREAT PEACE

During the period of the Taiping Rebellion, the leader of the revolutionary faction was Hung Hsiu-ch'üan and the leader on the government side was Tseng Kuo-fan. Hung's powerful collaborator was Yang Hsiu-ch'ing. Hence Hung and Yang were usually mentioned together and the Taiping Rebellion has often been referred to as the Hung-Yang Rebellion. Such rebels were also called "hair bandits" or "long-hair bandits" because they kept their hair long in protest against the Manchu custom of forcing the Chinese people to shave their foreheads as a sign of loyalty.

Tseng Kuo-fan, on account of his contributions in suppressing the Taipings, was canonized by the Manchus as Wen-cheng [a literary and upright man]. After the fall of the Manchu dynasty many regarded Hung

Hsiu-ch'üan as the forerunner of modern revolution and hence he was no longer called a bandit. On the other hand, Tseng Kuo-fan was later condemned by many Chinese as a counterrevolutionist. In Chinese literature there is no permanent definition of a bandit or nonbandit. The connotation depends on time circumstance, and subjective point of view. The merits or demerits of Hung Hsiu-ch'üan and Tseng Kuo-fan should not be judged and decided by the success or failure of the two parties, nor should we be affected by emotions which color historical facts.

Hung Hsiu-ch'üan and Other Revolutionary Leaders

Hung Hsiu-ch'üan and other leaders have become famous figures in folklore and historical fiction, though they were described slanderously by their conquerors before 1911. Hung, a native of Hua-hsien, Kwangtung, was born on January 1, 1814. He went to Canton to take the civil-service examination in 1836, but failed. Walking in his disappointment through the streets, he met a Chinese Christian, Liang A-fa, who gave him a book, *Ch'üan-shih liang-yen* [*Good Words to Exalt the Age*], which consisted of translations or summaries of chapters of the Bible as well as a number of sermons on texts from the Scriptures. Hung merely glanced at it.

In 1837 Hung returned to Canton for the civil-service examination, which he again failed. Once more he returned home. He fell seriously ill for forty days and during his illness dreamed that he entered a big mansion—a veritable palace. There he saw a venerable old man with a golden beard and a black robe who ordered him to go to the world below to stamp out demons and to save all mankind, all his brothers and sisters. In his dream he also saw a tall scholar who claimed to be his elder brother. He too urged destruction of demons, and he promised to assist Hung in destroying them.

Six years later, in 1843, Hung by chance read *Good Words to Exalt the Age*, which he had received previously. He suddenly recalled his dream and became aware that it was significant: the old man in the black robe and the tall scholar must be God and Jesus Christ, both of whom wished to stamp out demons and to save all brothers and sisters; that is, they wished him to believe in God and to save the world and its people. Taking the sermons perhaps as Divine Books expressing the will of Heaven, thereafter Hung enthusiastically believed in Christianity and advised others to believe in it.

In 1844 Hung went with his closest schoolmate, Feng Yün-shan, to Tzu-chin-shan [Thistlemount] in the district of Kweiping, Kwangsi. There they founded a Society of God-Worshippers. Later on, Hung heard that in Hong Kong there was a famous American missionary, Issachar J. Roberts. Hung went to him in 1847 to take lessons in Christian doctrine for two months. He left Roberts without being baptized and went to Kwangsi again to meet Feng Yün-shan. Upon reaching Kwangsi he found that there were nearly 2000 members of the Society of God-Worshippers. Hung was elected their leader, and the membership kept increasing daily.

The confession of a Taiping leader, Li Hsiu-ch'eng, provides further information concerning the life histories of Hung and other early leaders.

> The Heavenly King, Hung Hsiu-ch'üan, had two brothers. The eldest was named Jen-hua, and the second, Jen-t'a; both were born to his father's first wife, while the Heavenly King was born to his second wife: Both Jen-hua and Jen-t'a were farmers; Hsiu-ch'üan alone received education. The Southern King, Feng Yün-shan, was a schoolmate of the Heavenly King, and they were very close friends. In 1837 the Heavenly King was so seriously ill that he was unconscious for seven days. After awakening he suddenly uttered strange words advising people to believe in God, saying that he who believed in God could avoid misfortune, and those who did not

believe in God would be eaten by snails and tigers.

For the purpose of spreading Christianity he traveled hundreds of *li* to Kwangsi. His converts also went about doing evangelistic work. The Heavenly King frequently hid himself in mountainous areas, where after a few years he had gained many converts, most of them poor peasants. The majority of Confucian scholars did not believe in Christianity, while more than half of the farm people and povertystricken families believed in the religion.

Those who participated in the secret plot for starting a revolution included only six persons: Yang Hsiu-ch'ing, Hsiao Ch'ao-kuei, Feng Yün-shan, Wei Ch'ang-hui, Shih Ta-k'ai, and Ch'in Jih-ch'ang. All other followers were ignorant of the plot, being mostly concerned with their own livelihood.

Yang Hsiu-ch'ing, a native of Kweiping, Kwangsi, made a living by tilling hill land and making charcoal. He was fundamentally ignorant of military matters, but after he came to believe in God, he was deeply trusted by the Heavenly King, who let him take charge of all important affairs. Yang's orders were very stern; rewards and punishments were justly executed. Hsaio Ch'ao-kuei, a farmer of Wu-hsüan, Kwangsi, married the sister of the Heavenly King. He was very courageous and usually fought with the vanguard. Feng Yün-shan studied at home and was very capable. Among the six leaders who schemed to found a dynasty, it was Feng who initiated the idea and made all other plans. Wei Ch'ang-hui, a smart village leader of Chin-t'ien in Kweiping, was a man who when at home had frequented the office of the local city government. Shih Ta-k'ai, also a native of Kweiping, was a scholar from a rich family and was competent in both literary and military affairs. Ch'in Jih-ch'ang, another native of Kweiping, was a laborer on odd jobs; he had no particular ability, but since he was loyal, courageous, and honest, he gained the confidence of the Heavenly King.[5]

The Immediate Cause of the Rising

Before 1850 while Hung Hsiu-ch'üan and his followers propagated new religious tenets among the people of Kweiping, Wu-hsüan, and other districts, the bandits in Kwangsi and members of secret societies were also active; but Hung himself did not participate in their activities. In districts where Hung taught his religious principles, there existed a distinction between guest settlers and local people; the former were mostly migrants from Kwangtung, which was Hung's home. Those who joined Hung's church were largely guest settlers.

The local people and the guest settlers had frequent conflicts. At this time, when bandits were numerous, villagers had to train a militia for selfprotection. The power of the militia was wielded by the local people, who usually found some pretense to involve the guest settlers in trouble. The latter, for self-protection and in order to withstand the militia, also organized a Society for Protecting Good People and Attacking Bandits [*Paoliang kung-fei hui*], which was controlled by the leaders of the God Worshippers.

The local gentry was stirred to anxiety by this joint force, which was continually fomenting rebellion. They repeatedly demanded that the local governments arrest the leaders of the God-Worshippers. Both Hung Hsiu-ch'üan and Feng Yün-shan were arrested and imprisoned, but were set free as a result of a great demand for their release made by the society members. In Li Hsiu-ch'eng's confession he also says,

> In 1847 or 1848 bandits harassed cities and towns everywhere in Kwangsi. The militia and the God-Worshippers were separated. The God-Worshippers were organized into one group, the militia into

another. Each faction struggled against the other in order to spread its power, and this conflict resulted in the outbreak of the revolution.[6]

In 1850 a junior official sent a battalion of troops on a mission to arrest a notorious thief. On their way back they tried to coerce charcoal workers into giving them contributions. The workers, mostly members of the God-Worshippers Society, gathered many brethren to combat the soldiers. When the latter failed in their attempt to get a forced contribution, they withdrew, hurling threats as they retreated: "You God-Worshippers are rebellious bandits. A great force of government troops is coming here soon. You will see then whether you have to give them money or not."

Upon receiving this information, Feng Yün-shan summoned the charcoal workers to Chin-t'ien village, where they were incited to revolt. This incident, which marked the beginning of the Taiping Rebellion, occurred in the later half of 1850.

The Founding of the Heavenly Kingdom of Great Peace

When Feng Yün-shan, Yang Hsiu-ch'ing, and others held a conference at Chin-t'ien, Hung Hsiu-ch'üan was hiding in a friend's house. After the decision to start military action had been made, Hung was welcomed to Chin-t'ien and hailed as their leader. Messengers were sent to all villages and districts to summon members of the God-Worshippers Society. The chiefs of a number of secret societies—Lin Feng-hsiang, and others—each led a large group of their party members to affiliate with the God-Worshippers; gradually a force of nearly 10,000 was accumulated.

On account of the number of bandits in Kwangsi, the Ch'ing government commissioned a provincial commander in chief, Hsiang Jung, to lead troops from Hunan to suppress the insurrection. Li Hsing-yüan was appointed imperial commissioner to wipe out the bandits.

In November the imperial troops were defeated in their assault on Chint'ien. In February 1851 Hung Hsiu-ch'üan directed his troops to advance from Chin-t'ien to Ta-huang-chiang, where he won a decisive victory over the government troops. At that time he began to call himself the King of Great Peace. He appointed Yang Hsiu-ch'ing commander in chief of the left wing, Hsiao Ch'ao-kuei commander in chief of the right wing, Feng Yün-shan associate commander in chief of the vanguard, Wei Ch'ang-hui associate commander in chief of the rear guard, and Shih Ta-k'ai commander of the left route army.

The Ch'ing government did not pay much attention to the Taipings until this time. But shortly after Wu-lan-t'ai was appointed to join Hsiang Jung in directing the campaign, a special order was issued authorizing Grand Secretary Sai-shang-a to be an imperial commissioner. After the death of Li Hsing-yüan in April, Sai-shang-a took entire responsibility for quelling the insurrection.

The Taiping force, after defeating the Manchu troops at Ta-huang-chiang, suffered some minor setbacks. Their followers, however, were greatly augmented because many members of secret societies and numerous poor people were persuaded or compelled to join them. When Li Hsiu-ch'eng stated his reason for joining the Taiping army, he said that when the forces of the Heavenly King advanced to Yungan, they passed a place near his home. There Commander in Chief Yang Hsiu-ch'ing spread the word, "All those who believe in God should not be afraid or run away. We will all eat together as members of one family." When they moved on, all the houses of God-Worshippers were burned; they were not to be homesick. Since his indigent family had nothing left to eat, Li Hsiu-ch'eng joined the Taipings.

Organization of the Heavenly Kingdom

On September 25, 1851, the Taipings took Yungan, and there the national title, *T'ai-p'ing t'ien-kuo* [*Heavenly Kingdom of Great Peace*] was adopted. Hung was unanimously declared Heavenly King. The title of king was also conferred on Yang Hsiu-ch'ing and four others.

The national title, Heavenly Kingdom, was based on the God-Worshippers' religious doctrine that everything was dominated by heaven where God was the supreme ruler. God was Jehovah, the Heavenly Father; Jesus Christ was the eldest son of God; and Hung Hsiu-ch'üan was the second son of the Heavenly Father. Hence Jesus Christ was called the Heavenly Elder Brother. This was Hung's new Holy Trinity. Hung Hsiu-ch'üan had accepted the command of the Heavenly Father and Heavenly Elder Brother to descend to the mundane world to kill all demons, to save all brothers and sisters, and to cause all to enjoy the pleasure of great peace.

The new calendar proclaimed in 1851 by Hung was based neither upon the traditional Chinese lunar system nor upon the European solar system. A year was divided into 366 days; the odd months consisted of 31 days, and the even months of 30 days. February 4, 1852 was January 1 of the first year of the Heavenly Kingdom of Great Peace.

Hung appointed himself king [*wang*], not emperor [*huang-ti*]. Why was the title of king also conferred on Yang, Feng, and others? One can understand this after reading Hung's decree.

> The Heavenly King sends a circular notice to all military officers and soldiers urging each of them to act seriously in accordance with the truth. The Heavenly Father, the Supreme Lord, and the Almighty God is the genuine deity. Aside from Him there is no deity. The Heavenly Father, the Supreme Lord, and the Almighty God is omniscient and omnipresent; moreover, there is not a single

person who is not born and bred of Him. He is the highest Supreme Lord. No one can claim to be a supreme lord except the Heavenly Father, Supreme Lord, and Almighty God. From now on all officers and soldiers can only call me King; they cannot call me Supreme King [Emperor], for in doing so, they would transgress against the dignity of the Heavenly Father ....

Now I especially confer the title of Eastern King upon the commander in chief of the left wing, Yang Hsiu-ch'ing, who will rule the states in the East; I confer the title of Western King upon the commander in chief of the right wing, Hsiao Ch'ao-kuei, who will control the states in the South; and I confer the name of Assistant King upon Brother Shih Ta-k'ai, who will protect the Celestial Court. All kings will be under the supervision of the Eastern King .... Respect this! [7]

This decree was issued at Yungan on October 25, 1851, the first year of the Taiping dynasty.

In this decree there are two points which merit close attention. The first concerns the distribution of titles. When Hung began to spread his doctrines, all the men who joined his society were called brothers; women were called sisters. By means of this equality of treatment Hung probably secured many recruits. At the same time, this practice corresponded with the Christian tenet that all men are brothers. Shih Ta-k'ai, Yang Hsiu-ch'ing, and the other heroes were glad to cooperate with Hung, but all these men had great ambitions. Since they all were equal as brothers and Hung had become the king of the Kingdom of Great Peace, naturally they also wanted to be called kings.

This plan for equality was obviously not without its defects. If everyone were made a king, there would be no supreme commander. Yet if the title of emperor had been used to honor Hung alone, the others would have been displeased. For lack of another alternative Hung was honored with the title of Heavenly King, while the other heroes were referred to as Eastern, Western, Southern, and Northern King. This arrangement apparently did not seem presumptuous to Hung nor degrading to the other leaders.

When the God-Worshippers were at war with the Manchu government, it seems natural that they should have had a commander in chief as assistant to the Heavenly King. Feng Yün-shan was the earliest sponsor of the rebellion and was from the beginning closely related to Hung. But, as point two, we notice that Yang Hsiu-ch'ing, who was merely a farmer and charcoal maker, was the man, rather than Feng, to be appointed to the dominant position of Eastern King.

The fact of the matter was that Yang had learned to use Hung's own secret. Hung's power was entirely built upon his claim of having revelations from God, and men who wished to support Hung as their leader acknowledged his divine inspiration without question. Yang Hsiu-ch'ing alone frequently claimed that the Heavenly Father had descended to his person also and had ordered him to dominate and restrain Hung. Hung was afraid of Yang's cleverness. At the same time he was delighted with his wit. For both reasons, perhaps, he granted Yang great authority.

A biography of Yang Hsiu-ch'ing in the *T'ai-p'ing t'ien-kuo yeh-shih* [An Unofficial History of the Taiping Kingdom] states,

> Hung Hsiu-ch'üan frequently enticed people by his religious doctrine and divine authority .... Yang Hsiu-ch'ing understood his tricks and hence said that he also was able to comprehend the language of the Heavenly Father. Yang corroborated Hung by saying that Hung definitely had been ordained by the Heavenly Father to descend to the world as the Heavenly King. Thus more people were persuaded to believe in and worship Hung, and Hung was more than glad to have Yang's support. But one day Yang went so far as to

claim that the Heavenly Father, God, had descended upon his person and told him that the Heavenly King had made a mistake. Therefore he demanded that Hung kneel down on the ground and be whipped as a punishment. If Yang himself made a mistake, he let others whip him without complaint. Yang liked to watch the private actions of others and reveal their secrets. Even though Hung could hardly bear Yang's watchfulness, he could not do anything against him.[8]

From the two points mentioned above, one can readily see that from its beginnings the organization of the Heavenly Kingdom had internal weaknesses. Later on internal dissension increased.

The Taipings Make Nanking Their Capital

The Ch'ing government, upon becoming aware that Hung Hsiu-ch'üan had founded a dynasty and had established a new calendar system, realized that the God-Worshippers were different from ordinary bandits and urged Sai-shang-a to subdue them with all the forces under his command. Hsiang Jung and Wu-lan-t'ai concentrated their full strength upon surrounding and assaulting Yungan, but could not take it for many months. In April 1852 the Taiping force raised the siege of Yungan and moved northward toward Kweilin, the capital of Kwangsi. They were pursued by government troops, and Wu-lan-t'ai died on the march. The Taiping force attacked Kweilin for thirty-one days without success and then abandoned it in order to go northward to take Chuanchow. From there they entered Hunan, where they met the Hunan militia. These forces, trained by Chiang Chung-yüan, were the forerunners of Tseng Kuo-fan's Hunan braves. In an engagement between the two armies, Feng Yün-shan, one of the Heavenly Kingdom's ablest leaders, was killed by artillery fire and his forces decimated. This was the first major defeat which the Taipings suffered.

In spite of this frustration, the Taipings continued their campaign.

They took Tao-chou and other cities in Hunan, and soon reaching the provincial capital, Changsha, they heavily bombarded the city. It was here that Hsiao Ch'ao-kuei, the Western King, died in the battlefield. Finding the defenses of Changsha too strong, the Taipings withdrew in September and advanced northwestward to Changteh and Iyang. By means of several thousand boats captured at Iyang, they crossed Tungting Lake and progressed to Yochow. In Yochow they captured a huge amount of ammunition and cannon. Then, sailing down the Yangtze River, they seized Wuchang in January and February 1853. Here many government officials were slain. The Taiping force spent a month in Wuchang before they resumed their campaign by sailing eastward. Meeting no strong resistance, they took Nanking in March 1853.

After occupying Wuchang, the Taipings were for a time uncertain whether they should proceed to Nanking or Peking. The Chinese scholar, Ch'ien Chiang, who had earlier led one anti-British corps in Canton, is said to have offered the Taipings a fourteen-point plan including the capture of Nanking, where they could secure rich sources of provisions for their march to Honan and Shantung. According to Li Hsiu-ch'eng's later confession, an old sailor of Hunan, who manned a boat for the Eastern King, was said to have warned his commander in chief that in Honan there was a scarcity of supplies. After receiving this information, the Eastern King was reported to have decided to sail to Nanking instead of attempting to go from Honan to Peking. The authenticity of such stories is dubious. But Nanking was taken and its name changed to T'ien-ching [Celestial Capital].

In Nanking the Taipings put into practice their reform program. For this program the best source is the official documents which they published under the title *T'ien-ch'ao t'ien-mou chih-tu* [Land System of the Celestial Dynasty]. From this work we derive their theory of military, civil, financial, economic, judicial, and educational administrations.

Courtesy University of Wisconsin Press

NINETEENTH-CENTURY CHINA

The Taiping Military and Civil Administration

The smallest unit was the family. Every twenty-five families formed a larger unit, and among these twenty-five families there was a public storehouse and church. Military, religious, judicial, and social affairs involving this larger unit were managed by an officer who may be roughly called a master sergeant [*liang-ssu-ma*];[9] he seemed to serve as a military chaplain, an army officer, a teacher, and a judge. Above the liang-ssu-ma[9] there were several higher officials governing several larger groups of families up to the number of an army [*chün*]. According to the *Land System of the Celestial Dynasty*, "for every 13, 156 families there is one army commander [*chün-shuai*], under whom there are five division commanders [*shih-shuai*]. Below each division commander there are five brigade commanders [*lüshuai*], and under each brigade commander there are five captains [*tschang*]. Each captain commands four master sergeants [*liang-ssu-ma*], and under each master sergeant there are five corporals [*tsu-chang*]."[10]

When a new unit of twenty-five families was formed, an additional master sergeant was to be appointed. When five hundred families were organized, a brigade commander was to be chosen, and so on. All soldiers were to be supported by the nation. The orphans, the old, and the disabled were to be exempted from military service.

In an army there were two officers in charge of land, taxes, revenue, and expenditure. Each division commander reported in detail to the army superintendent [*chien-chün*] such matters as births, deaths, promotions and demotions, obedience, and even individual diligence in farming. The army superintendent forwarded this report up the line until it finally reached the Heavenly King. Decisions made by the Heavenly King were sent down through the ranks by the same process. Thus Hung was able to keep his fingers on the pulse of his entire nation.

The Taiping Tradition

This system is apparently derived from the *Chou-li* [Rites of Chou], a utopian book traditionally attributed to the Duke of Chou, who lived about the eleventh century B. C. Actually the book was probably compiled in the third century B. C. The Taiping legislators modified the original text slightly to strengthen their hierarchy and concentration of power, as well as in attempts to eliminate official corruption.

The Taiping government was theocratic, the Heavenly King being both the spiritual and temporal ruler. Since the original five kings and the hierarchy of officials beneath them had both civil and military duties, civil and military administrations were virtually identical. Soldiers were at the same time farmers. In this way also, the military organization over-lapped the political and social organization.

The Taiping Social System

The Land System of the Celestial Dynasty assigns to the master sergeant responsibility in such matters as marriages and all auspicious and inauspicious events within his twenty-five families. For all such matters it was necessary to pray to God. All traditional superstitions were to be entirely discarded. Young boys were to go to church every day to study the Old and New Testaments under the tutelage of the master sergeant. Every Sunday men and women were to go to the church. There they were seated in separated sections to listen to explanations of the truth and to sing songs eulogizing the Heavenly Father.

Among the twenty-five families, those who worked hard on their farms were to receive a reward, while those who were lazy were to be punished. If there were quarrels between two families, the master sergeant was to judge the right from the wrong. If the disagreement could not be settled, the case was submitted to a higher official who listened to the complaints and drew up a verdict. If his judgment was unsatisfactory, the case was presented to another higher official, who re-examined it. If the two parties were still discontented, the case was finally brought before the Heavenly King, who made a final decision.

The Economic and Financial System

The Taiping economic and financial system aimed at three goals: public ownership of land, equal allotment of surplus money and food, and a self-supporting economy. The text of *The Land System of the Celestial Dynasty* reads:

> The land is divided into nine grades, according to the utility of the soil, so that one *mou* of the first quality is equal to three *mou* of the ninth.
>
> Land shall be allotted according to population by simply counting the number of mouths in each family. The allotment will be composed of all nine grades of land. If the production of one place is insufficient, the production of other areas will be transported to it to make up the deficiency. Throughout the entire empire plentiful and sparse harvests are to be balanced. All people of the empire are expected to enjoy together the great fortune of the Heavenly Father, the Almighty God. Everybody shall have land to till, rice to eat, clothes to wear, and money to spend. All men and women sixteen or older will receive a share of land, while those below fifteen will be given one-half share.
>
> At harvest time the master sergeant is to leave enough grain to sustain each person in his group until the next harvest and to send the rest to the national treasury or public storehouse. Wheat, cloth, chickens, dogs, silver, and cash are to be handled in the same manner. The empire is like a large family of the Heavenly Father, Supreme Lord, and Almighty God; no one is selfish, and everything is turned over to the Supreme Lord, so that He will have goods at

His disposal. Equality is the ideal of the Almighty God, who has commissioned Hung Hsiu-ch'üan to save the world.

The master sergeant must keep a record of the money and grain received and present the account to those in charge of expenditure and income. All marriages, month-old birthdays, and other celebrations will be at the expense of the national treasury, but there will be a limit to expenditures for such occasions ....

Throughout the empire mulberry trees are to be planted. All women are to learn sericulture and to make garments. Every family is to raise five hens and two sows. Pottery making, smithing, carpentering, and masonry will be taken care of by the corporal and his five soldiers. [11]

The sources of these ideas embodied in the Taiping reform program are both the *Rites of Chou* and the *Works of Mencius*. These have been supplemented and interwoven with the tenets of Christianity.

Of these detailed organizational theories, the military and civil organizations were actually established. The financial program, however, especially the public ownership of land, remained for the most part untried. The Taiping army chiefly occupied cities and towns in which there was little arable land. Furthermore, in such countryside as was under the Taipings' jurisdiction, the people were resentful and uncooperative because of constant military turmoil. Nevertheless, public ownership of money and personal property was seriously enforced. When the capital was established at Nanking, the sacred treasury and sacred storehouses were erected. Everything secured from army expeditions was turned over to these two offices, from which goods were taken to pay the salaries of officers and soldiers. Anyone who privately concealed as little as ten ounces of silver or one ounce of gold was considered a violator of the law of the Heavenly Kingdom and was punished by the Heavenly Courts.

The Spirit of the Movement

The general spirit of the Taiping movement is portrayed in the Heavenly King's declaration against the Manchus:

> The empire is God's empire, not that of the barbarian Manchus; the people, their clothing, and their food belong to God rather than to the Manchus. Ever since the Manchus let loose their malignant influence, confusion has been rife in China, where much territory has been overrun by them and countless people have grown accustomed to their maltreatment. China is a sacred land; the barbarians are evil people. Why is China called a sacred land? Because the Heavenly Father, the Supreme Deity, and True God made its heaven, earth, mountains, and seas. Hence, formerly the name of China was Sacred Land [Shen-chou]. [12]

The declaration moves on to say that the Manchus changed the national dress, forced the Chinese to wear a queue, employed corrupt officials who robbed the masses, and compelled the Chinese to become demons. "The waves of the eastern sea cannot wash their sins away."

In Hung's diatribe one can see two fundamental themes: worship of God and rejection of the Manchus. The Taipings eventually made full use of both divine authority and nationalism.

At first Hung used only his claim to divine inspiration to attract followers. However, at this time there were many secret societies which fostered anti-Manchuism. These secret societies had considerable influence over the minds of the people. Hung wanted to overcome their influence and to absorb them into his own camp; but he could not do so unless he incorporated their anti-Manchu sentiments. He thought that it was wrong to attempt to restore the Ming dynasty. He therefore supported the nationalism and anti-Manchuism of the secret societies, but instead of using this spirit of nationalism to bring about the restoration of the Ming, he employed it to aid him in founding the Heavenly Kingdom of Great Peace.

When the Heavenly Kingdom was established, no opportunity was lost to stress the concept of divine authority. Decrees were called Heavenly Decrees; laws, Heavenly Codes; the imperial palace, Heavenly Palace; the treasury, Sacred Treasury; public storehouses, Sacred Storehouses; and civil-service examinations, Heavenly Examinations. The themes for civil-service examinations were ones such as "Discuss the Heavenly Father who built mountains and seas in seven days," and "Discuss 'Is the true doctrine the same as the worldly doctrine?'" The children's textbook compiled under the auspices of the Taipings opened with the phrase, "The Almighty God created heaven and earth."

Limitations of the Revolution

In form the Heavenly Kingdom of Great Peace seemed to carry out a total revolution against Chinese religion, politics, and economics. But this revolution actually was not in accord with modern revolutionary spirit. The Taiping leaders tried to put new wine in an old bottle; the flavor of the new was eventually soured by the old. The Taipings were soon permeated with old Chinese corruptions—nepotism and debauchery—and the old Chinese habit of conservatism and fixed ideas.

On the other hand, the innovations which the Taipings attempted to introduce into their political program, such as the equal distribution of land, the plans to build steamships, railways, factories, and modern industries, the demand for equality between nation and nation, as well as between man and man, and even for the simplification of the Chinese language, created an indelible impression in Chinese memories. Many of the ideas were remembered, and even carried through, after the Taiping kingdom itself had been destroyed.

THE RISE OF TSENG KUO-FAN AND HIS HUNAN ARMY

When Hung Hsiu-ch'üan started his initial military actions at Chin-t'ien, Tseng Kuo-fan was still a vice-minister of the board of ceremonies, rendering service to the court at Peking. As the Taiping force advanced toward Changsha in 1852, Tseng was sent to conduct a provincial examination in Kiangsi; but learning on his way south of the death of his mother, he was granted leave to return home to observe the customary mourning period. When the Taipings were assaulting Changsha, the emperor ordered him to train militia in Hunan. Unable to decline, Tseng in January 1853 assumed the responsibility of opposing Hung, whose forces by that time had already captured Wuchang.

At first the desire of the Manchu dynasty had been to have Tseng train militia to fight against the bandits in his own province. But when the Taipings moved to Hupeh and farther east without encountering resistance, the service of Tseng's "Hunan braves" was needed to replace the regular army in playing a major role in checking the Taiping onslaught. However, from the beginning, Tseng himself set out to train an army instead of a local militia.

In promoting a stronger organization of militias, Tseng Kuo-fan said, "It is better to have people protect themselves than to have officials protect them; and it is better to have mutual protection with others than to protect oneself alone. If the area is convenient and the financial resources abundant ... several hundred people may join together to build a fortress and to establish a militia."[13]

Chiang Chung-yüan's militiamen, in the district of Hsin-ning, Hunan, had already been called in 1852 by Sai-shang-a to Kwangsi, where they had won a victory greatly lauded by the Ch'ing court. When the Taipings progressed rapidly from Hunan to Hupeh and down to the lower

Yangtze Valley, the standing army of the Ch'ing dynasty, except for the troops commanded by Hsiang Jung, showed itself wholly incompetent. In 1852 Hsiang Jung was appointed imperial commissioner to replace Sai-shang-a and Hsü Kuang-chin, both of whom had been dismissed for incompetence. After the Taipings took Nanking, the imperial army, directed by Hsiang Jung, encamped in the suburb of Nanking called the Great Camp of Kiangnan.

Because of the repeated victories won by the Hunan militia under the command of Chiang Chung-yüan, Chiang was made judicial commissioner of Hupeh in 1853 and ordered to go to the Great Camp of Kiangnan to assist in military affairs. Thereupon for the first time a militia leader became an important figure in the regular army.

Tseng Kuo-fan reorganized these militiamen, already trained by Chiang Chung-yüan and Lo Tse-nan, to be the hard core of his future crack troops. From the outset he fostered *esprit de corps*. He wrote in a letter to a friend, "My humble idea is to train 10,000 militia ... whose pains and itches will be of common concern to one another, and who will even rush together into fire or into a pond of boiling water .... In retreat they will exert their strength until death to rescue all of their comrades." Tseng had discovered that the most flagrant weakness of the regular troops was: "In defeat the soldiers do not assist one another."[14]

When Chiang Chung-yüan was surrounded in the city of Nanchang, he sent letters to ask for aid from Hunan. Tseng Kuo-fan immediately ordered Lo Tse-nan to rush his militiamen to the rescue. These troops were called *Hsiang-yung* [the braves of Hsiang] from which *Hsiang-chün* [Army of Hsiang] as a name for the Hunan Army is derived. During this emergency the Hunan Army was moved from one province to another.

Tseng Builds a Naval Force

When the Hunan Army reached Nanchang, the Taiping force

seemingly could not be defeated. Kuo Sung-tao, who later became a famous diplomat, learned that the main strength of the Taipings lay in their naval force; hence, he suggested that the opposing troops establish a fleet on the Yangtze. In a letter to Chiang Chung-yüan he said: "The cities of many provinces in the southwest are near the river or lakes where, with good wind, the bandits' ships can sail in a short time. The government forces usually march by land to pursue them. Consequently, their speed is slower than that of the enemy. Thus the strategic spots along the Yangtze River have been entirely occupied by the bandits."[15]

Chiang Chung-yüan concurred with Kuo's suggestion and immediately memorialized the throne requesting that it order the authorities of Hunan, Hupeh, and other provinces to construct gunboats which would be assigned to the control of Tseng Kuo-fan. An imperial decree complied with this request, and Tseng Kuo-fan was authorized to build a water force on the Yangtze River.

Tseng Kuo-fan went to Heng-chou, southern Hunan, in August 1853 and obtained as right-hand man P'eng Yü-lin, who helped him carry out his navy program. At Heng-chou officers and sailors for the gunboats were selected, and guns were brought from Canton. At this time the Taipings abandoned Nanchang and prepared to attack Wuchang again. In October the Ch'ing court ordered Tseng Kuo-fan to move his naval force to Hupeh. Apparently the emperor had forgotten that he had once said that a militia "should not be sent to distant areas."

Tseng Kuo-fan cherished one purpose. He vowed that until he had built a solid foundation for his naval force and had wiped out the local bandits in Hunan so that his headquarters could be safe, he would not go out of the province to fight against the Taiping troops. The Ch'ing court repeatedly urged Tseng to go down the river to the succor of Hupeh; Tseng held adamantly to his original plan until finally Emperor Hsien-feng became impatient with him and rebuked him in his own vermilion handwriting, saying, "You think that you alone can handle all military affairs .... You are vain, considering no one better than yourself. You should try your best to go at once to the rescue."[16]

In spite of this reprimand from the emperor, Tseng was unmoved. Emperor Hsien-feng then consoled Tseng with kind words and assured him that he would not be punished as a coward. Even so Tseng did not immediately participate in the war as the emperor had expected.

During the spring of 1854 the Taiping army again entered Hupeh, where the governor-general died in battle. Wuchang was besieged for the second time; Yochow, Hunan, was also threatened. The emperor repeatedly issued decrees urging Tseng Kuo-fan to mobilize his troops, and made allowances for Tseng, saying: "I will not control him from afar in all military affairs." Tseng was ordered not only to take care of Hunan, but also to make general plans for the defense of the entire nation, especially northern China.

All these directives reveal the extreme anxiety of the Manchu dynasty, which no longer had any force able to suppress this rebellion of the Chinese people except as it used troops composed of Chinese soldiers.

After several months' preparation, Tseng Kuo-fan's force began to consolidate. In February 1854 he directed his army and navy to proceed down the river. In the first engagement Tseng suffered a setback, but later, on May 1, he gained a major victory at Hsiang-t'an. Encouraged by this, Tseng fought his way northward and recovered Hanyang and Wuchang in October.

Emperor Hsien-feng was greatly cheered by news of these naval successes. He told the grand councilors that he "had not expected that Tseng Kuo-fan, a studious scholar, could achieve such great merit." A grand councilor who was jealous of Tseng replied, "Tseng Kuo-fan ... a commoner, has stirred ten thousand people into action. I am afraid that this may not be a good omen for the dynasty." Upon hearing this remark, Emperor Hsien-feng changed color; but in spite of its dire implications, he continued to trust Tseng.

An imperial decree stated: "Tseng Kuo-fan should have overall authority; all officials in his military zone are to be under his control. If there is anyone who does not obey his orders or tries to put things off or is too timid, let Tseng Kuo-fan impeach him by special memorial in order to improve our military efficiency."[17] Thus, Tseng Kuo-fan's Hunan Army became the main force in the government's campaign against the Taiping rebels. The shifting of military power from the Manchu rulers to the hands of the Chinese people was accomplished.

The Spirit of the Hunan Army

The Japanese scholar Inaba Iwakichi has said that Tseng Kuo-fan's Hunan Army was not dedicated to helping the emperor, for Tseng's only object was the maintenance of Confucian doctrine; hence, his army was little different from a religious army. This statement is generally correct. But in implying that Tseng was not loyal to the emperor, Inaba is in error, for to aid and to be loyal to the emperor is part of the Confucian doctrine. Since maintaining the Confucian doctrine and respecting the emperor go hand and hand, it is wrong to say that Tseng's army had no intention of supporting the emperor, although it is correct to say that the Hunan Army had some religious spirit.

At this time, a majority of the Chinese scholar-official class were under the influence of customary moral standards and traditional religions, while the uneducated masses were indirectly influenced by the same beliefs. Even the famous Taiping general, the Loyal Prince Li Hsiu-ch'eng, may be said to have been a follower of Confucian doctrine rather than the theories of the Heavenly King. The effects of Confucianism upon Li Hsiu-ch'eng is revealed here and there in his long confession, from which some excerpts are worth quoting:

> My Lord and my mother had both been surrounded in the capital. At the time, I was in the Ch'üan-chiao district. I shed tears

day and night.

My Lord, the Heavenly King, did not bother to manage state affairs. He merely told his officials to recognize the heavenly principles and that there would be a time of great peace. He proclaimed severe decrees ordering me to command my soldiers and horses to take Soochow and Changchow; he set a time limit of one month for me to report the victory to him. A person living in this society is obliged to obey the Heavenly King.

... The Heavenly King was so superstitious as to say that the Heavenly Father and the Heavenly Elder Brother would help him out and that it was not necessary for him to put political affairs in good order .... Later on, the minds of the people were changed. Food was exhausted, but still the Heavenly King spoke the Heavenly language and relied entirely upon the will of God, which could not save the grave situation.[18]

After Li Hsiu-ch'eng captured Hangchow, the Chekiang governor, Wang Yu-ling, committed suicide. Li escorted Wang's coffin to the latter's native home and buried it with great ceremony, saying: "Each of us supported his master; each of us had to be loyal .... In our lifetimes we were enemies, but after death we are no longer enemies."[19]

Do these quotations not show that the Loyal Prince leaned more toward Confucianism than toward Christianity?

Tseng Kuo-fan was an exponent of traditional moral criteria, and the people who worked under him also possessed the same ideals. All took the maintenance of Confucianism as their primary duty and would not allow an unorthodox doctrine such as Christianity to destroy the social order. Men are evolutionary animals and the process of evolution has time elements. When one studies history, one should not forget these time elements. Since a majority of the Chinese people were under the influence of the Confucian doctrine, Hung's Christian teachings and communist beliefs could not be accepted by society at large. His anti-Manchuism, which seemed to be popular, faded shortly after the Opium War, when hatred of the "foreign devils" became the chief concern of the people. Using the "foreign devils'" religion to attack the Manchus only diminished the effect of the Heavenly King's anti-Manchuism. Therefore, the religious ideas of the Taiping force were doomed to failure because of the time element.

Moreover, Tseng's advantage was his interest in maintaining traditional civilization, which was a favorite idea of his era. Even as late as 1895 there were many people who attacked K'ang Yu-wei and Liang Ch'i-ch'ao, accusing the two scholars of misinterpreting sacred Confucian classics. It is no wonder that several decades before 1895 Tseng Kuo-fan could advantageously use traditional Confucian beliefs to resist the philosophy derived from a foreign religion.

ELEVEN YEARS OF THE TAIPING KINGDOM

The Heavenly Kingdom of Great Peace established its capital at Nanking in 1853 and remained at odds with the Ch'ing dynasty for eleven years until its overthrow in 1864. The history of the eleven years of hostilities can be divided into three periods. The first period centered upon a struggle for the control of the upper valley of the Yangtze (1853-1856). The second period was one of warfare in the middle part of the Yangtze (1857-1860); and in the third period the lower valley of the Yangtze became the stage for military operations (1860-1864).

The Warfare from 1853 to 1856

In the first period the Taiping forces moved rapidly from Yungan to Nanking, meeting little resistance. This may be considered the great initial success of the Taipings; but during the time of their victory they made a few serious errors. They failed to take Changsha, the capital of

Hunan, and thus allowed Tseng Kuo-fan to use this province as his headquarters while he organized the Hunan Army. All the cities which the Taiping forces captured were ransacked and abandoned; they left no garrisons to secure their victories. Further, after their occupation of Nanking, the Taipings did not quickly take the whole rich province of Kiangsu. Consequently, they were soon harassed by government forces from the Great Camp of Kiangnan and the Great Camp of Kiangpei.

The Great Camp of Kiangnan, under the command of Imperial Commissioner Hsiang Jung, was established near the Ming mausoleum in the outskirts of Nanking. The Great Camp of Kiangpei was composed of troops led by Ch'i-shan, who blocked the northward advance of the Taipings. Forces from these two camps were incapable of retaking the Celestial Capital, Nanking, but they were capable of threatening its safety. Fortunately for the Taipings, the Ch'ing dynasty had at this time no navy. The rebels had captured enough boats from the upper valley to enable them to sail in and out of Nanking freely on the wide Yangtze River; hence they were able to launch two further expeditions.

The northern expeditionary force crossed the Yangtze and moved through part of Anhwei to Honan and Chihli to harass the government troops in North China. It was conducted by Lin Feng-hsiang and Li K'ai-fang, both of whom were defeated and killed because of lack of reinforcements.

The other expedition was to reconquer the upper Yangtze Valley and take the Wuhan[20] cities again. Tseng Kuo-fan's naval force had not yet been formed, and this enabled the enemy to proceed from Wuhan to Hunan once more. By February 1854 Tseng Kuo-fan's "navy" was in action, forcing the Taipings to withdraw step by step to the east until the Wuhan cities were recovered by the Hunan Army. Taking advantage of the situation, the Hunan Army progressed further by land and by water, hoping to capture Kiukiang in order to regain the province of Kiangsi. The Taiping troops held Kiukiang so stubbornly that the Hunan Army could not take it. Tseng Kuo-fan's ships then hastily proceeded to enter Poyang Lake. The Taipings took this opportunity to cut the naval force into two parts. The part under Tseng's personal command was bottled up in the lake, while the other section, still in the Yangtze River, was decimated. Consequently, Tseng was confined in Kiangsi for two years without being able to accomplish much. On the other hand, the Taipings, desiring to weaken the position of the government, retook Wuchang for the third time in April 1855 and held it until December 1856.

From 1855 to 1856 the Hunan Army encountered great difficulties. In Kiangsi, Tseng Kuo-fan was often annoyed by the provincial governor, who by his jurisdiction restricted Tseng's exercise of authority. Kiukiang was frequently bombarded, but could not be taken. Transportation and communications were difficult. Reinforcements and supplies were frequently captured by the enemy. Because of the loss of the Wuhan cities, the Manchu court accepted Tseng Kuo-fan's recommendation to appoint Hu Lin-i as acting governor of Hupeh with instructions to recover the territory. Hu Lin-i, a very capable statesman, was one of the big four of modern Hunan.[21] To cooperate with Hu Lin-i, Tseng Kuo-fan ordered Lo Tse-nan to the rescue of Hupeh. After more than a year and while the goal was still not achieved, Lo Tse-nan died on the battlefield. Since most of the outlying districts had been taken by the Taipings, Tseng Kuo-fan was isolated in the city of Nanchang and was compelled to seek help from Hu Lin-i. The latter had to fight for the Wuhan cities, while at the same time sparing troops for the rescue of Kiangsi; for this reason he made slow progress in recovering the two cities.

Worse still was the crushing defeat sustained in August 1856 by the imperialist forces at the Great Camp of Kiangnan, where commander Hsiang Jung himself was seriously wounded and soon died. The Taipings succeeded in removing this constant threat to the safety of their capital.

Dissension Among the Taipings

This victory was followed by internal dissension among the followers of the Heavenly King which terminated in a series of murders. Of the five kings created at Yungan only three survived—the Eastern King, Yang Hsiuch'ing; the Northern King, Wei Ch'ang-hui; and the Assistant King, Shih Ta-k'ai. The authority of the Heavenly Kingdom was meanwhile almost completely monopolized by the Eastern King, Yang Hsiu-ch'ing.

Yang regarded the Heavenly King as a titular ruler. On the surface, he seemed to respect him as a sacred sage sent down to earth by the Heavenly Father. However, Yang would not allow court ministers to have direct contact with the Heavenly King. His pretext was that they might contaminate the Heavenly dignity. Yang also ordered Wei Ch'ang-hui and Shih Ta-k'ai on long expeditions far away from the capital.

The Heavenly King became more and more an isolated figurehead. After the destruction of Hsiang Jung's Great Camp, Yang Hsiu-ch'ing even attempted to usurp the position of the Heavenly King. Conscious of the increasing power of Yang, the Heavenly King secretly ordered Wei Ch'anghui and Shih Ta-k'ai to return to the capital in order to assassinate Yang. Since for a long time Wei Ch'ang-hui had been a victim of Yang's haughtiness, he hurried back from Kiangsi to the Celestial Capital. There, taking advantage of Yang's unpreparedness, he not only killed Yang but mercilessly slaughtered thousands of Yang's relatives and adherents. After this massacre, Wei became even more ruthless. When Shih Ta-k'ai also returned to the Celestial Capital from Hupeh and Anhwei, he was indignant about the cruel slayings. Wei, suspecting that Shih was a member of Yang's faction, prepared to take Shih's life. Visualizing the danger, Shih left Nanking quickly.

Everyone in the Celestial Capital lived under acute apprehension and mutual suspicion. Soon the Heavenly King managed to have Wei Ch'anghui murdered, after which he summoned Shih Ta-k'ai back to the capital. The court ministers unanimously accepted Shih as a person capable of conducting state affairs. The Heavenly King, however, feared that Shih might be as dictatorial as Yang and Wei. He dared not trust

Shih. Instead, he relied upon his two incapable elder brothers, Hung Jen-hua and Hung Jent'a. After Yang's attempt on his life, Hung had surrounded himself with a galaxy of relatives and fellow Cantonese. They in turn kept him from granting authority to other persons. Shih Ta-k'ai, realizing that his position was hopeless, left Nanking, taking an enormous number of followers.

This internal dissension weakened the Taipings tremendously. In December Wuchang was recovered by Hu Lin-i, and the Taiping force again lost the bases in the upper valley of the Yangtze. Henceforth, with Hu Lin-i occupying the Wuhan cities, the headquarters of the Hunan Army was secure, and victory was gradually decided in favor of the government's troops.

New Leaders Among the Taipings, 1857-1860

During the second period (1857-1860), the center of hostilities was shifted to Kiangsi and Anhwei. The Taipings lost control of Kiangsi, but still maintained their power in Anhwei and Nanking. Li Hsiu-ch'eng routed the reorganized Great Camp of Kiangnan and extended his force to Soochow and Changchow.

After Hu Lin-i recaptured Wuchang, he reorganized its administration and then increased his military strength in order to recover Anhwei and Kiangsi. The bases of the Hunan Army had been moved from Hunan to Hupeh. From February 1857 to May 1858 Tseng Kuo-fan was at home observing the mourning period after the death of his father. During his absence the central figure in the Hunan Army was Hu Lin-i, who governed Hupeh under the Manchu governor-general, Kuan-wen.

At first Hu Lin-i despised Kuan-wen, who was incapable, a nepotist, and a spendthrift. Hu even made plans to impeach Kuan before the throne. Hu was convinced by an advisor, however, to cultivate Kuan-wen's friend-ship in order to utilize him as his spokesman in dealing with the emperor. Because of Kuan-wen's requests, the Manchu court adopted all Hu's plans. Hu thus concentrated authority and executive power in his hands. Not only did Hu's personal position become firm, but the foundations of the Hunan Army became invulnerable.

As for the Taipings, after the departure of Shih Ta-k'ai from Nanking, the court of the Heavenly Kingdom lost its last able leader. Two young men, Li Hsiu-ch'eng and Ch'en Yü-ch'eng, were simultaneously selected and promoted to eminent positions.

According to Li's own confession, his family was extremely poor, making a living by tilling hilly land and by doing odd jobs. In his early years Li had received some schooling from his maternal uncle, but after he was ten he was forced to work with his parents in order to eke out a living. At twenty-five he became acquainted with the man named Hung who taught people to worship God. When the Taipings burned people's houses in Li's village, compelling the residents to join them, Li's entire family followed the crowd. After serving as a common soldier for a few years, Li was promoted to be a commander. Following the period of internal dissension in 1856, a search was made for capable men, and Commanders Li Hsiu-ch'eng and Ch'en Yü-ch'eng, among others, were recommended to take charge of military affairs. Later on, Li was given the title of Loyal Prince [*Chung wang*] and Ch'en was called Courageous Prince [*Ying wang*]. The Sphere of Ch'en's activities was mostly in Anhwei; Li's, in the area around the capital and the lower Yangtze Valley.

But though both men were invested with important military responsibilities, they had no authority to manage state affairs in the Celestial Court. Internal and external civil policy was still controlled by the Heavenly King's brothers and by a treacherous minister, Meng Te-en, who cultivated the two Hung brothers in order to usurp more power. Both Ch'en and Li had to obey Meng, who disrupted the court and disappointed the people to such an extent that according to Li Hsiu-ch'eng's confession, "at that time, all the people had some intention of going away, but no one dared do so because the officers and soldiers of the Ch'ing dynasty were mercilessly beheading all Taipings from Kwangsi; no pardons were given .... If the Ch'ing dynasty had been willing to excuse the Taipings, they might have been disbanded long ago." [22]

Li Hsiu-ch'eng reports in his confession that he himself earnestly admonished the Heavenly King "to select men of ability who could establish a definite administrative system which would be considerate of the people, to rectify conditions in the court, to determine clearly who should be rewarded and who should be punished, to give important assignments to Shih Ta-k'ai, and not to rely too much upon his two brothers." For this advice Li was reprimanded and degraded. However, he again sent a memorial to the Heavenly King. This time he was supported by Ch'en, who urged that Li's recommendations be considered and that his rank be restored.

Meanwhile, in May of 1858 a general of the Hunan Army, Li Hsü-pin, retook Kiukiang and steadily drove the Taiping forces from Kiangsi. One month after the recovery of Kiukiang, Shih Ta-k'ai began disturbing the border areas of Kiangsi, Fukien, and Chekiang with a formidable mobile force. Becoming alarmed, the Ch'ing court exhorted Tseng Kuo-fan to leave for Chekiang. When Tseng reached the boundary of Kiangsi, the situation in Chekiang had improved, and he was ordered to meet Shih Ta-k'ai's challenge in Fukien. Before long Shih moved to southern Hunan and to the borders of Kweichow, Kwangsi, and eventually to Szechwan, where he was arrested by a government force and executed in 1863.

From 1858 to 1859 the Hunan Army was transferred here and there. In November 1858 it suffered a major military defeat and lost Li Hsü-pin and several other outstanding generals. The combined forces of Li Hsiu-ch'eng and Ch'en Yü-ch'eng, along with the activities of the Nien-fei in northern Anhwei proved a severe menace to the Hunan Army. Tseng Kuo-fan was surrounded by the Taipings at Ch'i-men, Anhwei, from September 1860 for about a year.

Victories of Li Hsiu-ch'eng

Near Nanking the reorganized Great Camp under Ho-ch'un and Chang Kuo-liang (the latter had once been a chieftain of the secret societies in Kwangsi) was also tottering because Li Hsiu-ch'eng had been trying to get rid of this nuisance by new tactics. He knew that money and provisions for the Great Camp of Kiangnan came entirely from Hangchow and Soochow. He therefore attacked the two cities, anticipating that the enemy must come to their relief. He personally commanded an assault on Hangchow. Hoch'un, as Li expected, dispatched a strong force to relieve it. Li quickly withdrew his troops from Hangchow to storm the weakened Great Camp. Chang Kuo-liang stubbornly resisted the attack for eight days and nights. Both Chang and Ho-ch'un were killed on the battlefield, and the Great Camp of Kiangnan was completely destroyed. Li Hsiu-ch'eng used his advantageous situation to attack Changchow and Soochow; both cities were taken with little resistance, and the Celestial Capital was made secure.

The second destruction of the Great Camp of Kiangnan is the demarcation line between the second and third period (1860-1864) in Taiping history. After this event the conditions of both the government forces and the Taiping forces changed considerably.

The Ch'ing court relied more and more upon Tseng Kuo-fan, who had proved himself an indomitable commander. In 1860 Tseng was made governor-general of Kiangnan and Kiangsi [the Liang-Kiang provinces] and also imperial commissioner for the suppression of the Taipings in South China. He was given full power to deal with all matters relating to the campaign, including the levy of funds.

Formerly there had been two centers of government forces: the Hunan Army in the upper valley, and the Great Camp of Kiangnan. Now only the Hunan Army remained. A unified, over all military strategy was now possible. Formerly Tseng Kuo-fan was hampered both by local officials and by a clique in Peking who were very jealous of him. Now Governor Lo Ping-chang of Hunan and Governor Hu Lin-i of Hupeh were staunch supporters of Tseng; in the inner court he was highly praised by Su-shun, who had become his advocate before Emperor Hsien-feng. Therefore the emperor entrusted full authority to Tseng to wipe out the Heavenly Kingdom of Great Peace. This marks a significant turning point in the concentration of authority and military power.

Not long after Tseng received the appointment as Liang-Kiang governor-general, the allied forces of England and France occupied Peking; Emperor Hsien-feng fled to Jehol in September 1860. Both Tseng Kuo-fan and Hu Lin-i prepared to re-deploy troops northward to assist the emperor. However, the peace treaty with England and France was soon concluded, and Tseng did not advance northward.

On the Taiping side, Li Hsiu-ch'eng's activity was formerly interfered with by the Great Camp of Kiangnan; he could not make much progress in the lower valley of the Yangtze. After the death of Ho-ch'un and Chang Kuo-liang, Anhwei was still largely under the control of Ch'en Yü-ch'eng, who took full responsibility for the military situation there; Li Hsiu-ch'eng accordingly could concentrate his power in the lower valley of the Yangtze. The two provinces Kiangsu and Chekiang became the sphere of Li's activities. The complete destruction of the camp was also extremely beneficial to the Taipings. Unfortunately for them, the change came too late. While Li Hsiu-ch'eng was advancing toward Shanghai, another Li [Li Hung-chang] came upon the scene to become his stubborn opponent.

After Li Hsiu-ch'eng took Soochow, he advanced eastward along the Yangtze River and established his headquarters at Zikawei in the outskirts of Shanghai (August 1860). Strong resistance in the international city and a counterattack at Soochow by government forces compelled Li Hsiu-ch'eng to withdraw from Shanghai and to move elsewhere. In December 1861 he captured the Chekiang capital, Hangchow. Then a number of larger cities of Kiangsu and Chekiang fell into his hands.

In these victories, the behavior of Li Hsiu-ch'eng was very different from that of other Taiping leaders, who had devoted themselves to taking food and valuables from the people. Wherever Li went, he was very considerate of his enemies. He tried by every means to discipline his soldiers so that they would not disturb the people. All government officials who died on duty were buried with reverent ceremony, and their families were given financial support. Li's actions in Soochow and Hangchow were particularly esteemed by the people. Had all the actions of the Taipings resembled those of Li, the life of the Heavenly Kingdom might have been prolonged.

The Taipings at Shanghai

After Li Hsiu-ch'eng pacified various cities in Kiangsu and Chekiang, he concentrated once more, in 1862, upon taking Shanghai. In order to control the center of wealth in southeastern China he operated this time with greatly increased forces.

A few months after the Taipings settled down in Nanking in 1853, the leader of the Small Sword Society [*Hsiao-tao hui*], Liu Li-ch'uan, mustered a few thousand members of secret societies, including Triads, and occupied a considerable portion of the city of Shanghai. Manchu officials either fled or were killed. The English, Americans, French, and other foreigners observed neutrality. Liu Li-ch'uan sent an envoy to Nanking to make connections with the Taiping authorities, who declined his request because Liu and his secret-society members did not believe in Christianity. The government troops which had besieged and attacked Shanghai had been driven off by English and American sailors for violating foreigners' neutrality.

In 1853 the foreigners had entertained a friendly feeling toward the Taipings. If farsighted Taiping leaders had made use of Liu Li-ch'uan's occupation and sent heavy reinforcements to Shanghai, the city might have fallen under the control of the Heavenly Kingdom. Unfortunately the Taipings neglected this opportunity. Government troops, who were later joined by some French soldiers, continued to bombard Shanghai until February 1855. Then on account of the exhaustion of food supplies, the rebels surrendered. From that time on, Shanghai became a paradise for affluent Chinese, an asylum for those who wanted to take shelter from military devastation; it also became a reservoir of Chinese wealth.

When Li Hsiu-ch'eng attempted to occupy Shanghai in 1862, Chinese and foreign merchants were frightened. By this time foreigners had changed their attitude toward the Taipings. Natives of Kiangsu, who were refugees in Shanghai, were joined by other rich merchants in recruiting a volunteer corps for self-protection. Some adventurous Englishmen, Americans, and Frenchmen joined the Chinese merchants. The Americans F. T. Ward and H. A. Burgevine organized a volunteer army which served as the foundation of the later Ever Victorious Army, to repulse Li Hsiu-ch'eng's attack, but they had no real ability to check the assault. A number of the Kiangsu gentry and merchants went to Anhwei in 1862 to beg for Tseng Kuo-fan's aid.

The Rise of Li Hung-chang

In the meantime Tseng Kuo-fan's younger brother had taken Anking in September 1861 and used it as a springboard to reach Nanking. Tseng then ordered his brother Kuo-ch'üan to assail Nanking, entrusted Tso Tsung-t'ang with the duty of pacifying Chekiang, and gave Li Hung-chang the duty of relieving Kiangsu.

Tso Tsung-t'ang, a native of Hunan, was a man of great ability. Under the sponsorship of Tseng Kuo-fan and Hu Lin-i, he was rapidly promoted. He was appointed commander in charge of military affairs in Chekiang, and shortly after made governor of that province.

Li Hung-chang was Tseng Kuo-fan's disciple. Li had trained a militia in Anhwei and had also served in a secretarial capacity under an Anhwei governor. But unsatisfied with his superiors, he had gone to work under Tseng in order to receive the latter's training. Tseng, noticing Li's ability, had recommended him to the throne as able to shoulder the heavy responsibilities as governor of Kiangsu. When the representative had come from Shanghai to Anking to beg for help, Tseng Kuo-fan recommended Li Hung-chang to the throne to deal with the complicated situation. His request was complied with by an imperial decree, which also sanctioned Tseng's plan to let Li Hung-chang recruit several thousand soldiers from Huai-nan, the area south of the Huai River, including part of Anhwei and Kiangsu.

In organization and training, the Huai Army was patterned after the Hunan Army. Tseng also selected two veteran generals from the Hunan troops to serve Li Hung-chang. This was the nucleus of what was later known as the Huai-chün, loosely called the Anhwei Army.

The Shanghai merchants rented ten steamers from foreign countries and raised 18,000 taels of silver to be sent to Anking as a welcome for Tseng's relief force. In April, Li Hung-chang ordered his whole force to Shanghai. In June, Tseng Kuo-ch'üan's army forced its way into the suburbs of Nanking and began a long siege of the Taiping capital.

After the loss of Anking to the government forces, Ch'en Yü-ch'eng had fled to northern Anhwei. There he was betrayed by a Nien chief, Miao P'ei-lin, who arrested him and turned him over to the imperialists. Li Hsiu-ch'eng was now left without help. As the only able general of the Taipings, he could not repulse simultaneously the general attack of government forces in the upper and lower valley. The end of the Heavenly Kingdom was drawing near.

Li Hung-chang's newly organized force was assisted by the volunteer corps trained by F. T. Ward. After the death of Ward on the battlefield, Burgevine took over the command, but he defied Li Hung-chang's orders. Consequently, Li dismissed him, and Burgevine later joined the opposition, enlisting with Li Hsiu-ch'eng.

Li Hung-chang, to replace the American commanders, employed the English officer Charles G. ("Chinese") Gordon. With the Huai Army—the Ever Victorious Army—and new Western weapons, Li Hung-chang's force wiped out Li Hsiu-ch'eng's power and drove the enemy from Shanghai to Soochow.

Collapse of the Heavenly Kingdom, 1864

While the two Li's were waging war in the lower valley, the situation in the Celestial Capital became daily more precarious. The Heavenly King Hung Hsiu-ch'üan urged Li Hsiu-ch'eng to come back to relieve Nanking. Li was obliged to yield ground at the front in order to join the Heavenly King. He knew, however, that there was little hope of saving the capital. He therefore advised the Heavenly King to lead his followers to another base. The Heavenly King did not heed his advice, but reproved him saying, "I received the sacred decree from the Heavenly Father, Almighty God, and the Heavenly Elder Brother, Jesus Christ, to descend to the mundane world to be the lord of the ten thousand states of the universe. I am the only real king; why should I be afraid of anything? I will not heed your advice. My territory is as firm as an iron box. Why should I fear the demon Tseng?"[23] Hung's argument resembles that of Wang Mang, who some eighteen centuries earlier had said: "Heaven grants virtue to me. What can the troops of the Han dynasty do to me?"

Hung did not realize that the virtue of divine right had now lost its function. Li Hsiu-ch'eng had no way to carry out his own plans except to concentrate all his forces in many violent attacks on the headquarters of Tseng Kuo-ch'üan, near Nanking, even at the risk of losing his own life. He realized that there was no hope of raising the siege of the Celestial Capital.

Meanwhile his opponent Li Hung-chang took Soochow, while Tso Tsung-t'ang captured Hangchow. The Taiping relief forces outside Nanking were cut off. In June, Hung Hsiu-ch'üan committed suicide; his son, Hung Fu, succeeded him as the Heavenly King.

Tseng Kuo-ch'üan finally broke through the defenses of the Celestial Capital on July 19, 1864. Li Hsiu-ch'eng protected Hung Fu and managed to flee from the siege. However, in their flight the two lost track of each other. Li Hsiu-ch'eng was arrested in a village north of Nanking, while Hung Fu fled to Kiangsi, where he was arrested and executed. The Heavenly Kingdom of Great Peace was destroyed.

WHY THE TAIPING FORCES FAILED AND THE HUNAN ARMY SUCCEEDED

The failure of the Taipings and the success of the Hunan Army were caused by several factors. From the standpoint of military tactics, the tactical weakness of the Taipings was their concentration on forward movement with total disregard of security measures to hold the rear. In contrast, in the Hunan Army Tseng Kuo-fan and Hu Lin-i moved ahead cautiously, never neglecting security for their rear areas. Then, in regard to political policies the Taipings cared only about seizing territory. They were not much interested in making plans to govern it. Except for Li Hsiu-ch'eng, they had little regard for the feeling of the populace. Again in contrast, Tseng Kuo-fan appointed Lo Ping-chang and Hu Lin-i to the specific duties of ruling the recovered territory and governing the people in Hunan and Hupeh in the upper valley.

As far as leadership was concerned, though the Taipings had some good warriors, they suffered a great paucity of men with political talent. After the internal dissension of Yang and Wei in 1856, their only able man was the Loyal Prince, Li. In the court of the Celestial Capital everything was controlled by Hung's family and relatives, who were mediocre and covetous and without knowledge or ability. The Loyal Prince Li stood alone in a circle of mediocre individuals. "How can a single pillar support a great mansion?"

The warriors of the Hunan Army may not necessarily have been superior to those of the Taipings, but men with political ability and knowledge in the imperial camp far outbalanced those on the side of the Taipings. Tseng Kuo-fan in the earlier half of the war had suffered from the restrictions of local governors. In the latter part of the war he gradually gained the confidence of the Ch'ing court. He employed his keen observation of men to promote those of promise to duties which fitted the capacity or caliber of their individual talents. He made all his subordinates develop their individual powers.

As to political philosophies, Taiping pro-Chinese policies lost their effect when absorbed by their principle of Christian divine right. Moreover, their Christian principles at that time did not persuade the majority of the Chinese people. The Confucianism of the Hunan Army, on the other hand, had been firmly established in Chinese history for thousands of years. With the additional encouragement and promotion of such scholars as Tseng Kuo-fan and Lo Tse-nan, Confucian ideas became more continuously popular than Taiping Christianity.

Furthermore, the Christianity of Hung Hsiu-ch'üan and others was not authentic, while Tseng Kuo-fan's Confucianism was genuine. Hung and his followers paid lip service to Christianity without actual belief in the religion, in order to serve their personal ambitions and desires. Tseng's followers, on the other hand, were genuine believers in the Confucian faith. When the false carries on a struggle with the true, the former will certainly be defeated. Moreover, can a pretender maintain the spirit and faith of others?

When Tseng was first appointed to assist the militia he was unwilling to leave home where he was observing a mourning period for his mother. Before long his father died, and he insisted upon going home again to observe a mourning period of several months. This seems to be a very small matter, yet it proves Tseng's loyalty to the Confucian doctrine. Although he gained many victories for the Ch'ing dynasty, he declined reward. When granted great authority by the Manchu dynasty, he repeatedly declined and begged for retirement. After the recovery of Nanking he immediately requested the disbanding of the Hunan Army. Though these measures served to avert the suspicion of the Manchu court and the jealousy of others, such measures also show that Tseng earnestly sought to make his words and his actions agree. It cannot be said that all his subordinates were such consistent Confucians, but there were several leading men whose beliefs were very similar to Tseng's.

The Christianity of the Taipings

The Taipings claimed that they were brothers and equals, all children of the Heavenly Father. But these brothers killed one another. They said that women were equals and sisters, also children of the Heavenly Father. But two or three hundred women were enslaved by the Heavenly King as maidservants in his palace. Hung kept over sixty concubines. The other kings each had more than half a dozen. The Taipings held that all land and property were gifts of the Heavenly Father to be enjoyed in common by everybody. But the relatives of Hung Hsiu-ch'üan and all other dignitaries had accumulated enormous amounts of money, while the poor in Nanking had to eat "sweet dew" [grass].

Reports and comments of contemporary Europeans and Americans also illustrate the corrupt condition of the Heavenly Kingdom. Sir S. G. Bonham, former governor of Hongkong, after his investigation of conditions at Nanking in 1853, submitted to the British minister of foreign affairs a report pointing out that the Taiping pretenders used the Christian Scriptures to serve the end of personal aggrandizement and ambition. Eight years later, Frederick Bruce, the new British minister to Peking, sent the following report to Lord John Russell.

> We stayed a week in Nanking .... I will now give you, in as few words as I can, my general conclusions respecting the Tae-ping

rebellion .... They don't in any way encourage trade, excepting in firearms and gunpowder. These, as well as steamers, they are anxious to buy .... The fact is they live on loot, and so long as they can loot they will neither work nor trade.

The Tien Wang has a large palace. His attendants are females, 300 in number, besides 68 wives allowed to his rank. He is never seen by any but the Kings, and his person is held sacred. He is, however, by no means a puppet, for it is he alone who keeps the movement together ....

I have no hope of any good ever coming of the rebel movement. They do nothing but burn, murder, and destroy. Trade and industry are prohibited. Their land-taxes are three times heavier than those of the Imperialists. I must say, I cannot see any elements of stability about them, nor anything which can claim our sympathy.[24]

At this time the British were thoroughly disappointed in the Taipings.

The American missionary I. J. Roberts, under whom Hung Hsiu-ch'üan received some instruction in Christian tenets, was invited by the Heavenly King to Nanking, where he stayed fifteen months from 1861 to 1862. He wrote a report about the Nanking regime, part of which reads:

The bright side consists chiefly in negatives, such as, no idolatry, no prostitution, no gambling, nor any kind of public immorality allowed in the city ....

But when we come to the religious aspect of this revolution, together with other evils both political and civil, we have a very dark side ....

As to the religious opinions of Tien Wang, I believe he is crazy, especially in religious matters .... He calls his son the young saviour of the world, and himself the real brother of Jesus Christ ....

Their political system is about as poor as their theology. I do not believe they have any organized Government, nor do they know enough about Government to make one, in my opinion. The whole affair seems to consist in martial law, and that, too, runs very much in the line of killing men, from the highest to the lowest, by all in authority ....

He wanted me to come here, but it was not to preach the Gospel of Jesus Christ and convert men and women to God, but to preach his dogmas, and convert foreigners to himself.[25]

These quotations are sufficient to show a panorama of the Taiping kingdom; American and English eyewitnesses seem to have presented a true picture.

FOREIGN INVASIONS, 1856-1860

During the period of the Taiping Rebellion, English and French allies entered Peking. After this incident in 1860 foreign powers penetrated from China's main door to her inner halls. The central force in the government of the Ch'ing dynasty had also undergone a momentous upheaval.

The Delay in Opening Canton

What brought about this great foreign invasion? The immediate cause was the incident involving the *Arrow*, a lorcha [vessel with Chinese rig and foreign hull] challenged by a Chinese patrol; the remote cause was the baneful influences of the Opium War. After the Treaty of Nanking, European and American powers hurriedly sent envoys to China to request treaties for trade relations patterned after the one with England. In July 1844 the United States signed a friendly treaty with China, and in October France signed a similar treaty. The United States and France were to enjoy equal privileges of trade in the five ports opened by the Treaty of Nanking. Of the five trade ports, Shanghai, Ningpo, Amoy, and Foochow were in operation. Canton was in trouble. There the local people, harboring ill feeling against the British, requested the Chinese government to forbid them to enter the city. The governor-general, Ch'i-ying, was in a dilemma. Finally he obtained a two-year postponement for opening Canton's portals to the British by signing a convention with England promising "not to cede the Chusan islands to any other nation."

Before long, Ch'i-ying was transferred from Canton and Hsü Kuang-chin succeeded him as governor-general, while Yeh Ming-ch'en was the governor of Kwangtung. The British governor of Hong Kong, S. G. Bonham, renewed his request for fulfillment of the treaty obligation by opening Canton. Both Hsü and Yeh secretly incited the people of Canton to gather several ten thousands of militiamen to threaten Bonham when the latter was having a conference with Hsü. Since Bonham had no intention of starting hostilities, inasmuch as the two nations had signed a peace treaty only four years previously, he temporarily put off the problem of entering the city. Hsü and Yeh were greatly pleased with the results, and the Ch'ing court was so elated that the title of viscount was conferred upon Hsü, and that of baron upon Yeh. Both men considered that since they had the support of the populace, there was no reason to be afraid of the foreigners.

When the Taipings had entered Hunan in 1852, Hsü Kuang-chin was transferred to be governor-general of Hunan and Hupeh, and Yeh Ming-ch'en was promoted to take Hsü's position. The British governor of Hong Kong, Bonham, was also at this time removed from his post and replaced by Sir John Bowring. Bowring also requested entry to the city. Yeh Ming-ch'en, basing his decision on his agreement with Bonham, denied the request. Yeh was a favorite of the Ch'ing court because he had been successful in refusing to let the British into Canton, had ruthlessly slaughtered the Taipings in Kwangtung, and had enthusiastically raised funds to be used for suppressing the bandits. Yeh was very vain, however. He boasted that he himself would wash off China's humiliation and enhance its dignity. His attitude toward the British was very arrogant. Both Bowring and the British Consul at Canton, Harry Parkes, hated him.

The *Arrow* Affair

The *Arrow* affair occurred in 1856. At this time the pirates along the seacoast of Fukien and Kwangtung, as well as the treacherous merchants who smuggled opium, used Hong Kong as an asylum and flew the British flag to enable them to sail to all Chinese coastal ports. The lorcha *Arrow* was one of these boats, owned by the Chinese but flying an English flag on its mast.

When the *Arrow* was entering the Pearl River from the sea in October 1856 the Chinese water patrol learned that several notorious pirates were aboard relying upon the protection of the Union Jack. The patrol boarded the boat, arrested twelve Chinese sailors, and hauled down the British flag. Harry Parkes filed a protest with Yeh Ming-ch'en, pointing out that the lowering of the British flag was a great insult. Yeh's rejoinder was that the lorcha was owned and manned by Chinese and that the British flag was not flying at the time.

This explanation was deemed very unsatisfactory by Parkes and Bowring, who decided to resort to arms to put pressure on Yeh. At first Parkes demanded that Yeh hand over the arrested sailors to the British consul for questioning. If they were found guilty, they were to be returned to the Chinese government. Yeh replied that he had found by examination that three out of the twelve arrested were guilty; he agreed to hand the other nine over to Parkes. Parkes refused to accept the nine men. He accordingly consulted Bowring and made the following demands: (1) The twelve men must be escorted back to the original ship. (2) Yeh must submit a written apology acknowledging that he was at fault. (3) A guarantee should be given against similar actions in the future.

To these demands Yeh replied that the boat was a Chinese craft even though it was registered with the Hong Kong government, that its license had expired when it was searched, and that the people arrested were Chinese. Thus he refused the demands of the English.

Bowring and Parkes then went a step further. They set a limit of forty-eight hours for Yeh to give satisfactory answers. After this time limit, they announced, they would be free to take action. Yeh then sent the twelve men to the office of the consulate, but refused to acknowledge his actions as at fault. Parkes still regarded Yeh's actions as unsatisfactory. Yeh appeared indifferent to further action. The British then used their navy to bombard various forts along the Pearl River.

On October 23 the British force took the forts at Whampoa. Yeh Ming-ch'en sent a messenger to ask the reason for such action. Parkes answered that he would not say anything until he entered Canton because he desired to take this opportunity to solve the problem of entrance to the city. Yeh refused to take conciliatory measures. On October 27 approximately a thousand British troops seized Canton without British government sanction. They intended to use military force to subdue Yeh Ming-ch'en, but had no intention of occupying the city. For this reason they temporarily withdrew.

The Cantonese followed the retreating English troops. They burned all factories in the suburb of the city to express their hatred of foreigners without distinction as to nationality. But the English were not then in a good position to wage war against the Cantonese mob because a great mutiny had broken out in India in May 1857 and reinforcements had to be shifted from China to India.

During this period Great Britain, France, the United States, and Russia engaged in several actions against China. The United States and Russia sent envoys to the East with the intention of gaining commercial treaties with China. They showed no interest in taking military action. In France, Napoleon Ⅲ, who had just seized control of the government, wished to spread his power overseas in order to win the hearts of his people. After the murder of a French missionary in February 1856 in Kwangsi, the cradle of the Taiping Rebellion, France promised England to send troops to the East. The Anglo-French allied armies took Canton at the end of December 1857. They captured Yeh Ming-ch'en, who was escorted to India, where he died. Beginning in 1858 Canton was under the control of the military government of the British and French allies for three years.

The Treaties of Tientsin, 1858

After taking Canton the English and French authorities were free to turn their attention to the principal object of their mission: securing a revision of treaties. They invited the ministers of Russia and the United States to send simultaneous notes addressed to the chief grand councilor of the Manchu court and requested the latter to commission a sole plenipotentiary to confer with them at Shanghai.

The Manchu emperor, who was apparently unaware of the serious nature of the diplomatic situation and still maintained a contemptuous attitude toward the West, stated: "The grand councilors participate only in domestic administration; there is no precedent for them to concern themselves with diplomatic affairs, which should be discussed by the authorities at the national frontiers." [26] Thus the envoys of England, France, and the United States were informed that Huang Tsung-han, the newly appointed governor-general of Liang-Kiang, had been commissioned as imperial commissioner to open negotiations with them in Canton, while the imperial agent at Heilungkiang was to handle diplomatic matters with Russia.

The envoys of England and France, upon learning that their request was not complied with by the Ch'ing court, commanded their fleets in

April to go northward from Shanghai to the mouth of the Pei-ho River. They were joined by the envoys of the United States and Russia. After a month of fruitless negotiations, they sacked the forts at Taku on May 20. Thoroughly alarmed, the Ch'ing court sent the Grand Secretary Kuei-liang, and the Minister of Civil Appointments Hua-sha-nai as the emperor's plenipotentiaries to arrange a truce in Tientsin. There were no negotiations, however. England produced a list of fifty-six items, and France forty-two articles, which without discussion they compelled the Ch'ing government to accept. The Ch'ing court had no alternative but to yield to their demands and to sign the Treaties of Tientsin in June 1858.

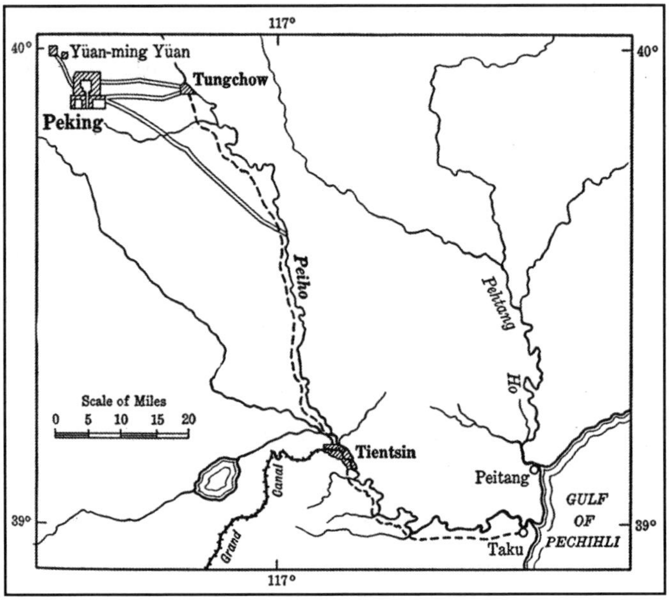

THE WAY TO PEKING, 1860-1900

The important points of the Anglo-Chinese Treaty included:

1. Great Britain was to have the right to maintain a resident at Peking, and China was permitted to send an envoy to reside in London.
2. Newchwang, Tengchow, Taiwan, Swatow, and Kiungchow were

to be opened as trade ports, and after the suppression of the civil war, the British were to have the right to select three more trade ports in the Yangtze Valley. [Hankow, Kiukiang, and Chinkiang, were later selected.]

3. The rate of tariff duties was to be revised and must be agreed to by the two nations concerned.
4. British subjects could travel in the interior of China.
5. Two million taels of silver were to be paid as reparation for the losses of British merchants, and two million taels as indemnity for military expenses.

The important points of the Sino-French Treaty were:

1. The main points in this treaty were to be the same as those in the Sino-English Treaty.
2. Tamsui (on Taiwan) and Nanking were to be opened as additional trade ports.
3. To all trade ports where French merchants were allowed to go, the French government could send warships, both to lie at anchor and to patrol.
4. French missionaries were to have access to all parts of the interior of China to spread Christianity, and French subjects could travel in the interior.
5. Legal suits in which the two parties concerned were French were to be judged by French consuls; if the French consul could not decide legal suits between French and Chinese, he would invite Chinese officials to assist in making a joint decision.
6. Hereafter, whenever China granted special privileges to other nations, France was to enjoy most-favored-nation treatment.

After the conclusion of these treaties, the envoys of England and France returned to Shanghai to decide, through concerted action, the rate for customs duties. During the same month the envoys of Russia and the United States also signed treaties at Tientsin with China. By most-favored-nation treatment, the two countries received the same privileges as those obtained by England and France.

The Treaties of Peking, 1860

The Ch'ing court was chagrined not only by the Treaties of Tientsin, which had been signed under military pressure, but also by the overbearing attitude of the British interpreters. Many scholar-officials and the Manchu emperor were outraged by this deep humiliation. As soon as the foreign fleets sailed from Taku, the famous Mongol Seng-ko-lin-ch'in was ordered to repair and strengthen the military defense works around Tientsin in order to bar the war vessels from the Pei-ho so that the safety of the capital would not be disturbed again. The envoys of England and France mistook this move as reluctance on the part of the Ch'ing court to ratify the treaties at Peking. In June 1859 they commanded their fleets to force their way into the mouth of the Pei-ho.

The Ch'ing authorities then requested the envoys to go ashore at Pei-t'ang, about ten miles north of the mouth of the Pei-ho, where Chinese representatives were ready to meet them. The request was not accepted. Instead, the Chinese defenses were fired upon. Seng-ko-lin-ch'in ordered the fortresses on both banks to return the gunfire. The British and French fleets suffered severe damage and withdrew southward.

Noticing the withdrawal of the British and French fleets, the Ch'ing court was greatly pleased, thinking that the foreigners would never dare to come again. The unrealistic scholar-official class also considered that the Treaties of Tientsin might be abolished. In March of the following year (1860), however, the British and French proceeded with reinforcements toward Tientsin and had their troops land at Pei-t'ang.

Seng-ko-lin-ch'in immediately commanded a large force which put up a vigorous resistance, but he was compelled to retreat step by step. The Anglo-French allies fought their way to Peking in September, and Emperor Hsien-feng fled to Jehol. Two envoys of England and France now separately signed treaties in Peking in October 1860, of which the main points were:

1. All articles of the Treaty of Tientsin except the points hereby revised were valid.
2. Tientsin was to be opened as a trade port.
3. The island of Kowloon, opposite Hong Kong, was to be controlled by England.

In the Sino-French Treaty of Peking, one point was added: French missionaries were to be allowed to buy land in the interior, to be used for any constructions they chose.

After the English and French allies withdrew from Peking, the Russian minister, who had served as arbitrator during the negotiations, requested that the territory east of the Ussuri River [which formed the Maritime Provinces] be ceded to Russia. The Ch'ing court signed a convention with Russia which gave her the territory which she wanted.

Besides losing territory and paying an indemnity, China sustained a great loss of sovereignty by permitting war vessels and commercial ships to navigate rivers in the interior, by the article guaranteeing most-favored-nation treatment, by the clause allowing consular jurisdiction, and by the fixing of tariff duties through concerted action. The main substance of the unequal treaties forced upon China by foreign powers was formed by the treaties of Tientsin and Peking.

Prior to these two treaties, Chinese diplomatic negotiations had been managed by provincial authorities. The Office of Colonial Affairs [*Li-fanyüan*] was the legitimate organ of the central government in charge of foreign affairs because all foreign nations were considered to be China's vassal states. After the conclusion of these treaties, a memorial of Prince Kung was adopted to establish a new office called *Tsung-li ko-kuo shih-wu ya-men* [Office in General Charge of Affairs Concerning All Foreign Nations], usually referred to as the Tsungli Yamen. Prince Kung, Grand Secretary Kuei-liang, Vice-Minister of Revenue Wen-hsiang, and others were in charge of this yamen.

At the same time Ch'ung-hou was appointed superintendent of trade for the three northern ports of Tientsin, Newchwang, and Chefoo. His title was later abbreviated to Minister Superintendent of Trade in Peiyang [*Peiyang ta-ch'en*]. The Kiangsu governor, Hsüeh Huan, was made a minister superintendent in charge of affairs at Canton, Amoy, Ningpo, Shanghai, Swatow, Kiungchow, Taiwan, Tamsui, and the three ports on the Yangtze River. He was later simply known as the Minister Superintendent of Trade in Nanyang [*Nan-yang ta-ch'en*]. The positions and functions of the two minister superintendents were like those of local ministers of foreign affairs in northern and southern China. The inauguration of the new yamen and the two superintendencies may be considered an unprecedented action, an indication of the Ch'ing government's change of attitude toward foreign countries.

THE RISE TO POWER OF EMPRESS DOWAGER TZ'U-HSI

During the time of the Taiping Rebellion and foreign invasion there was a major shift in the centers of political power. In the central government the power gradually fell into the hands of eunuchs and other favorites. In the local governments the power of provincial authorities was gradually increased.

The Death of Emperor Hsien-feng, 1861

When the English and French allies entered Peking, Emperor Hsien-feng fled to Jehol accompanied by a retinue of eight high officials, four adjutant-generals, and four grand councilors. These included three important imperial clansmen who were trusted by the emperor, Su-shun, Tsai-yüan, and Tuan-hua. These men, however, were not the emperor's closest relatives. The emperor's younger brother, Prince Kung, was ordered to stay in Peking to undertake peace negotiations with the English and French.

Su-shun, Tsai-yüan, and Tuan-hua were skilled in reading the mind of the emperor and in currying his favor through sensual pleasures. The emperor liked these men so much that gradually they participated in important political affairs and had more power than grand councilors. When they followed the emperor to Jehol, their power was further extended. After the conclusion of the peace treaty with England and France, Prince Kung requested the emperor and his retinue to return to Peking, but Su-shun and the others wanted the emperor to stay in Jehol. Thereupon, the Manchu court was divided into two centers of power. The one in Jehol was managed by Su-shun; the other, in Peking, was led by Prince Kung. Each organized a political faction to battle the other.

In 1861 Emperor Hsien-feng died in Jehol. His wife, who was later known as the Eastern Empress, had no son; but his concubine Yehonala, later known as the Western Empress or the Empress Dowager Tz'u-hsi, had one son named Tsai-ch'un. When the latter was only five years old, he was made heir apparent in accordance with his father's last will.

The Contest with Su-shun

During the minority of the child emperor, affairs of state were entrusted to Su-shun and the seven others in the retinue. This was in accordance with the late emperor's will, which provided for a regency composed of eight men. In issuing decrees, however, the eight regents were to obtain the consent of the two dowager empresses. Later this last will and testament was condemned as a forgery. Since Emperor Hsien-feng was so much swayed by favorites, the charge was quite possibly true. The regency forbade Prince Kung to go to Jehol to take charge of the funeral. From then on everything was decided by the eight regents under the leadership of Su-shun alone.

In Jehol the two empresses were very resentful of the overbearing attitude of Su-shun. In Peking Prince Kung and others who formerly harbored ill feeling toward Su-shun were also much mortified by the autocratic regency. About a month after Emperor Hsien-feng died, a censor in Peking submitted a memorial recommending that the two empresses listen to reports on state affairs from behind screens [*ch'ui-lien t'ing-cheng*] and also appoint the nearest related prince as assistant regent. After the empresses received this memorial, they put the recommendations into practice.

Su-shun protested, "There is no precedent in this dynasty for having an empress attend state affairs." Su-shun ordered the grand councilors in Jebol to draft an imperial decree to refute and reject this action. When the two empresses wished to defy Su-shun and the others, they accused the regents of rejecting orders from the empresses and not allowing the empresses to read memorials. Therefore, the two empresses would no longer tolerate them. When Prince Kung went to Jehol to pay his respects to the deceased emperor, he was summoned to an interview with the two widows. During this conference they apparently decided to execute Su-shun and his colleagues.

Prince Kung immediately returned to Peking to make careful plans. The two empresses prepared to return to the capital in spite of the objections of Su-shun and the other regents. In October Su-shun was commissioned to escort the coffin of the late emperor to Peking. On the following day the two empresses, taking the young emperor and escorted by Tsai-yüan and Tuan-hua, traveled to Peking hastily by another road. At this time in Peking, four Chinese ministers of state submitted a joint memorial requesting the two empresses to listen to state affairs from behind screens. The imperial commissioner and general, Sheng-pao, also requested the appointment of the closest prince to assist in state affairs in order to prevent the usurpation and monopolization of authority by powerful and treacherous ministers. Sheng-pao's military support was much needed.

As soon as the two empresses and the young emperor reached Peking, a decree was issued to relieve Su-shun and his party of regents from their duties. By a secret decree Prince Kung was made prince counselor. In addition, Grand Secretary Kuei-liang, the senior vice-minister of revenue Wen-hsiang, and two others were made grand councilors. Su-shun, still on his way to Peking, was completely ignorant of the plot. Soon the eight regents were arrested and imprisoned.

On November 8 a decree granted Tsai-yüan and Tuan-hua the privilege of committing suicide, while Su-shun was ordered decapitated immediately. The two empresses listened to state affairs from behind the screens, assisted by Prince Kung, who served as prince counselor. Their reign is referred to as the *t'ung-chih* [joint control] meaning that the two empresses jointly governed the empire.

This contest, which was originally a feud within the royal family, would seem to have nothing to do with China's general political situation. But it was of great significance. In the ancestral and family law of the Ch'ing dynasty there was no precedent for having an empress dowager manage court affairs. Since the Ch'ing dynasty customarily observed precedents and ancestral law, why did they not let Prince Kung execute state affairs directly on behalf of the child emperor by following the example of the regency of Dorgon, uncle of Emperor Shun-chih (1644-1661), during that emperor's minority? Family law was absolutely disregarded in allowing the two empresses to become so powerful; this was a momentous change in the political history of the Ch'ing dynasty.

Su-shun did not belong to the closest branch of the imperial family. Although he was not a man of ability, he knew that the Manchus were incapable. He admonished Emperor Hsien-feng to have great confidence in Tseng Kuo-fan, Hu Lin-i, Tso Tsung-t'ang, and others. From this fact, one can see that he did not lack discernment. The ability and political knowledge of the empresses and Prince Kung was probably not much superior to those of Su-shun. Su-shun was fond of visiting places of ill fame; but the Empress Dowager Tz'u-hsi herself was no stranger to licentious amusements. Su-shun's attempt to keep Prince Kung from participating in important state matters should be criticized; however, his restrictions which prevented the two empresses from handling government affairs were not particularly wrong or disadvantageous to the imperial family or to China.

After the death of Emperor Hsien-feng, Su-shun shifted the grand council's authority to the regents. After his downfall, political authority was not returned to the grand council. Instead, it was allotted to the two empress dowagers and to Prince Kung. In practice, both the prince regent and the grand council had to observe carefully every suggestion from the two empress dowagers and to act according to their wishes. As for the two empress dowagers themselves, the Eastern Empress was weak in ability and knowledge. She was aware of the fact that the child emperor was not her own son, and hence she adopted a retiring attitude, generally maintaining silence. The real power was held by the Western Empress.

Tz'u-hsi in Power

When the child emperor T'ung-chih had just reached the legal age at which he could govern by himself, he died in 1874 without an heir. A three-year-old child [of Prince Ch'un] was now made puppet emperor under the name Kuang-hsü. Before long, the Eastern Empress also died; the Western Empress Tz'u-hsi now dominated state affairs.

Tz'u-hsi gave rein to her passions without limit, and allowed her favorite eunuchs to participate in government. Gradually high officials within and without the capital were reduced to ingratiating themselves with her favorites in order to maintain power and position. From the 1860's on, the Manchu emperor became no more than a figurehead. From this time to the end of the Ch'ing dynasty, the real power of the central government was actually wielded by a woman and a few eunuchs. The downfall of the Ch'ing dynasty was thereby determined, while the future of Chinese government was left in a perilous position.

After the Heavenly Kingdom of the Great Peace had been successfully destroyed, the scholar-official class, whitewashing all court troubles, eulogized the T'ung-chih period (1862-1874) as one of national revival. They praised the sacred virtue of the two empress dowagers. They disregarded the fact that one leg of the dragon throne had been broken. They did not foresee the ruinous fate of four hundred million Chinese as the subjects of the former concubine Yehonala.

Shifts in Military Power

Before the Taiping Rebellion, provincial governors usually had had no military power. As to governors-general, though they were credited with military authority, in reality even their power was only nominal. The nerve center of military administration was entirely in the hands of the emperor; the forces of the whole nation were under his control. Whenever there was important military action, the basic decision was made by the emperor, who appointed an imperial commissioner to conduct the military campaign. Even in the early stages of the war against the Taipings, this kind of military command was still very important. Hsiang Jung, Ho-ch'un, and Kuan-wen were all imperial commissioners. Later, Tseng Kuo-fan was also an imperial commissioner.

Hsiang Jung and Ho-ch'un were supported by the troops of Chang Kuoliang. When Chang's troops were routed, the two imperial commissioners were killed. The power of Kuan-wen was maintained by the troops of Hu Lin-i, the governor of Hupeh. Then Kuan-wen became a puppet of the Hupeh governor. Tseng Kuo-fan alone was an imperial commissioner in fact as well as in name. And the troops he trained were his insurance of strength.

During the Taiping Rebellion, the national standing army was much weaker than the local temporary irregular troops. After Nanking was taken, Tseng Kuo-fan and his brother were accordingly envied and slandered by other military leaders. The Manchu court was also secretly suspicious of them. Perceiving the dangerous situation, Tseng requested to have his Hunan Army disbanded. The request was instantly approved by the court since it appeared no longer necessary to use these soldiers.

However, several provinces in northern China were still overrun by huge numbers of the Nien-fei rebels, whose power was second to none but the Taipings. The famous general Seng-ko-lin-ch'in was killed by them in 1865. Had there been no Nien movement after the suppression of the Taiping Rebellion, the Manchu government might have maintained its prestige and power and need not have relied upon Chinese forces any longer. Since the Ch'ing court was again forced to rely on Tseng Kuo-fan and Li Hung-chang, the Nien-fei, though suppressed in 1868 by Tseng, Li, and other generals, not only outlived the Taiping movement, but also exercised a continuing revolutionary impact on the Ch'ing regime. The Nien-fei struggle reinforced the shift of political and military powers from the Manchu to the Chinese. [27]

The main part of the Hunan Army had now been replaced by Li Hungchang's Anhwei Army. Li became famous as a protégé of Tseng Kuo-fan, while the Anhwei Army, patterned after Tseng's Hunan Army, also gained fame. Later on, Tseng and Li each served a term as governor-general of Chihli. There they organized new troops, following the pattern of the Anhwei Army. Still later, Yüan Shih-k'ai's inauguration of a new army was also derived from the system of the Anhwei Army. Therefore, the earliest ancestors of the Peiyang military clique, which played so large a role in the next political period, were Li Hung-chang, and before him, Tseng Kuo-fan, whose new armies had put down the Taipings and the Nien-fei.

Furthermore, during the Taiping Rebellion many more provincial positions were filled by Chinese who had attained prominence through military careers. While they served as governors or governors-general, they simultaneously commanded troops. Chiang Chung-yüan, Hu Lin-i,

Li Hung-chang, and Tso Tsung-t'ang played such dual roles. The command of troops by provincial authorities now became a matter of course.

In 1868 when Tseng Kuo-fan had been made governor-general of Chihli, he was summoned to Peking for an interview with the throne. His conversation with Empress Dowager Tz'u-hsi is very revealing:

> T'zu-hsi asked, "What matter is the most urgent in Chihli?"
>
> Tseng replied, "The training of soldiers has priority, and next comes the reorganization of administrative affairs."
>
> "Do you plan to train 20,000 soldiers?"
>
> "Yes, I plan to train 20,000 men."
>
> "Do you wish to have more regular soldiers or more militiamen?"
>
> "It is still uncertain. Probably there will be more militiamen than soldiers."
>
> "Have the provincial leaders recently spoken of coastal defense matters?"
>
> "Because the Long-haired and the Nien bandits have caused disturbances for so many years, the coastal defense measures have been slackened."
>
> The empress remarked, "This is an important matter."
>
> "This is a most important matter. Troops must be trained. Even though there might not be a war for a century to come, still it is necessary to train soldiers for defense. Soldiers must be well trained, although we should not open hostilities first. We should be serious in peace negotiations as well as in drilling soldiers. The two matters should not be neglected and both should be handled very carefully."[28]

After Tseng Kuo-fan took up his duties as governor-general of

Chihli, he memorialized the throne: "The training of troops in Chihli should follow the method used in the Southeast." An edict indicated approval.

Decentralization of Power and Its Effects

Clearly, after the Taiping Rebellion the Ch'ing court considered the training of soldiers to be one of the main duties of the provincial authorities. After the failure of China in the Sino-Japanese War, many governors and governors-general under the watchword "Self-strengthening" tried to organize new armies. Thus the Manchu's single, unified military system developed into a decentralized military establishment. These decentralized troops were subsequently used by revolutionists; they were also the ancestors of minor warlords in all the provinces. The history of the warlords began with the organization of temporary militias in different localities during the Taiping period.

The power of provincial authorities during the period of the Taiping Rebellion underwent two changes. The governors-general and governors secured real military authority and their power gradually increased. Also, the army was transformed from a single unified organization into a diversified and decentralized organization. Both changes weakened central government control over the provincial authorities and contributed to the downfall of the Ch'ing dynasty. They also aggravated that division and domination of the country which was exploited by warlords during the years of the Republic, especially 1916-1927.

During this same period, a new local force, the gentry, also emerged. At the time of the Taiping and the Nien-fei rebellion, the training of the militia in the Yangtze Valley and other provinces was entrusted to the outstanding gentlemen in these districts. By recruiting soldiers and raising funds to suppress bandits, these gentry gradually participated in important political affairs in their local government. Far-sighted governors-general and governors, visualizing that under difficult circumstances they must secure local assistance, consulted the opinions of the provincial gentry. Gradually in some provinces the increasing power of the gentry came to be accepted by the local magistrates as essential to security. Later on during the reform and constitutional movement, this auxiliary political force was used to serve both sides.

To sum up: Because of the shift in the location of military and political power which occurred during the Taiping period, the Taiping Rebellion provides the key to several critical changes in China in subsequent decades.

CHAPTER THREE THE PERIOD OF IMITATION OF WESTERN METHODS

The generation in China from 1864 to 1894 lived uneasily despite domestic peace. For the first several years of this period there were still disturbances by remnants of the Taipings in the South, by the Nien-fei in the North, and by the Mohammedans in the Northwest; but the important events in these thirty years mainly concerned diplomatic relations, particularly the loss of China's vassal states to foreign powers. During this difficult era some relatively far-sighted Chinese statesmen realized that threats of foreign aggression had become very serious. They therefore pursued with all their energy these "foreign matters" [*yang-wu*] by following a vigorous policy of westernization.

"Western methods imitation" became the crucial problem. This new focus of attention began with the establishment of the Kiangnan Arsenal in Shanghai (1867). It ended with the destruction of the Peiyang fleet by Japan (1894). To this inglorious end, thirty years of "imitation" seemed to have profited China only slightly. A few leaders then took steps to promote a more extensive reform movement.

The period of imitation of Western methods covered the two reigns of T'ung-chih [1862-1874] and Kuang-hsü [1875-1908]. In the last section of the preceding chapter, the shifts in political power have been briefly explained. In the following sections, court conditions and the central political figures during these two reigns will be briefly treated.

THE COURTS OF T'UNG-CHIH AND KUANG-HSÜ

After the execution of Su-shun, the political power of the central government was nominally shouldered by the two dowager empresses and by Prince Kung (I-hsin). Actually Empress Tz'u-hsi held the power and merely used the other empress and Prince Kung as her tools. One year after the suppression of the Taiping Rebellion, the Empress Tz'u-hsi deprived Prince Kung of all his offices, ostensibly because he had shown partiality to his relatives and because of his allegedly careless conduct at the court. Actually she was envious of him. She gave all of Prince Kung's offices to her favorite eunuch, An Te-hai, who was greedy for political power and hated the prince.

But at this time there were other princes and high officials in the court who pleaded for justice for the prince and joined together to submit memorials and to argue vigorously on his behalf. In his memorial the Supervising Censor Kuang-ch'eng spoke loudly against the prince's demotion, saying that people within and without Peking were surprised at the suspicion and disharmony in the court.

Confronted by the urgent pleas of officials, the empress showed apprehension of the public criticism. Soon she restored Prince Kung to the position of leader of the Tsungli Yemen and member of the Grand Council. His power, however, was much less than it had previously been. He no longer held the title of Prince Counselor. Henceforth, Prince Kung (I-hsin) had to be very docile and obedient to the Empress Tz'u-hsi. This achievement was the first step in her success in building herself up as an awe-inspiring power.

The Emperor T'ung-chih

The Eastern Empress, as the wife of Emperor Hsien-feng, should have had a more advantageous position than the Western Empress. But the Western Empress Tz'u-hsi was versed in literature, while the Eastern Empress was almost unlettered. Moreover, since Emperor T'ung-chih was the son of the Western Empress, the Eastern Empress dared not antagonize his mother. When Emperor T'ung-chih grew older, he came to realize the wrongdoings of his own mother and was so displeased that he began to side with the Eastern Empress.

When Emperor T'ung-chih approached a marriageable age, the Eastern Empress recommended an eighteen-year-old girl, while his mother selected another girl of only thirteen to be her daughter-in-law, so that she could easily control the young queen. She remained inflexible in her selection and the two empresses stood at odds without being able to make a decision. Finally, they had to allow the emperor to make his own choice. Emperor T'ung-chih concurred with the selection of the Eastern Empress; the eighteen-year-old girl was inaugurated as queen in 1872, while the younger lady was made a concubine of the first rank. The following year the emperor was regarded as mature enough to rule the empire personally. The regency was then terminated.

Empress Dowager Tz'u-hsi was chagrined because her suggestion was not accepted by the emperor. Utilizing her position as his mother, she interfered with state affairs and with the relationship between Emperor T'ung-chih and his wife. She forced a closer association between the young ruler and his concubine and induced him to go to various excesses. The emperor was so distraught that he began to live a solitary life and soon was led astray. He ruled the empire in name only for just over a year and then died.[1]

The Succession to T'ung-chih: Kuang-hsü

Emperor T'ung-chih left no heir and had no brother. When he was seriously ill, he summoned his tutor, Li Hung-tsao, for an interview, giving a verbal decree to him that he wished to have Tsai-chu, a prince of the third order, succeed to the throne. Li Hung-tsao took the decree to Empress Dowager Tz'u-hsi, who was enraged and ordered Li to leave the palace at once. When the emperor died and while people on the outside were not yet apprised of this occurrence, Empress Tz'u-hsi summoned the princes, the grand councilors, and ministers of the household to a confidential meeting and announced, "The emperor's illness is hopeless, and the successor has not yet been decided upon. Who is the right person?" After some discussion Tz'u-hsi said peremptorily that since the son of Prince I-huan was closely related to the imperial family, she intended to make him successor to the throne. The son of Prince I-huan was three years old. Tz'u-hsi refused to let anyone be selected who in rank or generation could be considered as the emperor's son.

If someone of closer rank and generation had been selected as the successor, Emperor T'ung-chih would be considered to have had an adopted heir. His widow would then have become the dowager empress, and the two senior empresses would no longer, from behind their screens, have had the right to listen to affairs of state. If a boy in his majority were established as the successor, the two empresses would have little chance of further domination. The three-year-old infant Tsai-t'ien, the son of the youngest sister of Empress Dowager Tz'u-hsi, was selected to succeed to the throne and became known as Kuang-hsü. By controlling this decision, the two dowager empresses managed to retain power in national affairs.

All princes of the imperial family were so afraid of Empress Dowager Tz'u-hsi that no one dared to oppose her choice even though it violated the dynastic law of succession, which provided that in case adoption was warranted, the one chosen should belong to the next generation below the deceased. A new precedent was established in the imperial family of the Ch'ing dynasty, the throne passing to a younger cousin and not to a nephew. Thereafter Emperor Kuang-hsü became the victim of Empress Dowager Tz'u-hsi, who resumed her regency with the other dowager empress.

The Court of Tz'u-hsi

In 1881 the Eastern dowager died, poisoned, according to Yün Yü-ting's account, by Tz'u-hsi.[2] Before her death the Eastern dowager had been the only person of whom the licentious Tz'u-hsi was afraid.

This fear had been intensified by the fate of Tz'u-hsi's eunuch, An Te-hai. The courtiers loathed this imperial favorite but dared not say anything against him. In 1869 An Te-hai, ordered by Tz'u-hsi to Canton to buy embroidered dragon robes, passed en route through Shantung. There Governor Ting Pao-chen, following a secret order from the Eastern Empress Dowager and Emperor T'ung-chih, arrested and killed him. This action was sanctioned according to the ancestral law of the Manchu dynasty, by which eunuchs were not permitted to go out of Peking; any eunuch who transgressed this law could be arrested and executed on the spot. When Governor Ting's report reached the court, the Eastern Empress Dowager spoke up in defense of Ting. She based her case on the ancestral law. Tz'u-hsi, the protector of the executed eunuch, could not refute the argument, but became thereafter very bitter. The death of the Eastern Empress, however, had removed the only person of whom Tz'u-hsi stood in awe.

When Emperor T'ung-chih came to power, a clever Cantonese merchant, who wished to secure a government position so that he could make a fortune, volunteered to contribute lumber for repairing the Yüan-ming Yüan[3] for the enjoyment of the dowager empress. Emperor T'ung-chih, who probably wished to take this opportunity to make his mother occupy the Summer Palace so as to avoid her interference in state affairs, accepted the offer. He conferred the title of *taotai* on the contributor, who was appointed superintendent of the repair work and was sent to buy more lumber from various provinces.

A censor submitted a memorial objecting to the plan, but it bore no fruit. Before long this Cantonese merchant not only extorted money but disobeyed the law in all the provinces. He was also involved in litigation with foreign merchants from whom he purchased lumber at 50 taels while reporting to the government that he had paid 300,000 taels. The investigation of the case by Li Hung-chang resulted in the dismissal and punishment of the Cantonese merchant. The reconstruction work of

Yüan-ming Yüan was temporarily suspended until the time of Kuang-hsü. Then Empress Dowager Tz'u-hsi appropriated a foreign loan, intended for use in naval construction, to build for herself the magnificent Summer Palace known as the I-ho Yüan, in the vicinity of Yüan-ming Yüan.

The next chief eunuch, Li Lien-ying, abused his power and accepted bribes even more than his predecessor, An Te-hai. Li Lien-ying was ordered by Tz'u-hsi to accompany the emperor's father, I-huan, on an inspection of the seaport near Tientsin in 1886. Thereupon a censor memorialized the throne urging strict suppression of the evils of eunuchs. On account of this memorial the censor was demoted.

Emperor Kuang-hsü was married in 1889. At this time he theoretically assumed personal control of governmental affairs. In practice he still had to report all appointments and administrative affairs to the empress for decision. In general the court after 1862 was the Empress Tz'u-hsi's court. The power of the chief eunuch gradually surpassed that of the princes and grand councilors.

When Su-shun had been in power, his opponents always requested the dowager empresses to attend court affairs lest too much authority should be yielded to unworthy advisors. Now the princes and high ministers witnessed the shifting of prestige into the hands of the eunuchs, and except by flattering the eunuchs they could do nothing.

The Character of Tz'u-hsi's Rule

What was the secret of Empress Tz'u-hsi's power? Tz'u-hsi relied entirely upon the influence of Confucian ethics. Although she herself did not pay much personal attention to Confucian moral principles, she always used the majestic power of the Confucian moral code when she dealt with others. She herself did not obey the law of her ancestors, but she always quoted the family law when arguing against the nobles of the imperial family, against the emperor, and against the imperial concubines. Any noble who hurt her feelings would be turned over to the imperial household for punishment. When the empress or an imperial concubine disobeyed her will, she would be scolded or whipped, according to the degree of punishment that was felt to be needed. The emperor dared not protect his wife or his concubine from this treatment, for he was morally obliged to obey his mother absolutely.

Empress Tz'u-hsi also used this obligation to cope with any objections that might be raised by the ministers. She supported the child emperor as a puppet before whom everybody had to stand in awe and whom all were bound to obey, according to the principle of loyalty to the ruler. At the same time everyone was obliged to obey her, the mother and the regent of the emperor. The proverb, "A sage uses filial piety to rule the empire" had now become the most precious law of Confucian morality. No one dared offend the Western Empress. During the lifetime of the Eastern Empress, the source of authority of this rule had been distributed between the two; there was still a balance of power. After the death of the Eastern Empress, Tz'u-hsi could do whatever she pleased.

Tz'u-hsi clearly perceived that the Taipings were the enemies of Confucian principles and that, until that enemy was vanquished, there was no chance for her to be happy. Among the great Manchu officials there was no one capable of subduing the Taipings. The Manchus were lucky enough, however, to secure the assistance of such men as Tseng Kuo-fan, Li Hung-chang, and Tso Tsung-t'ang, all of whom had been strongly influenced by Confucianism and were willing to fight at any cost to protect its principles. For this reason the Western Empress relied wholeheartedly on these men and entrusted them with enormous authority and responsibility. As long as they resisted the enemy, Tz'u-hsi could dominate court affairs quite easily and could enjoy herself lavishly.

Concerning this policy of using Chinese to control Chinese, the empress dowager saw eye to eye with Su-shun. Her view, however, was even more far-sighted than his. Tz'u-hsi followed this policy without modification, not only throughout the Taiping Rebellion but after its conclusion. By this policy she maintained her domination for a long time.

KEY MEN OF THE EMPIRE

During the suppression of the Taiping Rebellion, the central political figures, Li Hung-chang, Hu Lin-i, Tseng Kuo-ch'üan and Tso Tsung-t'ang all belonged to the group of Tseng Kuo-fan. Hu Lind died before the rebellion was suppressed; Tseng Kuo-fan, who had suffered much criticism and slander, disbanded his Hunan Army after the capture of Nanking and begged for retirement or for an insignificant position. Tz'u-hsi continued to make use of Tseng Kuo-fan, however, along with Tso Tsung-t'ang and Li Hung-chang.

Tso Tsung-t'ang was appointed in 1863 governor-general of Fukien and Chekiang and concurrently governor of the latter province. After the recovery of Chekiang, he resigned from his governorship and led his troops to Fukien and Kwangtung, where he annihilated the remnants of the Taipings in the following two years. Then he was transferred to the position of governor-general of Shensi and Kansu to undertake the suppression of the Western Nien bandits as well as of the Mohammedan Rebellion. Thenceforth Tso's service was limited to the Northwest of China until 1880. Then he was recalled from Sinkiang to Peking to serve in the Grand Council and the Tsungli Yamen. In the autumn of 1881 he was made governor-general of Liang-Kiang. After three years the Sino-French War brought Tso to a new appointment as the commander of military affairs in Fukien Province; shortly after this appointment he died.

At the time of the recovery of Nanking, Tseng Kuo-fan was governor-general of Liang-Kiang, and Li Hung-chang governor of Kiangsu. In 1865 Tseng was made imperial commissioner in Shantung and Honan for the purpose of suppressing the Nien rebels, and Li Hung-chang was ordained acting governor-general of Liang-Kiang. On account of slow military progress and poor health, Tseng begged for leave, but his request was refused by the throne. Instead, Li was appointed to succeed him as imperial commissioner and Tseng resumed his original position as the Liang-Kiang governor-general, with an additional responsibility of keeping a constant supply of ammunition and rations for Li's troops.

The Eastern Nien-fei were blotted out in January 1868, and after seven months the Western Nien-fei met the same fate. Tseng was then appointed governor-general of Chihli and his position in Liang-Kiang passed to Ma Hsin-i. When the Tientsin Massacre of a French consul and twelve missionaries occurred in 1870, Tseng's handling of the case was severely criticized by the chauvinistic scholar-official class; just at this same time Ma Hsin-i was assassinated. Thereupon the Ch'ing court made Tseng governor-general of Liang-Kiang and Li Hung-chang governor-general of Chihli. In 1872 Tseng died in office. Li Hung-chang remained governor-general of Chihli for nearly a quarter of a century, until 1895.

These various assignments involving eminent Chinese political leaders of the period not only indicate their status with the Ch'ing court but also help explain their influence on the modernization movement during this time. The three centers of the imitation of Western techniques were Shanghai in Kiangnan, Ma-wei [near Foochow], and Tientsin [in Chihli]; the three principal promoters were Tseng, Li, and Tso. However, Tso was soon obliged to concentrate his energy upon the campaign in the Northwest, and the management of the Foochow shipyard was handed over to Shen Pao-chen, who achieved very little. After Tseng's death no high official in Kiangnan took much interest in encouraging the adoption of Western civilization. The responsibility of promoting the imitation of Western methods was accordingly shouldered by Li Hung-chang, who retained his post as governor-general of Chihli.

After the suppression of the rebellions, the positions of the governors-general in the Southeast were not so important as that of the governor-general of Chihli. Chihli was closest to the imperial court and communication with the court was relatively easy. Li Hung-chang, the only progressive minister who made significant contributions to China's prosperity, was trusted by Empress Dowager Tz'u-hsi. He was not only superintendent of trade in the northern ports with the additional title of grand secretary, but he also had a large force of soldiers entirely at his disposal and was considered indispensable in handling diplomatic negotiations. His opinion on other important state affairs was frequently requested by Tz'u-hsi. Li had become the most influential man of his period.

In the eyes of foreigners there was only one person with whom they liked to deal when international problems arose, and that person was Li Hung-chang. The Chihli governor-generalship well-nigh became the second court of the Ch'ing dynasty. Nevertheless conservative scholar-officials, who opposed "foreign matters" and hated Western ideas, considered Li Hung-chang a monster. They even accused him of being a traitor. But though they were envious and resentful of him, they had no way to rob him of his prestige because Empress Dowager Tz'u-hsi had great confidence in him. Whenever an opportunity presented itself, however, the conservatives rose en masse to attack him. Although Li for many years seemed the most fortunate of men, his luck finally ran out.

THE IMITATION OF WESTERN METHODS

The earliest realization that China needed to imitate Western methods came after the conclusion of the Opium War. In the preface of the *Haikuo t'u-chih* [*An Illustrated Gazetteer of the Maritime Countries*] the compiler Wei Yüan says, "Why is this book written? The answer is, it is written to attack barbarians by using barbarians, and to learn the superior techniques of the barbarians in order to curb the barbarians." Because China suffered greatly from the Opium War, some Chinese became aware that their country could never control her invaders until she had mastered their superior knowledge of technology.

During the Taiping Rebellion, China suffered another great humiliation when the English and French allies occupied Peking. At this time the realization of the necessity of imitation became keener than ever. When Li Hung-chang and Tso Tsung-t'ang battled the Taipings in Kiangsu and Chekiang, they made use of foreign guns, ships, and other effective weapons in addition to the assistance of foreign soldiers. Hence from actual experience they learned to appreciate the superior equipment of the "barbarians."

In 1863 Li Hung-chang wrote a letter to Tseng Kuo-ch'üan saying that he had recovered Tai-tsang by using Gordon's artillery. In another letter to Tseng, Li says:

> The western cannon with explosive shells ... are matchless in the empire. Now I have hired several foreigners and have assigned them to instruct several battalions of our soldiers. I have also invited foreign mechanics to come to our camp and have purchased machines from Hong Kong for making guns. Ting Jih-chiang is coming soon to supervise the work. I have asked each of the admirals of France and England to buy several cannons for us to be sent from their countries .... The provisions of foreign countries are expensive and their number of soldiers small; but a mere ten thousand men can face a great enemy. The number of Chinese soldiers is many times larger than theirs, and yet ... they are incompetent ... owing to their poor and obsolete guns. If our weapons were as good as the Westerners', we would have more than sufficient power to pacify the rebellions in China, and we would also be strong enough to resist foreign aggressors. Russia and Japan knew nothing about gunnery until their emperors and officials became humble and open-minded enough to seek knowledge about the secret skills of England and France; soon Russia and Japan were able to make guns and steamships themselves

> and could fight for hegemony with England and France. If China follows their example, after a century she will be able to stand on her own feet for a long time. I beg you, my teacher, to lead us in this direction.[4]

In a further letter Li says:

> It is very difficult to commence to learn foreign ways. I only hope the rebellion will be quickly suppressed so that we can study foreign weapons. If only China had two items, guns with explosive shells and steamships, the Westerners would immediately behave themselves.[5]

Li Hung-chang's interest in Western ways is explicit in these two letters. His imitation of foreign methods was first ardently concentrated upon guns and steamships. When fighting against the Taipings, he bought machines for making guns and established factories for manufacturing these weapons. In 1865 Li and Tseng Kuo-fan jointly memorialized the throne requesting the establishment of the Kiangnan Arsenal. Before long a branch arsenal was set up in Nanking and the following establishments were also inaugurated:

1. A shipyard was established at Ma-wei, Foochow, as a result of Tso Tsung-t'ang's memorial in 1866.
2. A machine factory was established at Tientsin. The date of the establishment is uncertain; probably it was begun when Tseng Kuo-fan was governor-general of Chihli. In 1870 his successor Li Hung-chang memorialized the throne with a request that it be expanded and reorganized.
3. Students were selected and sent by the Chinese government to study in the United States. This action was brought about through a joint memorial of Tseng Kuo-fan and Li Hung-chang in

1872. Those sent were for the most part young boys who lacked a foundation in Chinese knowledge and thought.

4. The China Merchants' Steam Navigation Company was organized in 1872.
5. Preparation was made to build steel warships (1875).
6. Army officers were sent to Germany to learn about her army, navy, weapons, and other techniques; students from the Foochow naval academy were also sent to study abroad. The year 1876 was the first that China sent students to study in Europe.
7. The Kaiping coal mine was opened (1878).
8. A naval academy was established at Tientsin, and plans for telegraph lines were sanctioned by imperial decree (1880).
9. A harbor and shipyard were built at Port Arthur, and a cotton mill was planned by merchants at Shanghai (1882).
10. A military academy was established at Tientsin (1885).
11. The Peiyang fleet was formed (1888).

These undertakings were all carried on by Li Hung-chang except for the first three plans, which were jointly recommended by Tseng Kuo-fan, Tso Tsung-t'ang, and Li.

Li Hung-chang and His Critics

Li's attitude toward "foreign matters" and Western methods may be discerned from the last paragraph of his memorial requesting the establishment of the Kiangnan Arsenal. In this memorial he said that China's civilization and her political and social systems were better than those of the West; therefore, if anyone insisted that the only way to change China's precarious position into a secure position was to imitate the West and to become familiar with its machines, he would not agree with such a one-sided point of view; yet it was necessary to adopt, the superior techniques of foreigners. The scope of Li's plans was confined to the building of ships, the making of instruments, the construction of harbors, the establishment of telegraph offices, a merchants' navigation company, a cotton mill, a mine. In short, his plans were limited to military and economic affairs. Even the opening of schools and the sending of students abroad were part of a military plan to train interpreters so that they could become foreign envoys. Li Hung-chang had never dreamed of a fundamental reform of the Chinese political, educational, and social systems. He still believed that the Chinese culture was superior to that of foreign countries.

For this reason Liang Ch'i-ch'ao criticized him saying, "Li knows military affairs, but does not know civil administration; he is familiar with foreign affairs but does not know domestic matters; he cares for the court, but he does not care for the people; he understands some foreign matters but does not understand national problems." [6]

Li Hung-chang's industrial and military establishments were also criticized by Kuo Sung-tao, Chinese minister to England. Before the Sino-French War (1884) Kuo had already pointed out that Li's undertakings were not the fundamental and most reliable way to save China, and that China's imitation of the West was not so successful as that of Japan. In 1877 Kuo sent a letter to Li Hung-chang saying:

> There are more than two hundred Japanese studying technology in England, scattered in all the seaports; nineteen of them are in London. I have met more than twenty and all can speak English .... One, originally a feudal lord ... is studying law. Japan's Minister of Revenue ... is commissioned to study the [British] economic system and to imitate everything concerning the governing of income and expenditure .... There are very few who are studying military methods, because political and economic systems are more fundamental for developing a nation. The Grand Secretary [Li Hung-chang] is in charge of military affairs and therefore devotes attention to the investigation of military methods. In my humble opinion, I should

> like to have the government students abroad change their major subjects to metallurgy, railroad construction, and electricity. At the same time the governors-general and governors of all provinces should be ordered to select and support more intelligent youths to go to the various factories in Tientsin, Shanghai, and Fukien to study machinery and to learn foreign languages and then to be sent to foreign countries.[7]

At the time Kuo wrote this letter, Li Hung-chang had just sent for the first time some students to Europe to learn about military techniques and weapons. The several persons who were sent to Germany were selected from among army officers, while the others were selected from among the students at the school of naval administration attached to the Foochow shipyard.

Li's reply to Kuo's suggestion was:

> My humble duty is in military affairs, and therefore I must study military methods .... Weapons are the most important thing for a nation; if we look for other larger and more far-reaching plans, we can hardly achieve our purposes. The only thing I can do is to try my best to do what can be done.[8]

If Li had enlarged the scope of the Western imitation, he would undoubtedly have been more severely criticized by others and might not have been able even to maintain his own position.

Opposition to Reforms in Education

In 1867 a language school, T'ung-wen Kuan, was opened at Peking. Some courtiers, influenced by Tseng and Li, suggested that young and brilliant men be selected from the government ministries and the Hanlin Academy to study foreign languages, astronomy, mathematics, shipbuilding, machine making, and other subjects in the new school. A grand secretary, Wo-jen, who was a devotee of Neo-Confucianism, wrote a memorial to the emperor attacking this plan:

> According to my viewpoint, astronomy and mathematics are of very little use. If [these subjects] are going to be taught by Westerners as regular subjects of study, the damage will be great .... Even if we respect barbarians as teachers and even if the students faithfully study their teaching, we will only be training mathematicians. From ancient times to modern times, I have never heard of any one who could rely on mathematics to restore the strength of a nation .... If astronomy and mathematics must be taught, we can undoubtedly find some Chinese who has mastered both subjects, if an extensive search is made for such a person. Why is it necessary to learn from the barbarians? ... Since the conclusion of the Peace Treaty [1860] Christianity has been prevalent and half of our ignorant people have been fooled by it. The only thing [we can] rely upon is maintainance of our own scholars able to delve into Confucian principles by means of which they may keep the minds of the people quiet and harmonious. Now if these brilliant and talented scholars who have been trained by the nation and reserved for great usefulness in the future are converted [from their regular course of study] to follow the barbarians ... the multitudes of the Chinese will be tempted to give allegiance to the barbarians. [9]

A censor who was born in the same district as Wo-jen supported Wo's idea, saying:

> Astronomy and mathematics should only be studied by those working in the Board of Astronomy. Only the craftsmen and laborers of the Ministry of Public Works should be commanded to learn

> manufacturing. As for scholars and court ministers, they should not esteem such crafts, nor should they have barbarians as teachers.[10]

After these memorials were made known, the scholar-officials in Peking praised them wholeheartedly. Hence self-esteemed "scholarly gentlemen" considered the reading of foreign books shameful, and none of them was willing to enter the T'ung-wen Kuan. Consequently, the students of that language college were mostly mediocre people, lacking any lofty purpose, who wished to make a living from interpreting or from the drafting of diplomatic messages.

Opposition to Industrial Reforms

The shipyard established by Tso Tsung-t'ang in Fukien was given to Shen Pao-chen, who was to continue its management and development. After Tso was commissioned to the campaigns in the Northwest, Shen was directed to follow the same pattern of work set up by Tso. However, Shen lacked Tso's strong driving power and he was confronted by many difficulties. Because a great deal of money had been spent on the shipyard with insignificant results, while at the same time the nation was in financial straits, the throne was asked in 1872 to liquidate the shipyard. The Ch'ing court brought this suggestion before all of the provincial authorities for deliberation. Both Tso Tsung-t'ang and Li Hung-chang strongly supported its continuance; consequently, the life of the shipyard was prolonged. Part of Li's memorial attacking its liquidation reads:

> The Westerners rely expressly on the effectiveness of their guns and steamships to overrun China; and China with her obsolete weapons cannot oppose them and hence is controlled by them. For us to live today and to say "Let us reject the barbarians and drive them from our boundaries" is certainly absurd .... Our scholar-officials have been indulging in the practice of writing in fancy and flowery

language and are ignorant of the immense changes that have come about. They are accustomed to a fool's paradise and have forgotten how much they have suffered from defeats and insults inflicted by foreigners during the last twenty or thirty years. How can we maintain domestic security and at the same time resist the foreigners for a hundred or a thousand years to come? I humbly maintain that all other expenses of the nation might be curtailed, but as for supporting soldiers, planning defense measures, manufacturing guns, and making war vessels—these expenses should never be spared. If we try to be stingy with such funds, we will deprive ourselves of protection, our nation will have nothing to depend upon, and we can never be strong. [11]

Li Hung-chang was a man with a far-sighted point of view in comparison with that of his contemporaries. When foreigners built a section of railroad between Shanghai and Sungkiang, the Chinese government was urged by the scholar-official class to buy the railroad, have it wrecked, and to dump the wreckage into the sea. They considered railways and steamships to be objects of bad omen and the results of the ambitious designs of the foreign devils. Men who disagreed with the opinions of the majority were treated as pariahs.

The Fate of the Westernizers

Kuo Sung-tao, for instance, was fond of speaking about "foreign matters" and advising others not to denounce the barbarians in empty words. He was so harshly criticized by the conservative scholars and men of letters that there was almost no place for him to hide himself. He went abroad as the Chinese minister to England and France. Still people continued to accuse and criticize him. After his return to China, he dared not go to Peking. Kuo's correspondence with Li Hung-chang vividly illustrates current objections to Western methods. Kuo wrote:

On account of the prohibition of opium, conflicts arose; thereafter seaports [for trade] were multiplied until they reached the Yangtze River. The [foreigners'] power is becoming more oppressive by the day, and we suffer more and more from their disturbances. We should investigate carefully their entire history and itemize the actual causes of their becoming rich and strong and uncover their ambitions. Then China will know the essentials of how to stand on her own feet and how to deal with others.

I plan to compile a book and submit it to the Tsungli Yamen for distribution among the schools of the empire in order to dispel the doubts of scholars and officials. The idea of the court's polite treatment of people from afar certainly has its far-reaching and important implications, which officials and people should be enabled to understand. I think that if this principle is made clear, then the foundation for millions of generations of the nation can be firmly secured. En route to Tientsin I also explained this to the Grand Secretary [Li Hung-chang]. When I reached the capital I was frustrated by clamorous opinions and refrained from expressing myself.

Personally I think there is something in the minds of the Chinese which is absolutely unintelligible. Of the injuries visited upon us by Westerners none is more serious than the opium traffic. British gentlemen feel ashamed of having used this pernicious thing as an instrument to open hostilities with China, and they are making a strong effort to eradicate it. Yet Chinese scholars and officials are willing to indulge complacently in it without any sense of remorse. For several decades it has been the national humiliation; it has exhausted our financial power and poisoned and injured the lives of our people; yet there is not a single person whose conscience is weighed down by it. Clocks, watches, and toys are owned by all families. Woolen and cotton cloth and the like are prevalent in poor districts and the isolated countryside.

The practice in Kiangsu and Chekiang even goes so far as to put aside the national currency for the exclusive use of foreign banknotes; furthermore, they have raised their value and with such indifference that no one knows that this is wrong. Nevertheless, as soon as these people heard of the building of railroads and telegraph lines, they became sorely disturbed and enraged, and arose in multitudes to lay hindrances and difficulties in the way. There are even people who see foreign machines as objects of public hatred. Tseng Chi-tse to attend a family funeral took a small steamboat [instead of walking home with a sorrowful face according to custom] from Nanking to Changsha. This caused the local officials and gentry to raise a great uproar that lasted for several years .... I am too stupid to know their minds.

We have had relations with foreigners for thirty years, but the provincial authorities are entirely ignorant of them. These same authorities used to compel the court, as a facade, to do what they liked and called it public opinion .... The people's desires have been sadly suppressed and choked off for a long time. They have no means of expressing themselves to their superiors ....

I am a native of Hunan, born and bred in an undeveloped and conservative country. I have never engaged in business nor been close to foreigners. I have read books, observed the principles, and investigated changing events from ancient to modern times in order to obtain the truth. In the midst of the laughter and ridicule of the whole world, I have looked for the constant principle by means of which to protect the country and to regulate the nation, in order that it may become independent and may not decline. I speak frankly, in torrents of words, without the slightest reservation; yet no one has ever defended me. Even though I have fled 70,000 *li* away, in less than two months I have been impeached again and again.

Consequently I have suddenly changed my original stand, and do not presume any more to express my opinion.[12]

Li Hung-chang replied:

Although I have never been in Europe, I have been inquiring and investigating Western political and cultural conditions for nearly twenty years, and I have formed some general ideas. Ever since the discussion of coastal defense began in 1874, I have stated in detail the necessity of opening coal and iron mines, of building telegraph lines and railways, and of opening schools for pursuing Western knowledge and sciences in order to train men of ability. At that time Grand Councilor Wen-hsiang smiled in his eyes but kept silent, and in the Court conference most of the participants were noncommittal except for two members who strongly objected to my suggestions. I had the honor of meeting Prince Kung and explained to him thoroughly the advantages of railways .... Prince Kung agreed with my suggestion, but said that nobody dared to promote such action. I again begged him to watch for a chance to explain this point to the two dowager empresses, and he said that the two empresses could not initiate such a great plan either.

Thereafter I spoke no more .... My humble idea is that the prerequisites of building railways are the opening of coal and iron mines, because if iron must be bought from foreign countries for such work, it is too difficult to achieve. At present the coal and iron mines in Keelung, Taiwan, are already in operation, while two other mines are just now being opened here .... But the gentry class forbids the local people to use Western methods and machines, so that eventually the people will not be able to do anything. All these undertakings have been promoted by me alone; but it is as difficult to achieve a result as it is to catch the wind. Scholars and men of letters always criticize me for honoring strange knowledge and for being queer and unusual. It is really difficult to understand the minds of some Chinese.[13]

These two letters emphasize barriers stubbornly maintained by scholar-officials against China's Westernization movement. They also help us to understand part of the reason for its slow progress.

China Faces Western Expansion

The time of Li Hung-chang's imitation of Western methods coincided with the rapid development of imperialism. The period from 1865, when Li began to imitate Western methods, until 1870, when he became governor-general of Chihli, was one most noteworthy in the political history of the world. The Civil War in the United States ended in 1865 and the power of the federal government was gradually consolidated. The unifications of Italy and of Germany were completed between 1866 and 1870; the Third Republic of France was established in 1870, when her political system was fixed, civil war was allayed, and the foundations were established for foreign expansion. In 1868 Japan had restored Emperor Meiji, who moved the capital to Edo [now Tokyo], abolished the feudal system, launched a series of reforms, opened the nation to Western trade, and developed Japan's interest overseas. The spirit of imperialism was active and aggressive. Li Hung-chang's chief aim in imitating the West was no more than "improving the defense and consolidating the frontiers," a passive, defensive, and conservative aim.

In the last chapter the dialogue between Tseng Kuo-fan and Empress Dowager Tz'u-hsi was quoted: one must be able to fight before one can defend oneself, and one must be able to defend oneself before one can negotiate peace. Li Hung-chang's fundamental principles with regard to military and foreign policies were that he imitated Western methods on the one hand, and on the other, he tried his best to avoid war with foreign powers. China's conservative and passive spirit contributed to her own decline.

Members of the scholar-official class, with their limited, out-of-date knowledge, were nonetheless insurmountably proud of their superficial wisdom. Despising Western methods, they persistently advocated war against a foreign power whenever there was diplomatic controversy. The Ch'ing court mistook the scholars' high-sounding words for a reliable *esprit de corps* or for "public opinion." Therefore, Li Hung-chang and a few others, who were relatively clearheaded, had to cope with the invasions of the imperialists and at the same time deal with the misinformed court and people. As a result, during this period the imperialists were successful in carrying through their aggressive policy everywhere in China. China's efforts to "improve defenses and strengthen frontiers" were entirely unsuccessful.

During this period China's important diplomatic problems revolved about Russia in the Northwest, France in the extreme South, and Japan in the East and Northeast. The Sino-Russian problem, which involved the Moslem problem, developed first.

Russian Invasion of Ili and Sinkiang

In the Northwest when the Taiping Rebellion was about to be suppressed, Moslems in the two provinces Shensi and Kansu, influenced by the Taipings and the Nien-fei, started a rebellion which lasted for many years. It began when two Moslem chiefs, T'o-ming and T'o-lin, secretly went from Shensi to Urumchi, Sinkiang, where they tried to instigate a riot.

Just at this juncture they met a Manchu battalion commander who had for a long time cherished the idea of inciting a rebellion. The two Moslem chiefs allied themselves with this Manchu officer, killed the local commander in chief, and occupied Urumchi. Within a short time they took the important cities along the northern route of the Tien Shan.

Other factions of Moslems in the southern route of the Tien Shan got wind of the uprising and responded to its stimulus by capturing many important cities from the Manchu government. The big city Ili was lost to the rebels in 1866. Soon afterward T'o-ming was overrunning the northern route of the Tien Shan. Yakub of Kokand led his forces to invade Kashgar in the southern route of the Tien Shan and took all other important cities in the same route. Yakub then proclaimed himself *beg*, and in 1869 and 1870 advanced to the northern route, defeated the troops of T'o-ming, and expanded his power to the west of Urumchi.

At this time Tso Tsung-t'ang was suppressing the Mohammedan rebellion in Shensi and Kansu. The Manchu government had no more strength to take care of the area outside of Kansu. England secretly supported Yakub Beg; Russia, on the other hand, did not want Yakub Beg to expand his power. When the influence of T'o-ming was extended to Ili, Russia sent troops to the vicinity of Ili and occupied its strategic points. As soon as Yakub Beg's force advanced northward, Russia, under the pretense of maintaining peace along the border, openly occupied the city of Ili in 1871, subdued the Mohammedan chief, and moved troops toward Urumchi. The Russians were stopped, however, by a Chinese patriotic volunteer corps.

Russia then instructed her minister in Peking to inform the Ch'ing court of her occupation of Ili and to explain that she had no desire to annex the territory and that as soon as the power of the Chinese government could be extended again to Ili and the frontiers made secure, Russia would immediately withdraw. Actually, the Russian government, thinking that there was no longer a possibility of China's extending her power to Ili again, was willing to make the promise. After receiving this assurance, the Ch'ing government put the question aside.

Tso Tsung-t'ang's Pacification of Sinkiang

In 1873 the Mohammedan rebels in Shensi and Kansu were wiped out. The Ch'ing dynasty then decided to send troops to recover Sinkiang. The ambitious Tso Tsung-t'ang complied with an order to submit a detailed report on his military plans, provisions necessary for the undertaking, and all other matters connected with the campaign. In 1875 Tso was ordained imperial commissioner in charge of the Sinkiang military campaign. The members of the court were dubious about Tso's success, critical of the huge amount of military funds essential for this campaign, and inclined to favor giving up the eight cities in the southern route of the Tien Shan. The British minister in Peking, Sir Thomas Wade, also wanted Yakub Beg to be allowed to retain eight cities.

Tso Tsung-t'ang vigorously objected to these opinions, saying in a memorial:

> I am now sixty-five years old. How could I be so selfish as to want to obtain military glory in the frontier cities just to win Your Majesty's favor? But present events by all means should not be tolerated .... If we take no action while Ili is occupied by the Russians, and Kashgar and other cities by Yakub Beg, future troubles will be numerous, and our territory may be reduced a hundred *li* a day. Even after we recover these territories, rehabilitation problems will still require a tremendous amount of planning.[14]

The Ch'ing court heeded Tso's words and ordered him to proceed. Tso advanced his forces through different routes, recovered the northern route of the Tien Shan in 1876, and retook Turfan the next spring. Since Turfan is the gateway to the southern route of the Tien Shan, Yakub Beg became frightened. The English minister to Peking again tried to persuade the Ch'ing court to make Yakub king of the Tien Shan under Chinese suzerainty. This idea was opposed by Tso in a memorial:

Yakub is not without a place to live. Why is it necessary for the English to favor the establishment of a separate state for him? Even if this were deemed necessary, territory could be obtained from the boundary or the British colony or perhaps even by ceding India to Yakub. Why must the British minister ask that China relinquish fertile land in order to do Yakub a favor?

... England is covertly trying to create a buffer state for the protection of India, but outwardly she is compelling us to remove our protection from Sinkiang. Should we permit her to do so? The more we show our weakness, the more she will show her strength, and naturally there will be no end to our difficulties. I have heard that the English have sent an envoy to the headquarters of Yakub Beg, and I have hurriedly instructed my subordinates to treat the British envoy cordially. If he wishes to discuss the Moslem situation, they are to say that they were only ordered to suppress the bandits who occupied our territory and to recover our former dominion, and that they know nothing else.[15]

Being badly harassed, Yakub Beg realized that he had no future; he is reported to have committed suicide by swallowing poison in 1877. In the winter of this year the eight cities in the southern route were recovered one by one, and the whole province of Sinkiang was pacified except for Ili, which remained under Russian control.

When the eight cities in the southern route were on the verge of being recovered, the Ch'ing court ordered Tso to present his overall plans. Tso replied in a memorial containing the following lines:

To pay close attention to Sinkiang is to protect Mongolia, and to protect Mongolia is to shield Peking .... Russia has been expanding her territory continually and her territory borders ours from the west to the east for more than ten thousand *li*. The two nations are

> separated only by Mongolia, and we must take preventive measures lest we lose Mongolia. Now in the northern route only Ili has not yet been regained .... If we try now to recover our former territory, our soldiers will be spurred on by righteous patriotism .... I humbly maintain that our territory should not be given up and that our troops should not be left idle ....
>
> It is essential that we establish a new province, Sinkiang, with political subdivisions of counties and districts; this matter should be taken up without delay. [16]

Thus the recovery of Ili and the creation of a new province called Sinkiang from the territory which was formerly called Chinese Turkestan became the two chief issues before the central government at this time.

The Recovery of Ili

When the Russians occupied Ili, they promised to return it as soon as the Ch'ing forces had regained the Northwest. After Sinkiang had been pacified, the Ch'ing court asked Russia to fulfill her promise. The Russians, who were at war with Turkey, stalled by replying that it was necessary for China to guarantee peace and security at the frontiers in the future and to pay Russia for having guarded Ili on China's behalf. The Ch'ing court, then, in 1878 appointed Ch'ung-hou, who had accompanied Burlingame to the West and had served in the Tsungli Yamen, as minister plenipotentiary to negotiate with Russia. After waiting in St. Petersburg for a year without getting any results, Ch'ung finally concluded the Treaty of Livadia with the Russian government. This treaty provided that China was to pay the sum of five million rubles to cover the military expenses incurred by Russia during her occupation of Ili. China was also to cede to Russia the vast fertile lands along the Tekes River valley in the southern part of Ili.

Since Ch'ung-hou had not been authorized to cede territory to Russia, officials within and without the court were furious when the news of the treaty was conveyed to Peking. Empress Dowager Tz'u-hsi refused to sanction the treaty. Ch'ung-hou was immediately recalled to Peking and was thrown into jail as soon as he arrived, to await beheading. The Russian government considered this treatment of a diplomatic envoy by the Ch'ing court a great insult to Russia. Relations between the two nations were near a breaking point. Russia sent reinforcements to Ili and dispatched a fleet to patrol the Chinese seacoast as a demonstration of her power.

In heated discussions most Chinese scholar-officials advocated war against Russia. Chang Chih-tung, who was then a reader at the Hanlin Academy, was the spokesman for the war clique. A passage from a memorial he sent to the throne reads:

> Our resistance against Russia should be successful. Even if the Russians are victorious at times, they cannot shake the peace of the whole nation. After prolonged warfare they will have a food shortage, and their power will naturally decline. Why should we be afraid of them? If we fight against them now, the war will serve as a turning point at which China can become strong or weak .... Now our generals and ministers are at their prime. After a few years Tso Tsung-t'ang, though still living, will be declining and Li Hung-chang, though not yet declining, will be old; their energy and strength will be exhausted. Then even we who wish to fight will not be able to fight.[17]

This argument advocating war was ridiculously childish; nevertheless, the Ch'ing government gave heed to many such empty proposals. The court ordered Tso Tsung-t'ang to prepare for a war, and Tso went from Suchow to Hami in June of 1880. Li Hung-chang was ordered to strengthen the coastal defenses in the vicinity of Tientsin and other places, and he invited a German, C. von Hanneken, to build a fortress in Port Arthur. During the spring and summer of 1880 war between China and Russia seemed almost inevitable. Li Hung-chang did not want a war, but he was afraid of public opinion and did not voice any objection. However, he considered the preparation of defenses a necessity.

The Chinese minister to England, Tseng Chi-tse, did not favor war. The Englishman General Charles Gordon, because of his former connection with Li Hung-chang in suppressing the Taiping Rebellion, was invited to China. In a conference with Li Hung-chang at Tientsin, he advised Li not to resort to war carelessly. From there Gordon went to Peking, where he declared emphatically that China's preparation for both offensive and defensive warfare was far from adequate and that Russia would advance from the Amur River southward to threaten Peking. In his farewell speech Gordon even went so far as to say, "Those who advocate war while China is not yet ready to fight should all be beheaded .... So long as Peking is the capital," he added, "China should never wage war against a foreign country, because Peking is too close to the seacoast; China has no coastal defense, and it is too easy for foreign troops to invade the capital."[18]

In the spring of 1880 the Ch'ing court ordered Tseng Chi-tse to go from England to Russia to request the abrogation of the treaty concluded by Ch'ung-hou. After a great deal of argument and debate in St. Petersburg, he signed the Treaty of St. Petersburg with Russia in February 1881. This treaty provided for a changed indemnity of nine instead of five million rubles; China gained a large strip of territory including the Tekes valley and the mountain passes between Ili and Kashgaria, while the Russians secured various trade privileges and the right to establish consulates in China. In return, Russia gave Ili back to China. Thus the problem of regaining Ili was solved.

The Establishment of Sinkiang as a Province

The Ch'ing court paid considerable attention to Tso Tsung-t'ang's suggestion that Sinkiang be made a province, but it was an important matter which required much consideration, and many countries were dubious of its practicability. Tso, however, adamantly maintained his proposal. After the pacification of the southern and northern routes of Tien Shan and before the recovery of Ili, Tso made definite arrangements for this plan. His main objective was to have Chinese Turkestan made a province and to have all the particulars carefully arranged, including plans for its subdivisions, before the name for the province and districts was chosen.

The area of Sinkiang was called the Western Region during the Han dynasty; it had also been frequently referred to as Chinese Turkestan. For many centuries it had been under Chinese military governors. Most of these army officers were ignorant of civil and administrative affairs. Except for collecting taxes and suppressing riots, they had no conception of how to manage civil government, and a laissez-faire policy prevailed. In addition, since the inhabitants were of many different races, it was easy to start feuds or riots. As soon as a riot started, it usually got out of hand.

Tso Tsung-t'ang's administration of Sinkiang, by way of contrast, was not in accordance with the traditional laissez-faire policy. He paid great attention to civil affairs. Under his rule wells and ditches were opened in Sinkiang, land was extensively cultivated and surveyed, taxation was reorganized, currency was minted, sericulture was promoted, and free schools were established.

The last achievement was vitally significant. In a memorial, Tso said,

> In Sinkiang ... the Mohammedans and Chinese cannot get along together. The officers and the people keep a distance from each other, and it is extremely difficult to enforce a law or an order. All government regulations have to be explained and publicized by

Moslem chiefs and this is a considerable hindrance .... It will be necessary to have free public schools where Mohammedan children are ordered to study our written and spoken language ... to issue to them such books as *The One-thousand Character Essay*, *The Three Character Classic* .... And in addition we plan to issue *The Filial Piety Classic* ... for them to read .... After these works have been read, we will give them the *Six Classics* so that they can learn the meaning of Confucian ideas .... If they can be taught to read our books and ... understand our language it will be easy for us to achieve our goal of governing Sinkiang. [19]

Tso's policy consisted of assimilation by means of education. In this way Tso hoped to lay a good foundation for the organization of the province. His intention was to inaugurate a governor-general at Urumchi in the northern route of the Tien Shan. If this farsighted policy of Tso had been carried on with continued effort, the effects would have been considerable. Unfortunately, the plan was neglected by Tso's successors.

When the Ili problem occurred and China and Russia were on the verge of war, the Ch'ing court recalled Tso to Peking for consultation, leaving his enterprises in Sinkiang to be handled by his subordinate, Liu Chin-t'ang, who followed in Tso's footsteps. A couple of years after the regaining of Ili, the foundations for the organization of the province had been roughly laid down. In the winter of 1884 the Ch'ing court designated Liu Chin-t'ang governor of Kansu and Sinkiang, with Urumchi [now Ti-hua] as the provincial capital. Consequently, from the beginning Sinkiang was given the same administration as other provinces in the interior of China.

This should be considered as a great political success, although diplomatically China did suffer a limited loss in Ili. Sinkiang is at the present time still retained and has not met the same fate as Annam and Korea, because a solid foundation was laid down for it during the 1880's.

THE SINO-FRENCH WAR

Annam and China

At the beginning of the nineteenth century most of Indochina was ruled by the emperor of Annam. Historically speaking, the relation between Annam and China was established earlier than that between Sinkiang and China; and culturally speaking, Annam was more deeply influenced by Chinese civilization than Sinkiang. The political, social, and cultural systems of Annam were Sinicized. But politically speaking, Annam was sometimes within Chinese territory and under China's direct control, and sometimes independent, or at most only a tributary, vassal state. During the last centuries of the Ch'ing dynasty, it was a vassal state of China, presenting tribute to the Ch'ing court periodically.

The Ch'ing court did not interfere in Annam's domestic and foreign affairs, except that when a new king was enthroned, he received investiture from China, and whenever there was civil war in Annam, China sent troops to suppress it, leaving Annam afterwards to govern herself. Therefore, in political relations Annam was not so close to China as Sinkiang. For this reason when France began to gain the upper hand in Annam, the Chinese government did not pay much attention until French influence had been extended from southern Indochina to the northern part of Annam, thus affecting the frontier lands of Yunnan and Kwangsi. But by the time China realized the danger, the situation was already beyond control.

The French in Indochina

France had already been active in Annam before the French Revolution. After a long period of dynastic struggle and civil war in Annam during the latter half of the eighteenth century, French Catholic missionaries had already begun to take an active part in her national politics. In the last days of the Later Li Dynasty (1428-1789) two branches of the royal family of Annam strove for succession to the throne. In the 1780's a French missionary bishop espoused the cause of an Annamite claimant, to power in the southern part of the country. Through French support the prince established himself as Emperor Gialong, and from that time he and his successors were virtually under the control of France. Li Wei-ch'i, the last emperor of the Li dynasty, fled to China; in 1788 China sent troops to the rescue, but the expeditionary forces were routed.

During the Taiping Rebellion, France used military power to seize the three western provinces of Cochin China and to occupy Saigon. At this time the Ch'ing court was being harassed by the Taipings and naturally was too busy to take care of affairs in her vassal state. In 1868 the French explored the Mekong River as far as Yunnan. They hoped to find a useful route for penetration into southwestern China, but a large part of the Mekong River proved unnavigable. Therefore they began to turn their attention to the Red River of Tongking. French merchants such as Jean Dupuis were selling ammunition to the authorities in Yunnan to aid in the suppression of the Mohammedan rebellion, and they discovered that from the Red River they could navigate directly to Yunnan. Thus the French conquest of Hanoi and most of the Red River delta came about.

In 1874 deceitful means were employed to force the Annamite emperor to sign a treaty at Saigon with France. On the surface the treaty provided recognition of Annam as an independent state, but actually it was made a protectorate of France. The important points of the treaty were:

1. Should there be internal disorder or foreign aggression in Annam, France would do her best to help Annam with arms and army personnel.
2. The Annamite government was obliged to agree to conform its

foreign policy to that of France and to recognize French possession of Cochin China.

3. French ships were to be permitted to sail freely in the tributaries of the Red River to make connections with Yunnan and the other boundaries of China.

After the treaty was signed, the French minister residing at Peking presented the complete text in 1875 to the Tsungli Yamen of the Chinese government. Upon noticing the phrase in the treaty which stated that Annam was an independent state, the Ch'ing court refuted the two main points of the treaty, saying that Yunnan was not to be opened to foreign trade and that "Annam has since ancient times been a vassal of China, and accustomed to look to China for protection; therefore the Chinese government [could] not recognize this treaty." A secretary in the French legation translated the Chinese reply into very imprecise language,[20] which led the French minister to think that China had recognized the treaty. Since the Ch'ing court did not accept the treaty, it should have taken further positive action. But after its reply to the French minister, it did nothing.

Because of the Saigon treaty with Annam in 1874, France carried on her predetermined policy of invasion. In 1880 France quartered troops at Hanoi and Haiphong and built fortresses in strategic spots along the Red River. The Annamite government gradually realized fully the malign intentions of the Saigon treaty.

Annam, further, still desired to be under the protection of China. Even after she signed the treaty with France, she sent tribute to China twice, in 1876 and in 1880, an action which France could not prevent. Difficulties continued in Tongking and bandits made life in the delta insecure. The Annamite government wished to use the force of Liu Yung-fu's Black Flag to oppose the French. Liu Yung-fu, a former Taiping, led his party members, under the banner of the black flag which mourned the fall of the Heavenly Kingdom in China, to the frontiers of Annam and lorded over that area. French navigation in the upper reaches of the Red River was frequently menaced by Liu's men, and it was necessary for the French to build fortresses and to keep garrisons to protect themselves.

Embroilment with France, and the Li-Fournier Agreement, 1881-1884

While the French were building fortresses and stationing soldiers along the Red River, the Chinese governor-general of Yunnan, Liu Chang-yu, noticed the danger in the actions of the French. In 1881 he submitted a memorial to the throne suggesting that arms be used against the aggressor by employing the combined forces of Yunnan, Kwangtung, and Kwangsi. At this time, however, China was deeply involved in a serious dispute with Russia over the Ili problem. Tseng Chi-tse was on his way to Russia from England via Paris, where he attempted to get some information about conditions in Annam from the French government. The Ch'ing court, on account of its intensified negotiations with Russia, dared not take positive action.

After the Ili problem was solved, Tseng Chi-tse returned to Paris and filed a protest with the French government concerning the Annam affair, but it produced no result. In 1882 when France was engaged in warfare with Liu Yung-fu's Black Flag Party, Tseng Chi-tse again filed a protest with the French government. But France maintained that Annam was an independent state with which China had no right to interfere. Tseng argued that the French-Annamite treaty of 1874 had long before been denounced by China. However, the French government paid no attention to his protests. The Ch'ing court watched the ever-increasing military activities of the French in Annam and in 1883 ordered troops to advance from Yunnan and Kwangsi to the borders of Annam.

At this point the Ch'ing court urged Li Hung-chang, who was observing a mourning period at home, to hurry out to take up the arduous and complicated assignment of dealing with Annam and with difficulties between China and Japan over Korea, which also were mounting fast. On the French side, China also had trouble as a result of a change in the French cabinet. The policy of the new cabinet was relatively peaceful, and the French minister to China was ordered to find a peaceful method of solving problems with the Chinese government. During the conference between Li Hung-chang and the French envoy, Commander Fournier, the draft of a peace treaty between the two countries was drawn up, by which Li agreed to recognize French interests in Tongking, and to permit French trade in Yunnan and Kwangsi.

On the pretext of attacking the bandit Black Flag Party and forcing the Annamite government to fulfill its treaty obligations, the French carried on military activities. The military object of China, however, from beginning to end, extended only to protection for its borders. Li Hung-chang did not want war and the Ch'ing court also lacked the courage to open hostilities against France. Therefore, the Ch'ing court insisted on her suzerainty over Annam in the face of France's infringement, but at the same time did not actively oppose the enemy.

The troops sent to the borders of Annam were, for example, only used as secret reinforcements to Liu Yung-fu's Black Flags. By this time Chinese troops had reached Langson and other spots along the frontiers of Annam. Liu Yung-fu had also received his formal appointment from the Ch'ing court. His Black Flag soldiers had been recognized as part of the Chinese troops. The Ch'ing court, however, still expected a peaceful solution.

In the spring of 1884 the French troops progressed northward, defeated the combined forces of the Black Flag and the Chinese troops, and captured Chinese camps along the frontiers. Although hostilities between China and France thus actually commenced in 1884, the Ch'ing court still did not make up its mind to fight.

Upon hearing of the beginning of hostilities and the loss of a number of cities on the frontier, Empress Dowager Tz'u-hsi feared that the French fleet might take this opportunity to invade China's coastal provinces. Worried and angry, she put the blame on the courtiers for mismanaging the French affair, and she dismissed all of the grand councilors from Prince Kung (I-hsin) on down. I-hsin's position was filled by Prince I-huan, the father of Emperor Kuang-hsü. After some time, through the mediation of a German, Gustav Detring, who served as a commissioner of customs at Canton, the Ch'ing court ordered Li Hung-chang to open peace negotiations with Captain Fournier, and a preliminary peace treaty was signed in May 1884.

By the Li-Fournier agreement: (1) France pledged that she would not invade the southern boundaries of China. (2) China recognized all the treaties which had been concluded between France and Annam. All Chinese troops were to withdraw from Tongking to China before June 26 of that year. (3) France was not to demand any indemnity. (4) Hereafter, when France concluded new treaties or revised old treaties with Annam, no expression was to be used which might hurt the prestige of the Celestial Empire. And (5) ministers plenipotentiary were to be appointed by the two nations to discuss detailed articles based on this agreement.

After concluding this preliminary treaty, Li Hung-chang became the common target of attacks. There were as many as forty-seven memorials accusing him or demanding his impeachment. Li dared not reveal the date of the evacuation of Chinese troops from Annam.

The aggressive party in France ought to have been satisfied with this treaty, but because the fourth article still recognized China's suzerainty over Annam to some extent, the cabinet would not approve the treaty. Shortly after, on account of the withdrawal of Chinese troops from Langson, a skirmish developed which grew into a sizable fracas, and war between China and France became unavoidable.

When China's troops in Langson had not yet received orders to withdraw, an impetuous French officer attempted to force them to turn over the city to France. On the grounds that they had received no governmental order, the Chinese troops refused to budge. On June 23 at Bac-le (Pei-li) the French officer encountered a body of Chinese troops. In the resulting skirmish, the French troops were said to have suffered casualties of a few dozen soldiers. The French at home were greatly agitated, charging China with violating the article of the preliminary treaty which stipulated the time for withdrawal of troops. On July 12 France sent China an ultimatum demanding 250,000,000 francs indemnity and the immediate execution of the Fournier convention.

Because Li Hung-chang had been severely criticized by the public and was extremely unpopular, the Empress Dowager Tz'u-hsi dared not appoint him to negotiate with France. Instead she ordered Tseng Kuo-ch'üan, governor-general of Liang-Kiang, to have a conference with the French minister, Jules Patenôtre, at Shanghai. Since Li Hung-chang was censured and despised by a large number of scholar-officials for his weak foreign policy and since the ultimatum of the French was viewed as unreasonable, Tseng Kuo-ch'üan was inclined to adopt a stronger policy. The demands of the French minister were not complied with, because Tseng did not wish to pay the indemnity.

The French authorities then ordered their fleet to start military action in China with the intention of occupying strategic points along the coast in order to subdue the Ch'ing court. The latter, influenced by the clamors from many vociferous scholar-officials for military action against France, also issued orders to prepare for war as well as for defense. Basically, however, China still had no intention of fighting.

The War on the China Coast and Around Langson, 1884-1885

On August 5, 1884, warships bombarded Keelung on Taiwan, but the attack was repulsed by the Chinese garrisons. The French fleet then sailed into the Min River and destroyed more than ten Chinese ships which were protecting the Foochow shipyard, built by French engineers. The shipyard was destroyed on August 23. The Ch'ing court was now greatly alarmed and declared war against France. The French fleet continued to attack Taiwan and to blockade all important ports south of the Yangtze River in order to cut off the transportation of provisions between southern and northern China.

Robert Hart, an English subject who served as superintendent of the Chinese customs office, ordered his agent in England to find out whether the Paris government had any intention of negotiating for peace. The findings were encouraging. The French government, it appeared, had noted that after the destruction of the Foochow shipyard, the Manchu regime showed no sign of yielding. Besides this, the French domestic party struggle was keen, and the dispatch of reinforcements was greatly impeded. The request of a naval commander to attack Port Arthur had been vigorously rejected. The French government was clearly willing to call a halt to all hostilities. Robert Hart's agent cabled this information. Hart then acted as a mediator in conducting secret negotiations for peace on the basis that China still recognized the five articles of the preliminary treaty, and that France made no other demands.

The Chinese armies who fought with French forces at Langson were at first defeated. But in the spring of 1885, because of the great efforts of General Feng Tzu-ts'ai, the French forces suffered a great defeat at Langson. After the retaking of Langson on March 28, Feng Tzu-ts'ai held a military conference to discuss the strategy of the next advance. In the middle of this conference he received orders to stop fighting. He was greatly disappointed. The troops under the command of Shen Yü-ying had not yet received the order to stop the war and were still in hot pursuit of the French forces. Shen recovered all the territory lost in 1884.

The Annamese were now greatly cheered, but soon Shen also received his orders to stop fighting. He was forced to halt his progress, since the Ch'ing court had already approved the truce arranged by Robert Hart and his associates. In Peking the news of victory at Langson was taken by the court as an excellent bargaining point for peace negotiations; in Paris the news of the defeat caused the fall of the cabinet (March 30). Since the influence of the war faction in France was now greatly diminished, the Ch'ing court appointed the formerly unpopular Li Hung-chang as its minister plenipotentiary whose duty was to attend a peace conference at Tientsin with the French minister, M. Patenôtre. Li signed a peace treaty of ten articles on June 9, 1885.

The Peace Treaty and Its Aftermath, 1885

The battle of Langson did not seem to have any effect upon these peace terms, which harked back to the Li-Fournier convention (1884) by which China recognized all treaties signed between France and Annam and renounced her suzerainty over Annam. The treaty, however, amplified the Fournier convention by nominally opening Langson and Laokay as trade ports, but actually giving the two ports at the frontier to France. In addition, the two nations were to send a separate mission to investigate the boundary line between China and Annam and to negotiate a treaty concerning trade over the frontier. It was decided that if China should decide to build railways, the French government would use her "every facility to procure in France the personnel she might need."

China, however, did not fare very well in this treaty. The vassalage of Annam to China was completely ended. In addition, although China did not pay any indemnity, she suffered an economic loss totaling more than 100,000,000 taels. Also, this treaty opened a way for France to attack Yunnan through Annam.

The success of France was due to sheer luck, while the failure of China was brought about by indecision. The scholars who clamored for war were ignorant of domestic and foreign conditions. They could not comprehend the problems China would have to face after hostilities were opened.

The Chinese Debate over Foreign Policy

Among the men involved in the debate, Tseng Chi-tze was relatively clearheaded. Having spent years in Europe, Tseng had had a chance to make firsthand observations of domestic conditions in France and to know the weaknesses of the country. Because Li, on the other hand, only knew the conditions and the inadequacies of his own country, these two outstanding diplomats, though personal friends, had very different opinions on the question of French Indochina.

Foreign critics regarded Li as a leader favoring peace and Tseng as a leader championing war. As a matter of fact, Tseng did not necessarily advocate war; but he was inclined to be firm in his dealings with France. Because of the knowledge he had previously gained of China's adversary, he believed that France lacked the military and financial power to sustain a prolonged war and that the frequent party struggles which brought about the fall of the cabinet every two or three months would make it extremely difficult to continue any such undertaking. Tseng felt that if China adopted a strong policy against France from the beginning and prepared for warfare in advance, it would not be necessary to open real hostilities before the voice of the French invasion group was silenced. Tseng, therefore, for a long time wished his government to adopt a strong, unsubmissive policy.

On the other hand, Li Hung-chang believed that China lacked the power to fight against the French and that her weak fleet could not protect her long coastal lines. Nor did he believe that her army could be sent as far as Annam, because the Korean problem was also imminent and Korea was even more important to China than Annam. He recognized, too, that Chinese troops in Yunnan and Kwangsi could not be relied upon, since they did not know how to use their new weapons, and he felt that if hostilities started, the small Chinese navy, which had taken many years to build up, would be completely destroyed. Li did not know that France also had her weak points. His fear of her superior strength caused his disapproval of open warfare. Even when the French force bombarded Keelung, he did not want the Chinese navy in Foochow to take belligerent action.

Empress Dowager Tz'u-hsi approved the cautious attitude of Li Hung-chang, but she became easily agitated by the critics who shouted for war. Her policy, therefore, was sometimes strong and sometimes weak. Tz'u-hsi wavered indecisively between these two viewpoints until the Chinese navy in the area around Foochow had been routed, at which time she formally declared war. Hence, the Chinese failure in the Sino-French War may be attributed to this indecision and lack of determination.

Shifts in Power at the Court

Related to this indecision was a pertinent alteration in court personnel. As was pointed out earlier, Prince Kung and other grand councilors were dismissed in the year 1884. This abrupt act was not without its background.

When Prince Kung (I-hsin) was leader of the grand council, he was concerned with public opinion even though at the time conditions were corrupt and the members of the court were heedless of the opinion of the populace. The so-called pure and honest censors, who relied upon Li Hung-tsao as their supporter, liked to be courageous in their criticism of the government in order to incur a good reputation and quick promotion. Li Hung-tsao, who had been the tutor of Emperor T'ung-chih, was a grand councilor; he and Prince Kung tried to help each other.

When the Annam incident was imminent, another group of courtiers, working for their own ends and desiring to take this opportunity to expel Li Hung-tsao, became active. They tried to persuade the censors to impeach Li on the grounds that the Annam situation had been improperly directed by the grand councilors. Thus Empress Dowager Tz'u-hsi took this opportunity to dismiss all grand councilors under the leadership of Prince Kung, whom she disliked, and have him replaced by Prince I-huan. The latter introduced Sun Yü-wen to the grand council. Thereafter court conditions became even more corrupt, while the so-called pure and honest censors lost their backing. Open bribery prevailed among both the upper and lower ranks of officials.

THE NAVY YAMEN AND GOVERNMENT CORRUPTION

The inner weaknesses of the government were also a factor in the history of the Navy Yamen. After the Foochow shipyard and fleet were destroyed during the Sino-French conflict, the Navy Yamen was formed in Peking as a sign of the Ch'ing court's deep confidence in Li Hung-chang, who had for a long time advocated the expansion of the navy. Before the Sino-French War, Chihli, Kiangnan, Fukien, Kwangtung, and other provinces already had a number of small modern warships, which were purchased by funds raised by the provincial authorities and thus were at their disposal. In 1875 on account of the Tainanese episode, disputes with Japan occurred which gave rise to preparations for defense of the coast. Li Hung-chang advocated the purchase of large ironclad ships from foreign countries, and his suggestion was approved by the court. Thereafter, war vessels were ordered now and then, so that, by the time the Ili problem arose, a number of steel warships had been purchased from foreign countries, and many were still under construction by special order.

Gordon's Advice on the Armed Forces of China

When "Chinese" Gordon went home from Tientsin, he submitted twenty suggestions to Li Hung-chang as his farewell words. The seventh and eighth items advised China to reorganize her army before building up a navy. He warned that it would be a mistake to spend in haste a huge amount of money to buy war vessels. The fourteenth item advised that China should have a minister of the navy and that constant patrol should be maintained at all places of military importance.[21]

Gordon had discovered that one of the fundamental defects of Chinese government was the lack of an overall and unified plan for her military affairs. Li Hung-chang's official capacity was governor-general of Chihli. He had no authority to conduct the business of the entire nation. Although Li sent copies of Gordon's farewell words to the Tsungli Yamen, this office was not the place for making overall plans, either. Furthermore, most of the high officials in the Tsungli Yamen were shortsighted and mediocre. They paid little attention to Gordon's suggestions.

When the Sino-French War was impending and the French navy was appearing frequently in Chinese waters, the war vessels controlled by the provinces along the coast were counted upon to protect their own harbors. There was not, however, a single ship which could be freely transferred elsewhere; and there was no unified command. China's weak fleet fundamentally had no power to defend her seacoast. The court finally began to realize the validity of Gordon's proposals.

Problems of Organizing a Navy Yamen

At first the reader of the Hanlin Academy, Chang P'ei-lun, made the suggestion that a Navy Yamen be organized under the direction of the Tsungli Yamen, which would control the navy of the whole nation. Prince Kung heartily approved the suggestion and immediately hinted that Li Hung-chang should head this new office. Li took this opportunity to send a reply to the Tsungli Yamen supporting the creation of a naval ministry at Peking and stating that he himself probably might assist the new ministry. But the Grand Council was not ready to approve the plan promptly. It was while this case was being studied that Prince Kung and other grand councilors were summarily dismissed by the empress dowager. Consideration of the suggestion was suspended.

Before long, however, Chang P'ei-lun was appointed an associate director of naval affairs in Fukien. Upon his departure from Peking, he again requested through a memorial the organization of a Navy Yamen and the appointment of ministers to decide upon all relevant matters. An imperial edict called for a conference and a discussion by the authorities concerning the southern and northern ports. In the spring and summer of 1884 the Sino-French War had not yet formally been declared, but a declaration was imminent. Unfortunately, before the conferences accomplished any results, the Foochow fleet was destroyed. The warships ordered from foreign countries were, luckily, for the most part undelivered and there were still a few war vessels left in the northern ports and in the Kiangnan area. After the completion of peace negotiations, the establishment of a Navy Yamen was finally carried into effect.

An imperial decree of October 1885 reads:

> ... Formerly, on account of the great importance of coastal defense, the high ministers of the southern and northern ports were ordered to deliberate the case and report by memorial. Now, according to their memorials concerning an overall plan for the whole situation, it is requested that a well-trained navy for the northern ports be organized immediately and be used as an example. Henceforward, naval expansion will be undertaken every year. Their plan seems to be proper and practical. Let Prince Ch'un (I-huan) be the minister of the Navy Yamen to control and command all naval forces; let the Grand Secretary, Prince Ch'ing (I-k'uang) and the Chihli governor-general, Li Hung-chang, be the associate ministers; and let the Lieutenant General of the Chinese Red Banner, Shan-ch'ing, and the Junior Vice-Minister of the Ministry of War, Tseng

Chi-tse, be assistant ministers .... [22]

Organization of the Navy Yamen

This imperial decree was the formal announcement of the establishment of the Navy Yamen. Prince I-huan was to take general charge. Under him were two associate ministers and two assistant ministers, each rank consisting of a Manchu and a Chinese, a system corresponding to that of subordinates employed in the six ministries. But Prince I-huan's title was an empty one and I-k'uang and Shan-ch'ing were both ignorant of naval affairs. All the necessary plans were actually made by Tseng and Li. Li, however, was concurrently governor-general of Chihli and superintendent of trade for the northern ports, with offices at Paoting and Tientsin; he could not spend too much time in the Navy Yamen at Peking. Thus, later on, Tseng Chi-tse alone was the actual director of the Navy Yamen.

After the Navy Yamen had been decreed, Li Hung-chang wrote a letter to Tseng Kuo-ch'üan:

> When I was in Peking, I sojourned twenty days and had five audiences with the throne. As I reported current affairs I regretted that I could not help much those whose wisdom was too profound and unfathomable. My idea was entirely disagreeable to the highest authorities in the court. Generally speaking, the Sacred Empress and Prince Ch'un were vigorously working for better administration and for altering all the ingrained habits of procrastination and ostentation of the court, while the other courtiers seemed to cling to tradition without giving much hope that they could be stirred to action. Nor did they dare to make any suggestions .... Concerning naval affairs, there have been many proposals which seem to tend toward the concentration of power in the hands of one man. I have too many

duties and I am wearied. I declined the offer many times without success. Even though the two princes are to be the chief ministers, there is still not a single cent nor a single admiral for the navy. Thinking of the vast ocean, I am frightened. I wonder what you are going to advise me. [23]

In February of 1886 Li wrote a letter to Tseng Chi-tse:

> Concerning the matter of the navy I am counting on your help .... When I was just considering myself fortunate to have a chance to be relieved of my responsibility (on account of your assistance) you wish to avoid the duty on the pretext of illness. [24]

Tseng Chi-tse was then in Europe and had not yet returned to China. He had once, because of bad health, declined the offer to assist in the naval affairs.

> You have received great favor from the emperor [Li's letter continues] and should only do your respectful best and try to maneuver through the difficulties gradually. After the French incident is settled, a foreign loan of nearly twenty million taels must be paid by all the provinces. There are certainly no dependable funds for the navy, and we are still unable to buy many big warships. Men of ability for the positions of admirals and officers are particularly scarce. For the time being it will be hard for us to imitate one thousandth or even one millionth of the English naval system. But I earnestly hope that you will try to make a humble imitation in order to prepare for a gradual development for our country in the future. Would you be willing to do so?[24]

After reading these two letters we can see the great pains Li took in planning the navy single-handed and his earnest expectation of Tseng Chi-tse's assistance.

Although he told Tseng Kuo-ch'üan that the empress dowager was actively attempting to reform the government and strongly criticizing the former habits of procrastination and ostentation, the Navy Yamen became the "new Imperial Household" of the empress dowager. The minister of revenue, Yen Ching-ming, tried his best to save some money for the ill-fated Navy Yamen; but the empress dowager asked for money from Yen so frequently and insistently that he finally asked to be relieved of his post. No sooner had Yen left the ministry of revenue than the funds preassigned for the Navy Yamen were appropriated to build the Summer Palace, the I-ho Yüan, for the empress dowager. Tseng Chi-tse, when he served in the Navy Yamen, was so much impeded by his Manchu superiors and associates in everything he intended to do that he fell into a distress and melancholy which hastened his death.

The Northern Fleet was organized in 1888 with twenty-eight ships of various sizes. The fleet was still badly organized and poorly equipped. Li Hung-chang was, however, moderately satisfied when he, together with the Shantung governor, inspected the showy fleet on the sea in 1890. Who could predict that China's humiliation by Japan was soon to follow?

THE SINO-JAPANESE WAR

China and Japan have had contact, official and unofficial, throughout their histories. Ming dynasty officials perforce took cognizance of Japan because of the repeated harassment of the China coast by Japanese pirates. The Ch'ing court, however, had no official communication with Japan until Li Hung-chang became governor-general of Chihli in 1871. Li's political life began and ended in the period of China's first major open struggle with Japan. With the defeat of China in 1894 Li lost, to members of a more aggressive reform party, his pivotal position in Chinese politics.

Japanese Projects for Aggression

Although until 1870-1871 the Ch'ing court officially ignored Japan, several Japanese even before the Meiji period were already thinking about a conquest of China. In 1854 Yoshida Shoin, who was a Japanese Reform leader prior to the Meiji Restoration [1868], wrote while in jail a book entitled *Yūshū Roku* [*A Record of an Imprisonment*] in which he said:

> We should now speed up our military preparations with adequate supplies of war vessels and artillery, and then we should ... instruct the king of the Liuchiu [Ryukyu] Islands to send us tribute and order Korea to send her princes to Japan as hostages and to present tribute as she did in ancient times. The territory of Manchuria in the north should be ceded to us and that of Taiwan, Luzon, and other islands in the south should be annexed.

In another essay also written in jail, Yoshida said,

> We should build up our national strength, annex the weak, and attack the stupid, seize Manchuria and Korea, and conquer China. What we have lost to Russia and the United States may be made up by Korea and Manchuria.[25]

Another scholar, Sato Shinen, living in the Tokugawa period, wrote a book entitled *Kodo hisaku* [*A Secret Assimilation Policy*] in which he said:

> The method of invading other nations must begin with the one which is weak and easy to take. Now, among all nations of the world, there is no other territory easier for Japan to take than China's Manchuria, because the territory is near Japan, separated by water

> and a distance of less than 800 li .... Undoubtedly, sooner or later, the territory must belong to us. But are we to get only Manchuria? No. The decline and fall of the whole nation of China will begin with the loss of Manchuria. After we obtain Mongolia, then Korea and China will be secured in succession.[26]

When the English and French allies occupied Peking, a Japanese daimyo, Shimadzu of Satsuma, remarked that China was a large nation, yet she was subdued by England and France; hence for the purpose of self-protection, Japan should first send soldiers to invade one province of China—the best being Taiwan or Fukien—in order to extend her power to avert an eastward invasion by England and France. But at this time Japan was under the domination of her tottering Bakufu government. There were then heated arguments for and against the opening of the nation for international trade, with little spare time for the Japanese to invade China. Thus the opinion of Shimadzu was not widely supported. The people who favored the opening of Japan for international relations finally won the debate and the foundation of the Meiji Restoration was laid down.

The Opening of Relations with Japan

In 1870 Japan sent an envoy, Yanagiwara Sakimitsu, to China to seek a treaty of trade and friendly relations. At first the Tsungli Yamen only permitted Japan to trade. But then, as a result of Li Hung-chang's efforts, Japan was allowed to conclude a treaty with China. In the next year Japan appointed Date Muneki, who had been a minister of finance, to be envoy extraordinary to the court of Peking. In September 1871 at Tientsin he signed with Li Hung-chang a treaty of peace and amity to which were appended commercial regulations and a tariff table. This treaty marked the beginning of formal relations between China and Japan in modern times.

Before the treaty of 1871 was ratified and exchanged, more than fifty shipwrecked sailors from the Liuchiu [Ryukyu] Islands were killed by savages on Taiwan. The Japanese government, assuming suzerainty over Liuchiu,[27] demanded redress for the deaths of her subjects. Japan then incorporated Liuchiu and Taiwan within the jurisdiction of her empire. In 1873 the Japanese foreign minister himself, Count Soyejima Taneomi, journeyed to China to exchange the treaty signed in 1871 and to discuss the Liuchiu problem with the Chinese government.

According to a Japanese record,[28] Mao Ch'ang-hsi, a probationary secretary [*hsing-tsou*] of the Tsungli Yamen, wished to save trouble and to evade China's responsibility. He replied on June 21, 1873, that the savages of Taiwan were outside the sphere of Chinese government and civilization, and therefore, China was not responsible for their atrocities. The Japanese foreign minister did not offer any argument against Mao's reply, but in the next year the Japanese government sent Saigo Tsugumichi to command troops in a punitive expedition to "chastize" the savages in Taiwan.

Japanese Aggression in Liuchiu and Taiwan

According to a Chinese source, the Japanese foreign minister sent his assistant to the Tsungli Yamen to inquire about three points: whether Macao was under Chinese or Portuguese control; whether the king of Korea handled all administrative affairs without Chinese interference; and thirdly, the details concerning the murder of Liuchiu subjects by Taiwanese savages. There is no Chinese record available that gives the detailed conversation, which is said to have lasted not more than half an hour. The Chinese official said that Liuchiu was Chinese territory, but the savages in mountainous areas of Taiwan were allowed to live according to their own customs without forced interference from the Chinese administration.[29]

When the Chinese government indirectly learned from neutral sources of the Japanese expedition, it questioned the reason for the expedition from Japan on the one hand, and on the other hand, ordered Shen Pao-chen, who was then minister superintendent of the Foochow shipyard, to proceed with troops to Taiwan in an effort to compel Japan to withdraw her soldiers. Japan at first sent Yanagiwara and then Ōkubo Toshimichi to Peking for the negotiations, which were almost broken off. Later, through the mediation of the English minister to China, Thomas Wade, a compromise was reached whereby China was to pay a hundred thousand taels in compensation for those who had lost their lives at the hands of the savages, and four hundred thousand taels to the Japanese troops who built roads and military camps in Taiwan. In addition, China was to restrain the savages from doing any further harm to sailors in the future. When these conditions were met, Japan agreed to withdraw her soldiers from the island.

This settlement, though it helped China to secure protection for Taiwan for the time being, silently confirmed an agreement that the Liuchiu Islands belonged to Japan. The Japanese government immediately carried on its plans for the annexation of Liuchiu. Liuchiu repeatedly solicited help from China, and Tso Tsung-t'ang had intentions of going to the rescue; but on account of the Ili problem with Russia, the Ch'ing court had to keep silent. Thus Liuchiu became a Japanese district in 1879.

Korea and the Treaty of Kianghua

As Japan was advancing on Taiwan and Liuchiu, she was also preparing for aggression against Korea. When the Japanese envoy was negotiating with the Ch'ing court in Peking in connection with the Taiwan problem, he told the Tsungli Yamen of Korea's impoliteness toward Japan, implying that China should attempt to improve the relation between Korea and Japan. The members of the Tsungli Yamen, who only wanted to save themselves trouble, tried to dodge China's responsibility by replying that although Korea had been China's vassal state, had received investiture, and had adopted the Chinese calendar system, she was completely independent in her domestic and diplomatic affairs. The Japanese minister silently listened to this answer without producing any argument. After he returned, he urged his government to take open action.

The Korean king, who was only twelve years old, had succeeded to the throne in 1863 from an indirect branch of the royal family. Governmental power was wielded by his father, Tai-won-kun [Ta-yüan-chün], who was regent. Tai-won-kun was a very reactionary isolationist. At the beginning of the Meiji Restoration, messengers were sent to Korea to restore friendly relations. Tai-won-kun, when the Japanese gave him a letter in which the mikado referred to himself as Emperor of Great Japan, refused to accept it. He said that he hated Japan's Restoration and Japan's adoption of Western methods. He posted public notice to his subjects warning them not to have any contact with the Japanese; and for this reason the Japanese envoy had entered his complaint before the Chinese Tsungli Yamen.

Before the Japanese minister came to China, the aggressive party, headed by Saigo Takamori, had been loudly clamoring for a punitive expedition to Korea. As soon as the party heard the irresponsible reply of the Chinese Tsungli Yamen concerning Korea, they decided to follow the policy of positive aggression. In 1875 the Japanese government sent a war vessel to survey the harbors in Korea and the coast of China's Liaotung Peninsula. When the ship passed Korea's Kianghua Bay, a few small boats were sent off to sail to the Han River, the entrance of which was barred by the Koreans. The Japanese warship opened fire and destroyed the forts on the bank, thus creating a case for negotiations.

In the spring of the next year the Japanese government ordered Kuroda Kiyotaka and Inouye Kaoru to command the six war vessels and a battalion of the army in an expedition to Korea, forcing the Korean government to conclude in February 1876 a treaty of amity and commerce. In it Japan recognized Korea as an independent and autonomous state enjoying the "same sovereign rights" as Japan; ministers were to be exchanged between the two nations. Korea opened Fusan, Chemulpo, and Wönsan as trade ports; and all coastal ports of Korea were opened to the Japanese for free survey. This treaty, called the Treaty of Kianghua, was patterned after France's Treaty of Saigon concerning Annam.

When the Kianghua incident occurred, the Japanese government sent Mori Arinori to China telling the Tsungli Yamen about his country's action in Korea. Prince Kung replied that Japan should have discussed the Korean problem with China instead of directly sending troops to Korea. Mori replied that since China had given Korea autonomy in handling her own domestic and foreign affairs, Japan treated Korea as an independent and autonomous state. China did not take a positive action to dispute the treaty. Thus Japan was successful in the first step of her policy of expansion to Korea.

The Mutiny in Korea Settled by China

The treaty concluded between Korea and Japan was signed by the Koreans under duress. After the conclusion of the treaty, Korea still depended on China for protection. Now China tried to conduct Korean diplomatic affairs by inducing the United States and European nations to sign commercial and friendship treaties with Korea, by means of which Li Hung-chang attempted to have China's suzerainty over China affirmed. Japan, however, refused to permit China to meddle with Korean affairs any longer.

Japan's control of Korea led to further important developments, one in 1882 and the other in 1884. After the Treaty of Kianghua, the Korean court was divided into conservative and progressive factions. The conservatives, headed by Tai-won-kun, were pro-Chinese; the progressives, under the leadership of Kim Ok-kiun [Chin Yü-chün] and

Queen Min, were pro-Japanese. Tai-won-kun, who had been losing prestige, retired, after which event the power of the progressive faction expanded greatly and the Japanese were invited to train a new army. In July 1882 a great mutiny was caused by the partisans of Kim and Queen Min, who were embezzling funds intended for military purposes. Tai-won-kun took this opportunity to regain his political power by inciting the underpaid, hungry soldiers to invade the imperial palace, where they killed many important members of the Min faction. They also killed a Japanese who was training the new army. In the afternoon the mutineers surrounded and attacked the Japanese legation; the minister, Hanabusa Yoshitada, fled to Nagasaki. The Japanese government dispatched more than a thousand soldiers and marines to aid in returning Hanabusa to Korea and in punishing the Koreans.

As soon as the news of the mutiny was received in China, several thousand soldiers of the Peiyang army and navy, under the command of Ting Ju-ch'ang and others, were shipped to Korea. But on account of China's dispute with France over the Annam problem the Ch'ing court tried to settle the Korean matter quickly, so that the Japanese would have no pretext for opening hostilities. Chinese commanders were ordered by the court to punish the insurgents severely; they arrested Tai-won-kun and brought him to China. At the same time, negotiations with Japan were attempted, but Japan refused to hold any discussions. Since Chinese troops had already entered the capital of Korea and since the ringleader of the mutiny, Tai-won-kun, had been punished by China, the Japanese could only ask Korea to pay an indemnity and to apologize.

Shortly after, a peace treaty was signed, providing: (1) Korea was to pay \$50,000 as compensation for the Japanese killed in the mutiny and \$500,000 for Japan's military expenses. (2) Japan was to be permitted to have soldiers residing at the capital of Korea for the protection of her legation; the expense for the establishment of military camps was to be taken care of by Korea. (3) An envoy was to be sent to Japan to apologize for the incident. Hereafter, as a result of the mutiny of 1882, both China and Japan had soldiers encamped in Korea.

The Coup d'Etat of 1884

After this disturbance the Ch'ing court at last began to pay close attention to Korea. Yüan Shih-k'ai, who had accompanied the Peiyang army to Korea, remained there. He secretly made an alliance with Queen Min's faction in order to frustrate the ambitious of Japan. Japan used the pretext of assisting Korea's reform and independence movement in order to support the progressive party and to stir up internal conflict by setting the two parties at odds. The Min faction and the Kim Ok-kiun clique became now as incompatible as water and fire.

In December 1884 there was a *coup d'état* at Seoul. The Japanese minister to Korea, Takezoe Shinichiro, noticing that China had opened warfare with France over Annam, decided to take this opportunity to end Chinese power in Korea. On December 4 Takezoe secretly conspired with Kim's faction to assassinate the important figures of the Min clan. On the occasion of the opening of the post office of Seoul, Kim's followers set fire to nearby buildings. In the resulting confusion, Kim and others went to the imperial palace requesting the emperor to ask Japanese soldiers to protect the palace. These soldiers killed many members of the Min clique and forced the king to organize a new government.

The Min clique then appealed for aid to Chinese troops stationed in Korea. Yüan Shih-k'ai courageously led troops to the imperial palace to suppress the rebellious faction. Finding the palace occupied by the Japanese minister Takezoe, Yüan's men opened fire on the Japanese and defeated them. Takezoe forced the king of Korea to flee the palace. The Japanese fought their way out of the city of Seoul, where the civilians supported the Chinese. Even the king fled to Yüan Shih-k'ai's headquarters. Takezoe, having failed in his objective of gaining control of the government, burned the Japanese legation. He then went to Jinsen, a seaport in Korea; Kim and other members of his group escaped to Japan.

Early in January 1885 the Japanese government sent its foreign minister Inouye Kaoru as minister plenipotentiary to lead a military force to the rescue of Korea. The Ch'ing court also ordered Wu Ta-ch'eng as imperial commissioner to lead troops to Korea. As soon as Inouye reached the scene, Wu Ta-ch'eng also arrived. Inouye opened negotiations with the Korean government. Wu Ta-ch'eng intended to supervise the negotiations, but he was prevented from doing so by Inouye. A treaty was concluded by which the Korean government indemnified the Japanese for loss of life and property in the *coup d'état*. It also agreed to apologize to Japan, to punish the rioters, and to rebuild the Japanese legation. The incident of 1884 was thus concluded.

This incident was primarily a consequence of the conspiracy and adventurousness of Takezoe. He had received no order for such activity from his government, which at this time had no intention of opening hostilities with China. Hence the incident could be easily concluded.

The Tientsin Convention, 1885

In 1885 the Japanese government sent Ito Hirobumi to China to discuss the Korean situation. The Ch'ing court authorized Li Hung-chang to have a conference with Ito at Tientsin, where in April the Li-Ito, or Tientsin, Convention, was signed. By this agreement, troops of the two countries were to be withdrawn from Korea within four months. Neither China nor Japan was to train soldiers for Korea. Hereafter, in the event of any disturbance necessitating the dispatch of troops to Korea, each nation was to inform the other of its intention in advance, and troops so sent were to be withdrawn as soon as their objective was attained.

Apparently this convention recognized Korea as a coprotectorate of China and Japan. Because the Sino-French War had not yet been concluded and both the national treasury and military preparations of China were very inadequate, Li Hung-chang had to accept part of Ito's proposal concerning a balance of power between the two countries. This treaty served to light the fuse for the forthcoming Sino-Japanese War.

For eight years after the Tientsin Convention, China and Japan had no conflicts. Learning a lesson from the failures of 1882 and 1884, Japan concentrated upon consolidating her own power and seemed satisfied with her current treaty privileges. The Korean court, meanwhile, was prone to rely on China for protection. Yüan Shih-k'ai's prompt action in the incident of 1884 won recognition of his ability from Li Hung-chang, who recommended Yüan to the throne for an appointment as China's commissioner of commerce and resident official in Korea. All Korean commercial and diplomatic relations were to be under Yüan's supervision and direction. The Japanese were very jealous of him and insinuated that the Korean political refugees, Kim Ok-kiun and others, had instigated rebellions in Korea. They confidentially sent a number of young Japanese militarists to Korea to organize the so-called Heavenly Inspired Heroic Corps to disturb the peace so as to create a necessity for calling in troops.

The Tonghak Rebellion, 1894

In March 1894 the assassination of Kim Ok-kiun occurred. Both Kim and another leader, who had fled to Japan for shelter after the *coup d'état* of 1884, had urged their partisans in Korea to incite a revolution. This caused anxiety to the king, who sent assassins to Japan to take their lives. Kim was abducted to Shanghai, where he was murdered in a Japanese hotel. The assassin, Hong Cheong-wu, was arrested. At the request of the Korean king, the Shanghai authorities sent the assassin and the body of the victim to Korea. There the body of Kim was cut to pieces as a further punishment, while the assassin was set free. The Japanese were greatly agitated, and some of them advocated chastising Korea.

Immediately following these events occurred the outbreak of the Tonghak rebellion, the immediate prelude to the Sino-Japanese War. The Tonghak [*Tung-hsüeh-tang*] was a conservative party. Their ideas were a miscellany of Chinese Confucian, Buddhist, and Taoist theories combined in a doctrine which, as that of a Party for Eastern Studies, emphasized opposition to Western studies. This religious party was ethnocentric and chauvinistic. It also advocated the slaughtering of corrupt officials in order to save the lives of the people. Its members were persecuted by the government whenever they were discovered, but the Koreans had long been afflicted with misgovernment, and many of them were ready to revolt; it was easy for the Tonghak to stir up such people to a revolution. Their military actions were directed by officers of the Heavenly Inspired Heroic Corps secretly sent to Korea by Japan. Thus the Tonghak actually became an instrument manipulated by the Japanese to provide Japan with a further excuse to send troops to Korea.

The Tonghak insurrection broke out in one district in March 1894 and gradually spread to other areas. The Korean government tried in vain to suppress it and even solicited Chinese aid. When the assassination case of Kim was publicized, there was a rumor that Japan intended to send troops to Korea. Li Hung-chang cabled Yüan Shih-k'ai in Korea to investigate the source of the rumor. In reply Yüan said that the rumor might not be true, and at least there was no immediate danger. In another cable Yüan stated that he had had a talk with the Japanese minister to Korea, who said that there was no foundation for such a rumor. When Yüan asked him whether several Japanese war vessels were to come to Korea, the minister smiled and replied with a definite No.[30] At this time Yüan Shih-k'ai probably believed that there was no possibility yet of Japan's waging war in Korea.

When the rebellion of the Tonghak occurred, Li Hung-chang was inspecting the army at Hsiao-chan near Tientsin. He had no intention of sending troops to Korea to assist in the suppression of the revolt. On May 25 Li Hung-chang sent a telegram to the Tsungli Yamen, "The Korean king did not ask us to send troops to his aid, and I have not heard that Japan is going to send troops; hence it seems improper for us to take hasty action. We had better wait for further news before we make a decision."[30] Yüan cabled to Li again from Korea, assuring him that he had not yet heard that Japan intended to send troops.

In reality Japan actually intended to ship soldiers and also to persuade China to do the same. On June 1, Yüan Shih-k'ai cabled to Li Hung-chang saying that the translator from the Japanese legation had informed him that the prolonged disturbance of the Tonghak bandits had caused great commercial loss and other anxieties. The Koreans certainly could not terminate the rebellion, so why did not China suppress it quickly? The Chinese government, the Japanese translator suggested, would certainly have no objection.

On June 3 Yüan again reported to Li by cable: "Sugimura of the Japanese: legation came to see me to convey the idea that China is expected to suppress the rebellion quickly on behalf of Korea and he asked whether China will promise to do so or not .... Sugimura is my old friend and his conversation emphasized [the plight of] Japanese businessmen in Korea; it seems to me he has no other intention."[31] Li Hung-chang telegraphed the Tsungli Yamen saying that he was convinced by the Japanese consul at Tientsin, who came to see him and told him approximately the same thing that Sugimura had told Yüan. All these reports serve as evidence that Japan persuaded China to dispatch troops to Korea.

Both Li Hung-chang and Yüan Shih-k'ai still believed that Japan had no intention of resorting to war. The Korean government asked Yüan to suppress the Tonghak. Yüan said that it was necessary for the Korean government to make a formal official appeal, and at the same time he reported to Li Hung-chang:

> The Korean court asked China to suppress the rebellion on its behalf, and to maintain the dignity of a superior nation; the request should not be flatly refused. According to the Tientsin Convention of

> 1885, if China or Japan dispatched soldiers to Korea, the other country was to be notified beforehand by a diplomatic communication; originally the treaty made no mention of the proposal that whenever China sent troops, Japan should follow suit. If Japan is going to insist upon meddling in this revolt, the only excuse for sending more than a hundred soldiers to Seoul could be the protection of the Japanese legation, which is still far away from the center of the revolt. When Japanese soldiers come, they will cause trouble. The foreign ministry of Korea should not permit them to come.[32]

This is Yüan Shih-k'ai's judgment of his enemy.

After Li Hung-chang received the formal petition asking for troops for Korea, he immediately memorialized the throne asking that 1500 soldiers under the control of the provincial commander in chief Yeh Chih-ch'ao be sent to Yashan, a harbor in western Korea. At the same time the Japanese government was officially notified. Before the official note had reached the Japanese court, however, Li Hung-chang had received a notice from the Japanese consulate at Tientsin informing him that Japan had already ordered troops to Korea to protect her legation and merchants. The Tsungli Yamen in Peking and Yüan Shih-k'ai in Korea received this information almost simultaneously. While China sent only 1500 soldiers, Japan immediately dispatched 7000 in the first installment which sailed directly to Seoul.

Japanese Occupation of Korea

Japan's current parliamentary dissension was ironed out by this foreign crisis. Premier Ito and Foreign Minister Mutsu Munemitsu were at first sharply attacked by members of the Diet, which led Yüan Shih-k'ai to think that since the Japanese government was faced with hostile opposition from the Diet, it could not wage a foreign war. Unexpectedly, no sooner had Ito, Mutsu, and others decided to mobilize soldiers for Korea than the attention of all the Japanese immediately was concentrated on the diplomatic problem.

The Tonghak disappeared or disbanded themselves when they saw that China and Japan both were stationing a large number of troops in Korea. China thought that the insurrection had been suppressed. She requested Japan to withdraw her forces simultaneously with the Chinese troops, according to the provision of the Li-Ito convention. The Japanese government not only did not grant permission to withdraw troops, but took the further step of asking China to draw up procedures by which the two nations could reform Korea. Mutsu anticipated that China would not agree with Japan's suggestion, and if she did not, Japan would be at liberty to take independent action. Li Hung-chang and Yüan Shih-k'ai were alarmed at the suggestion.

Obviously the Ch'ing court could not agree with the suggestion of the Japanese government for joint action toward the reform of Korea's domestic administration. At first it argued that since Japan had recognized the independence and autonomy of Korea, she could not interfere with the country's domestic administration. Later on, learning that Japan was continually reinforcing her troops in Korea, Li Hung-chang requested that her forces be withdrawn before the discussion of reform. Japan firmly maintained her original position without yielding any ground and speeded up her reinforcements. The European and American ministers in China also thought that the action of Japan was too harsh. The only hope of Li Hung-chang and the important members of the Tsungli Yamen was interference by European nations and the United States.

Russia was particularly expected to become involved in the Korean dispute because the Russian minister had already expressed his intention to Li of taking positive measures of intervention. Li thought the words of the Russian minister very reliable. England, meanwhile, promised to do her best to bring about mediation, and the United States admonished

Japan. Nevertheless, after the Japanese government decided its policy, it was not moved by the mediation of other nations. After Japan's assurances to Russia that Japan had no desire to occupy the territory of Korea, Russia took the position of bystander in the affair.

The Ch'ing court, watching the overbearing and domineering attitude of the Japanese in Korea, was frightened and perplexed. The armchair scholars reprimanded Li Hung-chang and urged the dispatch of a large force to Korea. The Tsungli Yamen was in a dilemma. If China sent large reinforcements, it would mean overt hostilities; if no reinforcements were sent, China would have to rely on the mediation of England, Russia, and other nations. The outcome was unpredictable, but it was still hoped that mediation might bring about the desired results. Li Hung-chang, who had been misled by the assurances of the Russian minister, was particularly reluctant to reinforce the Korean garrison, lest a war be stirred up. Yüan Shih-k'ai and Yeh Chih-ch'ao, who noticed that the Japanese troops had been increasing continually and occupying many strategic points, ordered Yeh's troops to go from Yashan to the vicinity of Seoul. At the same time they cabled the Tsungli Yamen for additional troops. In a reply by telegram, Li still forbade hasty action and told them that there was still a ray of hope for a peaceful solution.

As soon as a large Japanese force had occupied the Korean capital and all adjacent strategic points, Japan at once put her reform plan before the Korean court. She hinted to the English minister in Japan, who was trying to mediate, that since China disapproved of reforming the Korean domestic administration, Japan would reform it independently and that China's reinforcements to Korea meant a challenge to war. Obviously this was a strong hint that war would be declared against China.

Outbreak and Course of the War

But Li Hung-chang still hoped that there might be a peaceful solution. Not until the imperial court of Korea fell completely into the hands of the Japanese and the latter began to expel all Chinese officials from Korea did Li Hung-chang request the throne to order 8000 soldiers to Pingyang. The reinforcements arrived on July 16, one and a half months after the beginning of the negotiations. Li Hung-chang cabled Yeh Chih-ch'ao warning him against unnecessarily starting a shooting war. On July 20 Li instructed Yeh that regardless of Japan's energetic preparations for war, if China did not start the fighting, Japan would probably not take the initiative and that according to international law, whoever started a war was at fault. Li added, "You must remember this carefully and must not forget it. You should not be short-tempered." This seems to indicate that the Ch'ing court and Li Hung-chang had no intention of fighting.

The mediation of the ministers of England, Russia, and other nations was not yet completely suspended, and Li still awaited an amicable solution. This hope he held to the very last. Only when the transport ship *Kowshing*, carrying troops to Korea, was sunk in the Korean Bay by the Japanese navy, July 25, 1894, and the troops under Yeh encamped at Yashan were surrounded and attacked by the Japanese army, did Li begin to realize that war was inevitable.

Hostilities lasted from the formal declaration of war by Japan on August 1, 1894, to the next March; but China's fate had been determined long before. Japanese forces had long held all the strategic military points; China could only advance troops from Pingyang in the north of Korea. Using Seoul as a base, Japan surrounded Pingyang and in the middle of September forced the Chinese army to withdraw. A Chinese fleet consisting of twelve ships under the command of Admiral Ting Ju-ch'ang confronted the Japanese fleet near the mouth of the Yalu. After a bitter combat for half a day, only eight ships of the Chinese fleet remained. These were all damaged and had to withdraw to the shipyard at Port Arthur for repairs. Later on, the remnant fleet was used for garrison purposes at Weihaiwei and dared not sail out of the harbor any more. After this the Yellow Sea was entirely under Japanese control.

After naval and military successes, the Japanese forces advanced toward Manchuria and in November occupied Ta-lien [Dairen] and Lü-shun [Port Arthur]. All important places in southeast Fengtien Province were subsequently taken. In January of the following year a Japanese fleet landed at Yungcheng Bay, Shantung, for the purpose of assaulting Weihaiwei. Ting Ju-ch'ang led the remaining Peiyang fleet in a desperate attempt at defense. Unfortunately, both officers and soldiers refused to take his orders.

In February the Japanese force invited the Chinese garrisons to surrender. This invitation was refused by Ting Ju-ch'ang, who sabotaged the ships' engines and committed suicide by swallowing poison. His subordinates then surrendered themselves, together with their fleet and Weihaiwei, to the Japanese.

Negotiations for Peace

These battles had a pronounced effect on China. China's warmongers, who had clamored loudly at the time of the negotiations and had attacked Li Hung-chang severely, were disheartened. Li Hung-chang was punished by dismissal from the official ranks, but was allowed to continue making plans for war and defense. Li kept on urging the European and American ministers in China to mediate with Japan and to negotiate a truce, but his efforts were fruitless. Finally, through the good offices of the United States, Japan began to show some interest in a peace. At first the Ch'ing court commissioned two men as ministers plenipotentiary to inquire what terms Japan demanded to bring the war to an end, but the Japanese government refused to discuss anything with them because their credentials were insufficient to qualify them as plenipotentiaries. For this reason the two men returned without achieving any results.

Then Li Hung-chang was appointed ambassador extraordinary for the peace negotiations and was accepted by Japan. Li arrived at Shimonoseki on March 19.

The Japanese plenipotentiaries, Count Ito and Foreign Minister Mutsu, set very severe conditions for a truce. While the negotiations were in progress, Li Hung-chang was suddenly wounded in an attempted as-sassination by a Japanese fanatic; the bullet entered an inch below the left eye. The Japanese government, fearful of the criticism of the world because of this occurrence, agreed to an unconditional armistice for twenty-one days. On April 17, 1895, the end of the time limit, the peace treaty was signed at Shimonoseki.

The Treaty of Shimonoseki, 1895

By the treaty China was required to recognize the full independence and autonomy of Korea. She was to cede the Liaotung Peninsula, Taiwan, and the Pescadores Islands to Japan, and she was to pay an indemnity of two hundred million taels. All treaties between China and Japan previously concluded were to be abrogated and replaced by a new treaty based on the treaties China had signed with European nations. Four cities, Shasi, Chung-king, Soochow, and Hangchow, were to be added to the list of trade ports.

In the subsidiary treaty of commerce signed at Peking in July 1896, Japan gained a new privilege which China had not granted to any of the Western powers: in all trade ports in China the Japanese were to have the freedom to engage in carrying on trade, manufacture, and industry. Furthermore, all kinds of machines, after the payment of a customs duty upon entrance into China, could be shipped to other ports freely. The commodities which were manufactured by Japanese in the interior of China were to be exempted from all taxes.

The last article listed above dealt the national economy of China a great blow. Western imperialists, though repeatedly forcing China to sign humiliating peace treaties, never demanded such privileges. After this article had been provided in the treaty with Japan, all other nations secured the same privilege. Thus China's industry was entirely under the control of Japanese and Western imperialists. In this situation China could never develop a prosperous industry for herself. Since his nation had suffered a crushing defeat, Li Hung-chang could do nothing but accept the demands submissively.

However, Li Hung-chang knew that Russia cherished ambitions toward Korea and China's Three Eastern Provinces. While Li was negotiating peace, he was also keeping all the foreign ministers in Peking well informed about the demands put forth by Japan. He hoped to incite the jealousy of the other nations and bring about their intervention. Eight days after the Treaty of Shimonoseki had been proclaimed, Russia allied herself with Germany and France to deliver a joint note to the Japanese government "recommending" the return of the Liaotung Peninsula to China. Japan was then not in a position to resist the triple intervention; though reluctant, she had to give in.

Throughout his life, Li Hung-chang's diplomatic policy was "to use one barbarian to check another barbarian." This policy now appeared to have produced results; but the aftermath became even more complicated for him to face. The Liaotung Peninsula was nominally under Chinese control; but before long, Russia entreated that Port Arthur and Dairen be rented to her. Then Germany demanded Kiaochow Bay, France Kwanghow Bay, and England Weihaiwei. China had to yield to all these demands. The Japanese-Russian War was also hereby engendered.

Reasons for China's Defeat

The causes of China's failure in the Sino-Japanese War are manifold if they are minutely analyzed, but generally speaking they may be grouped under the following three heads:

1. *Prevalence of Corruption*. The depravity and corruption of society affected all strata of officials from Empress Dowager Tz'u-hsi

down to minor clerks.

The Empress Dowager, apart from appropriating national military funds for her personal pleasure, permitted a group of eunuchs and maidservants in the inner court to sell official posts. Since the people of high rank did this, those below them naturally followed suit. Bribery was rampant. Most of the personnel who served in various offices of the government tried their best to offer bribes in order to gain or maintain their positions or to get promotions. Most of the important generals and personnel of the Peiyang army and navy bent their knees before the eunuch Li Lien-ying and proclaimed themselves Li's pupils. The source of money for gifts and bribes was mainly the embezzlement of military rations and public funds; consequently, there was unbelievably poor equipment for military establishments.

According to the account of the Englishman J. O. P. Bland, two years before the outbreak of the Sino-Japanese War C. von Hanneken, working under Li Hung-chang, suggested to Li that China should buy a large number of explosive shells manufactured by the Krupp factory in Germany for the use of large cannon on warships. Li did put in an order through official channels. But it was never carried out, because it was objectionable to Chang P'ei-lun, an important man then in charge of military supplies. Chang thought it was a sheer waste of the funds allotted to him to buy explosive shells for which there appeared to be no use. As the war grew near, Li Hung-chang hurriedly purchased military supplies from England, Germany, and other nations in spite of the fact that these countries wanted to maintain neutrality and could not sell arms openly to China. Shipping of the necessary equipment to China, therefore, was difficult. At the time of the naval battle with Japan in the Yellow Sea, China's two steel warships had only three explosive shells suitable for large cannon, and because of the shortage of ammunition, only the small guns were used. According to the statement made by the English-trained navy man Yen Fu, some of the torpedoes which China herself had made were even filled with scrap iron instead of gunpowder.

Moreover, since corruption was even more rife in the army than it was in the navy, Li Hung-chang was extremely hesitant, at the inception of the Korean difficulties, to resort to arms. He tried desperately, by one means and then another, to settle the question diplomatically and peaceably. The scholar-officials criticized him, scorned him as a coward, and urged him to send troops to Korea. But always conscious of China's weaknesses, Li was slow to relinquish the method of procedure which he thought best.

2. *Lack of Unification*. Lack of unification weakened the various administrations, political, diplomatic, financial, and military. The administrative system resembled a sheet of scattered sand. Theoretically, the emperor had absolute authority and it looked as though there was complete national unification under his rule. In fact, with the emperor a mere figurehead, Empress Dowager Tz'u-hsi sold official posts and promoted or degraded officials. The Tsungli Yamen pondered diplomatic problems, but had to depend upon the advice obtained from the superintendents of trade in the northern and southern ports, both of whom were far removed from Peking. Li Hung-chang had the courage to shoulder responsibility for diplomatic affairs, but he lacked the authority to execute his policies. Besides the superintendents of the ports, there were many grand secretaries, censors, the state minister, the vice-minister, governors-general, and governors. All of them had the right to express their ideas about various diplomatic problems. It was hard to know who actually did control foreign policy.

In Japan, by way of contrast, there was only one premier and one minister of foreign affairs, each of whom had only to deal with one governmental organ, the Diet. Li Hung-chang, in China, was neither premier nor minister of foreign affairs, and he had to deal with many irresponsible, unruly, powerful, and petty officials. In China even the emperor and the empress dowager were usually unable to decide whose ideas were the best. Throughout the Sino-Japanese conflict, not a single person could understand one day what course was to be taken the next; from the beginning to end there was no firm policy.

From the military standpoint, the Navy Yamen was said to control and direct the entire navy, but actually this office only commanded the Peiyang [the northern] fleet. If the Navy Yamen wanted to direct the Nanyang [the southern] fleet, it had to consult by telegraph the superintendent of the southern ports first. Even in the Navy Yamen itself, which was under the direction of the Tsungli Yamen, there were two associate directors and two assistant directors. The director had authority but no ability, while, among the associate and assistant directors, some had great ability and some had little; yet all had equal authority. Even within this one Yamen there was no unification of authority nor any single policy.

The organization of the army was even worse than that of the navy. The ministry of war was a government department which had no function at all, aside from being decorative. The provincial troops had been for a long time the personal troops of the governors-general and governors. Those soldiers who could be ordered by Li Hung-chang were limited to the Peiyang army. Other provincial troops lacked unification in organization, training, and military equipment, and their commanding officials were uncongenial and far distant from one another.

As for China's financial condition, the ministry of revenue supposedly controlled the finances of the whole nation, but in fact the offices which actually possessed the money were the provincial treasuries over which the provincial governors-general and governors had more authority than the ministry. Li Hung-chang had the responsibility of appropriating military funds, but he had no power to make use of the financial resources of the whole nation. Only the income of the one province of Chihli, which was under his jurisdiction, could be directly appropriated by him. If he wished to ask for money from other provinces, he first had to memorialize to the throne; the emperor, after receiving his memorial, as a rule turned it over for consideration and discussion to the ministry of revenue. After such a request was approved, the provincial authorities sometimes could avoid fulfilling it by tactfully reporting to the emperor lack of funds in their respective treasuries. The person seeking funds still had to beg personally for friendly help from those in charge of financial resources in the provinces.

When diplomatic problems came up, there were many governors-general and governors who enjoyed voicing high-sounding words favoring war. But if military funds were invoked, they would say that their compliance with the request would depend upon whether the unexpected expenditure would impede the financial activity of their provinces. Thus Li Hung-chang himself said, "The one province, Chihli, is dealing with the whole nation of Japan." This was not an expression Li used to whitewash his own faults; it was the truth.

3. *A Modernized Nation Opposed to an Old Kingdom*. Corruption and disunity were two causes of the failure of China during this period. China's old-style concept of a kingdom was a third cause.

China's opponent, Japan, had modernized herself. Her government was a single unit commanding its subjects directly, as nerves direct the five senses and the four limbs. China, on the other hand, was still feudalistic. The central government and the people were separate entities, with little or no direct contact. The throne could not inspire virtue among the people. Those who served under the throne resembled slaves in a decadent family. Each sought personal profit and pleasure and was addicted to slovenliness, stealing, and bickering. Even if among them there were one or two out-standing faithful and able persons who wished to support the decadent family, they could not do very much.

When Li Hung-chang and Ito Hirobumi had a conference at Tientsin, Li said, "But your honorable minister has done all that he would like to do. If you took my position in China, you would understand that the difficulties which I have faced are beyond description." Ito replied, "If I were in your honorable country, I'm afraid I could not become an official."[33]

Although these are remarks in social conversation, they speak the truth. Fundamentally, the reason that Japan could win the war was that she had undergone a bloodless political revolution. The reform party, which first gained a victory in domestic affairs, took charge of Japan's foreign policy. What was most needed in China also was a political revolution, but forward-looking individuals who promoted China's adoption of Western methods were restrained by the conservatives, and the Chinese people generally had no spirit of adventure. How could they avoid failure in dealing with foreign countries? However, after the fiasco of the Sino-Japanese War, the prestige of the traditional leaders could not be maintained any longer. A political revolutionary force began to emerge.

CHAPTER FOUR THE REFORM MOVEMENT: THE FIRST STEP

Continuing though sporadic imitation of Western methods beginning with the 1860's finally brought forth a reform movement which culminated in the work of two great leaders. As early as 1885 Sun Yat-sen had made up his mind to overthrow the Ch'ing dynasty; and in 1889 K'ang Yu-wei attempted to submit a petition to the throne requesting reform. Both of these men were born near Canton, where people had had the earliest contact with Western culture and where the Opium War had taken place. The two men in consequence received a common stimulus. Their family backgrounds and childhood education, however, were quite different and from the beginning their purposes diverged.

TWO REFORM LEADERS—SUN YAT-SEN AND K'ANG YU-WEI

Sun's Early Years

Sun Yat-sen's original name was Sun Wen, and his *tzu* [courtesy name] was I-hsien, of which a Cantonese pronunciation is Yat-sen. Later, on one of the occasions when he fled to Japan, he took the name Chung-shan-ch'iao [the Wood Cutter of Chung-shan] in order to conceal his identity, and thus he was known as Chung-shan. He was born in 1866 in the district of Hsiangshan, Kwangtung. His father was Sun Tao-ch'uan; his mother was a Yang. They had three sons. The eldest one was Te-chang; the second died prematurely; Yat-sen was the youngest.

For generations the poor family had made a living through agriculture; in childhood Sun Yat-sen had to assist in farm work. From the villagers he learned the stories of Hung Hsiu-ch'üan and Yang Hsiu-ch'ing, and his early ambition was to become a second Hung Hsiu-ch'üan. At the age of twelve, having received some schooling from his uncle, he was sent to Hawaii where his elder brother, Te-chang, fifteen years his senior, had for a long time been a prosperous cattleman on a small island. Sun Yat-sen while in Hawaii attended a missionary school in Honolulu from 1879 to 1882.

By the late fall of 1883 Yat-sen was back in China, in Hong Kong for the first time. There he attended briefly the diocesan school of the Church of England. He soon changed to Queen's College, at which the instruction given was not above a high-school level. In 1886 he entered the Po-chi Hospital School at Canton, where he made friends with Cheng Shih-liang, a member of a secret society, the San-tien Hui [known among Occidentals as the Triad].

In the following year Sun transferred to Alice Memorial Hospital, Hong Kong, where he became acquainted with Ch'en Shao-po, Lu Hao-tung, and two others. They discussed revolutions so much and so often that their relatives and friends in Hong Kong and Macao began to call Sun, Ch'en, and two others the Rebel Quartet. As early as 1885 at the age of nineteen, Sun Yat-sen says in his autobiography, "I began to make up my mind to overthrow the Ch'ing dynasty, and from that time on I was using the [Pochi Hospital] school as headquarters for propaganda and using medicine as a medium for entering the world."[1]

K'ang the Scholar

As for K'ang Yu-wei, his first given name was Tsu-i. He was born in 1858, in the district of Nan-hai, Kwangtung, into an old and aristocratic family which for generations had been noted for its Neo-Confucian scholarship. His great-grandfather was a private tutor and a respected, dedicated scholar. His grandfather, Tsan-hsiu, director of studies of Lien-chou and a promoter of the doctrine of the Neo-Confucianism of the

Sung dynasty, commanded great respect from the young scholars of Kwangtung. His grandfather's brother, K'ang Kuo-ch'i, had served in the army under Tso Tsung-t'ang in the latter half of the nineteenth century, and as a reward for merit had been made Governor of Kwangsi. His father, Ta-ch'u, died young, but not until two sons had been born—Yu-wei and Kuang-jen.

Since K'ang Yu-wei was an orphan, he received his education from his grandfather. At seven he could write good essays and was considered a precocious child. During his boyhood his mind was fixed upon knowledge of Confucius, the sage, and Mencius, the wise man; the village boys laughed at him and gave him the nickname, "Sage Wei."[2]

At the age of eighteen K'ang began to study under Chu Tz'u-ch'i [*tzu* Chiu-chiang], a great scholar of Kwangtung. Chu's knowledge was based on the Neo-Confucianism of the Sung and Ming dynasties, and he concentrated on the guiding principle of usefulness to society. He made great advances in his research into Chinese history and the political evolution of all dynasties. K'ang studied under him for six years until Chu's death, and the foundation of his knowledge in Neo-Confucianism and government was acquired from this famous teacher. After the death of the teacher, K'ang lived alone and studied assiduously for four years in a quiet studio on a mountain of Nan-hai. Then he went to Peking.

At this time Western sciences were being introduced into China, but scholars all over the country paid little attention to them. Living in an isolated countryside, K'ang had no chance to participate in the pursuit of Western knowledge until he was en route to Peking via Hong Kong and Shanghai. In these two places he saw efficient and honest municipal administrations among the Westerners and deduced that if their colonies and foreign settlements were so well governed, their home countries would be even better managed. Accordingly, he tried to discover the reasons for the efficiency of Western administrations. He concluded that Westerners must have a solid foundation of moral principles as well as a knowledge of political and natural sciences. He purchased and read all the Western books prepared by the translation bureau attached to the Kiangnan Arsenal and by Western missionaries—books of popular knowledge about industry, military science, medicine, and the Bible. There was little on Western politics and philosophy. K'ang, however, had unusual understanding and could easily make analogies from one point to another, from small to large issues, and soon was opening a new dimension in his pursuit of knowledge.[3]

A Comparison of Backgrounds

In comparing the early lives of K'ang Yu-wei and Sun Yat-sen we might conclude that, since Sun emerged from an old agricultural family in which existence was a struggle and thought was simple, he could hardly have avoided the pressures of traditions several thousand years old. Nevertheless he was comparatively free from the constricted views typical of Neo-Confucianism. Even at the age of twelve or thirteen he showed a naturally active and inquiring mind and he was not embarrassed to talk of becoming Hung Hsiu-ch'üan the Second. By contrast K'ang Yu-wei from early boyhood was trapped by Neo-Confucianism and aspired to become, in the traditional sense, a sage.

From the beginning Sun Yat-sen received a modern Western, scientific education and had direct contact with European culture. His thoughts concentrated upon immediate practical aspects of political and social problems. K'ang Yu-wei received an old-fashioned and characteristically Oriental education. He was absorbed in abstruse inquiries and was inclined always to examine affairs in terms of comprehensive systems and universal meanings. His acquaintance with Western culture was only indirect. K'ang's opinions, when people first encountered them, appeared to be fresh and original; but actually he never freed himself from traditional assumptions which hampered his power to deal with changing times and new circumstances.

Early Activities of Sun and K'ang

The years from 1894 to 1898 may be considered as the initial stage of the reform movement in China. In this movement, the two leaders, Sun and K'ang, were very active. After the outbreak of the Sino-Japanese War in 1894, Sun Yat-sen went to Hawaii to found the Hsing-Chung Hui [Revive China Society]. In December he returned to his homeland. In the following January he organized his Hsing-Chung Hui headquarters in Hong Kong and made the first attempt to organize a revolutionary army in Kwangtung.

K'ang Yu-wei received the *chü-jen* degree by passing a provincial examination in 1894 and in the following year took the metropolitan examination, where he submitted a joint petition to the throne signed by hundreds of examination candidates. This petition was subsequently called *Kung-che shang-shu* [Petition Presented by the Examination Candidates]. It was written by K'ang, who strongly urged reforms in order to keep China from perishing as a nation.

Circumstances in 1894 were more suitable for K'ang than for Sun, because this was a period ready rather for reform than for active revolution. Sun's activities were acceptable to few people other than the members of secret societies, whereas K'ang's stand was accepted and supported by many. When Sun organized the Hsing-Chung Hui in Hawaii, his only followers were his elder brother Te-chang, together with Teng Yin-nan and some ten others. On the other hand, the joint petition by the metropolitan examination candidates led by K'ang is said to have been signed by twelve or thirteen hundred candidates. With the first failure of the revolutionary army in Canton, Sun became notorious throughout China, and newspapers spoke of him in derogatory and scurrilous terms; he was described as a gangster, a rebel, indeed a dreadful monster with red eyebrows and green eyes. No one then could have imagined that Sun was both handsome and a gentleman, a man whose appearance warranted the name Sun Wen ["refined" or "elegant"].[4]

Sun Yat-sen went to Hawaii again in 1896, and thence to many large cities in the United States and England to promote the Hsing-Chung Hui. Only a handful of people, hardly more than ten in each city, welcomed his revolutionary ideas. Since people outside China who had contact with Westerners and had seen better governments were still indifferent to Sun's program, it goes without saying that the number of sympathizers Sun could find within China was extremely small.

It was in 1896 that Sun Yat-sen was kidnapped and confined in the Chinese legation in London. At this time he attracted considerable public attention in England. In China his reputation remained negligible; he was still the great monster with red eyebrows and green eyes. Even K'ang Yu-wei's follower Mei Meng-hua wrote an article in a newspaper branding Sun a bandit, a member of secret societies, and a man who had caused China great humiliation because he obtained his freedom from the Chinese legation through the interference of the Earl of Salisbury. This was indeed the prevailing Chinese attitude toward all reform leaders at the time. Sun's activities thus far had produced little effect on the Chinese government except to stir up a little diplomatic storm in London.

K'ang's Appeal to Scholar-Officials

K'ang Yu-wei's activity caused a much greater political storm in China. Because his ideas suited the temper of the times, K'ang was able to rouse the emperor, many high officials, and many scholars. Chinese political thinking still was largely the preserve of the scholar-official class, which was deeply affected by the results of the fiasco of the Sino-Japanese War. K'ang Yu-wei had just obtained the *chin-shih* degree in 1895 and had become a dignitary among scholars.

Such scholars had little use for Sun, a man trained only in the techniques of Western medicine. As Wu Chih-hui said, "At first I despised Sun Wen simply because he was not a man who had passed the high official examinations, nor was he a classical scholar and a man of letters; I suspected that he was illiterate."[5] K'ang Yu-wei, however, as both a classical scholar and a man of letters, could submit to the emperor a very emotional, persuasive, fluent petition ten thousand words long, and therefore he was recognized as a leader by his own scholar class. The Chinese populace still regarded the emperor as the Son of Heaven, with divine right, while the scholar-official class, which had been strongly influenced by the agelong Confucian ethics of loyalty, felt even more respectful toward the Dragon Throne. According to Wu Chih-hui, "Although at that time I had made some progress by changing from a mild-reform to a radical-reform party, I still could not disregard Emperor Kuang-hsü. ... I felt that revolutionary action might be taken, but after all it seemed improper, and I frequently thought I would simply let Sun Wen carry on the revolt, while I myself would not do it."[5] On the other hand K'ang Yu-wei said in his petition that the relation between an emperor and a minister had long been fixed, "like the horizon between the sky and ocean which can never be crossed. ... The populace eat the food of the emperor and the land they walk upon is the emperor's land. Who is not his servant or son?"

K'ang frequently voiced such traditional eulogies as "the kindness of all imperial ancestors, the former rulers, and our present majesty, who have bestowed on us profound benevolence and unfathomable favor in feeding us generously for the last several hundred years." He said, "According to Kung-yang's commentary on the *Spring and Autumn Annals*, *minister* and *son* are synonyms, and now that the Ch'ing dynasty has suffered the greatest humiliation which has ever been experienced in more than two hundred years of the dynasty, people should be sympathetic with instead of rebellious against the regime."[6]

Such expressions sounded so proper and loyal that they could not fail to move the minds of the entire scholar-official class. Wu Chih-hui, who had no personal respect for K'ang, was so inspired by K'ang's writings, that he paid him a visit in his lodgings in Peking in order to see this patriotic and heroic scholar and to talk about reforms. Under such circumstances, it is easy to see why the leadership of the reform movement in China naturally fell into the hands of K'ang Yu-wei.

REFORM BASED ON THE CLASSICS: THE INTERPRETATIONS BY K'ANG YU-WEI

It was certainly easier for K'ang Yu-wei to secure leadership of the reform movement than for Sun Yat-sen. But in the scholar-official class, why could K'ang alone become the leader of reform?

Let us look at a phrase in his petition to the emperor: "I presume to think that the present government should rule the empire by a new power [as at the beginning of a dynasty] and should not rule by perfunctory authority."[7] Such an idea no other member of the scholar-official class who held a government position at the time dared to express, for the "new power" referred to could be interpreted as a contempt for the later rulers of the Ch'ing dynasty. But K'ang proceeded to promote such fundamental proposals for reform by presenting them as a recovery of the classical tradition. In Chinese politics Confucian classics had been traditionally respected as a criterion of good government, and the Six Classics were in fact China's constitution. K'ang Yu-wei's political ideas derived from the Six Classics, and the reason why he could become a reform leader and stir up a great storm at the time was simply that he had done some revolutionary work on the Six Classics.

K'ang's disciple Liang Ch'i-ch'ao said in 1902: "In China today a majority of the people would still not be terrified at the mention of constitutional or republican government; but unless such ideas can be quoted from the early sages as a basis, how can we set up a fortress to fight against the formidable enemy with a tradition of two thousand years?" For the purpose of promoting political reform K'ang Yu-wei had tried long before to find a basis for reform in the Confucian classics. Liang Ch'i-ch'ao traced the sources of the academic ideas of his teacher back as far as Kung Tzu-chen and Wei Yüan, both of whom adhered to the "Modern Text School"of classical criticism. [8]

This Modern Text School cast doubt on the central idea of academic thought in the Ch'ing dynasty. As Liang Ch'i-ch'ao reports:

> Kung and Wei and their followers were inclined to clever arguments, and yet a change was made in our thinking world. ... Their approximate contemporary ... was Shao I-ch'en (Wei-hsi) ... who was an eminent professor of classics. ... Wei Yüan was the first specialist in the modern text of the *Book of Odes* and the *Book of History*, while Shao expounded the theory of the modern text of the *Book of Rites* and wrote a book, *Li-ching tung-lun* [A General Discussion of the Book of Rites] in which he alleged that thirty-nine chapters of the recollected version of the *Book of Rites* had been forged by Liu Hsin [*ob.* 23 B. C.]. Thereafter the modern texts of all the classics were issued. Wang K'ai-yün (Jen-ch'iu) and his disciple, Liao P'ing (Chi-p'ing) were the two great exponents of the modern text. Wang interpreted the Six Classics according to Kung-yang's commentaries, and Kung-yang was really the center of the Modern Text School. Liao followed his teacher's doctrines and enlarged them. My teacher, K'ang Yu-wei, studied in his boyhood under Chu Tz'u-ch'i of the same district, Nan-hai Chu was fond of the philosophy of Lu Hsiang-shan [1139-1193] and Wang Yang-ming [1472-1529], whose theory was not spoken of by his contemporaries, and Chu particularly enjoyed discussing the advantages and disadvantages of various political and legal systems in Chinese history. Chu's method of studying the classics was an overall scrutiny of the methods of the Han and the Sung schools, the modern

and ancient texts, without adhering to any particular school. K'ang's special study of the Kung-yang commentary was to follow the modern text, and his interpretation was undoubtedly derived from that of Liao P'ing. Although both Liao and K'ang made a special study of the Kung-yang commentary, the objectives of their research were not the same. All specialists on the Kung-yang spoke of his guiding principles in judgment, but K'ang alone perceived his most profound ideas. ...[9]

K'ang Yu-wei was the first man to interpret the ideas of reform as he believed he found them in the *Spring and Autumn Annals*. From this text he explained the three stages of political evolution, a progression from the existing stage of disorder through a local peaceful stage to the stage of world peace. K'ang Yu-wei considered the *Spring and Autumn Annals* a work purposely intended to curb the power of the emperor, to limit the claims of the nobility, to enlarge the rights of the people, to honor equality, remove domestic struggle and bring unification, abolish bad customs and develop respect for government by law.

The traditional attitude of Chinese scholars toward a legal system was that it might be revised but not reformed. Their attitude toward the government was that they should obey it or occasionally admonish it, but they should never rebel against it. Although trained to think in this way by the pressure of tyrannical rulers, they were also misled by their study of Confucius, who, they believed, advocated this attitude toward government. K'ang Yu-wei sought to alter this interpretation of Confucius, which he believed to be an erroneous one.

After establishing the idea of three stages, K'ang used his evolutionary theory to explain the intention of Confucius to render service to society. This theory could be verified in the classics without difficulty, and it could inspire both hope for the future and the scholar's understanding of his present duty to society. K'ang cherished a great ambition to change the Chinese mind, though he knew that Chinese thinking had been rigid for a long time and could hardly be changed suddenly. He therefore used the generally respected Confucius as a means to lead other scholars to reform. This was the subtle and profound intention of K'ang Yu-wei's new interpretation of the classics.

K'ang Yu-wei esteemed the idea of a cosmopolitan world [*ta-t'ung*] described in the chapter "Li-yün" of the *Book of Rites*. The profound ideal mentioned in this chapter refers either to a cosmopolitan society and an age of great peace or to a peaceful society and an intermediate period of security between chaos and world peace. From an analysis of this passage K'ang went on to discuss political problems and to expound the reason why the government should progress from despotism to a constitutional republic.

K'ang's Early Writings

Before 1894 K'ang wrote two books, one entitled *Hsin-hsüeh wei-ching k'ao* [A Study of the New Dynasty School's Forgeries] and the other *Kung-tzu kai-chih k'ao* [A Study of Confucius as a Reformer]. In the first book K'ang charged that all those classics which Liu Hsin fought to have registered by the government as orthodox works—including the *Chou-li*, *Ili*, *Tso-chuan*, and Mao's *Commentary on the Book of Odes*—were forged by Liu Hsin, the imperial tutor of Wang Mang. Thus, according to K'ang, the ideas of these classics current in the Eastern Han dynasty should not be considered Han scholarship but merely ideas promoted by Wang Mang. The purpose of the book *Hsin-hsüeh wei-ching k'ao* was to break down the prestige of the popular Han School interpretation of classics and to open a whole new realm of thought.

In the *Kung-tzu kai-chih k'ao*, K'ang says that all the philosophers in the Chou and Ch'in period claimed that there had been a golden age in ancient times because they wished to promote a reform movement by their contemporary rulers patterned after the ancient exemplary rulers. For instance, Lao-tzu created an ideal ruler, the Yellow Emperor; Mo-tzu created the Great Yü; and Hsü-hsing created Shen-nung [the Divine Husbandman]. K'ang further asserts that the method Confucius used in writing the *Spring and Autumn Annals* implies to competent readers great principles and profound ideas of reform which the general public could not understand. Emperors Yao and Shun were, in K'ang's opinion, merely figures originated by Confucius. Whether there were actually such figures or not in ancient times is hard to ascertain; but their great achievements and brilliant virtues depicted in the classics all corresponded, in K'ang's opinion, to the ideas of Confucius. The Kung-yang interpretation of the three periods of unity [*T'ung san-t'ung*] meant that the three dynasties, Hsia, Shang, and Chou, were different from one another, and that reforms were made from time to time. The interpretation of the three stages [*Chang san-shih*] also explains the essential ideas of the Confucian reform movement. The function of K'ang's book was to paste a label of "precedents and examples of reforms" on old classics, using the prestige of the most accomplished sage, Confucius, to subdue all those who might object to reform.[10]

K'ang's Bid for Imperial Attention

As for K'ang Yu-wei's method of promoting reform, it was fundamentally different from that of Sun Yat-sen. Sun started his revolution from the lower stratum of society, whereas K'ang began in the upper stratum. K'ang's first step was to attempt to influence or control the emperor to act as his puppet; another step was to secure as many partisans as possible within the scholar-official class. He knew that because in the political organization of China the principle of despotism had been intensively developed, all authority was concentrated in the throne. It was therefore necessary to win the heart of the emperor first. If K'ang could not do this, he could do nothing, no matter how perfect his doctrine or how superior his ability. He therefore worked hard toward this goal.

His first petition failing to reach the emperor, he tried again and again. He tried altogether seven times, with the determination that not until the emperor appreciated his opinions and accepted his suggestions would he call a halt to his efforts. Finally, through the recommendation of Hsü Chih-ching and others, the emperor summoned him for an interview and actually liked him.

The popular story is not true that K'ang was introduced by Weng T'ung-ho, for in Weng's diary one can see that Weng and K'ang were of different opinions. Here are a few excerpts from Weng's diary:

> On June 21, 1894, I read K'ang Yu-wei's *Hsin-hsüeh wei-ching k'ao*, in which he asserts that the old texts of classics established by Liu Hsin were forgeries and interpolations, and that all scholars beginning with Cheng K'ang-ch'eng [of the Han dynasty] were fooled by the spurious Six Classics. K'ang is really a wild fox among classical scholars. I am surprised by his work. [On May 26, 1898] the emperor ordered me to look for the K'ang books which had been presented to the court by the author and to make another copy to submit to His Majesty. I replied, "I have never had any contact with K'ang." His Majesty asked why. I said, "This man's heart cannot be fathomed!" And the emperor said, "Why did you not say this before?" I replied, "Your minister did not know until he recently read K'ang's *Kung-tzu kai-chih k'ao*."
>
> [May 28] the emperor inquired again about K'ang's books and the minister's reply was the same as yesterday's. The emperor was angry and scorned him. The minister replied, "It is better to order the Tsungli Yamen to submit the books." The emperor did not approve of this suggestion and insisted that the minister must go to see Chang Yin-huan in the Yamen to convey the order. I replied, "Chang comes to see your majesty every day. Why did you not

instruct him to do so?" The emperor still insisted. I withdrew from the interview and conveyed his request to Chang.

[On December 23, 1899] an imperial decree of the twentieth was published in a newspaper *Hsin-wen pao*, reading, "Vigilantly arrest the two rebels K'ang and Liang" and also referring to Weng T'ung-ho's strong recommendation of K'ang Yu-wei avowing that K'ang's ability was a hundred times better than his own. I read this decree with fear and trembling. I recalled that when the rebel K'ang entered the court, I had been dismissed and sent home [to Kiangsu] from the capital; moreover, I had repeatedly said that that man's [K'ang's] mind was unfathomable and I dared not associate with him. The emperor asked for his books again and again and eventually a decree was conveyed to Chang Yin-huan to search for them and present them to the Grand Council, where the grand councilors jointly sealed and submitted them to the throne. Nobody knew the content of K'ang's books. Thereafter, had I still been in the court, I would never have let the rebel be so unruly and influential, yet I am now blamed for it. I can do nothing but have pity for myself.[11]

From these excerpts we may conclude that K'ang was not recommended to the throne by Weng T'ung-ho. The statement that he was recommended by Hsü Chih-ching is based on the account given by Yün Yü-ting in *Ch'ung-ling ch'uan-hsin lu*.[11]

Eventually K'ang's writings were read by the emperor. In June 1898 the emperor appointed K'ang second-class assistant secretary of the ministry of public works, to serve in the Tsungli Yamen. From that time on he gradually received opportunities to approach the emperor, and it was not difficult for him soon to make the emperor his puppet.

Having placed himself in contact with the emperor, K'ang sought allies among the scholar-official class to propagate his doctrine and to help form a party. He knew that although the emperor theoretically wielded universal authority, in actuality the emperor alone had no ability to exercise this authority, for there were too many people who could send memorials and suggestions to him and his point of view was constantly being changed.

Before 1894 K'ang had already obtained several disciples, of whom the most influential was Liang Ch'i-ch'ao. After K'ang achieved new dignity by passing the metropolitan examination, he made friends with official circles, including Hsü Chih-ching, a reader of the Hanlin Academy; Yang Shen-hsiu, a censor; Kao Hsieh-tseng, a supervising censor; as well as Chang Yin-huan, Li Tuan-fen, Yang Jui, Liu Kuang-ti and others. Among the governors-general and governors, he obtained the support of Ch'en Pao-chen and Chang Chih-tung, who at first sympathized with him. Many other scholar-officials, like Huang Tsun-hsien and T'u Chou-jen, served under his leadership. Among K'ang's comrades, T'an Ssu-t'ung of Hunan was the most ready for open agitation to promote K'ang's ideas.

The Spread of K'ang's Reform Movement

K'ang's method of propaganda was at first to organize study clubs and to open newspaper offices. When he taught in Kwangtung and Kwangsi he sponsored a learned society at Kweilin (*Kuei-hsüeh Hui*). When in Peking in 1896 he met a galaxy of famous scholars including Wen T'ing-shih, and organized the *Ch'iang-hsüeh Hui* [Society for the Study of National Rejuvenation]. He saw to it that the society seized the opportunity to elect Chang Chih-tung as its head. Yüan Shih-k'ai (who was then a *taotai*) was also a supporter of the Ch'iang-hsüeh Hui, which had a branch in Shanghai. The Ch'iang-hsüeh press which was attached to the headquarters of the society at Peking published a newspaper called *Chung-wai chi-wen* [*Chinese and Foreign News Chronicle*]. Another paper, called *Ch'iang-hsüeh pao*, was published in Shanghai, but because the paper was dated according to the birth of Confucius, it somehow frightened Chang Chih-tung, who caused its suppression. A censor, Yang Ch'ung-i, who was influenced by an unknown person, accused the *Ch'iang-hsüeh Hui* of improper purposes and requested the throne to seal up the society house at once. Later on the Ch'iang-hsüeh press was transformed into a government printing office and Li Tuan-fen requested that more schools be opened and the site of the government printing office be enlarged and made into the Imperial University [*Ching-shih ta-hsüeh*, later referred to familiarly as *Pei-ta*, the university in the North, at the capital].

The branch society in Shanghai was also closed down and the house converted into a newspaper office. Huang Tsun-hsien, Wang K'ang-nien, Liang Ch'i-ch'ao, Mei Meng-hua, and others then organized the *Shih-wu pao* [*Current News*] which was warmly received, and its editor, Liang Ch'i-ch'ao, built up a good reputation.

In Tientsin, Yen Fu, Hsia Tseng-yu, and others issued the *Kuo-wen tsachih* [*Magazine of National News*]. Its circulation was as large as that of the *Shih-wu pao*. Yen Fu's famous translation of Huxley's *Social Evolution* [*T'ien-yen-lun*] was published in this magazine. Although this magazine was not under K'ang Yu-wei's control, it was sympathetic with K'ang's reform program.

The dissolution of the Ch'iang-hsüeh Hui tended to curb K'ang's reform movement slightly; nevertheless, before long, the seizure of Kiaochow by the Germans occurred, and Chinese scholars of the whole empire were as excited as if they had taken morphine injections. K'ang availed himself of this opportunity to establish in Peking a National Protection Society [*Pao-kuo Hui*]. His slogan was national salvation, and his method was to stir up the spirit of the scholars by asking farsighted students to set up study clubs in the provinces in order to discuss ways of saving the nation from foreign aggression and conquest. There were in Peking the Kwangtung Study Club, the Szechwan Study Club, the Fukien Study Club, the Chekiang and Shensi Study Clubs. By means of these clubs, the scholars of all provinces were utilized as a basic force in the spread of K'ang's influence to their native provinces.

Of all the provinces, the one most affected by the reform movement was Hunan, where in the period from 1895 to 1897 there was a very enlightened director of studies, Chiang Piao, who promoted a new academic spirit. The acting judicial commissioner, Huang Tsun-hsien, the provincial governor, Ch'en Pao-chen, and his son, San-li, enthusiastic for reform, cooperated with the native scholars T'an Ssu-t'ung, Hsiung Hsi-ling, T'ang Ts'ai-ch'ang, and others in opening an Academy of Current Affairs [*Shih-wu hsüeh-t'ang*], in which Liang Ch'i-ch'ao was the director. A newspaper, *Hsiang-hsüeh hsin-pao*, was published, and a learned society, *Nan-hsüeh Hui* [Southern Studies Society], organized. Chiang Piao left his office in the winter of 1897 and was succeeded in the position of provincial director of studies by Hsü Jen-chu (son of Hsü Chih-ching), a man also interested in promoting reform. Later on another newspaper, *Hsiang-pao*, was issued in the spring and summer of 1898 when the new reform spirit became very strong in Hunan.

THE HUNDRED DAYS' REFORM, 1898

The reform movement reached its climax in the late spring and early summer of 1898. In Peking K'ang Yu-wei's powerful supporters were Hsü Chih-ching, Yang Shen-hsiu, and Yang Jui. Yang persuaded the supervising censor, Kao Hsieh-tseng, to submit a memorial to the throne recommending the reformers very highly. This action resulted in the imperial decree to the princes and high ministers summoning K'ang to the Tsungli Yamen to ask him about the reform situation. The princes and high ministers then presented to the throne K'ang Yu-wei's letter, which had been submitted in 1897 through the minister of public works. Upon reading the letter the emperor pointed out the sentence: "It may be too late for him to beg to become a commoner of the capital Ch'ang-an, and I could not bear to see such an event recur as when the last emperor of the Ming had to hang himself on Coal Hill." The emperor said to the grand councilors: "How daring is K'ang, who writes such expressions to me without thinking of his own safety!"[12] Nevertheless he did not punish K'ang but instead ordered that thereafter if K'ang presented memorials, they should be forwarded to the throne immediately and not be put aside. The emperor also asked for K'ang's books dealing with the Meiji Restoration in Japan and a biography of Peter the Great.

As a result of successive memorials by Hsü Chih-ching and Yang Shen-hsiu, an imperial decree was proclaimed on June 11 to decide upon these national affairs. This decree marked the beginning of the reform movement. On June 16 the reader of the Hanlin Academy, Hsü Chih-ching, was ordered to bring the assistant secretary of the ministry of public affairs, K'ang Yu-wei, and others to court to have an interview with the emperor. After the interview K'ang was immediately appointed probationary secretary [*hsing-tsou*] in the Tsungli Yamen. At first the emperor intended to appoint K'ang to a high position, but at this time, even though nominally he ruled the nation, actually all promotions and demotions of any high officials had to be decided by the empress dowager, who was living in the Summer Palace. The emperor could not decide such matters alone, and as a result, could only appoint K'ang to the office of a secretary.

Proposed Reforms

Nevertheless the new administration began auspiciously, with the following reforms.

1. Beginning with the next examination, topics for themes in the district, provincial, and metropolitan examinations, which had been heretofore selected from the Four Books, were to be changed

to topics on current problems.

2. Liang Ch'i-ch'ao, who had been a *chu-jen*, was to be granted a sixth-rank position in charge of the affairs of the Translation Bureau.
3. The method of grading the candidates after each test in the provincial and metropolitan examinations was to be extended to districts and lower examinations, and the palace examination was to be revised.
4. A bureau of agriculture, industry, and commerce was to be established in Peking.
5. Orders were proclaimed abolishing the sinecure appointments in the imperial supervisorate of instruction, office of transmission, court of imperial entertainments, court of state ceremonial, court of equerries, and grand court of revision. The governorships of Hupeh, Kwangtung, and Yunnan and the director-generalship of the Yellow River were to be abolished as well as the *taotai* for grain transportation, which did not take charge of transportation affairs, and the salt *taotai*, which heretofore had no salt fields.
6. On the question of whether the other civil and military posts within and without the capital should be abolished or not, the grand secretaries, the six ministries, the governors-general, and governors of all provinces were ordered to ponder carefully and report.

There were many other reforms, which need not be listed here. From June 11 to September 16 was a span of about one hundred days—called "the Hundred Days' Reform." This was K'ang Yu-wei's happiest and most powerful period.

The Reformers in the Grand Council

In many respects K'ang Yu-wei had realized his dreams; but in others he was under a cloud. He controlled only the emperor. The empress dowager, the Grand Council, and the governor-general of Chihli, who wielded the military power, were beyond his control. K'ang himself was merely probational secretary in the Tsungli Yamen. How could he control those many august personages and offices? No sooner had he been assigned errand duty in the Tsungli Yamen than the empress dowager bade Emperor Kuang-hsü appoint Jung-lu to the position of governor-general of Chihli; and Yu-lu, a confidant of the empress dowager, was made a secretary in the Grand Council to serve as a spy. K'ang Yu-wei had no way to dominate the Grand Council.

In August 1898 as a result of political maneuvers and recommendations from many sides, Emperor Kuang-hsü was persuaded to bestow the fourth official rank on Yang Jui, Liu Kuang-ti, Lin Hsü, and T'an Ssu-t'ung, and to appoint them probationary secretaries in the Grand Council; the emperor dared not replace the grand councilors, and so he especially appointed these four persons to be actual executives to do the work of the Grand Council, with the hope that they could take over the real power of the council. According to Liang Ch'i-ch'ao: "After the four dignitaries entered the Grand Council, communication between the emperor and K'ang improved, and thereafter they resolutely carried out the great reforms." From now on, the four dignitaries read all important memorials and drafted all the imperial decrees. It was natural that the other grand councilors were very jealous of them; but in less than ten days their exercise of power was terminated by *coup d'état*.

Before the four dignitaries—T'an, Yang, Lin, and Liu—entered the Grand Council, there had been another important instance of dismissal in which the six officials of the ministry of ceremonies were relieved of their duties. This was effected by Wang Chao, a secretary of the ministry of ceremonies, who had sent a petition to the emperor, but which the ministers Huai-t'a-pu and Hsü Ying-k'uei refused to forward. Wang openly criticized them, saying that they had disobeyed the imperial decree. A great turmoil was caused in the ministry and was heard by the emperor. The emperor was looking for an excuse to get rid of several conservative ministers in order to build up his own prestige, and he therefore dismissed the six ministers and vice-ministers, including Huai-t'a-pu and Hsü Ying-k'uei. As a reward Wang Chao was granted a button of the third rank and was appointed candidate for vice-minister.

Wu Chih-hui said that the names of the six ministry officials to be dismissed were written by K'ang Yu-wei on the reverse side of a visiting card and submitted to Emperor Kuang-hsü, who issued the order according to K'ang's list. This visiting card was later found in the chamber of the emperor by the empress dowager, who was infuriated. The inside story further revealed that Huai-t'a-pu's wife had frequented the Summer Palace to serve the empress dowager and had become her favorite. When the dismissal of the six ministry officials was announced, she complained to the empress dowager and insinuated that the emperor was trying to get rid of all Manchus.[13] Upon hearing the complaints from Huai-t'a-pu's wife, the empress dowager disapproved the action of the emperor.

The four new dignitaries who had entered the Grand Council, aggravating the jealousy of the other councilors, were so aggressive and energetic that it looked as though everything was to be changed at once. "The four dignitaries," Yün Yü-ting has written, "were angered by and critical of the control of the emperor by the empress dowager and other important officials. The emperor gave them instructions in his own handwriting, stating briefly: 'I can do very little against the stubborn, conservative high ministers; but you people should tactfully get along with them in order to make the nation rich and strong, and you must prevent these high ministers from placing obstructions before that goal. If you will do this, I will not hurt the feelings of my mother [the empress dowager]. Otherwise, I cannot even protect my own position, so what can I do for the nation?'"[14] This instruction was later called "the decree written on a piece of cloth from the emperor's coat or belt"[*i-tai-chao*]—that is, a top-secret decree. In reality, though the decree gave the impression that the emperor might be able to protect his own position, it is obvious that there was no intention of getting rid of the empress dowager. This is also implicit in a copy of the instructions from the emperor to T'an Ssu-t'ung, found in the diary of Yüan Shih-k'ai. T'an had shown the directive to Yüan, and the empress dowager managed to know the content of the emperor's instructions.

Reaction Against the Emperor

A plot to depose the emperor was to be carried out during the military inspection at Tientsin in October. Jung-lu, then governor-general of Chihli, controlled the three Peiyang armies (the Kansu army of Tung Fu-hsiang, the Wu-i army of Nieh Shih-ch'eng, and the Hsin-chien army of Yüan Shih-k'ai). The empress dowager, dissatisfied with the reform activity of the emperor, plotted secretly with Jung-lu to hint to Censor Li Sheng-to that he should submit a memorial requesting the emperor to accompany the empress dowager on an inspection of the army at Tientsin, where the emperor would be compelled by military force to abdicate.

When Li Sheng-to's memorial was received, the emperor invited the empress dowager to go to Tientsin and she consented with pleasure. An imperial decree was issued to the effect that the emperor was to accompany the empress dowager in October on a journey to Tientsin to inspect the troops. After proclamation of the decree, rumors of the forced abdication of the emperor became stronger day by day.

Demotion of the Emperor

The reform leaders tried to find a way to save the emperor from this danger. After the four dignitaries received the instruction of the emperor mentioned above, they knew that his position was extremely precarious, and in their panic they did not know what to do. Their chief hope was to persuade Yüan Shih-k'ai to control Jung-lu and through the latter to control the empress dowager. According to Liang Ch'i-ch'ao's biography of Lin Hsü, only Lin disapproved of the plan. The other reformers thought that since Yüan Shih-k'ai had been an envoy in Korea for a long time, carrying on diplomatic negotiations and reforms, and since he was a supporter of the Society for the Study of National Rejuvenation [*Ch'iang-hsüeh Hui*] he might be persuaded to come over to the reformers' side. They secretly requested the emperor to make an ally of Yüan Shih-k'ai by granting him special favor. On June 16 Yüan Shih-k'ai was summoned for an imperial interview in which he was dismissed from the post of judicial commissioner of Chihli and promoted to be vice-minister in charge of military training. On the following day Yüan was summoned again. On the night of September 18, T'an Ssu-t'ung visited Yüan to urge that at the time of military inspection Yüan should "protect the sacred emperor, restore his great authority, clear out the bad people around the emperor, and restore order in the imperial palace."

Yüan Shih-k'ai was so strongly pressed by T'an Ssu-t'ung that he had to go through the motions of consenting.[15] Nevertheless, before he returned to Tientsin, the *coup d'état* had occurred. On September 21 an imperial order was issued to search the Nan-hai-kuan where K'ang lived; and the emperor was reported to be ill. Taking the emperor's alleged illness as a pretext, the empress dowager resumed control of court affairs and the entire imperial administration.

Since the month of May there had been a rumor in Peking that the emperor was seriously ill. Yet the fact that he had been summoning high officials for interviews every day indicated that he was in good health. When the six high ministry officials were dismissed and the four new dignitaries were appointed, Huai-t'a-pu and Censor Yang Ch'ung-i and others in succession went to Tientsin to call on Jung-lu and the plot was decided.

Five thousand soldiers from Nieh Shih-ch'eng's army were ordered to encamp at Tientsin, while Tung Fu-hsiang's army was shifted to quarters at Ch'ang-hsin-tien, about ten miles south of Peking. Three high-priority telegrams went to the Tsungli Yamen, reporting that England and Russia had opened hostilities in Vladivostok and that seven English warships had anchored at Tientsin. Yüan Shih-k'ai was requested to hurry back to defend the latter city. When Yüan Shih-k'ai reached Tientsin, Jung-lu immediately took an express train to Peking and thence to the Summer Palace with Huai-t'a-pu, Hsü Ying-k'uei, and Yang Ch'ung-i to submit a joint petition to the empress dowager begging her to conduct all state affairs.

The empress dowager immediately ordered Jung-lu's bodyguards to garrison the palace and ordered Jung-lu to return to Tientsin to await further instructions. The meeting did not adjourn until midnight. The following morning there was a rumor that the reform party planned to lay siege to the Summer Palace. At first some eunuchs spread the story in a teahouse that the emperor had plotted to overthrow and physically harm the empress and that he had secured the help of some foreigners. This rumor was firmly believed by many scholar-officials, who helped it along. In this atmosphere there appeared the decree authorizing the empress dowager to resume conduct of state affairs.[16]

According to Yün Yü-ting, however, Censor Yang Ch'ung-i and others who had perceived the intention of the empress dowager confidentially planned, with Prince Ch'ing (I-k'uang), to send a secret message telling the empress about this plot against her and requesting her to manage court affairs again. The secret message was carefully delivered by I-k'uang to the Summer Palace. On the dawn of September 21 when the emperor went to the palace gate to perform the perfunctory ceremony of bidding good morning to the empress dowager, the latter had already gone to the Hsi-chih Gate of the city of Peking through a small passage; the emperor hurried back to the palace. He found that the empress dowager had hastened directly to his living room and taken all the memorials away. Soon he was summoned to see her and she scolded him angrily:

> "I have been feeding you and taking care of you for more than twenty years, and yet you listen to the words of these churls to plot against me." The emperor trembled without uttering a single word, but after a long time he stuttered, "I have no such intention." The empress dowager spat at him. "Stupid son! If I do not exist today, how can you exist tomorrow?" And then the empress's decree was issued to the effect that the emperor was so ill that he could not manage affairs of the state and thus it was necessary for her, the empress, to attend court affairs and to instruct the administration.[17]

K'ang Yu-wei had already left Peking. At the beginning of September the political atmosphere daily became more and more tense, and Emperor Kuang-hsü secretly and repeatedly instructed him to leave Peking at once; finally he did, on September 20. When his arrest was ordered the next day, he already was on an ocean-bound ship.

The scapegoats were Chang Yin-huan, Hsü Chih-ching, Yang Shen-hsiu, Yang Jui, Lin Hsü, Liu Kuang-ti, T'an Ssu-t'ung and K'ang's brother, Kuang-jen, who were arrested. Chang was exiled to the frontiers, Hsü received life imprisonment, while the others were all executed. As martyrs, these were later to become known as the Six Gentlemen [*Liu Chün-tzu*]. K'ang's reform movement was thus at an end. His later organization, the Emperor Protection Society [*Pao-huang Hui*], and his attempt at a restoration were merely minor swells after the high waves of the great reform.

AFTERMATH OF THE REFORM MOVEMENT

The superficial cause of the failure of the 1898 reform movement seemed to be that Emperor Kuang-hsü and K'ang Yu-wei were no match for the power of the empress dowager, whose decisive action determined the failure of reform. Those who dreamed of peaceful reform criticized the empress dowager because, they said, had it not been for her interference, Emperor Kuang-hsü would have become the Emperor Meiji of China and the great anti-Manchu revolution would have been avoided. Such thinking over-simplified the situation. The failure of Emperor Kuang-hsü and of K'ang Yu-wei was caused only in part by the unwillingness of the empress dowager to relinquish her power.

K'ang Yu-wei's reform theory had brought disgrace to the Confucian classics and irritated a majority of classical scholars and men of letters. They regarded the protection of Confucian ethics as their duty and considered K'ang a demon and a monster. Chu I-hsin, for example, wrote a letter to K'ang Yu-wei:

> Now you call the uncrowned prince [Confucius] a reformer in order to facilitate the promotion of your own reform movement. Even though the sage Confucius really had a reform intention, he only desired ... to restore the ancient systems of the Sage Kings of the Three Dynasties; he had no intention of replacing Chinese institutions with barbarian systems. [18]

Weng T'ung-ho, too, was an advocate of reform, but as soon as Weng saw K'ang's books (*Hsin-hsüeh wei-ching-k'ao* and *Kung-tzu kai-chih-k'ao*) he immediately labeled K'ang a "wild fox among classical scholars" and informed the emperor that "This man's mind is unfathomable." As soon as K'ang had achieved great popularity in Peking and his disciple Liang Ch'i-ch'ao had propagated his doctrines in Hunan, the conservative scholars in a body severely attacked him. A Hunanese, Tseng Lien, then in Peking, submitted a letter to the emperor, containing the suggestion that "K'ang Yu-wei should be beheaded."[19]

When K'ang's supporter, Liang Ch'i-ch'ao, was lecturing in the Academy of Current Affairs at Hunan and speaking of K'ang's political theories, he brought down upon himself the bitter hatred of the conservative scholars like Wang Hsien-chien and Yeh Te-hui. In a letter by Yeh to two students, he said that "K'ang Yu-wei ... imitates Confucius in his external appearance, but follows the barbarians in his inner mind." In addition to arguments against K'ang published in the Hunan newspaper, K'ang's enemies sent letters to their conservative disciples and friends in Peking, in an effort to exert all their energies against the monster who had insulted and rebelled against the sage and had blasphemed Confucian doctrine. It is clear, therefore, that the reform movement of 1898 in no sense failed merely because of imperial intrigue at the Peking court.

Moreover, the conservative scholars were afraid that the reform movement would break their rice bowls [traditional means of livelihood]. Heretofore scholar-officials made a living by their knowledge of Confucian classics. With the new emphasis on Western sciences and with the abolition of sinecures (such as the six bureaus in Peking, offices of governor in the three provinces in the Northeast, and many other posts within and without the capital) many scholar-officials found themselves already unemployed or in immediate peril of losing their rice bowls. Officials in general were greatly alarmed. Saying that the emperor was altering the political systems of his ancestors, they requested that the empress dowager protect them and rescind his orders.

Anger at K'ang did not confine itself merely to those who already held appointments. There was also bitter disappointment among students who hoped to receive government posts. Changes in the civil-service examination and abolition of the eight-legged essay blocked the opportunities of thousands of students who had been counting on entering officialdom. They had no hope for the traditional recompense in return for the energy and time they had spent imitating traditional essays and memorizing the classics. Thus the students in the Yo-lu Academy [*Yo-lu shu-yüan*] in Hunan viewed askance the students in the new Academy of Current Affairs. They considered the latter to be "foreign slaves" and "Chinese traitors."

According to Liang Ch'i-ch'ao,

> The conservatives ... had previously relied upon the eight-legged essays to pass the civil-service examination, and now they were to be tested on their practical knowledge; that meant that the steppingstone for their advancement was blocked. What they had formerly depended upon to secure high position was their academic degrees and careers; but now this was changed to the emphasis on real abilities, and the instrument supporting their pride was broken. Graft was the means by which they enriched themselves in former times, but the new reforms required that all accounts be checked very carefully, thus cutting off the resources which used to provide for the comfort of their descendants.
>
> K'ang Yu-wei's reforms hurt the feelings of several hundred members of the Hanlin Academy, several thousand *chin-shih*, several scores of thousands of *chü-jen*, and several millions of *hsiu-ts'ai* and licentiates. Those people joined together to attack the reforms.[20]

For this reason, primarily, K'ang failed in his direction of the reform movement of 1898.

Nevertheless the reform movement produced some continuing effects. First and most important, the movement stimulated the thinking of Chinese youth and of the intelligentsia in general. Whether his specific ideas were accepted or rejected, K'ang did teach people a critical attitude toward the Confucian classics. Moreover, K'ang's use of arguments based on the classics affected the reactionaries by rousing their own self-interest in maintaining Chinese traditional civilization, with fatal results for the reactionaries themselves. Just as unexpectedly, despite the fact that in both K'ang's memorials and in Liang Ch'i-ch'ao's writings the idea of erasing the barriers between the Chinese and the Manchu was clearly expounded, K'ang's reform proposals stimulated a revival of ill feeling between the Chinese and the Manchu. This newly roused critical attitude very soon produced fateful consequences for the Manchu dynasty.

CHAPTER FIVE THE REACTION TO THE REFORM MOVEMENT

The history of the reaction against the reformers begins with the *coup d'état* of 1898 and ends in the summer of 1900 with the great Boxer Uprising in Peking. As for the composition of this reactionary movement, it consisted of three classes of people: (1) powerful nobles who, along with the empress dowager, intended to make use of the Boxers to drive out the foreigners; (2) scholar-officials who encouraged the Boxers to drive out the foreigners; and (3) unemployed mobs, including the Boxers. Although all these people composed the reactionary group, their purposes and methods were noticeably diverse.

ANALYSIS OF REACTIONARY FORCES

The Self-esteem of the Chinese People

In general a people does not like to admit its inferior position in the international family. For several millenniums the Chinese people had regarded itself as superior to other peoples. After 1894, however, a small part of the Chinese awakened to the fact that the foreigners they were confronting at that time could not be compared with the barbarians of former times. Nevertheless, a majority of the Chinese were bigoted, limited by their traditional, historical conceptions. Such Chinese still thought of the foreigners with blue eyes and red beards whom they were now encountering as identical with the Hsiung-nu, Khitan, Turfan, or Uighur of the past. They were confident that, even though the Chinese were currently being oppressed by Western military power, eventually the foreigners would yield to the influence of their sages. Those scholars who, instead of teaching the essential elements of Chinese civilization to the barbarians by means of the writings of Confucius, were themselves converted to the ways of the barbarians were regarded as a disgrace to China.

As Yeh Te-hui writes, in a letter to P'i Hsi-jui:

> Nowadays progressive scholars are trying to break the boundary line between barbarian and Chinese and to combine the civilization of China with that of foreign countries; but I can never agree with them. ... If they say that there should be no distinction between the Chinese and foreigners, can they also say there is no east and west? ... Westerners have distinguished the Chinese as a yellow race, which implies that from the beginning, when the heaven and earth were created, the Chinese were given a central position. When Westerners laugh at Chinese egotism, why can we not explain it by this reasoning? ... The civilization of Yao, Shun, Yü, T'ang, Wen, and Wu was inherited by the Duke of Chou and enlarged by Confucius. Since the Three Dynasties the civilization of our sages has conquered or absorbed innumerable alien cultures. ... Buddhism was popular in the period of the Six Dynasties [221-588] and yet the Sanskrit Buddhist sutras were spread and handed down through the medium of Chinese. The Khitan, Juchen, and Mongol invaded and ravaged the kingdom of the Sung dynasty, and yet there is not a single work left in these three alien languages. ... The powerful and intangible influence of our sages can absorb cultures without the people being aware of what is happening and will influence, undoubtedly, those books which are written in illegible horizontal lines. ...
>
> ... When strong neighbors infringe upon us, their criticism of us is by no means reliable. Had France been defeated and China victorious in the war of 1884, China would have been considered more civilized; when China was defeated and Japan was successful in

the war of 1894, then China was despised as a semicivilized nation. Such criticism ... is hardly worthy of attention. Just as silkworms eat mulberry leaves, foreigners treat a weak nation like a piece of meat to be eaten or like prey to be swallowed by whales. It is no surprise that they, being of an alien race, are hostile to us. I am surprised, however, at our own progressive scholars who seem to enjoy our misfortune and agree with the foreigners. Such scholars disregard the fact that their grandfathers and fathers were subjects and officials of China, and that their sons and grandsons will be China's citizens. How can we determine the reason for this attitude?[1]

Such expressions of egotism and pride reveal the actual psychology of the great majority of the people.

One outgrowth of this attitude was the *I-ho-t'uan* [Righteous and Harmonious Society] generally known as the Boxers. This society included such branches as the K'an Boxers and the Ch'ien Boxers, which in turn were branches of the Eight Diagrams.[2] Founded toward the close of the Ming dynasty [1368-1644], the Eight Diagrams Society finally grew to be one of the largest and most widespread of the secret sects. The K'an and Ch'ien branches were still active in northern China during the time of the Boxer Uprising.

The leader of the I-ho-t'uan, Ts'ao Fu-t'ien, in a statement revealing the Boxer attitude toward foreigners, said: "I have reverently received a decree from the Jade Emperor [a Taoist deity] ordering me to command the Celestial soldiers and officers in the annihilation of all foreigners; how do I dare disobey His order?"[3] Such superstitious beliefs among the Boxers were supported by conservative and narrow-minded officials. A censor, Hsü Tao-hun, for example, submitted a memorial to the throne in which he said: "The Taoist patriarch Hung-chün ordered that five dragons guard the Taku Bar and that all barbarian soldiers be entirely exterminated." Another censor, Ch'en Chia-yen, said that he had obtained "a letter on silk written by Kuan Kung [Kuan Yü, the god of war] who predicted that the barbarians will destroy themselves." A compiler of the Hanlin Academy, Hsiao Jung-chüeh, asserted, "The barbarians have recognized no ruler and no fathers for more than two thousand years, and Heaven by means of our righteous Boxers will wipe them out completely."[4]

From the intellectual scholar-official class to the ignorant multitudes, all believed that the Chinese were especially esteemed by heaven, earth, and other enlightened deities. Though the Chinese must temporarily endure the humiliations of foreigners, they believed that heaven, earth, and other deities would eventually establish China's honorable position permanently. Such psychology is pitifully foolish, but one may find some excuse for its existence in the need of a nation for self-respect.

The Accumulated Anger of the Public

The proud Chinese people were now seething with an anger building up day by day as a result of ill treatment which they were receiving from the foreigners. From the Opium War to the Sino-Japanese War and the continued aggressions of Germany and Russia, China had been repeatedly oppressed by powerful foreign countries. The situation was further aggravated by the haughtiness and unruliness of Christian missionaries, who relied on European imperial power to support missionary interference with China's civil administration. For several decades, anger, melancholy, and resentment had accumulated in the minds of both the upper and lower classes of Chinese. Local accounts of events which occurred during the Boxer Rebellion help us understand the situation:

> After the Allied Forces took Tientsin and Peking and came to Paoting, T'ing-yung, the acting governor-general of Chihli, who had commanded the Boxers in the slaughter of Western missionaries and of those Chinese who were promoters of the study of new knowledge,

was arrested and examined. During the examination T'ing-yung frankly admitted that he had burned the churches and killed the people. When asked why he did so, he replied, "Ever since the Tao-kuang period you people have insulted us too much, so who would not take revenge when he gets the chance? But now, whether you cut me by ax or by sword, the decision is entirely yours. Why is it necessary for you to question me?" Then he was executed, and even now there are still many people of the locality who feel sorry for him. [5]

Another typical view is expressed by Hsü T'ung, who was promoted from being a Chinese bannerman to appointment as a member of the Hanlin Academy and Grand Secretary. Regarding himself as a staunch supporter of Neo-Confucianism, he was antagonistic to the new knowledge. Though his house was close to the Legation Quarter [*Tung-chiao min-hsiang*], he hated so much to see foreigners that he made long detours around the foreign buildings in order to avoid passing through them on his way to visit his friends. Hsü T'ung was happy when the Boxers first appeared in Peking and believed that hereafter China would be strong.

Hsü T'ung eulogized a leader of the Boxers:

> You have made unusual news such as has not been heard in a thousand years; you are neither heretic nor heathen but attack the unorthodox sects [Christians] in order to set the minds of the people right. ... Your loyalty, filial piety, integrity, and honesty will thereby exist forever. Your actions will result in good stories which will make some people happy and will alarm others. You use magic power to intimidate the barbarians and to work off the anger and hatred of our farmers, our workers, and our merchants. [6]

The voices of T'ing-yung and Hsü T'ung may serve to express the state of accumulated anger in which many people found themselves. At the same time another high official requested that the bones of Kuo Sung-tao be cut to pieces as an apology to the nation because Kuo had favored the Chinese westernization movement. Still another official said that the sixteen persons who were killed by Tseng Kuo-fan on account of the Tientsin massacre of 1870 should be accorded honors as posthumous consolation. Such proposals reflect the popular opinion that China's repeated humiliations were directly caused by Kuo, Tseng, and other traitors.

The Insecurity of Life

The opening of the five trade ports in 1842 and the resultant penetration of foreign economic power into China put pressure on her indigenous and traditional industry. The percentage of unemployment gradually began to increase. Further, heavy taxation was required to support the troops fighting domestic and foreign wars and to pay indemnities to foreign nations. After the wars were over, insecurity increased. Defeated troops had become vagabonds. Soldiers were disbanded without adequate pay. Moreover, especially in the northern provinces, for more than twenty years after 1875 no single year was free from natural catastrophe such as great floods, severe droughts, or inundations of river banks. [7]

As for the three classes of people mentioned in the opening paragraph of this chapter, neither the powerful nobles nor the scholar-official class was greatly affected by this economic insecurity. The third class, an unemployed populace created by economic insecurity, was severely afflicted. The unemployed, ignorant of the real cause of their hardships, realized only that they had no means of livelihood. They thought illogically that the sources of their poverty were wars caused by foreigners' insults and the building of railways and the opening of mines which, according to their superstitions, meant cutting of the veins of the dragons of their earth and permitting the precious air to escape. Moreover, the establishment of churches seemed to them to humiliate their deities and ancestors. In order to avoid further misfortune they felt that they must drive out all foreigners from China and kill all the traitorous Chinese who believed in foreign religion and read foreign books.

But the people were fearful of the effectiveness of foreigners' warships and guns. They hoped more and more to destroy the enemy by means of magic power. Such power was described in novels like the *Fung-shen*, in which people could fight in the sky or under the earth, and the *Hsi-yu-chi*, in which the monkey could fight with all sorts of magic power against demons. To the Chinese populace such magic power was dependable. At first a small number of cunning fellows exaggerated this power to fool a large number of people. Magic power began gradually to be believed in more and more. Soon even those who were exploiting the belief began to believe in it as the one hopeful weapon of the antiforeign movement.

As a result, during a period of eighteen months beginning with the seizure of Kiaochow Bay by Germany and the diplomatic troubles in connection with railways, mines, and churches, the number of Boxers in the Province of Shantung, at first totaling something more than a thousand, rose sharply. From the winter of 1899 to the summer of 1900 this number increased to hundreds of thousands.

Plots to Depose the Emperor

As for those Chinese who favored political reforms, after the *coup d'état* of 1898 the empress dowager had an intense aversion to Kuang-hsü, K'ang, and Liang. All her adherents cherished the same ill feeling in order to maintain their political positions.

K'ang and Liang were able to escape imminent danger with the aid of foreigners. K'ang was helped by the English consul general at Shanghai, and Liang escaped in a Japanese warship. Later on K'ang and Liang established the *Pao-huang Hui* [Emperor Protection Society] in foreign countries, where they received help rather than interference. From this point on, hatred of K'ang and Liang was enlarged to a hatred of all foreigners.

In Lo Tun-yung's *Ch'uan-pien yü-wen*, he says:

> Kang-i was ordered to go to Kiangnan to investigate a certain case. ... Here he found a copy of Liang Ch'i-ch'ao's *Ch'ing-i pao* [*Public Opinion Press*], which was presented to the empress dowager. Upon seeing it, she shouted invectives against the two men and against the foreign countries which protected them. She was so determined to avenge herself on these enemies and on the emperor, whom she hated even more, that she plotted to depose the emperor by February 1900 and to make P'u-chün prince regent. P'u-chün was the son of Prince Tuan (Tsai-i). The plot was suggested by Kang-i, who strongly recommended that Tsai-i, P'u-chün's father, should occupy an important position and receive from the empress higher favor than all other princes. Worried that the deposition of Kuang-hsü might cause criticism from the foreign powers, she ordered Jung-lu to inform Li Hung-chang to consult privately with the diplomatic ministers in Peking concerning the deposition of the emperor; but the result was that all the ministers objected to the plan. The empress dowager became angrier. Every day Kang-i spoke of hatred against the foreigners and accused as traitors those who even discussed foreign matters. When he passed through Nanking and saw the Ch'u-ts'ai College, established by Liu K'un-i, he immediately ordered it closed. ...
>
> Tsai-i was very happy and proud because he knew that he was to be the father of the new emperor. When he heard that foreign nations

were impeding the progress of the plot, he was extremely resentful against the foreigners and sought an opportunity to take revenge. Just at this time the I-ho t'uan claimed that it was able to obliterate the foreigners and he was greatly pleased.[8]

Yün Yü-ting's *Ch'ung-ling ch'uan-hsin-lu* also comments:

> Although the I-ho t'uan was a heretic religion ... there were other reasons for the court to believe in it. The intention of deposing the emperor had been cherished for two years, but on account of the objection of China's neighbors on all sides, the court dared not put its plan into effect immediately. Tsai-i was very anxious to have his son obtain the position of emperor, and he reasoned that unless he relied on military power to intimidate the foreign ministers, he could hardly achieve his aim. At this juncture the Boxers appeared ... and Tsai-i utilized them to start a great uprising. In spite of the fact that some courtiers strongly argued that the magic power was untrustworthy and that military hostilities should not be opened, these arguments were as ineffective as scratching an itch from the outside of one's boots.[9]

In sum, the attitudes which formed the basis for the reactionary activities which followed the reform movement included ethnocentric self-esteem and resentment against war, against foreigners who caused wars, and against Chinese who advocated foreign ideas. The extreme hatred of foreigners and reformers found expression in the plot to depose the emperor. But this reaction was peculiar to the empress dowager and to the high officials. Reaction was nevertheless a common tendency, even though the demands of each class were different. The demands of the people, however, tended toward the benefit of the nation; in contrast, the purposes of the high government officials were selfish in the extreme.

But the combination of the people's insecurity and the palace plotting created a formidable force.

TWO YEARS OF REACTION, 1898–1900

In September 1898 when the empress dowager again attended court to direct the government, the reactionary period began. Having attempted to arrest K'ang and Liang, having executed the six martyrs, banished Chang Yin-huan, and imprisoned Hsü Chih-ching for life, she also dismissed all officials who were connected with the reform movement, including the Hunan governor, Ch'en Pao-chen. She placed her personal favorites in key positions. Kang-i, Jung-lu, and others, for example, were appointed to the Grand Council, and Yü-lu was made governor-general of Chihli. The Peiyang Army was formerly under the direct control of the Chihli governor-general. After Jung-lu had been transferred from the governor-generalship to the Grand Council, however, he still controlled the army, while Yü-lu was only its assistant commander. Thus the empress dowager consolidated her power in the nerve center of the government.

Reforms Rescinded

Thereafter all the innovations announced during the Hundred Days' Reform were within one month entirely rescinded: (1) The Imperial Supervisorate of Instruction and other offices for maintaining the rice bowls of sinecure officials were ordered reopened. (2) The governorships of Hupeh, Kwangtung, and Yunnan, as well as the director-general of the conservation of the Yellow River, were to be restored. (3) The order to transform the *shu-yüan* [academies] of all provinces into modern schools was rescinded. (4) The eight-legged essays and the examinations on the memorization of the classics were to be used again for all levels of examinations. (5) The special examination on economic affairs [*ching-chi t'e-k'o*] was abolished. (6) The Bureau of Agriculture, Industry, and

Commerce was to be abrogated. (7) The Government Press was to be closed. (8) All people, including scholars, were forbidden to submit memorials to the throne discussing state affairs. (9) Public meetings were forbidden. (10) Newspaper offices were to be closed and their editors arrested.

In a word, everything was to be resumed as before. At the beginning of 1899 the newly appointed Hupeh governor memorialized the throne requesting cancellation of these reactionary orders. He was impeached and accused of "presumptuously requesting a change of laws and disturbing the government by malicious words." He was immediately punished by dismissal from office and was denied any further employment by the government. Thereafter not a single soul dared speak again the two words "new administration."

But in the mind of the empress dowager and her trusted favorites the great unsolved problem was the position of Emperor Kuang-hsü. During the two-year reactionary period, from the autumn of 1898 to the summer of 1900, this problem was pondered and worked upon day and night.

Plans Against the Captive Emperor

Before the *coup d'état* in September, it had been confidentially decided to carry out the plot to depose the emperor during the ceremony of military inspection at Tientsin. After the *coup d'état*, since the emperor was imprisoned in Ying-t'ai in the palace, it was no longer necessary to have the military inspection. A rumor of the emperor's serious illness was widely circulated so that he might be deposed at the discretion of the empress dowager.

Experienced in the ways of government, she understood nevertheless that the great political power was in the provinces, not in the court. Even though she controlled the Chihli governor-general and the Peiyang Army, she recognized that she could not be sure of the opinion of the governors-general of all provinces in southern China. Accordingly she ordered the

Grand Council to send secret telegrams to the southern governors-general and governors to ask their opinion of the emperor. One governor-general of Liang-kiang, Liu K'un-i, said frankly that "the rightful position of the emperor and ministers had been firmly established, and the criticism of both Chinese and foreigners should be avoided." This warning frustrated their plot, and the position of the powerless emperor was maintained for the time being.

In the winter of 1899, however, the empress dowager, along with Kang-i and others, was out of patience. Trouble was being stirred up in foreign countries by K'ang and Liang, who were advocating the protection of the emperor. Jung-lu, however, was more cautious. There was also an old Neo-Confucianist, Hsü T'ung, who was highly respected by the empress and who, together with Ch'i-hsiu and Ch'ung-ch'i, understood very clearly the intention of the empress dowager. In Yün Yü-ting's *Ch'ung-ling ch'uan-hsin-lu*, there is a vivid description of the maneuvers of this group:

> At this time Duke Ch'ung-ch'i had been retired at home for several years. The Grand Secretary Hsü T'ung, who was eager to grasp political power, was on good terms with the State Minister Ch'i-hsiu. These three persons hoped to receive credit for dethroning the emperor. The Grand Secretary Jung-lu held the position next to the highest among the ministers. Even though his rank was beneath that of the prince, he was very close to the empress dowager, who believed whatever he said and gave him a great deal of authority. The three men, Ch'ung, Hsü, and Ch'i, had completed elaborate preparations before they made an appointment to visit Jung-lu in his private mansion to tell him the procedure to be followed in deposing the emperor. Ch'ung and Hsü drafted a confidential memorial to that effect and asked Jung-lu to be a cosignatory and submit it to the empress dowager in the Yung-ning Palace. ... Jung was greatly

surprised. ... On the next day after the court interview Jung-lu requested to see the empress dowager alone and asked her if the rumor that the emperor was to be dethroned were true. The empress dowager replied, "No. Can such a thing be done?" Jung-lu remarked, "If the empress dowager does it, who dares say no? Nevertheless, since the case against the emperor is not strong, the foreign ministers will interfere, so for that reason we must be cautious." The empress dowager said, "The plan has been uncovered. What can we do?" Jung-lu replied, "That does not matter. The emperor at his prime of life still has no son. It is better for us to select a child from a close branch of the imperial family and make him the heir apparent—not to Kuang-hsü, but to the preceding emperor T'ung-chih. The child should be bred in the palace with the intention that he should take over the throne gradually, and then this action will be legitimate."

After long silence and meditation the empress dowager concluded, "You are right." Then on January 24, 1900, the princes of the close branches of the imperial family, grand chamberlains, ministers of the imperial household, directors of the imperial colleges of inscriptions, the Hanlin Academy, and all the ministers were summoned to a meeting at I-luan Hall. An alarming rumor was spread among the people to the effect that the emperor would be deposed soon ... However, the imperial decree proclaimed P'u-chün to be the heir apparent.[10]

The establishment of the heir apparent at the end of 1899 was carefully planned by Jung-lu. Afraid that the powerful governor-general, Liu K'un-i, might object again, Jung called Liu to Peking in advance for an interview with the empress dowager.

As for Li Hung-chang, in the low ebb of his political influence, he did not object to the heir apparent. He was then appointed governor-general of Kwangtung and Kwangsi because the two Cantonese—K'ang Yu-wei and Liang Ch'i-ch'ao—were very active among the Chinese emigrants in other countries and trying to organize a party to protect the emperor. Since most of these Chinese were Cantonese, it was feared that something might happen in Kwangtung; as a diplomat, Li Hung-chang was appointed to go there to take preventive measures.

Trouble arose, however, when a number of patriotic scholars like Chang Yüan-shan, Ts'ai Yüan-p'ei, and others, who were hiding out in Shanghai, unexpectedly joined forces with more than a thousand prominent businessmen in sending a telegram to protest the establishment of an heir apparent. Several hundred thousand overseas Chinese also cabled to voice a similar disapproval. Although the heir apparent had already been established, his inauguration was being delayed until an appropriate moment.

The empress and her supporters were not intimidated by the telegrams. They were more fearful of the opinion of foreign nations. In order to test the foreigners, messengers were set to the Legation Quarters to hint to the foreign ministers that they should come to the court for a celebration. It was thought that their readiness to celebrate the establishment of the heir apparent would be an indication of their approval of the dethronement. However, the foreign ministers did not come. The conservatives then utilized the Boxers of the Eight Diagrams sect to further their scheme.

THE BOXER UPRISING

The Boxers [*I-ho t'uan*] within the Eight Diagrams Society originated in the Chia-ch'ing period (1796-1820). The high officials who first used Boxers as an instrument of antiforeignism were Li Ping-heng and Yü-hsien. Later T'ing-yung, Yü-lu, Kang-i, Tsai-i, and finally the empress dowager employed them.

In 1895 Li Ping-heng was governor of Shantung, where members of an anti-Christian group, the Big Sword Society, were being encouraged. In November 1897 the society's members killed two German missionaries. This brought about the occupation of Kiaochow Bay by Germany, and in response to Germany's request, Governor Li Ping-heng was dismissed from office. In March 1899 Li's close subordinate Yü-hsien was made governor of Shantung. He followed Li's old policy of giving encouragement to the Big Sword Society. It was Chu Hung-teng, the leader of this society, who selected the new name *I-ho ch'üan* [Righteous and Harmonious Fists] and set up its slogan, "Protect the Ch'ing and annihilate the foreigners." Governor Yü-hsien, in his official notice, changed the name *I-ho ch'üan* [Righteous and Harmonious Fists] to *I-ho t'uan* [Righteous and Harmonious Society] as a more elegant term. The Boxers then flew a banner inscribed with the character *yü*, which stood for Yü-hsien.

The Boxers' activities in killing Christian converts and burning churches were now protested by the French minister. As a result Yü-hsien was called to Peking and his position as governor of Shantung was assumed by Yüan Shih-k'ai. The new governor vigorously suppressed the Boxers, arrested and executed Chu Hung-teng, and drove his followers from Shantung to Chihli.

After Yü-hsien came to Peking from Shantung, he gave exaggerated accounts of the loyalty, bravery, and dependability of the I-ho t'uan to Prince Tuan (Tsai-i) and to Grand Secretary Kang-i, who retold the legends to the empress. For this reason, Yü-hsien was transferred to the governorship of Shansi. Here he declared to his subordinates: "There are two leaders of the I-ho t'uan: one is Li Ping-heng and the other is I."

In the spring of 1900 the Boxers were rampant in the province of Chihli. There they received encouragement from the governmental authorities. One magistrate, Lao Nai-hsüan of the Wu-ch'iao district, sternly curbed their activities and petitioned the governor-general to suppress them. But the governor-general, Yü-lu, was sympathetic with the Boxers, and the judicial commissioner, T'ing-yung, had secretly allied himself with this group. They decided to ignore Lao's petition. By June the Boxers had spread to all districts of Chihli, and Yü-lu had given them open support.

The Empress Favors the Boxers

While the Boxers were killing Christian converts and burning churches in various districts of Chihli, the empress dowager was playing a dual role. She ordered their arrest, while at the same time dispatching Kang-i and the Minister of Punishment, Chao Shu-ch'iao, and others to disband them. In reality, however, these men were not instructed to disband the outlaws. Rather they were to investigate the conditions of these "righteous people." Chao Shu-ch'iao noticed that the so-called righteous people were mostly untrustworthy rascals, but perceiving the real intention of the empress dowager, he lacked the courage to do anything except to report that they were "very dependable, righteous people." Kang-i not only spoke of their usefulness to the country, but in cooperation with Tsai-i and others, he helped lead the Boxers into Peking itself.

The manner in which the government dealt with the Boxers after they entered the capital has been reliably recorded by Yün Yü-ting. He was one of the participants in the four confidential meetings before the empress dowager. Yün wrote:

> On June 11, 1900, Mr. Sugiyama, a secretary of the Japanese Legation, was murdered. Christian converts, including many innocent people, were daily put to the sword. On June 16 a fire was set to burn the houses west of the Cheng-yang Gate. ... At this time the Western soldiers in the Legation Quarter were fully armed in self-defense.

Suddenly at noon of the sixteenth, the princes, high officials, and heads of the six ministries and the nine bureaus were summoned by the empress to a meeting in the eastern chamber of the I-lüan Palace. There more than a hundred officials participated and the room was filled with kneelers while the latecomers knelt outside the door. ... The emperor was very serious and he first blamed the officials for their failure in suppressing the rioters. A reader of the Hanlin Academy, Liu Yung-heng, knelt in the back near Yün Yü-ting. ... He moved forward on his knees and said, "Your servant has just seen Tung Fu-hsiang, who wishes to receive orders to drive away the rioters." He had not finished his sentence before Prince Tuan (Tsai-i) raised his big thumb and interrupted in a sharp voice, "Well! This is the best way to disappoint the people!" Liu Yung-heng was so frightened that he could not finish his speech. The empress dowager was silent.

The director of the court of sacrificial worship, Yüan Ch'ang, who was outside the room, said loudly, "The minister Yüan Ch'ang also has something to report." The emperor ordered him to come to the front. He then reported in detail that the Boxers were really rebellious and unreliable people and that even if they possessed magic power, this power had never been able to achieve a success from ancient to modern times. The empress dowager interrupted, "Magic power may be unreliable; but are the patriotic minds of the people also undependable? Today China's power is declining and she is extremely weak; only the minds of the people can be depended upon. If we dishearten the people, what then can our nation depend upon?" And again she said, "Now the capital has been disturbed and there is a rumor that the foreigners are asking for reinforcements. How should we deal with them? If anyone has anything to say, he should at once express his point of view."

All the officials hurriedly made their reports. Some said that the

Boxers should be suppressed, while others said that they should be controlled in a friendly and encouraging manner; some said that the foreign reinforcements should be quickly intercepted while others stated that troops should be called to protect the foreigners. Subsequently, the vice-ministers Na-t'ung and Hsü Ching-teng were dispatched to go out of Peking at once to stop the advance of foreign soldiers and at the same time to soothe the rebels and to disband them tactfully. Then the meeting was adjourned.

Chang Heng-chia, the subdirector of the Grand Court of Revision, Chu Tsu-mou, a reader of the Hanlin Academy, and Yün Yü-ting observed that the empress dowager was still inclined to protect the Boxer bandits, that the day's meeting had not reached any important conclusion, and that the rebellion would be endless. Therefore, they purposely remained after the meeting to present another report. Chang Heng-chia strongly urged that the Boxer bandits be suppressed, arguing that if only a few leaders were killed, the rest would be easily disbanded ... Chu Tsu-mou said that the empress dowager trusted rebellious people to fight against foreign countries, and he wondered who should be relied upon to handle such tremendous affairs. The empress dowager said, "I have been relying upon Tung Fu-hsiang." Chu Tsu-mou abruptly replied, "Tung Fu-hsiang is most unreliable." In great wrath the empress dowager changed her tone and said in a severe voice, "What is your name? ... You say that Tung Fu-hsiang is unreliable. You recommend to me someone else!" Panic-stricken, Chu could not give a reply, but Yün Yü-ting responded, "The Shantung governor, Yüan Shih-k'ai, is loyal, courageous and farsighted; he could be called to Peking to suppress the rebels." ... Yün added, "It is rumored that the court is to be moved to Sian. The capital is the center of gravity and as soon as a step is taken to move it, the whole nation will be disturbed." The empress dowager strongly denied the rumor. Then the ministers stood up. After Chu Tsu-mou had left the room, the empress dowager looked after him with wrathful eyes.

About 2 P. M. , June 17, another urgent meeting was held in the I-lüan Palace. The emperor at first questioned Hsü Yung-i, a minister of the Tsungli Yamen. ... The emperor beat the desk and rebuked him sharply, "You have tried to put this important matter off. Do you think you can conclude it now?"

The empress dowager subsequently announced: "Recently I have received four demands from the foreigners. They ask first that a place be designated for the Chinese emperor to live; second, that all provincial taxes be collected by them on our behalf; third, that the control of our military power be put in their hands. Now hostilities are opened by them first, and the end of our nation is near at hand. If we courteously yield to their demands, I cannot face our deceased emperors of the past. Our nation may be conquered by foreigners; but it is better to fight to the finish than to be conquered without resistance."

All the ministers touched their heads to the floor and said, "We will render our services to our country until death," and some of them even shed tears.

But what was the fourth demand? After the meeting, I asked minister Jung-lu, who said it was to compel the empress dowager to hand over her administrative power to the emperor and that was why she did not mention it.

At this time Tsai-i and Vice-Minister P'u-liang expressed their desire for war in stirring and exciting words. The empress dowager again loudly instructed, "The matter under discussion today has been heard by all high officials. I can not help declaring war for our territory and our ancestral altars, but the outcome is unpredictable. If after this war our territory and ancestral altars still cannot be protected, all you officials present now should understand my difficulties and not blame me alone by saying that the empress dowager has put an end to the dynasty handed down to her from her ancestors for three hundred years." All the officials again touched their heads to the floor saying, "All your ministers to the man are ready to suffer for the nation."[11]

Thereafter three officials were immediately sent to the Legation Quarter to inform the foreign ministers of the serious developments and to tell them that if they wished to open hostilities, they must lower their flags and return to their nations instantly. Jung-lu was then instructed to prepare his Wu-wei army for war.

But no official [Yün Yü-ting continues] of the Tsungli Yamen knew who had delivered the demands of the foreign nations. Some speculated that they came from the commander of the Peiyang Army, Yü-lu, but that was not true. After some time I [Yün Yü-ting] learned that deep in the night of June 16 a certain Mr. Lo, who was grain *taotai* of Kiangsu, sent his son to knock on Jung-lu's door and say that there was a confidential matter to report to him. At this interview the four demands were presented. After he had been informed of the demands, Jung-lu was frightened and paced around his house for the rest of the night. At dawn he went to give the demands to the empress dowager, who was embittered and outraged. Thus the war was decided. In reality there were no such demands from the foreign nations. The Kiangsu grain *taotai* may have been deceived by irresponsible rumors. Another statement indicates that Lien-wen, a secretary of the Grand Council, acting on orders from Tsai-i, forged these demands. Possibly because of their obscure origin, they were not mentioned in the declaration of war on June 20.[12]

Meanwhile, from 1 to 3 P.M., June 19, another meeting was

held in the I-lüan Palace, at which time the empress dowager decided to declare war. She ordered the ministers of all nations to leave Peking within twenty-four hours. Chinese soldiers would escort them.

The emperor did not want to precipitate a war. He held Hsü Ching-teng's hands: "You must deliberate the matter thoroughly." The empress dowager rebuked him, "Hands off, emperor! Don't invite trouble!" And Vice-Minister Lien-yüan admonished, "France is protecting the Roman Catholics, and the Boxer trouble started with France. If we declare war, we can afford to fight only France; there is actually no reason for us to be hostile to the other eleven nations. If we are, our nation will be in great danger." While he was talking, he shed tears, and the perspiration on his forehead dropped like pearls; I have not heard that there was anyone who argued against him.

... Shortly after, an instruction was given, early on the morning of the twentieth. A communication from the Legation Quarter was received asking Prince Ch'ing and Prince Tuan to go there for a discussion, but the Tsungli Yamen was directed to reply that they could not attend. Kang-i, who had just returned to the court, was also summoned to participate in the morning interview. When the decision in favor of war had been made, the important ministers and all other officials whose advice was no longer needed were dismissed.

Since the imperial plan had probably been predetermined, the court meetings were held partly to obtain support for the plan and partly to secure collaborators to share the blame. The plan was first suggested by Prince Tuan and agreed to by the empress dowager. But when the Boxer movement developed into a serious affair, even the empress dowager could not control it.[13]

Intrigues of the Court and the Generals

For nearly two months, from June 20 to August 14, the Kansu army of Tung Fu-hsiang and hundreds of the "righteous people" flourished all sorts of magic weapons such as soul-absorbing banners, sky-covering flags, thunderbolt fans, hooks, and flying swords. They succeeded in killing only one important person, the German minister, Von Ketteler. They could not even break into the garrison of the Legation Quarter. During these same two months most of the governors-general and governors gave no support to the declaration of war. Further, the Allied Powers had taken Taku, Tientsin, and Peking. The empress dowager compelled Emperor Kuang-hsü to go to the Northwest to enjoy the landscape. This concluded the notable performance staged by the court reactionaries. There remained to be performed the tragedy of the Peking Protocol.

During the time of the reaction, Shantung and South China were not involved in the Boxer movement. The four high provincial authorities, Yüan Shih-k'ai, Li Hung-chang, Liu K'un-i and Chang Chih-tung (of Shan-tung, Kwangtung, Chiang-nan, and Liang-Hu, respectively) tried their best to maintain order and peace in the coastal provinces. They took concerted action to ignore the imperial decree of June 20; they also wired to Jung-lu to save the situation in Peking from becoming worse. They negotiated with the consuls of all nations in Shanghai. They also continued their discussions with Chinese diplomatic representatives abroad in order to explain the nature of the uprising and to confine it to the province of Chihli alone.

In the Chihli action, the behavior of Jung-lu was the most reprehensible. Originally the military power of the Peiyang army had been completely in his hands. He was not only a member of the Grand Council but also a confidant of the empress dowager. In addition, he knew that the Boxers could not be effectively utilized and that it was dangerous to precipitate a foreign war. When the Boxers spread to the boundary of Chihli, he could have suppressed them instantly, as Yüan Shih-k'ai did. For selfish and opportunistic reasons he refrained from taking any kind of action until the Boxer trouble was right at his doorstep. Even then he was undecided whether he should encourage them or fight against them.

For a better understanding of this situation we may turn to Tung Fu-hsiang's letter reproaching Jung-lu, part of which reads:

> Your letter to comfort me in imprisonment makes me feel grateful to you and also ashamed of you. If I do not express my inmost sentiments, I cannot control myself from extreme wrath and bitter weeping. I had the honor to serve under your command in the management of military affairs. ... During the Boxer Uprising, I repeatedly received instructions from you to order my subordinates to attack the Legation Quarter. I was reluctant to assume this gigantic task. But when you prodded me, how could I disobey? I also repeatedly received your oral instructions to lay siege to and bombard the Legation Quarter. I could not be sure whether a foreign minister in Peking should be killed or not, but you said that we should do everything to oust the barbarians, and that you would share the outcome with me. Being a military man, I am fundamentally ignorant. I simply relied on you, my superior, and followed you like a dog or a horse. Now while you are still loftily in charge of state affairs, I am being punished. I begin to have great doubts about you. [14]

But Jung-lu's telegram report to Liu K'un-i, governor-general of Liang-kiang, gives a quite different impression:

> A weak nation is fighting against several strong powers; the peril will be evident immediately. Since ancient times it has been the custom to see to it that diplomatic envoys of belligerent nations are not injured. The ancestors of our dynasty underwent great hardships

to create our empire. How can we unwarily destroy it in such a gamble as we are now taking because of the heretic Boxers?[15]

Jung-lu on the one hand had ordered Tung Fu-hsiang to bombard the Legation Quarter, and on the other hand, said that he wished to protect the diplomatic envoys. For his opportunism and two-faced policy, the weight of the blame for the Boxer Uprising should be placed squarely on the shoulders of Jung-lu.

THE STRUGGLE BETWEEN THE REVOLUTIONARY PARTY AND THE EMPEROR PROTECTION SOCIETY

As Sun Yat-sen said in his autobiography, "The five years between 1895 and 1900 constituted the most difficult period of my entire revolutionary career. During this time there appeared the Emperor Protection Society, which fought against revolution and republicanism for the Ch'ing much more vigorously than the dynasty itself." The situation within the revolutionary groups themselves, in other words, was also very complex.

Before 1900 the only supporters of Sun Yat-sen's revolution were overseas Chinese and members of the secret societies in China, while the backbone of the reform party of K'ang and Liang was the scholar-official class. Before 1898 K'ang and Liang had not paid much attention to the overseas Chinese or to secret-society members. They turned to these groups after the *coup d'état* of 1898, when both K'ang and Liang were forced to flee to foreign countries and lost their original support within China. The result was that Sun Yat-sen lost to K'ang and Liang a large part of the support for which he had been working many years. The contest between the two reform groups themselves was a further significant development during the reactionary period.

Sun and Kang as Rivals Overseas

The two main branches of the Hsing-Chung Hui [Revive China Society] in foreign countries were in Honolulu and Yokohama. After Sun's failure in 1895, Yokohama was used as his headquarters to prepare for a second revolt. Most of his party members in Yokohama, numbering more than a hundred persons, were prominent Chinese merchants in Japan. There in the winter of 1896 Kuang Ju-p'an organized a school for the children of Chinese residents.

With the intention of inviting teachers from China, Kuang consulted Sun Yat-sen, but Sun felt that the members of his Hsing-Chung Hui were too active in their revolutionary work to occupy themselves with teaching. Sun also believed that K'ang and Liang should be considered their patriotic colleagues. Since K'ang had many disciples, Sun wrote a letter of recommendation asking Kuang Ju-p'an to discuss the matter with K'ang personally in Shanghai. He also named the contemplated school, *Chung-hsi hsüeh-chiao* [Chinese-Western School].

After Kuang met K'ang in Shanghai, the latter recommended Hsü Ch'in and others to go to Japan to teach in the school. He felt that the name *Chung-hsi* was unrefined and that it should be replaced by *Ta-t'ung hsüeh-chiao* [Cosmopolitan School]. K'ang personally wrote four large characters to be used as a signboard for the school.

In Japan Hsü Ch'in and Sun Yat-sen often saw each other and regarded themselves as comrades. But Hsü and the others, taking advantage of their positions as teachers in the new school, associated constantly with Chinese merchants in Japan. Eventually they gained control of these businessmen. When K'ang and Liang fled to Japan after September 1898, Sun Yat-sen treated them as friends who had also failed in their attempt to reform the nation. He paid K'ang a visit. The latter, however, who considered himself teacher of the emperor, refused to receive Sun's visit. Association with a revolutionary leader, K'ang thought, might harm his own future activities. His Emperor Protection Society appeared in Yokohama, and a majority of the Chinese merchants who belonged to the Hsing-Chung Hui changed sides to the new society. In the Ta-t'ung School was posted the slogan: "Sun Wen is not permitted to come to this school."

At this time Liang Ch'i-ch'ao was not so haughty as K'ang Yu-wei. Liang, associating himself closely with Sun Yat-sen, who trusted him, expressed himself as a supporter of the revolution. Liang discussed with Ch'en Shao-po, a member of the Hsing-Chung Hui, the idea of combining the two parties into one, and Ch'en and Hsü Ch'in were asked to draft procedures for the incorporation.

Hsü, however, privately objected to such a combination. He wrote to K'ang Yu-wei, then in Singapore: "Liang is gradually falling into the pit of Sun. We must quickly determine a way to save him." Upon receiving this letter, K'ang immediately sent to Japan someone with money to urge Liang to go to Honolulu as promoter of the Emperor Protection Society. Before Liang set out for Honolulu, he made another visit to Sun Yat-sen, at which time he continued the discussion of the consolidation of the two parties. Because Honolulu had been the cradle of the *Hsing-Chung Hui*, he asked Sun to write letters of recommendation for him. Without any hesitation, Sun complied with letters introducing Liang to his elder brother, Sun Te-chang, and to his other relatives and friends. Liang later used these letters not merely to meet Sun's elder brother but chiefly to meet many Chinese merchant leaders, who gave him an enthusiastic welcome.

After spending several months in Honolulu, Liang organized a branch of the Emperor Protection Society. He did this by persuading the local Chinese merchants to join, on the assumption that the society nominally stood for protecting the emperor but actually intended to carry on a revolution. The local Chinese merchants, trusting him because he was recommended by Sun Yat-sen, gave him considerable sums of money to be used for an uprising in Hankow. By the time Sun had become aware of this and had written a letter reprimanding Liang for bad faith, it was already too late to stop a large number of members of his Hsing-Chung Hui in Honolulu from joining the Emperor Protection Society. In this way Sun's base of operations in Honolulu was taken over by the local society.

Revolutionary Organization in China

The next arena in which Sun was attacked by the K'ang-Liang group was among the secret societies. Liang Ch'i-ch'ao had become acquainted with T'ang Ts'ai-ch'ang and Lin Kuei, two men influential in the secret societies, when he taught at the Academy of Current Affairs in Hunan. After the *coup d'état*, T'ang Ts'ai-ch'ang had been so dismayed that he attempted to start an uprising. At this time his friend Pi Yung-nien had gone to Japan. There he made friends with Sun Yat-sen, Miyazaki Yazo, and Hirayama Shiu. Since Pi was also acquainted with the leaders of secret societies in Hunan and Hupeh, Sun Yat-sen sent Hirayama to accompany Pi to Hunan to make connections with secret societies, and they traveled many times between Hunan and Hupeh. Meanwhile, to discuss a plan for an uprising with K'ang and Liang, T'ang Ts'ai-ch'ang also went to Japan in 1899. By means of a letter of recommendation from Pi Yung-nien, he was also able to discuss with Sun Yat-sen a plan for cooperation in the provinces along the Yangtze River and in Fukien and Kwangtung.

Lin Kuei, Liang's other acquaintance, who from the Hunan days had been connected with the Hunan leaders of secret societies, also came to Japan. He studied in the senior division of the Ta-t'ung School. At this time Chinese students in Japan numbered no more than seventy or eighty persons. Among them less than half had revolutionary ideas. Among the latter may be listed, however, such names as Ts'al Ao, Wu Lu-chen, Ch'in Li-shan, and Ch'i I-hui.

To speak candidly, Pi, Lin, T'ang and other revolutionary students in Japan, including even Liang Ch'i-ch'ao, had no intention of sparing the Manchu. However, their attitudes differed to a large degree. Liang's relation with K'ang Yu-wei, for instance, and his previous affiliation with Emperor Kuang-hsü had brought him under the standard of the Emperor Protection Society. Those who were close to Liang, such as T'ang Ts'al-ch'ang, Lin Kuei, Ch'in Li-shan, did not find it easy to follow a very different course. T'ang Ts'ai-ch'ang, in particular, found himself in a difficult position. Pi Yung-nien tried to enlist him under Sun Yat-sen's banner, while K'ang and Liang were pulling him firmly to their side. He finally began to side more and more with Pi. In the winter of 1899, T'ang led Ch'in Li-shan and more than twenty other Chinese students in a return to China. There they planned to initiate a great uprising along the Yangtze Valley in the section of Hunan and Hupeh.

Arriving at Shanghai, T'ang with Lin Kuei and the others secretly sponsored an organization called the *Cheng-ch'i Hui* [Righteous Spirit Society] to execute their activities. Soon Lin Kuei went to Hankow to invite secret-society members to join them by means of a sort of lottery [*fu-yu p'iao*]. Pi Yung-nien, meanwhile, invited the secret-society members to go in the direction of Hong Kong and Kwangtung. Pi strongly advised T'ang Ts'ai-ch'ang to sever all his connections with K'ang and Liang. T'ang could not do so, however, because all expenses for his activities depended upon the money raised by K'ang and Liang in foreign countries. Worse still, the chiefs of the secret societies, who had been invited by Pi to go to Hong Kong, were induced by K'ang Yu-wei's money to change their allegiance from the Hsing-Chung Hui to T'ang's leadership. Pi was so dismayed at this turn of events that he shaved his hair and became a monk.

This was the first attempt that the Emperor Protection Society had made to recruit members from among secret societies, and the drastic measure was taken only after the dismal failure of the Hundred Days' Reform.[16]

Uprisings in Central and South China

All three events mentioned above occurred during the reactionary period. Here were the roots for the later growth of incompatibility between the Revolutionary Party and the Constitutional Party, since the latter was derived from the Emperor Protection Society.

A series of uprisings were attempted by two revolutionary groups in the 1900's. T'ang Ts'ai-ch'ang and Lin Kuei were fomenting the uprising along the Yangtze River. Sun Yat-sen and his comrades of the *Hsing-Chung Hui* planned a revolution in Kwangtung. The Boxer Uprising in the early summer of 1900 was taken by both T'ang and Sun as the best opportunity to start a revolution. An attempt was made to start two revolts: one at Hankow and Tatung along the Yangtze River in September, and one at Huichou, Kwangtung, in October.

At Huichou the rebels attacked an enemy greatly surpassing them in strength. They gained four victories, but in the end the odds went against them. They were unable to bring sufficient military supplies through to the front. As a coordinate action with the attack at Huichou, Shih Chien-yu attempted to assassinate Te-shou, governor-general of Kwangtung, by bombing his office on October 26. This plan also failed, and Shih lost his life.

In the Yangtze Valley a plan had been made to take simultaneous revolutionary action at Hankow, Tatung, Anking, and elsewhere, under the direction of T'ang Ts'ai-ch'ang and Lin Kuei. Money to be remitted by K'ang and Liang did not come, however, and the plan had to be postponed again and again. The plot was ultimately discovered by the government—just two days before the scheduled attacks. The attempt, made on September 8, was already doomed. In Hankow action was postponed until September 16. By this time the headquarters of the rebels had already been discovered by Chang Chih-tung. Twenty persons, including T'ang Ts'ai-ch'ang and Lin Kuei, were arrested and executed.

Other riots planned for Changteh, Hsinti, and Anking had to be called off. After these failures, the loyalists K'ang and Liang made no further use of the members of the secret societies. Thereafter they were also afraid to give the emperor any assistance except for a few useless words of eulogy in their periodical, *Hsin-min ts'ung-pao*.

Though its military revolts had been unsuccessful, the popularity of the Revolutionary Party had been increased considerably. The governor-general of Liang-kuang, Te-shou, in his public notice and memorials to the throne referred to both Sun and K'ang, branding K'ang, Liang, Sun Wen, and others as agitators of the Huichou uprising. "The monster with red eyes" and the "emperor's tutor" were mentioned together in the same line of the memorial—Sun and K'ang were paired as agitators.

Sun Yat-sen says in his autobiography: "After my first failure in 1895, the whole nation regarded me as a bandit or a rebel, an unprincipled man guilty of rank treason. ... But after my failure in 1900, not only did the people stop cursing me, but the progressive elements were actually sympathetic with me in my misfortunes."[17] Sun's position at this time is an indication of the changing attitude of the great majority of the people, who were now more cognizant of the many evils of the Manchu court. The original intention of T'ang and Lin had been not to protect the emperor but to utilize his name to fire others with enthusiasm for a revolution. After their military failure this time, the number of people utilizing the slogan "Protect the Emperor" gradually decreased. This may be regarded as one fruit of the reactionary period.

YÜAN SHIH-K'AI AND THE PEIYANG MILITARY CLIQUE

It is commonly known that the power of the Peiyang warlords has been of tremendous importance in Chinese political history of the last several decades. It is well known, too, that Yüan Shih-k'ai was the founder of the Peiyang military clique. During this reactionary period, Yüan's position seemed to be insignificant. Together with Li Hung-chang, Chang Chih-tung, Liu K'un-i, and others, he tried to maintain order in the coastal provinces south of Shantung. During these same years, nevertheless, Yüan built a foundation for his warlord clique.

Yüan Shih-k'ai's great ability won recognition first from Wu Ch'ang-ch'ing, then from Li Hung-chang, and later from Jung-lu and Li Hung-tsao. Yüan served under Wu Ch'ang-ch'ing, of the Anhwei Army [*Huai-chün*] in 1880. Two years later he followed Wu to Korea, where his actions were subsequently admired by Li Hung-chang. After the Treaty of Tientsin was concluded between China and Japan in 1885, Yüan remained in Korea as a third-rank *taotai*, to take charge of diplomatic and commercial affairs. In 1895 after he precipitated the Sino-Japanese War in Korea, he was recalled to China to do transportation work for the eastern expedition. At this time Yüan's friends respected him as a military expert. Hu Yü-fen, a salt controller, recommended Yüan to train a special army to be used for the war. Yüan insisted, "The prerequisites of a new army are adequate rations, good weapons, and thorough disciplining for many months in order to assure its invulnerability before I can commence this new undertaking; otherwise I do not wish to flee after the others." Apparently the recommendation was not accepted.

Yüan Shih-k'ai as a Builder of Armies

Shortly after, someone else memorialized the throne requesting that troops be rapidly trained in the foreign style. As a result Hu Yü-fen, with the help of a foreign officer, C. von Hanneken, was appointed to recruit soldiers from Tientsin. The new training program drafted by the foreign officers proved impractical and was suspended. Finally Hu Yü-fen devised another plan to recruit and train ten battalions of the Pacification [*Ting-wu*] Army, including 3000 infantrymen, 1000 artillerymen, 250 cavalrymen, and 500 engineers, a total of 4750 men to be drilled partly by

Western methods.

After the Sino-Japanese peace treaty in 1895, Yüan, who held the official rank of *taotai*, was serving in Peking in the Office for the Promotion of New Military Affairs. He attracted the attention of the grand councilors Li Hung-tsao and Jung-lu, who asked him to draft a program for training a new army. It was then that K'ang and Liang also tried to win Yüan's friendship by inviting him to support the Society for the Study of National Rejuvenation. In November of the same year, Prince Ch'un, Prince Ch'ing, and the grand councilors submitted a memorial to the throne begging for a reform of the military system, the organization of a new army at Tientsin, and the appointment of Yüan Shih-k'ai to supervise military education.

Just at this moment Hu Yü-fen was put in charge of the construction of a railroad from Tientsin to Lukouchiao, and someone had to replace him in the training of the Pacification Army, which Hu had been training since 1894. Hu recommended Yüan to take over his military duty and to recruit additional soldiers to enlarge the ten battalions of the Pacification Army to 7000 men. If the result of the training was satisfactory, the number was to be further increased. The memorial was sanctioned by an imperial decree. At the same time, a petition was filed to appoint the *taotai*, Yin-ch'ang, to select robust sons from the Eight Banners to study in the Military Preparation Academy at Tientsin. From this academy, established by Tseng Kuo-fan and Li Hung-chang, most of Yüan's subordinates were emerging. The preparation of Manchu officers was a parallel action with Yüan's training of the army.[18]

After accepting the appointment, Yüan carried on his work according to his plan. The Pacification Army was trained at Hsiaochan, a former station of the Anhwei Army which was located seventy li from Tientsin, between Tientsin and Taku. The officers under Yüan's command were partly veterans and partly graduates from the Tientsin Military Academy. Chiang Kuei-t'i, Tuan Ch'i-jui, Wang Shih-chen, Feng Kuo-chang, Ch'en

Kuang-yüan, Wang Chan-yüan, Ts'ao K'un, Tuan Chih-kuei were among these officers; Hsü Shih-ch'ang served as his military adviser.

During the *coup d'état* of 1898, because he wished to utilize Yüan as an intimate official of Emperor Kuang-hsü, T'an Ssu-t'ung was offered the rank of expectant vice-minister of state. Yüan himself preferred to curry favor with the empress dowager. He was made acting superintendent of trade in the Northern ports [*Pei-yang ta-ch'en*][19] for ten days during Jung-lu's absence. He received 4000 taels of silver as a reward for his Newly Created Army [*Hsin-chien lu-chün*]. But after ten days, when Yü-lu came to take up the position of governor-general of Chihli, Yüan had to go back to his military camp at Hsiaochan.

Yüan and the Boxers 1900

Yüan's new army, after training for nearly three years, gained a reputation. In the spring of 1899 an imperial decree ordered him to lead his troops to the area of Techow and Ichow, Shantung, for military maneuvers. In Ichow the Boxers were in conflict with the churches. Yüan asked that the central government pay careful attention to this matter and then returned to his camp in June. By December, Governor Yü-hsien, criticized by foreigners for his toleration and encouragement of the Boxers, was trans-ferred to Peking. Yüan was then made acting governor of Shantung. In March 1900 he assumed full governorship of the province. To this sphere of jurisdiction he took his newly trained army, the name of which had been changed from the Newly Created Army to the Right Division of Guard Army [*Wu-wei yu-chün*]. The original troops at Shantung, still numbering more than thirty battalions, were subsequently reorganized into twenty battalions, called the Vanguard of the Right Division of the Guard Army. These battalions were trained by the officers of the new army.

Yüan's military strength thus augmented, in a short time his troops drove all the Boxers out of Shantung. Yüan was accordingly praised by resident foreigners. When the Boxer Uprising was at its height, Shantung was quiet and peaceful, a shelter for the many refugees fleeing from Chihli.

On June 17, 1900, Yüan was ordered by imperial decree to transfer his army to Peking. This was a turning point in the fortunes of Yüan and other warlords. The empress dowager intended to have Yüan come into the capital to assist the "righteous people"; but Jung-lu's intentions were not very clear. Among the governors-general in the Southeast, a few suggested that Governor Yüan should immediately lead his troops from Shantung through Paoting to Peking to drive corrupting elements from the court and to protect the emperor and the dowager empress. But after dispatching a part of his troops to the border between Shantung and Chihli, Yüan stopped them from going further. Later on he was blamed by some people for defying orders and for detaining his troops to enhance his own reputation.

The fate of Nieh Shih-ch'eng and his Tenacious Army [*Wu-i Chün*] may help us to understand Yüan's fortune. When the Tenacious Army was attacked by both the Boxers and the Allied forces, the commander lost his life and his army was annihilated. If Yüan had led his troops into Peking, he would not only have been an enemy of the "righteous people" but would also not have received friendly treatment from the Allied Powers. Should Yüan fight against the "righteous people" or should he fight against the Allied Powers? Realizing that the fate of his army might be the same as the fate of Nieh Shih-ch'eng's, he did not follow orders.

Yüan held a pivotal military position. After the 1860's the military power was in the hands of the provincial governors and governors-general. The governor-general of Chihli was the most important because Chihli was the site of the imperial capital. During the Sino-Japanese War, Li Hung-chang had been sharply criticized, and consequently in August 1895 Li had been transferred to the Grand Secretariat. His position as governor-general of Chihli was assigned to Wang Wen-shao. In May

1898, however, to break up the power of Emperor Kuang-hsü and the Reform Party, the empress dowager had to control the Peiyang Army. She therefore transferred Wang Wen-shao to Peking and appointed her intimate and trusted Manchu, Jung-lu, to the governor-generalship of Chihli. After the *coup d'état*, Jung-lu was transferred to the Grand Council. The Chihli position was filled by another intimate and trusted follower, Yü-lu. He served until the Boxer Uprising was beyond control and met death at the hands of the Allied Powers. Only then was Li Hung-chang again invited to Peking and once more made governor-general of Chihli.

Yüan Governor-General of Chihli

Just after the Boxer Protocol was signed, and on the day before his death, Li dictated a memorial to his secretary, Yü Shih-mei, recommending Yüan Shih-k'ai to succeed him as governor-general of Chihli. Li said: "I have looked for men of ability all over the nation. I can find no one better than Yüan." During the Boxer Uprising, Li Hung-chang had noticed Yüan's exceptional work and esteemed his ability.

Receiving the posthumous memorial, the empress dowager gave some consideration to it, since except for Yüan Shih-k'ai, it was difficult to find another competent person for the Chihli post. She had had heretofore some confidence in Yüan, and realized that now only Yüan's troops could maintain order in North China. Hence Yüan was given the position of governor-general of Chihli and at the same time made superintendent of trade in the Northern ports [*Pei-yang ta-ch'en*]. This appointment, a further by-product of reactionary politics, laid the foundation of the Peiyang military clique.[20]

CHAPTER SIX REVIVAL OF THE REFORM MOVEMENT

In the revived activity of the reform movement, Liang Ch'i-ch'ao was one of the most influential publicists in modern China. Before 1898, while he was editor of *Current Affairs* [*Shih-wu pao*], he had already built a reputation for himself. He was then, however, merely a following of K'ang Yu-wei, and the ideas he promoted were K'ang's. For K'ang Yu-wei the teachings of Mencius and the Kung-yang theories concerning the moral and cyclic aspects of history together provided essential doctrine; Liang promoted the same views. K'ang advocated the protection of Confucianism and reverence for Confucius; and with this cult of Confucius Liang also, until 1898, concurred.

LIANG CH'I-CH'AO—A STAR OF THE PRESS

Before 1898 K'ang Yu-wei held the spotlight. Liang Ch'i-ch'ao had at this time no independent position. After the failure of the first attempt at reform, K'ang's ideas remained the same as before; Liang's opinions, however, changed in many ways. In Japan, where he was writing newspaper articles, he was at the same time studying Japanese and reading new books. He gradually gave up discoursing on the Kung-yang and Mencius and the protection of Confucianism. He turned instead to the philosophy of Rousseau and Montesquieu.

The name of Liang's periodical in Japan was changed three different times. Beginning with November 1898 it was called the *Public Opinion Press* [*Ch'ing-i pao*]; in 1902 it acquired the name *New People's Magazine* [*Hsin-min ts'ung-pao*]; from 1910 on it was called *The National Spirit* [*Kuo-feng pao*]. From the academic point of view, his later writings were better than his earlier ones. From a political and social point of view his essays appearing in the *Public Opinion Press* and in the *New People's Magazine* between 1902 and 1903 were more influential. Even though his periodical was published in Japan, it had an extraordinary influence on China's intellectuals. Freedom of the press on the continent was closely restricted in 1899 and 1900. In Shanghai several periodicals were discontinued shortly after their first appearance. But the *Public Opinion Press* circulated for more than three years; the life of the *New People's Magazine* was even longer. Liang, a very effective publicist, became a star of the public press.

Liang as a Literary Influence

Liang's journalistic style was far superior to that of many of his contemporaries. It was emotional, often powerful in firing the minds of his readers with great enthusiasm. After the abolition of the eight-legged essay and its replacement by discussions on events of current interest, students had lost their standard models. They now began to imitate Liang's journalistic style as it appeared in his periodicals. Though the government forbade the circulation of his journal in China, numerous copies were sold. They were widely read and imitated by other scholars.

Liang's progressive ideas suited the young intellectuals and had considerable influence in bringing on needed political and social changes. Except that he still referred to Kuang-hsü as "My Emperor" or "My Sacred Ruler," Liang advocated a violent anti-Manchu movement, a revolution, involving destruction and assassination.

In his essay, "Allow Me Respectfully to Tell My Fellow Journalists," in the *New People's Magazine* of 1902, he states:

> A newspaper writer must serve the needs of the time and must propagate a single idea. ... Even if his writing is somewhat radical, it does not matter. Why? Because if I take a firm stand, at the same

time there will be people who take the opposite stand just as firmly in order to correct me, and there will also be other people who take a middle course or an eclectic view between the two extremes. ... It is human nature to be content with what one is accustomed to and to be surprised at what one has never heard before. We must therefore acquaint the people with the unfamiliar and in this way their wisdom may be gradually increased. Twenty years ago many people were astonished at hearing about Western knowledge, but when they heard of the reform movement, they were no longer astonished at Western knowledge. Ten years ago many were amazed at the reform movement until they listened to talk of a democratic revolution, and then they were no longer amazed at the reform idea. One or two years ago many people were alarmed at the mention of democratic government until they heard talk of a revolution, and then they had no objection to democracy. Today in the thinking of the academic people of our nation, we can generally find only one out of every thousand who is not afraid of a revolution; but we can find one out of every hundred who is afraid of revolution, but not of democracy. There is almost no one who is still afraid of reform or of Western knowledge. Accordingly, gentlemen, you can understand the function of newspapermen as the guides of our people. If you wish to conduct the people toward reform, you must startle them by democracy; if you wish to lead them to democracy you must intimidate them by revolution. When a revolution is advocated, the people will not feel strange about reform and democracy. ... If our newspapers are to be the guides of the people we must understand this technique. [1]

Liang's *Public Opinion Press* used this kind of strategy in 1902-1903. His fundamental objective was a constitutional monarchy, but the opinions expressed in his newspaper went to much greater extremes.

Except for the governmental authorities his readers were delighted with his advanced ideas. Because the reactionary period had oppressed the intellectual class, many aspired to break down the *status quo*. Liang's colorful, emotional, and persuasive writings were exactly what they needed. During the five or six years after 1898 his contributions roused his younger readers to take action.

THE FERMENTATION OF NEW INTELLECTUAL FORCES

At the turn of the century China was in a transitional stage between an old and a new civilization. The Boxer Uprising in 1900 marked the climax of the reactionary forces. In the succeeding year and when the Boxer Protocol was signed, the new reform force emerged and grew steadily for five years—until the Russo-Japanese War. These five years differed greatly from those of the initial stage of the reform movement (1894 to 1898). In this earlier period the Sino-Japanese War had completely exposed China's weak points and precipitated the numerous invasions by Western imperialists. A majority of Chinese scholars still abhorred the Westerners but still dared not despise the Manchu court. After the Boxer Uprising, the imperialists modified their methods. They put pressure on the Manchu government, but also protected and supported it. A majority of Chinese scholars, in their hatred of foreigners, now began to hate the Manchu court even more—as incapable, infamous, and without prestige. It was still evident that China must reform and there were now fewer scholars ready to object. But could the method of the Hundred Days' Reform of 1898 meet the needs and satisfy the will of the people? An examination of the achievements by the new reform force may help to answer this question.

Revolutionary Agitation on the Mainland

When T'ang Ts'ai-ch'ang was planning a riot along the Yangtze

River, the Boxer Uprising was at its height. Famous scholars in North China such as Yen Fu and others fled to Shanghai. There T'ang Ts'ai-ch'ang, utilizing the slogan "Save the nation from the current trouble," called the liberal-minded scholars of all provinces to a conference. Among the eminent participants at this meeting were Yung Wing, Yen Fu, Chang Ping-lin, and Wen T'ing-shih. Altogether several hundred people attended. Yung Wing was elected chairman, Yen Fu vice-chairman, and T'ang Ts'ai-ch'ang general secretary. Only a few knew T'ang's secret motive. A majority of the participants attended the conference only as a pastime. During the conference, however, Chang Ping-lin cut off his queue before the crowd in order to show that he was determined to sever all his relations with the Manchu dynasty.

In September when T'ang Ts'ai-ch'ang's independent army failed in Hankow, Chang Chih-tung asked Liu K'un-i, governor-general of Liang-Kiang, to arrest the important members of the Shanghai conference. The prominent participants, frightened, hid themselves in the foreign settlement in Shanghai or fled overseas. This occurred in 1900.

The next year was fairly uneventful. Even so, several books and periodicals appeared, advocating a revolution. In 1902 the Chinese Education Society was organized in Shanghai by Chang Ping-lin, Ts'ai Yüan-p'ei, and others. In the same year some Chinese students in Tokyo had a skirmish with Ts'al Chün, the Chinese minister to Japan, as a result of which the student leader Wu Chih-hui was driven back to China. Students of the Nanyang Academy in Shanghai went on strike to support the Tokyo conflict. The members of the Chinese Education Society formed a Patriotic Society [*Ai-kuo hsüeh-she*]. This was joined by a number of students who had withdrawn from the Army Academy in Nanking. Thereupon the Patriotic Society became the headquarters of revolutionary ideas; the site of the Shanghai conference became the lecture hall for revolutionary agitation; and the newspaper *Su-pao*, then very popular, served as the organ for revolutionary propaganda.

In the spring of 1903 a meeting at Chang-yüan decided to oppose Wang Chih-ch'un, governor of Kwangsi, because he planned to borrow money and troops from France to suppress bandits. In May another convention at Chang-yüan passed a resolution to protest against the Russians in the Three Eastern Provinces. In June 1903 the governor of Kiangsu wrote a letter to the authorities of the foreign settlement at Shanghai saying that young people who had held meetings at Chang-yüan, nominally to protest the actions of France and Russia, were actually attempting to start a rebellion. He requested that the leaders be secretly arrested and severely punished.

While all the foreign consuls were reported to have endorsed the arrest, the municipal government did not support it. The *Shanghai Times*, an English paper, published an editorial praising the municipal government for its ability to maintain justice. The Western newspapers in Shanghai generally published a detailed record of the affair and those whose arrests were imminent were asked to report their names and addresses to the municipal government in order to receive special protection. Even so, near the end of June Chinese authorities, who claimed to have received an imperial decree from the Manchu emperor, negotiated with authorities in the foreign settlements to effect the arrest of the allegedly subversive Chinese. Consequently these authorities sent a number of Chinese and Western detectives to the Patriotic Society to arrest Chang Ping-lin and others; however, only Chang was arrested. Ts'ai Yüan-p'ei fled to Berlin, and Wu Chih-hui to London. Both the *Su-pao* office and the Patriotic Society were dissolved.

Chang Ping-lin was imprisoned for three years. When his case was examined at the Mixed Court of the International Settlement, the attorney representing the Chinese government accused the editors of the *Su-pao* of despising the emperor, agitating a revolution, and defaming the Manchus. For instance, in the first chapter of *The Revolutionary Army*, there were such lines as "The Manchus, who are like animals, should all be killed. ... How wonderful and how glorious is revolution!" In the second chapter there were such expressions as "Let us revolt and revolt! There is no justification for having a Manchu ruler. The Manchus are only about fifty thousand in number. Many of their princes and high officials are illiterates and are amateur opera singers."[2] These comments, from a book published by the *Su-pao*, indicate something of the content of this newspaper which reflected some of the ideas of the new party in China.

In 1899 the patriotic scholars of Shanghai, led by Chang Yüan-shan and Ts'ai Yüan-p'ei, considered the abdication of Emperor Kuang-hsü as the central problem; now they even referred to the Manchu emperor as the "little comic figure." Public sentiment toward the Manchu, in other words, had by this time undergone a pronounced mutation. After the dissolution of the Patriotic Society and the sealing up of the newspaper office of *Su-pao*, Chang Shih-chao and Chang Chi organized in November 1903 the *National Daily News* [*Kuo-min jih-pao*] in Shanghai. Its reputation and influence equaled that of *Su-pao*. During the two years 1904 and 1905 there were more than a hundred other Shanghai revolutionary publications. Revolutionary ideas were being spread, and sporadic revolutionary actions taken.

Chinese Students Abroad

At this time Japan was the center for Chinese students abroad. Their total number was less than a hundred in 1899-1900, but they increased to several thousand in the following two years. In the spring of 1901 Cantonese students in Japan, including Wang Ch'ung-hui and Feng Tzu-yu, formed a Kwangtung Independence Association. They advocated that a declaration of independence from the Manchu government should be made by the provincial authorities. Some Cantonese immigrants to Japan also joined the association. Sun Yat-sen, who was then living in Yokohama, gave his wholehearted support to the movement. Thus began the close relation between Sun Yat-sen and the Cantonese students abroad.

In 1902 Chinese students, who had come to Japan from all the provinces, organized a Chinese student club in Tokyo. At its opening Wu Lu-chen made a speech in which he compared the clubhouse with Independence Hall in Philadelphia. In April a commemoration of the 258th anniversary of the Manchu conquest of China was prepared and a declaration was written by Chang Ping-lin. Several hundred students signed their names to attend the service. The Chinese minister to Japan, Ts'ai Chün, hearing the news beforehand, requested that the Japanese government stop the meeting. When the time came, Japanese police intervened and those who had gathered were quickly dispersed. After several months the Chinese students and Minister Ts'ai had another quarrel because Ts'ai Chün refused to recommend a military academy which they had intended to enter at their own expense. Wu Chih-hui led more than twenty students to the Chinese legation to request the recommendation. Here they remained until midnight when Ts'ai summoned Japanese police to drag them away. The Chinese students then banded together in groups to argue with Minister Ts'ai for several days in succession. Ts'ai, persuading the Japanese government to arrest Wu Chih-hui and others, compelled them to return to China as punishment for their disturbance of order and peace. This incident aggravated the intense hatred of the Chinese students for the Manchu officials.

On New Year's Day of 1903 more than a thousand Chinese students in Japan held a celebration meeting at their clubhouse. Minister Ts'al also participated. The history of the Manchu annexation of China was the subject of a speech written by Ma Chün-wu and Liu Ch'eng-yü, who advocated the overthrow of the Manchu and the restoration of authority to the Chinese. When the speech was loudly applauded by the whole audience, a Manchu imperial member, Chang-fu, stood up to argue. He was shouted down by the multitude without being able to finish a sentence. Minister Ts'ai was angry but dared not utter a single word. He was unable to take any revenge except to dismiss Liu Ch'eng-yü from school.

In May 1903, because the Russians had occupied the Three Eastern Provinces by force, Chinese students in Japan organized a volunteer corps to fight against Russia. This corps was called the Association for Universal Military Training. Lan T'ien-wei was elected commander of the more than one thousand student members. Every day they drilled assiduously until they were prohibited from doing so by the Japanese government. They sent Niu Yung-chien and another man as their representatives to China to see Yüan Shih-k'ai, the governor-general of Chihli, to ask for the mobilization of troops to oppose Russia and to offer their services as assault troops. But Yüan refused to receive their representatives.

Furthermore there was a rumor that the lives of the representatives were in danger, and the Chinese students in Japan became excited. In the winter of that year a secret revolutionary military school was formed, for at this time only the government-supported students could enter a Japanese military college. Those who were suspected of having revolutionary inclinations were not given the opportunity to enter military institutions. Sun Yat-sen had a Japanese friend, Major Hino, a military expert, who was invited to direct the secret military school in the vicinity of Aoiyama near Tokyo. The school existed for five months before it was closed.

During the years 1903 and 1904 many revolutionary publications prepared in Japan by Chinese students appeared: the *Hupeh Student's Circle*; the *Voice of the Han*; the *Tide of Chekiang*, *Translations by Chinese Students Abroad*; the *New Hunan*; the *Military History of the Heavenly Kingdom of Great Peace*; *Twentieth-Century China*. They sprang up like bamboo shoots after an abundant shower. Then in the spring of 1904 Huang Hsing organized in Japan the China Arise Society [*Hua-hsing Hui*].

The Chinese students in Europe were, according to Wu Chih-hui, very few before 1898. With the exception of the thirty students sent two decades before by the Peiyang Navy Academy, no further Chinese students were sent to Europe until 1902. When Wu Chih-hui went to England in 1903, he found a few students from the Nanyang Academy; and in France, Belgium, and Germany there were a few students sent by Chang Chih-tung from Hupeh. Sun Yat-sen said, "When I visited Europe again in the spring of 1905, most of the Chinese students there supported a revolution, because ... during the last two years they had already been deeply affected by the revolutionary tide."[3]

A general review of student attitudes and publications, however, indicates that the reform pattern of the Hundred Days of 1898 could not by any means cope with the present tide of the expectant Chinese people.

A SHOW OF REFORM BY THE MANCHU GOVERNMENT

An official [Tsai-i] who followed the empress dowager and Emperor Kuang-hsü in their flight said later:

> When the empress dowager escaped from the danger, she often told her officials in attendance, "I did not expect that I would be ridiculed by the emperor." When they reached Taiyuan, the emperor was able to express some of his opinions. One day he summoned Tsai-i, and Kang-i and reproached them severely, with the intention of punishing them according to law. The empress interrupted "If we punish them first, our enemies will demand much more severe punishment." The emperor retorted, "According to our national law their crimes are inexcusable. Why should we care what our enemies think?" Tsai-i and the others quickly kotowed.[4]

The empress dowager at this time could not hide her humiliation even before Emperor Kuang-hsü and could not expect to hide it from her people and from foreigners. Therefore, during her flight, as a self-criticism she proclaimed decrees blaming herself for what had happened and reproving her own actions. In January 1901 orders were issued for reforms. In April a new office *T'u-pan cheng-wu ch'u* [Office for Promotion of State Affairs] was organized to take over the promotion of a new administration. It looked as though she really meant to reform. Upon hearing this news, the foreigners remarked that her increased wisdom and knowledge was compensation for the huge indemnity paid for the Boxer Rebellion. But it is more accurate to say that the empress dowager had no means of disguising her shame except to pretend reforms by issuing all sorts of decrees. The new office was no more than a branch of the Grand Council. It actually had no new administration to promote.

The so-called new administrations and changes announced during the five years after 1901 amounted to the abolition of some old positions, including those of some clerks and government servants in all offices; of the governorships of Yunnan, Hupeh, and Kwangtung; and of the director-generalship of the river conservancy. The selling of official posts was discontinued. The Imperial Supervisorate of Instruction was annexed to the Hanlin Academy. Of the new offices organized, the ministry of foreign affairs (July 1901) had been demanded by the Allied Powers as a replacement for the Tsungli Yamen. A ministry of commercial affairs annexed the bureau for railroads and mining. The bureau for military training, a ministry of police, and a ministry of education were set up.

New military reforms included a twenty or thirty per cent disbanding of the Army of the Green Standard [Chinese troops organized by provinces, a system the Manchus had maintained since the seventeenth century]. Each province was ordered to establish a military academy. All military units stationed in the provinces were to be strictly sifted and distributed, some to the standing army, some to the reserve forces, some to the police force. T'ieh-liang and Yüan Shih-k'ai were made directors of military training of the Manchu Banners [military groups in which membership was inherited] around Peking. An autumn military maneuver was ordered to take place at Ho-chien, and Yüan Shih-k'ai and T'ieh-liang were appointed commissioners of military inspection (October 1905).

Reforms in Education

Among the education reforms, the special state examination on economic affairs was restored (May 1901). The Hanlin Academy was reorganized, now to give instructions to the Hanlin compilers and graduates. High officials were ordered to return to China for government service. The eight-legged essay was permanently abrogated [1901] and replaced by themes on current affairs in both provincial and metropolitan examinations. All military examinations were canceled in 1902.

An order was issued to all provinces to reform the *shu-yüan* [academies]. In the capital these were to become universities; in the prefects and counties, high schools; and in the districts, grade schools. As an encouragement to the students, regulations [November 1901] for conferring degrees were formed to the effect that titles of licentiates, *chü-jen*, *chin-shin* and others would be conferred upon all upper-school graduates after they had passed an examination. The provincial authorities were again ordered to select and dispatch students to European nations to pursue special courses of study. Beginning with 1902 all Hanlin compilers and graduates of the third degree and those graduates of the lowest degrees who were to be employed as secretaries in government ministries were to be ordered to study in various departments in the imperial university. Finally, various school regulations were proclaimed. Examinations were to be given to returned students from foreign countries; examinations were to be set annually. All provincial, metropolitan, and other lower-grade examinations were to be abolished.

The number of reforms listed here seems to be greater than that of the Hundred Days' Reform of 1898. In reality their scope and content do not exceed the previous reforms. During the first five years of the twentieth century the reforms effected were no more than the abolition of civil-service examinations, the establishment of schools, and the dispatch of students to study abroad.

Manchus versus Chinese in Government

A further reform permitted marriage between the Manchus and Chinese. This extremely liberal move by the Manchu authorities was one which K'ang Yu-wei had strongly advocated, without success, in 1898. Unfortunately this move now came too late to have any favorable effect. Manchu authorities, while working toward harmony between the Manchus and Chinese, at the same time were taking vigilant defense measures against the Chinese. In any significant office the Manchus must still be placed in a superior or at least an equal position with the Chinese. Of the six ministers in the bureau for the promotion of new state affairs, the ratio was still three Manchus to three Chinese; and the actual power was in the hands of Jung-lu.

The newly established ministry of foreign affairs was under the directorship of I-k'uang, whose position was above the Chinese associate ministers. The new bureau of military training was also under the guidance of I-k'uang. Military inspection and the military drills of the Banners around Peking were jointly managed by T'ieh-liang and Yüan Shih-k'ai. Even the imperial university had also to be managed by the Manchu, Jung-ch'ing, while a Chinese, Chang Po-hsi, served as associate director. Suppression of the Chinese and the discrimination against them continued to be severe. An order permitting interracial marriage between the Manchu and Chinese was not enough to produce harmony.

The Role of High Officials in Reform

Of the governmental personnel of this time, a leader of the

reactionary faction, Kang-i, died, supposedly of anger and disappointment, during his flight with the court to Sian. Prince Tsai-i was banished upon the demand of the allied powers. The central power of the government was then left entirely in the hands of I-k'uang and Jung-lu. The former, with Li Hung-chang, stayed at Peking to negotiate peace with the Allied Powers. The latter, following the court to Sian, acquired even greater power than he had previously possessed. The first decrees which served to disguise the humiliation and shame of the court and the proposal for the establishment of the bureau for the promotion of new state affairs were both suggested by Jung-lu.

Among the important governors-general were Li Hung-chang, Yüan Shih-k'ai, Chang Chih-tung, and Liu K'un-i. After Li Hung-chang went to the North, he became so deeply involved in complicated diplomatic problems that he had no time to ponder other reform plans. Shortly after the signing of the peace treaty he died.

The first proposals for an effective reform were the memorials of Liu K'un-i and Chang Chih-tung. These were called "the three joint memorials for reform presented by the governors-general of Chiang and Ch'u." A favorable attitude toward them may be found in these words from the special decree of the empress dowager issued in September 1901: "The officials within and without the capital are entrusted with the duty to consider what should be reformed, and what ingrained habits should be disposed of, in order to correct the current predicament. The essential reforms outlined in the joint memorials of Liu K'un-i and Chang Chih-tung should be put into practice from time to time."[5]

Fundamentally, the new reforms during the five-year period for "the abolition of civil-service examinations, the establishment of schools and the dispatch of students abroad" were actually derived from suggestions in the joint memorials of Liu and Chang. After the death of Li Hung-chang, Yüan Shih-k'ai succeeded him as Chihli governor-general. After Liu K'un-i's death in October, 1902, Yüan Shih-k'ai and Chang Chih-tung became the leading governors-general. Jung-lu also died in April 1903, leaving I-k'uang the pillar among the nobles.

In former times Yüan Shih-k'ai had flattered Jung-lu in order to secure special favor from the empress dowager. After Jung-lu's death, I-k'uang was used similarly. In addition, his position as governor-general of Chihli brought Yüan very close to the imperial court. I-k'uang and Yüan Shih-k'ai became the two most important figures of the nation, with power con-siderably greater than that of Chang Chih-tung.

I-k'uang, in his indecisiveness and greed for power, closely resembled the late Jung-lu, but lacked his predecessor's ability and knowledge while surpassing him in corruption and covetousness. Chang Chih-tung had more book knowledge than Yüan Shih-k'ai, but he was inferior to the latter in ability and understanding of political tactics. Therefore, though in the control of the present situation Yüan Shih-k'ai's position was greater, his lack of education was a hindrance to him. He wished to imitate Li Hung-chang, but lacked Li's integrity and experience. During the five years of reform, Yüan nevertheless contributed in effecting reforms and the final abolishment of the civil service examinations was a direct result of a joint memorial of Yüan Shih-k'ai and Chang Chih-tung. Yüan paid most attention to the raising of funds and the training of soldiers, just as Li Hung-chang had done during his tenure as superintendent of trade in Northern ports. The new military reforms should be credited mostly to Yüan's efforts. The power and prestige of the Peiyang military clique accordingly increased a great deal during these five years. Manchu suspicion of Yüan also increased.

THE RUSSO-JAPANESE WAR AND THE CRY FOR CONSTITUTIONAL GOVERNMENT

While the Manchu government was carrying on its reforms, aggressive imperialists were losing no time in using the territory in

Northeast China as a battleground. Two remote causes of the Russo-Japanese War of 1904-1905 were the Sino-Japanese War of 1894 and the Boxer Uprising of 1900. The Sino-Japanese peace treaty at Shimonoseki had ceded the Liaotung Peninsula to Japan, but because Russia, Germany, and France had compelled her to return it to China, Japan was determined to avenge herself. During the Boxer Uprising, Russia had seized the opportunity to send troops and occupy the Three Eastern Provinces and she was now unwilling to withdraw. Furthermore, it was evident that Russia intended to invade Korea.

In February 1904 as a result of many fruitless negotiations concerning the problems of the Three Eastern Provinces and Korea, Japan formally declared war on Russia. The Japanese forces gained one victory after another. In May 1905 when the Russian Baltic fleet was completely annihilated, the world-shaking war came to an abrupt end.

This war stirred the Eastern peoples to fight for independence from the Westerners. It also gave the Chinese a new faith in political reform. The Japanese constitutional government, though it had not yet given its people real freedom, had enabled this small country to defeat a gigantic despotic nation, China; after a decade Japan had again defeated a similar enemy—Russia. Thereupon it became the general belief among the Chinese people that a constitutional monarchy could automatically make a nation strong as soon as a constitution was declared. Now that Japan actually had defeated Russia, conservative Chinese who were antireform and anticonstitution had nothing more to say.

By this time the people of Russia were also beginning a revolution and the Russian government was also obliged to show its intention of adopting a constitution and a *duma*, or parliament. Could China afford to remain alone as a despotic nation? Before the peace treaty between Japan and Russia had been concluded, a famous Kiangsu scholar, Chang Chien, wrote a letter advocating a constitutional monarchy which is reported to have influenced Yüan Shih-k'ai. Part of Chang Chien's letter to Yüan reads:

> Sir, now you are commanding the important troops of the empire and shouldering the heavy responsibility of the nation. You should take grave concern for the life or death, the rise or fall, of the nation; and you should also realize that now the danger to our nation is not the same as it was in 1894 and 1900. It would be futile to change a little bit here and there without having a fundamental reform of the political body, and it would be useless to attempt a humiliating appeasement policy while the Russo-Japanese War has not yet been concluded. ... The outcome of this war depends on which nation has gained a constitutional government. ... In Japan Ito, Itagaki, and others worked out a constitution and magnificently achieved the great goal of respect for their emperor but at the same time protection of their people; that is really fortunate for Japan. As far as your ability is concerned, you are not inferior to them. [6]

During the tenure of Sun Pao-ch'i as Chinese minister to France he also requested that the Chinese government work toward constitutional monarchy. And since most of the famous members of the old and new parties in South China were influenced by Liang Ch'i-ch'ao's ideas, two or three local governors also jointly requested a constitutional monarchy. Manchu nobles in the central government were also aware that constitutional monarchy should not be opposed any longer. The empress dowager, firmly holding political power in her own hands, not even yielding authority to her own nephew, who was merely occupying the throne, was naturally reluctant to yield any power to the people. Thus she used a policy of procrastination: "You say a constitutional monarchy can really make the nation strong; I will immediately send high officials to make a careful study of all constitutional monarchies."

Following this pronouncement, in the months of July and August

1905 the five high ministers Tsai-tse, Tai Hung-tz'u, Hsü Shih-ch'ang, Tuan-fang, and Shao-ying were commissioned to go abroad and investigate various constitutional administrations. This was supposed to be an indication of the actual intention of the government. While the government created this appearance of intending to set up a new political system, other people besides the dowager empress were working against the intention. An attempt was made by Wu Yüeh to assassinate the five high officials at the railroad station in Peking as they were setting out on their journey abroad. Two of them, Hsü Shih-ch'ang and Shao-ying, were frightened by their narrow escape and withdrew from the mission. Later they were replaced by two other appointees. Wu Yüeh's bomb was an attempt to show that some Chinese citizens would not accept as reform the sugar-coated constitutional monarchy intended by the Manchu regime.

CHAPTER SEVEN THE STRUGGLE BETWEEN THE REVOLUTIONARY AND THE CONSTITUTIONAL MOVEMENTS

Emperor Kuang-hsu and the empress dowager died—on November 14 and 15, 1908, respectively. After their deaths the central government was controlled again by the Manchu royal family, leaving few important positions for the Chinese. The time for the overthrow of the Ch'ing dynasty was at hand.

THE FOUNDATION OF CHUNG-KUO T'UNG-MENG HUI

The bomb thrown by Wu Yüeh in his attempt to assassinate the five high ministers was an individual action. It was not an organized plot of a revolutionary party. As a matter of fact, before 1905 all anti-Manchu activities within and without the nation were local and disorganized. But when the Manchu government dispatched the five ministers abroad to investigate constitutional monarchies, the *Chung-kuo T'ung-meng Hui* [Chinese Covenant Society] was organized in Tokyo. Henceforth, the anti-government revolutionary force had a unified organization. Thereby also, Sun Yat-sen's influence increased among the young intellectuals. No longer need he rely solely upon overseas Chinese and secret-society members for his support. He now was generally recognized as a revolutionary leader of the whole nation.

Sun himself said, "The founding of the revolutionary T'ung-meng Hui opened to me a new era of hope. ... I began to have confidence that revolution could be achieved during my lifetime. I therefore dared to select the title of *Chung-hua min-kuo* [Republic of China] and declare it to my party members, who were ordered to return to their respective provinces to advocate my revolutionary principles and to spread the idea of the Republic of China."[1] Thus in the same year, 1905, while a constitutional monarchic movement was prepared by the Manchu government, the T'ung-meng Hui was founded to direct the forthcoming revolution.

The Foundation of the T'ung-meng Hui

Exactly ten years elapsed between the founding of the Hsing-Chung Hui in 1894 and the T'ung-meng Hui in 1905. In the first half of this decade the extension of revolutionary ideas to the intellectual class was very limited. In the latter half of the period, revolutionary ideas gradually ripened among the educated class within and without China, and a close relation formed between Sun Yat-sen and the advanced Chinese students abroad.

Sun Yat-sen stayed in Yokohama from 1901 to 1903, frequently associating with Chinese students in Japan and discussing revolution, although during these years he had no organization except a small number of Cantonese students who wished to form an independent association. In 1903 Sun went to Annam. In the following year he returned to Japan and prepared to make a return trip to the United States and Europe. At this time he met Liao Chung-k'ai, Ma Chün-wu, and others who were supporters of revolution; and he entrusted them with the job of seeking revolutionary students in Tokyo to organize a party. In the spring of 1905 Sun Yat-sen went to Europe, where a large number of Chinese students were beginning to come from Hupeh. Some were distributed to Germany, some to Belgium, some to France. To show their admiration for the revolutionary leader they raised money to cover Sun Yat-sen's traveling expenses from the United States to Europe.

After receiving the money Sun Yat-sen immediately went to Brussels to discuss revolutionary methods with Chinese students there. Some maintained that they should essay a conversion of the new army to their revolutionary purposes, following the example already set up by Wu Luchen with considerable success in Hupeh. Sun Yat-sen, on the other hand, insisted that the best way to start a revolution was to improve the organization of a party. After long discussion they agreed to do the two things simultaneously.

Sun Yat-sen's suggestion for the organization of a revolutionary party was accepted almost unanimously and each of the adherents pledged an oath which read as follows:

> The person writing this statement of determination, by name, has sworn before heaven to drive out the Manchu barbarians, restore China to the Chinese, create a republic, distribute the land equally, and keep his good faith and maintain his loyalty from beginning to end. If he breaks this promise, he should be punished by other members as they see fit. [2]

This oath was followed by the date upon which it was made, after which it was signed and fingerprinted.

The oath was administered by Sun himself. After it was made, he shook hands with the participants one by one and congratulated them, saying, "Hereafter, you are no longer subjects of the Manchu dynasty." These events in the capital of Belgium make up the story of Sun's first congress of the revolutionary party.

Sun Yat-sen subsequently went to Germany, England, and France, in each of which countries he persuaded some Chinese students to join his party. Thus branches of the party were formed in four European countries, and the first steps had been taken in the foundation of the T'ung-meng Hui in Europe.

In August 1905 Sun returned to Tokyo. The revolutionary spirit among the Chinese students in Japan was now high. The Hunanese were particularly active, because Huang Hsing and others had organized a revolutionary party, called Hua-hsing Hui and had sent its members back to Hunan to start an uprising. This attempt, though abortive politically, was effective as a surprise tactic to stir the people.

Huang Hsing, also known as Huang K'e-ch'iang, was a good student of the Liang-hu Academy, Hupeh, and an admirer of T'an Ssu-t'ung and T'ang Ts'ai-ch'ang. He had been sent by means of government funds to study in Japan, where he enrolled in a short course at a normal school. In 1903 he was one of the sponsors of a volunteer corps to fight against the Russian occupation of Manchuria. In the spring of the following year he organized the Hua-hsing Hui, which was joined by most of the Hunanese students in Japan. Their strategy was to agitate the learned circles in China on the one hand, and on the other to make alliances with secret societies.

Because of Liu K'uei-i's friendship with Ma Fu-i, the head of the Elder Brother's Society, Huang returned to China with Liu. In Changsha he invited Chang Chi and others to teach in the Ming-teh middle school, and Wu Lu-chen to direct physical education. An academy for studying of the Japanese language was opened in the Hsiao-wu Gate of Changsha to serve as secret headquarters for the revolutionists. Liu K'uei-i was responsible for an alliance with the secret society members, while another leader, Yang Tu-sheng, resided at Shanghai as a liaison officer. Soon several hundred students had joined the party.

Because of some difficulty in allying themselves with the secret-society members, the Association Against the Common Enemy [*T'ung-ch'iu Hui*] was established solely to appeal to these secret groups and to enlist their support. This new society was said to have gained approximately 100,000 members. Uprisings were then planned in five cities, including Changsha and Yochow, on the empress dowager's birthday in 1904. Following Huang Hsing, Sung Chiao-jen returned from

Japan to Hunan to direct the uprising in Changteh. Unexpectedly, ten days before the empress dowager's birthday, November 29, the plot was revealed and the Hunan governor ordered the arrest of the rebels. Huang Hsing narrowly escaped through the protection of two priests of the Roman Catholic Church and fled to Shanghai. Sung Chiao-jen, who was in Changsha on a business trip, also fled to Shanghai upon learning of the incident.

When Sung reached Shanghai, he discovered that Huang Hsing, Ch'en T'ien-hua, Chang Chi, Chang Shih-chao, and about ten others had been jailed on account of their involvement in an assassination attempt. Sung immediately went to Japan and was followed by Huang and the others, after their release from prison through the help of some influential Hunanese. Arriving in Japan, they were all admired by Chinese students. Huang now published in Japan a magazine entitled *Twentieth-Century China* [*Erh-shih shih-chi chih Chih-la*]. Sun Yat-sen's arrival in Japan at the end of August occasioned a meeting, in the clubhouse of Huang's magazine, at which Sun discussed some problems of the organization of a revolutionary party.

On September 9 the T'ung-meng Hui was at last formed in the headquarters of the Japanese Black Dragon Society in Tokyo. On September 29 the constitution of the T'ung-meng Hui was distributed and a formal inauguration meeting was held, in which Sun Yat-sen was elected general director [*tsung-li*]. Among other officers Huang Hsing was treasurer; Ch'en T'ien-hua, secretary; Sung Chiao-jen and Cheng Chia-sheng, membership directors; Wang Ching-wei and Feng Tzu-yu, counselors. The membership represented all provinces of China except Kansu.

The Three Principles of the People

The platform of the T'ung-meng Hui was Sun Yat-sen's Three Principles of the People, which had been previously formulated. When Sun Yat-sen had organized the earlier Hsing-Chung Hui [1894] he had

had only the two principles—nationalism and democracy—in his mind. During his three years in Europe (1896-1898) his ideas expanded:

> After I was set free from the kidnapping in London I sojourned in Europe for a while in order to make an investigation on the spot of its politics and customs, and here I made friends with eminent citizens within and without government circles. In two years I learned a great deal from what I saw and heard. I began to realize that to make a nation rich and strong, or to promote democracy as had been done in European nations, was not sufficient to make the people really happy. And that is why the progressive thinkers of Europe are still carrying on a movement of social revolution. I wish to make one all-out effort and be forever at ease by adopting the principle of people's livelihood (*min-sheng*) in order to solve the problem of nationalism and democracy simultaneously.[3]

This statement confirms the fact that the Three Principles of the People were conceived during Sun's sojourn in Europe. Sun did not announce these new ideas, however, until 1905, when the oath for the formation of the party was made in Brussels. Such phrases, from this oath as, "Let us drive away the Manchu barbarians, restore China, create a republic, and equally distribute the land," were a crude form of the Three Principles of the People. When the T'ung-meng Hui was formally organized in Tokyo, the oath was still exactly the same as it was in Europe. The name of the party and the wording of the oath were then discussed with several members, who suggested that the name be "Revolutionary Covenant Against the Manchus" [*Tui-Man T'ung-meng Hui*]. However, after Sun Yat-sen remarked that the aims of the revolution were not limited to anti-Manchuism but included the dissolution of a despotic monarchy and the creation of a republic, the name *Chung-kuo T'ung-meng Hui* was decided upon.

Next the wording of the oath was discussed. Several members disagreed with "the equal distribution of land" and demanded the elimination of that phrase; but Sun's patient explanation and argument eventually won their assent. It is evident that many T'ung-meng Hui members at the time of its founding believed only in nationalism in the narrowest sense—that is, anti-Manchuism. They had no clear conception nor any genuine belief in the principles of democracy and the people's livelihood. For this reason it was easy to gain support for the overthrow of the Manchu regime; but for this same reason, the organization of the T'ung-meng Hui was very weak.

After the founding of T'ung-meng Hui, Sun Yat-sen published an editorial in the first issue of his party organ the *People's Tribune* [*Min-pao*]. He said in that essay:

> I consider that the evolution of Europe and America was based on three leading principles, namely nationalism, democracy, and socialism or people's livelihood. The fall of the Roman Empire gave rise to nationalism and independence in various nations of Europe. When these various nations became monarchies, with despotism and intolerable distress inflicted upon the people under their jurisdictions, the principle of democracy was aroused. At the end of the eighteenth and the beginning of the nineteenth century a number of despotic monarchies were replaced by constitutional monarchies. The more the world progressed, the more did human wisdom. When, out of the experience of a thousand years, material inventions were made during the last hundred years, economic problems succeeded the political problems and thus socialism or people's livelihood emerged; the twentieth century may be considered the era of socialism. The three major principles were all concerned with the people, and through the development of these principles, the Europeans were largely well governed. ...

Now China has been plagued by despotism for over a thousand years. She has been afflicted with alien races, encroached upon by foreign nations. The principles of nationalism and democracy are indispensable for us, while the principle of people's livelihood or socialism, which the Europeans and Americans are worrying about, has not yet affected China very much and it is easy for her to remove its defects. [4]

This is the first time that Sun Yat-sen expresses his ideas of the Three Principles in his writings. Later on, in the anniversary issue of the *People's Tribune*, Sun Yat-sen's long speech on the Three Principles was printed and the editor also discussed the problem of people's livelihood. But the majority of the T'ung-meng Hui members paid most attention to nationalism or anti-Manchuism.

REVOLUTIONISTS VERSUS CONSTITUTIONAL MONARCHISTS

The Revolutionary Party had published a newspaper in Hong Kong (from 1899 to 1903) to argue against the Canton newspaper and a Hong Kong daily, both of which were owned by the Emperor Protection Society. In Honolulu the *Daily News of People's Life* [*Min-sheng jih-pao*], first published in 1904, carried on arguments against the *New China* of the Emperor Protection Society. In San Francisco a revolutionist paper [*Ta-t'ung-pao*] carried on debates with the *Literature Star* [*Wen-hsing*], which was an organ of the same society. In Japan the *Twentieth Century China*, which had changed its name to the *People's Tribune*, continued its revolutionary propaganda. All these arguments, however, had little effect on the young intellectuals in the interior of China. But when the *People's Tribune* was published by the T'ung-meng Hui as an organ for debate with the *New People's Miscellany*, edited by Liang Ch'i-ch'ao, the arguments between the Revolutionary Party and the Constitutional Monarchist Party became increasingly more vehement. Liang Ch'i-ch'ao had now met a formidable enemy and his predominant position in public life was gradually shaken by the Revolutionary Party.

The editors-in-chief of the *People's Tribune* were Wang Ching-wei, Ch'en T'ien-hua, Hu Han-min, and Chang Ping-lin. In less than one month after the newspaper's first issue, Ch'en T'ien-hua was so infuriated at the announcement by the Japanese minister of education of his intention of eliminating the "unprincipled Chinese students in Japan" that he committed suicide by jumping into the ocean. When the *Tribune* was first published, Chang Ping-lin was still in a Shanghai prison and he remained in custody until the middle of 1906. When he had served his sentence he was escorted by T'ung-meng Hui members to Tokyo, where he edited the *Tribune* for a time.

Soon after the publication of the *People's Tribune*, the abilities of Wang Ching-wei and Hu Han-min as writers and leaders were recognized by a large number of young intellectuals. Wang frequently challenged Liang Ch'i-ch'ao, and their arguments grew more and more heated. By 1910, when Liang's new magazine, the *National Spirit* [*Kuo-feng-pao*] was being published, the Revolutionary Party had already entered a period of direct action.

The heated arguments between the revolutionary *People's Tribune* and Liang's *New People's Miscellany* included the whole scope of the Three Principles of the People. The general readers, however, were chiefly interested at this time in the arguments concerning nationalism and democracy. The *Tribune* made a greater impression on the youth than did the *Miscellany*. The young people applauded innovation and opposed any form of conventionalism or conservatism. The *Tribune* was consistent in propagating the Three Principles, whereas the position of the *Miscellany* fluctuated.

Liang Against the Revolutionists

Liang Ch'i-ch'ao's feeling was that a newspaper should serve as a guide to the people and should change its stand according to the needs of the time. The readers, however, regarded this flexibility as contradictory and opportunistic, as "a pile of broken glass, some of which is red in color and some white, but no one can determine the real color and shape of the whole piece." Liang himself frequently said, "I do not mind challenging my own ideas of today with those I had yesterday."

Liang claimed to be a follower of Wang Yang-ming's principle of conscience. "If my viewpoint guided by my conscience today is like this, then I do according to my conscience of today; if my conscience of tomorrow receives some further enlightenment, then I will do according to my conscience of tomorrow." What Liang did not realize was that conscience has no absolute standard, that it is vacillating, and that the conscience of the majority could not always be consistent with his own.

Although Liang Ch'i-ch'ao predicted bad effects from a revolution and a republic—such as internal dissension, struggle for power among the revolutionary leaders themselves, and endless disorder—to people having no previous experience of such a radical change such effects were inconceivable. On the other hand, as described by the *People's Tribune*, the corruption of the Manchu government, the insincerity of the reform, the falsehood of the constitutional monarchy, the malign intent of the monarchy's anti-Chinese actions were facts understood by everybody. The revolutionists criticized the government for such policies. Even Liang himself frequently attacked the government for its corruption. Young people tend to see present evils clearly but are slow in discerning the evil which may come in the future. Thus it was easier for them to be swayed by the *Tribune* than by Liang's articles.

Nevertheless, Liang's words sometimes served to promote the idea of revolution. For instance:

> If the nation is doomed, it would be better to have a revolution with the hope that the nation may be saved from destruction. ... If these revolutionists are truly punishable, the government should be punished first. ... The government still seems unaware of its corruption: the ruthless slaughter of the people continues and some government officials still use the murder of revolutionists as a short cut to promotion. The government has even requested that revolutionary leaders be returned from the foreign countries where they are seeking refuge, thus breaking the precedent of international law, which offers asylum to political offenders. Alas! Can this be stopped?[5]

Thus Liang revealed his strong resentment against the Manchu government. He also said:

> I have no affection for the Manchus. Whenever I read the *Ten Days' Diary of Yang-chow* and the *Massacre of the City of Chia-ting* by the Manchu conquerors, my eyes overflow with warm tears. Therefore, several years ago, I advocated anti-Manchuism; even though my teacher and friends reprimanded me every day, I refused to change my mind, and even today my feeling is still the same. ... If there is a way which can save the nation and at the same time help us to take revenge against the Manchus, I would certainly be delighted to follow it. ... Unfortunately, the two, the saving of the nation and the revenge, are incompatible, for to take revenge it is necessary to have violent revolution, and a violent revolution must ... necessarily terminate the life of the nation. ... I prefer to bear humiliation under the Manchu regime rather than to become a man without a nation.[6]

Liang intended to admonish the people for their anti-Manchuism, but unconsciously he admitted the existence of a racial prejudice and hatred which could not be entirely eliminated, a fact which the revolutionists wished to have reiterated constantly and loudly.

While the anti-Manchu sentiment did not wane, the anti-Chinese feeling was stimulated. The revolutionary tide became increasingly stronger and anti-Chinese demonstrations by the Manchus became daily more conspicuous.

After all, the most important problem separating the Manchu and the Chinese could not be solved by written debates. In his last testament, Ch'en T'ien-hua wrote:

> The Manchus and the Chinese can never stand together on the earth. While we oppose them with words, they fight us with action; while we have only recently been against them, they have been our enemy for the last two hundred years; while we withdraw, they advance. How can we expect them to give up their jealousy and suspicion and willingly cooperate with us in national affairs? If we desire to save China, the only way is to sever completely our relations with them and govern the people with Chinese alone.[7]

Herein is revealed Ch'en's deep understanding of the current problem concerning the Manchus and the Chinese. A glance at the many instances of anti-Chinese discrimination by the Manchu government during the preparatory period for constitutional monarchy confirms the truth of his words.

A SUGAR-COATED CONSTITUTIONAL MONARCHY: THE COVERT STRUGGLE BETWEEN MANCHUS AND CHINESE

After the five ministers had been sent abroad to investigate government structures, other high officials from time to time submitted memorials to the throne requesting the adoption of a constitutional monarchy. After the five ministers had returned to China with the suggestion that a constitutional monarchy be established, an imperial conference announced, on September 1, 1906, that the government was preparing a constitution and was initiating a reform of the administration. Immediately Tsai-tse and others were appointed to draft a plan for a new administrative system, and I-k'uang and Ch'ü Hung-chi were appointed to review it.

In October the revised governmental system was proclaimed. The Bureau for the Promotion of Political Affairs [*T'u-pan cheng-wu-ch'u*] was changed to Bureau for the Discussion of Political Affairs [*Hui-i cheng-wu-ch'u*]. In August 1907 the Bureau for Political Investigation was changed into the Bureau for Constitutional Compilation, which was to be under the direction of the Bureau for Discussion of Political Affairs. This, in turn, was to be under the control of the Grand Secretariat. In September several high officials were commissioned to investigate further the constitutional systems of Japan, England, and Germany. P'u-lun and Sun Chia-nai were made president and vice-president of the National Assembly to prepare for such an organization. Provincial and district assemblies were also ordered for discussing local governmental affairs.

An information bureau was to be established in each province and a statistical office in each ministry. In July 1908, regulations for the provincial assemblies and for the election of their members were proclaimed. In September, outlines for the constitution, the parliament, and the election law were submitted by I-k'uang and others. An imperial decree sanctioned these outlines, and orders were given for their completion in nine years.

The Bad Faith Underlying Government Reforms

What was the real intention of the Manchu government in preparing a constitutional monarchy? As for the empress dowager's policy, her intention was procrastination. In 1908 she was seventy-four years old, and she wanted to keep a firm hold on her authority for the rest of her life. Her anticipation was that at the end of nine years she might no longer be alive. If this were the case, then she would not care what sort of government the people had. A local French newspaper of that year correctly analyzed the empress dowager when it commented, during the visit of the investigating ministers from China, that her expressed intention to create a constitutional monarchy was her method of fooling the people.

As for the policy of the Manchu nobles, their intention was simply to concentrate all authority in the hands of the Manchus. They knew that the tide of constitutional monarchy could not be repulsed. They knew, too, that the power of the governors-general was so great and the political ability and numerical strength of the Chinese so far superior to that of the Manchus that once a real constitutional monarchy was effected, the Chinese would gain absolute control. Therefore the nobles, under the name of a constitutional movement, actually struggled to concentrate the power in their own hands.

As for the policy of the high Chinese officials, although a few of them were still loyal to the imperial family, they intended to use the constitutional movement as a means of breaking up the Manchu monopoly of political power. The majority of these Chinese believed the words of Liang Ch'i-ch'ao: "In free political competition, whoever has superior ability must occupy the superior position. Since the political ability of the Chinese is far greater than that of the Manchus, there will be no problem whether the Manchus or the Chinese will have the predominant position under a constitutional government."[8]

With these various selfish motives at work behind the scene, it was no wonder that a constitutional monarchy could not be put into practice. The result was a mere show of preparation for this new form of government. In actuality the Manchus and the Chinese were struggling for power within the court. Nevertheless, in spite of their individual ability and numerical strength, the high Chinese officials were unable to gain a victory in their struggle against the Manchus, as the following governmental reorganization reveals.

Struggles Over Reorganization

The reorganization of the governmental system was based on the report of Tsai-tse and Tuan-fang to the empress dowager, after their investigative trip. They strongly recommended that Japan's constitution serve as a model for China and stressed the urgent need for reform of the official system. An imperial conference determined four major policies: (1) In accordance with the wishes of the empress dowager a constitutional government was to be put in effect within or after ten years. (2) The constitutional government was to be patterned after that of Japan. (3) The power of the present governors-general was to be reduced to that of Japanese magistrates in prefects or districts, and the military power of the former governors-general was to be yielded to the central government. (4) The central government was to be reorganized to correspond to the Japanese governmental structure.

These general policies had been predetermined by the Manchus. During the conference for the reorganization of the administration there were many struggles and disagreements. Tsai-tse, T'ieh-liang, and others pleaded vigorously for a reduction of the powers of the governors-general; but, unexpectedly, the first dissenter was Yüan Shih-k'ai, who was a participant in this conference. According to a Chinese newspaper, the purpose of the imperial court in reorganizing the local government was to curb the authority of the governors-general, but Yüan Shih-k'ai considered this motion unfavorable to his own authority. I-k'uang urged that the main problem of the central government be discussed first and that this local problem be left until later.

During the discussion of the central-government organization there were also many struggles over the loss of jobs. Consequently, any discussion of the Grand Council, the Imperial Household, the Eight Banners, the Hanlin Academy, and the eunuchs was assiduously avoided. Finally, on November 6, 1906, the reorganized governmental system was proclaimed by an imperial decree.

The essential ideas of this reform system were concentration of responsibility, elimination of defects, and promotion of real efficiency in order to eliminate the incompetence which weak officials had tried to cover up by false and exaggerated reports of their accomplishments. The Grand Secretariat, the Grand Council, the Ministry of Foreign Affairs, and the Ministry of Civil Appointments were to remain as before. The police office was to be called the Ministry of Civil Affairs. The Ministry of Public Revenue was to be changed into the Ministry of Income and Expenditure, to which the Office of Financial Administration was to be annexed. The Court of Sacrificial Worship, the Court of Imperial Entertainments, and the Court of State Ceremonials were to be incorporated into the Ministry of Rites. The Ministry of War would be renamed the Ministry of the Army, to which the Office for Military Drill and the Court of the Imperial Equerries would be attached. A Ministry of the Navy was to be established, and the Office for Military Consultation was to be managed for the time being by the Ministry of the Army. The Ministry of Punishment was to be changed into the Ministry of Law to take charge of judicial affairs. The Ministry of Work was to be incorporated into the Ministry of Agriculture, Industry, and Commerce. Special offices were to be opened to take charge of steamships, railways, telegraphs, and the postal system. These offices would be under the Ministry of Post and Communications. For each ministry there was to be one minister and two vice-ministers, with no preference shown for either Chinese or Manchus.

New offices to be organized were the National Assembly [*Tzu-cheng yüan*][9] for the organized expression of public opinion, and an Audit

Department [*Shen-chi yüan*] for checking expenditures. As for the Imperial Clan Court, the Grand Secretariat, the Hanlin Academy, the Imperial Board of Astronomy, the Imperial Equipage Department, the College of Imperial Physicians—these remained unchanged.

After the proclamation of this new official system, the staunch advocates of a constitutional government were greatly disappointed. An editorial in the *Shanghai Times* said: "This reform is nothing but a change in the names of several offices and an elimination of a few old and powerless officials. Nothing else has been accomplished." Japanese newspapers were particularly satirical. Said the Tokyo *Daily News* [*Asahi Shimbun*]: "This kind of cabinet reorganization does not appear in any other nation. It can hardly avoid the criticism that it makes a big noise with little substance." The most notable aspect of the change was the redistribution or reassignment of personnel to key position.

The new list of cabinet members named seven Manchus, four Chinese, one Mongol, and one Chinese Bannerman. Since the Mongols and the Bannermen were usually partisans of the Manchus, the result was that now only one-third of the key government positions were retained by Chinese. Formerly the posts had been divided equally between Manchus and Chinese. Naturally the Chinese officials, who had expected a real constitutional government, were disappointed. Quite as naturally, from the viewpoint of the Manchu nobles, the reform was a success.

Efforts to Weaken the Governors-General

The powers of the governors-general posed the most difficult and vital problem, for the Manchus, in the entire reorganization scheme. On this problem a Japanese newspaper commented:

> The prerequisite for the solution of China's constitutional problem is the discontinuation of the governors-general system. These governors-general are actually vice-emperors. So long as this

system continues, concentration of power in the central government is out of the question and China will have to imitate the federal government system. The struggle between T'ieh-liang and Yüan Shih-k'ai centers upon this fundamental problem.[10]

The Manchu nobles were well aware of this, but found difficulty in getting to the root of their problem. Although in June 1907 the reorganization of the local governmental system was proclaimed, there was no change at all in the military and financial authority of the governors-general. The only changes made involved the names of minor officials, an increase in the police organization and in the office for promoting industry, and the abrogation of the *taotai*.

Later on, two methods for solving the governor-general problem were evolved. One provided for the collection of taxes by financial supervisors appointed by the central government in order to gain greater control of provincial finances. The other transferred the most powerful governors-general to the central government under the guise of promotion, but with the actual purpose of gaining more control over them.

The general intention involved absorbing the military powers of all governors-general into the ministry of the army. The four strategic positions in North China were transferred to the direct control of the army ministry. Financial supervisors were appointed, and the most powerful governors-general, Yüan Shih-k'ai and Chang Chih-tung, were transferred to Peking as Grand Councilors in August 1907, with Yüan Shih-k'ai concurrently holding the office of minister of foreign affairs. It was openly declared that the pivotal positions in the central government had been given to the Chinese to show that there was no longer any distinction between the Manchus and Chinese. In actuality it was planned that the two dominant governors-general, Yüan and Chang, would be demoted first and that gradually the power of the other governors-general would be eliminated.

Contrary to expectations, the success of these plans was negligible. Eventually they ended in failure. From our point of view, it would seem that military and financial power should unquestionably be in the hands of the central government. Unfortunately, in China at this time the concentration of such power served the purpose of anti-Chinese discrimination and it was no wonder that even the advocates of a constitutional monarchy were opposed to it.

Manchu-Chinese Feuds Intensified

The covert struggle between high Manchu and Chinese officials became very tense. There was constant antagonism between the Chinese and Manchu office seekers. According to an eyewitness: "On the waiting list for each ministry are more than a thousand persons, and the Manchu and Chinese office seekers will not even talk to each other. In the offices the Manchus are very domineering and arrogant toward their Chinese associates, and the latter can only bear their insults in silence. Outside the office, the resounding anti-Chinese talk fills the people's ears."

Because of the rumor spread by Kang-i that when the Chinese were strong, the Manchus would be killed, anti-Chinese sentiment had become firmly implanted in the minds of the Manchu nobles. Stories of the conflicts between high Manchu and Chinese officials were common, such as the struggle between Jung-ch'ing and Chang Po-hsi and between I-k'uang and Ch'ü Hung-chi.

In the early years of Peking University [*Ching-shih ta-hsüeh*], Chang Po-hsi was the only person to be appointed a member of the committee of educational affairs [*kuan-hsüeh tn-ch'en*]. He was inclined to be a reformer and was fond of using men skilled in the new ways and known to be liberalminded. Since this galaxy of men trained in modern ideas passed judgment freely, they incited the hatred of the Manchus, who tried to involve Chang in trouble. Chang was frightened and requested the empress dowager to appoint her confidant Jung-ch'ing to be cosuperintendent of the university. Jung-ch'ing was strongly anti-Chinese and wished only to develop the academy for the Eight Banners. He proved to be a stumbling block to Chang and Chang could do nothing without sending him a petition first. Even so, Jung-ch'ing was dissatisfied; his ambition was to monopolize the educational superintendency. Carrying out this scheme, Jung-ch'ing suggested the establishment of a ministry of education with himself as sole minister. This ministry came into existence in the autumn of 1905.

Another case involved Ch'ü Hung-chi, who had previously been a favorite of the empress. He and I-k'uang were both Grand Councilors. Ch'ü's student Wang K'ang-nien, however, was both a member of the reform party and editor of a Peking newspaper, *Ching-pao*, in which he frequently made slurring remarks against I-k'uang and his son Tsai-chen. At this time a censor accused both the father and the son of taking bribes; their case involved numerous other people. Since the teacher-student relation between Ch'ü and Wang was known to everybody, I-k'uang immediately suspected that Ch'ü had instigated the newspaper satire written by Wang, and other Manchu nobles shared this suspicion.

One day when Ch'ü went on duty in the Grand Council, the empress dowager casually revealed her dissatisfaction with I-k'uang's service and her intention of dismissing him from the Grand Council because of the many accusations made against him by numerous people. Upon returning home Ch'ü told his wife of these remarks in the Grand Council. The news spread, reached the ears of a London *Times* correspondent residing in Peking, and ultimately appeared in his newspaper. Infuriated with Ch'u for divulging the conversation, the empress dowager immediately seized the opportunity to demand the impeachment of Ch'ü on the charge that he had had secret communications with both the Peking paper *Ching-pao* and with a foreign correspondent. Consequently Ch'ü was allowed to retire, while I-k'uang remained in his post.

Manchu Intrigue Against Yüan Shih-k'ai

As for the feud between Yüan Shih-k'ai and T'ieh-liang, its development was even more significant. After Yüan had been appointed simultaneously governor-general of Chihli and trade superintendent of the ports in north China, he established in Tientsin several departments such as the offices of military, educational, and agricultural affairs. Under the department of military affairs Yüan imitated the Japanese military organization by setting up three offices: for the general staff, for military training, and for military preparation. This move created a second central government under Yüan; his power was second to none but the throne's.

Nevertheless the Manchu court was not at this time jealous of Yüan and the latter showed no ambition to be independent of the court. In 1903 he sent a memorial to the throne requesting the unification of military administration:

> The military system of the various provinces is not the same. The discipline is not uniform, and rations and weapons differ. The drills are so disparate that in time of peace there is no communication between various provincial army units and in time of war there is neither cooperation nor coordination. It is therefore very difficult to achieve military success unless we plan a military unification.[11]

Previously, in 1902, Yüan had been chosen to train the Bannermen, and he had even requested that the able Manchu T'ieh-liang be appointed director of the Bannermen around Peking. After a few years T'ieh-liang became minister of the army. These events amply attest to the concord which then existed between Yüan and T'ieh.

In the winter of 1903, however, after the bureau of military drill in Peking was organized, the anti-Yüan movement emerged. The bureau had been organized for the purpose of unification of military power under the central government, and at its inception I-k'uang was appointed its director, although the actual power was still wielded by the Peiyang military clique. Among the high officials in the bureau, Hsü Shih-ch'ang, Tuan Ch'i-jui, and Wang Shih-chen were Yüan's subordinates.

At this time most of the Chinese military cadets in Japan had returned to China. Those who had originally been sent abroad by the Peiyang clique were made low-ranking officers. Among the cadets, Liang-pi, an outstanding Manchu noble and graduate of a military school in Japan, pretended to be very friendly to Wu Lu-chen, a member of the revolutionary party. Liang-pi was in reality an active member of the anti-Chinese faction which, involving one group of the cadets returned from Japan, secretly planned, with T'ieh-liang as their leader, an anti-Yüan movement. The struggle between Yüan and T'ieh began with these rivalries and plots among the returned cadets.

Impressed by Liang-pi's gallant appearance, Yüan had hoped to control him for future use by making him colonel of the Twenty-third Division of the Sixth Army, an attractive rank not usually granted so quickly to a returned cadet. But though Liang-pi received a colonel's pay, he never reported to duty. Instead, anti-Yüan sentiment in Peking was becoming more evident daily. Two strong factions now opposed him: the conservative officials who envied his many positions, and the cadets who were seeking military strength for their revolution. Liang-pi was delighted to make an alliance with the revolutionary-minded cadets in order to cover up his anti-Chinese plot. Thus it appeared on the surface that the struggle was between the cadets and the Peiyang military clique, while in reality it proved to be another fight to the finish between the Manchus and the Chinese.

When the reorganization of the official system was discussed and the problem of reducing the power of the governors-general arose, Yüan Shih-k'ai became a needle in the eyes of the Manchu nobles. The proclamation of the new official system coincided with the autumn military maneuvers at Changteh at which both Yüan and T'ieh were ministers of the military inspection. At this moment the anti-Yüan movement in Peking suddenly reached its peak. The censors requested the throne to impeach Yüan, and the Manchu nobles also stirred up trouble. Realizing his position, Yüan begged the throne to dismiss him from all his posts, saying, "The First Division of the army was trained jointly by me and T'ieh-liang; the Second, Third, Fourth, Fifth and Sixth Divisions were commanded and trained by me alone; but since T'ieh-liang has now been made minister of the army, all these divisions should be under the direct control of the ministry except for the Second and Fourth, now stationed in the vicinity of Tientsin where the foreign troops have not withdrawn entirely; since ... it is necessary to have sufficient troops to maintain peace, I therefore request that the Second and Fourth remain under my control in order that I may cope with this situation."[12] The memorial was approved.

Thus only two out of the six divisions of the Peiyang Army were retained by Yüan; the other four were given to T'ieh-liang. This step is considered the first in the success of the anti-Yüan movement. But the Manchu nobles were not to be satisfied until Yüan had relinquished all the divisions over which he had any control.

Yüan also became involved in a minor skirmish with Tsai-chen, son of I-k'uang. When the ministry of commerce was first established, Tsai-chen was its minister. He attempted to seize control of the railroads for this ministry, both by appointing his own secretaries to positions in all the railroad offices and appointing the supervisors and managers of the railways to serve as consultants of the ministry. At this time Yüan Shih-k'ai was a minister-superintendent of one railroad, and his stubborn objection to this plan resulted in imperial disapproval of Tsai-chen's attempt and its eventual frustration. Tsai-chen, who held a prominent position among the nobles as the new minister of agriculture, industry and commerce, was ready to have Yüan dismissed from the governor-generalship of Chihli for his part in this affair. Since many members of the inner court were Yüan's supporters, it was not easy for Tsai-chen to shake his position. Nevertheless, in August 1907, Yüan and Chang Chih-tung were both transferred to the Grand Council—another coup for the imperial nobles in their anti-Yüan movement.

At this time, the Peiyang military circle sympathized with Yüan. That group thought that Yüan's misfortune was caused by the Chinese military cadets just returned from Japan where they had had close associations with Liang-pi. But they did not know that this was a part of T'ieh-liang's plan to get rid of Yüan.

Another far-reaching plan of T'ieh-liang in carrying out his anti-Chinese movement was the establishment of a college for the Manchu nobles. It was his hope that all Chinese soldiers would be placed under the command of Manchu officers, after which the Chinese could be herded like a flock of sheep and the worries of the Manchus would be over. For this reason a college for Manchu nobles was established with the hope that the academic standard would be comparable to that of a military college in foreign countries, and that thereafter high military officers would have to be graduates of this college, while the graduates of the provincial military colleges could only serve as minor officers. Only the descendants of the imperial family and the Eight Banners were to be admitted to the college. Nevertheless, the military college for Manchu nobles did not produce the desired results. The nobles, accustomed to a lascivious and easy life, were not amenable to military discipline.

In sum, these years were a tangle of jealousies and struggles between the Manchus and the Chinese. To hide this tangle the perfunctory preparation for the constitution was an attempt to pull the wool over the eyes of the Chinese. Obviously, there was little hope for an actual constitutional monarchy. In spite of this fact, the members of the Constitutional Party were not discouraged, and as we shall see, continued their activities.

ACTIVITIES OF THE CONSTITUTIONAL PARTY

Theoretically speaking, since the Manchu regime had adopted as its platform the preparation for constitutional government, the Constitutional Party seemed to be in a more advantageous position than the Revolutionary Party, and the advocates of a constitutional monarchy were still exceedingly optimistic. The most popular and influential man in the Constitutional Party was certainly Liang Ch'i-ch'ao. In the summer of 1907 he organized a Political Information Club [*Cheng-wen she*] and issued a declaration outlining its programs, which included a responsible cabinet system, a revised legal system with independent judicial authority, a sound local government with a clear-cut division of authority between central and local governments, and a careful handling of diplomatic affairs so as to maintain China's equality among foreign powers.

In the last paragraph of this declaration Liang further enunciated his methods and expectations:

> The methods of the Political Information Club are proper petitions and orderly actions without the slightest intention of violating the dignity of the imperial family or disturbing the peace of our society. That is the normal behavior for citizens of any constitutional state. Now the decree for constitutional monarchy has been proclaimed and the freedom of public assembly has been proclaimed and political organization has been recognized as the right of the people. ... If some government officials do not obey this imperial decree and stubbornly object to constitutional rights, then such officials are not responsible either to the people or to their emperor.[13]

Liang seems to anticipate governmental interference. He uses "the freedom of assembly" to intimidate meddlesome officials and to encourage his club members to work together toward their aim of a constitutional government.

Though Liang Ch'i-ch'ao had many supporters, he also had many formidable enemies. His first great enemy was the empress dowager. Next were Yüan Shih-k'ai and Chang Chih-tung, with whom Liang was completely incompatible and whom he had repeatedly attacked in his writings. Despite Liang's statement that he had not the slightest intention of violating the dignity of the imperial family, there was a widespread rumor that he wanted to protect the emperor, not the empress dowager, and to preserve China rather than the great Ch'ing dynasty. This dreadful rumor had deeply impressed the Manchu nobles. No matter how hard Liang tried to assure them of his loyalty, they did not trust him.

Within the Constitutional Party there were a great many people who were very enthusiastic and worked hard toward a constitutional government, yet their efforts were viewed by the revolutionists as extremely foolish. Though the way to a constitutional monarchy seemed smooth sailing, in reality rough seas were ahead. From the beginning the Political Information Club had to face attacks from both the Manchu nobles and the revolutionists.

A deliberate interference by the revolutionists in the inauguration meeting of the club in Tokyo is vividly penned by Chang Ping-lin:

> On August 25 the Political Information Club held its first congress to work for constitutional government, with Liang Ch'i-ch'ao as the club leader and with nearly two hundred members and one thousand participants present. A few eminent Japanese such as Inuka Hatasu, who were sympathetic with the aims of the club, had also been invited. Chang Chi, T'ao Ch'eng-chang, and others who advocated immediate revolutionary action attended the meeting too.

> Anticipating some trouble, Liang Ch'i-ch'ao had employed a few strong Japanese fighters as his bodyguards. On the speaker's stand Liang spoke of the parliament, the diet, and so on, and he said, "Now our court has issued the decree and set up a time limit for enforcing a constitution; you people should rejoice." No sooner had he finished this sentence than Chang Chi derided him ... and shouted, "Beat him! Beat him!" Several people rushed at Liang; he jumped to the stairway, ran, and fell on the steps in his haste. Someone threw a sandal at him and hit his cheek.[14]

Thus the meeting was interrupted and ended. When Liang Ch'i-ch'ao subsequently returned to China, however, he promoted with considerable success a constitutional movement in the actual political arena. A number of overseas Chinese submitted a joint petition to the Manchu court requesting the implementing of a constitutional government. Several Hunanese in China also presented a joint petition to the throne asking for a parliament with members elected by the people. Here and there students held frequent meetings and made public speeches eulogizing constitutional government. All these demonstrations were worked out by the members of the Political Information Club.

The Manchu government considered such mass demands, whatever their nature, to be improper. It maintained that the emperor had already announced his preparatory plans for a constitutional monarchy and that there was no legitimate reason for these nonsensical requests from the populace. In December 1907 an imperial decree prohibited students from interfering with political affairs and another severe decree banned public meetings and political speeches in Peking.

Before long the platform of the Political Information Club had been published in many places in China; the Manchu government could no longer tolerate its existence. On July 25, 1908, a member of the Political Information Club who held the government position of secretary in a ministry was dismissed. In August all provincial governors-general and governors were sternly ordered to arrest the entire membership and to allow not a single one to escape prosecution. The Political Information Club, as an organization, then dropped completely out of sight.

Although this club of the Constitutional Party disappeared, there were other organizations working for the same purpose. These included the Association for Preparation of Constitutional Monarchy in Kiangsu and Chekiang, and in Kwangtung the Self-government Association. The members of these associations included many outstanding political and industrial leaders in Kiangsu, Chekiang, and Fukien. They shunned any overt association with K'ang and Liang in order to avoid pressure from the Manchu government. In July 1908 Chang Hsiao-hsü headed the list of names of a union of constitutional associations in a petition to the throne which requested the convening of a parliament. This union, joined in the petition by some members of the Eight Banners, asked the government authorities of Hunan, Hupeh, Kwangtung, Honan, Anhwei, Chihli, Shantung, Szechwan, Kweichow, and other provinces to send delegates to an assembly in Peking.

The throne neither accepted nor suppressed these petitioners, because many of them had some reputation in the traditional society and also had little relation with K'ang and Liang. Moreover, just at this time the Bureau for Compilation of the Constitution had completed and submitted an outline of the constitution and of the laws governing the parliament and the election to the throne. These documents were proclaimed on September 22. In addition, a limit of nine years was fixed for preparing the constitution.

THE CONSTITUTION OF 1908

The outlines of the constitution were very disappointing. It was entirely copied from the Japanese constitution with one modification: the great power of the Chinese emperor was even more unrestricted than that of the Mikado. Such a constitution protected the emperor's authority and rights but offered little benefit to the people.

The Emperor's Authority

According to this constitution, the emperor's authority, in the royal family of the great Ch'ing dynasty, was to control the empire for ten thousand generations to come and was to be respected and obeyed by all the people; the emperor was to be regarded as sacred and inviolable; the emperor had the right to sanction or proclaim a law and to transfer it to the parliament (a law passed by the parliament could not be put into effect until it had been sanctioned by an imperial decree); furthermore, the emperor had the right to open, close, prolong, or disband the parliament; he had the right to open new offices, decide salaries, and promote or degrade all officials without any interference from the parliament; had the power to command the army, navy, and other military organizations, including the mobilization of the standing army, the fixing of the number of soldiers, and all other military matters, none of which could be interfered with by the parliament. The emperor also retained the right to declare war, conclude peace, sign treaties, send envoys, and receive diplomatic ministers. Diplomatic affairs were to be decided by the emperor personally, not by the parliament. He had also the authority to declare martial law; and during an emergency the freedom of the people could be restricted by an imperial decree. He had the right to confer titles, rewards, and amnesty.

With regard to judicial authority, this was to be exercised by the emperor's entrusted judicial office, according to the code sanctioned by him; the code, furthermore, could be changed from time to time by imperial decree. The emperor had the right to issue orders or to authorize others to issue orders. Although the established law could not be changed or abrogated by his order, when urgent matters occurred during a parliamentary recess, the emperor could proclaim a decree which was equivalent to law and could raise necessary funds to meet the exigency—with the provision that these cases were to be turned over for the consent of the parliament when it reconvened in the following year. As to the expenditures permitted to the imperial family, these were to be established by the emperor and withdrawn from the national treasury; with these sums the parliament could not interfere. Great ceremonies involving the imperial family were to be decided upon by the emperor in consultation with the members of the imperial family and with specially appointed ministers; in these matters the parliament also could not interfere.

Articles Concerning the Rights and Duties of the People

All those people who met the standards set up by law or by imperial orders could become civil or military officers and also become members of parliament. Within the sphere of law, officials and common people were to enjoy freedom of writing, publication, public assembly, organization, and so on. An official or a common person was not to be arrested, imprisoned, or fined unless this was done in accordance with the law. The property or house of an official or of the common people was not to be violated without particular reason. Both officials and the common people had the duty of paying taxes and serving in the army according to the law.

The outline of this constitution is not worth comment. Its board of compilers was entirely controlled by the Manchu imperial family. While Tsai-tse was investigating the constitutional government in Japan, Ito Hirobumi explained to him the Japanese constitution by emphasizing the great authority of the Japanese emperor, with no mention of the limitations of the position.[15] Tsai-tse, who was ignorant of Japanese, had to rely upon information supplied through inaccurate translations or interpretations and believed that the Japanese constitution was exactly as Ito had explained it. Tsai-tse, therefore, happily supported the empress dowager's scheme for constitutional government and drew an outline of the constitution as given above.

VICISSITUDES OF THE REVOLUTIONARY PARTY

As for the Revolutionary Party, after the organization of the T'ung-meng Hui, this group had a unified central organ, but it encountered far greater difficulties in carrying on its activities than did the Constitutional Party. The Revolutionists could not act openly and could not set up headquarters in any city of the vast empire; above all, they lacked the means of obtaining the enormous amount of money and material essential for building up military strength. For these same reasons the Constitutionalists continued to believe that there was no way to start a revolution.

Only two fields were open for revolutionary activity: one was to make alliances with the members of secret societies; the other was to stir up mutiny among the soldiers. Such work had already started before the organization of the T'ung-meng Hui. Through the assistance of the French minister of war, Sun Yat-sen had obtained the aid of seven officers of the French military advisory staff who were stationed at Tientsin. After the establishment of the T'ung-meng Hui, Sun ordered Liao Chung-k'ai to set up a secret liaison office at Tientsin. From there members were sent to accompany French military officers on investigations of the conditions in Kwangtung, Kwangsi, Szechwan, and Kweichow as well as in the cities of Nanking and Wuchang in the lower Yangtze Valley, with special attention paid to contacting the local troops. This mission marked the beginning of activities directed by the T'ung-meng Hui.

Seven Uprisings Quelled

From 1906 to 1908 seven attempts were made to overthrow the

Manchu regime by military strength:

1. The attempt at P'ing-hsiang and Liu-yang, Hunan (1906).
2. The attempt at Chaochow and Huang-kang, Kwangtung (1907).
3. The attempt at Huichow, Kwangtung (1907).
4. The attempt at Anking, Anhwei (1907).
5. The attempt at Ch'in-chou and Lien-chou, Kwangtung (1907).
6. The attempt at Chen-nan-kuan, Kwangsi (1907).
7. The attempt at Hokow, a frontier town in southeastern Yunnan (1908).

Of these seven attempts, all except the first and fourth were made wholly by members of the T'ung-meng Hui.

The first attempt, launched at P'ing-hsiang and Liu-yang, Hunan, occurred during a famine in central China. Since hungry vagrants were everywhere, the leaders of the secret societies cooperated with the T'ung-meng Hui to start a riot. Unfortunately, the plot leaked out and the soldiers in Liu-yang mutinied in advance of the determined time and occupied several towns. In response to this success, the soldiers and the miners of P'ing-hsiang also seized a few important spots. Alarmed by the news, the authorities of Hunan, Hupeh, and Kiangsi quickly summoned troops and the rebels were quelled.

Although this riot had been planned by members of the T'ung-meng Hui, its participants formed a motley group. Some followed the standard of the T'ung-meng Hui, hoping to set up a republic of China; others were merely fighting against the Manchu and for the restoration of the Great Chinese Empire. Since the weapons they used were miscellaneous and inferior, the rioters were no match for the government forces. They were doomed from the outset to fail, even though they appeared formidable at first. The headquarters of the T'ung-meng Hui in Tokyo was not aware of this revolutionary attempt until news of its failure was spread abroad.

A number of T'ung-meng Hui members then hurried back to China to agitate among the soldiers along the Yangtze Valley. On account of this P'ing-hsiang and Liu-yang incident the government took vigilant preventive measures, and consequently many T'ung-meng Hui members in Hunan, Hupeh, and Kiangsu were arrested, imprisoned, or executed. These were the first martyrs for the T'ung-meng Hui cause.

After this failure the revolutionary base along the Yangtze Valley was lost. Meanwhile in the Wuhan area a revolutionary organization under cover of church sponsorship and called the Society for Daily Increase of Knowledge [*Jih-chih Hui*], was being used as a headquarters for agitation among the local troops. This agitation was directed by one Revolutionist and by a French military officer in Hupeh. Because of a revolutionary speech made by the Frenchman, however, their secret was discovered by a government spy. The society was subsequently routed and many of its members were arrested. In Nanking the newly organized troops had also been influenced and a number of the army officers had gradually joined the T'ung-meng Hui. A subordinate of Sun Yat-sen, accompanied by a French military officer, came to Nanking and maintained close contact with the military circles. Their plot was also uncovered by spies. The Nanking government arrested the Chinese leaders, and the army officers who had joined the T'ung-meng Hui were dismissed.

All of these failures in China naturally had a severe impact on the T'ung-meng Hui headquarters in Tokyo. When the Manchu government learned that the central organization of the Revolutionary Party was in Tokyo, it requested the Japanese government to deport the prominent leaders of the group. In order to secure advantages for itself the Japanese government complied with the request and ordered Sun Yat-sen to leave the empire in February 1907. Having no choice, Sun left; but, taking with him Hu Han-min and Wang Ching-wei, he next established headquarters in Hanoi, Annam. The sphere of his revolutionary activity was now confined to the bordering areas of Yunnan, Kwangtung, and Kwangsi.

Two riots, one at Chaochow and another at Huichow, occurred in May and June 1907. The secret-society members of Huang-kang district in Chaochow Fu, Kwangtung, had now allied themselves with the Revolutionary Party. Sun Yat-sen had sent his followers to work out an uprising for the purpose of seizing the government arsenal at Huang-kang. A member of the secret society was caught by the police and kept in the military government office. His fellow members surrounded the building and killed several Manchu officials, after which they occupied the fortified city. But this was a temporary success, for reinforcements from Chaochow quickly subdued the rebels. Another revolt at Ch'i-ju-hu, twenty li from the city of Huichow, Kwangtung, was also rapidly put down by government forces.

In August 1907 there was another upheaval, at Ch'in-chou and Lien-chou, Kwangtung. A few months before, a Ten Thousand Men Club had been organized in this area to put up strong opposition to government taxation. The Manchu officials called troops to suppress them, but no sooner had the government forces withdrawn than the club members returned. In Ch'in-chou also restlessness was growing among secret-society members, and the government sent three or four thousand soldiers there to stamp them out. In command of these government forces were two officers, one of whom had already joined the Revolutionary Party; the other had promised to do so when the proper time arrived. Counting on their help when the time came, Sun Yat-sen schemed to enlist the help of club members in Ch'in-chou and Lien-chou and of many retired French army officers and to purchase weapons from Japan in order to organize a great revolutionary army with which to launch an expedition from Ch'in-chou and Lien-chou to Canton, where he hoped to set up his headquarters. But the military supplies from Japan were not obtained and the great expedition had to be supplanted by an attack at Ch'in-chou. The two government commanders, realizing that the party army was weak and that it was under close surveillance by the government, dared not openly change sides. Additional troops were sent by the Manchu officials and the rebels were crushed.

Unsuccessful in Kwangtung, Sun Yat-sen reorganized his forces to attack Kwangsi from Annam. In the vicinity of Chen-nan-kuan there was a group of poorly organized but very brave soldiers. Sun Yat-sen frequently sent messengers to contact them, intending to use them as a vanguard in the attack on Chen-nan-kuan. On the evening of November 18, 1907, a surprise assault on three forts was undertaken, intended to unite those members of the secret societies who had been defeated and who had withdrawn to mountainous areas. After the two forces were joined, the next move was to have been a bombing of Lungchow.

Unfortunately, the members of the secret societies in the more distant mountainous areas could not reach the rendezvous. Sun Yat-sen and Huang Hsing personally led more than a hundred soldiers in holding the three fortresses and withstanding for seven days and nights an attack by several thousand Manchu government soldiers. Finally Sun's rebels were over-whelmed by the government troops and were forced to retreat to Annam.

When Sun Yat-sen passed through Langson, he was discovered by spies of the Manchu government and reported to the local authorities. Later on, the Manchu court negotiated with the French government to expel Sun from Annam. When he left Annam, he ordered Huang Hsing to reenter Ch'in-chou and Lien-chou to gather his comrades in these areas. At the same time Sun ordered another comrade to attack Hokow in order to take Yunnan for a base of operations.

Huang Hsing then moved more than two hundred soldiers from Annam to Ch'in-chou and Lien-chou, where he could move freely, and his reputation as a good fighter became a threat to the local Manchu officials. Unfortunately Huang was compelled to withdraw on account of the shortage of reinforcements. In April 1908 an officer of the revolutionary force attacked Hokow, killed the Manchu government commander at the frontier, and accepted the surrender of part of the government troops. Hsi-liang, governor-general of Yunnan, was greatly alarmed and immediately mobilized crack troops to recapture the city. Shortly thereafter, Huang Hsing also arrived at Hokow, and a combined revolutionary force desperately fought the government troops against great odds. Eventually, however, the revolutionary troops lost Hokow. Huang and others led their forces, more than six hundred strong, in a new retreat to Annam.[16]

But in Annam the revolutionists were not tolerated by the Annam government and the rebel leaders were sent to Singapore. The viceroy of Singapore, who regarded them as insurgents, refused them permission to land until the French government intervened, explaining that they were a legitimate revolutionary force that had been recognized by the French government.

Hereafter, Annam could no longer be used as their base of operations. Sun Yat-sen, who no longer could travel freely to any areas on the border between China and French Indochina, was obliged to return to Europe. During his absence, he entrusted Huang Hsing and Hu Han-min with the burden of his revolutionary projects. Repeated failures, however, with an acute shortage of financial resources and the difficulty of securing a revolutionary base, compelled them to suspend action temporarily. At this point Sun's party had reached its lowest ebb.

The uprising at Anking, in which the famous woman Ch'iu Chin was involved, occurred in June 1907, when Hsü Hsi-lin assassinated the governor of Anhwei, En-ming. Although this uprising was also unsuccessful, it had an invigorating effect on the people. Hsü Hsi-lin, a native of Chekiang, had for a long time cherished the idea of deposing the Manchu and restoring the Chinese to power. He had set up the Ta-tung

Academy at Shaohsing, whence he communicated with many leaders of secret societies in the surrounding districts, planning to initiate a revolution. Shortly thereafter he was sent to Japan to take an entrance examination for a Japanese military academy. Because of his physical condition he was rejected and received police training instead. Upon his return he organized a Restoration Society [*Kuang-fu Hui*]. With him were Ch'iu Chin (who, having also spent several years with the revolutionists in Japan, was now on the staff of Hsü's Ta-tung Academy), T'ao Ch'eng-chang, and others.

Purchasing the government post of *taotai*, Hsü now went to Anhwei to await his appointment. The governor, En-ming, deceived by Hsü's smooth talk, appointed him associate director of the provincial police department and concurrently principal of a police academy. With utmost secrecy Hsü distributed his party members in various key positions and planned a riot in Anhwei. Because he appeared to be a serious worker, En-ming liked Hsü very much and did not suspect his revolutionary purposes. Of Hsü's group T'ao Ch'en-chang tried to establish contact with secret societies of Wu-i and other districts of Chekiang, while Ch'iu Chin served as principal of Ta-tung Academy at Shaohsing. Here she contacted secret societies in the neighboring districts, organized a restoration army, and kept Hsü informed of her activities.

At this period a member of the Revolutionary Party arrested in the lower valley of the Yangtze River was found to be carrying a list of the names of his party members. From this list the governor-general of Liang-Kiang learned that important Revolutionary Party members were assembling in the province of Anhwei and he warned Governor En-ming by telegram to take precautions. En-ming, not knowing that the party leader was Hsü Hsi-lin, his favorite, ordered Hsü to make a confidential investigation. Hsü, fearing discovery, planned to act first. July 24 was graduation day at the police academy. Hsü invited all the high officials of the provincial government to take part in the commencement exercises, hoping to kill them all at once before assembling soldiers and police to start a riot. In this attempt, however, only the governor was shot; the rest escaped. When Hsü commanded his police students to occupy the ammunition storehouse, they were surrounded by government troops. During the fighting several revolutionary leaders were killed, and several others were arrested and subsequently executed.

Upon receiving a telegram from Anhwei, the governor of Chekiang instituted a search for other party members. A man of the gentry class of Chekiang who bore ill feeling toward the family of Ch'iu Chin reported the secret to the governor, who in turn sent troops to the Ta-tung Academy to arrest Ch'iu Chin. Ch'iu Chin was eventually executed and many others were also involved in her case. Later Sun referred to them as the "patriots, such as Hsü Hsi-lin and Ch'iu Chin, inspired by the principles of revolution, who arose to fight for its cause without hesitation."[17]

This particular revolutionary attempt had a profound effect in that it accelerated the steadily increasing antipathy between the Manchus and the Chinese. En-ming was a Manchu. When the other Manchu officials of both high and low rank heard of his assassination, they began to fear for their very lives. On the other side, the ire of the Chinese was aroused by the case of Ch'iu Chin, who was tried before a Manchu judge, Kuei-fu, the prefect of Shaohsing. No evidence of her revolutionary activities was brought out during her trial nor did she confess to any such activity. (While in jail Ch'iu wrote that the autumn wind and the autumn rain would make her die of melancholy.) Ch'iu Chin was executed; also many innocent people who were involved in her trial; furthermore, Kuei-fu's legal assistant and a fellow judge were both dismissed because they protested the injustice of the sentence.

The people of Chekiang were even further aroused when a commissioner from the provincial government, Ch'en I-tung, who came to Shaohsing to re-examine the case, openly criticized the procedures of Kuei-fu, the Manchu judge. After this, the governor of Chekiang, Cheng Tseng-t'i, felt so uneasy that he requested a transfer, as did Kuei-fu also. As to the betrayer of Ch'iu Chin, this enemy of her family was later mysteriously murdered. This phase of the revolution indeed had a great and far-reaching influence affecting all parties.

CHAPTER EIGHT
REVOLUTION VERSUS CONSTITUTIONAL MOVEMENT, 1908 TO 1911

THE SUCCESSION OF HSÜAN-T'UNG

Although the empress dowager Tz'u-hsi played a major part in hastening the fall of the Ch'ing dynasty, at the same time she did much to hold the Manchu regime together during its declining stage. Her experience and political resources were far more powerful than those of the young Manchu nobles. Although she had no real intention of initiating any reform, she was able to control the situation completely even while reform was being demanded from many sides. With many high-sounding phrases she was able to disguise her anti-Chinese sentiments. Before her death every Chinese and Manchu official, whatever his rank or position or his connection with the imperial family, was in her clutches. There was no question but that a Chinese official had to obey her orders and even the proudest and most arrogant princes of royal blood dared not disobey her.

After the death of the empress dowager, however, the fall of the Manchu court was inevitable. Its life might have been prolonged by a few years had Emperor Kuang-hsü lived. Though he lacked great ability and any far-reaching plan, he had already shown himself able to weather storms and misfortunes. He probably would not have been so narrow-minded and harsh as other Manchus like Tsai-feng. Though he might have had no way to resolve the enmities between the Chinese and the Manchus, the chances are that he would have known better than to try to concentrate state power in the hands of a few members of the royal family, a move which further aggravated the ill feeling between the two factions. This is, of course, mere speculation. But the emperor did not outlive Tz'u-hsi. Their deaths marked a significant turning point in the political status of the Manchus.

The death of Emperor Kuang-hsü and of the empress dowager occurred in November 1908 two months after the imperial constitution was proclaimed.

Strange Death of the Emperor, 1908

There is no question but that the empress dowager died of illness on November 15; but the exact date of and the reason for the death of the emperor are still in question. One rumor asserts that he died of an illness on November 14. Another rumor maintains that he died at the hands of the empress dowager. Still another rumor suggests that even Yüan Shih-k'ai participated in the plot to end his life. Although none of these rumors can be verified, there are many suspicious aspects to the case, as may be seen in the account in Yün Yü-ting's *Ch'ung-ling ch'uan-hsin lu*:

> The emperor enjoyed such excellent health that for thirty-four years he was never ill and never absent from court functions for even a single day. ... After his return from Sian he lived in compulsory retirement without interfering in state affairs. The eunuchs who surrounded him were replaced by the confidants of the empress dowager. He sat idly in a small room, spending his life in melancholy solitude. In the autumn of 1908 the news of his illness was suddenly spread, and famous physicians were summoned to treat him. When the physicians came to feel his pulse, he put his two hands on the desk without uttering a single word. ... If any physician tried to ask him a question, he would grow very angry. ... Those physicians who examined him agreed unanimously that his health was normal. On November 3 he led all the high courtiers in the birthday celebration of the empress dowager. The officials in attendance, who were responsible for keeping a record of the emperor's daily life [Yün Yü-

ting was one of these], had been assembled first at the threshold of the empress's palace. The emperor walked to that spot. ... The keepers noticed that the emperor tried to open the gate and that he exercised his legs to prepare himself for long kneeling during the celebration.

After a while, a decree from the empress dowager was suddenly proclaimed to the effect that the emperor was sick in bed and that he should be excused from leading the courtiers in performing the ceremony.

Upon hearing this the emperor cried bitterly. At that time the empress dowager had been suffering from diarrhea for several days, and someone had slanderously accused the emperor before the empress dowager of being elated when he heard of her illness. The empress dowager said in anger, "I cannot die before him." ...

On November 11 Prince Ch'ing [I-k'uang, the emperor's father] was ordered by the empress dowager to leave the palace to investigate something, and he did not return until November 14. It was thought by some that he had been purposely sent out of the way. On the twelfth, imperial guards were increased at all gates of the palace, and people who entered and left the palace were very carefully examined. ... It was rumored that the emperor had died. On the thirteenth all was quiet, but in the afternoon a decree was proclaimed to the effect that Prince Ch'un [Tsai-feng] was to be regent. On the fourteenth the queen, going to see the emperor in his bedroom, found that he had died, the exact time of his death being unknown. She rushed out, crying, and reported the sad news to the empress dowager, who said nothing but heaved a great sigh. ... The empress dowager died one day after the emperor's death.[1]

The Influence of Yüan Shih-k'ai

Judging from the history of the relations between Emperor Kuang-hsü and the empress dowager, one cannot help being suspicious of the real cause of his death. In particular Yüan Shih-k'ai, who had been deeply involved in the *coup d'état* of 1898, would have found his life in great danger if the emperor had survived the empress dowager; for this reason he was suspected of having had a part in the plot. It was rumored that Yüan supported and even suggested P'u-i's succession to the throne and the appointment of his father, Prince Ch'un [Tsai-feng, a younger brother of Emperor Kuang-hsü] to be regent.

According to the account of Yüan Shih-k'ai's life by his students, *Jung-an ti-tzu chi*:

> When Emperor Kuang-hstü's illness became daily more serious, the empress dowager called a conference to discuss the problem of finding, in advance, a successor to the throne. Yüan was then in a very important position and was much trusted by the empress dowager; he could advise the empress as intimately as if he were a member of the same family. The eldest son of Prince Ch'un [Tsai-feng] was frequently carried to the inner court, and the empress dowager confidentially consulted Yüan about the possibility of making the child emperor. Yüan supported her idea wholeheartedly. ... When Emperor Kuang-hsü passed away, the young child was made his successor under the title Hsüan-t'ung. Yüan worried because the empress dowager was old and members of the royal family were fighting for the succession; thus it appeared clear that a disturbance would naturally occur while the new emperor was yet an infant unless there was somebody to steer the affairs of the state. He therefore suggested that Prince Ch'un [Tsai-feng] be made regent. On November 15 came the sudden death of the empress dowager, and Yüan, in cooperation with two or three courtiers, was able to decide on state policy at leisure and without any trouble.[2]

It is to be noted that Yüan Shih-k'ai had been compelled to relinquish his military duties, and at the command of several court nobles, had been transferred to the posts of minister of foreign affairs and grand councilor. On the surface, Yüan's military power was taken away, but in reality the officers of the six divisions of the Peiyang Army, who were his old subordinates, still kept in close touch with him. The chief grand councilor and the head of the ministry of foreign affairs, I-k'uang, and the vice-minister of the army, Yin-ch'ang, were both close associates of Yüan, and both tried to support him. Since the empress dowager had much confidence in Yüan, he therefore wielded great power in the nerve center of the government. It is quite conceivable, therefore, that Yüan would participate in the discussion of such pivotal problems as finding a successor to the throne.

The Dismissal of Yüan Shih-k'ai

Yüan knew that immediately on the death of the empress dowager his own position would be in danger. Even if he relied expressly on the protection of I-k'uang and Yin-ch'ang, he could not withstand the young nobles among the Manchus. He therefore tried his best to make an alliance with Tsai-feng in the hope that the latter would be grateful enough for his support to forget the previous enmity over Tsai-feng's deceased older brother, Emperor Kuang-hsü. This too is understandable.

But Tsai-feng sided with the young Manchu nobles. In less than a month after Emperor Hsüan-t'ung ascended to the throne, Yüan Shih-k'ai was dismissed by an imperial decree which was very obviously the idea of the regent. Yüan was sent home "to recuperate."

When Yüan was still working in the ministry of foreign affairs, he had advocated an amicable policy toward the United States and a plan for the exchange of ambassadors between the two countries. After consulting I-k'uang, Yüan had taken upon himself the privilege of reporting alone to the empress dowager and managed to secure her approval of this plan. It was regrettable that Yüan did this without even mentioning his colleague I-k'uang, who was of equal rank in the ministry, for this incident provided a reason for several officials to seek his expulsion from the government. (This incident has been cited by Yüan's apologists as the main cause for his later expulsion, but in all fairness it can only be regarded as a subsidiary rather than a main cause.)

When Yüan was driven from office, a rumor was current that a member of the royal family had suggested that he be put to death, but that fear of a revolution by the Peiyang Army prevented the plan from being carried out. Another rumor asserted that the regent had sent telegrams to consult the six divisional commanders of the Peiyang Army and that most of them had requested permission to resign their commissions rather than face a mutiny among their own troops. The nobles who had suggested that Yüan be executed were discouraged and had to abandon their plan. But such rumors can never be fully verified. Had Yüan been put to death, the history of China's politics in the following twenty years might have been different. But the fall of the Manchu regime would still have been inevitable because the ill will between the Manchus and the Chinese was too deep-seated to be pacified easily. Furthermore, men of ability among the Manchu authorities were indeed extremely scarce.

The New Regime and Reformist Hopes

When the news of Tsai-feng's regency and of Yüan Shih-k'ai's expulsion spread over the country, speculation on Tsai-feng's course of action and on the possible outcome of the political situation varied. The Constitutionalists for their part believed that since Tsai-feng was the younger brother of Emperor Kuang-hsü, he would be able to carry on the ambitions of his deceased brother and promote the reform programs effectively; that he must be a determined and resolute person for daring to expel Yüan Shih-k'ai without hesitation; and that he would restore to important positions all the reform leaders who had been dismissed in the antireform *coup d'état* of 1898. Hence the outlook for a constitutional government seemed to the Constitutionalists to be very hopeful.

But unhappily Tsai-feng, after all, was only the younger brother of Emperor Kuang-hsü and not the emperor himself; his rejection of Yüan was motivated by his scheme to prevent the Chinese from wielding state power. The expectations of K'ang and Liang were not to be fulfilled until the revolution of 1911 in Wuchang and Hankow.

According to Yün Yü-ting the people in general also had great hope at first that the regent would carry out the unaccomplished task of the former emperor. Through two years of Tsai-feng's regency K'ang and Liang had been repeatedly recommended for recall from foreign countries to government positions, but they were never reinstated by the regent; the blood of the six martyrs for reform continued to go unavenged. The attitude of the Constitutionalists changed perforce from hope to disappointment.

The Revolutionists, on the other hand, had not originally expected the regent to carry out plans for a constitutional government nor to restore the reformists to government positions. But after Yüan's expulsion they changed their minds and assumed that Tsai-feng was determined to carry out the reform program and to use K'ang and Liang again. From their point of view Tsai-feng would still be a great hindrance to the revolution. However, their conclusions were just as wrong as those of the Constitutionalists.

There was a small group within the Revolutionary Party who wished that some of the governors-general might become Revolutionists. Several members of this group, who had returned from their study in Europe, had sent letters to Yüan Shih-k'ai inviting him to become a member of their party. Upon learning of Yüan's dismissal, some of this group regarded it as a great loss to the revolutionary forces. Others, more optimistically, regarded Yüan's expulsion as an excellent opportunity to persuade his troops, who might be strongly resentful of the dismissal of their superior, to start a revolution. That these two attitudes were neither entirely correct nor entirely wrong may be seen in the lukewarm reaction of the Peiyang Army toward the Manchu government in 1911.

All in all, Tsai-feng's regency and Yüan Shih-k'ai's expulsion fed the imaginations and hopes of the people; these two events had a vital connection with the future of the Manchu government.

CONCENTRATION OF POWER IN THE ROYAL FAMILY

During his regency, Tsai-feng seemed to be enthusiastic for the preparation of a constitutional monarchy. In December of 1908 he proclaimed that any decree must be countersigned by the Grand Councilors, just as the cosignature of the premier is required in European countries which have constitutional monarchies. In March of the next year another decree was issued announcing that the government had determined to adopt the constitution. In October the provincial assemblies [*tzu-i-chü*] were organized, and in January 1910 regulations for local government and for the compilation of the legal code were announced. In October the National Assembly [*Tzu-cheng-yüan*] was inaugurated and a law court was introduced in each of the provincial capitals and trade ports. In November, P'u-lun and Tsaitse were appointed high officials in charge of the compilation of a constitution.

During these same two years a governor-general of Shen-Kan [Shensi and Kansu] was dismissed because he had sent a memorial to the throne denouncing the preparations for constitutional reform; and, for the same reason, a few other minor officials were also discharged. All of this indicates that the regent took the preparation for a constitution seriously. Nevertheless, his zeal for the constitution was entirely different from that of the Constitutionalists, who wished to establish a parliament with real power and a cabinet which would be responsible for the parliament. These two government organs, they believed, would be the only means of saving China.

Tsai-feng, meanwhile, was cognizant only of the dangerous position of the members of the imperial family and the other Manchus. He was deeply concerned because, with the fall of power from the hands of the Manchus, his people would be under the control of the Chinese and have no means of maintaining even a bare subsistence. His hope was to create a constitution that would still fool the Chinese and protect the great power of the royal family. In such a spirit he took the lead in the preparation of another constitution.

Tsai-feng Seeks Military Power

The first step in Tsai-feng's plan for concentration of power in the royal family was the control of the military. In 1901 he had served as special envoy to Germany to apologize on China's behalf for the murder of a German envoy to China during the Boxer Uprising. Recognizing the great power and prestige of the German royal family, he asked Kaiser Wilhelm how he himself could enjoy such power. The Kaiser told him that the most important thing was to grasp military power, and to build up military strength. The regent remembered this very well, but during the lifetime of the empress dowager he could not follow the advice. He had therefore tried to keep himself from interfering in state affairs; now that he was regent, however, he immediately began to put the German Kaiser's advice into effect. In January 1909 he organized under his command a new army of Imperial Guards and appointed Tsai-t'ao, his younger brother, and Yü-liang, who was also a member of the royal family, together with T'ieh-liang, to train the newly organized army.

Following out his general plan, in March Tsai-feng ordered Prince Su [Shan-chi], Tsai-tse, T'ieh-liang, and Sa Chen ping to make preparations for a navy. In June the regent announced himself concurrently commander in chief of the army and navy. He next established a bureau of military supply under the direction of Yü-liang. In July he was made minister in charge of preparation of the navy. In August Tsai-hsün and Sa Chen-ping were ordered to inspect the military defenses of all the provinces along the Yangtze River and shortly after were sent to inspect the navies of various European nations. In May 1911 a general staff council was inaugurated, headed by Tsai-t'ao.

All these changes were made to concentrate military power further within the hands of the royal family. The three brothers, Tsai-feng, Tsai-t'ao, and Tsai-hsün, had become, respectively, chief of staff, head of the army, and head of the navy. They believed themselves to be following the letter of the imperial constitution, which granted the emperor the authority of a commander in chief of the army and the navy and the power to rearrange the military system. The emperors of the constitutional monarchies of Germany and Japan also had such power; and not one of their subjects dared criticize them.

DISILLUSIONMENT OVER CONSTITUTIONAL REFORMS

At this time the Constitutionalists in all the provinces were more active than before, because a provincial assembly was to be inaugurated in each province as well as a National Assembly in Peking. Liang Ch'i-ch'ao, a theoretician or authority on constitutions, published several long articles explaining the various problems concerning the organization and the functioning of a parliament and a cabinet and their official and financial problems. His articles had great influence on the activity of the Constitutionalists in China. The famous scholar Chang Chien, then the leader of the provincial assembly of Kiangsu, sent circular telegrams to other provincial assemblies and dispatched representatives to persuade them to make a joint petition to the emperor requesting an early adoption of a constitutional government, because foreign encroachments upon China were creating a serious threat and the ministers had made too many mistakes in their policy. Hence, he argued, it was necessary to open parliament and to organize a responsible cabinet in order to save the nation. Soon after, three representatives from each of the sixteen provincial assemblies met at Shanghai to organize a petition club to work for the opening of a national parliament in Peking.

In February 1910 the representatives met in Peking to submit a joint petition through the office of the Censorate under the chief signature of Sun Hung-i. At the same time they visited the princes and high officials, asking for their assistance. Before long they received an imperial decree rejecting their request. This was the first petition during the reign of Emperor Hsüan-t'ung.

In May the representatives of the provincial assemblies allied themselves with the provincial governments, the chambers of commerce, and the overseas Chinese, asking each of these groups to send delegates to organize an Association of Petition for the Convention of the National Parliament. Sun Hung-i and nine others were chosen as members of an executive committee, which worked together with other representatives in preparing matters relating to the petition. Other representatives went out of Peking to make public speeches designed to incite the populace to work toward the same goal. The result was that ten public petitions were submitted to the throne through the Censorate, but the reply, by imperial decree, was still negative.

In October the National Assembly was established in Peking. The representatives again submitted a petition to this new organization, requesting that it make a move towards the establishment of a responsible cabinet and that it open a parliament immediately. A large proportion of the assembly sympathized with the provincial assemblies and a resolution was passed to ask the emperor to open parliament quickly.

At this time the governors-general and governors, who were either urged by the provincial assemblies or embittered by the attempt to concentrate power in the central government, were also anxious for the creation of a responsible cabinet. Accordingly, they dispatched a joint telegram to the Grand Council suggesting an early inauguration of both parliament and cabinet. In November 1910 an imperial decree stated that the period of preparation for a constitutional monarchy was to be shortened and parliament was to be convened in 1913. Before the opening of the parliament the official system was to be reorganized; at the same time a cabinet was to be established.

Some of the petitioners were apparently satisfied with this minor concession and thought it best to go no further. Others, like T'ang Hua-lung of Hupeh and T'an Yen-k'ai of Hunan, still insisted upon an early opening of the parliament. They split off from the satisfied group, and working hard for another petition, had their efforts reinforced by additional new representatives who came from the Three Eastern Provinces. In December the government moved against the petitioners. First, the metropolitan police office was ordered to arrest the representatives of the Three Eastern Provinces and to escort them home. Then the governors-general and governors of all provinces were instructed to explain matters to and restrain the provincial assemblies from sending any more representatives. Whoever disobeyed the imperial order was to be punished. A leader in Tientsin was exiled to Sinkiang because of his attempt to prepare a fourth petition at Tientsin. Thus the storm of petitions for the opening of a parliament was silenced.

But there was no way of dissolving either the national assembly in Peking or the assemblies in all the provinces, and they continued to cause trouble for the Manchu government. After the convening of the national assembly its members repeatedly wrote letters questioning the authority of the grand councilors. The latter openly replied that they were not responsible for anything. Thereupon the assembly, accusing the grand councilors of incompetence and ignorance of their duties, requested the organization of a responsible cabinet to replace the Grand Council.

In response to this request an imperial decree read:

> I think that the organization of the official system and the promotion and the demotion of officials are the prerogatives of the court and that these have been clearly stated in the statutes of the dynasty. Whether the grand councilors were responsible or irresponsible and whether a responsible cabinet should be organized or not, are problems to be decided by the court and should not be interfered with by the chief members of the assembly. Therefore the request is to be dismissed without any further discussion.[3]

This decree was signed by a grand councilor on the emperor's behalf.

The Royal Cabinet, 1911

In April 1911 Tsai-feng actually fulfilled his promise of the previous November by proclaiming the regulations governing the organization and personnel of the cabinet. The old cabinet, the grand council, and the national assembly were all abolished. In the new cabinet there were two vice-premiers. Among the thirteen cabinet members, all of whom had cabinet rank, there were only four Chinese. Of the eight Manchus, five were members of the royal family. The thirteenth cabinet member was a Mongolian Bannerman. This cabinet, called by contemporaries "the royal cabinet," clearly revealed to everyone Tsai-feng's real intention.

Had the members of the royal family been men of ability, the selection still might have been justified, but practically all of them were inane, unprincipled muddlers, ignorant of world affairs. Yün Yü-ting says:

> Formerly the Imperial Study for Princes was directed by choice members from the Hanlin Academy. In the middle of the Kuang-hsü

> period no tutors were appointed and the study was empty. Princes of royal blood up to fifteen or sixteen years old were made imperial guards to follow the suite of the emperor and march back and forth from one palace to another in smart uniforms. When they were unoccupied by these duties, they amused themselves in horseback riding or in taming birds.[4]

Tsai-feng had confidence only in his own brothers and nephews, and especially in I-k'uang, whom he regarded as the only person qualified for the premiership. But I-k'uang was extremely covetous and his son very corrupt; both father and son were notorious and had been frequently denounced by the censors.

The regent's restriction of the censor's right to criticize corrupt officials stirred up a great storm. In 1910, Censor Chiang Ch'un-lin twice attempted by submitting memorials to the throne to have I-k'uang impeached. In one memorial he said:

> Now the parliament has not yet been opened and imperial decrees have forbidden censors to be too critical. But your servant worries that those who have the responsibility of reporting matters to the emperor tend to think that it is not necessary for them to point out small matters, and they dare not say anything about larger issues; so they have acquired the habit of keeping silent.[5]

For this the censor was sternly rebuked and ordered by imperial decree to go home without causing further trouble in the capital. A group of other censors asked that the throne rescind the order, but their request was not granted.

This greatly disturbed the members of the entire Censorate, and a petition was sent to the throne saying that since there was no definition of the censors' duties, these should be clearly defined by an imperial instruction. Other petitions were made to protest overtly the restriction of public opinion as voiced by the censors, but none of these requests was effective. Many censors at that time begged to be relieved of their duties with the government.

After the organization of the new cabinet and the announcement of its members by the throne, many Constitutionalists were extremely dissatisfied. In July 1911 a group petition of the provincial assemblies was submitted to the throne through the Transmission Office to the effect that since the cabinet consisted mainly of members of the royal family, unlike the cabinets in other constitutional monarchies, it should be reorganized and its members should be re-elected. This request was rejected by an imperial decree on the familiar grounds that promotion and demotion of officials were the prerogatives of the emperor and were not to be interfered with. This reply did little to boost the spirits of the already disillusioned advocates of constitutionalism.

FRUSTRATIONS OF ATTEMPTED REVOLUTION, 1908-APRIL 1911

The activities of the Revolutionary Party during the three-year period before the Revolution were considerably restricted. Among the numerous difficulties which the Revolutionists had to confront were the severe preventive measures which the Manchu government took against them. Also the sugar-coated constitution had fooled a large part of the people. The appearance of the royal cabinet finally awakened them to a realization of the true state of affairs and the people began to grow restless once more.

During the last three years of the Manchu dynasty there occurred, along with several minor riots, the following attempts at revolution:

1. On November 19, 1908, Hsiung Ch'eng-chi started an uprising at

Anking.

2. In February 1910, the new army started a mutiny at Canton.
3. In March 1910, Wang Ching-wei attempted to assassinate the regent Tsai-feng.
4. On April 27, 1911, seventy-two martyrs shed their blood for the revolution in an unsuccessful attempt at Huang-hua-kang.

Of these attempts, only that of Hsiung Ch'eng-chi was not planned by the T'ung-meng Hui, although this leader was what Dr. Sun called "an independent admirer of the revolution." Hsiung was a commander of an artillery battalion of the new Anhwei army. In the autumn of 1908 the new armies of Hupeh, Kiangsu, Kiangsi, and Anhwei had planned huge military maneuvers around the Great Lake of Anhwei. Hsiung and his followers planned to take the opportunity there to launch an uprising.

Just at that time occurred the deaths of Emperor Kuang-hsü and the empress dowager. As the news spread, the people became increasingly alarmed that there would be great unrest all over the country. A number of foreigners in China had the same apprehensions. The provincial authorities showed unusual severity in arresting members of the Revolutionary Party. On November 19 (four days after the death of the empress dowager) Hsiung, fearing that his plot might be discovered, commanded his soldiers in the artillery battalion in alliance with a detachment of cavalry to initiate a riot. But the governor of Anhwei, Chu Chia-pao, had taken very strict precautions against such activities. Hearing of the riots, he had the city gates shut. Planning to make a stubborn stand against any assault, he also sent appeals for help to some of the troops on maneuvers and to the navy along the Yangtze River.

Hsiung could not take the city, and government reinforcements were gathering from all quarters. Nothing was left for him but retreat to Luchow, where he was routed and his followers scattered. Although this riot was not successful and was carried on as an action independent of the

T'ung-meng Hui, it did help to prove that revolutionary ideas had become deeply rooted in the new armies and that the Manchu officials were now constantly uneasy.

After Hsiung's failure and several defeats suffered by the T'ung-meng Hui at Chen-nan-kuan and Hokow, the Revolutionary Party remained inactive during 1909. Sun Yat-sen had left the headquarters for Europe and entrusted Huang Hsing and Hu Han-min with the continuation of his revolutionary work. Huang and Hu were sometimes in distress, in the South Sea Islands or hiding in Hong Kong, with very meager financial resources. Because the previous failures were still fresh in their minds, they were now much more cautious, preferring to wait for a good opportunity before taking any action.

Since 1907 Wang Ching-wei had nurtured a different plan—to achieve revolution by assassination; but this violent method was opposed by Huang, Hu, and others. In 1909 while Huang and Hu were traveling secretly between the South Sea Islands and Hong Kong sowing the seeds of revolution among the people and especially in the new army in Canton, Wang determined to carry out his plan.

Wang Ching-wei attempted to assassinate the regent in Peking, but his plot was discovered and he was arrested. During his trial Wang's eloquent confession ran into several thousand words, not a single word of which was published by the Manchu dynasty because they feared it would incite the people. The original sentence against the culprit was capital punishment. Later on, taking the advice of a few veteran statesmen, Tsai-feng changed it to life imprisonment in order to gain a reputation for benevolence and also to soothe the rebels. But the rebels were unappreciative. Although Wang's plan was abortive and another plan of mutiny by the new army of Canton worked out by Huang and Hu was also a failure, the rebels continued to seek an opportunity for future attempts.

At this time Sun Yat-sen was in San Francisco. Upon hearing the bad news from China, he went to Penang, via Hawaii and Japan, with the intention of summoning Hu Han-min, Huang Hsing, and others to a conference. Their discussion was recorded by Sun himself as follows:

> I tried to encourage them, saying that formerly I was deeply disappointed, that I had been ostracized by almost the whole world, and that the difficulties I faced then were much greater than those which they face today. Although we are poor now, the storm of revolution is at its height and the thinking of Chinese abroad has made progress. Hereafter we shall only worry if we lack plans and courage. Were all our comrades more optimistic, I should try my best to be responsible for the financial resources.
>
> In spite of my encouragement all the comrades could personally see was the poverty-stricken predicament of the local revolutionaries. We refugees had been in distress ourselves, with meager resources providing bare subsistence, so how could we have money left over to support revolutionary activities? I said again and again that I must be able to find some way. ...
>
> Then I called my comrades among the local overseas Chinese to a meeting in which I urged them to support our high principles, and within one evening I had accumulated more than eight thousand dollars. I ordered a number of comrades to go to different cities to raise funds. Within a few days the collection from contributions was about fifty or sixty thousand dollars, while the contribution from distant areas had not yet been calculated. With these funds we were able to carry on our activities in various places and thus bring about the uprising at Canton on April 29, 1911. [6]

From this account one can see that the famous incident at Canton in the spring of 1911 was brought about by the Revolutionary Party working under extreme difficulties. Even so the outcome was again a fiasco.

The Canton Uprising, April 1911

The eventual failure of the Canton uprising did not come about for any lack of careful planning. The three causes of the failure were: (1) lack of weapons for the new army; (2) precautionary measures of the governor-general of Kwangtung, who had received information from reactionaries living in the South Sea Islands where the rebels had raised money; and (3) the assassination of a Manchu official by Wen Sheng-ts'ai on April 8, which precipitated thorough search efforts on the part of the Canton authorities. This assassination and its sequel were the most important causes of the failure.

The time of the uprising had been fixed for April 13. The party selected eight hundred reliable men, who were divided into ten assault groups. Huang Hsing commanded a hundred of them in an attack on the offices of the governor-general; Chao Sheng led another hundred in an attack on the office of the provincial navy, while four other leaders took four hundred to make four separate assaults elsewhere. The remaining two hundred were divided into four groups of fifty men and assigned to further raiding points.

Even while the rebels were awaiting the arrival of weapons, the governor-general and the admiral had already learned their secret. Moreover, on April 8, after Wen Sheng-ts'ai had assassinated the Manchu official, martial law was declared and additional soldiers were brought in to guard the city. Orders were issued to institute a thorough search for the rebels.

On April 23 Huang Hsing entered Canton, but during the next two days the branches of the party were discovered and a number of the comrades arrested. The atmosphere within the city was very tense. Thereupon some party members suggested a delay of the contemplated riot and ordered the assault groups to stay away for the time being. Huang Hsing, however, was desperate to fight against the admiral Li

Chun, even at the risk of his own life. It had not been easy to raise money, and he was afraid that the comrades in the South Sea Islands might lose confidence. But it was finally decided by a majority of members to issue orders postponing the uprising.

On the twenty-sixth and twenty-seventh it was reported that the guards transferred to Canton from other places by the governor-general were the comrades of the Revolutionary Party and that the situation would still be favorable for the revolutionists. As a result an order was issued to start the uprising at midnight on the twenty-seventh. On the morning of that same day, however, some of the party branches in the vicinity of Huang Hsing's residence had already been discovered, and Huang was afraid that the intense search would soon be extended to his own house and that all he had planned would come to naught. Many comrades asked permission to act immediately. Some, like Chu Chih-hsin, threatened to commit suicide if their request were refused. Therefore at 5:30 P.M. Huang Hsing, commanding one assault group of a hundred men, began an attack on the office of the governor-general. Some of the ten groups originally assigned were not yet assembled because of the repeated change of orders and the suddenness of the decision to take action earlier on the twenty-seventh. Consequently there were only four hundred men out of the original eight hundred to start the uprising with Huang. The detachment which was to provide weapons for the new army was unable to deliver all of them because of the change of plans. The result was that the new army was left without arms and had to watch the progress of the uprising from outside the city.

The assault group under the command of Huang Hsing advanced to the government buildings of the governor-general, Chang Ming-ch'i, who escaped by digging a hole from the back wall to the headquarters of the admiral. Huang then commanded his men to attack other points. On his way he met Wen Tai-hsiung, who commanded several hundred city guards in an attack on the office of the admiral at 5:30. Wen intended to arrest the admiral, who had just previously ordered him to go to the city to ward off the rebels. Very happily he detained the admiral's messenger and commanded his followers to attack the office of the navy.

Unfortunately Huang Hsing did not know that Wen's men had joined the rebels because they did not show the white-cross armbands which would have identified them. Huang's force at once opened fire upon Wen and killed him. Soldiers of the two sides then exchanged rifle fire and both groups were dispersed. Huang ran alone to a small shop. There he kept shooting from a chink in the door until the enemy was driven away. When he finally noticed blood on his clothes, he realized also that he had lost three fingers. He later managed to flee to Hong Kong.

If Huang's men had not fired on Wen's followers, the governor-general and the admiral might have been killed or arrested by Wen's guard and Canton might then have been occupied by the revolutionary army. With such a victory all the revolutionaries would have arisen and the mandate of the Manchu dynasty could perhaps have ended six months earlier. But to keep their secret, Wen's soldiers could not wear a white band on their sleeves beforehand, and Wen himself had not reported this in advance to the executive committee. The two main revolutionary forces thus fought against each other and destroyed themselves.

The revolutionaries suffered a good deal from this failure. The famous seventy-two martyrs at Huang-hua-kang (actually more than seventy-two party members lost their lives) represented the elite of the party membership and were at the same time solid citizens. Some of them, like Lin Chüeh-min, were famous writers. Although the suffering was great, the reaction to this failure was widespread. The fate of the seventy-two martyrs served to awaken the great majority of the Chinese people to the fact that all hope for China's future lay in the formation of a republic, rather than in a constitutional monarchy. It paved the way for final success of the October revolution of 1911.

REACTION AGAINST NATIONALIZATION OF THE RAILROADS

An immediate cause of the 1911 revolution was the railroad-nationalization problem. The policy of nationalizing the railroads resulted from the struggle and competition among imperialistic powers for making large investments in China. After defeating Russia, Japan's national power was so greatly enhanced that she became herself one of the world's imperialist powers and competed with the rest for a dominant position in China. Diplomatic acts such as the renewal of the Anglo-Japanese alliance (August 1905), the Franco-Japanese Treaty (June 1907), the Russo-Japanese Treaty (July 1907) and the American-Japanese agreement (November 1908) indicated the willingness of the Western powers to compromise and cooperate with Japan. When Japan and Russia were too aggressive in their cooperative invasion of Manchuria and Mongolia, the United States was concerned and suggested that the railroads in Manchuria should be placed under international control so as to curb the actions of Japan and Russia.

The failure of this plan for the neutralization and internationalization of the railroads in Manchuria stimulated closer cooperation between Japan and Russia and brought about the second agreement between them. This demarcated a sphere in Manchuria and provided for common action in defense of their interests. It caused great alarm among the Chinese, making both the Revolutionary Party and the Constitutional Party work hard to avert the danger which this agreement posed.

After the failure of her move to have the Manchurian railroads internationalized, the United States changed her policy to that of making joint investments with other powers. The Manchu government had almost exhausted its original financial resources in keeping up the show of a progressive government and was very glad to see foreign capital being used to develop some of her industries. The covetous young Manchu nobles were also delighted at the prospect of being able to divert much of this foreign capital into their own pockets.

With such encouragement, foreign investments in China increased to about $200,000,000 within a few months in the spring and summer of 1911. The larger investments were £10,000,000, borrowed from the consortium of the banks of the four powers (England, Germany, France, and the United States); $10,000,000 borrowed from Japan for railroad construction (March 24); and £6,000,000 from the consortium of the four powers for building the railroads between Szechwan and Hankow, and Canton and Hankow.

The important men responsible for these loans were Tsai-tse and Sheng Hsüan-huai. Tsai-tse's wife was the sister of Emperor Kuang-hsü's wife, who was then the dowager empress, and Tsai, who held the most powerful position among the nobles, was minister of finance, with full authority over financial matters. During the Sino-Japanese War of 1894, Sheng had been a customs *taotai* at Tientsin, had been bitterly criticized for accepting bribes, and finally was suspected of being a traitor. He was dismissed by imperial order and now was awaiting an official investigation by Wang Wen-shao, the minister superintendent of the trade ports in northern China, and Chang Chih-tung, who held a similar position in the ports in southern China. Sheng could count on Wang's protection, but Chang disliked him. At that time Chang himself had been severely reprimanded by the ministry of finance for a deficit of more than six million while he was in charge of the iron industry of Hanyang, the forerunner of the Han-Yeh-Ping Company.

Under these conditions, Chang asked Sheng to assume his position as director of the iron industry and make up the deficit for him. Sheng replied that, since there had been a deficit in the iron industry and there was no market for the iron produced, the responsibility was too great for him to assume; nevertheless, if Chang could recommend that Sheng be placed concurrently in charge of railroad construction, then it would be an easier task for him to undertake. Chang accepted Sheng's counterproposal, and Wang Wen-shao and Chang Chih-tung submitted a joint memorial to that effect.

This marked the beginning of Sheng's connection with the railroads. Sheng made a great fortune through his management of the iron industry and the railroads, while the losses of the Han-Yeh-Ping Company were mounting daily. Money had to be borrowed frequently from Japan, and so the ownership of the company soon passed into the hands of the Japanese. This was the handsome contribution that Chang Chih-tung made to the promotion of Chinese industry.

Sheng Hsüan-huai, meanwhile, proceeded to bribe the Manchu nobles and to curry favor with Tsai-tse so that he was made minister of the postal administration. His aim was to borrow money for railroad construction to increase his own private wealth as well as to consolidate his position of power. To satisfy the prevailing desire to concentrate power in the hands of the royal family, he suggested the policy of nationalizing the railroads. This policy was declared by an imperial decree on May 13, 1911. On the twentieth of the same month, Sheng signed a contract with the consortium of the banks of the four foreign nations for a loan to build the Szechwan-Hankow and Canton-Hankow railroads.

During these five years, the Revolutionary and the Constitutional movements had been closely linked to rebellion against economic invasion by the imperialists. The people had become greatly concerned over the lavish waste by the government of the money borrowed from foreign nations; and when the loans from the consortium and the $10,000,000 borrowed from Japan were made public, they became enraged. However, no action was taken because these two loans had little direct impact on the merchants. When the policy of nationalizing the railroads was proclaimed, however, and knowledge of the loans borrowed for building the Szechwan-Hankow Railroad became public, a storm of objection arose.

Originally it had been decided to build the Canton-Hankow section of this railroad with the aid of an American concern. Later, because this American firm would not observe its agreement, the Chinese people strongly urged the government to terminate the contract and to hand the job over to the Chinese merchants. But without the Canton merchants, who were relatively affluent, the financial power of the merchants of Szechwan, Hunan, and other provinces was limited, and it was difficult for them to collect the full amount of ready money from the shareholders. For this reason special taxes on rice, salt, and rents were assessed in Szechwan, Hunan, and the other provinces. The section of the railroad passing through the province of Kwangtung had been constructed long ago and that in Szechwan was also under construction.

But when suddenly the contracts for the construction of the railways by the merchants were canceled and railroads were proclaimed the property of the nation (which had no money to carry on the work except by floating loans from foreign powers) the interests of the merchants in these several provinces were directly affected. Their vehement objection to railroad nationalization spread like wildfire. Railway protection clubs were organized in Szechwan, Kwangtung, Hunan, Hupeh, and other provinces, and the provincial assemblies were used for planning protests against the government. At the same time representatives were sent to Peking, and telegrams were delivered to high officials in the capital requesting their support. The result was that numerous memorials and petitions rained upon the court, demanding the impeachment of Sheng Hsüan-huai.

Sheng, relying upon the support of the royal cabinet, had no fears for his position. Instead, the provincial authorities of Szechwan and Hunan, who sympathized with the merchants, were reprimanded by the central government, and orders were issued to put to death without hesitation all those who were holding resistance meetings in the provinces. Chinese students in Japan and Cantonese in the United States strongly supported the claims of the merchants, urging the latter to fight for their rights over the railroads.

Discontent in Szechwan

The most vehement objectors in the storm over the railroads were the natives of Szechwan. The representative of this province in Peking, Liu Sheng-yüan thinking that all high ministers of state had the same aims as Sheng Hsüan-huai, tried to file petitions directly with the regent. He went to the office twice, but on both occasions he was rejected by the janitor. Then he knelt on the ground outside a city gate, awaiting Tsai-feng's passing, and stopped the regent's sedan chair to deliver the petition. He was immediately arrested, but was later released. Next he tried to send a petition to I-k'uang, who then ordered the police to escort him back to Szechwan. Other Szechwan residents in Peking gathered together, shedding tears of farewell.

The struggle in Szechwan itself over rights in the railroad continued. On August 24 the Railroad Protection Club determined to arrange for all merchants to go on strike. Merchants of every description performed worship at the tablet of Emperor Kuang-hsü and lamented loudly. The consuls of all foreign nations in that province saw the gravity of the situation, and communicating with the provincial government, requested protection of their nationals. The governor-general, Chao Erh-feng, was also alarmed lest a great uprising should take place. He and the Tatar general submitted a joint memorial to the throne requesting that the merchants in Szechwan be permitted to take control of the railroad, at least for the time being. This request was not approved and they were rebuked by an imperial decree. Tuan-fang, governor-general of Hupeh, took this opportunity to accuse Chao Erh-feng before the throne of being timid and incompetent and of bungling the imperial railroad policy. Thereupon Tuan-fang was ordered to command the troops from Hupeh to Szechwan to investigate the case.

On the seventh of September upon hearing this news the natives of Szechwan chose four representatives to the governor-general's office who were to beg that Tuan-fang's trip of investigation be canceled. Chao Erh-feng, recalling his past trouble with Tuan-fang, declared that he would have nothing to do with the case. These four representatives, the elite of the locality, persisted and were imprisoned. The people went in large groups to the governor-general's office requesting their release. Many were killed or wounded by the guards. Thereupon Chao sent a telegram to Peking reporting that the people of Szechwan were using the struggle for railroad rights as a pretense to further work toward political independence. The Manchu government ordered Chao to use both old and new armies to suppress rioters as he saw fit. As a result, the militia near the provincial capital was practically wiped out by the government forces.

The struggle for the railroad rights was certainly incited by some members of the Revolutionary Party. Had the merchants not had a direct interest in the railroads, however, the propaganda of the Revolutionists could not have been so effective. After this struggle the merchants, who heretofore had had little connection with them, began to lean more and more toward the Revolutionary Party. Meanwhile the Revolutionists continued to watch for a good opportunity to start a revolution and the Constitutionalists were also disappointed in the results of the petitions. All these groups accordingly joined forces to overthrow the Manchu dynasty, which had now been in power for 268 years.

CHAPTER NINE
THE OVERTHROW OF THE MANCHU GOVERNMENT AND THE ESTABLISHMENT OF THE REPUBLIC OF CHINA

From 1894 to 1911 there were three large political groups in China—the radical Revolutionists, the mild Constitutional Monarchists, and the realistic Yüan Shih-k'ai faction. The first of these three had clearly declared itself to be an enemy of the Manchu government; the second wished to maintain a reformed version of the existing administration; the third had not yet shown any clear-cut political inclination. The supporters of Yüan Shih-k'ai were primarily office seekers. When Hsüan-t'ung succeeded to the throne, the Revolutionists were vigorously antagonistic toward the Manchu regime; but they were not alone. The other two groups, long opposed by the Manchu nobles, were also dissatisfied; both joined in the ultimate overthrow of the Manchu.

THE WUCHANG REVOLUTION AND THE RESPONSE OF ALL THE PROVINCES

For several years the attempts at revolution had been made mostly in southern China. Before the Canton uprising of April 1911 T'an Jen-feng had pointed out to Huang Hsing that Hunan and Hupeh occupied such focal positions in the country that they could control even the Manchu court, and that the revolutionaries could not hope to achieve very much unless they occupied these two provinces. To this effect he suggested financing Chü Cheng and his comrades, who had been planning a riot in Wuchang. Members in that area, united to work for the cause of the revolution, were reinforced by the new army and by members of the secret societies, who had now been persuaded to cooperate actively.

The staff members of the T'ung-meng Hui, meanwhile, were so dejected after the great fiasco in Canton that Chao Sheng died of worry and melancholy. Huang Hsing and Hu Han-min went into hiding in Hong Kong. Sun Yat-sen was in the United States. Ch'en Ch'i-mei, Sung Chiao-jen, T'an Jen-feng, and others then went from Hong Kong to Shanghai in order to organize a regional headquarters for the T'ung-meng Hui in central China. They planned to shift the center of the revolution from southern China to the lower valley of the Yangtze River, with the focus at Wuhan. T'an Jen-feng, who was an untiring member of the Revolutionary Party of Hunan, commanded great respect from the youth in the two provinces; Sung Chiao-jen also kept in close touch with the youth in his native Hupeh. After the organization of the headquarters, T'an and Sung made frequent trips between Hankow and Shanghai to unite further the various revolutionary elements.

At that time a newspaper, the *People's Independence Press* of Shanghai under the managing editorship of Yü Yu-jen, was an important propaganda instrument of the party. To this newspaper Sung Chiao-jen, under the pseudonym of Yü-fu, frequently contributed forceful and convincing articles. Sung's original belief had been that the revolution should not take place for several years. After the storm brought on by the nationalization of the railroads, he saw that the wave of revolution could no longer be stemmed. In August and September, members in the Wuhan area sent representatives to Shanghai and Hong Kong urging the party headquarters to appoint important men to direct their activities.

The Sudden Crisis in Wuhan

The correspondence between the revolutionary leaders has revealed that the members in the area of Wuchang requested that the revolution start in that spot and invited Huang Hsing to direct the rising. Governor-General Jui-ch'eng at Wuchang learned of the plot (just when the news reached Huang in Hong Kong) and strict precautions were taken at all important points along the river as well as inland. The revolution, originally planned for October 6, was then postponed to the sixteenth because of insufficient preparation and the failure of several prominent people to arrive. On the afternoon of the ninth, however, some party members who had hidden themselves in the Russian concession at Hankow inadvertently set off a loud charge from among those explosives which they were preparing for the revolution. Sun Wu was wounded in this accident; police were attracted to the spot, and two partisans were arrested during the subsequent investigation.

Upon hearing of this, Manchu officials sent soldiers and policemen to search for the rebels. A few clandestine organizations of the party were uncovered in the British concession at Hankow as well as in the city of Wuchang. Several score party members of both sexes, including some policemen who had been persuaded to join the revolutionary cause, were arrested. A number of insurgent flags and seals and some stationery were seized. Most important of all, a list of the party members was confiscated.

Hu Ying, who heard in prison all this bad news, managed to warn Ch'en Ch'i-mei and the others in Shanghai against coming to Hupeh. He suggested that the revolt be postponed, since Sun Wu was wounded, Chiang I-wu had been taken to Szechwan by Tuan-fang, and Chü Cheng was in Shanghai. But because many of the names on the party rolls seized by the police were those of soldiers, the party members were worried that the government would have them arrested. Accordingly, Hsiung Ping-k'un, a sergeant in an engineering battalion, insisted upon immediate action. At nine o'clock on the night of October 10, he gathered his army comrades and occupied the ammunition dump after a fierce assault. The army service corps fought its way from the suburbs to the city to join Hsiung's men, the artillery battalion, and the cavalry in an attack on the governor-general's office. Frightened by this show of strength, the governor-general's army under the command of Chang Piao abandoned the city and fled in disorder. Wuchang was in the hands of the revolutionary army. Hanyang and Han-kow fell soon after.

The sudden beginning of the revolution at Wuchang was just as disorganized as the April 27 uprising at Canton had been. Largely, however, because of the cowardice and incompetence of Governor-General Jui-ch'eng and Commander Chang Piao, this uprising succeeded. According to Sun Yat-sen:

> The success at Wuchang was accidental and was mainly due to the flight of Jui-ch'eng; if he had not fled, Chang Piao undoubtedly would have stayed and kept his troops together and in order. At that time most of those in the new army at Wuchang who supported the revolutionary cause had been sent away to Szechwan. The few who remained made up only a very small part of the artillery and engineering battalions, while the other soldiers in the new Wuchang army had little appetite for the new cause. It was that small group which was prompted, by the police discovery of the revolutionary headquarters, to make the attempt without much thought for its chances of success.[1]

Military Government Established at Wuchang

After this overwhelming success a military government was inaugurated at Wuchang. But the immediate and pressing problem was to find a leader for the revolutionary army. The assistant commander of the new army, Li Yüan-hung, an honest man well-liked by the soldiers, was compelled to assume the leadership of the revolutionary army in Hupeh, under the military government of the Republic of China. Eight days after Li had taken office, he wrote a letter to Admiral Sa Chen-ping, urging the latter to surrender to the new government. At the same time he frankly confessed the manner in which he himself had come to be the commander of the Hupeh army. Part of the letter reads:

> At the time of the Wuchang incident, all the troops under my command had been sent away, and I had to stay alone in the camp without knowing what to do. After the revolutionary army drove governor-general Jui-ch'eng away from the city, soldiers surrounded my camp and made a thorough search. ... I was quickly arrested and asked to become the commander of this revolutionary army. I was surrounded by guns at the time, and I might have been killed instantly if I had not complied with their request. ... Even though I undertook this new task, I did not dare take any action for the first several days. ... It was eight days ago that I took over the military duties, and I have found that thousands have fought against the same enemy with high spirits. ... The soldiers fought as individuals and even without commanders they rushed courageously into battle. Many of our fellow Chinese ... with empty hands destroyed a large section of the railroad. Women brought bread and tea to the soldiers in the battlefield. This situation is encouraging to us. ... Who wants to be a slave to the Manchus, or to injure his own brothers? For these reasons I can see great hope in our undertaking, and I therefore swear to God that I intend to restore this territory to the Chinese.[2]

This is a true record of Li Yüan-hung's undertaking of the command. Since a non-party-member like Li Yüan-hung could become the commander of a revolutionary army, T'ang Hua-lung, a Constitutionalist, was recommended to become the minister of civil affairs in the military government. This was the first instance of a Constitutionalist joining the Revolutionists. After the establishment of the military government at Wuchang, peace and order were maintained in the city. The foreign consuls at Hankow got a good impression of the behavior of the Revolutionary Party. Realizing that this movement was different from the Boxers' antiforeign activities in 1900, the consuls declared a neutral policy toward the revolutionaries.

The Provinces Join the Revolt

Beginning October 10, the authorities of many provinces responded to the revolution by declaring their independence of the Manchu government. With the exception of the provinces of Chihli, Honan, Shantung, and the Three Eastern Provinces, which were still under the control of the Manchu government, all other provinces had now joined the Republic of China. On November 11 the navy surrendered to the Republic. Szechwan, which had originally been the fuse of the revolution, was not declared independent until November 27. It was controlled by Chao Erh-feng, and not until Chao and Tuan-fang were killed could independence be declared.

Changsha, which is to the south of Wuchang, and Kiukiang, to the east, were two strategic cities which declared their independence first. No longer threatened from those directions, Wuchang could concentrate its efforts on fighting the Manchu troops coming in from the north. The declaration of independence of Shansi and Shensi, which were comparatively close to Peking, was also important. These two provinces diverted the military force of the Ch'ing court so that it could not concentrate its power to fight the rebels in the Wuhan area.

In the lower valley of the Yangtze, particularly at Nanking, the important officials of the Manchu dynasty, Chang Jen-chün, Chang Hsün, T'ieh-liang, and others, offered stubborn resistance to the revolutionaries. However, when Soochow, Shanghai, Chekiang, and other cities declared their independence in succession and the forces of all these cities were combined for the attack on Nanking, the Manchus were forced to yield the city to the revolutionary forces on December 12, despite the fact that Hanyang had been reoccupied by the Manchu forces only four days before. Nanking was a significant gain for the revolutionaries because they had lost Hanyang in central China and their position in Wuchang was in great peril. Nanking, therefore, could serve as a second base for the provisional government.

Another remarkable fact about this revolution was that, although the declarations of independence were made by the Revolutionists, the Constitutionalists in the provincial governments quite willingly joined in the revolutionary activities and accepted positions from the new government. In no single province were the Constitutionalists still at odds with the Revolutionists after 1911. All of the Chinese people had by now revolted against the Manchus.

THE REAPPOINTMENT OF YÜAN SHIH-K'AI AND THE GRADUAL SURRENDER OF THE MANCHU COURT

When the news of the revolution at Wuchang reached Peking, the Manchu government was greatly alarmed. On October 12 Jui-ch'eng and Chang Piao were dismissed by imperial decree but were allowed to retain their posts temporarily to have a chance to redeem themselves. At the same time the minister of war, Yin-ch'ang, was ordered to take command of two divisions of the Peiyang Army and to go south. Two days later came Yüan Shih-k'ai's reappointment as governor-general of Hunan and Hupeh and his orders to take charge of the suppression of the "bandits." The appointment provided that Yüan was to control not only the entire military force already in Hupeh but was also to be co-commander, with Yin-ch'ang, of all reinforcements. The original suggestion of this reappointment had come from the chief minister of the cabinet, I-k'uang, an old friend of Yüan, and many foreigners in China had voiced immediate and strong approval of the plan. Tsai-feng, yielding to this pressure, offered the position of power to a man whom he could not trust.

Yüan, unlike Tseng Kuo-fan and Li Hung-chang, was not a genuinely devoted supporter of the Manchu dynasty nor was he able to forget so soon his ignominious expulsion from the court by Tsai-feng, who had ordered him home to "recuperate from the leg ailment which affected his gait." With this insult fresh in his mind, he declined the offer on the pretext that his leg had not yet been cured.

Back of Yüan's reluctance to resume his former position was a cunning scheme. He had been awaiting the opportunity to avenge himself for the ill-treatment he had received from the Manchus. His plan was to wait until the situation became so grave that Tsai-feng would be unable to handle it and would yield to conditions demanded by Yüan. When the associate premier, Hsü Shih-ch'ang, Yüan's protégé, reported the rejection of the offer, Tsai went in person to Yüan's hometown to persuade him to change his mind. After repeated urging from the Manchu court, Yüan produced six important demands which he announced through his friends Hsü Shih-ch'ang, and I-k'uang. He made the acceptance of these demands the condition for his resumption of the task.

Yüan Demands Concessions of the Manchus

Yüan demanded (1) the opening of parliament in the following year; (2) the organization of a responsible cabinet; (3) amnesty for all those who were connected with the revolution; (4) the granting of legal recognition to the Revolutionary Party; (5) the granting to himself of full authority over, and the power to reorganize, all the armed forces; and (6) adequate military funds.

These six demands reveal Yüan's great personal ambition. Of the six demands, the first four were essentially for the purpose of soothing the feelings of the Revolutionary Party and the people at large, with a view to arriving at a compromise agreement with them. The purpose of this compromise was obviously to serve not the interests of the Manchu court, but rather his own. He did not want to incur the hatred of the Revolutionists by using arms against them. Moreover, he realized that if the revolutionary force were wiped out, his power over the Manchu nobles would be considerably diminished. If on the other hand the revolutionary army were allowed to remain in existence, and he as a middleman tried to arrange a compromise between the two sides, then he could gain the favor of the Revolutionary Party. At the same time he could convince the Manchus that they had to give him their undivided support. In addition Yüan reasoned that if he did not seize for himself full military power, the revolutionary force might become so powerful that it would refuse to permit him to mediate, and in this event he would be unable to control even the Manchu court. For this reason he emphasized the importance of his last two demands.

There was yet another important reason for his request for a "responsible cabinet," which the Constitutionalists had also long been demanding. His purpose was to replace the cabinet of nobles in the hope of reducing the political power of the royal family and, in so doing, to render the position of the regent, Tsai-feng, useless. Yüan was well aware that if this demand were granted, not only would his personal grudge against Tsai-feng be settled, but the premiership of the "responsible cabinet" would assuredly fall to himself, because at this time there was no one in public life more popular or more capable than he was. Regardless of whether the Revolutionary Party accepted the compromise or not, or whether the Manchu throne was maintained, power would eventually rest in his own hands.

Tsai-feng was at first very reluctant to accede to Yüan's demands. Yüan, on the other hand, stubbornly refused to resume his official duties until his demands had been accepted in their entirety. But things were not going well with the Manchu army. All the soldiers sent south with Yin-ch'ang to fight against the rebels had formerly been under Yüan's command. Even though Yin-ch'ang spent most of his time at the front lines, he was unable to fire them with the enthusiasm to fight and to work, as Yüan had done before him. During the long march the commander and his officers did not get along well together and the soldiers remained disorganized until October 27, when Hunan, Shensi, and Kiukiang responded to the revolutionary army. Then Tsai-feng grew so worried that he was forced to appoint Yüan Shih-k'ai imperial commissioner in command of all the armies, of which Feng Kuo-chang was commander of the First Army and Tuan Ch'i-jui commander of the Second Army; Yin-ch'ang meanwhile was recalled to Peking. The army in the south, upon hearing the news that Yüan would soon resume his duties, immediately began to fight with great eagerness against the revolutionary army, and Hankow was retaken a few days later. Thus again external pressure had forced the regent to submit to Yüan's power.

With regard to Yüan's other demands, Tsai-feng had as yet given no sign of acceptance, and Yüan had not yet come out of retirement. On the very day that Yüan was made imperial commissioner, the Constitutionalists in the National Assembly [*Tzu-cheng-yüan*] announced their four demands: namely, that the cabinet composed mainly of nobles be abolished; that some representatives of the people be allowed to participate in the preparation of the constitution; that an amnesty be extended to political offenders; and last, that the parliament [*kuo-hui*] should be immediately convened. When these demands were passed in the Assembly, they were immediately submitted to the throne.

Demands of the Military Party

While the Manchu nobles were pondering the four demands, another thunderbolt struck. On October 29 five or six army officers from the Twentieth Division, including Chang Shao-tseng and Lan T'ien-wei, wired the following twelve requests to the throne:

1. The Manchu emperor was to rule the country forever.

2. The parliament must be convened within the year.
3. The constitution should be drafted by the parliament and proclaimed in the name of the emperor, although the latter should have no right to revise or reject it.
4. The signing of treaties and the declaration of war should be decided by the parliament, but announced in the name of the emperor.
5. The emperor was the commander in chief of the armed forces, but in the event of civil war his jurisdiction must be subject to the approval of the parliament.
6. The emperor was to have no power to order an immediate execution nor any execution without further legal inquiries.
7. A special pardon should be extended to all political offenders.
8. A responsible cabinet should be organized, of which the premier should be elected by the parliament and appointed by the emperor, while other members should be recommended by the premier. Members of the royal family were to be considered ineligible.
9. The parliament was to have the right to suggest a revision of the constitution.
10. When a budget for the current fiscal year had not been approved by the parliament, the expenditures of the preceding year should not be met.
11. All acts which might result in an increased burden on the people must be submitted for parliamentary consideration.
12. Military men should have the right to participate in the compilation of the constitution and parliamentary laws.

Between the Constitutionalists in the National Assembly and the military party, the movement behind the scenes was complicated. After Yüan Shih-k'ai was removed from the commandership of the Twentieth Division, some members of the Revolutionary Party, such as Wu Lu-chen and Lan T'ien-wei, returned from Japan and infiltrated the division. The revolutionary elements in the army intended to take Peking, but a majority of other army officers, who had been loyal to Yüan Shih-k'ai, refused. The members of the Revolutionary Party had to modify their plan. They stationed the army at Luanchow, halfway between Mukden and Peking, whence the twelve requests had been submitted to the throne. If the Manchu court did not accept them, the Revolutionary Party would have grounds for attacking Peking.

The Manchu Rulers Make Concessions

Unexpectedly, the day for them to deliver the requests was also the time for the province of Shansi to declare its independence. Were their request not granted, the threat of an advance from Luanchow, together with a pincer attack from Shansi, would have placed Peking in an extremely grave position. Caught in this trap, Tsai-feng issued a decree on October 30 abolishing the present regulations governing the cabinet. In addition, the national assembly was authorized to draft a constitution, and the political offenders, Wang Ching-wei and others, were released. In addition the Revolutionary Party was recognized as a legal political party. Army officers, including Chang Shao-tseng, were praised by the decree, while the regent spoke of himself in derogatory terms.

Prince Ch'ing I-k'uang's cabinet was thus dissolved on November 1, 1911, and Yüan Shih-k'ai was appointed on the following day to replace him and to serve as prime minister. On November 3, nineteen articles of the draft constitution prepared by the Assembly were submitted to the throne. Tsai-feng immediately ordered them to be printed, announced, and read before the ancestral temple. This represents the first step in the surrender of the Ch'ing to the demands of the Chinese people. It was the third step in Tsai-feng's surrender to Yüan Shih-k'ai.

When news of the demands from the Twentieth Division and of the independence of Shansi reached Peking, the capital was filled with rumors. Families of officials and many citizens fled in panic to Tientsin. The empress dowager, with Emperor Hsüan-t'ung, was preparing to flee to Jehol, supposing Peking might fall immediately into the hands of the revolutionary army.

At this time Yüan Shih-k'ai was still "recuperating" at home, but news was being supplied to him very promptly by his protégés Hsü Shih-ch'ang and Chao Ping-chün in Peking, and by Feng Kuo-chang and others in the South, where Yüan's arrival was eagerly anticipated. Upon hearing the astounding news of the army officers' requests and of the independence of Shansi, he realized that Tsai-feng must now surrender. Consequently, on November 1 he began his journey from Changteh to assume command of the troops in the South. Meanwhile lest he lose his best pawn in the game, he sent a telegram advising the court to remain in Peking rather than try to escape to Jehol. When Yüan resumed his military duties, no more than twenty days had passed, since the successful revolution at Wuchang. More than half of the nation had fallen into the hands of the revolutionary army. On November 8 the national assembly elected Yüan Shih-k'ai premier, and the Manchu court subsequently reappointed him according to the new law. The day before Yüan's election to the premiership, however, another important incident occurred—the assassination of Wu Lu-chen.

Assassination of Wu Lu-chen

When the revolt at Wuchang started, Wu Lu-chen, commander of the Sixth Division, asked to be allowed to lead his division to the front to suppress the rebellion, whereupon the Manchu court became suspicious of him. After Chang Shao-tseng and the other officers had sent their strong demands to the Ch'ing faction, Wu went to Luanchow to discuss with them the taking of Peking. Upon discovering his plot, the Ch'ing faction ordered all trains along the Peking and Fengtien railway to be concentrated in the vicinity of the capital so that Chang's troops should have no means of transportation, and Wu was ordered to lead his troops in an attack on the revolutionary army in Shansi. When his army arrived at Shih-chia-chuang, Wu gave orders not to attack the enemy. Alone, he rode to a meeting with the representative of the Shansi army at Lang-tzu-kuan, and they agreed to unite in attacking Peking. To begin with, Wu's army intercepted the ammunition and provisions for the troops of the Ch'ing, which were being transported south. In the meantime Wu reported to the court that the Shansi army had surrendered to him. But the Manchu court was aware of the deception. While they officially appointed him governor of Shansi, they made arrangements to have him assassinated.[3]

The assassination did very little to increase the stability of the Ch'ing dynasty. It did, however, have a great effect on the power and prestige of Yüan Shih-k'ai. After Wu's death all the other army officers who did not belong to the Peiyang military clique were promptly purged or annihilated. Had Wu's plans for the seizure of Peking succeeded, the Ch'ing dynasty most likely would soon have been overthrown, and there would have been no need for the peace negotiations. Since negotiation now became necessary, Yüan played politics in order to seize the great power of the Ch'ing for himself.

Yüan Heads the Government

On November 11 while Yüan was with the army at Hsiao-kan, he received the imperial decree appointing him premier of the cabinet, but he declined the offer. Upon repeated urging from the court, however, he changed his mind and on the thirteenth of the month started for Peking with his bodyguards. On the sixteenth he announced the names of his cabinet members, calling Liang Tun-yen as minister of foreign affairs; Chao Ping-chün, minister of civil affairs; Shen Chia-pen, minister of justice; Liang Ch'i-ch'ao, vice-minister; and T'ang Shao-i, minister of post and transportation. Although this list of cabinet members seemed to indicate Yüan's intention of securing men of ability from all circles, in reality he was assuming that several of them, such as Liang Ch'i-ch'ao, would not accept the positions. This assumption proved to be correct, and as a result of these refusals the cabinet positions remained primarily occupied by Yüan's own partisans.

Yüan had previously secured full authority over all the troops in the vicinity of the capital. Consequently, after the organization of the cabinet, the real authority of the Manchu dynasty fell completely into his hands. Nevertheless, the regent could even now be an obstacle in Yüan's way. There were also the so-called Imperial Guards, nominally under the command of Tsai-feng but actually under Tsai-t'ao, whom Yüan had some reason to fear. Before long, however, the regent resigned, and Yüan organized a new corps of guards to oppose the original one.

Yüan now made great play of persuading Tsai-t'ao to lead his guards out of Peking on the punitive military expedition against the rebels. Tsai-t'ao was a young noble, lacking military experience, who had heard a great deal about the revolutionary army. He was considerably awed by this army and lacked the courage to lead the expedition. Yüan, perceiving this weakness, had deliberately placed him in this embarrassing position. The upshot of the whole affair was that Tsai-t'ao requested of his own accord to be relieved of his command of the Imperial Guards. Yüan gladly complied and immediately replaced him by his own protégé Feng Kuo-chang, while Yüan's duties at the head of the imperial troops at Wuhan were handed to Tuan Ch'i-jui. Soon after that the Imperial Guards were moved out of the city of Peking, on the pretext of preparing for the expedition, and were replaced by Yüan's newly organized corps. The Manchu court was now entirely deprived of military protection. An infant emperor and a widow were left in the palace to be used as pawns in Yüan's political maneuverings.

THE ORGANIZATION OF THE PROVISIONAL GOVERNMENT AT NANKING

The Taking of Nanking

In mid-November 1911 the territory still under the jurisdiction of the Manchu dynasty was limited to Chihli, Shantung, Honan, and the Three Eastern Provinces. The real power, after the formation of the cabinet, was concentrated in Yüan's hands. Yet despite the fact that they controlled two-thirds of China, the revolutionary armies still had no unified organization. Sun Yat-sen was still abroad, and Huang Hsing did not arrive at Wuchang until November 3, when Hankow had just been retaken by the Manchu forces. Upon his arrival Huang became commander in chief of the revolutionary army in Hupeh and led his forces in a desperate struggle near Hanyang against the northern army.

Although opposition to the Manchus was widespread, there was no cooperation between the provinces, and each province had been fighting in its own way with no unified plan of action. The provincial authorities in the upper and lower valleys of the Yangtze were, however, aware of the great need for organization. On November 9, the military governor [*tutu*] of Hupeh dispatched telegrams to all of the provincial governments asking that delegations with full authority be sent to Wuchang to organize a provisional government. Since plans for an organizational meeting in Shanghai were already well under way, there was some disagreement over the location of the general meeting. By compromise it was decided on November 23 that the representatives of all the provinces should go to Wuchang, where the central military government of the Republic of China was located.

Since Hanyang had already been reoccupied by the imperial forces, the whole city of Wuchang was under fire from the government bases across the river by the time the representatives reached their destination. They finally assembled in the British Settlement at Hankow. The conference was called to order on November 30 under the chairmanship of T'an Jen-feng. On December 2 Ma Chün-wu, Wang Cheng-t'ing, and others were elected to a committee to draft an outline for the organization of the provisional government. A resolution was passed to the effect that Yüan Shih-k'ai should be elected president if he changed allegiance from the Manchu to support the revolution and the republic. On the following day twenty-one articles of the outline were approved and proclaimed.

On the next day when the news of the capture of Nanking was received, this city was designated the capital for the provisional government. All representatives were to assemble there within seven days. As soon as the representatives of more than ten provinces arrived in Nanking, the president and vice-president should be elected. Most of the representatives took a particular interest in the importance of the president's position and retained a blind and adamant faith in Yüan Shih-k'ai's ability. Yet opinion varied even at the outset. The representatives who had formerly assembled at Shanghai favored Huang Hsing as commander in chief and Li Yüan-hung as associate commander in chief, while the representatives invited by the military government to Wuchang were strongly in favor of Yüan Shih-k'ai. Still others preferred to have Li Yüan-hung as commander in chief, and Huang Hsing as associate commander.

This diversity of opinion not only delayed the creation of the provisional government but also made more apparent the weak points among the revolutionaries. One was the arrogance of the militarists; each of them thought that he personally had made a great contribution to the defeat of the crack Peiyang Army. The second was the opportunism of the politicians. Lacking sound purpose and firm revolutionary principles, they changed their opinions readily.

The Republic, 1912

Fortunately, Sun Yat-sen arrived at Shanghai on December 25. It was he who managed to put aside for the time being the problem of the election of the commander in chief and the associate commander in chief. It was he also who decided the election of a provisional president. At the time of the election, December 29, sixteen out of the seventeen provincial representatives voted for Sun Yat-sen. On January 1, 1912, the delegation passed a resolution proclaiming the new year the first year of the Republic of China and prescribed the solar calendar in lieu of the lunar calendar. Delegates were promptly sent to Shanghai to welcome Sun Yat-sen at his inauguration in Nanking on the first day of this first year.

On the inauguration day the delegation held no session. On the following day, when meetings were resumed, arguments arose concerning the revision of the organization of law of the provisional government, the addition of a vice-president, and the question whether the authority of the new president should resemble that of the American or of the French president. On January 3 Li Yüan-hung was elected vice-president. The first cabinet of the Republic, presented by President Sun and approved by the representatives, included Huang Hsing, minister of the army; Huang Chung-ying, minister of the navy; Wang Ch'ung-hui, minister of foreign affairs; Wu T'ing-fang, minister of judicial affairs; Ch'en Chin-t'ao, minister of finance; Ch'eng Te-ch'üan, minister of domestic affairs; Ts'ai Yüan-p'ei, minister of education; Chang Chien, minister of industry; T'ang Shou-ch'ien, minister of communication.

As set forth by Dr. Sun, the organization of the government during the process of revolution should undergo three distinct stages:

> The first stage is a military government. After the outbreak of revolution all provinces will follow suit ... all soldiers and civilians should be under military rule ... all local government should be under

> the control of the military authority. ... Each district should be ruled in this manner for a period of three years ... at the end of this period, the military rule will be replaced by a constitutional administration.
>
> The second stage is a provisional constitutional government. After each district has undergone the period of military rule, the central authority should grant the people self-government. ... After six years, when the country has been pacified, the administration will be replaced by a formal constitutional government.
>
> The third stage is a constitutional government. After the provisional constitution has been put into practice by the whole nation for six years, a formal constitution should then be compiled and the military and the political power of the military government should cease functioning. The president and the congressmen should be chosen by public election to form a parliament. The political affairs of the whole nation should be conducted according to the constitution.[4]

This process had already been determined by the T'ung-meng Hui in 1906 and 1907. If the Revolutionary Party near the end of 1911 had observed this order, a strong military government would have been the initial order of organization. Although the revolutionary army had fought itself to a standstill with the imperial forces and a peace had already been negotiated, the outcome was still unpredictable. It was too early to be arguing the problem of the president's authority and cabinet system matters, which properly belonged to a constitutional administration. Nevertheless, at this time the members of the Revolutionary Party had already forgotten their theory of the revolutionary process, except for Sun Yat-sen himself, who said:

> At the beginning of the first year of the Republic I resolutely watched over the revolutionary process in order to achieve the goal of

> revolution and reconstruction ... but most of my comrades did not agree with me. Even though I repeatedly explained matters to them and argued with them, it was of no avail. Most of them thought my ideas were too advanced. Alas, was it really that my ideas were too advanced or was it that the knowledge, of my comrades was too limited? I could not help feeling disappointed. ... For this reason I intended to retire.[5]

The people, hating the Manchu dynasty, hoped that once it was overthrown, they could all enjoy peace and happiness. The delegates, all intellectuals despite individual diversities in background, still anxiously anticipated the realization of a constitutional government under a republic. They could not recognize that Dr. Sun's "revolutionary process" was necessary for a nation seeking to change overnight from monarchism to republicanism.

In brief, when the provisional government was organized, the attention of the public was directed toward the peace negotiations between North and South China, and toward Yüan Shih-k'ai, who held the life of the Manchu emperor in his hands. They were ready to give the provisional presidency to Yüan Shih-k'ai as a reward for his part in the overthrow of the Manchu court and believed that as soon as Yüan Shih-k'ai became president, it would be time to create a republican constitutional government. Even before the peace negotiations between the North and the South were successfully concluded, the newborn Republic of China had already fallen into the hands of Yüan Shih-k'ai.

THE PEACE NEGOTIATIONS OF YÜAN AND THE REVOLUTIONARIES

From the very beginning Yüan Shih-k'ai adopted a policy of compromise with the revolutionary faction. After the Ch'ing dynasty acquiesced in Yüan's demands, he wielded full power over the destiny of the Manchu court, and on the revolutionary side it had long been agreed that Yüan would be the president of the Republic. It would thus seem to have been a very easy matter to conclude the peace negotiations successfully. Many difficulties occurred, however, because of the fundamental difference in purpose between Yüan Shih-k'ai and the Revolutionary Party. The latter had consented long before to make Yüan the president of a republic which was to transfer to the people the former powers of the emperor and which was to be based upon popular suffrage. But Yüan, to the contrary, expected the presidency to resemble exactly the position of an emperor. He expected to have for himself complete and absolute control over the entire nation.

The first part of the negotiations was conducted by T'ang Shao-i and Wu T'ing-fang. On November 1 Yüan set out on his journey to the south. On the sixth he received an imperial order to strengthen the attack against the revolutionaries. Yüan chose at this point to try to persuade Li Yüan-hung to come to terms. Having received no response, Yüan sent two representatives to Wuchang on November 11 to ask Li for peace. Bolstered by the support of Sung Chiao-jen, who had arrived by this time at Wuchang, Li rejected the proposal. Instead, the revolutionary leaders invited Yüan to change sides and to fight against the remnants of the Manchu faction and announced that Yüan had been appointed tutu of the revolutionary army of Honan and Hopei.

Yüan, realizing that the central figure of the revolutionary army in the Wuhan area was Huang Hsing, then ordered his son to make a secret journey to Hanyang to contact Huang, as if to hint that he would like to cooperate with the revolutionary leaders. Yüan was also aware that in order to conclude the peace on his own terms, he would have to deal the revolutionary army a severe blow. To this end he ordered a fierce assault on Hanyang, which was captured on November 27. Had the imperialists continued their attack across the river, Wuchang would have been taken.

Yüan used this propitious moment to reopen negotiations and asked the British minister in China to arrange a meeting. Because England had the lion's share of the foreign trade in China and needed peace to do business, the British minister gladly instructed the British consul general at Hankow to mediate between the two parties.

At this moment, the field commander of the imperial armies, Feng Kuo-chang, who was still ignorant of Yüan's designs, asked the revolutionary army to surrender. But this army, though it had suffered a recent setback, was not willing to surrender. An unconditional truce was declared for three days, beginning December 1, and was later prolonged for another three days. On December 5 Yüan Shih-k'ai's proposals for an armistice reached Hankow. When the last three days of the truce expired, it was extended for another fifteen days, while negotiations were carried on at Hankow between Yüan's representative, T'ang Shao-i, and Wu T'ing-fan on the revolutionary side. After prolonged discussions, the peace conference was broken off because of Sun Yat-sen's election to the presidency of the provisional government of the Republic.

Actually, all discussions between T'ang and Wu had been mere formalities. The real purpose of the revolutionaries in the negotiations was to persuade Yüan to overthrow the Manchu emperor, and to offer him the presidency as a reward. But suddenly, on the twenty-ninth of December, the representatives in Nanking had elected Sun Yat-sen president, and he was inaugurated on January 1, 1912. Yüan Shih-k'ai regarded this action of the revolutionaries as a breach of agreement and felt that he had been cheated. Furthermore, after the establishment of the provisional government at Nanking, he could hope to control only a very small part of the parliament to be convened and thus he could hardly expect to exert much power over the government. Now he schemed to ask the Manchu emperor to abdicate voluntarily and to grant Yüan the authority to organize a provisional government.

If this plan worked, it would not be necessary to have the National

Assembly, and Yüan would have the entire administration under his control.

Sun Offers the Presidency to Yüan

Sun Yat-sen, meanwhile, was insisting that so long as the Republic, as a government of the people, accorded all the rights appropriate to a democratic government, the position of the presidency could safely be yielded to Yüan. On the very day that he himself was elected president, Sun immediately dispatched a telegram to Yüan Shih-k'ai which read:

> I beg to call the attention of Premier Yüan in Peking to the fact that when I reached Shanghai two days ago my comrades entrusted me with the responsibility of organizing a provisional government. ... Although I have accepted this position for the time being, it is actually waiting for you, and my offer will eventually be made clear to the world. I hope that you will soon decide to accept this offer. [6]

The purpose of Sun's telegram was to satisfy Yüan that the presidency would be given to him as soon as the Manchu throne was overthrown. Yüan could not believe it, but was reluctant to reveal his suspicions. After receiving Sun's telegram, he sent a reply on January 2:

> I have received your telegram of the first. The choice between monarchism and republicanism in the political system is to be decided by public opinion and there is no way to predict what the decision will be. I dare not participate in the provisional government. You have been kind to offer me such great honor, but I am sorry to say that I dare not accept it; I hope I shall be excused from doing so. [7]

Sun Yat-sen knew that Yüan was not yet completely reassured and hence another telegram was sent:

> Your telegram of the second has been received. Since I could not bear to see a war between the South and the North because the people would suffer so tremendously, I have no objection to peace negotiations. ... If war can be avoided through your efforts and the people's desire for peace can be satisfied ... it would certainly be only fair for me to give you full credit and to yield [the presidency] to you as the most capable person. Since I have been elected by the representatives of all the provinces and have been formally sworn in, my sincere intention for peace should thus be made plain before both God and our people. If you think that I am trying to tempt you with this offer, you are certainly laboring under a misconception.[8]

Sun Yat-sen was entirely sincere in his promises. Even though Yüan might still not believe him, Yüan realized that there was no possible way to overthrow the provisional government at Nanking. If he resorted to military force, he would be faced with lack of funds to finance an expedition; foreigners dared not at that time lend any money to the Manchu dynasty. Not even funds from previously arranged loans were available to the moribund regime, for Sun Yat-sen had arranged with the British government to freeze all loans made to the Manchu dynasty.[9]

Although it was obvious that Yüan could not at this time break with the revolutionaries, he did hold stubbornly to his own position. On the day of the inauguration, Yüan suggested to Tuan Ch'i-jui, Feng Kuo-chang, and others that they should join with forty officers of all ranks submitting a joint telegram to the cabinet urging the retention of the constitutional monarchy, expressing their strong opposition to republicanism, and threatening that if the will of the minority was to be imposed upon them in the form of a republic, they would certainly resist it to the death. This message was conveyed to Wu T'ing-fang, the representative of the revolutionary government at the peace negotiations. It was the first time that Yüan had used the military power of the Peiyang

Army clique as an instrument to menace Sun's Kuomintang [see Chapter Ten]. This political maneuver also served to strengthen the confidence of the Ch'ing dynasty in Yüan's loyalty.

Taking advantage of this situation, Yüan proceeded to secure for himself funds from the imperial treasury, ostensibly for military operations against the revolutionaries. On January 2 in an interview with the court, he submitted the telegram of Tuan and Feng with the remark that the demands of the revolutionaries had been so heavy that the punitive expedition suggested in the telegram should be equipped at once. Because of the shortage of military funds, it proved to be impossible to take such action. He therefore threatened to resign his premiership. The new empress dowager then tried to dissuade him by warm and comforting phrases and by giving him eight thousand ingots of gold from the imperial treasury. Yüan proceeded to sell these to foreign bankers.

THE ABDICATION OF THE MANCHU EMPEROR

In the first ten days of January, an agreement was reached during secret negotiations that under certain favorable conditions, the Manchu emperor would abdicate, after which Sun Yat-sen would resign his position as provisional president and be replaced by Yüan Shih-k'ai. Now Yüan was confronted with a most difficult and embarrassing situation. He had formerly insisted that the choice of a political system be left up to the national assembly. He had taken enormous sums from the Manchu imperial treasury for military expenditures to oppose the revolutionaries. Now he was suddenly requesting the voluntary abdication of the Manchu emperor.

Debate at the Manchu Court

At this point Yüan again had to make use of I-k'uang. In confidence he showed I-k'uang the conditions for the abdication of the emperor and convinced him that it was the best way to work for the safety of the dynasty. On the twelfth the nobles held a secret meeting at which I-k'uang advanced the idea of voluntary abdication by the emperor. The nobles, with the exception of a few of the younger ones, were violently opposed and refused to discuss the suggestion, and the conference bore no fruit. The next day Tsai-feng consulted Yüan on this matter, but Yüan refused to commit himself. However, as the rumor of the emperor's possible abdication spread, some of the nobles, especially Tsai-t'ao, Liang-pi, and T'ieh-liang, grew angry with Yüan. The direct result of this discontent was the appearance of the Imperial Clan Party [*Tsung-she Tang*]. On the sixteenth, Yüan had requested an interview with the empress dowager in order to ask her advice on the final decision regarding the abdication. Her reply was that she would have to wait until the meetings of the nobles and high officials to be held next day before she could voice any opinion.

As Yüan was leaving the court, an attempt was made on his life. He was unhurt, but a few of his bodyguards and several policemen were killed. Three suspects, arrested on the spot, all confessed to being members of the Revolutionary Party and were all subsequently executed.

At this time the news of a possible abdication had been spread far and wide. The Revolutionists, unaware of the scheme, blamed Yüan for keeping the emperor on the throne. But though their plot backfired, it proved useful for Yüan. After this incident, the empress dowager had complete trust in him. Thereafter she ignored all the slanderous tales against him which were hawked around court by the nobles.

On January 17 the first imperial conference was held. I-k'uang, speaking first, declared that the only solution was voluntary abdication. The empress dowager began to sob and the conference room was silent. Suddenly a Mongolian prince began to argue with I-k'uang and suggested that the whole idea of abdication be rejected. Tsai-feng and the others remained silent. The meeting adjourned without reaching any decision.

The second imperial conference was held on the eighteenth; I-kuang still insisted on his original suggestion. The Mongol prince objected even more strenuously, but received little help from other nobles, and again nothing was decided. Later some thirty nobles congregated around the mansion of I-k'uang to demonstrate their vehement objections to his proposal and to demand the reason why Tsai-t'ao and his brother, who had formerly been strongly opposed to abdication, had not uttered a single word during the last two imperial conferences. On the morning of the nineteenth, they issued a strong statement of their views under the name of "A Society for the Maintenance of the Constitutional Monarchy." Thus came into existence the Imperial Clan Party.

At the third conference, held on January 19, all the Mongolian and Manchu princes participated and Yüan Shih-k'ai ordered Chao Ping-chün, Liang Shih-i, and Hu Wei-te to be his representatives there. First Chao Ping-chün made a motion to have the current problem decided by the cabinet. He suggested that the monarchical government in Peking and the provisional government at Nanking should be dissolved simultaneously and a provisional integrated government be established at Tientsin instead. When this motion had been put before the conference, it was also wired by Yüan's cabinet to Representative Wu, who was to transmit it to the Nanking government, requesting that two days after the abdication of the Manchu emperor this government should be discontinued. Although Yüan Shih-k'ai was scheming to seize power by organizing such a new provisional government, he now discovered himself in a position more difficult than ever.

When the motion was put before the third imperial congress, it was unanimously rejected by the Mongolian and Manchu princes. They said that the simultaneous dissolution of both the governments, in Nanking and Peking, and the establishment of another unified government would change the monarchy into a republic, something which could never be done. I-k'uang also changed his attitude, saying that it might be all right to establish another unified government, but that it was absolutely necessary that the throne be retained. Liang Shih-i replied that since financial resources were so meager, it was hard for the government to meet military expenditures for one month, while Hu Wei-te mentioned possible interference by England, Russia, and Japan. But the nobles paid little attention to what these people said.

Then Chao Ping-chün added that this motion had been made after painstaking study by the premier, who was trying his best to discover a way out of the myriad difficulties, and if it were not carried, there would be no alternative for Yüan's entire cabinet except to resign. Consequently, Liang, Hu and others withdrew from the meeting, which was subsequently adjourned without any result. Two more imperial conferences were held on the twentieth and the twenty-second, but again with no success.

Yüan was now in a predicament. The leader of the Imperial Clan Party was Liang-pi, who was planning to have a new cabinet organized by Yü-liang, Tsai-tse, and others as soon as Yüan Shih-k'ai's resignation should be approved, and to have. T'ieh-liang appointed commander in chief of the Manchu army, which would make one final and decisive fight against the enemy. This was the trouble brewing for Yüan in Peking.

Sun Makes Public the Negotiations Involving Yüan

Nanking, meanwhile, received the news conveyed by their representative, Wu, which unveiled Yüan's secret plot to seize power. The republican authorities immediately ordered Representative Wu to inquire into Yüan's real intentions by telegram and to present him with the following four demands:

1. The Manchu emperor should abdicate and relinquish all powers.
2. The Manchu emperor should not interfere in any matters

concerning the organization of the provisional government.

3. The location of the provisional government should be in Nanking.
4. President Sun's resignation should come only after the provisional government had been recognized by all powers, the domestic reform had been achieved, and peace well established; Yüan Shih-k'ai should not interfere in any matters of the provisional government before the resignation of President Sun.

On the twentieth, Representative Wu again telegraphed to Yüan the conditions for favorable treatment of the Manchu emperor after his abdication, as well as for the treatment of the Manchus, Mongolians, Mohammedans, and Tibetans. There were ten articles, five of which applied to the emperor. On the twenty-second, President Sun again asked Representative Wu to convey to Yüan the last five articles, which were being published in the newspapers. Sun explained his position as follows:

> Formerly I said that I would resign from the provisional presidency after the abdication of the Manchu emperor. By this I meant that Yüan Shih-k'ai must have severed all his relations with the Manchu government and become a citizen of the Republic of China, since only then would he be qualified to be elected president. Later on, I unexpectedly learned from his telegrams that not only has Yüan no intention of getting rid of the Manchu government, but he is attempting to abolish or destroy the republican government and to organize a provisional one in North China. There is no indication whether he means this provisional government to be republican or monarchical, and even if he says that it will be republican, there is no guarantee that it will be so. That is why I have said that I must wait until the government has been recognized as republican by all powers before I can relinquish my duties.
>
> ... I am now setting up the following arrangement: (1) The

> Manchu emperor must abdicate, and Yüan must at the same time inform all foreign ministers in Peking, asking them to convey the news to the Republican government, or to transmit it directly through the consuls of the various nations in Shanghai; (2) Yüan must at the same time announce his political position, and he must declare absolute support of republicanism; (3) When Sun Wen has received assurance of the abdication of the emperor from the legations or from the consuls in Shanghai, he will resign from the provisional presidency immediately; (4) Yüan will be elected provisional president by the senate [*ts'an-i-yüan*]; (5) After his election, but before he is given actual power and authority, Yüan must swear to observe the constitution prepared by the senate.
>
> The first two articles are for the purpose of making Yüan sever his relations with the Manchu government and become a republican citizen. That was the final and last arrangement. If Yüan cannot carry out these two articles, it means that he does not support republicanism and that he has no real intention of solving the problem peacefully, if this is so, the favorable treatment promised the emperor and the Manchu and Mongolian races cannot be guaranteed. Yüan would have to take the blame for the resumption of hostilities, which would bring about tragic bloodshed in the country.[10]

Sun Yat-sen announced to the public the results of the conferences and the exchange of these telegrams in order to show his firmness with Yüan, realizing very well that Yüan dared not break off relations with him and could not afford to play politics as he had previously been doing. If Yüan did not comply with the five demands, he had no other way to deal with Sun; on the other hand, if he acquiesced, the Imperial Clan Party would cause him trouble because he had not yet secured the consent of the Manchu emperor with regard to the abdication.

Another difficulty Yüan Shih-k'ai confronted was that he had been bargaining semisecretly to get the position of the presidency for himself. After Sun Yat-sen announced the five articles to the newspapers, this bargaining became completely public. Since now the Imperial Clan Party had more reason than ever to hate Yüan and even foreigners criticized him, Yüan had halted all dealings with the Manchu court on the pretext of illness. With regard to foreigners, he ordered the ministry of foreign affairs to issue a statement to the effect that the negotiations between the South and the North were neither being directly conducted by him nor approved by him, nor had he any intentions of becoming president. At the same time he had the rumor spread that he was about to resign and that there would be a great riot in Peking; to avoid possible danger, all foreigners were advised to move to the quarters of their respective legations.

Yüan's Use of Military Threats

The Nanking government urged Yüan to reply. Yüan at first ignored them. Later on, after much urging, he replied that he had never discussed matters concerning the abdication of the emperor with the representatives of the Nanking government. When the latter reprimanded him, he again refused to reply. By now he was forced to resort to his ultimate weapon—the threat of the power of the Peiyang military clique.

Just as Yüan began to exploit this resource, he received some unexpected assistance from a Revolutionary Party member; on January 26, P'eng Chia-chen threw a bomb that killed Liang-pi (and P'eng himself). Thereupon, the members of the Imperial Clan Party were so frightened that some fled from Peking while others went into hiding in the city.

The speculation by some Japanese, however, that Yüan himself ordered the assassination is quite absurd. On January 27, Yüan's own chief weapon was employed: more than forty officers of various ranks, headed by Tuan Ch'i-jui, sent a long telegram to the cabinet, the military advisory council, the ministry of war, and all the princes, urging the immediate adoption of a republican government in order to insure the security of the royal family and of the nation, and requesting them to report this to the emperor on behalf of the army officers. This was the second time that Yüan Shih-k'ai had resorted to the Peiyang military clique for a show of power to threaten the Manchu government.

This device was used again later on to frighten the parliament and the committee which was drafting the constitution. Tuan Ch'i-jui, after he became premier, was a master of this technique fathered by Yüan Shih-k'ai. In sum, Yüan was the creator of the Chinese warlord. The warlords of the Peiyang clique were shamefully lacking in patriotism and used all their influence to meddle in political affairs in order to gain power and advantage for themselves. Twice already they had interfered during the negotiations with the Manchu court; in their New Year's Day telegram they had said that they would fight to the death the adoption of a republican system; but a month later, when they became aware that the majority of the people were supporting republicanism, they accepted the convention of the national assembly and agreed that it was necessary to adopt the republican system immediately. Members of Tuan's faction afterward boasted frequently of the many contributions that they had made to the creation of the Republic. In actuality, the only accomplishment which they could honestly claim was that they had helped to further Yüan Shih-k'ai's personal ambitions. When their telegram arrived, the Imperial Clan Party dared object no longer to the abdication of the emperor.

The End of Manchu Rule

On January 29 another imperial conference was called. I-k'uang and Yüan Shih-k'ai were both absent on account of "illness," and there appeared to be no more need for debate. On the thirtieth the empress dowager summoned I-k'uang and Tsai-feng for an interview, during which both men agreed that "since the imperial force had no intention of fighting, abdication will ... obtain the advantages of favorable treatment." On February 1 an imperial decree from the empress dowager ordered Yüan Shih-k'ai to negotiate with the revolutionary army the conditions for the abdication. Yüan, now completely recovered from his illness, two days later dispatched a telegram to Representative Wu saying, "I now have the power to negotiate the matter of favorable treatment of the royal family." After the conditions were agreed upon and approved by the provisional senate of the Nanking government, consent was sent on the sixth of February to Yüan Shih-k'ai. On February 12 the Manchu emperor relinquished his throne.

He said, in his decree of abdication:

> Yüan Shih-k'ai was formerly elected premier by the national assembly (*Tzu-cheng yüan*) and now, in the interval between the old and the new political systems, a method is needed which will bring about the unification of South and North China; Yüan Shih-k'ai should have full power to organize a provisional republican government to negotiate with the revolutionary army for unification measures.[11]

These few sentences Yüan Shih-k'ai interpreted as proof of his inheritance of power from the Manchu emperor—the final achievement of his life's ambition. There was, however, still the senate of the Nanking government, which Yüan had no way of destroying and with which he would have to contend for the time being.

The conditions for the abdication were three: (1) Favorable treatment was to be extended to the emperor after abdication in that he would retain his original title of emperor, would be cordially treated by the Republic as the ruler of a foreign country, would be supported in his annual expenses, amounting to four million dollars, by the Republic of

China, would continue to live in the palace, be allowed to keep his guards, and be assured of protection for his ancestral temples and the private property of the imperial family. (2) Favorable treatment would be extended to the members of the royal family, who would continue to enjoy their hereditary titles, the same privileges as Chinese citizens, protection of their private properties, and exemption from military service. (3) The Manchus, Mongolians, Mohammedans, and Tibetans were all to have equal rights with the Chinese, to receive protection of their original private property, to enjoy their hereditary titles, and to receive subsidies for their poor. In addition, all of these peoples were to enjoy freedom of worship.

All these articles were listed in official documents the contents of which were made known to the foreign ministers in Peking.

RE-ELECTION OF THE PRESIDENT

When the provisional government was established in Nanking, the function of the senate was performed by the delegation made up of the provincial representatives. Before long, however, the senate members elected by all the provinces reached Nanking. They formally convened on the twenty-eighth of January. Soon after the abdication of the Manchu emperor, Yüan Shih-k'ai sent a telegram to the Nanking provisional government, part of which reads:

> That a republic is the best political system is generally recognized by the world. It is really due to the energy and blood given by you gentlemen over a period of many years that the nation has been enabled to make the change from a monarchy to a republic, which will be an endless blessing to the people. ... We should now work hard to promote its progress ... and we should never allow the monarchic system to be restored in China. ... I am quite willing to go

> to the South to hear your ideas and to work with you but ... because it is not easy to maintain order in North China and because it is necessary to control the soldiers with their divergent backgrounds, ... I am afraid that if I go elsewhere, any trouble which may occur here will affect the whole nation. All you gentlemen are thoroughly clear about the situation, and you should be able to excuse my not being able to go to the South.[12]

When Sun received this telegram, he tendered his resignation of the presidency to the senate and recommended Yüan as his successor. On the fourteenth, Sun Yat-sen personally went to the senate to express his support of Yüan Shih-k'ai and won the agreement of the senate. On the same day Yüan Shih-k'ai was unanimously elected provisional president by the representatives of seventeen provinces and Li Yüan-hung was re-elected vice -president. Although both Yüan and Sun had kept their promises, there were still a few important matters in which Yüan did not wish to yield.

To his letter of resignation to the senate, Sun Yat-sen attached three conditions:

1. The location of the provisional government should be in Nanking, as had been decided by the representatives of all the provinces, and that should not be changed.
2. After his resignation and the election of the new president by the senate, the latter should come to Nanking to take up his new position, and only then should the duties of the former president and of the members of the National Assembly be terminated.
3. The constitution of the provisional government was to be prepared by the senate (at that time the constitution had not yet been proclaimed), and the new president must obey it; all laws and regulations which had been proclaimed were to continue in effect

unless revoked by the senate.

These conditions were set up because it was impossible for the people to trust Yüan Shih-k'ai entirely. From the time when he trained soldiers at Hsiao-chan to the time he overthrew the Manchu dynasty, all his actions had been equivocal. But because of the real necessity to use Yüan at this time to put an end to the Manchu regime and to get him to work under the banner of the Republic, the presidency had been given to him. The first two conditions set forth by Sun were designed to force Yüan to leave Peking, the nest of emperors, thus separating him from corrupt, conservative forces; the third was to curb his ambition by legal restrictions. In short, Sun planned to have the foundation of the republic firmly built.

Framing a Constitution

The framing of the provisional constitution, mentioned under the third condition, had started before the abdication of the Ch'ing emperor. While the earlier outlines for the organization of the provisional government were being revised, Sung Chiao-jen had insisted on modifying it to a "responsible cabinet" system so as to eliminate the power of the president. Those who were jealous of him had stubbornly objected to his move and had blocked the modification. But between February 7 and March 8 the necessity for such a change became fully evident and the responsible cabinet system was set up in order to curb Yüan's ambition.

In the responsible cabinet system of the provisional constitution, all cabinet members had to be approved by the senate before they could be appointed. This legislation was passed under unusual circumstances and was designed for only one person—Yüan. Such legislation must be considered erroneous, from the legal point of view, because a really ambitious man would not pay attention to legal restrictions, while a conscientious official might be misled by such a law originally intended for one individual. Later on the constitution was repeatedly disregarded or violated. Yüan and the other warlords of the Peiyang military group were arrogant. The constitution itself was, moreover, not very sound. Unfortunately also, most of the members of the senate believed that once black words were written on white paper and passed by a majority of the parliament, those words would become sacred law which could suppress all devils and like iron cages could confine all fierce beasts. The beasts would later regard the constitution as merely paper to be torn to pieces.

Yüan Shih-k'ai, however, seemed for the moment to be willing to tolerate the constitutional restrictions. He had made up his mind, long before, to respect whatever charms were drawn on paper until he had a firm grasp on all real power. For the time being he would accede to the constitution prepared by the senate. It was very difficult for him to comply with the first and second conditions, however, which required him to leave his headquarters in Peking.

Yüan Avoids Coming to Nanking

Yüan Shih-k'ai's reluctance to leave Peking for Nanking had been revealed in the telegram of February 13. Some of the Nanking senators, among them Ku Chung-hsiu and others who were sentimental about the city which had been a capital for more than six centuries, moved that the seat of the provisional government be changed to Peking. After due consideration, this motion of February 14 was passed by a majority of twenty votes to eight, showing that a majority of the senators did not understand the real intention of Sun Yat-sen in giving up the old capital for a new one.

Sun Yat-sen was outraged to learn of the decision of the senate. Immediately he requested a rediscussion of the bill and insisted that the provisional government be at Nanking. When it was rediscussed by the senate on the fifteenth, the arguments were unusually vehement, but a number of senators eventually came to understand Sun Yat-sen's idea after he had plainly explained it to them. The result of the new vote was a 19-to-7 reversal of the original voting.

Two influential groups stood by Yüan Shih-k'ai in opposing the transfer of the capital to Nanking. One group was composed of the military and official cliques, who considered Peking their well-established headquarters; the other was the diplomatic corps of the imperialists, who enjoyed special privileges in the Legation Quarters. Yüan relied on these two groups to increase his influence. After repeatedly urging Yüan to take up his new post in the South, Sun Yat-sen openly warned him that there would be trouble if he tried to follow the orders of the Manchu emperor to organize a provisional government in Peking; Sun impatiently assured him that if he, Yüan, feared that there would be no one to maintain order in North China, he should leave someone else with full authority to maintain order there before he went South. Yüan, however, was planning to be elected president by the army in North China and by the representatives of Mongolia if Sun did not permit him to follow the emperor's order.

For the moment, Yüan found it essential that he play along with the Nanking government. There was danger that China would be divided into two parts; he did not feel happy about being president of only one part of the country. Yet the Legation Quarters in Peking, as well as the army in North China, wanted him to remain where he was, for his power and prestige could maintain order and peace in the North; as soon as he went to the South, the foreigners and the army would become restless.

But Sun Yat-sen refused to be threatened and still insisted on his original plan. Immediately Ts'ai Yüan-p'ei, Wang Ching-wei, Sung Chiao-jen, and others were dispatched to Peking as special envoys to welcome and accompany Yüan to the South. They arrived at Peking near the end of February. Yüan showed no signs of canceling his projected trip and extended an unusually enthusiastic welcome to the envoys. The Legation Quarters, acting on a hint given them secretly by Yüan, voiced loud objections to his leaving, but to this the envoys paid no attention.

On the night of February 29, the Third Division stationed at Peking under the command of Ts'ao K'un mutinied by setting fire to many houses in the residential and business districts in the heart of the capital. Several thousand commercial firms and civilian families suffered heavy losses as a result of fire and pillage. The lodgings of the envoys were also broken into by the rioters, but the victims managed to escape. Troops in Tientsin and Paoting also rioted on the following day.

These mutinies were generally known to have been plotted by Yüan or by his closest supporters, even though he himself did not take the initiative. The members of the Peiyang military clique later tried to gloss over Yüan's part in the uprisings by alleging that the real cause of the mutinies was that the special grant of one tael of silver, which each soldier was supposed to receive every month during time of war, had been suddenly stopped. Although no definite evidence can be found that Yüan gave the order to mutiny, it does seem suspicious that the special grant was not at that time being given to the Second and Fourth divisions, while the Third Division was still receiving it; yet it was that very division which mutinied. Yüan's followers seem to have been feebly trying to disguise the real cause of the riots.

These military riots caused the foreigners in the Legation Quarters of Peking to fear a recurrence of the Boxer Uprising of 1900. They decided to call protective reinforcements to Peking. The first to do so were the Japanese, who summoned more than a thousand soldiers to Peking from Shanhaikwan and southern Manchuria. Thus, Yüan Shih-k'ai's objective was achieved. The envoys Ts'ai and Wang sent a telegram to the Nanking government and the senate on March 2:

> The military riots in Peking greatly excited the foreigners, and Japan has already sent many soldiers to the capital. Should such incidents recur, the foreigners will certainly take free military action. Observing this situation, we have decided that the crux of the

problem is the need for establishment of a unified government. Other objectives may be compromised.[13]

Ts'ai and Wang were very patriotic, but they were also timid. They fell into Yüan's trap. The provisional government at Nanking made the same mistake, and Sun Yat-sen was unable to do much alone. The Japanese imperialists, in order to augment their own private schemes, were trying to split China. With so much at stake, it seemed not very sensible to squabble with Yüan. On March 6 the senate decided on six measures which consented to Yüan Shih-k'ai's inauguration to the presidency at Peking, and provided that he was to report the names of his premier and cabinet members to the senate in order to secure their approval; after this occurred, President Sun would resign.

Yüan Takes Over the Presidency

Yüan Shih-k'ai was delighted. On March 10 he was inaugurated at Peking, at which time the welcoming envoys Ts'ai and Wang participated in the inauguration ceremonies. The words of his oath were as follows:

> At the beginning of the establishment of the Republic of China, numerous affairs are awaiting to be administered. I, Yüan Shih-k'ai, will exert my energies to the utmost in order to develop the spirit of the republic, to eliminate the defects of the monarchy. I will carefully observe the constitution and follow the desires of the people to steer the nation to a strong and secure position so that our five great races may enjoy together its benefits and pleasures. I will work faithfully to achieve this goal, and I will wait until the convention of the national assembly, by which the first president is to be elected, before I resign. I sincerely swear to announce my true intentions to all the people.[14]

After the inauguration ceremonies Yüan Shih-k'ai wired this oath to the senate at Nanking, and the latter expressed its satisfaction. On March 11, President Sun Yat-sen proclaimed the constitution prepared by the senate. After his approval by the Nanking senate, the premier of Yüan's cabinet, T'ang Shao-i, went to Nanking to organize the new cabinet, the members of which included Lu Cheng-hsiang, minister of foreign affairs; Chao Ping-chün, minister of domestic affairs; Tuan Ch'i-jui, minister of war; Wang Ch'ung-hui, minister of justice; and Ts'ai Yüan-p'ei, minister of education. Ch'en Ch'i-mei, who had been offered the ministry of agriculture and forestry, did not accept his appointment and was replaced by Wang Cheng-t'ing. It was first suggested that the ministry of the army be given to Huang Hsing, but how could Yüan Shih-k'ai give such a pivotal position to a leader of the Revolutionists? Yüan controlled the three most important ministries: domestic affairs, the army, and the navy; the less important ministries were given in appeasement to members of the Revolutionary Party.

On March 29 the new premier, T'ang Shao-i, went to the senate to express his political position and to take charge of the provisional government of Nanking. President Sun formally resigned on the first of April. Four days later the senate decided that the provisional government should be transferred to Peking. Thus came about the first unification of North and South China under the Republic.

THE PROVISIONAL CONSTITUTION

A résumé of the Provisional Constitution of the Republic of China may be appropriate here. The authority of the Republic of China was to be exercised by the senate, the provisional president, the parliament, and the court. All the peoples of China were to be equal, without racial, caste, or religious discrimination. They were to enjoy personal safety and legal protection of their homes and properties, which could not be infringed upon except according to law. They were to enjoy freedom of business enterprise, of the press, of assembly, of private correspondence, movement, and worship. They were to have the right to appeal to the parliament or administrative officers or judges. They were also to have the right to participate in civil-service examinations, to vote, and to stand for election. They were to be obliged to pay taxes and to serve in the army. All civil rights, however, could be restricted by law in times of emergency in order to maintain the peace.

The legislative power of the Republic of China was to be wielded by the senate, which was to consist of representatives of all the provinces as well as of Mongolia and Tibet. Its functions were to approve all laws, the budget, rates of taxation, and standards of measurement, to issue currency, to consider petitions from the people, to make written inquiries of parliamentary members, and to request the provisional government to punish any high officials who accepted bribes or otherwise broke the law. The minutes of the senate were to be published, but they could be kept secret at the request of the parliamentary members, provided more than half of the members of the senate approved. All the decisions of the senate were to be announced and put into effect by the provisional president. The senate was to be dissolved as soon as the parliament [*kuo-hui*] was organized, and its functions were to be carried out by that new organization.

The provisional president and the vice-president were to represent the provisional government, to take general charge of political affairs, and to proclaim laws. The president was to be the commander in chief of the army and navy of the whole nation. He could decide upon official military organization and regulations and appoint all high civil officials and military officers, but the appointment of diplomatic envoys and of ministers had to be approved by the senate. This approval was also necessary when the provisional president declared war, negotiated peace, and signed treaties. He could also receive foreign envoys, bestow decorations, grant amnesties, and so forth. The provisional vice-president was to perform the functions of the president if the latter was for any reason removed from office or unable to perform his duties.

The cabinet, consisting of the premier and the ministers, all of whom were called cabinet members, was to assist the president and was to be directly responsible to him. The cabinet members were to cosign all laws and were to explain political problems before the senate (Articles 43-47).

The court was to be composed of the provisional president, the minister of justice, and the judges, who were to be appointed by the president and the minister of justice. The judges were to handle all cases in open courts, except those which might disturb the security and peace of society, and they were to be free from interference from higher government circles (Articles 48-52).

The supplementary rule provided that the parliament was to be convened within ten months of the proclamation of the provisional constitution, and was to draw up a formal constitution [*hsien-fa*]. The provisional constitution, which was to remain in effect until the completion of this formal constitution, could be neither amended nor revised except by a two-thirds vote of the senate or upon motion of the provisional government supported by four-fifths of the membership of the senate (Articles 53-55).

This, in sum, was the constitution which Yüan Shih-k'ai and T'ang Shao-i had taken an oath to defend. Its provisions, in large part, were lost sight of in the subsequent conflicts between the Kuomintang and the Peiyang military clique.

CHAPTER TEN THE STRUGGLE BETWEEN THE KUOMINTANG AND THE PEIYANG MILITARY CLIQUE

The first decade after the establishment of the Republic saw much activity by these groups: the Revolutionists, the Constitutionalists, and the Peiyang warlords and officials. They differed fundamentally in spirit as well as in method of action. The Revolutionists were interested in radical action, regardless of immediate results. The warlords and politicians were relatively inactive and conservative, showing careful consideration of immediate results. The Constitutionalists, who were less apprehensive of immediate results than the warlords, provided the mean between conservative and radical action. The goal of the Constiutionalists was peaceful reform. When they were allowed to act freely, they were alway reasonable and easy to compromise with; however, when their actions were circumscribed, they occasionally joined the Revolutionists.

Because the Constitutionalists were somewhat unpredictable, the Chinese political struggle, after the overthrow of the Manchu emperor, was always basically between the Revolutionists and the warlords. This general pattern had already been formed at the time of the 1911 revolution. For example, when the riot started at Wuchang, the leaders of the Constitutionalists in the provincial parliament immediately joined the revolutionary activity. The bitter war at Hanyang was on the surface a war between the revolutionary army and the imperial army; actually, it was a struggle between the revolutionary army and the Peiyang military group. Similarly, during the peace negotiations, the arguments were, on the surface, between the revolutionary army and the Manchu court; actually, they marked the beginning of the undercover struggle between the republicans and the Peiyang militarists. During the initial period of this struggle the Constitutionalists were dissatisfied with the Revolutionists and they inclined to the military group.

The years from the time the provisional government was moved to the North until the first dissolution of the parliament (1912－1914) may be called the first period of the struggle of the Kuomintang against the Peiyang clique. During this period, the Constitutionalists and large numbers of politically inert individuals turned to the militarists. This shift caused the Revolutionists to fail for a time to gain popular support.

THE DEVELOPMENT OF POLITICAL PARTIES

Before the fall of the Manchu dynasty, the T'ung-meng Hui had been a secret revolutionary organization rather than an open political party. During the last three years of the Manchu regime, only the Comrades' Association for Petition for a Parliament [*Kuo-hui ch'ing-yüan t'ung-chih Hui*] which later became the Friends of the Constitution [*Hsien-yu Hui*] was an open political party. In 1910 when the national assembly [*tzucheng yüan*] was established, the members elected from the provincial assemblies [*tzu-i-chü*] belonged mostly to the Comrades' Association, and their interests diverged widely from those of the members of the national assembly, who had been appointed by the regent. The two groups were strongly opposed to each other, with the result that the former organized the Friends of the Constitution while the latter organized the Society for the Realization of Constitutional Government. In addition, another small group organized the 1911 Club.

Although these three political organizations acted within the sphere of constitutional monarchism, the last two parties consisted entirely of veteran politicians. As soon as the monarchy collapsed, they also disappeared. Only the Friends of the Constitution may be considered to have been a forerunner of the Progressive Party [*Chin-pu Tang*] which was not only a political party in the national assembly but also had many members outside the assembly as well as branches in many provinces, under the leadership of such men as Sun Hung-i of Chihli, T'ang Hua-lung of Hupeh, and T'an Yen-k'ai of Hunan.

Changes in the T'ung-meng Hui

From the 1911 uprising in Wuchang until the establishment of the provisional government of the republic, the revolutionary T'ung-meng Hui and the Friends of the Constitution both underwent considerable change. The T'ung-meng Hui changed from a secret society to an open party. The other society was dissolved because its stand for a constitutional monarchy had become outmoded. The greatest change, however, was the division and reshuffling of the two big parties to create many small political parties, which again gathered into two great political camps, the Kuomintang for the Revolutionists and the Progressive Party for the Constitutionalists. This shift had occurred before the opening of the first formal parliament. This complicated relationship deserves some further explanation.

The principles of the T'ung-meng Hui at first incorporated the Three Principles of the People (*San-min chu-i*): people's race, or nationalism; people's rights, or democracy; and people's livelihood, or socialism. The T'ung-meng Hui at first also accepted the concept of the revolutionary process through a military administration and political tutelage up to the final goal of a constitutional government. But by the time of the organization of the provisional government, the three phases of the revolutionary process had been completely forgotten. Even the Three Principles of the People were no longer stressed.

At the formation of the T'ung-meng Hui many members believed only in a narrow nationalism, that is, in simply rescuing China from the domination of the Manchus. No sooner had the Manchu dynasty been destroyed than many such members withdrew, seeing no further reason for the continued existence of the party. Misunderstanding between Sun

Yat-sen and some important members of the T'ung-meng Hui, such as Chang Ping-lin, had also been simmering even before the 1911 revolution. These men later split with the T'ung-meng Hui to organize the Union of the Chinese Republic. In the Hupeh area, Sun Wu, Liu Ch'eng-yü, and others who had also been originally members of the T'ung-meng Hui now split off and cooperated with some veteran politicians to organize a political party called the People's Society [*Min-she*] with Li Yüan-hung as their leader and Hupeh as their headquarters.

Other Parties and Their Mergers

The Friends of the Constitution, who had aimed at a constitutional monarchy during the time of the national assembly, now also split up. T'ang Hua-lung, Lin Ch'ang-min and others led a group in organizing a Society for Discussing the Reconstruction of the Republic [*Kung-ho chien-she tao-lun Hui*]. Sun Hung-i and others led a separate group in forming the Republican Unification Party [*Kung-ho tung-i Tang*]. Still others abandoned the Friends of the Constitution to organize the Citizens' Harmonious Progressive Society [*Kuo-min chieh-chin Hui*].

The various parties mentioned above all stemmed from the Revolutionist and the Constitutionalist groups. However, these divisions did not remain apart for long. In reunification the first step was taken by the Unification Party [*Tung-i Tang*], composed of non-T'ung-meng-Hui members, such as Chang Ping-lin and other scholars, mainly from Kiangsu and Chekiang. The second combination was the Republican Party [*Kung-ho Tang*].

In the provisional parliament (*lin-shih ts'an-i yüan*)[1] there were only the two large parties fighting against each other: the T'ung-meng Hui and the Republican Party. The T'ung-meng Hui considered itself to be campaigning for People's Rights, or democracy, while the Republican Party stood for National Rights. The former tried to curb the ambition of Yüan Shih-k'ai; the latter supported him. The former slandered the latter as Yüan's "slave party"; and the latter retaliated by calling its opponents a "mob party." Although the members of both parties constituted less than one-half of the membership of the provisional parliament, the Republican Party was frequently in control of the parliament because it was protected and supported by Yüan Shih-k'ai's military officers and his politicians.

Gradually an important third group emerged, the Unified Republican Party. This party, some of whose members had formerly belonged to the T'ung-meng Hui, gave support to Ts'al Ao, a hero who was to fight against Yüan Shih-k'ai in the winter of 1915. It occupied twenty-five seats in the provisional parliament in Peking (the T'ung-meng Hui and the Kuomintang each occupied more than forty seats) which gave it considerable power in the parliament; it also had six or seven branches in the provinces. During this period, many other political parties, some of which had considerable power, also sprang up, but they were too ephemeral to be listed here.

The great reorganization of the revolutionary forces was initiated by the T'ung-meng Hui leader, Sung Chiao-jen. Next to Sun and Huang, Sung was then the most prominent and active person in politics and was respected by the other parties, especially by many leaders in the United Republican Party. Through his personal influence, the famous Kuomintang was formed in August 1912 by a combination of the T'ung-meng Hui and the United Republican Party, together with other smaller parties.

Other parties were also reshaped, notably the Democratic Party [*Minchü Tang*] headed by Liang Ch'i-ch'ao. At the first election for the members of the parliament, four political parties were active. The largest, the Kuomintang, was opposed by the other three, the Republican, Unification, and Democratic parties. These three parties were no match for the larger one. Since many provincial governments were at that time still in the hands of the revolutionaries, the Kuomintang was very successful in the election.

Chinese political parties, at the beginning of the republican period, had some characteristics without parallel in Europe or America. It was, for instance, possible for a man to belong to several parties at the same time. Prominent people did not easily refuse to accept the offers of several parties who might want them for their leader. Membership in several political parties was also used by unscrupulous men for advancing their own interests. However undesirable, there were many such party members in the early period of the Republic, especially after 1916.

Party Platforms

Party principles amounted to no more than trademarks or slogans. After the fall of the Manchu dynasty and the formation of a number of minor parties, the platforms of the Revolutionary and Constitutional parties became increasingly vague. Hardly any distinctions existed between the political platforms of the T'ung-meng Hui and the Unified Republican Party, except that the T'ung-meng Hui advocated equality between men and women, which no other party at that time was willing to tolerate.

As the parties underwent divisions and recombinations, their statements of principles altered. The most conspicuous change common to all parties was that announced principles were now worded in short, extremely vague sentences capable of very flexible interpretation.

The Kuomintang claimed promotion of political unification, the development of local self-government, the abolition of racial discrimination, emphasis on the improvement of the standard of living, and the maintenance of international peace.

The Republican Party claimed such goals as the maintenance of national unification and the adoption of nationalism, the encouragement of the people's progress by the government, adherence to prevailing international tendencies, and the use of peace and the benefit of the people as the guiding principles of the nation.

The Progressive Party aimed at the adoption of nationalism, establishment of a good and strong government, respect for public opinion, and freedom within the letter of the law. It also intended to follow prevailing international tendencies and to promote peace and the benefit of the people.

In order to attract members from other parties, the Kuomintang increasingly generalized its platform, gave up entirely its stand for equality between men and women, and modified "the strife for international equality" into "the maintenance of international peace." Only on one point, insistence upon "the development of local self-government," did the Kuomintang differ from the Republican and the Progressive parties. However, the Republican Party also advocated "political unification," which was not very different from the "strong and good government" of the Nationalists.

The announced platforms of the current political parties did not, in fact, encompass all of their ideas. Even within the Kuomintang there were two factions, one favoring concentration of power and one preferring decentralization. Sun Yat-sen did not approve of decentralization. At the same time he was absolutely opposed to concentrating tremendous national power in the hands of one unreliable and ambitious man. The two rival parties had no objections to local self-government as such. They believed, however, that unification could be maintained only as the central authorities had absolute power. Actually, this entire problem was a matter of handling just one person—Yüan Shih-k'ai. One party was trying to curb him; the other two were supporting him.

Not one of these parties had the support of the populace. The Chinese people had characteristically remained aloof from party politics for the last several thousand years, refraining from positive action except during their most distressing moments, when they had made a slight show of resistance to governmental force. Because of the general economic backwardness of China, there were no sharply defined castes or classes; there was little struggle of interests between different castes. Political parties were entirely monopolized by the intelligentsia.

After the overthrow of the Manchu government, political parties still lacked popular support. They existed like duckweed, without firm roots. Some of the T'ung-meng Hui members were so ignorant and overbearing that they actually invited resistance rather than support to their cause. The people were tired of war and longing for peace; they trusted their hero, Yüan Shih-k'ai, to give them peace and security without any interference in their daily lives. Trying to curb Yüan, the Kuomintang was the first party to find itself in a precarious position. After its collapse other parties such as the Progressive Party also found themselves losing ground.

In the first few years of the republican period in China, and especially after Yüan Shih-k'ai's abortive attempt to become emperor, China was divided, the North from the South. Political parties changed their emphases. During the period of chaos that followed the division of China and the weakening of the prominent political parties, further new parties grew up, serving merely as instruments of individuals. They carried such names as "Tao-yüan," "Chien-she," "Number Twelve of Thirteenth Street," or "Number Two Hundred of Thirteenth Avenue." They possessed no principles apart from the inducements to financial gain and official position.

CABINET CHANGES AND THEIR RELATIONS TO POLITICAL PARTIES

The transfer of the provisional government and the provisional parliament from Nanking to Peking on April 4,1912, was a great triumph for Yüan Shih-k'ai. The only weapon with which the revolutionaries could fight Yüan was the cabinet system, which had been provided for in the provisional constitution. But from the time of the T'ang Shao-i cabinet until the Chao Ping-chün cabinet, that institution had become absolutely powerless. The cabinet system lacked the support of the populace, who were ignorant of its importance. Its partisans had worked out the system of a party-supported cabinet, but did not understand that this political party must in turn have the support of a large percentage of the population.

During the period from the T'ang to the Chao cabinet, the members of the T'ung-meng Hui became increasingly aware of their inability to dominate the cabinet. The members of the other political parties, fearing that the cabinet might fall entirely into the hands of the T'ung-meng Hui, attempted to create strong parties of their own to fight against the T'ung-meng Hui. This controversy exactly suited Yüan Shih-k'ai. A look at the fall of the T'ang cabinet, and its reorganization under premiers Lu and Chao, shows clearly how the cabinet system, moving with difficulty under the iron heel of the Peiyang Army and the police, soon became helpless and powerless.

The New Cabinet

When T'ang Shao-i was recommended as the premier of the first cabinet, both the Revolutionary Party and Yüan Shih-k'ai considered him most suitable. During T'ang's peace negotiations in the South he had shown sympathy with the Revolutionary Party; after the abdication of the Manchu emperor, he had joined the T'ung-meng Hui. Accordingly, the Revolutionary Party strongly supported him for the premiership. On the other hand, Yüan felt sure of T'ang's support because of a long-standing personal friendship.

T'ang, along with Chao Ping-chün, had long been regarded as Yüan's protégé, always at the call of the master. They had first become close friends in Korea, when Yüan was in charge of military affairs there and T'ang was a customs official. Later on, when Yüan was training soldiers at Hsiao-chan near Tientsin, Hsü Shih-ch'ang was the camp commander and T'ang Shao-i was his assistant. Again, when Yüan became governor of Shantung, he took T'ang along to handle diplomatic affairs and to take general charge of commercial matters. When Yüan was transferred to Chihli as governor-general, he recommended T'ang to a higher position because of his distinguished service and extraordinary ability. Shortly thereafter Yüan asked to take T'ang along with him to his new post, after which he recommended T'ang as acting *taotai* of customs at Tientsin. During Yüan's tenure as governor-general of Chihli, Chao Ping-chün had helped him in handling police administration, while T'ang was the right-hand man in international dealings, thus gaining for himself a prominent name in diplomatic circles. As Yüan progressed up the political ladder, this friendship became even more closely knit.

T'ang Shao-i, however, had received a Western education in the United States. Also, unlike the other politicians of the Peiyang military clique, he was farsighted and concerned not so much with his own political party as with his duty to his country. Despite his friendship with Yüan and the fact that he was not a veteran member of the T'ung-meng Hui, T'ang was not likely to yield meekly to Yüan. This independence of thinking was later to bring the two into conflict.

The ministerial appointees comprised elements of the old and new parties: the ministry of the interior, the army, and the navy were headed by Yüan's henchmen, while a member of the Republican Party was given the ministry of finance; the ministries of agriculture and forestry, justice, education, and industry and commerce were under the control of the T'ung-meng Hui. The various ministers, of course, had numerous disagreements. Chao Ping-chün, minister of the interior, never participated in any cabinet meetings. On being asked the reason for his absence, he would say only that the matters discussed did not concern his ministry, and that he was so busy trying to keep peace for the whole nation that it was better for him not to participate in any of the cabinet meetings.[2]

The first tough task the T'ang cabinet faced was finance. There had been no previous financial administration worth mentioning. The monarchy merely made various attempts to borrow money from foreign countries. The imperialist consortium of banks, which consisted of Britain, the United States, Germany, France, and near the end of the Manchu period Japan and Russia, was trying to dominate the course of Chinese financial affairs because China desired to borrow money from them. T'ang wished to break away from the control of the consortium. He essayed to raise a small loan from a Belgian bank, thus enraging the powerful foreign nations. The finance minister, Hsiung, who had originally opposed the Belgian loans, was terrified when he saw the anger of the consortium. This led to frequent disputes with T'ang and added to the silent conflict between the president and the premier which contributed to T'ang's eventual resignation from the cabinet.

The Resignation of T'ang

When T'ang became premier, he was very strict in his dealings with Yüan, not even permitting the latter's first inaugural message, which had been read before the parliament, to be published until he himself had edited it. Occasionally, official documents issued from the president's office were returned when T'ang disapproved of them. He refused to yield even when secretaries from the president's office or Yüan himself disputed his decisions. Yüan tolerated this stubbornness of the premier only until their disagreement over the governor-generalship of Chihli.

The provisional parliament had agreed that the title of governor-general should be changed to tutu [military governor] and that the provincial assemblies, who should be given the power to elect the tutu, should be changed to provincial parliaments. The Kuomintang members of Chihli had successfully campaigned for the election of Wang Chih-hsiang as tutu of Chihli. To secure this position for him was to enable him to watch Yüan Shih-k'ai, who had refused to go to Nanking. T'ang Shad-i, who was organizing the cabinet in Nanking, also supported this election and informed Yüan Shih-k'ai of the result. Yüan opposed the election, but the Kuomintang members of Chihli insisted that it be recognized. After T'ang went to Peking, he personally requested Yüan to inaugurate Wang; Yüan gave his verbal assent. Wang was summoned to Peking and the news of the election was announced in Chihli.

As soon as Wang Chih-hsiang reached Peking, however, a circular telegram signed by the leaders of five military divisions in Chihli was sent from Peking objecting to the appointment. Yüan seized this chance to send Wang to Nanking to disband troops there. When Premier T'ang refused to cosign the Wang commission, on the grounds that the government should not use such excuses to break its promise to the people, Yüan argued that he was entirely willing to accept the premier's opinion on all other matters except this one; he sent Wang's commission to him without the premier's signature.

The next day T'ang resigned and left Peking. This was the first occasion after he became president on which Yüan used the Peiyang military clique to override the restrictions of the provisional government. Many parliamentary members and newspaper correspondents who hated the T'ung-meng Hui, ignorant of the true state of affairs, ridiculed T'ang's resignation. Even the T'ung-meng Hui members of the parliament regretted only that Wang Chih-hsiang had not succeeded in becoming tutu of Chihli. They paid no attention at all to the document which conspicuously lacked T'ang's signature. It appears that Yüan was not alone in his disregard of the constitution.

After T'ang Shao-i's departure from Peking, the four T'ung-meng Hui members of the cabinet also resigned, and two other ministers, Hsiung Hsi-ling and Shih Chao-chi, who were closely associated with the T'ung-meng Hui, began to feel uneasy in their positions. The T'ung-meng Hui members of the parliament now suggested a one-party cabinet.

The Republican Party knew that they could have no hope of organizing a cabinet. Fearing that the parliament would come to be entirely dominated by the T'ung-meng Hui, they suggested that the parliament should be headed by a nonpartisan premier. This principle was heartily welcomed by Yüan Shih-k'ai, and a docile diplomat, Lu Cheng-hsiang, was chosen as the new premier.

Lu Cheng-hsiang had spent a long time abroad, spoke foreign languages fluently, and was skillful in social affairs. He was welcomed by foreigners as a veteran diplomat. Yüan, too, praised his ability and versatility in foreign affairs. The people therefore looked up to him and failed to recognize him for what he was—a good-natured mediocrity. On party principles the T'ung-meng Hui members objected to Lu's appointment. But on the eighteenth of July, Lu released the names of his candidates for the six ministries (the four ministers of Yüan's clique had not resigned) and at the same time announced his own political opinions. His speech, vulgar and insignificant, brought on such widespread disgust among the members of the parliament that a great turmoil broke loose; all six of his candidates for the vacant ministries were disapproved.

Weakness of the Government in Dealing with Yüan

Immediately afterward a tremendous diplomatic threat appeared in the form of the Russo-Japanese alliance and the decision of Great Britain to take free action in Tibet. Yüan Shih-k'ai again began to play his old tricks. First a special conference of soldiers and police in Peking issued a statement to all the provinces accusing the senate of ignoring the imminent peril of the nation. This was followed by a joint letter written by the generals of South China, who had sold out to Yüan, criticizing the senate. On the twenty-third, Yüan Shih-k'ai selected six cabinet members and asked the senate to approve their appointment. The following day many other letters, signed and anonymous, were sent to the members of the senate either slandering them or threatening their personal safety.

The rumor spread that if the six cabinet members were not immediately approved, the senate would be dissolved by military force and its members might be murdered.

Even the famous scholar Chang Ping-lin, sharply criticizing the senate, threw his support to Yüan Shih-k'ai. He requested that the president be given the power to act according to the exigencies of the time, without constitutional restriction. On July 26 the senate approved all of Yüan's six cabinet ministers except the one for industry and commerce. Thus Yüan Shih-k'ai retested his military strength against the power of the parliament and discovered his might to be supreme.

At this point the Republic of China became a republic utterly dominated by soldiers and police. This coup was possible because of lack of judgment among both the so-called leaders of political parties and the newspapermen. Perfectly willing to become phonograph records for the military group, they reiterated further threats to the senate without any understanding of the importance of this branch of the administration.

Actually, disapproval of all six cabinet ministers by the senate would have been childish. Nevertheless, it was a mistake to conjecture that the appointment of the six cabinet ministers would help float a loan from foreign countries. Nor could the power policy of foreign empires fishing in the troubled waters of China be changed by a Chinese cabinet.

Though the constitution could no longer be used as an effective weapon for the appointment of the president, the senate still insisted that the cabinet ministers should have their approval. On July 27 the senate charged Premier Lu Cheng-hsiang with neglect of duty. Lu, pleading illness, went to a hospital. His sick leave was renewed again and again. Finally the duties of the premier were performed by Chao Ping-chün, the minister of the interior.

After Premier T'ang's resignation, the cabinet actually became the secretariat of the president. All cabinet members had to take orders from the president; it did not matter whether there was a premier or not. On

September 24 the acting premier, Chao Ping-chün, was formally appointed. The other cabinet members remaining unchanged; the Lu cabinet became the Chao cabinet. The Chao cabinet also marked the end of Kuomintang attacks on the Peiyang military clique. A kind of cooperation between the Kuomintang and the Peiyang militarists came to be expected. At least this was the hope of Huang Hsing.

The Fate of Sun's Policy

Though he did not approve of this kind of cooperation, Sun Yat-sen still held to his intention of yielding political power to Yüan Shih-k'ai as soon as the provisional government had been transferred from Nanking to Peking. Sun intended to lead his comrades in forming the opposition party and in devoting their energies to developing education and industry in order to establish a stable foundation for the nation. However, his comrade Ch'en Ch'i-mei objected to this kind of fanciful ideology.

Had the Kuomintang adopted the policy of Sun Yat-sen—that is, refraining from fighting with Yüan, but working on the basic level of the people to implant democratic ideas—they would have been more effective. But the ambitious Sung Chiao-jen and others refused to follow Sun's policy. Huang Hsing acted in complete independence. He asked to be relieved of his duties as commander of the Nanking garrison, and thereupon disbanded his revolutionary troops without pay. Since he cleverly exploited the fact that imperialist banks had refused to grant him a loan, his soldiers were told to go home without pay to show their patriotism and to admire his support of the central government.

After the termination of the Lu cabinet, Sun Yat-sen and Huang Hsing went to Peking to iron out the differences between the parties. Yüan Shih-k'ai, treating them courteously, soon had a single political platform proclaimed. Eight points were announced as having been decided upon through the cooperative efforts of Sun, Huang, Li Yüan-hung, and Yüan Shih-k'ai himself. The Kuomintang had been reorganized to favor cooperation of the old and the new forces. Sun and Huang did their best to remain on good terms with Yüan.

Nevertheless, Kuomintang leaders did not agree among themselves. Sun Yat-sen, yielding all his political powers to Yüan, hoped to lead his party members toward a movement for the modernization of China. His declared policy, to build 200,000 miles of railroad, was regarded by most people, however, as nothing but high-sounding words fired from a big cannon—hence his nickname "Cannon Sun" [*Sun Ta-pao*]. Sun Yat-sen, sincere in his desire for modernization, felt that cooperation between the government and the opposition party was essential. Sung Chiao-jen interpreted cooperation, however, as cooperation solely with President Yüan Shih-k'ai and the party cabinet.

The naive Huang Hsing could believe only good about everyone. Taking for granted that party membership meant party loyalty, he spent his time soliciting new members for the Kuomintang, including the reactionary Yang Tu. But all his efforts were in vain.

Yüan's suggestion to Huang Hsing that Shen Ping-k'un, presumably a loyal member of the Kuomintang, be made premier while all the other cabinet members should remain unchanged was rejected by the party leaders of the Kuomintang. They felt that such a cabinet, headed by a man who had had few connections with them, would be their party cabinet in name only. Hence they agreed to let Yüan Shih-k'ai make Chao Ping-chün the real premier instead of merely the acting premier. Huang transmitted this suggestion to Yüan, who then sought the consent of the senate. Since two-thirds of the senate was controlled by Kuomintang members, because of the combination of the T'ung-meng Hui and the Unified Republican Party, the motion on September 24 was easily passed.

This Chao cabinet was not yet a cabinet of the Kuomintang. Honest Huang Hsing, believing in miracles, tried to persuade all the cabinet members to join the Kuomintang. He even advised Yüan Shih-k'ai to become its leader on the grounds that such action would give support to the government and political security. Yüan, of course, never joined the party. Cabinet members, with the exception of Chou Hsüeh-hsi, Fan Yüan-lien, and the ministers of the army and the navy, did file application blanks for the Kuomintang. Thus in theory the Chao cabinet became the Kuomintang cabinet.

In practice, according to contemporary newspapers, it was a political rather than a party cabinet. Huang Hsing's desire was to obtain political security. He hoped that the officials and warlords of the Peiyang military group could be assimilated and could be persuaded to cooperate with the Kuomintang members. Sun Yat-sen adopted a policy of surrender, for the time being, having no intention of declaring war on Yüan Shih-k'ai.

Herein lies the weakness of the Kuomintang from its very beginnings. It was also the gravestone of Sung Chiao-jen. His concept of the cooperation between the old and the new was to yield only the formal presidency to Yüan Shih-k'ai, an exponent of the traditional forces, while the cabinet was to be controlled by the members representing the new force. After the Kuomintang won its next battle, the war to elect parliamentary members, there occurred the notorious murder of Sung.

SUNG'S MURDER AND THE GREAT LOAN STORM

After the appearance of Chao Ping-chün's "cabinet party," the Kuomintang opposition to Yüan Shih-k'ai in the senate ceased. The members of the Provisional Parliament were all busy campaigning for formal parliamentary positions. In the spring of 1913 there was little notable political news in Peking, but a great confusion of the election activity in all the provinces. The Kuomintang, reputedly the most successful revolutionary party and moreover absorbing a large number of opportunistic politicians, had great advantages in the election.

The First Election

Except for the small nucleus of faithful members of the Kuomintang, a great many other members belonged to several parties simultaneously. In the first election it was announced that the Kuomintang gained more than 360 seats in the house of representatives. The Republican Party had 250-odd seats, and the Unification Party well beyond a hundred; the Democratic Party also claimed to have more than a hundred seats. However, there were only slightly more than 500 seats in the house; the seats claimed by the various parties totaled over 700. There could be only one explanation of this—the parties were sharing their membership.

The success of the Kuomintang in the election, even including those members who had also joined other parties, was still sufficient to enable it to command a majority. This majority, however, led to its failure.

Sung Chiao-jen had tried his best to form a strong party, hoping to launch a vigorous but legal struggle within the framework of constitutional government. After the successful election of the Kuomintang, he campaigned from Hunan to Hupeh, Anhwei, Nanking, and Shanghai for his own appointment to the cabinet. Wherever he went, he made speeches criticizing the administration very sharply and advocating the control of the cabinet by the majority party. But he still maintained that the future president should be Yüan Shih-k'ai.

Yüan and the Murder of Sung

To Sung Chiao-jen criticism was normal in a constitutional nation; but to the officials and the warlords of the Peiyang military clique such actions, even within the framework of constitutional government, were absolutely intolerable. On March 20, 1913, Sung Chiao-jen, on his way to catch a train northward from Shanghai, was shot and killed at the railroad station.

Immediately after Sung's death the assassin, Wu Shih-ying, and his accomplice, Ying Kuei-sheng, were arrested and many documents relating to the conspiracy were found in their homes. These documents indicated that with the conspirators there were also included the secretary of the cabinet Hung Shu-tsu, the Premier Chao Ping-chün, and even President Yüan. This news stirred a great furor among the people.

When the murder occurred, President Yüan ordered the Kiangsu tutu, Ch'eng Te-ch'üan, "to investigate thoroughly the leading conspirators and obtain the exact facts in order to punish them severely according to the law." On April 26, Ch'eng reported to Yüan Shih-k'ai as follows:

> The case of the assassination of Sung Chiao-jen, the former minister of agriculture and forestry, has been thoroughly examined by the two mixed courts of the municipal government of the International Settlement and the French Concession in Shanghai, and the plan of the assassination has been clearly established. On the sixteenth and seventeenth of April, the murderers, Wu Shih-ying and Ying Kuei-sheng, were transferred to this government. On the eighteenth, the Mixed Court of the International Settlement sent over a five-shot pistol... also three copies of a secret telegram code, and two packages of carefully sealed telegraphic correspondence... In addition, there were five packages of correspondence and telegrams discovered in the culprit Ying's house by the police of the Shanghai International Settlement.
>
> On January 14 of this year Premier Chao sent a letter to the culprit Ying: "The secret telegram code has been sent. Please keep it carefully, and hereafter your telegrams may be addressed to the cabinet directly." Under separate cover there was a secret code labeled "Ying, the Cabinet, Confidential, January 14, 1913..."
>
> On February 1 Hung Shu-tsu sent a letter to the culprit Ying, saying: "The most valuable thing for us to do is to write a violent

essay on a great theme."

On February 2 Hung wrote a letter to the culprit Ying, saying: "I have hinted at the writing of the most important essay, and have told him there must be violent action. You must send a telegram to old Chao before writing the essay and ask him what the amount will be." In these telegrams the phrases "important essay," "violent action" implied the assassination.

On the twenty-first, Hung sent Ying another telegram: "As soon as the Sung case has been handled, you can ask for money at once."

On February 22 Hung sent a letter to Ying, saying: 'Your letter has been personally handed over to the president, who has read it. Hereafter, please do not send any telegrams to the cabinet, because Chao Ping-chün has sent me the secret code, and it is feared that the secret might be revealed.'"[3]

Chao Ping-chün appears to have been an accessory to the murder; even Yüan Shih-k'ai could not but be recognized as such, judging from the sudden deaths of Ying Kuei-sheng and Chao Ping-chün. Hung Shu-tsu was sought by the government, but he fled to Tsingtao, where he lived comfortably. Chao Ping-chün tried to resign, but Yüan Shih-k'ai only permitted him to ask for temporary leave. Chao continued to enjoy life in Peking. Ying Kuei-sheng, escaping from jail in Shanghai, sent a telegram to the government in Peking on October 1, 1913, begging for a review of his case. In January 1914 Ying went to Peking; but he was assassinated on January 19 in the train from Peking to Tientsin. The assassination was said to have been ordered by Yüan.

At that time Chao Ping-chün was the tutu of Chihli. He dispatched a circular telegram to search for Ying's assassin. Shortly afterward Chao Ping-chün also died suddenly, with the blood gushing from his five orifices. It is reported that when Chao heard of Ying's death, he picked up the telephone and complained to Yüan, saying that hereafter no one would want to do anything for the president. A few clays later Chao died suddenly. Probably Yüan was afraid that Chao would reveal his secret. After Yüan's death in 1916, Hung Shu-tsu was arrested by the son of Sung Chiao-jen, and was tried in a court of law, where he was sentenced to death. Thus the Sung case was concluded.

Yüan's motive in taking Sung's life was, very likely, his recognition that since the Kuomintang had been successful in getting votes in the parliament, Sung would make use of this majority to compel Yüan to reorganize the cabinet; to destroy the Kuomintang, it was necessary to destroy its leaders first. There were, however, many other leaders. Why was Sung alone assassinated? Because Yüan knew that Sun Yat-sen at that time had no intention of antagonizing him, Huang was too naive and honest, while a few others with rank equal to Sung in the party had either been bribed by Yüan or did not wish to draw unfavorable attention to themselves.

It was common for Yüan to bribe members of the Kuomintang. He had even tried to purchase Sung Chiao-jen by giving him a checkbook for a bank in Peking and allowing him to write checks for any amount he desired. Sung, drawing a little money to show his appreciation, then returned the original checkbook to Yüan. This action undoubtedly contributed to Sung's early death.

Yüan Shih-k'ai hated people with ability and integrity; such people were difficult to order around. During his entire life Yüan's ability lay in cheating and in placing his own partisans in lucrative positions. He fostered such habits in society, thus driving the entire populace to corruption, covetousness, and fraud. In comparison with this basic jealousy and dishonesty his usurpation of power was a lesser fault.

When the evidence for the Sung case was announced in Shanghai and the local court insisted on summoning Chao Ping-chün to the examination, both Yüan and Chao were alarmed. They spread the rumors at once of further assassinations in Peking to justify the government's arrest of many suspects. They announced that a list of the names of a bloodthirsty organization had been discovered, that a parliamentary member of the Kuomintang had been arrested, and that a self-confessed member of this bloodthirsty society had voluntarily surrendered to the government and confessed that Huang Hsing was the murderer. When the Shanghai court summoned Chao Ping-chün, Peking threatened to arrest Huang Hsing in retaliation. The judicial problem thus became a political one; the Shanghai court could not achieve the expected result according to proper procedure.

Yüan and Foreign Loans

Thereafter, the underhand struggle became more severe. Yüan anticipated that a civil war was inevitable. He secretly endeavored to float a large loan to finance his military preparations as well as his bribes. On the same day, April 26, that the evidence of the Sung case was announced, the contract for the great loan for £25,000,000 was also signed.

The arrangements for this loan were begun when T'ang Shao-i was premier, but were not completed until December 1912. The imperialistic capitalists, who aimed at an economic invasion of China, refused to lend money until this aim was fulfilled. The important items of the loan were reported by Chou Hsüeh-hsi, minister of finance, to the provisional parliament, and the latter indicated its approval in principle. But the government did not bring the loan up for discussion in a formal session of the parliament. Neither did the parliament approve the loan through a majority resolution.

This great loan, after it had been reported to the senate in December, underwent some new changes on the part of the bank corporations. The ministers of Russia and France objected to the items concerning the employment of foreigners by the Chinese government and insisted that each of their nations must have one person thus employed. Later on, a compromise was made in the Legation Quarters to the effect that an Englishman must be invited by the Chinese government as the controller of the salt taxes, to be assisted by a German, while the Bureau of International Loans was to be under the general directorship of a German, with a Russian and a Frenchman to serve in the capacity of auditors and advisors. The Legation Quarters conveyed this plan on March 3, 1913, when the Sung case had not yet occurred, to the Chinese authorities, who considered such an arrangement disadvantageous to China and so rejected it. The American government, considering the demands of the international bank corporation for the power to supervise Chinese financial authorities to be unreasonable, ordered its own banks to withdraw from the corporation and encouraged American businessmen to make investments in China at low interest rates.

The five-nation bank corporation now seemed frightened. If Yüan Shihk'ai had not tried to create a civil war and had not counted on a foreign loan to suppress that civil war, it would have been a great opportunity for him to break the control of the five-nation bank corporation. However, after the Sung case came up, Yüan secretly consulted the five-nation bank corporation, which, recently alarmed by the withdrawal of the United States, welcomed Yüan's request. The contract for the big loan, which had required over a year of negotiations, was now signed in a few days. Afterward, Yüan stated that though the floating of the loan had been approved by the senate the previous December, he now wished to have the parliament reaffirm the case. The members of the Kuomintang arose in a great uproar. The supporters of Yüan Shih-k'ai admitted that the procedure for arranging the loan had been irregular, even though they still strongly objected to the Kuomintang's anti-Yüan movement. Some of the provincial tutu sent telegrams charging that the procedure of Yüan was illegal; however, many of them, bribed by Yüan, later gave him their full support.

The previous July another secret loan from Austria had been arranged by the Yüan government. On April 20 before the signing of the great loan, this Austrian loan had still not been approved by the parliament, nor was the parliament informed until some members repeatedly inquired about it. Thereafter, even those members who campaigned for Yüan could no longer speak out for their government. Consequently, Chao Ping-chün and Chou Hsüeh-hsi resigned. After securing these two loans, Yüan Shih-k'ai was prepared for any new action.

THE FAILURE OF THE ANTI-YÜAN ARMY

After the murder of Sung, Yüan Shih-k'ai prepared for war against the Kuomintang without any further hesitation and without regard for law or parliament. After the truth about the Sung case had been revealed, Sun Yat-sen returned from Japan to Shanghai. He was now aware that the heavy responsibilities of the reconstruction of China should not be entrusted to Yüan. Since it was of no use to oppose Yüan either by law or by argument, Sun, too, now favored early warfare against him. But at this time the members of the Kuomintang were a motley crowd, and there was not even any agreement of opinion among the old T'ung-meng Hui members. The opinions of the Kuomintang members in the parliament in North China were different from those held by the members of the party organization in South China. Some favored a peaceful policy, while others advocated violent action. Among the party bosses in the southern provinces, some advocated quick action, while others suggested gradual action against Yüan.

Confusion in the Kuomintang

In his correspondence published on May 27 of that year, the newspaperman Huang Yüan-yung gives a useful description of the state of the Kuomintang. He says:

> At the time of the Sung case, the Kuomintang members were almost at the primitive stage of the T'ung-meng Hui, and even the group of members who were jurists in North China kept silent, lacking the courage to form any opinion different from that of the government...On account of the influence of the second revolution in 1913, many members of the Kuomintang withdrew or organized a third party. Now because of the distressing situation created by the failure of the second revolution and the stronger attitude of the government, the radical elements of the Kuomintang in South China began to soften and the jurists also regained their influence by announcing a sincere report of Kuomintang opinions: (1) that President Yüan should stop his military expeditions; (2) that the great loan should again be handled by the government, through which all negotiations with foreign banks were to be conducted, while the Kuomintang members in the parliament would guarantee their approval of the loan, though the additional articles concerning the use of the loan should be slightly modified; (3) that the cabinet must be reorganized. If these three requests were complied with, the Kuomintang would promptly approve the loan recommended by the new cabinet, and if the new cabinet were organized by the Progressive Party, which had been combined with the Kuomintang, the additional articles would not be mentioned at all. [4]

The once arrogant Kuomintang was now very meek. The military clique of the Kuomintang insisted on overcoming Yüan by force. At the beginning of the Sung case, the power of the parliamentary clique had been inferior to that of the military clique, and the former had had to keep silent. Now, even though Kuomintang military power had not been used on a large scale, it was clearly ineffective. Therefore the parliamentary clique, again active, determined to wrangle with Yüan through the law, to defeat him legally, and later to defeat him by military force.

Their plan was to accuse Yüan of having illegally negotiated the great loan, to demand the reorganization of his cabinet, and possibly to bribe the members of the Progressive Party, with the promise of such a reorganization, thus putting a stop to the cooperation between this party and Yüan Shih-k'ai. After T'ang Hua-lung was elected speaker of the parliament, this plan was unanimously adopted by the Kuomintang, which was ready to support the Progressive Party in organizing a new cabinet.

Military Resources of the Kuomintang

The domestic condition of the Kuomintang was in a great confusion. Sun Yat-sen and Li Lieh-chün insisted on removing Yüan by military power. Some of the other leaders objected to Yüan, while others were hesitant and indecisive. In Peking a majority of the partisan members in the parliament wished to cooperate with the Progressive Party in order to control Yüan by constitutional means.

In the southern provinces, Wuchang, although it was the cradle of the 1911 Revolution, was then entirely under the control of Li Yüan-hung, Yüan Shih-k'ai's former henchman. Although Hunan was under the control of the Kuomintang, T'an Yen-k'ai was irresolute and his officers were at odds with one another. Po Wen-wei, the tutu of Anhwei, was similarly undecided, and his subordinates were also in a state of disharmony. In Nanking, the Kiangsu tutu, Ch'eng Te-ch'üan, played politics between the two sides, and his troops were not united. Kwangtung, under Hu Han-min and Ch'en Hsiung-ming, was even more chaotic. Only in Kiangsi did Li Lieh-chün hold real power. The other provinces, though they had less relation with the forthcoming war, were full of unrest and disorder.

Under such conditions, there was very little chance to combat Yüan Shih-k'ai by military force. The Progressive Party supported Yüan Shih-k'ai, and so did all the foreign imperialists.

Yüan Breaks with the Kuomintang

Although the speakers of the senate, Chang Chi and Wang Cheng-t'ing, had sent telegrams overseas to delay the payment of the great loan, the parliamentary members of the Progressive Party, supporting Yüan Shih-k'ai, compelled Chang and Wang to issue another telegram voiding their previous telegrams and declaring that what they had said previously represented only their personal opinions. As to the imperialists' support of Yüan, while Sun Yat-sen earnestly advised the consortium of the five nations to stop the loan and the latter promised that no money would be paid for two weeks after the signing of the agreement, in reality £2,000,000 had already been paid on April 29, only four days after their promise. Even the *London Times* made sarcastic comment on Sun Yat-sen's objection to the loan.

Yüan Shih-k'ai, strengthened by the financial support of the imperialists as well as by the moral support of the Progressive Party, began scheming to rid himself of several of the arrogant tutus, including Li Lieh-chün, Po Wen-wei, and Hu Han-min. Yüan made an important and surprising announcement to the correspondent Huang Yüan-yung:

> You may tell the Kuomintang members that I have made up my mind. Sun, Huang, and the others aim at nothing but trouble. I, who have been entrusted with the safety of the four hundred million people and their property, cannot tolerate the actions of these troublemakers. They all say that I am contesting for the presidency. As a matter of fact, I would be glad to yield the position to a competent man, if there is one; but I believe that my own political and military experience and personal credit in diplomatic circles are not inferior to those of any other man... If they can organize another government, I certainly have the power to destroy it.[5]

Three days later Yüan issued the orders severing relations with the Kuomintang.

On the pretext that Li, Po, Hu and others had disobeyed the central government by sending telegrams to oppose the loan, they were all dismissed in June from their positions as tutu. Since Yüan feared that the authorities of Hunan might attack Hupeh, he bribed some treacherous persons to destroy the Hunan ammunition dumps so that more violent elements in that province would have no means of action. Yüan was not afraid of Kwangtung because of its distance from Peking and its internal strife, nor was he afraid of Anhwei, which was also having domestic trouble. As to Kiangsi, he advanced troops to Kiukiang, under the command of Li Shun, long before any action was taken by the Kiangsi military leader.

The dismissal of the three tutus, Li, Po, and Hu, aroused no repercussions. Troops of the Peiyang military clique continued to advance toward Kiangsi until July 12, when Li Shun was appointed by Yüan Shih-k'ai to be the garrison commander of Kiukiang. There his troops clashed with the provincial troops. On the same day, Li Lieh-chün started his military action by occupying Hukow and declared war against Yüan. Huang Hsing went to Nanking on the fifteenth and compelled the Kiangsu tutu, Ch'eng Tech'üan, to announce his intention to fight against Yüan in support of Li Lieh-chün's Kiangsi army. Military authorities of Anhwei, Hunan, Kwangtung, Fukien, and Szechwan declared sympathy with Li Lieh-chün, but only halfheartedly. This war, which lasted a little longer in Kiangsi and Nanking, was called the Second Revolution of 1913.

After the initial military action, many newspapers controlled by the Progressive Party favored Yüan and criticized the Kuomintang. To make a good impression on Yüan, some of the parliamentary members of the Progressive Party even made a move for a punitive expedition against the rebels. Only the powerless Chiang Chih-yu, who did not belong to any political party, suggested that Yüan Shih-k'ai should resign from the presidency. His declaration of this conviction, regarded by Yüan's partisans as pro-Kuomintang, was therefore ignored.

Two famous leaders of the Kuomintang, Wang Ching-wei and Ts'ai Yüan-p'ei, had consistently objected to the war. Progressive Party members who usually cherished friendly feelings toward them now wished to make use of them. Wang and Ts'ai each issued a declaration requesting Yüan's resignation and the re-election of a president in order to prevent a war. Their request, of course, went unheeded.

Nearsighted newspaper critics assumed that the Kuomintang had taken up arms first. They insisted that even if Yüan had been in the wrong, he ought to have been reprimanded by the proper legal methods and not by military power. However, the so-called legal procedures were illusory, since at that time the criminal Chao Ping-chün had declined to appear in court, and the parliament had lost its free powers of election.

This illusion was not shattered until the parliament was dissolved and Yüan proclaimed himself emperor. Meanwhile, most of the intelligentsia argued that no one but Yüan could be the president because, without him, the foreign powers would not recognize the Republic, because he possessed the most powerful army, and because his subordinates gave their allegiance only to Yüan, not caring whether the nation was a republic or a monarchy. The people at large still could not understand why Yüan should be removed from his office; they still could not believe that Yüan intended to become emperor.

Military Defeat of the Kuomintang

The war was formally begun on July 12. The anti-Yüan army from Hukow, Kiangsi, was attacked by Yüan's force from both water and land, and was routed on July 25. On August 18 the capture of Nanchang, the provincial capital, by Yüan's forces was followed by their complete occupation of the province.

On the Nanking front, because a part of the troops had been

purchased by Yüan with the money borrowed from the imperialist nations and a riot took place, the Eighth Division of the revolutionary army had to withdraw from the front in order to protect its headquarters. Thus the troops fighting against Yüan's army on the Hsuchow front were also forced to retreat because of the lack of support. The dangerous situation inside and outside of Nanking compelled Huang Hsing to leave the city on July 29, and Ch'eng Te-ch'üan canceled his declaration of independence. Resistance against Yüan's army continued until September 1; then Nanking was taken by Chang Hsün, a general whose soldiers were ordered to keep their pigtails as a sign of loyalty to the Manchus.

While Huang Hsing was still in Nanking, Ch'en Ch'i-mei, Niu Yung-chien, and others had made an abortive attack on the Shanghai arsenal. On August 13 they were also forced to give up the fort at Woosung. When the independent government of Po Wen-wei in Anhwei was also destroyed by Yüan's soldiers, the whole Yangtze Valley was again under the control of the Peiyang military clique. Shortly thereafter T'ang Hsiang-ming was appointed tutu of Hunan, Tuan Ch'i-jui tutu of Anhwei, Li Shun tutu of Kiangsi, and Feng Kuo-chang tutu of Kiangsu.

Hunan now became the source of inflammation from which war between North and South China spread repeatedly. Hupeh, Anhwei, Kiangsi, and Kiangsu remained under the oppression of the Peiyang clique for more than ten years. The Peiyang warlords were not driven away until the attacks by the Kwangtung revolutionary army in 1926.

The failure in 1913 of the anti-Yüan army was perhaps due to lack of support from the people at large. Tired of war, they could not see that an operation for a cancer should be performed early rather than at the last moment.

THE DESTRUCTION OF THE PARLIAMENT AND THE END OF THE "FIRST-CLASS CABINET"

The anti-Yüan campaign had resulted from the Sung murder case, which in its turn derived from the fact that a majority of the seats in the first formal parliament were occupied by the Kuomintang. But between the Sung case and the dissolution of the parliament the situation of the various parties had undergone some changes. Facing the superior position of the Kuomintang, the three parties, the Republican, the Unification, and the Democratic, were combined into the Progressive Party, and T'ang Hua-lung secured the position of speaker of the house of representatives. The assassination of Sung Chiao-jen was a great loss to the Kuomintang, since he had been very active and influential among his fellow members in the parliament. Under Yüan Shih-k'ai's policy of bribery and pressure, the Kuomintang partially disintegrated, breaking into factions such as the Constitutional Friends and the Political Friends Society.

The center of gravity in the parliament was thus shifted to the Progressive Party. This now included, among others, some of the eminent members of the old Constitutional Party, whose actions and words were very mild but always different from those of the Kuomintang, whose members were considered to be a mere mob. On account of this, the Progressive Party was supported by current public opinion. Fundamentally, Yüan Shih-k'ai had no particular affection for them. Nevertheless, in order to control the Kuomintang, he had to make use of them for the time being. The milder elements of the Kuomintang, realizing their dangerous situation, cooperated with the more moderate members of the Progressive Party in order to prolong their own political lives in the parliament.

Hsiung Hsi-ling's Cabinet

The most fortunate achievement of the Progressive Party appeared to be its success in organizing the so-called "first-class cabinet." During the anti Yüan expedition, there was virtually no premier because Chao Ping-chün had not paid attention to his duties for some time, and Tuan Ch'i-jui had been made acting premier. When the secret loan from Austria was revealed, even the Progressive Party tried to impeach some of the cabinet members, and Yüan thereupon decided to reorganize the cabinet.

Yüan's original intention was to have Hsü Shih-ch'ang head the list. Some remnants of the Kuomintang still existed in the parliament, however, and Hsü dared not take the responsibility. Yüan, hoping to use the Progressive Party, suggested that either Hsiung Hsi-ling or Hsü Shih-ch'ang be made premier and allowed the Progressive Party to take its choice between them. A prominent member of that party suggested that it would be easier to win acceptance for Hsiung in the parliament, and again another member suggested to Yüan that the first choice, no matter who it was, would meet opposition, and that it was therefore better to try Hsiung first, and if he should prove unacceptable to the parliament, then to call on Hsü. Yüan accordingly recommended Hsiung Hsi-ling as premier near the end of July and sought the consent of the parliament.

At this time, the moderate wing of the Kuomintang was trying to cooperate with the Progressive Party, hoping that the Progressive Party would organize the cabinet. Hsiung Hsi-ling was exactly the man to have close dealings with the Progressive Party. Since he was then supported by that party, he would at least be better than Hsü Shih-ch'ang, a warlord of the Peiyang machine. Hsiung was accepted by both houses of the parliament.

Since Yüan's original intention had been to propose Hsiung first only to test the intentions of the parliament, this unexpected approval of Hsiung drew Yüan into a trap. The Progressive Party hoped to support Hsiung Hsi-ling in organizing a cabinet which would consist entirely of its own members, except for the ministers of the army and the navy. On July 31, Hsiung was formally appointed premier. Still retaining his office as governor of Jehol, he declined again and again to come to Peking. After repeated urging from Liang Ch'i-ch'ao, he was finally installed as premier on August 28.

After a week in this new post, Hsiung still could not organize a cabinet because Yüan Shih-k'ai had already appointed the important ministers before Hsiung came to Peking. Only the insignificant ministries of education, justice, agriculture, and commerce were given to him to dispose of. Hsiung, who had declared beforehand that he would organize a first-class cabinet with the most capable and experienced ministers, now found that the experts had been selected for him by Yüan.

Hsiung's plan had been to head his "first-class cabinet" with Liang Ch'i-ch'ao, whom he wished to appoint minister of finance so that he might fulfill his plan of financial reorganization. Chang Chien and Wang Ta-hsi, the second and third most capable persons on Hsiung's list, refused to enter the cabinet unless Liang did so. The members of the Progressive Party, hoping to have the cabinet posts occupied by their members alone, did not want Liang Ch'i-ch'ao in the cabinet. After much persuasion by Hsiung and Yüan, Liang eventually accepted the ministry of justice. The list of cabinet members was rapidly completed and announced on September 11:

Hsiung Hsi-ling, premier and minister of finance
Tuan Ch'i-jui, minister of war
Liu Kuan-hsiung, minister of the navy
Chu Ch'i-ch'ien, minister of domestic affairs
Sun Pao-ch'i, minister of foreign affairs
Chou Tzu-chi, minister of communications
Liang Ch'i-ch'ao, minister of justice
Wang Ta-hsi, minister of education
Chang Chien, minister of agriculture and commerce

At first glance, this cabinet appeared to be similar to that headed by T'ang Shao-i in the first year of the Republic. The ministers of T'ang's cabinet, apart from the warlords and the officials of the Peiyang militarists, had included a few famous members of the T'ung-meng Hui, who filled up the various cabinet sinecures. Hsiung's cabinet, apart from the members of the Peiyang clique, included a few members of the Progressive Party in similar positions. The major difference was that the T'ang cabinet had dared to refuse to cosign an appointment with the president, and after it was dissolved, activity by the Revolutionists and Constitutionalists was still possible. The Hsiung cabinet, on the other hand, was willing to cosign Yüan Shih-k'ai's orders to drive out the Kuomintang parliamentary members and to dissolve the parliament. After the fall of this cabinet, there was no more freedom of action for the political parties; there was no more opportunity for activity for even the most outstanding members.

The Formal Election of a President

As the war against Yüan Shih-k'ai continued, the more aggressive Kuomintang members recognized that the parliament in Peking had lost its freedom to perform its duties and suggested that all the Kuomintang members should leave Peking for the South. The speaker of the senate, Chang Chi, who had left Peking long before, persuaded two of the military governors, Ch'eng Te-ch'üan and T'an Yen-k'ai to send telegrams to the parliament requesting their members to go South. A majority of their parliamentary members, however, did not wish to do so, although Wang Ching-wei and Ts'ai Yüan-p'ei also advocated this move. A rumor was thereupon spread that the more obstreperous of the Kuomintang members were planning to bomb the parliament.

Yüan Shih-k'ai shared the desire to destroy the parliament, but at that very moment he realized the necessity of maintaining it, since he had not yet secured the formal presidency, which had to be voted by the parliament. If the parliament were destroyed, he would have to create another body to insure his election, and that would take time; if a large number of the parliamentary members should go to the South, they would be utilized by Sun and Huang, his enemies. Therefore his solution was to arrest and imprison members of the parliament, while issuing at the same time a special bulletin assuring their protection. Because he desired to obtain the formal presidency, he was forced for the time being to maintain the parliament and to rely on the Progressive Party. Neither the Progressive Party nor the moderate Kuomintang members perceived his scheme. But the Progressive Party, while hoping to make a constitution which would be ideal to guide the traditional force of the Peiyang warlords gradually to constitutional government, certainly had no desire for Yüan Shih-k'ai's formal election to the presidency.

The moderate wing of the Kuomintang naturally did not trust Yüan, and they were unwilling to elect him formally as president. They had difficulty, however, in finding another suitable candidate, because neither Sun nor Huang nor Li was acceptable to the Progressive Party. The moderates desired to follow the normal procedure for writing the constitution and then formally electing a president in accordance with its provisions. In this way they could watch Yüan's activity during the period of constitutional codification, and if Yüan did not interfere with the parliament illegally, he might be elected president; at the same time they would have a formal constitution which, they believed, Yüan would not dare to flout.

In short, the moderate wing of the Kuomintang planned to overcome Yüan by constitutional restraint and by the presidential election. But if the provisional constitution could not control Yüan, how could a later permanent constitution do so? Actually the articles governing the presidential election were just one part of the constitution; it was a normal procedure to draw up the constitution first and elect the president later. The leader of the Progressive Party, Liang Ch'i-ch'ao, favored this procedure. Nevertheless, the people at large considered the recognition of the Republic of China by the foreign powers to be the big problem. If the republic were not formally recognized by the foreign powers, she would not have a legal standing in the international family; and unless there was a formally elected president, it would not be easy to gain this recognition.

Yüan Shih-k'ai, utilizing this popular opinion, ordered his partisans to advocate the necessity of electing a president before the drawing up of a constitution. The Progressive members of the parliament preferred to confirm the leading position of Yüan. They feared that postponement of the election might give the Kuomintang members of the parliament the opportunity to cause more trouble. The Kuomintang members, unable to insist on their original intention, had to yield.

The constitution committee, selected from among the members of the parliament to draw up the articles governing the election of the president, announced these articles on the sixth of October. A committee on presidential elections was organized by the members of the two houses to elect the president. On election day, however, the situation was farcical.

Originally, Yüan Shih-k'ai had planned to be formally inaugurated as president and to receive the congratulations of foreign diplomats on the national holiday of the Double Tenth [the tenth of October]. He did not propose to be prevented from receiving the foreign diplomats on that day merely for some delay in the election date which might be forced by the Kuomintang. He was further afraid that the other factions in the parliment might ask for favors in exchange for their electing him president. He therefore ordered in advance several thousand secret police, disguised as an independent Citizens' Corps, to surround the parliament building after the members had entered. Then this group announced that unless the right president was elected that day, no electors would be allowed to go out of the door.

Members of the parliament remained in session from eight in the morning until ten at night, when their business was finally concluded. Strong-willed members who desired to follow the electoral laws announced that a three-fourths majority was required to elect the president. If no candidate attained this after the second ballot, the candidate with the most votes after the second ballot was to be elected, provided the votes cast for him were more than one-half of the total votes. That group of determined members, angered by the so-called Citizens' Corps, purposely refused to vote for Yüan. It was only on the third ballot that Yüan received the required number of votes. Only after the announcement of the election had been welcomed by the "citizens" with the shout of "Long live the president!" were the members allowed to leave.

Before his formal election as president, Yüan already understood that he could not trust the Progressive Party. He therefore ordered his chief secretary, Liang Shih-i, who was concurrently the head of the Bank of Communication, to bribe a few members of the parliament to organize a Citizens' Party [Kung-min Tang]. All persons who were under Liang's influence (Liang had been minister of post and communications and head of the Bank of China) were ordered to join his Citizens' Party, and formed what was later called the "Communications clique." The functions of this party were to campaign for Yüan's formal election as president and to supervise the codification of the constitution. While the constitution committee was working, the Citizens' Party caused trouble in every possible way, including the publication of derogatory articles in newspapers claiming that the constitution being drafted by the committee would be unfavorable to the president. Yüan's legal advisors also took this opportunity to explain to Yüan that the article in the draft constitution concerning his term of office would be harmful to him.

The article concerning the term of office of the president, as first proposed, set the term at six years, with a one-term limit. Yüan declared: "I desire very much to have the term limited to three years, and the shorter the better. But there should be no limitation on re-election, lest my army officers and soldiers should not obey my restrictions." Another problem was the definition of the "responsible cabinet." A third point was that after the relinquishment of his office, the president should face criminal prosecution for any misdeeds he committed during his tenure. This article was suggested by a member of the Progressive Party. Before the election of the president had been decided, Yüan showed no signs of objecting. He tried his best to suppress the rumors that soldiers and police might interfere with the parliament. He also instructed his close assistants that they should not interfere with the constitution nor take any futile action.

When the constitution committee announced the articles governing the election of the president, Yüan was already unhappy. He lamented that a president had not even the authority to proclaim a constitution. Afraid that his inauguration might be delayed beyond the Double Tenth, he dared not argue at this time. But after the Double Tenth and his formal inauguration, he informed the constitution committee that it should be within his rights to proclaim the constitution. He also demanded that the constitution be revised by the house of representatives. At that time the draft Constitution was about to be read for the third time before the committee members, and they ignored demands for its revision.

On October 18 when the draft committee was hearing the third reading of the draft constitution, eight new members, appointed by Yüan Shih-k'ai, suddenly appeared at the conference room. The committee members protested that according to law, only recognized members of this present parliament could be permitted to attend; other persons, no matter what their background, could not be admitted even to listen, and certainly they could not express any opinion. The constitution committee refused to admit the eight men.

As a matter of fact, the draft constitution prepared by the committee did represent the consensus of opinion among the members of the Kuomintang and the Progressive Party. How good the draft constitution was need not be discussed right now, but great improvements had been made over the provisional constitution and there were no great restrictions placed on the authority of the president.

Yüan Shih-k'ai, however, had determined that he would like to be a president who could have power as great as that of an emperor. On October 25 he issued a circular telegram to all provincial generals and governors. The general ideas of the circular telegram were that the drawing up of the constitution was directly related to the rise and fail of the republic; that many Kuomintang members intended to harm the nation and ruin the republican government; that the constitution committee consisted of a majority of Kuomintang members; that their draft constitution was absurd and, put into effect, would prove very detrimental to the nation. "All your army and civil officials are citizens of the nation and should not keep silence with regard to the fundamental laws. You should study the articles one by one and tell me your reactions to them by telegram within five days."

This telegram was meant to excite Yüan's followers in each province to respond as his parrots. In response, all of them, including the governors, tutus, and army officers of various ranks, unanimously criticized the constitution. Almost unanimously also, they neglected to discuss the contents of the draft constitution itself, but instead concentrated their suggestions on dissolving the Kuomintang and canceling the parliamentary seats of its members, withdrawing the draft constitution, and dissolving the constitution committee. The people at large were not appealed to by Yüan and they were ignorant about the whole affair. Had weapons been resorted to, merchants would be the first to suffer and the various merchants' associations would have something to say about this suffering. But as it was, nobody paid any attention to what was going on.

Dissolution of the Parliament

Some of the Progressive members in the parliament, realizing that the situation had gone from bad to worse, were very willing to cooperate with the moderate wing of the Kuomintang in working for sound constitutional government. They organized a new party called the People's Constitution Party [*Min-hsien Tang*] which included many eminent figures of the Kuomintang and the Progressive Party. They declared their purpose to be the maintenance of the democratic spirit and the protection of the draft constitution against any pressure of money or force. Unfortunately, their efforts came too late.

On November 4 came Yüan Shih-k'ai's *coup d'état*. The order of the president, cosigned by the premier, was issued for the dissolution of the Kuomintang and the cancellation of its parliamentary membership. Certificates and Badges were revoked for more than 350 persons whose names had been listed in the Kuomintang since the military uprising against Yüan in 1913. Since there were still enough members left in both houses to make a quorum, Yüan now revoked a further 80 badges. Thus even members who had renounced their connection with the Kuomintang and had registered in another party lost their positions in the parliament. A total of 438 persons who had some affiliation with the Kuomintang lost their parliamentary seats.

On the fifth, when the two houses were convened, Yüan sent soldiers and police to check the names of those who had been suspended from the parliament and to check carefully all those present. They found that the number of members present was not enough to form a quorum, and the parliament could no longer function. Most of the remaining members, except a small part of the Citizens' Party, were enraged, but they could do nothing against Yüan. After a long time, two long letters of inquiry, signed by the members of the two houses, were presented to the cabinet, and replies were requested within a time limit. There was no response. After another long interval Premier Hsiung Hsi-ling wrote a letter to the speakers of the two houses, saying that the president had had to take unusual action in response to the exigencies of the situation; he could not be restricted by ordinary parliamentary procedure, and he was clearly justified in his actions. Before long, there was another joint telegram from the military and civil officials of all the provinces requesting the president to dissolve what remained of the parliament.

Yüan, however, was careful; he did not disperse the members immediately. Instead, he turned the request over for discussion by what was called the Political Conference [*Cheng-chih hui-i*]. The result of the discussion was not reported until January 10, 1914, when it was requested that the duties of the remaining members of the two houses of the parliament be suspended, and only then was the parliament formally dissolved. Yüan removed this great obstruction through the assistance of the "first-class cabinet," but the cabinet itself was doomed.

Dissolution of the Cabinet

Shortly after the organization of the cabinet headed by Hsiung Hsi-ling, it suffered direct pressure from the Peiyang warlords: Hsiung, as a native of Hunan, disapproved of the garrisoning of that province by the Peiyang Army. He planned to shift the appointment of Ts'ai Ao from Yunnan to the post of *tuchün* [title of military governor of a province] of Hunan so that Ts'ai Ao, who wished to go home, could superintend affairs in his native province. For this Hsiung secured Yüan's consent, but it was merely a token consent. Although the Hunanese unanimously welcomed the appointment, Tuan Ch'i-jui and Tuan Chih-kuei, insisted on dispatching the Peiyang Army to Hunan. Tuan Ch'i-jui argued against Hsiung in the cabinet, saying that Hsiung's objection to sending the Peiyang Army there was nothing but timidity, while Tuan Chih-kuei told Hsiung that unless Hunan received a thorough cleanup there was danger of a rebellion. He added that "We cleaned it up once," by which he meant the warfare in Kiangsi and Nanking in 1913, "and we would be very unhappy if it were necessary for us to clean it up again."

Neither of the Tuans said clearly that they objected to Ts'ai Ao's becoming the tuchün of Hunan. They implied it, however, in urging the control of the province by the Peiyang Army. Although because of his appointment to Hunan, Ts'ai Ao, as he wished, was able to leave Yunnan, he was required to come directly to Peking. There he remained under the heel of the Peiyang Army led by T'ang Hsiang-ming for more than two years. This was the first victory of the warlords against Hsiung Hsi-ling.

The second triumph of the militarists concerned financial matters. Telegrams from all the provincial military leaders asking for military aid rained down upon his office. Hsiung tried to transfer some money from the ministry of communications. Liang Shih-i, finance minister, who controlled both the Bank of Communications and the Communications clique, purposely rejected Hsiung's request, saying that the Bank of Communications had been overdrawn and could not pay out more. When a man has no money he has no power. Hsiung was already handicapped. At that time the Progressive Party still applauded him in the parliament and he tried his best to keep up a front. In cooperation with Liang Ch'i-ch'ao and others, Hsiung planned a great political platform to be announced to the parliament. Its most important point was the reform of the provincial system by the abolition of the provincial divisions in order to consolidate the central government and to strengthen national unification. Since Yüan Shih-k'ai's method of unification was fundamentally different, he secretly ridiculed their plan as pure bookish fancy.

Yüan did not express himself publicly to this effect, except to say that the problem was too big and could be solved only after the convention of the representatives of the local governments, a gathering which he saw could be cleverly turned to his own advantage. Hsiung concurred in Yüan's proposal to organize an Administrators' Conference [*Hsing-cheng hui-i*]. This order was issued concurrently with the suspension of the parliamentary membership of the Kuomintang.

After the dissolution of the parliament, Yüan Shih-k'ai changed this Administrators' Conference into a Political Conference in which the leading participants included the so-called "political elders," who were appointed by the president's office and the cabinet. Others were delegated by the heads of all the provinces or special political divisions. The chairman of the Political Conference was Li Ching-hsi, who opened the meeting on December 15. The great political platform prepared by the "first-class cabinet" had to be announced before this Political Conference.

Consequently, the representatives of the provinces heard that the provincial divisions were to be abolished. Since this affected their personal positions, they objected to the new political platform. Hsiung retired under a barrage of sarcasm.

Near the end of the year Hsiung had to face a large number of people asking for money. Those in the president's office who had formerly praised the cabinet, as one made up of people of first-class ability, were now disgusted with it. The president said: "The cabinet is too slow in handling state affairs." By February 1914 the Hsiung cabinet had cosigned Yüan's orders suspending the national parliament, the provincial assemblies, and the local governments, as well as the new lawmaking institutions. Hsiung became aware that soon a cabinet, even though "first-class," would have no room for existence. Hsiung Hsi-ling, Liang Ch'i-ch'ao, and Wang Ta-hsi resigned in succession, thereby marking the end of the "first-class" cabinet.

Hsiung, Liang, and others had honestly intended to guide the Peiyang military clique into the road of constitutional government and to reform the Chinese system of local governments. But Yüan Shih-k'ai had his own way, concentrated all power in his own hands, and bribed the devotion of his subordinates by means of the vacancies in the central and provincial governments. He would not even accept the plan for the abolition of the provincial system. T'ang Shao-i and Yüan Shih-k'ai had been friends for twenty years, but because Yüan refused to follow the rules of constitutional government, T'ang preferred to give up his personal friendship and break with Yüan. Hsiung, Liang, and others had already been cheated by Yüan Shih-k'ai in the 1898 reform movement;

they should have known their enemy.

Even though the organization of the parliament may have been imperfect, the Hsiung cabinet, in trying to guide Yüan toward a constitutional government, should have been sufficiently aware of his ambition to refuse to cosign so many of his orders. Their actions reveal the short-sightedness of the eminent members of the Constitutional Party; they were not as enlightened as T'ang Shao-i, who was not a dedicated member of the T'ung-meng Hui. Not until Yüan Shih-k'ai's attempt to become emperor did Hsiung and others finally relinquish their firm belief that no one but Yüan could head the government. Realizing now that there was no hope until Yüan was out of the way, they began to cooperate again with the Kuomintang.

CHAPTER ELEVEN MONARCHICAL AND ANTIMONARCHICAL MOVEMENTS

When the power of the kuomintang was at its height, the Progressive Party supported Yüan Shih-k'ai wholeheartedly in his fight against the Kuomintang. After the defeat of the Kuomintang in the winter of 1913 the political stage of China was monopolized by the Peiyang warlords and their politicians. The Progressive Party then threw its whole support to the Kuomintang camp. We have seen that while Yüan was trying to revise the provisional constitution, the leaders of the Progressive Party still cooperated with him in every way in the hope that by means of the constitution Yüan's enlightened despotism would save China. But Yüan's ambition was to progress from despotism to monarchism, not enlightenment. He had soon achieved this aim.

This drastic reversal of the hopes of the Chinese patriots caused even the most conservative leaders of the Progressive Party to turn against him. Dissension among the Peiyang warlords was another serious problem for Yüan. The monarchical movement was a great danger to the Republic. It also marked the disruption of the Peiyang clique. The campaign of the National Protection Army (*Hu-kuo chün*) in December 1915 until Yüan's death in June 1916 is as significant as the revolution which overthrew the Manchu dynasty.

REVISION OF THE PROVISIONAL CONSTITUTION

Yüan's Ambitions

We may rightly ask just when Yüan conceived the idea of becoming emperor. Shortly after the 1911 revolution when he was interviewed by G. E. Morrison, a *London Times* correspondent in Peking, Yüan was quoted as saying: "I firmly believe that seventy per cent of the Chinese people are conservatives … only thirty per cent are progressive. If we overthrow the Manchu family now, the conservatives must, before long, try to restore the monarchical system." Again, he was supposed to have said: "I am very much afraid that the democratic polity cannot be stable … It would be better to preserve the Manchu regime, at the same time depriving it of its actual authority, so that it exists merely in name. Thus the security of the nation can be maintained."[1]

These words were interpreted as a hint of Yüan's plan to restore the monarchical system. More probably they indicate merely Yüan's untrustworthiness. They do not prove that he had already decided to make himself absolute monarch. As he talked to Morrison, he was carrying on negotiations with the Chinese revolutionary army in order to secure the position of the presidency as a basis for overthrowing the Manchu family. Even when Yüan was about to interfere with the codification of the constitution, he still warned his close subordinates that: "We must maintain a policy of noninterference." When he was about to carry out his monarchical movement, he swore to God that he would uphold the republican system.

As to when Yüan first conceived the idea of his monarchical movement, we know only that he always coveted high positions and that he was very skillful at usurping power. In seeking for power his tactics were to keep under cover all evidence of his intentions until the actual power was in his grasp.

The open activity of the monarchical movement began in the early autumn of 1915 under the name of the Peace Planning Society [*Chou-an Hui*] which claimed to be working for peace under a monarchy in lieu of disorder under a republic. But the real inception of that movement dated from the time of the constitutional revision; hence, the story of Yüan's monarchical scheme properly begins with the revision of the constitution.

The Political Conference Becomes the Constitutional Conference

Yüan had two instruments for constitutional revision: one was the Political Conference, and the other was the Constitutional Conference, both mentioned in the preceding chapter. At first he planned to use the Political Conference. Some members of the conference, realizing that the qualifications of its members were too ambiguous, proposed, in answering Yüan's inquiries as to the proper procedure for constitutional revision, "a special legislative body, distinct from the consultative organization and ordinary legislative bodies, to work on the fundamental laws for the Republic of China." Following this suggestion, Yüan ordered the Political Conference to reorganize itself into the Constitutional Conference, using exactly the same membership.

The members of this new conference were nominally elected from among those members of the parliament in the capital as well as in all the provinces who had high qualifications and administrative experience. Actually they were all appointed by Yüan's government to serve him as his instruments. Newspapers at the time reported, "The Political Conference is an extension of the secretariat; the Constitutional Conference is an extension of the legislative bureau." Important members of the Political Conference were also important figures in the secretariat; leading figures in the Constitutional Conference were also the outstanding members of the legislative bureau.

The articles of organization of the Constitutional Conference were pro- claimed on January 26, 1914, and the first meeting was held on February 18. Yüan saw to it that Sun Yü-yün was elected chairman. Since Sun Yü-yün had formally been a member of the Kuomintang but had secretly changed sides, his name could be used to confuse the people. On March 20 Yüan wrote in an official letter requesting the revision of the provisional constitution:

> For the purpose of national reconstruction… it is proper to have two periods for the preparation of the fundamental laws: one for the revision of the provisional constitution, and the other for the codification of a formal constitution; that is to say, there should be a period for the application of the provisional constitution and another period for the enforcement of the formal constitution. Since the revision of the provisional constitution and the application of the constitution belong to two entirely different periods, we should understand that the application of the provisional constitution was to be our concern from the very beginning, whereas the enforcement of the formal constitution is something which must come about after everything has been well organized. The two constitutions are entirely different. [2]

Sun Yat-sen's period of political tutelage to be followed by a period of constitutional government had been given up by the Kuomintang in 1912 and 1913. Now Yüan adopted it for his own use. For Yüan, the period of applying the provisional constitution was his time to usurp the real authority of the emperor; the period for enforcing the formal constitution was his time for announcing the monarchical system.

The Revised Constitution

Let us examine the seven items which Yüan requested as the basis for the revision of the provisional constitution: (1) All diplomatic power should be in the hands of the president, who could declare war, conclude peace, and negotiate treaties without the consent of the senate. (2) The president should have the right to decide official systems and government regulations, as well as to appoint cabinet members, ambassadors, and ministers, without the consent of the senate. (3) The presidential system of the central government should be adopted. (4) The formal constitution should be passed by a national people's assembly [*kuo-min hui-i*], not by the parliament, and proclaimed by the president; and the authority for drafting it should belong to the president and the senate. (5) The president should have full freedom of action with regard to the withdrawal or restoration of the privileges of citizenship. (6) The president should have authority to issue emergency orders. (7) The president should have full fiscal authority in time of emergency.

The above seven items gave the president even greater power, except for the despots, than the ruler of any modern monarchical nation. The members of the Constitutional Conference could do nothing except copy these items into the new constitution which they were supposed to be discussing at their meetings. In the new constitution, proclaimed by the president on May 1, the power of the president was extended to the utmost; the responsible cabinet was discarded and replaced by the so-called presidential system. The presidential system, in Yüan's new constitution, even put the legislature under the control of the president.

Lawmakers in the Constitutional Conference had several extraordinary ideas regarding the presidential system. Since they knew a Japanese translation of the American term for secretary of state as *kuo-wu ch'ing*, this secretarial position was adopted in the new constitution in the following way: "The president is the chief executive; he is to be assisted by one secretary of state." Since in classical Chinese, however, the word *ch'ing* usually means "servant of the emperor," this tactfully indicated that the position of the president was similar to that of the emperor. According to Article 27 of the new constitution, the president had the right to confer the five ranks. The mention of *ch'ing* and also the five ranks gives a further clear indication of the monarchical system. When the title of secretary of state (*kuo-wu ch'ing*) was introduced in the new constitution, Yüan immediately appointed Hsü Shih-ch'ang to the post and established the council of state [*cheng-shih t'ang*], which was to be attached to the office of the president.

The council of state was headed by the secretary of state, under whom there were two *ch'ing* [secretaries] under whom, in turn, there were five offices: official documents, promotions and appointments, strategic affairs, accounting and auditing, and printing of currency. The power of the office of strategic affairs was much greater than that of the state ministers. The office of accounting and auditing took over completely the duties of the ministry of finance and the bureau of auditing. All state ministers had to take their orders from the secretary of state in dealing with any affairs of importance, and only the routine of their offices was left to them to handle. In short, the importance and the duties of the council of state were approximately the same as those of the Grand Council of the Manchu dynasty, and the position of the secretary of state corresponded to that of the grand councilor.

According to the new constitution, legislative power was concentrated in the hands of a single *yüan* [council]. But the constitution still authorized the senate to act as a consultative body to the president, and it fulfilled the duties of the Legislative Yüan before the latter was established. The rules of organization for the Legislative Yüan and the senate were decided upon by the Constitutional Conference. It first announced the rules for the senate on May 24, according to which the senators were to be appointed by the president. The senate was established on June 20 under the chairmanship of Li Yüan-hung, with Wang Ta-hsi as vice-chairman; Liang Ch'i-ch'ao's name was also listed. The Political Conference was then dissolved.

On June 29 Yüan Shih-k'ai proclaimed a law stating that according to the new constitution, the senate was to take the place of the Legislative Yüan. The latter, which was authorized in the new constitution and had also had its rules of organization and election proclaimed on November 27, was never organized. The senate was at all times a substitute for the Legislative Yüan. Working for Yüan's monarchical movement, it lasted until his death.

New Laws for the Election of a President

In accordance with Yüan's intention, the senate requested that the laws governing the election of the president, which had been proclaimed in October 1913, be revised. In compliance with this request the Constitutional Conference worked out a set of revised articles on December 28, and they were announced in Yüan's name on the following day.

The important points of the revised laws governing the election of the president were as follows: (1) The term of office of the president was changed to ten years, with no limitation on the number of terms. (2) During presidential election years the senate, if it saw the "necessity for political reasons," could permit the president to continue for another term without the formality of an election. (3) Presidential candidates were to be nominated by the president to the election committee, and the number of nominees was not to exceed three; their names were to be inscribed in advance on elaborately decorated documents by the president, and they were to be stored in a vault or safety box and not removed until the election committee was convened.

Even under such conditions, the president in office could still be re-elected. With the new constitution, which was proclaimed in May 1914, Yüan Shih-k'ai became a dictator, *de jure* and *de facto*; with the revised laws governing presidential elections, which were proclaimed in December, Yüan became a dictator for life. If the candidates nominated by him were his sons, the dictatorship could become hereditary, since the new election laws placed no restriction on the nomination of the president's relatives. Yüan had virtually all possible titles and authority, except that of *huang-ti*[emperor].

Had Yüan been just a little more astute, he would have stopped at this point. He would have played the role of Chou Wen who planned the triumph of the Chou dynasty [usurping the powers of the Shang dynasty, eleventh century B. C.] and left to his son, Yüan K'o-ting, the role of Chou Wu, as first king of a new dynasty. But Yüan lacked even so much patience as was shown by Ts'ao Ts'ao, the usurper of the Han throne at the beginning of the third century. Ts'ao Ts'ao had made his son emperor. Yüan insisted on making himself emperor.

OPEN ACTIVITY OF THE MONARCHICAL MOVEMENT

Yüan's precipitateness may have been encouraged by his oldest son, Yüan K'o-ting. Between 1913 and 1914 it was rumored in Peking that "republicanism does not suit the national condition, as people have seen from the rebellions and troubles during these past two years. Unless there is a great change of polity, it is impossible to save the nation." This rumor was reportedly spread by Yüan's oldest son, but of course there is no way to verify this report.

There were two recognized groups of people who worked for the restoration of the monarchical system. One consisted of the members of Yüan's family; the other included remnants of the Manchu imperial family. After the proclamation of the new constitution Yüan began to assert the prerogatives of an emperor. In September he ordered the worship of Confucius throughout the empire. He also prepared himself to offer that winter the imperial sacrifices to heaven. This aroused the jealousy of the remaining officials of the Manchu dynasty, such as Lao Nai-hsüan, who sought an opportunity to restore the abdicated Manchu emperor to power.

First Lao Nai-hsüan published in June 1914 his short book (less than 10,000 words) *An Explanation of Republicanism, with a Supplement* [*Cheng-hsü kung-ho chieh*]. Lao himself said that he had given the book to Chao Ping-chün, who in turn submitted it to President Yüan. The main tenet of the book, based on stories of the Chou dynasty, was that when the Emperor Hsiang was unable to carry on administrative duties, his ministers cooperated in attending to matters of state, and that this system was called monarchism [*kung-ho*]. Readers with only a smattering of knowledge misinterpreted this term as meaning republicanism. In the supplement Lao suggests to the president that a Chinese *kung-ho* constitution should be established which would fit the definition as he had just described it, and that China should once more be called *Chung kuo* [Middle Kingdom] and not the Republic [*Min kuo*]—in order to indicate that the monarchical system was preferred.

Following Lao's book, Sung Yü-jen and other conservatives of the Editorial Board of National History submitted a letter to Yüan requesting the restoration of monarchical government. As a matter of fact, by early November, even before the preparation of this letter, the rumor of the restoration had already been widely spread in Peking. Soon after, Sung Yü-jen was suspected of being involved in the restoration movement and was arrested by the police of Peking and escorted back to his native district. This was a temporary blow to Yüan's monarchical movement.

The members of Yüan's family were becoming impatient. In the early spring of 1915 the monarchical movement was still being carried on despite lack of support from the people. Liang Ch'i-ch'ao said:

> In January, last year [1915] Yüan K'o-ting suddenly invited me to dinner, and I found Yang Tu there also [Yang was to be the campaign manager for Yüan, the emperor]. During the conversation, they enumerated the weaknesses of republicanism, implying that they wanted to change the national polity and were seeking my consent. To their displeasure I explained to them the probable diplomatic and domestic dangers. I anticipated disaster and moved my family to Tientsin, and thence southward.

This personal report by Liang indicates that the move by Yüan K'o-ting and Yang Tu to make Yüan emperor took place before the open movement of the Peace Planning Society [*Chou-an Hui*].

Yüan and Japan's Twenty-one Demands

The European War broke out in August 1914 and the Western Powers had no time to look after their interests in the East. Japan, the only remaining powerful nation in Asia, was like a tiger ready to prowl over the tempting area between Kiaochow and Tsinan in Shantung. On January 18, 1915, Japan delivered her famous Twenty-one Demands, and all the members of the Revolutionary Party sensed the dangerous position of China. Fearing that the Yüan government, facing both internal and external difficulties, could not concentrate on the invasion, they accordingly dispatched telegrams announcing the cessation of all revolutionary activities and advocating a united front against the foreigners.

The members of Yüan's family unexpectedly regarded the Japanese aggression as a good opportunity for the monarchical movement. When the Japanese delivered their Twenty-one Demands, Yüan Shih-k'ai's son gave dinner parties to campaign for the monarchical system. They thought that since the European powers had no time to interfere in Chinese affairs, Japan could be pacified if she were conceded a few small privileges. According to Yu Hui-yüan's *History of China's Rebirth* [*Chung-kuo ts'ai-tsao shih*], Yüan tried to negotiate with Japan to the effect that he would comply with the Twenty-one Demands if Japan would support China's monarchical system. However, these diplomatic discussions were conducted in secret, so this charge is not easy to verify. A Japanese newspaper published an interview with Premier Okuma, who said that since Japan was a monarchy, the political systems of the two nations would coincide if China too were to become a monarchy, and that Japan would be glad to support China. He added, moreover, that since Yüan Shih-k'ai had virtually dominated the political scene, a change to the monarchical system would be closer to reality.

This was obviously meant to lure Yüan Shih-k'ai into the net of the

Japanese premier. Yüan thought that he would succeed if the Japanese premier supported his monarchical government. In this he was somewhat like the man who saw gold lying in the street and picked it up, failing to realize that the owners of that gold were standing beside him. He agreed to the Japanese demands on May 9. Although the Chinese people considered this a great humiliation, some of his supporters eulogized him. Yüan's own newspaper put out special issues, saying: "Both sides yielded ground, insuring good fortune for eastern Asia." The provincial governors under Yüan's influence even sent him telegrams of congratulations, and some suggested a lantern parade in celebration.

When Japan presented the ultimatum, these Twenty-one Demands were divided into five groups. The first four had to be accepted, but the fifth, which had purposely been made very serious, was set aside to provide some leeway in the negotiations. When Yüan rejected the last group, Japan did not urge him strongly, and his supporters considered that as his great success. Why should not Yüan's supporters feel the same humiliation as the rest of the people? Because the prestige of the presumptive emperor had been somewhat injured during the negotiations between Japan and China, and his henchmen wanted to use his so-called diplomatic success to repair the damage.

During May and June while Yüan's supporters were eager for action, he himself still strongly denied the existence of any monarchical ambition. He told an American correspondent: "Since my national system is the same as that in the United States, I will try my best to advance toward the development of a genuine spirit of democracy." When it was widely rumored in Japan that Yüan sought to restore monarchy, he again declared:

> During the 1911 revolution, members of the Manchu royal family intended to yield the throne to me, but I did not accept it. Why should I now suddenly take it? If I were to do so, I would be

> cheating my innocent people, I would be unkind to them and unrighteous; how could I bear to do so? Furthermore, judging from Chinese history, there has always been a revolution after a few generations of a dynasty, the royal family has been wiped out, and immeasurable disaster follows… Were I to become emperor, it would mean that I would be cutting off my own descendants, and that would benefit neither the nation nor my family. Even an extremely foolish man would not do this. [3]

According to the *Mai-nichi Shimbun* the monarchical plan was suggested by Yang Tu and Sun Yü-yün. Yang sent a cable to the Chinese minister in Japan asking him to place a denial of that story in the paper.

Feng Kuo-chang heard this rumor and went to Peking with Liang Ch'i-ch'ao to find out the inside story. Yüan again unhesitatingly denied it before the two inquirers, asserting that, "If the Chinese people compel me to take up the throne, I will flee to London."

Nevertheless, in the early part of August, Yüan's constitutional advisor, Frank J. Goodnow, later a president of Johns Hopkins University, presented a memorandum on republicanism and monarchism which declared that republicanism did not suit the condition of China. In less than a week six gentlemen took Goodnow's opinion as the basis for sponsoring the Peace Planning Society. Thereafter the monarchical movement entered a stage of open action.

The Peace Planning Society

The six gentlemen who sponsored the Peace Planning Society were Yang Tu, the central figure, Sun Yü-yün, Yen Fu, Liu Shih-p'ei, Hu Ying, and Li Hsieh-ho. Of these, the names of Sun, Yen, and Li were used because they had been early members of the old Revolutionary Party [*Ko-ming Tang*]. Liu Shih-p'ei was listed because he was a great scholar with profound classical knowledge. Yen Fu was listed because he had been well educated in China as well as in Europe. According to Yen's letter to his friend Hsiung Shun-ju, which appeared in the *Hsüeh-heng* magazine, he was "abducted" by Yang Tu, who had listed his name as one of the sponsors of the Peace Planning Society. Although Yen himself believed in theory in constitutional monarchism, he was puzzled as to who should be the constitutional monarch.

Yang Tu had been a successful candidate for the special examination in economic affairs held during the time of the 1898 reform movement. After 1898 he was in close association with the revolutionary leaders Huang Hsing and others. Later on, he felt that the Revolutionary Party was more destructive than constructive, and so he made up his mind to join the Constitutional Party, to share the ideas of Liang Ch'i-ch'ao. Upon realizing later that since Liang Ch'i-ch'ao was disliked by the empress dowager, cooperation with him would be harmful, he entered into his political activities alone. While the [1907-1908] constitution was being prepared, Yang was honorably promoted from a low fourth-rank officer to a compiler of the constitution, and it was during this period that he developed a close association with Yüan Shih-k'ai.

Yang was fortunate not to have been dismissed when Yüan was driven out of the government by Tsai-feng in 1908. When Yüan was recalled from retirement in 1911, Yang rejoiced at the chance for renewed activity. The so-called Association for Assisting National Affairs, headed by Yang Tu and Wang Ching-wei, existed at that time, and these two were instrumental in making the arrangements for the abdication of the Manchu emperor and for Sun Yat-sen's yielding the provisional presidency to Yüan Shih-k'ai. Had Yang Tu really believed that republicanism did not suit China, he should have taken the same position as Liang Ch'i-ch'ao, who strongly advocated constitutional monarchism. Yang's excuse for not doing this was that relations between the Manchus and the Chinese had been injured beyond repair, so that it was necessary to create a new monarchy.

If Yang had been as farsighted as Liang Ch'i-ch'ao, he would have agreed with Liang that the president should first have an efficient government, he should make everybody prosperous, and he should reorganize the army in order to have the chance to win an international war. Then all the people would admire him and would be glad to support him as emperor, so that he could bequeath the empire to his descendants. Unfortunately, Yang insisted on making Yüan emperor at a time when China was not prospering and was even being humiliated by a strong neighbor.

After the establishment of the Peace Planning Society, Yang published an essay on "National Salvation by a Constitutional Monarchy" [*Chün-hsien chiu-kuo lun*] arguing that only under a monarchy could the constitution be enforced and that a constitutional government under a monarchy would be more desirable than despotism under a republic. His purpose seemed to be to convince his readers that Yüan, because of the inefficiency of the republic, should be given the hereditary throne of an emperor and that the bare title of president would be insufficient to secure constitutional government.

This was obviously a move on Yang's part to enhance his own position. Despite the fact that he had done a great deal for Yüan after the 1911 revolution, his influence had never been so great as Liang Shih-i's. He had, however, perceived Yüan's secret ambition and that of Yüan's son. Yang accordingly cultivated a close friendship with Yüan K'o-ting and tried his best to make Yüan Shih-k'ai emperor. Thus Yang hoped that he himself might secure the premiership of Yüan's first imperial cabinet. The Peace Planning Society consequently may be said to have arisen from Yüan's desire to make use of Yang, and from Yang's desire to achieve his personal goal through Yüan.

According to *A Short History of the Peiyang WarLords* published in a newspaper in Tientsin, Yüan severely rebuked all those who tried to persuade him to support the monarchist movement. But after being reminded that his generals had only been faithful to him in the hope of leaving their descendants wealth and position under his influence, he gave his consent. Although we have no way now of ascertaining who offered this reminder, the man who persuaded him was probably Yang Tu.

An organization meeting of the Peace Planning Society scheduled for August 21 was canceled for fear it might be attended by some troublemakers. An announcement was made on the nineteenth that since there were so many things to be discussed, it would be necessary, before calling a general meeting, to elect Yang Tu director of the society, Sun Yü-yün associate director, and Yen, Liu, Li, and Hu executive members.

A circular notice to the members said, in brief: "The purpose of the Peace Planning Society is to study whether monarchism or republicanism is more suitable for China, devoting its discussion solely to the academic question of which is right or wrong, and which is advantageous or harmful in practice; other matters are in no way connected with our society." At the same time, a circular telegram was sent to the military and civil authorities of all provinces asking them to send representatives to Peking. To this telegram were attached Goodnow's report, application blanks for membership in the society, ballots asking for expression of a preference for either monarchism or republicanism, and a request for the recruiting of other members.

At that time Yüan's attitude appeared to change gradually. When asked whether the actions of the Peace Planning Society should be forbidden, he replied:

> I have long since heard the opinion of this society but I can under- stand the organization only of republicanism, and I therefore have no other choice. I desire neither to be emperor nor president. Those who are studying the two political systems, and whatever conclusion they reach, have nothing to do with me. On the other

> hand, our citizens and I all have families, properties, descendants, and relatives. If citizens wish to devise an adequate method for protecting their safety permanently, they should do so. How dare I, who have been entrusted with the presidency by the citizens, interfere in this discus-sion? … If I do not let the scholars enjoy freedom of discussion, then those who strongly favor monarchism may use military power to shake the foundations of the nation; it would be much better to permit them to continue talking, so that they may not go to extremes.

When the provincial authorities asked the opinion of the central government by telegram, Yüan replied:

> The Peace Planning Society consists of learned scholars, who are studying the political system of the nation; so long as they do not disturb the order and peace of society, the government has no right to interfere in their discussion.

When the censors, as a body, requested the government to dissolve the society, Yüan merely advised the ministry of domestic affairs: "Hereafter, some limitation should be set on the scope of the discussion and activity of this society." Thereafter petitions addressed to the Censorate and police headquarters of the ministry of domestic affairs for the dissolution of the Peace Planning Society received no reply.

The headquarters of the society in Yang's private mansion was carefully guarded by armed soldiers and police. Under such conditions all provincial, civil, and military authorities had to respond quickly to all letters and telegrams issued by the society, and representatives were sent from all provinces to Peking. In October the society sent a notice, which included a ballot, to all its members, saying:

> This society originally planned to wait until all the representatives had arrived in Peking and then to set a date for a final conference. The membership of the society numbers is about ten thousand now, and it is difficult to find a place to accommodate them all; it is necessary to present the enclosed ballots on which each of the members may state whether he favors monarchism or republicanism. The head- quarters will take the majority opinion as the basis for action.

The Peace Planning Society, which claimed to be making a purely academic study of the problem, actually never held a meeting.

Yüan "Chosen" Emperor

The original intention of the Peace Planning Society was to wait for a decision by all the provincial representatives, and then to request the government to put their decision into effect. But this request could not be made directly since the society was not a legal organization. The society arranged for petitions by the representatives of all the provinces to be submitted to the Political Council [*Ts'an-cheng yüan*], which was then performing the functions of the Legislative Yüan. Through this organization decisions might be forwarded to the chief executive as advice to establish the monarchy. But the Political Council announced its meeting for September 1. Since provincial representatives of the Peace Planning Society could not now reach Peking in time, in this emergency the directors of the society organized the natives of the various provinces who were living in Peking into various citizens' groups. These groups were to send the petitions drafted by the Peace Planning Committee.

After the opening of the Political Council on September 1, the petitions were still pouring in, On the sixth Yüan Shih-k'ai delegated Yang Shih-ch'i to read a statement to the Political Council, saying: "The change of national polity should be made with extreme care. If someone wishes to make such a change hurriedly and carelessly, I am afraid that there will be a great deal of trouble, and I, as president, do not consider such action proper. However, the petitions of the citizens are plainly concerned with fundamental procedures for the security of the nation. If the opinion of the people is widely represented, some suitable method should be offered." Yüan, understanding that the Political Council might make an immediate decision to ask him to establish the monarchy, indicated by this statement that he wished its members to go through the motions of having the problem appealed to the people.

Some of the members of the Political Council voiced the opinion that with respect to the authority of the Legislative Yüan they should not accept petitions concerning the change of the national polity. As a result of this discussion a vote was cast on September 20 urging the government to call the national assembly within a year to make a fundamental change in the political system, or to devise some better method of determining public opinion.

The real intention was revealed in the last phrase. It would be very troublesome to call the national people's assembly [*kuo-min hui-i*]. This decision and eighty-three petitions were sent to the government. Thus the first suggestion was made by the Political Council.

On September 25 Yüan Shih-k'ai replied that he preferred calling the national people's assembly at an early date to any other method, but his impatient monarchist supporters feared the complicated procedure involved. The result was that Liang Shih-i sponsored an organization called the Union of Petitioners, under which all groups who had sent petitions were incorporated into one body. In the name of this new organization a petition was submitted to the Political Council objecting to both solutions and suggesting that the Legislative Yüan find some other method or create an office to gather information on public opinion.

This petition was discussed on September 28. Liang Shih-i, Sun Yü-yün and others suggested acceptance of the method proposed in the petition, creating a meeting of the representatives of the national people's assembly. The rules of organization for this meeting, drawn up on October 2 and submitted to the government, followed the suggestion made by the Political Council. On October 8 these rules of organization were proclaimed under Yüan's name.

According to the regulations the procedure for electing the representatives would take a long time, representatives throughout the vast country being elected and then traveling to Peking. Nevertheless, the elections took place on October 25. Ballots presenting votes for monarchism or republicanism were already being collected on the twenty-eighth. In less than one month, eighteen provinces had declared in favor of monarchism. Before the deadline on November 20, all the ballots had been collected. The result was 1993 votes unanimously supporting constitutional monarchy, and not a single one against it. Yüan Shih-k'ai's prestige was, so to speak, twice as high as Napoleon's, whose own elevation was ratified by a plebiscite 3, 572, 329 in favor and 2, 569 against him.

Moreover, according to the rules of organization, the national assembly was authorized only to decide the political system of the nation. The selection of the chief executive was to be made later. Nevertheless, when the representatives of the national people's assembly cast their votes as to the political system, they also selected their emperor. They made a unanimous declaration:

> Reverently representing the public opinion of the nation, we request that the president, Yüan Shih-k'ai, be made emperor of the Chinese empire. He will have the highest and most complete authority and sovereignty over the nation. The throne will be handed down in his royal family from generation to generation through ten thousand generations.[4]

Miraculously, all the ballots were identically inscribed.

While the national people's assembly cast votes and selected the emperor, they authorized the Political Council to act as their deputy. Through the Council, a petition was submitted to Yüan Shih-k'ai welcoming him as the new emperor. On December 11 after a meeting of the Political Council, an elaborately prepared eulogy was submitted to Yüan Shih-k'ai, begging him to ascend the throne. Yüan declined the request. The Council submitted at once a second letter reiterating their request. On December 12 Yüan accepted the throne. This was the third act of the monarchical play.

The Story Behind Yüan's Popular Support

A bureau for the preparation of Yüan's enthronement had already been established in September, though it had not been announced to the world. This promptness may be better understood from the following confidential dispatches by Yüan's supporters to provincial authorities. Tuan Chih-kuei and nine others issued a telegram on August 13:

> Now we are presenting our first procedure, that of using the names of the citizens of all the provinces to submit a petition to the Political Council, which is fulfilling the function of the Legislative Yüan. Each province must send a petition, which has been prepared by this office here and is enclosed. Please sign your name and the names of the gentlemen and influential merchants of your province.

On September 26, Sun Yü-yün sent a telegram:

> We are now planning methods of representing public opinion. The general, governor, and other officials of each province should order each district to elect one person as a participant in the provisional assembly.

On September 27 a telegram was issued by the Peace Planning Society stating:

> Although the participant from each district is actually appointed by civil or military officials, he should nominally be elected, and this procedure should be set up by the magistrate, though on the date you arbitrarily assign.

On October 7 another message stated:

> In the telegrams from the representatives of the national assembly requesting Yüan to become emperor it is necessary to say, "We reverently request that the president, Yüan Shih-k'ai, be the emperor of the Chinese empire." There should be as many other telegrams as possible with a like request from commercial and military establish-ments.

On October 29 a telegram was sent from the office for preparing the national people's assembly:

> Your last telegram has been received. Hereafter you should tell us confidentially how much money you need and whether you have difficulty in getting it. This office will do its best to help you financially, so that you can go ahead making all arrangements without any hesitation.

On November 11 the same office issued another telegram:

> All telegrams between Peking and the provincial authorities discussing confidential matters are of great concern to order and peace; if any such discussion should become public, it might reveal our

whole plan and prove detrimental to the fundamental problem of the nation … It is earnestly hoped that all of you will dispatch trusted sub-ordinates to exercise very particular care with these confidential dispatches.[5]

It thus appears that the vote for the monarchy and for Yüan was carefully directed by the Peace Planning Society. The provincial authorities were apparently well paid for their services. Some of these telegrams were later published in a newspaper [*Yunnan Cheng-pao*] in facsimile. Later Liang Ch'i-ch'ao collected them and wrote a note on Yüan Shih-k'ai's creation of public opinion, by confidential telegrams. A perusal of Liang's collection helps us understand why the movement achieved such rapid success.

In his note Liang Ch'i-ch'ao said:

> Ever since the beginning of the political system, what was called *discussion* was the discussion led by Yüan himself, and what was called *support* was the support given by Yüan and his partisans. What was called *petition* was petitioned by Yüan's adherents; what was called *vote* was the vote of Yüan's adherents … Yüan held a sharp knife in his right hand and plenty of money in his left, gathering a few of the meanest and most shameless politicians to work for him as pup-pets; through these a large number of other poorly educated, shame-less puppets were recruited, and claimed to be the representatives of the people at large.[6]

THE UNITED ANTIMONARCHIST FRONT

The puppet show had been so well arranged by Yüan's followers that, in their minds at least, their position was unassailable. They knew for certain that the populace expected a genuine emperor, that though the constitutional monarchists would not help them, they would not strongly oppose them, since they lacked the power to do so, and that the revolutionists, who would have liked to cause trouble, could do them no real damage. In addition, the influence of the Peiyang warlords had spread all over the nation. Even the few generals who might not be entirely enthusiastic about a monarchy would not dare to oppose it. But the situation of China in 1916 was quite different from that in 1913.

Yüan's Government Unpopular in the Provinces

The common people of China were usually indifferent to politics, but when they suffered, their passive resistance was a formidable force. This had been demonstrated during the 1911 revolution against the Manchus and against the Kuomintang's anti-Yüan movement in 1913. Yüan's partisans thought that the sentiments of the people were still the same as in 1913. But even in 1913 the people were not especially in favor of Yüan; they mistakenly blamed the Kuomintang for their troubles, believing that once these troublemakers were disposed of, they could return to a peaceful life.

Now that Yüan's partisans were, in 1916, trying to restore monarchism, the people considered this certain to incur more trouble from the revolutionists. Had Yüan's government itself done more for the people, Yüan might have been able to gain their support, but the people had received no favors from Yüan's government. Graft among officials and the savage behavior of the Peiyang Army were much worse than the behavior of the partisans of the revolution. These facts were known among the people, even though the newspapers dared not report them. A letter, a résumé of which follows, was written at this time by Wu Chih-yu to the editor of the *Chia-yin* magazine, accurately describing the political corruption:

I returned to my home several months ago and since then have quietly observed the local administration. I have noticed that nine out of ten officers in the counties and districts are the notoriously corrupt officials of the late Ch'ing dynasty, but no local newspaper dares to report candidly on what they are doing. The local gentry are also afraid to speak of public affairs lest they be accused of being rebels. Such is the corruption that even conservatives, surprised to find a situation more disastrous than under the late Manchu dynasty, pray that the Yüan government may perish. I saw more than ten grade-school students arrested by the police in connection with revolutionary activities. How could a teenage grade-school student know much about revolution? They had simply learned one of their Chinese lessons, entitled "The Revolution at Wuchang," in which there is a reference to a man by the name of Li Yüan-hung, and they talked about this revolution with their playmates on their way home from school. No sooner did the police hear the word "revolution" than they arrested the children, regardless of whether they were talking about the Wuchang revolution or any other. Were all these children shot? No, but they were put in jail until ransomed by their parents. When the parents had experienced such procedures several times, most of them dared not allow their children to go to school, and the enrollment of the grade schools in the last two years has dropped sharply.

When the government issued bonds twice last year, the magistrate each time compelled the people to buy. If after the money was paid they actually received the bonds, they might still have some vague hope of future repayment. But in the actual transaction the magistrate merely sent a notice to wealthy people, saying: "Give me your cash first, so that I know how many government bonds you are planning to buy; then I can report to the governor, and the latter can report to Peking, where the bond will be prepared and mailed to the district to be distributed to the creditors." Since communications in our country are very slow, it usually takes several months for the process from the district to the province, to Peking, and back again to the original district. During this long interval, the magistrate has been replaced by a new one. The new magistrate behaves similarly, and the creditor asking about his bonds is told that they have not yet arrived. Creditors are told by the new magistrate that he does not know how his predecessor handled their cases, and that the inquirers' names are not listed in the book for government bonds. I dare not say that bonds throughout the country have been handled in this same way, but from what I have seen, a majority of the people who have paid money to the government have not yet received any bonds. Though the so-called credit bonds were never cashed under the late Manchu dynasty, the people could at least use the uncashed bonds to purchase a brevet title. Now the people do not even receive bonds; they merely give to the magistrate money which is used for his own selfish purposes. These are merely two small examples to show how badly the people are misgoverned.[7]

Under the pressure of such administration, the people naturally did not support Yüan's government. Reluctant to support the central administra- tion, they were also under the constant threat of being accused as rebels. Their universal hatred and anger, reinforced by this terror of accusation, afforded a strong passive resistance to the government.

Before the organization of the Peace Planning Society, Lao Nai-hsüan and Sung Yü-jen had already been taught a lesson by Yüan Shih-k'ai. Yüan attempted to make himself emperor in less than half a year after Sung was arrested. But even though Sung and the other restoration leaders were much chagrined, they had no power to oppose Yüan. There was still the famous K'ang Yu-wei, however, with his very influential writings. And Chang Hsün had strong military power. Both these men were awaiting an opportunity to restore the Manchu emperor to the throne.

Antimonarchist Forces Around Yüan

At the same time there was dissension within the Peiyang military clique. Yüan Shih-k'ai's power lay entirely in his warlords, who were in turn entirely dependent upon him. Mutually dependent though they were, each had a somewhat different purpose, and this was a source of dissension. The two pillars of Yüan's military support were Tuan Ch'i-jui and Feng Kuo-chang, and his leading civilian supporter was Hsü Shih-ch'ang. Hsü's purpose was to maintain his position as premier under Yüan Shih-k'ai for the rest of his life, but he was reluctant to support Yüan's ambition to become emperor. Tuan and Feng hoped to succeed Yüan as president some time in the future, but they did not mind serving Yüan during the time that he remained president.

After the Revolutionary Party was defeated in 1914 and the influence of the Progressive Party also declined, the military and civilian factions of the Peiyang clique found themselves at odds; Liang Shih-i and Tuan Ch'i-jui had frequent private quarrels; and Yüan K'o-ting envied Tuan lest the latter should succeed Yüan to power. Liang and Yüan K'o-ting worked, accordingly, to undermine the very close relations between Yüan Shih-k'ai and Tuan Ch'i-jui.

Formerly, major military power had been completely delegated to the ministry of war, headed by Tuan Ch'i-jui, whose authority was almost unrestricted. After the establishment of the headquarters for the army and navy in 1914, some of this military authority had been taken away from the ministry of war. Tuan, although he said nothing, certainly resented this.

Soon thereafter Yüan used the low morale and corrupt elements of the Peiyang troops as a pretext to organize in their stead a model corps in Peking. Distinct from the old Peiyang Army, this corps consisted of his best and most trusted officers. Later on, Yüan's intimate advisors criticized General Hsü Shu-cheng, who was Tuan's right-hand man. When Yüan alluded to possible dismissal of Hsü, Tuan responded angrily: "This can easily be done! You, sir, should dismiss me first!" Thereafter, the rift between Yüan and Tuan was complete.

Resigning from the ministry of war, Tuan went to Shensi just before the appearance of the Peace Planning Society. Yüan approved Tuan's resignation when that society was organized. Tuan was replaced by Wang Shih-chen, who had carefully avoided expressing opinions during the early days of the monarchical government.

Feng Kuo-chang went to Peking in June 1915 to inquire into Yüan's intentions, but Yüan remained mute. Realizing that he was no longer in Yüan's confidence and that when Tuan's resignation was accepted, his future with Yüan too was doomed, Feng also grew very cool toward Yüan. When the support of these two pillars of the Peiyang military clique was lost, the rest of the warlords began to give only superficial support to Yüan. Although most of the Peiyang militarists felt very unhappy with Yüan K'o-ting, who had been arrogant even before his father became emperor, none of them dared to oppose Yüan and his son openly.

The Chinese Revolutionary Party

In the anti-Yüan groups there were various other elements. Chief among these elements were members of the Kuomintang organized now in a radical wing and a moderate wing.

After the failure of the campaign against Yüan Shih-k'ai in 1913, the Kuomintang leaders had fled overseas. Other party members who held positions in the army had all been purged, and the Kuomintang itself was dissolved through Yüan's pressure. Sun Yat-sen, knowing in advance that sooner or later Yüan would try to make himself emperor, accordingly regrouped his party members and in 1914 organized the Chinese

Revolutionary Party [*Chung-hua ko-ming tang*]. Its purpose, even though located in Japan, was to carry out the two principles of "the people's rights" and "the people's livelihood"; the progress of revolutionary government was still to be divided into three stages: military conquest, political tutelage, and constitutional government.

The process of becoming a member of this party was very strict. All members had to be absolutely obedient to the orders of the party, and the head of the party was to have absolute power over the organization. As soon as the headquarters were established in Japan, members were sent to all the provinces of China to organize secret branches of the party; similar branches were established in foreign countries. Revolution was the party goal. Regardless of whether Yüan tried to make himself emperor or not, the Peiyang warlords had to be blotted out before the party could achieve its purpose. Since at this precise time the monarchical movement came out into the open, the new revolutionary party was given fresh impetus to positive action.

Some members of the Kuomintang moderate wing, however, though invited by Sun Yat-sen to join the Chinese Revolutionary Party in Japan, were not satisfied with Sun Yat-sen's methods. According to Articles 11 and 12 of the party constitution, for example, party members would eventually enjoy all sorts of privileges in the revolutionary government, whereas nonmembers would not even have the status of free citizens. Sun's purpose was the protection of revolutionary leaders so that they might not be suppressed, as in 1913, by large groups of pseudorevolutionaries. In other words, Sun intended this Revolutionary Party to be a dictatorship during the revolutionary period. Kuomintang moderates opposed this, maintaining that there should be no caste distinctions and pointing out that the T'ungmeng Hui members were forced out in 1912-1913 because they had been too dogmatic. If now special rights or privileges were granted under the party constitution, objections from the people would inevitably be aroused. Furthermore, the moderates particularly objected to the rule providing that a member had to be fingerprinted upon joining the party. Consequently, members of the moderate wing of the Kuomintang refused to join the Chinese Revolutionary Party. Huang Hsing not only refused to join but departed for the United States.

When Japan's Twenty-one Demands were presented, the Kuomintang moderates in Japan were afraid that if Yüan Shih-k'ai had to deal with both foreign aggression and the new Revolutionary Party, China herself might suffer tremendously. To prevent this, a circular telegram signed by Li Ken-yüan, Niu Yung-chien, Ch'eng Ch'ien, Ch'en Hsiung-ming, Chang Shih-chao, and others—twenty-eight all together—was issued asking the suspension of all revolutionary activities so that a united front might be presented against the Japanese aggression. These moderates then organized themselves into a group to discuss diplomatic matters as they occurred. Because the European War was then in progress, this organization was called the Discussion Group for European Affairs [*Ou-shih yen-chiu hui*]. At its inception no one was elected leader, nor was there any political program. Moreover, since the name itself did not draw the attention of the government, connections could be made with Chinese on the mainland without government censorship. Eventually, however, Li Ken-yüan decided to try to make use of the organization to support Ch'en Ch'un-hsüan. Ch'en had had no relations with any revolutionary party, but he had had disagreements with Yüan Shih-k'ai and had been persuaded by Chang Shih-chao to join the anti-Yüan movement in 1913.

The rumor that the Discussion Group for European Affairs had been sponsored by Huang Hsing to fight against the Chinese Revolutionary Party was without any basis. During the monarchical movement the activity of the Discussion Group for European Affairs extended to China, where it included cooperation with the most moderate wing of the Kuomintang in the fight against Yüan Shih-k'ai.

The Progressive Party Opposes Yüan

This moderate wing of the Kuomintang was already cooperating with a segment of the Progressive Party before the dissolution of the parliament. When the monarchical attempt became overt the relations of these two parties became much closer. Their publications included the *Righteous Magazine* [*Cheng-i tsa-chih*] under the influence of the moderate Kuomintang members; the *China Magazine* [*Chung-hua tsa-chih*] of the Progressive Party; and the *Chia-yin Magazine* of the Discussion Group for European Affairs. Later on, the latter two periodicals combined to form the *New China Magazine* [*Hsin Chung-hua*].

The Progressive Party, developing as it did from the Constitutional Monarchy Party, knew that a statue, once thrown down, no longer commands the people's respect; the Progressives knew that since the Ch'ing dynasty had fallen, to create a new image to replace the Manchu emperor would take time. They gave no support to Yüan's monarchical movement. Yüan himself they hated violently. Under his regime they had either lost their jobs or were eking out only very humble livings under the rule of politicians and warlords of the Peiyang clique. They knew, moreover, that the political *status quo* could no longer be maintained. If they did not fight the monarchical movement, the Kuomintang would act alone and receive sole credit for any successful campaign against Yüan. Then as in 1911, the Progressives would have no position in the government. Therefore, Liang Ch'i-ch'ao, the leader of the Progressive Party, who had expressed no opinion of Yüan since returning from Japan in 1912, decided now upon open opposition; he published his famous article in refutation of Yüan's theory of a suitable political system for the nation.

Yüan, knowing of the article before it was published, offered a $200,000 bribe to Liang not to publish it. This being declined, Yüan tried to use force. Nevertheless, the article was published.

The participation of the Progressive Party in the anti-Yüan campaign was a blow to Yüan. First of all, the leaders of the Progressive Party had been very closely associated with the chiefs of the Peiyang clique. Now such chiefs as Feng, Tuan, and Hsü, for example, became even more actively opposed to Yüan than before. Secondly, the leaders of the Progressive Party had gained a reputation for careful action. Now their open opposition to Yüan led the usually lethargic populace to think that the Revolutionary Party might also have good reason for causing trouble. Thirdly, the Progressive Party, able to maintain relations with all the officials, was allied also with the mild wing of the Kuomintang, which in turn could obviously make an alliance with the Chinese Revolutionary Party. Thus all the active elements of the antimonarchists could form a united front.

THE DIPLOMATIC SITUATION

The diplomatic situation, too, was now very different from the situation in 1913-14. Yüan's victory over the anti-Yüan campaign in Kiangsi and Nanking [1913] had resulted from the great loan he had obtained from foreign imperialists. England was then particularly in favor of Yüan. The British minister to China and Yüan's advisor, Morrison, of the *London Times*, having seen their chance to utilize Yüan for the benefit of the British Empire, seized every opportunity to maintain good relations with Yüan and to give him help when he needed it.

After the outbreak of the European War the European nations, as we have already noted, had no time or energy to look after their interests in the East. They left Japan as the sole remaining power in the Eastern Hemisphere. If Japan had chosen this time to pounce upon all the available privileges in China, neither Britain nor Russia nor any other nation could have threatened her. Therefore, when the monarchical movement was uncovered, England, Russia, and the other nations all objected for fear of what Japan might do during the upheaval. Japanese authorities as well as the Japanese press initially expressed delighted approbation of the new monarchical campaign in China. Later, Japan began to issue its own warnings against the activities of the monarchists.

Yüan's Failure with Japan

The opinions of the Japanese authorities on the Chinese situation were divided into two factions led by, respectively, the ministry of foreign affairs and the ministry of war. According to Yoshino Sakuzo's *China After the Third Revolution*, the former advocated Yüan's overthrow, while the latter proposed to assist him. Yet another source indicates that these positions were exactly the reverse. It is difficult to ascertain which of these sources is correct, but at least it is a fact that Japanese opinion toward Yüan was not at first unified.

Early Japanese estimates of the power of Yüan and of the anti-Yüan movement were not very clear. Support of Yüan would be profitable to Japan if he were to win, but would strengthen Chinese ill feeling if he should lose. The policy of the Japanese government was not yet entirely settled upon when the first warnings were delivered on October 28. It was only decided that Japan should interfere one way or another. When Japan saw that the antimonarchists' power was increasing day by day, a second warning was presented on December 15. England, France, Italy, and Russia then followed suit. By this time Yüan had begun to realize that the British minister and Morrison, on whom he had relied as his helpers, were unable to prevent Japanese intervention. He decided to deal with Japan alone.

Yüan dispatched Chou Tzu-chi to present China's belated good wishes on the coronation of the Japanese emperor. The announcement of this diplomatic mission was made in early January 1916, but the negotiations had taken place a month earlier. The secret was revealed unexpectedly, and the jealousy of England, Russia, and the other nations was aroused to such an extent that they abandoned their undercover support of Yüan.

After this became public, Japan feared that she would incur the active resentment of the Chinese people and that the chances of success for the monarchical movement were very slim. Thereupon, she abruptly rejected even Chou Tzu-chi's diplomatic mission, though the arrangements had already been completed. Yüan's treacherous diplomacy had failed and his monarchy was already doomed.

THE RISE OF THE NATIONAL PROTECTION ARMY

The vanguard of the antimonarchist movement was certainly the Chinese Revolutionary Party, which had undergone extreme hardships after the failure of its attempt to overthrow Yüan in 1913. Before 1911 the troops in the provinces along the Yangtze River had been the instruments of the Revolutionists. Now, except for the provinces of Yunnan, Kweichow, Kwantung, and Kwangsi, all the provinces were garrisoned by Peiyang troops. Even in Kwangtung, Lung Chi-kuang and his troops had been bought by Yüan's money and patronage. Lu Jung-t'ing, though not bought by Yüan, was kept under close surveillance by Lung, and it was not easy for him to take any military action. Only the two provinces of Yunnan and Kweichow could be used as a starting point for an anti-Yüan campaign.

These two provinces, however, had heretofore been the headquarters of the Progressive Party. At the time of the 1911 Revolution, when Ts'ai Ao had been elected tutu of Yunnan, he ordered T'ang Chi-yao to lead the troops to Kweichow, placing that province within the influence of Yunnan. Although Ts'ai Ao had some dealings with the Kuomintang in 1912-13, he was a faithful student of Liang Ch'i-ch'ao and was a protégé of the Progressive Party. For a long time the two provinces of Yunnan and Kweichow had been the sphere of activity of the Progressive Party. During the anti-Yüan struggle of 1913, Li Lieh-chün invited Ts'ai by telegram to take simultaneous action, but the latter, thinking the time was not yet ripe, did not respond. Shortly thereafter, ordering T'ang Chi-yao to replace him as tutu of Yunnan, Ts'ai Ao left the province but his latent power in Yunnan continued, and the Progressive Party still relied on this province to shelter their activities.

This background made it almost impossible for the Revolutionary Party to persuade the authorities of Yunnan and Kweichow to take action against Yüan. The only one who could force the authorities of these two provinces into action was Ts'ai Ao. Although the Revolutionary Party was the ostensible leader of the united anti-Yüan forces, the operative power of the movement actually depended on Ts'ai Ao, who led the National Protection Army [*Hu-kuo chün*].

Before the rise of the National Protection Army, the Chinese Revolutionary Party under Ch'en Ch'i-mei's leadership accomplished the assassination of the commander of Shanghai, Cheng Ju-ch'eng, on November 10 and attacked the warship *Chao-ho* on December 5. Ch'en, who had discussed military plans with Sun Yat-sen in Tokyo, originally planned to start an uprising in Canton; but when he passed through Shanghai, he was persuaded by his comrades that if the garrison commander, Cheng Ju-ch'eng, were assassinated, Shanghai could easily be occupied. Shortly after the assassination of Cheng Ju-ch'eng, Yüan Shih-k'ai appointed Yang Shan-te garrison commander of Sungkiang and Shanghai. Yang at once proceeded to vigilant supervision of all local forces. Even though the Revolutionists had attacked the warship *Chao-ho* and occupied the telegraph and other offices, their forces were no match for Yüan's troops. This attempt by the Revolutionists to occupy Shanghai soon petered out.

Thereafter, the major activities of the Chinese Revolutionary Party concentrated in the South in Canton under the leadership of Chu Chih-hsin with another concentration in the North under Chü Cheng in Shantung. These two could shackle Yüan while the National Protection Army also started its activities. A few days before Yüan's accession to the throne, which was planned for January 1, 1916, the National Protection Army launched its anti-Yüan expedition from Yunnan.

Founding the National Protection Army

Concerning the beginning of the National Protection Army in Yunnan, Liang Ch'i-ch'ao said:

> The day after the establishment of the Peace Planning Society, Ts'ai [Ao] paid me a visit in Tientsin to discuss his plans. I said, "My responsibility is to the press, and I must therefore write an article to protest, openly and with dignity, against Yüan's action. You are an important military man and you should be very careful to avoid Yüan's hatred and envy while you secretly try to fight against him." Agreeing with my statement, Ts'ai played along with Yüan for two months in Peking so that Yüan might not suspect him. At the same time, he sent confidential telegrams to military leaders in Yunnan and Kweichow to discuss with them the implications of Yüan's treachery. He also invited Tai K'an to come to Peking to discuss with him personally. Tai was a native of Kweichow and a member of the Progressive Party; later he fought under Ts'ai in Szechwan and other provinces. In October 1915 Tai arrived in Peking from Kweichow accompanied by Wang Po-chou, and they made all their plans at my residence in Tientsin; all these plans were the results of several conferences. Thereafter Ts'ai and Tai left for the South, and I followed them to Shanghai.[8]

This account is certainly reliable as far as it goes, but it is oversimplified in its implication that Liang, Ts'ai, and Tai were the only promoters of the great operation. Liang, it would appear, indulged in considerable propaganda promoting his own importance.

Actually, the older Kuomintang members, Li Lieh-chün, Li Ken-yüan, and others, had long before turned their attention to Yunnan. Li Lieh-chün had served near the end of the Manchu dynasty as director of the army's "middle school" in Yunnan, and as a teacher in the military academy of that province. He therefore stood in a teacher-student relation to many of the military officers of Yunnan. After the failure of his anti-Yüan attempt in 1913, many of his subordinates fled from the Kiangsi army to Yunnan and enlisted in the Yunnan army. When Yüan's monarchical plans gathered momentum, Liang, Ts'ai and others were already having confidential communications with Yunnan. Li Lieh-chün, at the same time, dispatched representatives from Japan to Yunnan to carry on his anti-Yüan activities.

The first of these to arrive in Yunnan was Fang Sheng-t'ao, who had been a classmate of Li Lieh-chün in a Japanese military academy and had served as Li's subordinate while Li was tutu of Kiangsi. They had both fled to Japan after the failure of their anti-Yüan fight in 1913. With the full knowledge of T'ang Chi-yao, then tutu of Yunnan, Fang held many confidential conferences with the army officers of that province. Although Li Keng-yüan did not return to Yunnan personally, he kept in constant touch with T'ang, urging him to start a revolution. It is therefore clear that those who tried to persuade Yunnan to start a revolution against Yüan were not limited to members of the Progressive Party.

Several army officers of Yunnan took the initiative. According to Ts'ai Ao's letter to Liang Ch'i-ch'ao, dated January 5, 1916,

> Many middle-ranking officers were greatly angered by the establishment of the Peace Planning Society, and they frequently urged T'ang Chi-yao to take action. Since T'ang knew neither the full intentions of the Progressive Party nor the real attitude of the other

provincial authorities, he followed a cautious policy for several months, showing no noticeable inclination toward either course. The news that Yüan's police had searched my Peking residence and of my absence from Peking on the pretext of illness excited the public here. As soon as I reached Yunnan, T'ang made up his mind.[9]

From Yunnan the inciter of the revolution was, however, by no means T'ang Chi-yao, who was simply an opportunist. T'ang's determination to start the revolution was influenced by Ts'ai Ao and others. If Ts'ai had not gone to Yunnan, the attitude in the province would have remained unpredictable. According to Yoshino Sakuzo's *China After the Third Revolution*, the promoters of the movement in the Yunnan army were three officers, Huang Yü-ch'eng, Teng Tai-chung, and Yang Tseng. They compelled T'ang to take action, threatening to mutiny if he did not.

Cooperation between Ts'ai Ao and Li Lieh-chün had begun before Ts'ai reached Yunnan. While Ts'ai was traveling from Tientsin to Japan, to Taiwan, to Haiphong, and thence to Yunnan, he kept in touch with the army leaders and politicians of the old Kuomintang. In Taiwan he had an interview with Li Lieh-chün, but in order to avoid arousing suspicion, they proceeded to Yunnan separately.

In short, the beginning of the revolution by the National Protection Army in Yunnan was the result of cooperation between the old Kuomintang, especially the moderate wing, and the Progressive Party. The first stirrings of the movement appeared simultaneously in Peking, Tientsin, Tokyo, and Yunnan. Gradually all the plotters were concentrated in Shanghai and Hong Kong: Liang Ch'i-ch'ao and Ku Chung-hsiu were in Shanghai; Li Ken-yüan and Lin Hu in Hong Kong. The important army officers who were concentrated in Yunnan took action shortly after the arrival there of Ts'ai Ao.

Action in Yunnan

Ts'ai Ao reached Yunnan on December 19. On the twenty-third a telegram signed by T'ang Chi-yao and Jen K'e-ch'en was sent to Peking demanding that Yüan give up the monarchical plan and punish its instigators. If no reply was forthcoming by 10 P. M. on the twenty-fifth, their wire asserted, they would immediately declare their independence.

They had originally planned to move the Yunnan troops secretly to the border of Szechwan and then send the above telegram to Peking. The Yunnan army hoped to take Szechwan before any reinforcements could come from the North, and to organize their anti-Yüan headquarters in that province. But Yüan Shih-k'ai's preparations for signing a treaty with Japan necessitated prompt and immediate action. Because the declaration of independence of Yunnan took place three weeks earlier than originally planned, the military situation in Szechwan became extremely difficult.

After Yunnan declared its independence, T'ang Chi-yao was made tutu, while Ts'ai took the responsibility of commanding an expeditionary army, which was at first called the Republican Army [*Kung-ho Chün*]. Because Li Lieh-chün pointed out that it might be confused with the Republican Party, the name was dropped. In the meantime a conference held at the Hu-kuo Ssu [Nation-Protection Temple] asserted that the purpose of this war was to protect the nation [*hu kuo*]. Therefore, the expeditionary army was renamed *Hu-kuo Chün* [National Protection Army]. The National Protection Army had three divisions: the first was led by Ts'ai Ao to Szechwan; the second by Tai K'an to Kweichow; the third by Li Liehchün to southern Yunnan.

Ts'ai Ao's division had three regiments, totaling only 3130 men. When he launched his campaign, there were (according to a facsimile reproduction of General Ts'ai's writings) provisions to last only two months. The future of the National Protection Army appeared dubious if the other provinces did not respond. His army advanced very slowly. Yüan Shih-k'ai's strong forces had already gathered to meet him before he could reach the province of Szechwan.

Originally Kweichow had intended to declare its independence of the central government at the same time as Yunnan, and Kwangsi and Kiangsu were expected to respond immediately. But General Lung Chi-kuang of Kwangsi stubbornly refused to act along with Yunnan and insisted that Yunnan must declare its independence first. Because Yunnan made its declaration of independence early, Kweichow did not have enough time to prepare for a similar step and did not formally declare its independence until the Yunnan army under Tai K'an reached Kweiyang, the capital. Kwangsi did not indicate its support of the revolutionary movement until the middle of March. Feng Kuo-chang of Kiangsu failed to respond at all, except for presenting passive resistance to Yüan by refusing to fight for him.

On the border between Yunnan and Szechwan the several thousand hunger-stricken soldiers of the National Protection Army under Ts'ai Ao and Tai K'an fought bitterly against the more powerful Yüan Shih-k'ai army under Ts'ao K'un and Chang Ching-yao. Much to the credit of Ts'ai Ao's leadership and to his army's courage, they resisted all efforts by the over- whelmingly more numerous enemy to push them back, despite the fact that they were unable to reach Szechwan. When Kwangsi declared its independence, giving moral as well as actual support to the National Protection Army, Yüan Shih-k'ai's army grew disheartened.

Lu Jung-t'ing Declares Kwangsi Independent

Yüan's strategy was to surround the two provinces of Yunnan and Kweichow. He sent Ts'ao and Chang with a large army to attack Yunnan from Szechwan. He ordered Ma Chi-tseng with his forces to enter Kweichow from Hunan. He assigned Lung Chin-kuang, Lung Chi-kuang's younger brother, to lead a detachment of Cantonese troops to attack the southern part of Yunnan jointly with soldiers from Kwangsi. Because Lu Jung-t'ing's dubious attitude worried him, Yüan appointed Lu overseer of Kweichow on March 7. He also appointed Ch'en Ping-k'un, a division commander of the Kwangsi army, to serve as overseer of the troops in Kwangsi for the purpose of controlling Lu.

However, this plan backfired. Friendship existed between these two men. On March 15 they jointly declared their independence of the central government and immediately disarmed Lung's troops, which were marching towards the south of Yunnan. Lu Jung-t'ing was again made tutu of Kwangsi. He had long wanted to fight against monarchism, but for several reasons had not dared to take open action.

Lu had been closely watched by the governor of Kwangsi, Wang Tsu-t'ung, Yüan's faithful spy, whom Yüan had made codirector of military affairs in Kwangsi. The contents of most of the letters and telegrams of the Kuomintang members to Lu were known to Wang. But chiefly because Lu's son had been kept in Peking as Yüan's bodyguard, serving as a hostage to ensure Lu's loyalty, the father dared not risk open action. When Lu asked for two months' sick leave, this request was taken as an indication of his support of the antimonarchists. When his sick leave was up, Lu unexpectedly changed his attitude and sent telegrams to Peking, assuring Yüan of his loyalty and begging that his son be returned to his home to serve him during his sickness. Yüan complied with the request. Strangely enough, Lu's son suddenly died of an illness when he reached Hankow, giving rise to rumors of all sorts. Yüan's telegrams of condolence to Lu were overtly appreciated, but now Lu's covert feelings toward Yüan had developed into fierce hatred.

After the generals of Yunnan started the uprising, the Kuomintang members again tried to persuade Lu to participate in the revolution. Lu was sympathetic toward the cause; but he begged to be allowed to maintain his neutrality for some time before declaring his independence, because the extreme poverty of the province of Kwangsi made it difficult to raise military provisions, and the province was controlled by Kwangtung; he also asked that the Yunnan soldiers should not violate the boundaries of Kwangsi. One of his secretaries was dispatched to Yunnan, however, to take part in the military planning, and the people came to expect the three provinces of Yunnan, Kweichow, and Kwangsi to take simultaneous action against Yüan.

After the revolution started from Yunnan, Yüan planned to send his troops from North China to attack that province from Kwangsi. Lu encouraged merchants to send telegrams to Yüan protesting the action as highly detrimental to commerce. When Yüan asked him to send troops to attack Yunnan, Lu declined on the ground of the shortage of military provisions and the urgent need for local garrisons. Yüan took the opportunity to order Lung Chin-kuang to lead some Cantonese troops to Kwangsi to help Lu attack Yunnan, leaving Lu with no further pretexts to defy orders. Yüan secretly ordered Lung to wait until Lu had left Nanning, and then to try to take the latter's position as tutu.

Lu and Lung were related through the marriage of their children, and Lu had therefore sent a representative to Lung for confidential discussions regarding a joint declaration of independence. Lung, however, did not agree with Lu and continued his preparations to lead his troops from Kwangsi to Yunnan. Using the argument that soldiers could easily be recruited in Kwangsi, Lu managed to persuade Lung to bring fewer troups and more weapons. Since there were many revolutionaries hidden in Kwangtung, Lung Chi-kuang, the tutu, could not spare many soldiers to send to other provinces; so his brother, Lung Chin-kuang, could take only a few to Kwangsi, where Lu assigned a number of his soldiers to join Lung and urged them to proceed toward Yunnan. He even ordered another son to lead a regiment of soldiers to go along with Lung; more than that, he asked to be allowed to attack Yunnan himself, but he asked Yüan to give him more arms and one million Chinese dollars for provisions. Yüan gave Lu half the amount he requested, but Lu sent a telegram insisting on the full million. Yüan finally gave in. In a few days Lu asked for more weapons, and Yüan's suspicions increased. Yet since Lu had asked to attack Yunnan, Yüan appointed him tutu of Kweichow and appointed Ch'en Ping-k'un overseer of military affairs in Kwangsi. These appointments were made on March 7.

Shortly thereafter Lu was ready to start his expedition. On the twelfth, Yüan received a telegram from Wang Tsu-t'ung, who reported that Lu was about to side with the revolutionaries. On the fifteenth, Kwangsi formally declared its independence, and all the troops of Lung Chin-kuang were disarmed. The declaration itself was signed by Lu Jung-t'ing, Ch'en Ping-k'un, and others; even Liang Ch'i-ch'ao's name was included because both Lu and Ch'en admired Liang. The declaration of Kwangsi alarmed Yüan's government and upset Yüan's plan for attacking Yunnan with the joint armies of Kwangtung and Kwangsi. In addition, the security of the rich Province of Kwangtung was endangered.

ABANDONMENT OF THE MONARCHICAL SYSTEM

The influence of the National Protection Army was constantly expanding. Yüan's hopes for its suppression grew dimmer and dimmer. Kwangsi gave the National Protection Army in Yunnan and Kweichow enormous support and dealt Yüan a heavy blow. *Hung Hsien* [Glorious Constitution], the title of Yüan's reign, was shortly to be canceled. The abandonment of the monarchical plan was rumored a fortnight after the National Protection Army launched its campaign from Yunnan.

Japan's rejection of Yüan's special envoy Chou Tzu-chi indicated to Yüan that he had lost his diplomatic support. But since the change of national polity had been publicized as a response to the will of the whole nation, Yüan stood to lose face if he suddenly ordered an end to the monarchist movement. Moreover, Yunnan was the only province that was openly antimonarchist. If peace could be restored in Yunnan, the diplomatic situation might be yet improved. With this in mind, Yüan did not order the abandonment of the entire movement, but rather postponed the date of his accession to the throne. Resources assigned for the great ceremony were shifted to the suppression of the "rebellion" in Yunnan.

Kweichow formally declared its independence in the latter half of January 1916. Within a month the situation in Szechwan and Hunan was getting out of hand. For the great ceremony of accession no more money was appropriated after March 1. There were rumors that the title of the reign, *Hung Hsien*, would be abandoned, and that the Political Council would be dissolved along with the Bureau for the Preparation of the Ceremony. Frequent conferences were called in Yüan's government. To save face, abandonment of the monarchical movement had to come through some organization which appeared to represent public opinion. Consequently, on February 28 a meeting of the Legislative Yüan was called for May 5. The members of the Political Council, which had been acting for the Legislative Yüan, were ordered to act as members of the latter body since the election of members was so complicated. In this manner the convention could be held on the date specified.

Telegrams were also sent from the central government to all the provincial authorities and Chinese diplomatic officials abroad requesting them to give their views on the monarchical system. Some of the replies subsequently received expressed hope that Yüan would soon ascend the throne but the majority were, directly or indirectly, unfavorable. Dispatching requests for expression of opinion was primarily intended to prolong the announcement of the abandonment of the monarchical system as long as possible in order not to shake the morale of the soldiers at the front and thereby hurt the prestige of the government; but if the war against Yunnan should last long and prove difficult to win, then the announcement of rejection of the monarchy would be made through the Legislative Yüan.

Early in March reports of several victories at the front greatly encouraged the watchdogs of the monarchists. They immediately tried to persuade Yüan to continue preparations for his ascension to the throne. Unexpectedly, however, the news of Kwangsi's declaration of independence was followed by still another warning from the diplomatic corps, which had already delivered two such warnings to Yüan before the revolution broke out in Yunnan.

Yüan's Diplomatic Difficulties

This latest warning from the diplomatic corps took the form of an inquiry as to how Yüan meant to suppress the revolution. Yüan had told the diplomatic corps that the troubles in Yunnan could easily be suppressed in two or three months; now Kwangsi had declared its independence and the disturbance was spreading. It was said that a certain minister received instructions from his government as follows:

> China's civil war is spreading, and Yüan's government lacks the power to suppress it. The actions of Yunnan and Kweichow are meant to ensure the continuance of the Republic, and they should not be considered to be merely the actions of rebels. The monarchy in Peking has not yet been recognized by any nation, and it has lost its standing as the representative of the Chinese nation. Hereafter the governments of both North and South China are to be treated as merely belligerent parties.

It was said that the minister delivered a note conveying the substance of this to Yüan, who was much perturbed by it. The minister alluded to here is obviously the Japanese minister, whose country had by then decided to help overthrow Yüan in order to gain the confidence of the more successful Kuomintang, in hopes of receiving certain concessions.

Yüan was also hampered by the lack of military funds. His hopes of raising loans abroad were thwarted by the fact that only Japan and the United States were then in a position to lend him money. Now that Japan's position had changed, she not only refused to make a loan herself, but even obstructed a possible loan from the United States. Yüan obviously could not hope for funds from foreign sources; his only remaining chance was a compromise with the antimonarchists.

Yüan Relinquishes His Pretensions to the Throne

Before any compromise could be reached, Yüan would have to abandon first his monarchical system; otherwise he could not hope to placate his opponents. The only men he could find to negotiate such a compromise were Li Yüan-hung, Hsü Shih-ch'ang, and Tuan Ch'i-jui, with whom he was certainly no longer on good terms. On March 21, five days after Kwangsi declared its independence, Yüan called a conference during which these three men applauded Yüan's expressed intention of abandoning monarchism. But Chu Ch'i-ch'ien, Liang Shih-i, and several others for selfish reasons expressed strong objections. Yüan showed them telegrams from five generals, including Feng Kuo-chang, Li Shun, and Chin Yün-p'eng, urging him to abandon monarchism in order to placate the people in Yunnan and Kweichow. Even staunch monarchists fell silent. Ni Ssu-ch'ung, the governor of Anhwei, then became very excited and cried, "Monarchism has been practiced in China for several thousand years. How dare these churls demand its abandonment? I swear upon my life to wipe them out!"

Despite such heated protests, the conference ordered Chang I-lin to draft a document, to be made public on the twenty-second, announcing that Yüan's acceptance of the throne on December 12 was revoked. Yüan did not use the Legislative Yüan to gloss over the procedure, and he immediately appointed Hsü Shih-ch'ang minister. On the twenty-third, Tuan Ch'i-jui was appointed chief of staff. *Hung Hsien*, the title of the reign, was formally discarded. The year 1916 resumed its notation as the fifth year of the Republic of China.

The original draft of Chang I-lin's document was written in the first person and contained no such terms as "this great president." The draft was modified by Hsü Shih-ch'ang and others; Yüan finally made a few modifications of his own, omitting the accusations against his monarchist supporters. At the end of the document he added, "It is the duty of this great president to rule over the entire country." The expression "great president" had been noticeably absent from official documents for more than three months. It is said that when Yüan picked up a pen to add it, he hesitated again and again as if even he were a little ashamed. Had he not taken this opportunity to use the term, he might have been thought to have no title whatsoever. The political problem, however, was not to be solved so easily.

THE SOUTHERN AND NORTHERN GOVERNMENTS

The most remarkable events after the abandonment of monarchism were Tuan Ch'i-jui's reorganization of the cabinet in North China and the enforced independence of Kwangtung in South China. Feng Kuo-chang sponsored a conference at Nanking for the purpose of settling the political situation between the South and the North. On June 6, 1916, Yüan died and the curtain on his great drama fell. Let us look at these events in some detail.

Efforts to Compromise

After Yüan's abandonment of monarchism, which was intended to effect a compromise with South China, it became apparent that several persons must be found who could deal with the Southern authorities. For this purpose a joint telegram, ostensibly from Li Yüan-hung, Hsü Shih-ch'ang and Tuan Ch'i-jui, was sent to Ts'ai Ao, T'ang Chi-yao, Lu Jung-t'ing, and Liang Ch'i-ch'ao, requesting a truce and a discussion of the problems which now existed. Actually Hsü had taken the initiative and tried to get Tuan to sign it. Tuan, although he knew of the telegram, did not sign it; Li was not even aware of its existence.

In other ways too Hsü tried to enlist the aid of these men and tried to solve the problem of South China. He asked his friends to offer Li the command of the military government, to which Li replied that he would accept no position other than the vice-presidency, to which he was constitutionally entitled. At the same time Hsü urged Tuan to accept the position of chief of staff, but it was said that Tuan named three factors upon which his acceptance would be contingent: (1) solution of the South China problem by peaceful means; (2) temporary suspension of the further expansion of the model army (Yüan intended to expand it into ten regiments); and (3) restoration of the full authority of the chief of staff. Since Yüan preferred not to give the chief of staff much power, Tuan did not take up the position.

Only Hsü Shih-chang performed his functions, as prime minister, sending telegrams to the authorities of every province pleading for the preservation of order and security in each locality and making suggestions to Yüan with regard to possible problems that might arise in the future. Also, he recruited K'ang Yu-wei, Wu T'ing-fang, T'ang Shao-i, T'ang Hua-lung, and others to serve as mediators and ordered Lung Chi-kuang and Lu Jung-t'ing to bring about a compromise. (Liang Ch'i-ch'ao, fearing that Lu might be confused, sent him a telegram urging him not to be swayed by Lung.) But all of Hsü's efforts were in vain. The commanders of the National Protection Army refused to suspend their military operations until Yüan stepped down from his position.

A *de facto* truce had already been reached in the battle zone of Szechwan and Kweichow because the regiments of the National Protection Army wished to rest and regroup; while the troops of Yüan Shih-k'ai had been greatly discouraged by the abandonment of monarchism. The tutu of

Szechwan, Ch'en Huan, realizing that Yüan was no longer a solid support, tried to keep on good terms with the National Protection Army. Through his secret negotiations with Ts'ai Ao, the latter agreed to a week's truce to begin on March 31. By mutual agreement of both parties, this was later extended so that there was virtually no warfare in Szechwan and Kweichow after March.

Ts'ai Ao's reply to the joint telegram, however, emphatically insisted that Yüan should go, since he had been discarded by the populace and was completely untrustworthy. In mid-April, a joint reply from all the independent provinces, indicating that no compromise was feasible and that Yüan must retire immediately, was even stronger in tone.

Yüan Yields Further Authority

It was evident to Hsü Shih-chang that it would not be easy to conclude this matter. Although a truce had been reached in Szechwan and Kweichow, Kwangtung declared its independence on April 6, and Chekiang followed suit on the twelfth. Tuan Ch'i-jui was giving only lukewarm support to the compromise, implying that he would refuse any responsibility unless Yüan gave him a great deal of authority. Yüan, also realizing that the situation was a difficult one to handle, tried to change the structure of the government back to the responsible cabinet system, both to attract Tuan to his side and to satisfy the Kuomintang. On April 21 he issued this order:

> Because of numerous affairs of state which require direct attention, this president, with the assistance of the prime minister, formerly assumed all political authority. During the past two years, however, procedures have been inadequate for want of a responsible cabinet, and prompt reform is now desirable. In accordance with the constitutional organization of the government I have now designated a prime minister who will take charge of affairs of state and reorganize

procedures to set an example of responsible government and to take the first steps toward improvement of administration. [10]

This order was intended to indicate that Yüan now retained only the titular presidency and had handed his political powers over to the responsible cabinet. This, he hoped, would placate his enemies. After the proclamation of this order he accepted the resignation of Premier Hsü Shih-ch'ang on April 22 and designated Tuan Ch'i-jui to organize a cabinet, appointing him concurrently minister of war. On May 4 the laws governing the organization of the government were revised. The council of state [*cheng-shih-t'ang*] was changed into the cabinet [*kuo-wu yüan*]. The designated wording for official stationery was also proclaimed by the president. Now Tuan Ch'i-jui accepted this new appointment.

After assuming the premiership, Tuan requested the president to give the cabinet great military and political authority and to abolish the office of strategic affairs and the bureau for military administration. Yüan gave his verbal consent, without actually abolishing the two offices or transferring to Tuan any real power; the cabinet could still command neither the bodyguards nor the model corps. Yüan was certainly much more capable than Tsai-feng and far cleverer than Tuan. But despite his continued grip on the central government Yüan still had no means of subduing the National Protection Army in the South.

The Organization of the Military Government in the South

Kwangtung formally declared its independence on April 6. The organization of the military government of Kwangtung and Kwangsi was not announced until the first of May. Kwangtung's declaration of independence was made by Lung Chi-kuang in response to pressure from all sides, although he considered it contradictory to the purposes of the National Protection Army. (At this time the Revolutionary Party of China and some members of the old Kuomintang, e. g., Li Ken-yüan,

Lin Hu, and Ch'en Hsiung-ming, concentrated on taking Kwangtung by force.) According to *An Account of the National Protection Army* [*Hu-kuo-chün chi-shih*] compiled by the newspaper office called *Chung-hua hsin-pao*, thirty-one places had been occupied by the Chinese Revolutionary Army, which had two warships; seven places had been occupied by the National Protection Army under Ch'en Hsiung-ming, who possessed one warship; the generals in the other parts of Kwangtung declared their independence in response to Kwangsi's action. Lung was thus isolated and could not extend his power beyond the metropolitan area of Canton. Moreover, since he had killed many members of the Kuomintang, the party hated him with an intransigent hatred. Both Lu Jung-t'ing and Ch'en Ch'un-hsüan tried to persuade him to declare his independence, but Lung would not change his mind. Li Ken-yüan, in his official capacity as representative of T'ang Chi-yao, tutu of Yunnan, went to Canton personally to carry on negotiations with Lung.

Since Lung's position was greatly endangered by the pressure from all directions, he secretly telegraphed Yüan Shih-k'ai's government, calling urgently for heavy reinforcements for the local garrisons. When Yüan sent reinforcements, the Cantonese in Shanghai were greatly disturbed, and they warned the China Merchants' Navigation Company against transporting the troops to Kwangtung. The members of the Kuomintang in Kwangtung were even more outraged by Lung's covert methods. Several warships which had been anchored in the river near Canton sailed suddenly on April 4, and the flags which were carried by the army bore the inscription "We are waiting for Lung Chi-kuang to declare independence."

Lung, now convinced that he could not maintain the *status quo*, telegraphed the Yüan government for directions. Yüan replied, "Declare independence, but continue to support the central government." Lung accordingly proclaimed, on the sixth, the independence of Kwangtung, though without a single word of criticism of Yüan. But the Kuomintang members who had been arrested by him had not yet been freed, and Ts'ai Naihuang, a man deeply loathed by the Kuomintang, was still protected by Lung. It was immediately apparent to the Kuomintang that Lung's declaration was nothing but a ruse to prevent military action. Their decision to drive him away was also supported, before his entry into Nanning, by the moderate leader Liang Ch'i-ch'ao.

In a telegram to Lu Jung-t'ing from Lungchow, Liang Ch'i-ch'ao said: "The position of Kwangtung is of great importance to the fate of the nation. If Lung still insists on his stand, we must make him surrender to us, and even the protection of his present position should not be thoughtlessly granted if he requests it." In another telegram to T'ang Chüeh-t'un, he stated: "Unless Yüan abdicates, there is no room for mediation in Peking; unless Lung resigns, there can be no compromise in Kwangtung."[11]

Nevertheless, Lu Jung-t'ing did not wish to break off relations with Lung Chi-kuang. He urged Ch'en Ch'un-hsüan to go south, hoping that Ch'en could use his influence to control Lung, a former subordinate, and to persuade him to participate in the northern expedition. After Liang Ch'i-ch'ao reached Nanning, he too supported Lu's idea, and he even tried to alleviate the ill feeling toward Lung on the part of the members of the Kuomintang, requesting them to avoid military actions against Lung so that the peace and order of Kwangtung might be preserved as a headquarters for the northern expedition. After sending this telegram, Liang journeyed from Nanning to Kwangtung, accompanied by the tutu Lu Jung-t'ing.

Lu's representative, T'ang Chüeh-t'un, going to Kwangtung from Wuchow to negotiate with Lung, conferred at Haichow with Lung's subordinates and some Kuomintang members. During the conference Lung's subordinates assassinated T'ang, Hsü Ch'in, and several others. This act infuriated Liang and the Kuomintang members in Kwangtung. Frightened, Lung sent Governor Chang Ming-ch'i to Wuchow to explain the situation to Lu and Liang. Lu, producing seven demands which were accepted by Lung, immediately led his troops to Kwangtung.

When Lu and Liang reached Chao-ch'ing in the west of Kwangtung, they received many letters and telegrams from the provincial politicians and generals expressing unanimous objection to Lung's retaining his position as tutu of Kwangtung, although this had been one of the seven demands. Lu and Liang advised Lung to lead troops to join the northern expedition and recommended that Ch'en Ch'un-hsüan take his place as tutu. Realizing that his forces could not match that of Kwangsi and determined to do his best to retain his position, Lung went to Chao-ch'ing on April 19 to seek a compromise with Lu, offering cooperation under the following conditions: (1) Lung Chi-kuang would continue as tutu of Kwangtung. (2) A temporary military government under the tutu Ch'en Ch'un-hsüan would be set up at Chao-ch'ing. (3) Ts'ai Nai-huang should be punished. (4) The northern expedition should be promptly carried out. (5) The local militia should be better controlled after Ch'en entered Kwangtung. These measures presented a compromise rather than a thorough solution of a problem, as Liang later told Ts'ai Ao, but there was no alternative. There was urgent need for cooperation between Kwangtung and Kwangsi in the northern expedition in order to reduce the pressure from their enemies in Szechwan and Kweichow.

Near the end of April, Ch'en Ch'un-hsüan went to Chao-ch'ing. He was favored for appointment as commander of the National Protection Army of Kwangtung and Kwangsi, of which Liang Ch'i-ch'ao was made chief of staff. The military government was set up at Chao-ch'ing, in order not to encroach on Lung's position. It was established to solve the Kwangtung problem, but there was still no unified organization for other independent provinces.

The supreme military government of the National Protection Army was organized and represented by the four tutus of Yunnan, Kweichow, Kwangtung, and Kwangsi, and by Ts'ai Ao, Liang Ch'i-ch'ao, Li Lieh-chün, and others, who issued five declarations. The first was to disqualify Yüan Shih-k'ai from the presidency of China; the second was to support Li Yüan-hung, the vice -president, for the presidency, in accordance with Article 5 of the laws published in October 1913 for election of the president. The third declaration announced that since Li Yüan-hung was unable to escape from the control of the "bandits" to perform his duties as legal president and since there was no way to form a cabinet, a Military Council under the president was to command the military affairs of the whole nation and to look after civil affairs; this council would include a number of directors appointed as a committee to execute state affairs and would serve as the highest authority of the country, but would be abolished as soon as a cabinet could be organized. The fourth declaration comprised the rules for the organization of this Military Council. The fifth announced the appointments, in accordance with the rules of organization, of T'ang Chi-yao, Lu Jung-t'ing, Lung Chi-kuang, Ch'en Ch'un-hsüan, Liang Ch'i-ch'ao, Ts'ai Ao, and others as councilors. T'ang Chi-yao was elected chairman, Ch'en Ch'un-hsüan vice-chairman, and Liang Ch'i-ch'ao chairman of the committee of political affairs. The Military Council was formally established on May 8 and located at Chao-ch'ing. Because T'ang Chi-yao could not come to Kwangtung, Ch'en Ch'un-hsüan was made chairman of the council.

The Nanking Conference Sponsored by Feng Kuo-chang

In order to protect his position as president, Yüan asked Tuan Ch'i-jui again to reorganize the cabinet, but the organization of the Military Council in Southern China was itself a strong rejection of Yüan. Even Feng Kuo-chang, once a strong supporter of Yüan, had been maintaining contact with the antimonarchists. When Yüan Shih-k'ai, having tendered his resignation to the Political Council, was urged to stay on, some members of the Council were conscientious enough to feel ashamed of their action. They sent a petition to Yüan requesting the dissolution of that body. Yüan then tried to utilize the governors of those provinces which had not yet declared their independence. He asked his secretary to compose a telegram urging Yüan to retain the presidency, and he asked Feng Kuo-chang in Nanking to persuade all the governors to sign that telegram. On the pretext that it would be better to await a more opportune time, Feng, who was no longer a Yüan supporter, refused to comply.

Nevertheless, Feng intended to fish in these troubled waters. Relying on his connections with the leaders in South China in his dealings with Yüan, and on his relations with the Northern authorities in bargaining with the National Protection Army, he acted exactly as Yüan had done in bargaining with the Manchu dynasty and the revolutionary army in 1911. Feng, having learned all of Yüan's tricks, kept his position ambiguous. On April 16 Feng urged Yüan not to concentrate power in the hands of the central government, not to deprive the provincial generals of their authority, and not to resort to war against South China at a time when Yüan was so unpopular with the people. He also suggested that Yüan yield his position to some other capable person. Moreover, Feng sent telegrams to Hsü Shih-ch'ang and Tuan Ch'i-jui, asking them to urge Yüan, as a means of selfprotection, to give up his position.

But in another telegram on April 17, Feng said: "The president's term of office is four years, and he is depended upon by the people. During this period, his position is safe from objectors and he cannot resign." Attached to this telegram were eight proposals, including suggestions that Yüan's position as president be maintained and that members of the parliament be carefully elected and the parliament reopened.

Yüan, having long since lost all confidence in Feng, wished to use Tuan. Tuan in accepting the premiership had stipulated neither that Yüan should resign the presidency nor that he should retain it. After the cabinet was reorganized, however, Tuan immediately sent a telegram to the authorities in South China, informing them that the responsible cabinet had been reestablished, that Yüan was president only in name, and requesting them to send a delegation to Peking to carry on direct negotiations. Tuan further stated that (1) the responsible cabinet was merely in a transitional period and was not a military government; (2) it was responsible to all circles of government, not to the president alone; (3) since it took full responsibility, it certainly had a political authority which could be affected neither by the president nor by any other organization; (4) the cabinet had no intention of disregarding the parliament, since the latter would be carefully constituted; and (5) since the important members from South China were not there, the cabinet members had been selected from among the representatives actually in the capital. When it became evident that the Southern authorities would continue to insist on Yüan's retirement, Tuan began to give them open support.

Yüan then began to think of dismissing Tuan and preparing for war against his enemies in South China. He avoided transferring to Tuan the great political and military authority which he had promised him. Seeing no hope for either peace or actual power, Tuan tendered his verbal resignation to Yüan. The latter was not free, however, to get rid of Tuan immediately. Since Feng, too, objected to the resumption of military measures and there was no way to solve the financial predicament, Yüan could not accept Tuan's resignation; but the Peking government was completely paralyzed.

In order to monopolize the political situation in North and South China, Feng Kuo-chang now tried to create a neutral force under his own control in order to gain the support of all the provincial authorities for his own candidacy for the presidency. His method was to organize a new parliament, to which Yüan should send his resignation and by which a new president would be elected. That is why he issued the above-mentioned eight proposals in the middle of April. On the twenty-fifth he sent another statement to the provinces which had not yet declared their independence,

> The four provinces, Yunnan, Kweichow, and others, continue to go to extremes. It is best for the other provinces to make alliances for self-protection and for the extension of their military power in order to control both the central government and the four provinces. We can then adopt the proper policies, based on the law and on our own estimate of the national situation, in order to establish a strong foundation and bring the two parties into harmony. Should the four provinces act in a manner contrary to our opinions, we must consider them our common enemy. Should the central government differ with our ideas, we must insist on our own. [12]

Favorable response to this telegram was soon received from the provinces, but Feng reorganized his eight points in another circular telegram to the provinces on May 1. In this document Feng admitted that China did not then have a legal government and said that it would be better to recognize Yüan for the time being in order to maintain peace until the opening of the parliament, which would elect a new president before Yüan's resignation. The election of the president should be carefully carried out in accordance with both the rules governing it and those governing the organization of the parliament.

This telegram was highly disturbing to the political leaders. A strong refutation, representing the opinion of twenty-two provinces which had resident representatives in Shanghai, was proclaimed under the leadership of T'ang Shao-i. Feng, ignoring the rebuke, went to Hsuchow on May 5 to have a conference with Chang Hsün and Ni Ssu-ch'ung. Ni was fundamentally a loyal partisan of Yüan, and Chang was also eager to secure Yüan's favor. They immediately sent a joint telegram, with Feng, to the central government and another telegram to all the provinces which had not yet declared their independence, requesting each of them to send a delegate to the meeting at Nanking on May 15.

Yüan, delighted with the turn of events, believed that he could use this meeting for his own benefit. He declared that though he would not try to retain the presidency, he would await the outcome of the Nanking conference before resigning.

On May 18 twenty-three representatives convened under the chairmanship of Feng Kuo-chang. The first item on the agenda was the problem of the president. The Shantung representative, Ting Shih-i, first suggested that Yüan should immediately retire because there was great danger that some international imbroglio might be fomented in Shantung, where the Chinese Revolutionary Party was planning to start an uprising with the support of some Japanese. The Hunan representative seconded this motion. A majority of the representatives seemed to favor Yüan's resignation. Realizing that the decision would be of major concern, Feng adjourned the meeting without putting the motion to a formal vote. That evening, Ni Ssu-ch'ung ordered three battalions of his bodyguards to hurry from Pang-pu to Nanking.

At the next day's meeting, Ni spoke first, proposing that the president should not retire immediately. Ting Shih-i objected, but Chang Hsün's alternate seconded Ni's proposal. A number of other representatives who were intimidated by Ni's military forces were found to constitute only a minority in favor of Yüan's retirement. However, the matter was not put to a formal vote. When the conference resumed next day, Feng Kuo-chang moved that "President Yüan should retire, but his retirement should be approved by the parliament, and it is improper for this conference to make a suggestion in the matter." Ni requested that Feng's motion be put to a vote, and it was passed. Feng's secretary was immediately directed to draft a telegram to all the provinces, and the draft was taken under discussion on the twenty-second.

Some of the representatives expressed objections. Ting Shih-i took this opportunity to say:

> There are only three possible measures: no retirement, immediate retirement, delayed retirement. This telegram, leaving the problem to be decided by the parliament, actually suggests delayed retirement. Even if all the provinces were to agree to Yüan's immediate resignation, the process would take a couple of months; even if we prefer delayed resignation, the first issue to be raised when the parliament convenes will be the impeachment of the president. This process will inevitably lead to his retirement in three or four months. The difference between immediate and delayed retirement will be only one or two months; it is not worth arguing with the independent provinces about this brief period. [13]

Feng Kuo-chang, persuaded by Ting's words, suggested that telegrams be sent to invite the independent provinces to send their representatives to the meeting in order to solve the problem that would follow Yüan's resignation. This was approved, and the telegram was dispatched. After receiving it, Chang Hsün was so angry that he immediately sent a circular telegram to rebuke all the representatives. Worse yet, he preferred the resumption of warfare.

Yüan Shih-k'ai noticed that the Nanking conference was unfavorable to him and that he could no longer rely on Feng Kuo-chang. He therefore tried to entice Feng by offering him the premiership, while his position as tutu of Nanking would be filled by Chang Hsün. If Feng rejected this arrangement, Chang Hsün and Ni Ssu-ch'ung would jointly attack Kiangsu. Chang Hsün's sudden support of Yüan was intended to enable him to secure the position of tutu of Kiangsu, and Yüan's plan was therefore heartily welcomed by him. Liu Kuan-hsiung and Tuan Chih-kuei were also strongly in favor of war, and Yüan therefore made up his mind to fight. On May 29, a proclamation was issued revealing the entire history of the monarchical movement, attempting to remove from Yüan the blame of being a traitor to the nation, and providing a prelude to the use of arms.

Before long, the independent provinces telegraphed their refusal to participate in the Nanking conference, which was then dissolved by Feng. He sent a telegram to Peking,

> At present, the conference is suspended, since the independent provinces refuse to send representatives unless the president resigns. It is thus very difficult for the conference to achieve the expected result. There are only three possibilities: first, the president must announce his resignation, whereupon the conference may be reopened; secondly, some other method might be found to break the deadlock; thirdly, lacking another method, I am able only to maintain the order of Kiangsu and cannot take on any other posts.[14]

While Yüan was resolving to resume warfare, the Military Council of South China stated its minimum requirement for peace—the immediate resignation of Yüan. The southern independent provinces pressed strongly for Yüan's retirement.

As to the possibility of resuming warfare, government banks in North China had already announced on May 12 that they would not honor banknotes—an obvious indication of the government's financial predicament.

In South China, even though the Military Council had been established at Chao-ch'ing, the Kwangtung problem had not yet been solved. Though the Kwangsi army was on its way to Hunan, the Kwangtung soldiers under Lung still concentrated their energies on guarding Kwangtung, and Lung's promise to send soldiers to join the northern expedition was not kept. Although Li Lieh-chün commanded a regiment of the Yunnan army which was on its way from Yunnan to Chao-ch'ing, and thence planned to go to Kiangsi, this regiment, suspected of trying to seize the territory guarded by Lung, had conflicts with Lung's troops. T'ang Chi-yao promised to reinforce the Yunnan troops, but he did not do so, because he was jealous of Ts'ai's success in the Szechwan-Hunan border campaign.

Other circumstances were favorable to the Southerners, however. Szechwan on May 22 unexpectedly declared its independence. Hunan also declared its independence on May 25, just as Yüan was revealing the whole history of the monarchical movement; Shensi had made a similar declaration on May 9. The tutu of Szechwan, Ch'eh Huan, and the tutu of Hunan, T'ang Hsiang-ming, had both once been faithful supporters of Yüan; they now went over to the side of the National Protection Army. The tutu of Shensi, Ch'en Shu-fan, was compelled to declare independence by his subordinates, who had long had secret communications with General Ts'ai Ao. One of these subordinates was Feng Yü-hsiang, a brigadier general, who tried to overthrow Yüan in order to support Feng Kuo-chang. Feng Yü-hsiang had once started an uprising at Luanchow, Chihli, but had been dismissed by Yüan, whom he hated for that reason. In 1916 Feng and his subordinates in Szechwan had long been inclined to favor the anti-Yüan campaign. In addition Hunan also declared independence.

THE DEATH OF YÜAN SHIH-K'AI

Ever since the inception of the National Protection Army, Yüan's constant worry and his disgrace had made him ill. He could no longer control his temper and anxiety when he heard of the successive declarations of independence by Hunan and Szechwan. His death on June 6, 1916, brought on by his disappointment and excitement, provided an automatic solution to the problem of his retirement.

The agony Yüan suffered just before his death was commensurate with what he had himself inflicted on the Manchu imperial family. Even the method he used to deal with the Southern rebels were somewhat similar to those which had been used by Tsai-feng against the revolutionists in 1911. Tsai-feng had promised the people constitutional government in order to protect the throne; Yüan tried to abandon the monarchical system in order to protect his presidency. Tsai-feng had surrendered to Yüan by abolishing the cabinet dominated by members of the royal family and by reappointing Yüan to organize a responsible cabinet; Yüan likewise yielded to Tuan by abolishing the council of state [*cheng-shih-t'ang*] and recalling him to organize a responsible cabinet. Just as Yüan repeatedly demanded from Tsai-feng great authority and would not take up his duties until he had secured all he demanded, Tuan also made similar demands and his resumption of the premiership was contingent upon their fulfillment. Just as Yüan had had secret communications in 1911 with the revolutionary army, Feng Kuo-chang and Tuan Ch'i-jui also had confidential contact with the National Protection Army. In 1911 public opinion among the foreigners had been unanimously critical of the Manchus; now public opinion was also opposed to Yüan.

Nevertheless, Yüan Shih-k'ai was much more capable than Tsai-feng. All the demands he had made of the Manchu royal family had been complied with, but he himself did not give Tuan all that the latter requested. In 1911 Liang-pi and others of the Imperial Clan Party delayed the abdication of the Manchu emperor; now the faction of Tuan Chih-kuei and Ni Ssu-ch'ung also protected Yüan and delayed his retirement. Moreover, Yüan was not only more determined and strong-willed than Tsai-feng had been, but the problem of his retirement posed much greater difficulty than that of the abdication of the Ch'ing emperor. Finally, the implement which evoked the abdication of the Manchu emperor was a telegram signed by Tuan Ch'i-jui and more than forty other generals; although such a joint telegram was now lacking, the declaration of independence by Szechwan and Hunan achieved the same result.

After Yüan's death, Vice-President Li Yüan-hung succeeded him as president, as provided by the constitution. When Tuan reorganized his cabinet, the new president announced the restoration of the old constitution of 1912, and the Military Council in South China was dissolved. The war against monarchism had ended.

Yüan Shih-k'ai had been in power for four and a half years. With regard to his political maneuvers and his pernicious influence, Liang Ch'i-ch'ao's criticism is apposite:

> Yüan thought that it was human nature to tremble before a flash- ing knife and to go wild for yellow gold, both of which weapons he used to rule the empire, and by means of which he thought everything could be done. For over four years there was nothing that might be called administration in the Peking government, save the activities of these two elements … Yüan occupied the highest position of the nation, and yet he daily placed yellow gold before people to entice them, while the knife flashed behind them. He hoped to enslave all the people, either by soft bribery or by hard military pressure. Few who lacked strong determination could escape these two weapons … The morale of our scholar-official class has dropped ten thousand feet in the last few years, and the consciences of a majority of people have been numbed. Yüan perceived a common weakness of human beings, and he devoted himself to using this weakness for his own personal benefit. Those who could overcome this common weakness and refuse to be utilized by Yüan were murdered, driven away, or pressed so hard that they could no longer survive … The corrupt and filthy atmosphere of Chinese political circles was created by Yüan's administration. [15]

BY-PRODUCTS OF THE MONARCHICAL WAR

The purpose of the monarchical war was to overthrow Yüan Shih-k'ai, and Yüan's death may be considered a direct result of this war. But his death deprived the Peiyang military clique of a leader and caused internal dissension. Furthermore, the practice of the occupation of provinces by generals, set up during the war, resulted in the building of many military bases for smaller warlords.

Chang Tso-lin's Occupation of Fengtien

Near the end of the Manchu dynasty, Chang Tso-lin was merely a minor officer of the old garrison battalion in the Northeast. During the 1911 revolution Governor-General Chao Erh-hsün of the Three Eastern Provinces, lacking confidence in the New Army, summoned Chang and the garrison battalion to the provincial capital as a preventive measure and allowed Chang to participate in the administration of the province. In 1912 the Second Regiment of the New Army in Fengtien started a mutiny. The garrison battalion was then expanded to form the Twenty-seventh and Twenty-eighth Divisions, the first of which Chang Tso-lin commanded, while Feng Te-lin became commander of the other.

When Chang Hsi-luan was governor-general of Fengtien, the two divisional commanders showed him great respect because they were old friends, but when Yüan tried to become emperor and appointed his confidant Tuan Chihkuei to replace Chang Hsi-luan as governor-general, Chang Tso-lin began to show disobedience to his new superior. When the National Protection Army started its campaign, Chang tried to attract Yüan's favor by ostensibly issuing a telegram requesting that Yüan be enthroned at an early date, and he volunteered to lead an army on a punitive expedition to southwestern China. Tuan Chih-kuei promptly took this opportunity to get rid of Chang, and he secretly requested Yüan to order Chang to lead troops to Hunan. Chang, however, aiming to seize the position of tutu of Fengtien, requested a great quantity of arms and provisions from Tuan, upon receipt of which he secretly hinted to the Merchants' Association of Fengtien that they should send a telegram to the central government requesting that Chang be kept in that province and that other troops be ordered to Hunan instead. Tuan Chih-kuei's plot thus foiled, Chang became even haughtier than ever, spreading word that his Fengtien troops would declare their independence if Yüan did not resign.

Tuan Chih-kuei had a bodyguard of about 1000 men, but there were nearly 20,000 troops under Chang's command. Tuan's power was no match for Chang's, and the Peking government could send no reinforcements to Fengtien. There were also rumors that numerous members of the Revolutionary Party had come from Dairen to Fengtien. Yüan could do nothing except to grant the position of tutu to Chang, in the hope that this title would placate him and keep him in a friendly camp. Chang was therefore made tutu of Fengtien and, concurrently, acting governor.

Feng Te-lin had heretofore enjoyed a position equal to Chang's. Afraid that Feng would be jealous of his sudden promotion, Chang therefore re- quested Yüan to appoint Feng associate chief of military affairs.

At the same time, Hsü Lan-chou, who wielded the military power in the province of Heilungkiang, also took the declaration of independence as a pretext to drive away the provincial tutu, Chu Ch'ing-lan. Superficially, this action was taken to insure the continued dependence of the province; in actuality it was a private war for the position of tutu. The Peking government quickly appointed Pi Kuei-fang tutu and, concurrently, governor of Heilungkiang. In order to appease Hsü, they appointed him associate di- rector of military affairs. Since Hsü was not satisfied, Chang Tso-lin, wish- ing to bring Hsü over to his camp, sent a telegram to Peking opposing Pi Kuei-fang's new appointment and requesting that Hsü be appointed tutu. Yüan Shih-k'ai's government had no other choice. The northeastern military clique thus acquired a firm foundation.

Ch'en Shu-fan's Occupation of Shensi

The tutu of Shensi, Lu Chien-chang, was Yüan's confidant. The com- mander of the garrison of southern Shensi, Ch'en Shu-fan, was, however, not a member of the Peiyang military machine. After the beginning of the monarchical war Lu, afraid that he could not control Ch'en, ordered him to take command of the garrison of northern Shensi. Unknown to Lu, that area harbored a number of members of the Chinese Revolutionary Party, with whom Ch'en made connections, and he was made commander in chief of the National Protection Army in Shensi. Independence was declared on May 9. The subsequent war between Lu and Ch'en led to the defeat and arrest of Lu's son. Lu was forced to plead for peace on condition that he leave the province and surrender his position as tutu to Ch'en.

At first Yüan Shih-k'ai, considering Shensi an isolated area, gave only the title of associate director of military affairs to Ch'en, who declined it. When Yüan died, Ch'en, planning to show allegiance to the central govern-ment as a means of seizing the territory of Shensi, conceded his declaration of independence. Premier Tuan actually let Ch'en have what he wanted.

The Beginning of T'ang Chi-yao's "Greater Yunnan" Plan

T'ang Chi-yao had no great desire to fight Yüan Shih-k'ai, but his inability to resist the influence of Ts'ai Ao secured for him an unexpected reputation as a leader of the anti-Yüan movement. From the beginning he intended to preserve Yunnan as his headquarters. At the outset of the National Protection Army's campaign, Ts'ai Ao gave T'ang the choice of staying in Yunnan or leading an expeditionary army. T'ang elected to stay. His only donation to Ts'ai was 3000 soldiers, provided with rations for only two months. Later T'ang evaded Ts'ai's repeated requests from the front for reinforcements, refusing to give him additional money, soldiers, or weapons. T'ang not only envied Ts'ai's career but was also afraid to weaken the defenses of his own headquarters. After Yüan's death and the conclusion of the war, Yunnan reinforcements were pulled into the province of Szechwan. Since there was not at that time any difficulty in protecting Yunnan, T'ang attempted to expand his territories into Szechwan by sending a large number of Yunnan troops there. But the Szechwan troops were also anxious to protect their own territory, and a great conflict arose between the two provinces.

Ts'ai Ao did not aim at governing Szechwan; his intention, instead, was to put himself within the Peiyang military clique in order to reform it. In a telegram to Liu Hsien-shih, Ts'ai Ao said:

> I intend to decline the appointment as tutu of Szechwan, partly to fulfill my avowed purpose of not becoming a high official and partly because my poor health does not permit me to shoulder the heavy re- sponsibilities of that position. My serious throat condition could easily be aggravated and I might entirely lose the use of my voice. Besides I would have to rule Szechwan for more than ten years before any achievement could be expected … That is why I am indifferent to that appointment. The army in North China is the best in the country so far as prowess and endurance are concerned; however, it lacks a nationalist orientation and has few able officers. If there were a good commander to lead and reform this army, it might prove to be the foundation of a truly national army. I would like very much to lay the foundation for a national army and prepare its future effectiveness, but I am so ill at present that this is impossible. [16]

This telegram reveals Ts'ai's farsightedness and affirms his lack of territorial ambitions.

The impoverished province of Kweichow was occupied by Yunnan troops under the command of Tsai K'an. Tsai did not wish to return to Yunnan to be fed by the provincial government. The province of Kweichow was not happy with the continued presence of Yunnan troops, but Tsai, having made important contributions during the anti-Yüan campaign, could not be left without an important position. So Kweichow too became involved in the struggle between the troops of Szechwan and Yunnan.

The Contest for Kwangtung

When the campaign of the National Protection Army began, Lu Jung-t'ing had wanted to keep his territory exclusively in Kwangsi. He adopted a conciliatory and peaceful attitude in his alliance with Lung Chi-kuang. Lu did dispatch some of his troops to Hunan, but because he had no intention of seizing any territory, he ordered them to withdraw after Yüan's death. Nevertheless, Lung's stubborn hold on Kwangtung gave Lu a chance to expand. When the Military Council was established at Chao-ch'ing, and a northern expeditionary force was organized from the troops of Yunnan, Kwangtung, and Kwangsi, Li Lieh-chün, the commander of the Second Division of the Yunnan army, was ordered to lead his soldiers from Kwangtung to Kiangsi. Suspecting Li of planning to occupy Kwangtung, Lung objected to the passage of the Yunnan army. After long negotiations, Lung allowed the Yunnan army to march along the border of Kwangtung to Shaochow, but its advance was impeded by Lung's troops along the entire way. When the Yunnan troops reached Shaochow, not a single soldier was permitted to enter the city. Lung's garrison opened fire from the city wall. This, of course, led to a battle. When Yüan died, Lung immediately, without consulting the Military Council, announced the cancellation of the independence of Kwangtung.

Tuan Ch'i-jui tried to use Lung to fight against the Kuomintang by immediately appointing him tutu and governor of Kwangtung. Lung was well satisfied, but the people of Kwangtung were angry. Sun Yat-sen, T'ang Shao-i, Wang Ch'ung-hui, and others, as well as many organizations of the people, sent circular telegrams expressing their objections. Even Liang Ch'i-ch'ao, the most moderate leader, voiced his objection to Lung's prolonged stay in that province.

The old Kuomintang members, Li Ken-yüan and his faction, wished to keep Ch'en Ch'un-hsüan as tutu of Kwangtung, but Tuan strongly disapproved of such a move. Liang Ch'i-ch'ao wished to make use of Lu, but he did not want to see the territory of Kwangtung fall into the hands of the Kuomintang. He therefore worked for the appointment of Lu. On July 6 Lu was named tutu of Kwangtung, but Lung was ordered to act in Lu's behalf until the latter could assume his new office. At this time Lung himself was appointed director of mineral affairs of Kwangtung and Kwangsi.

The people of Kwangtung criticized Tuan for showing special consideration to Lung, particularly since Lung still had not called a halt to the fighting. Lu's return to Kwangsi, to take command of a large number of troops to support his inauguration to his new office, finally compelled Lung to go to Hainan. At first Lu planned to yield the position of tutu to Ch'en Ch'un-hsüan, but Ch'en declined. The province of Kwangtung remained under Lu's jurisdiction, becoming the base of the old military clique of Kwangsi.

Effects of Shifting Power on Cliques and Parties

Though these were the outstanding events in the struggle of the small warlords, the dissensions among the great warlords of the Peiyang military clique were not immediately evident. All these warlords, however, either fought against the Southern army or communicated with it in order to insure the safety of their own holdings. By the defection of the tutu of Shensi, Lu Chien-chang, the tutu of Szechwan, Ch'en Huan, and the tutu of Hunan, T'ang Hsiang-ming, the Peiyang warlords appeared to have lost three provinces. Since Ch'en Huan soon turned to the Peiyang military clique, only Szechwan and Hunan were actually lost. But the Peiyang clique, once a unified group, was now unified in form only.

As to the shifts of power between the Progressive Party and the Kuomintang, after the outbreak of the war the four provinces of Yunnan, Kweichow, Kwangtung, and Kwangsi became the sphere of joint activity of the two parties. The Progressive Party had more influence in Yunnan and Kweichow; the Kuomintang had more power in Kwangtung and Kwangsi. After Lu Jung-t'ing invited Liang Ch'i-ch'ao to Kwangsi, the power of the Progressive Party was also extended to the other two provinces.

Because of the positive activity of Li Ken-yüan and others, the potential power of the Kuomintang in Yunnan, Kwangtung, and Kwangsi seemed to be greater than that of the Progressive Party. When Ts'ai Ao left Kweichow because of mortal illness, the Progressive Party was left without its protector.

Before Yüan's death, Liang Ch'i-ch'ao tried his best to consolidate the influence of the Progressive Party in South China and to build his head- quarters in Szechwan, Yunnan, and Kweichow. He wished to use Ts'ai Ao's power to occupy these provinces as a field of experimentation for his political reforms as well as to establish a balance of power with Northern China. When Yüan died, however, Liang tried his best to establish close relations with Tuan Ch'i-jui to abolish the Military Council. At the same time, he tried to support Tsai K'an to go to Szechwan to continue Ts'ai Ao's influence.

The radical wing of the old Kuomintang (the Chinese Revolutionary Party) had meanwhile failed in all its revolutionary plans in Shantung, Kwangtung, and other areas along the Yangtze Valley. Furthermore, the assassination of Ch'en Ch'i-mei in Yunnan deprived the Chinese Revolutionary Party of one of its strong members.

The upshot of the monarchical war amounted to political maneuvers through which both the Progressive Party and the moderate wing of the old Kuomintang tried to secure support from various warlords both in the South and in the North. In order to dominate the political situation, both these parties appeased the warlords and in so doing helped to extend the power of the warlords.

CHAPTER TWELVE INTERNAL DISSENSION OF THE PEIYANG MILITARY CLIQUE, AND THE WARLORDS IN SOUTH CHINA

After the dissolution of the parliament for the second time (1917) and the brief restoration of a Manchu emperor (1917) the Constitution Protection Army emerged. The Constitution Protection Movement had started when disputes over the parliament and the restoration of the old constitution arose. These constitutional disputes brought no result other than the splitting of the Peiyang military clique into two factions—the Chihli faction and the Anhwei faction. By the summer and early autumn of 1920, the two factions were at war with each other.

During these convulsive years there was at first a stubborn war between the radical wing of the old Kuomintang and the Peiyang military clique, while the old Progressive Party tried its best to establish close relations with the Peiyang group. The moderate wing of the old Kuomintang stood irresolutely between the two factions. During the Manchu restoration incident, the Progressive Party was united with the Peiyang military clique, and both wings of the old Kuomintang were also ostensibly united in the Military Government at Kwangtung, so that the governments of North and of South China were at loggerheads.

During the strife between the Southern and Northern governments, there was also constant division within the Peiyang military clique, which soon dropped the Progressive Party. The old Kuomintang in South China preserved a semblance of unity for some time; but when the members of the moderate wing allied themselves with the warlords of Kwangsi to suppress the radical wing, and when the Chihli and Anhwei troops fought against each other in North China, the two wings of the old Kuomintang irrevocably split apart.

THE STRIFE OVER THE OLD AND NEW CONSTITUTIONS

After Yüan Shih-k'ai's demise, Vice-President Li Yüan-hung became president, as had been suggested long before by the Military Council of South China. Li's qualification to become president was based on the presidential election laws set forth in the old constitution and proclaimed in October 1913. But the North China government recognized Li's qualification for the presidency on the basis of the revised presidential election laws of 1914, based on the new constitution prepared under Yüan Shih-k'ai's direction.

The Succession to Yüan Shih-k'ai

According to *An Account of the National Protection Army* [*Hu-kuo-chün chi-shih*], Yüan had entrusted Hsü Shih-ch'ang with his family affairs just before his death, without mentioning his successor as president. His death actually occurred on June 5; it was not announced until the following day because the government leaders of North China had not made the necessary arrangements. Immediately some people began to advocate the restoration of the Manchu emperor; some, the succession of Yüan's son, Yüan K'o-ting; and still others, that of Tuan Ch'i-jui. Hsü Shih-ch'ang believed that only Tuan was capable of maintaining peace in Peking and was willing to cooperate with him. Tuan decided that the new constitution should be observed, and that Li should be the nominal president while he himself would take over all political responsibility.

Tuan accordingly tried to persuade Li to accept the presidency. At first Li declined because he lacked the power to maintain order, but when Tuan said: "If you take up the office, I alone will be responsible for order in Peking," Li accepted the presidency.

The death of Yüan Shih-k'ai was then announced, and a last will and testament was composed for him. It contained such sentences as: "According to Article 29 of the constitution, when the president must, for some reason, vacate his position or cannot look after his duties, the vice-president must take over his functions. On the basis of this article, I announce that Vice-President Li Yüan-hung shall act as the president of the Republic of China." The subsequent dispute over the old and new constitution arose from debate over the presidential qualifications of Li, and this debate raised the curtain also on the Constitution Protection Movement.

The Northern government faced difficulties with regard to accepting the vice-president as the acting president. According to Yüan's new constitution and the revised presidential election laws, the period of Li's acting presidency was limited to three days. Within that time a committee for presidential elections was to be organized and a new president was to be selected by the committee from a list of names recommended by the former president. Actually this committee could not be organized within three days, and the term of the acting president therefore had to exceed the limit set by law. As a matter of convenience, the Northern government tried to avoid all mention of the time limit.

On June 6 when Yüan's death was announced, Tuan Ch'i-jui preempted use of the name of the cabinet in issuing a circular telegram to the whole nation, saying: "President Yüan died of illness on the morning of the sixth and has left orders to follow Article 29 of the new constitution in announcing the appointment of Vice-President Li Yüan-hung to be acting president of the Republic of China. ..." On the seventh, Tuan dispatched another circular telegram: "At 7 A. M. of the seventh, Vice-President Li, in accordance with the constitution, has taken over the presidency of the Chinese Republic." "To take over an office" may be interpreted to mean either "to act in" or "to succeed to." [1] Playing with such ambiguities in their documents appears to be a traditional amusement of Chinese secretaries.

Li Yüan-hung's oath of inauguration was even more confusing and vague, saying in the first part: "I will follow the provisional constitution proclaimed in 1912 and continue the function of the president. ... "In the latter part he stated: "I swear that during the time when I am acting president, I shall firmly observe the constitution of the nation." Li actually did not know what position he was taking. Li intended to use the 1912 constitution, but his secretary failed to distinguish clearly the presidential election laws of the two constitutions, a misunderstanding which fitted Tuan Ch'i-jui's plan perfectly.

The leaders of South China and its members in the parliament could not tolerate such confusion. After receiving the telegram from the cabinet on the sixth, the parliament members first declared:

> The so-called constitution of the Republic of China, proclaimed by Yüan Shih-k'ai in 1914, was drawn up by Yüan and carries the impress of his personal ideas. All the procedures of the revision were contrary to the laws provided in the provisional constitution of 1912 and it therefore is not valid as a state document. The provisional constitution made at the beginning of the Republic should continue in effect. Li's continuation in office as president is actually based on Article 5 of the presidential election laws passed by the parliament in October 1913, which provide that President Li shall remain in office until October 1918 to complete President Yüan's seven-year term. Yüan's last will and testament was based on Article 29 of the new constitution, by which the vice-president becomes acting president. But we do not accept that constitution. [2]

Tuan Ch'i-jui's plan to use Li as his puppet and eventually to grasp all the power of the president in his own hands would be endangered if the provisional constitution of 1912 were to be revived, giving complete control to the parliament. Though Tuan had no objection to Li Yüan-hung's becoming Yüan Shih-k'ai's successor, he objected very strongly to reinstatement of the provisional constitution.

Southern Efforts to Restore the Parliament

The leaders of South China in their anti-Yüan movement recognized the importance of the restoration of the parliament and the protection of the provisional constitution. A communiqué issued by the Military Council asserted:

> A nation relies upon a constitution to maintain its life. For the protection of the provisional constitution, which provides for a parliament as the highest legislative office to enact all laws, the parliament must be promptly restored; otherwise administrative affairs cannot be properly handled. All the provincial members of the dissolved parliament are asked to reconvene in order to solve all the many threatening problems. [3]

Advocating the restoration of the parliament was for the Southern leaders no more than a political scheme dictated by their own exigencies at that moment. They faced many legal difficulties because the parliament, which had been dissolved by Yüan Shih-k'ai, had passed the end of its legal three-year term, having begun on April 8, 1913. By this time all the members of the house of representatives should have relinquished their duties. Even if the old constitution were restored, new members would have to be elected according to its provisions. A new election, however, would take a long time, and since the power of the Kuomintang extended only to a few provinces in southwestern China, such an election could very easily be controlled by the Peiyang clique. For this reason, the Southern leaders insisted that the representatives to the last parliament should continue in their positions. This dispute was a matter of political expediency between the Kuomintang and the Peiyang militarists.

Between June 7 and 25 the two parties argued without reaching any agreement. Among the leaders of the independent provinces there was no consensus. Ts'ai Ao, always a prominent figure, declared that the problem of the parliament should be settled according to the precedent set by the provisional senate [*lin-shih ts'an-i-yüan*] in 1913, which was to elect between five and ten persons from among the former parliamentary members of each province to act temporarily. He did not insist on restoring the old parliament entirely.

Finally, Ch'en Ch'un-hsüan, the vice-president of the Military Council, declared his acceptance of four proposals made by T'ang Chi-yao as representing the consensus of the Southern military leaders, as well as the final stand of all the independent provinces. The proposals were:

1. President Li was to be requested to announce that the fundamental laws for the nation would be the ones which had been proclaimed before the dissolution of the parliament.
2. The president was to be requested to recall the former members of the two houses of parliament to convene immediately at Tientsin so as to elect a vice-president according to law and to approve members for a formal cabinet.
3. The president was to be requested to recall the Northern army which had been sent to check the advance of the National Protection Army.
4. An order was to be issued immediately for a special military conference at Shanghai, consisting of representatives of all the provincial tutus, to decide on all military problems.

A postscript read: "The Military Council is to be dissolved after the formation of the cabinet, which must be approved by the parliament." President Li completely agreed with these proposals.

Tuan's followers at once insisted that laws should not be abolished or amended simply by order of the president. Tuan dispatched on June 22 a circular telegram which protested the dangerous precedent which had just been established by the president, who had presumed to issue an order to abandon the revised constitution of 1914, which had been so long in use, and to restore the constitution of 1912. A joint telegram from T'ang Shao-i, Liang Ch'i-ch'ao, Wu T'ing-fang, and others challenged Tuan's argument and explained the presidential alteration of the law by the fact that the 1914 constitution was basically illegal. Tuan's followers of course still continued to hold their own views.

The Navy Supports the South

On June 25, Li Ting-hsin declared the independence of the navy. A move in this direction had started before the anti-Yüan campaign from Yunnan. After the failure of the riot on the warship *Chao-ho*, the Chinese Revolutionary Party continued to work on the navy, but could achieve little, owing to the vigilance of Admiral Liu Kuan-hsiung. With the death of Yüan Shih-k'ai, the efforts of Revolutionary Party members began to show results. Li Ting-hsin, who had been secretly elected leader of the movement, had been in close touch with the Shanghai representative of the Military Council, T'ang Shao-i, and others. When no decision was reached in the dispute over the constitution, Li Ting-hsin, commander in chief of the navy, Commander Lin Pao-i of the first fleet, and Tseng Ch'ao-lin, commander of the training fleet, concentrated all the large warships off the mouth of the Woosung River, and issued this declaration:

> Although President Li has taken up his duties, the Peking government is still using the constitution which was illegally devised by Yüan… How can such a document win the hearts of the nation? We are leading the officers of the navy to join the National Protection

Army on June 25, in order to support the president. Our purpose is to protect the Republic, and unless the 1912 constitution is recognized, the parliament reopened, and a cabinet formed, the orders from the ministry for the navy in Peking will not be obeyed.[4]

Feng Kuo-chang, fearing that the navy might take action against him because Sungkiang and Shanghai were under his jurisdiction, urged Tuan, by telegram, to seek a quick solution. Tuan realized that he had to yield to the demands of the Southerners. Thereupon the president issued an edict on June 29:

In a republic, the will of the people should be respected first, and the will of the people is summarized in the constitution as drawn up by the parliament. The parliament of our Republic, since its suspension of January 10, 1914, has not been reconvened for more than two years. The constitution of 1916 has not yet been decided upon, and the great foundation of the nation has not yet been established. There is no way to carry on a civil administration. The parliament must be summoned quickly to decide on the constitution, in order that the will of the people may be followed and the foundations of the nation consolidated. Until a decision is reached about the constitution, the provisional constitution proclaimed on March 11, 1912, is to be observed. The presidential election laws announced on October 5, 1913, which are a part of the provisional constitution, will continue in force.[4]

Troubles in Organizing the Cabinet

Thus the position of President Li as successor to Yüan was finally affirmed. The remaining problem was that of the organization of a cabinet. On August 1, the day the parliament reconvened, the president issued another decree reappointing Tuan Ch'i-jui as premier, and on the thirtieth the names of the members of the cabinet were announced:

Minister of foreign affairs—T'ang Shao-i
Minister of domestic affairs—Hsü Shih-ying
Minister of finance—Ch'en Chin-t'ao
Minister of judicial affairs—Chang Yao-tseng
Minister of education—Sun Hung-i
Minister of agriculture and commerce—Chang Kuo-kan
Minister of communications—Wang Ta-hsi
Minister of the navy—Ch'eng Pi-kuang
Minister of war—Tuan Ch'i-jui

From Tuan's point of view, this organization indicated the president's acceptance of the men of ability in the Kuomintang, but the leaders of Southern China were not satisfied. T'ang Shao-i, Sun Hung-i, and Chang Yao-tseng firmly declined appointment. Wang Ta-hsi and Chang Kuo-kan also declined, observing they were not welcomed by public opinion. Hsü Shih-ying was later given the ministry of communications, while Sun Hung-i was made minister of domestic affairs, Fan Yüan-lien minister of education, and Ku Chung-hsiu minister of agriculture and commerce. Because he was secretly opposed by the Peiyang military clique, T'ang Shao-i never took up his duties as minister of foreign affairs, which were performed first by Ch'en Chin-t'ao and later by Wu T'ing-fang.

The abolition of the Military Council was announced on July 14. The leaders of South China had originally intended to dissolve it after the parliament had formally convened on August 1; but Liang Ch'i-ch'ao, anxious to establish close relations with Tuan Ch'i-jui, sent telegrams from Shanghai asking the councilors in Kwangtung to advance the date originally scheduled. Although the telegram was said to have been signed by all the councilors, many of them were not consulted. Realizing there was no longer any reason for the continued existence of the Military Council, they did not try to repudiate the telegram, but many of them were now annoyed with Liang. Later the members of the Progressive Party under Liang Ch'i-ch'ao allied themselves with the faction of the Peiyang military group which was led by Tuan Ch'i-jui, thus causing a major split with the old Kuomintang.

THE CONFUSION OF THE POLITICAL PARTIES AFTER THE RESTORATION OF THE PARLIAMENT

The second unification of North and South China was marked by the abolition of the Military Council, the convening of the parliament on August 1, 1916, and its approval of the cabinet appointments. During this short period of unification, however, the tide of political affairs ran even more violently than before.

During the anti-Yüan campaign, the old Kuomintang and the Progressive Party had presented a united front. After Yüan's death some leaders of the Progressive Party, such as Liang Ch'i-ch'ao and T'ang Hua-lung, tried vigorously to cooperate with Tuan Ch'i-jui. In this effort they maintained that there should no longer be political parties and that they wanted no cabinet positions for themselves or their party; and as a result, only one member of their party, Fan Yüan-lien, was included in the newly organized cabinet. Sun Hung-i, who had once been a member of the Progressive Party, had more recently joined another group.

The Research Clique

When the parliament convened, those members of the Progressive Party who maintained that there should be no political parties split into two factions: the Constitution Discussion Society [*Hsien-fa t'ao-lun Hui*] headed by T'ang Hua-lung, and the Constitution Research

Association [*Hsien-fa yen-chiu Hui*] led by Liang Ch'i-ch'ao and Lin Ch'ang-min. What the difference was between "discussion" and "research" and why the two factions were organized are unanswerable questions. Later, when the old Kuomintang was reunified and became the dominant power, T'ang and Liang reunited as a "research" group and the former Progressive Party became the later famous Research Clique [*Yen-chiu Hsi*].

On the Kuomintang side, the Chinese Revolutionary Party, as a secret revolutionary organization, could not openly enter the political arena. The moderate wing of the Kuomintang planned to organize a "Research Society for European Affairs," with Ch'en Ch'un-hsüan as its leader, but this name was soon discarded since it did not attract many supporters. Nevertheless, the party had to develop some method of participating in the parliament. Therefore Chang Chi, the leader of the old Kuomintang, gathered a group of his old comrades from Japan to form a Society for the Discussion of Constitutional Government [*Hsien-cheng shang-chüeh Hui*]. The moderate and the radical wings of the Kuomintang now appeared to be united, but there were actually four groups within the Kuomintang.[5] Though in parliament the Kuomintang occupied a majority of the seats, internal dissension made the party even less effectual than the opposing Research Clique.

Within the parliament there were also many minor political organizations. Some attached themselves either to the Kuomintang or to the Research Clique. Others existed merely for Tuan Ch'i-jui's personal use.

The Provinces: Reorganization and Intrigue

The major parties listed were all active in the parliament, but although the important political parties in 1912-1913 had branches in all the provinces, this was not now the case. They had not abandoned their earlier spheres of influence in the provinces; however, they now concentrated their attention on influencing the provincial governors. The central government ordered, on July 6, that all the provincial military governors be given the title of *tuchun* [military governor, directing military affairs] and each chief civil officer of a province be called *shêng-chang* ["governor," senior administrator for the province]. [6] Officials for these posts were all to be newly appointed. These reappointments became an important problem.

Except for the four provinces of Yunnan, Kweichow, Kwangtung, and Kwangsi, only the provinces of Szechwan and Hunan were freed from the domination of the Peiyang military clique as a result of the monarchical war. When he appointed the provincial tutus and governors in July, Tuan Ch'i-jui adopted a policy of fomenting jealousy between the provincial authorities of Szechwan, Hunan, Kwangtung and Kwangsi. To add further fuel to the fires of jealousy and distrust, he appointed Ch'en Huan governor of Hunan; the acting governor of Hunan, Lu Jung-t'ing refused to leave his post until Ch'en's arrival. Lu Jung-t'ing was, at the same time, appointed governor of Kwangtung, where Lung Chi-kuang was to act as chief administrator until he arrived. Tuan first appointed Ts'ai Ao both tuchun and governor of Szechwan, but Ts'ai declined on account of illness. Lo P'ei-chin, who had been appointed governor of Kwangsi, was then made acting tuchun of Szechwan, where Liu Ts'un-hou was opposing troops from other provinces. Tuan ordered Lo to curb the antagonism of the Szechwan troops; at the same time he incited Liu Ts'un-hou to fight against Lo. This led to a civil war in Szechwan.

When Ch'en Huan was unable to take up his post as tutu of Hunan, Tuan ordered Wu Kuang-hsin to keep troops at Yochow as a threat to the provincial capital. Later, taking the opportunity afforded by the civil war in Szechwan, he ordered Wu Kuang-hsin to march into Hunan. In short, Tuan's policy toward Southwest China was to divide and rule.

This policy was successful only in Szechwan, but even that province did not fall into the hands of the Peiyang clique. In general, the highest authorities of the Southwest worked only to achieve their selfish purposes. Their attitude toward the provincial representatives in the parliament was decided by their personal interests rather than by their political affiliations.

The Hsuchow Conferences

The provinces within the influence of the Peiyang clique had, however, an organization which had been promoted by Chang Hsün, with the assistance of Ni Ssu-ch'ung, but had been utilized by Tuan Ch'i-jui's confidant, Hsü Shu-cheng. After the dissolution of the Nanking conference, Chang Hsün dispatched the delegates to invite the representatives of all the provinces in that conference to another meeting at Hsuchow, where he had his headquarters. The Hsuchow meeting began on June 9. Chang Hsün proposed a ten-item agenda, the most attractive items of which were: absolute exclusion of all rebellious and radical members from political affairs; concerted action on the part of the provinces to advise the central government against steps which might harm the people; and formation of a solid organization to take united action with regard to state matters. The participants suggested in addition that an executive office be established with a prominent person as its leader.

Hsü Shu-cheng and others secretly agreed with Ni Ssu-ch'ung to support Chang Hsün as executive director. Chang Hsün then ordered all the provinces to send representatives to a subsequent meeting in Hsuchow and this joint meeting was opened on September 21. Nine provinces were originally represented, but the number later increased to thirteen, including even Kwangtung, which was represented by Lung Chi-kuang. At this conference, twelve major regulations were established for the Interprovincial Association, including: (1) Support of national defense, consolidation of military power, and support of the central government. (2) Control of insurgent members who were trying to seize political power, the union having the power to call a meeting to take united action against any members who caused trouble. (3) Election by the association of a leader to conduct warfare within the areas of the member provinces if it proved necessary to resort to arms to protect the safety of the nation. (4) The leader thus elected to be regarded as the head of hegemony with executive power to enforce all the decisions of the association. (5) Election by the association of Generalissimo Chang Hsün to represent the views of the group on important matters when there was insufficient time to consult the members; it was to be his duty, however, to inform the members afterwards of his actions. (6) Regarding as a common enemy anyone who tried to undermine the unity of the nation, made unreasonable demands on the government, or proved intolerable to the people. (7) Aid to the central government in subduing any province which was not a member of the association if it opposed the central government and jeopardized the peace of the nation.

Such an interprovincial alliance may be considered a conscious attempt at self-preservation on the part of the Peiyang military clique. But even this new organization was no more than a formal gesture, lacking any real *esprit de corps*. Among its members, Ni Ssu-ch'ung and his following planned to use the organization to support Tuan Ch'i-jui; Chang Hsün tried to use it to restore the Manchu emperor to power; Feng Kuo-chang, who had a representative in the organization, intended to use it to further his ambition for the presidency. In spite of these divergent elements, however, the organization proved to be a serious menace to the parliament.

The Cabinet and Hsü Shu-cheng

Along with these intrigues outside the parliament, there were conflicts between the president's secretariat and the cabinet. The cabinet was a combination of elements of the Research Clique, represented by Fan Yüan-lien, and the left and right wings of the Society for the Discussion of

Constitutional Government, the former represented by Sun Hung-i and the latter by Ku Chung-hsiu and Chang Yao-tseng. Nevertheless, the cabinet was dominated by its own secretariat chief, Hsü Shu-cheng, who represented Tuan's military clique. The chief of the secretariat of the president's office, Ting Shih-i, frequently resented the haughtiness of Tuan and Hsü; the president's secretariat was inclined to favor the Research Clique.

In this political situation the dispute over the constitution, the struggle between the president's office and the cabinet, the threatening power of the tuchuns, and the controversy over China's participation in the war against Germany stirred up a strong drive within the Peiyang military clique to defeat the parliament.

In this great political storm the Kuomintang was sometimes criticized as too radical. As a matter of fact, the first challenger of the Kuomintang was the Peiyang military group. In Tuan's cabinet, for example, the appointed minister of foreign affairs was T'ang Shao-i. When T'ang started his journey from Shanghai to the north, however, the Peiyang military clique, headed by Chang Hsün, circulated a telegram objecting to him. Handbills slandering him were distributed in the names of the local gentry and people on his arrival in Tientsin. He had no choice but to resign. This surrender marked the first direct challenge to the Kuomintang by the Peiyang military clique.

After the organization of Tuan's cabinet, the minister of domestic affairs, Sun Hung-i, quarreled with the chief of the secretariat of the cabinet, Hsü Shu-cheng. Strictly speaking, the chief of the cabinet secretariat had no right to speak in a cabinet meeting. Nevertheless, during the discussion of the war between Li Lieh-chün and Lung Chi-kuang in Kwangtung, Hsü Shu-cheng suggested that the four provinces of Fukien, Kwangtung, Hunan, and Kiangsi be ordered by telegram to launch a joint expedition against Li Lieh-chün. Sun Hung-i's proposal that a reconciliation be effected was favored by a majority of the cabinet members, but no one tried to question Hsü's right to speak. After the meeting and without authorization, Hsü sent a telegram to the four provinces, advising the expedition against Li. When the replies of the four provinces reached the cabinet, Sun rebuked Hsü, who continued to insist that his action was proper. This quarrel precipitated a lasting hatred between Sun and Hsü.

Tuan's presumptuous actions and the disagreement between the office of the president and the cabinet were all directly caused by the arrogant attitude of Hsü Shu-cheng. As minister of domestic affairs, Sun certainly had control over the appointments and transfers of provincial governors. Relying on Premier Tuan's backing, Hsü Shu-cheng tried to dominate all the affairs of the cabinet, without regard to legal restrictions. Sun, who refused to yield any of his authority, was dismissed by order of the president on November 20. Thus the second attack by the Peiyang militarists against a member of the Kuomintang was successfully concluded.

Feuds in Parliament

In the parliament the Research Clique and the right wing of the Society for the Discussion of Constitutional Government supported Tuan and his cabinet; the left wing advocated the overthrow of Tuan. These two factions also disagreed on several points regarding the constitution.

The Research Clique, for example, maintained that the bicameral system of the provisional constitution should be changed into a unicameral system, and that even if it was necessary to retain the old system, the organization of the senate should be greatly altered. The majority of the Society for the Discussion of Constitutional Government insisted on the retention of the bicameral system without change. The Research Clique maintained that the provinces should be governed by common law; and they objected to the election of the governor by the people. The Society for the Discussion of Constitutional Government insisted that a general outline of provincial government should be defined in the constitution, and that the governors should be elected by the people. Lesser matters, such as the necessary procedure for the dissolution of parliament and votes of confidence in the cabinet, also gave rise to differences between the two factions.

When the parliament convened on September 15, the question whether the provincial system should be defined in the constitution brought about a fight between the two political factions. The Research Clique then sent to all the provincial tuchuns telegrams attacking the Clique's parliamentary rivals. These rivals promptly sent circular telegrams to the whole nation. This squabble marked the beginning of the interference of the provincial warlords in parliamentary affairs. On the twenty-first there appeared in Peking the so-called Society for the Promotion of the Constitution [*Hsien-fa ts'u-ch'eng Hui*], which was secretly sponsored by the Peiyang military clique as a warning to the parliament.

The president's secretariat and the cabinet also resumed their open feud which had been caused by Premier Tuan's excessive reliance on Hsü Shu-cheng. Ting Shih-i was selected chief of the secretariat of the office of the president lest President Li's simplemindedness place him under the thumb of the Peiyang military clique. Hsü Shu-cheng's haughty actions became almost intolerable to the president, and he became more and more reluctant to approve requests that came to him through Hsü. Hsü's arrogance was later detailed in the letter of resignation written by Secretary Ting Shih-i:

> Before the meeting of the cabinet there is no agenda, and after it there is no report to the president, who therefore has to sign orders without knowing their meaning and who must approve an official appointment without knowing anything about the appointee. ... The premier [Tuan] frequently does not have an interview with the

president for as long as ten days, communicating by messages carried to and fro by his chief secretary [Hsü]. If the office of the president attempts to make inquiries, the cabinet secretary says that the matter has been discussed in the parliament, to which the cabinet is responsible. The president is limited in his contacts with the people and he is not well informed, but he is seen every day in his office fulfilling his duty by placing his seal on state documents. ... For instance, when Ts'ao Ju-lin was to be appointed Chinese minister to Japan, the choice had been accepted and announced by the Japanese minister of foreign affairs one month before, but even when the appointment was made, our president knew nothing of the matter.[7]

A joint telegram of advice to the president and the parliament, signed by the civil and military authorities of twenty-two provinces (headed by Feng Kuo-chang), appeared in the last ten days of December. The gist of the telegram was that the president should have confidence in the premier, who should manage state affairs, while the parliament should decide on the constitution at an early date and should not meddle in administrative affairs. This joint telegram was a prelude to an alliance of tuchuns which was to provide a further serious threat to the president and the parliament.

In other words, the political situation rapidly deteriorated in the autumn and winter of 1916. After the dismissal of Sun Hung-i, the government first recommended as his successor Jen K'e-ch'eng and then Chang Kuo-kan, both of whom were officials close to the Progressive Party, but the parliament did not approve either of them. Finally on January 1, 1917, Fan Yüan-lien was appointed acting minister of domestic affairs, in addition to his position as minister of education. Liang Ch'i-ch'ao reached Peking from Shanghai on January 5. Rumors immediately arose that his arrival would be followed by major changes in the political situation, and that the parliament would even be dissolved. Actually, though Liang was at that time close to Tuan, he was still trying to effect a compromise between the two political factions.

Liang had definite opinions on such constitutional problems as the reorganization of the upper house and the exclusion from the constitution of any mention of the provincial system; at the same time, he was repeatedly declaring his intention not to enter politics but to work instead at educational tasks. That he still often supported Tuan and his following made him even more unpopular. The opposition had been antagonistic toward him ever since the debates over the abolition of the Military Council.

But Liang Ch'i-ch'ao could not alter the actions of Tuan's military clique. On January 9 Chang Hsün, Ni Ssu-ch'ung, Chin Yün-p'eng, Hsü Shu-cheng and others called another meeting of the Interprovincial Association at Hsuchow to discuss the methods of coping with the president and the parliament. At Feng Kuo-chang's birthday party at Nanking, to which many provincial authorities dispatched representatives, Chang Hsün took the opportunity to invite the representatives to Hsuchow for a further meeting of the Interprovincial Association.

Breaking Relations with Germany

At this moment occurred the problem of war against Germany. When that country announced that beginning on February 1, 1917, she would use her submarines to blockade the Allies, the United States severed diplomatic relations with her. Invited by the United States to do the same, China issued her protest on February 9. The formal severing of relations between China and Germany was announced on March 14, but the problem of the declaration of war on Germany was not presented to the parliament until May 7. Many members objected to China's participation in the war. On the tenth the so-called Citizens' Corps surrounded the house of representatives and insulted a number of the members.

Tuan used the Citizens' Corps to force the house of representatives to vote for China's declaration of war. Another important problem before the parliament at the same time was the second reading of the constitution, which began on January 26. During the second reading, no proposal made by the Research Clique was adopted, and hence this clique was strongly opposed to the constitution.

The problem of the war with Germany was very complicated. First, President Li and Vice-President Feng (the latter had been elected to that post in October 1916) and a majority of the tuchuns opposed China's joining the allied powers; many of the parliamentary members, too, were quite dubious concerning any such action on China's part. Secondly, such famous leaders not in the government as Sun Yat-sen and T'ang Shao-i, and also civic and commercial organizations, voiced objections to China's participation; but Liang Ch'i-ch'ao was strongly in favor of it. Thirdly, all the members of the Research Clique in the parliament supported the proposal of Liang, their leader, while the old Kuomintang group strongly objected to it. Nevertheless, one Kuomintang faction under Chang Chi and the Political Study group supported Liang.

At least for once they all appeared to be thinking of the advantage of the nation rather than acting solely along party lines. On March 10 all the cabinet members attended meetings of the two houses and reported on the diplomatic policy. On the same day, the house of representatives passed a resolution declaring war on Germany by a vote of 331 to 82; the senate passed the resolution on the following day by a vote of 158 to 72. Coincidentally, on the tenth the German minister in Peking tendered his government's reply to the protest of February 9, and on the fourteenth, relations between the two countries were formally broken.

Before the severing of diplomatic relations, Premier Tuan and President Li had an argument. On March 3 Tuan, going to the office of the president with all the members of his cabinet, presented a draft telegram of instructions to the Chinese minister in Japan, Chang Tsung-hsiang, and requested that the president sign and dispatch it. The telegram stated:

> The Chinese government has decided to break off relations with Germany and will now proceed toward accomplishing the following aims: (1) complete cancellation of the Boxer indemnity payable to Germany and Austria, and a ten-year postponement of further payments to the Allied Powers; (2) raising the present five per cent customs duties on imported goods to seven and one-half per cent, and to twelve and one-half after China's abolition of the likin system, or transit dues; (3) cancellation of the provision in the Boxer protocol that no Chinese soldier be stationed within twenty li of Tientsin, and of the foreign privileges of stationing troops along the Peking-Tientsin railroad and around the Legation Quarter in Peking. Relying on the sincere friendship of the Japanese government towards China, Japan's assistance and cooperation in the above three points is requested.

President Li thought it unnecessary to inform foreign countries of decisions in matters of such vital importance before the parliament had given its approval, and he therefore refused to sign. Tuan instantly became angry and said: "If the president believes the actions of the cabinet to be improper, he should select other capable men." The upshot of the quarrel was that Tuan resigned that afternoon and went to Tientsin.

Through a great deal of effort on the part of Feng Kuo-chang, who had come to Peking the previous month, a compromise was later reached between the president and the cabinet in which the president agreed hereafter not to interfere in diplomatic affairs with Germany and to dismiss his chief secretary. After this, Tuan returned to Peking to resume his duties. When the president sent the telegram to Minister Chang Tsung-hsiang in Japan, the two opponents were brought together, but only temporarily.

The main diplomatic policy toward Germany had been approved by the cabinet and the parliament. There should have been no further problem. But leaders both within and without the government were still divided on this matter. Chang Shih-chao, a member of the senate, suggested that a few members without portfolio be added to the cabinet to give several leaders then outside the government a voice in state affairs, but the suggestion was not adopted. However, a Committee for Commenting on International Affairs was organized under the cabinet, and ten important persons from several influential circles were invited by the premier to be commentators; but outstanding leaders of the main factions were still not included.

Liang Ch'i-ch'ao on March 26 wrote a letter to this committee asking an early declaration of war against Germany and Austria. Liang's letter was unacceptable to several persons, among whom was Feng Kuo-chang, who telegraphed his objection to the government from Nanking. Opinion within the Committee for Commenting on International Affairs was also diverged on the war issue. By and large, the only strong advocates of war were Premier Tuan and Liang Ch'i-ch'ao. Liang's motive was to imitate the statesman Cavour, who insisted on Italy's participation in the Crimean War in order to enhance Italy's international position. Tuan had long made clandestine connections with Japanese militarists through the introduction of Chang Tsung-hsiang and Lu Tsung-yü and he had fallen into the trap of the Japanese. Tuan, on the one hand, hoped to improve China's international reputation by relying on Japan's assistance; and on the other hand, he hoped to get Japanese money and weapons in order to strengthen the power of the Peiyang military clique against his rivals in China. Liang could not discern Tuan's real intentions and the tuchuns supporting Tuan were also mostly ignorant of Tuan's underhand dealings with Japan. Accordingly many of them expressed doubt regarding Tuan's proposed policy of participating in the war.

Tuan called all provincial tuchuns to a military conference in Peking in order to unify their opinion and to frighten the parliament. The conference, opened on April 25 and presided over by Tuan, effected a unanimous vote for war. The tuchuns signed their names to attest their decision.

Growing Opposition to Tuan

On May 3 the Tuchuns Association, as a body, entertained the parliamentary members with a banquet for the purpose of persuading them to act according to Tuan's wish. On the seventh the bill for participating in the war was introduced. On the following day a confidential meeting held in the house of representatives was attended by all members. If the Peiyang military clique had not used harsh methods, the bill would have passed without trouble. In the parliament all parties (except the 1916 Club, a leftist wing) intended to pass the bill. The warlords, however, chose to use threats. While the house of representatives was convening, there appeared suddenly the "Citizen's Petition Corps", "The Five Races Petition Corps" the "War Petition Corps of Peking Citizens" and the "Petition Corps of Military Political and Commercial Circles"—all together about 3000 people, directed by army generals such as Fu Liang-tso and Chin Yün-p'eng. They surrounded the house of representatives, beat or insulted many members, and declared that until the bill was passed, they would not disperse.

The representatives were angered; the meeting was suspended. Cabinet members tendered their resignations, except for Premier Tuan. Having played such a stupid game, Tuan himself intended to resign; but this intention was abruptly put aside by his close assistants, who encouraged him to continue the harassment of the parliament. The extreme left wing in the parliament had always been dissatisfied with

Tuan. Now many other factions, except the Research Clique, also favored the fall of Tuan's cabinet.

The anti-Tuan sentiment was accelerated by the publication, on May 18, of Tuan's secret connections with Japanese militarists. An English newspaper, the *Peking Daily*, reported that Tuan had just borrowed a hundred million dollars from Japan through the arrangement of Lu Tsung-yü and Ts'ao Ju-lin for the reorganization of three arsenals by Japanese and for the training of soldiers by Japanese officers, among whom Adviser Tanaka had already arrived. The editor of this newspaper, Eugene Chen (Ch'en Yu-jen), was arrested on the following day and imprisoned by Tuan's government.

This action stirred a majority of parliamentary members to final disgust with Tuan. On the nineteenth a resolution passed by the house of representatives to the effect that the great diplomatic issue should be debated in a reorganized cabinet, meant that the war-participation bill could be passed, but Tuan must resign first.

The tuchuns understood that they could expect nothing from the parliament, and they now determined to destroy it. But they had no excuse to do so since the parliament was to be blamed for passing the bill for severing relations with Germany. The Research Clique was outraged and disappointed by its failure to enforce its ideas concerning the constitution. Noting that Premier Tuan could not maintain his position much longer, they decided to use the tuchuns to bring about a change in the parliament by pointing out to them that the articles of the draft constitution were not suited to the present state of the nation. Accordingly, the tuchuns requested that the government dissolve the parliament. President Li, summoning to his office the tuchuns, Meng En-yüan and Wang Chan-yüan, told them that the president had no constitutional power to dissolve the parliament, and that the only way to solve the problem was to ask Premier Tuan to resign. The tuchuns, recognizing that President Li stood by the parliament, left Peking to hold conferences at Tientsin, Hsuchow, and elsewhere. On May 23 President Li issued an order, cosigned by Wu T'ing-fang, a member of the cabinet, to the effect that Tuan Ch'i-jui was dismissed from the post of premier, which was to be filled by Wu. The immediate results of this dismissal were a rebellion by the union of tuchuns and the second dissolution of the parliament.

THE DISMISSAL OF TUAN AND DISSOLUTION OF THE PARLIAMENT

Intrigue to Restore the Manchus

Although the ensuing comedy of the restoration of the Manchu emperor began with the great dispute concerning the declaration of war on Germany, it had a long prefatory history. Sung Yü-jen and Lao Nai-hsüan had made the first attempt to restore the Manchu regime before Yüan Shih-k'ai tried to make himself emperor. When the antimonarchical war was at its peak, K'ang Yu-wei was again very active toward that goal, but after the National Protection Army launched its expedition from Yunnan, Yüan Shih-k'ai and K'ang Yu-wei became extremely unpopular. K'ang had written two scathing letters to Yüan voicing his disapproval of Yüan's action, but at the same time he essayed to put the Manchu emperor on the throne again. After Yüan's abandonment of the monarchical system, K'ang raised his banner of Manchu restoration openly, publishing a long discourse under the title of *A Plan for National Security*. Liang Ch'i-ch'ao published a prompt refutation of the argument; but fearing that he would be unable to convince his teacher, Liang asked the tuchuns of the four provinces of Yunnan, Kweichow, Kwangsi, and Kwangtung to issue a telegram denouncing K'ang's plans. The telegram read: "Refusal to change the national polity is the unanimous determination of the people. They did not permit Yüan, the traitor, to become emperor. Would they permit another to do so? … If there is anyone who still wishes to restore the Manchu emperor, T'ang Chi-yao and others will consider him a common enemy and a traitor and he will be treated as such." After this telegram, K'ang appeared to abandon the restoration movement completely.

Chang Hsün must long have had connections with K'ang Yu-wei, but because he was being watched by Yüan Shih-k'ai, he dared take no action. When Feng Kuo-chang sponsored the Nanking conference, Chang Hsün thought that he could use that opportunity to gain favor with Yüan and secure his confidence in order to establish a foundation for his plot to enthrone the Manchu emperor. Unfortunately for Chang, Yüan died, and the Nanking conference proved fruitless. Chang next induced the representatives to the Nanking conference to go to Hsuchow to form the Interprovincial Association that has already been described. Nominally in favor of consolidation of the Peiyang military clique, Chang actually wanted to establish it as a foundation for his own plans to restore the monarchy. The opportunity to unveil this plan was luckily provided by Tuan Ch'i-jui's dismissal.

Effects of Tuan's Dismissal

On the day of his dismissal, Tuan Ch'i-jui announced that the order for his dismissal and for the appointment of Wu T'ing-fang to succeed him as acting premier had not been cosigned by himself, the premier, and that he therefore would not be responsible for the outcome. This was tantamount to an invitation to the Association of Tuchuns to start a war against the president. Having dismissed Tuan, President Li recommended Li Ching-hsi as premier and secured the approval of both houses of parliament. On the following day, the twenty-sixth, he also intended to appoint Wang Shih-chen minister of war, and the latter had even declared his acceptance. As chief of staff, Wang issued an order to all military officers to the effect that the term, Peiyang military clique, should be discarded and that the nation should be protected.

In response to Premier Tuan's hint, Ni Ssu-ch'ung severed his relations with the central government. Declarations of independence were also made by Chang Tso-lin, tuchun of Fengtien, Chang Huai-chih, tuchun of Shantung, Li Hou-chi, tuchun of Fukien—eight provinces altogether. But Chang Hsün, at this time tuchun of Anhwei, had made no such declaration; instead, in the name of the Interprovincial Association of Thirteen Provinces he requested President Li to resign.

Several factors combined to bolster President Li's courage in dismissing Premier Tuan. (1) He thought that the tuchuns of the Tuan clique would not dare to take open action against him and that the Chihli clique could control them even if they should attempt an uprising. (2) Although the names of the Chihli and Anhwei cliques had not yet become established in use, the army officers of Chihli clearly objected to cooperating with Tuan's Anhwei officers. Sun Hung-i, a native of Chihli, hinted that he was planning to unite the Chihli army officers in order to control the Anhwei army group. (3) Wang Shih-chen had the same seniority in the Peiyang clique as Tuan Ch'i-jui. Even though the Chihli army officers could not control Tuan's clique, Wang Shih-chen himself could do so. Everyone, including even Ts'ao K'un, a head of the Chihli clique, declared his independence, except for the three Chihli tuchuns in the Yangtze Valley.

After his declaration of independence, Ni Ssu-ch'ung detained the trains in Peng-fou [Anhwei], intending to use them to advance his troops toward Peking in a joint attack with the soldiers coming from Honan, Shantung, and Fengtien. His announced reason was that the president was surrounded by knaves, and that the parliament was dominated by rascals who maintained close contact with the personnel in the president's office for the purpose of seizing political power.

Dissolution of the Parliament

Upon hearing of Ni's declaration of independence, President Li invited Hsü Shih-ch'ang to mediate; Hsü replied no mediation was possible unless the parliament was dissolved. Li then asked Liang Ch'i-ch'ao to come to Peking to mediate, but Liang replied that he had retired to live as a recluse on the seashore. T'ang Hua-lung next resigned as speaker for the house of representatives. Members of parliament belonging to the Research Clique stayed away from the parliament and so made it impossible to assemble a quorum. Moreover, a good many members tendered their resignations. Because of threats from the tuchuns, Premier Li Ching-hsi, though approved of by the parliament, dared not assume office. Finally on June 2 when Li Sheng-to came to Peking from Hsuchow with Chang Hsün's offer to mediate, the president deduced that Chang Hsün was not a partisan of Tuan's clique. He hoped that Chang, as chairman of the Interprovincial Association, might achieve some solution if he should come to Peking. Hence President Li ordered Li Sheng-to to return to Hsuchow and welcome Chang Hsün's offer.

At this time the military men of Tuan's clique, assembled in Tientsin, hoped to organize a government there with Hsü Shih-ch'ang as its generalissimo; they invited the important members of the Research Clique to join them. Hsü Shih-ch'ang, however, did not approve. He insisted that foreigners would not allow them to establish a government at Tientsin. Thus there was internal friction among the army men themselves.

When Chang Hsün led a large number of troops from Hsuchow to Peking via Tientsin, Tuan's military followers took the opportunity to persuade Chang Hsün to support them in the capital. Although Chang Hsün too wanted to dissolve the parliament, he agreed to cooperate only if Tuan's men would agree to restore the Manchu emperor. Tuan's clique consented. In one of his telegrams Chang Hsün says: "Although Tuan Ch'i-jui did not personally express his consent to the restoration, he did not disapprove of it. When I reached Peking, he again sent delegates saying that Tuan would certainly like to talk over the matter of the restoration after the dissolution of the parliament and the overthrow of the president. "

Instead of going to Peking immediately, Chang remained in Tientsin until his troops had arrived. He then demanded that President Li dissolve the parliament at once; otherwise he would not take up the responsibility of mediation. On June 13, 1917, after much confusion and harangue, the president, using as a cosignatory Chiang Chao-tsung, whom he appointed acting premier for just this purpose, dissolved the parliament for the second time during the republican period.

On the following day Chang Hsün went to Peking, accompanied by Li Ching-hsi; on June 28 K'ang Yu-wei went to live secretly in Chang Hsün's home in Peking.

CHANG HSÜN'S RESTORATION OF THE MANCHU EMPEROR

Chang Hsün on July 1, 1917, announced the restoration of the Manchu emperor. During the interval before this announcement, Li Ching-hsi fulfilled his dream of becoming premier, and many tuchuns, after the dissolution of the parliament, retracted their declarations of independence. A number of tuchuns, however, refused to support Li because he had refused to cosign the order dissolving the parliament. Li, now relying solely on the military power of Chang Hsün, formally assumed the premiership on July 24 and requested that Wang Shih-chen be made minister of war. Chang Hsün did not meddle in Li's organization of the cabinet, but he recruited new troops and had interviews with the abdicated emperor, Henry P'u-i, and with the former high officials of the Manchu regime. Subsequently, Li was asked to return the sovereignty to the former emperor. It was now quite clear what Chang's intention had been when he offered to mediate. Although Li spurned the request, he was powerless now to resist the tiger which had entered his house.

Chang Hsün used the names of Feng Kuo-chang, Lu Jung-t'ing and others to memorialize the throne on July 1 asking that Li Yüan-hung be permitted to turn his authority over to His Majesty, and the former emperor P'u-i was thus restored to power. On the same day, many decrees were issued, including the ones which designated July 1 to be considered May 15 of the ninth year of the period Hsüan-t'ung, bestowed the rank of duke of the first class on Li Yüan-hung, and appointed Feng Kuo-chang governor-general of Liang-Kiang and superintendent of trade for the southern ports, Chang Hsün governor-general of Chihli and superintendent of trade for the northern ports, and Lu Jung-t'ing governor-general of Liang-Kwang. Furthermore, the title of *tuchun* was changed to *governor* in all provinces, although no changes were made in the original personnel. Hsü Shih-ch'ang and Wang Shih-chen also received appointments; but the imperial government gave no post to Tuan Ch'i-jui.

K'ang Yu-wei, Last of the Court Literati

K'ang Yu-wei, who wanted to support Chang Hsün, drafted a number of imperial decrees in highly polished classical style, but none of them was adopted. K'ang's drafted decrees carried such titles as "Announcing the Enthronement", "Convening the National Assembly to Discuss the Constitution", "The Convening of the Parliament", "For Religious Tolerance", "For Abolishing the Kotow Ceremony", "For Abandoning the Observance of Tabooed Characters." Another forbade the members of the royal family to interfere in state affairs. K'ang tried to avoid the kotow ceremony, but Chang Hsün liked people knocking their heads on the floor. K'ang was so dismayed that after a few days, he declared that he would shave his head and become a monk. After the failure of the restoration he fled to the Japanese legation, where the Japanese minister, impressed by his calligraphy, had K'ang recopy for him the drafted decrees.[8]

Li Yüan-hung also fled to the Japanese legation. He then sent an envoy, Ting Huai, southward secretly, to carry the government seals to Vice-President Feng Kuo-chang for the attempt to restore the republic.

End of the Restored Monarchy

Upon receiving the news of the restoration, all the provincial military leaders and other important persons sent telegrams unanimously condemning Chang Hsün. The troops of the Peiyang clique in the vicinity of Peking were in a good position for an attack on the capital. Chang Shao-tseng, Feng Yü-hsiang, and Ts'ao K'un were among the first to start the war. Tuan Ch'i-jui, making himself commander in chief of the antirestoration army, personally presided over a ceremony initiating a punitive war at Ma-chang on July 5. His headquarters were established at Tientsin. As a result of hard fighting directed chiefly by Feng Yü-hsiang, the antirestoration army advanced to Peking on the twelfth. Chang Hsün was forced to flee to the Dutch legation and all the other leading figures of the restoration also disappeared. Two days later Tuan Ch'i-jui entered Peking. Within two weeks the restoration was at an end.

Chang Hsün had only about 20,000 troops (with queues). Most of these remained in Hsuchow, where they mutinied and dispersed early in July. Chang had undertaken large-scale action with such meager forces, apparently, on the basis of his previous understanding with Tuan's military clique. He evidently did not recognize that this agreement had been merely a plan to cheat him, just as Li Yüan-hung had earlier been cheated by the army men of Chihli, who had promised to support him in dismissing Tuan, and thus gave Feng Kuo-chang a chance to seize the presidency.

The Return of Tuan

At the conclusion of the comedy of the restoration, Tuan's followers and the Research Clique were exuberant. On July 5, the same day that

Tuan Ch'i-jui performed his antirestoration ceremony, he declared by telegram: "Today a secretary of the cabinet brought an order from the president dated July 2, appointing Tuan Ch'i-jui premier. It is my duty not to decline the appointment when the situation is so pressing, but to take up my duties immediately." On July 6 there was another presidential order, which read: "Premier Li Ching-hsi has asked to resign. Let him be relieved of his duties, and let Tuan Ch'i-jui be appointed as the new premier." This order was cosigned by Fan Yüan-lien.

The anti-Tuan group suspected that the two orders must have been forged by Tuan's followers and the Research Clique. But at that time all the newspapers printed a message from President Li to Vice-President Feng, saying:

> Since I am not virtuous and am already unable to perform my duties, the life span of the Republic seems to be approaching its end. You and I have been entrusted by the people with heavy duties, and we should follow the constitution in having you, as vice-president, perform the duties of the president. Since communications have been severed, it is difficult and dangerous to send you the state seals, and I have therefore appointed Tuan Ch'i-jui premier and allowed him to act as president for the time being.[9]

From these lines it would appear that the two orders announced by Tuan were not forged. But it also appears that Li gave the state seals to Tuan and entrusted him to forward them to Feng. Why, then, had Ting Huai been dispatched to bring the seals southward? (Later on, Tuan ordered Lu Yung-hsiang to arrest and imprison Ting Huai.) The anti-Tuan group deduced that President Li's message to Feng Kuo-chang was also forged by Tuan's followers. Although Tuan attained the premiership, the origin and procedure of his appointment, the inside story, is doubtless now beyond discovery.

Even in the official telegram that Tuan issued on his dismissal, he claimed that no order was effective in a government with a responsible cabinet unless cosigned by the premier. The order for his own dismissal was cosigned only by Wu T'ing-fang; the order reappointing him as premier was cosigned only by Fan Yüan-lien, who was minister of education and of domestic affairs. Tuan perhaps claimed allowance for the exigencies of the time.

On July 7, before the recovery of Peking, Feng Kuo-chang announced that he was assuming his duties as acting president and invited all the important officials to go to Nanking to organize a government. On the same day Tuan discussed moving the government to Tientsin, where a provisional office for national affairs was soon opened. On the fourteenth, Tuan entered Peking, accompanied by many important figures of the Research Clique, including Liang Ch'i-ch'ao and T'ang Hua-lung. On the seventeenth, Tuan announced his list of cabinet members, obviously drawing on Tuan's own following as well as on both Research and Communications men. Tuan persuaded ex-President Li Yüan-hung to return to his own home from the Legation Quarter and to announce by telegram his retirement as well as his recommendation of Vice-President Feng Kuo-chang for president. After an attempt was made on his life, Li planned to retire to Tientsin. Tuan did not give such permission, however, until he was assured that Li had no other plans.

Feng Kuo-chang had no desire to yield his territories around Nanking to others, but rather wanted the entire Yangtze Valley brought under his control so that he might not be isolated and oppressed by Tuan as Li had been. Feng therefore modestly declined the presidency. While on the one hand he requested Li to resume it, on the other hand he secretly negotiated with the central government regarding the selection of a successor as tutu of Kiangsu. On August 1 when these negotiations were concluded to his satisfaction, he went to Peking to assume the presidency.

A few days after Feng Kuo-chang reached Peking, the government announced that Li Shun, as tutu, would be transferred to Kiangsi, and Wang Chan-yüan was to become tutu of Hupeh. These three provinces formed the base of the Chihli clique. Each of the two great Peiyang leaders, Tuan and Feng, as well as the heads of the Research Clique, had now obtained prominent positions. But many other ambitious and prominent men were left without satisfactory positions. These prevented the government leaders from carrying their plans through peacefully.

THE SEPARATION OF NORTH AND SOUTH CHINA

The Research Clique Reorganizes the Parliament

Two of the most important problems facing Tuan's government were China's participation in the European war and the reorganization of the parliament. Tuan planned to use the foreign problem to control the domestic situation. His policy has been humorously described as a declaration of war abroad without fighting, and a fight at home without declaration of war. China declared war against Germany and Austria on August 14; but during the last ten days of July, troops had been sent to Hunan where there was no war. When Tuan's cabinet was inaugurated, the leading figures of the Research Clique suggested a meeting of the provisional senate [*lin-shih ts'an-i yüan*]. Sun Yat-sen accordingly organized the Military Government at Canton under the banner of "protection of the constitution." Thereafter North and South China once more fought each other.

Liang Ch'i-ch'ao, T'ang Hua-lung, and others expressed in the following terms the need to reorganize the parliament: "The Republic of China was overthrown by Chang Hsün in his restoration movement, and now the government has been entirely reorganized. According to the precedent of the first revolution of 1911, a provisional senate should be convened in order to draw up new regulations for the organization of the senate, as well as for elections. A new parliament may then be opened." Since the existence of the old parliament was a thorn in the flesh of the Peiyang militarists, they undoubtedly supported this plan of the Research Clique.

The arguments of the Research Clique were certainly full of contradictions. Just how legally, we may ask, did the members of parliament occupy their seats? On what basis did Feng Kuo-chang attain the presidency? If, as they claimed, the Republic of China had been overthrown by Chang Hsün and reconstructed by them, their new government was clearly only provisional, and the appointment of the new premier should not have been based on President Li's order, cosigned by Minister Fan. Moreover, Feng should not have become president on the basis of the old constitution which provided that the vice-president should succeed the president. The clique cited the old constitution to secure its own positions, but also claimed that the republic had been destroyed and a new government constructed.

If they claimed that the parliament had been reconvened because Yüan's dissolution of it had been illegal, then was Li's dissolution of the parliament legal? These Research Clique leaders must have known that their reasons were unsound. They continued to maintain that the members of the old parliament were very corrupt. Lacking a legal basis, however, for reorganizing it, the clique advanced any argument which seemed serviceable.

The parliament had, to be sure, wasted time on arguments for private ends and neglected to complete a second reading and discussion of the draft constitution. For this neglect, however, members of the Research Clique were to blame along with other members of the parliament. It is true, also, that members of the extreme left wing refused to accept reasonable suggestions made by the Research Clique; but the latter's secret connections with the warlords were certainly outside the proper sphere of parliamentary activity, In short, it was a fact that there were many incompetent and untrustworthy members in the parliament; but the argument for reorganization was nonetheless illogical.

Some people advocated following the regulations for the organization of the parliament and for elections as provided by the old constitution, in order to allow the people to decide whom to elect. This group, however, recognized no grounds for convening a provisional parliament and their compromise proposal was rejected not only by the left-wing members but also by the Research Clique. This group insisted that the dissolved "old" parliament must have a fundamental reorganization; otherwise this dissolution, resulting from the interference of the Tuchuns Association, would turn out to be meaningless. From the point of view of the Research Clique, the provisional parliament was to carry through a thorough parliamentary reorganization. Their actual purpose, however, seems much like the purpose of the tuchuns, when they persuaded themselves to interfere with the parliament.

Reorganized under pressure, the parliament of North China finally came under the control of the Anhwei and Fukien or An-fu militarists, who were actually much haughtier and more overbearing than their predecessors, whom they regarded as rascals. This reorganized parliament in North China was never recognized as legal by the authorities in South China, and thus a prolonged war over the problem of the constitution developed. Earlier, when the Association of Tuchuns had interfered with the parliament, Sun Yat-sen, Ch'en Ch'un-hsüan, T'ang Shao-i, and others had telegraphed to President Li asking him to protect the constitution and thereby hold firm the foundations of the republic. When Ni Ssu-ch'ung and others declared their independence, the chief spokesmen of South China again dispatched telegrams expressing their desire to fight against the rebel leaders. After the dissolution of the parliament the tuchuns of Kwangtung and Kwangsi immediately declared that the two provinces would for the time being be autonomous. Since the parliament had been dissolved illegally, they also refused to recognize a parliament reorganized to conform with the personal desires of a small group.

Southern Leaders Repudiate Peking

During the restoration period the military leaders of Southwest China were more than ready to fight against the monarchist traitors. But Tuan Ch'i-jui wanted all the credit for recreating the republic. Tuan understood the danger of his position if the troops from the Southwest should move north toward Peking. Appointing such commanders as Ni Ssu-ch'ung and Tuan Chih-kuei, who lacked any real power, he telegraphed at the same time to the authorities of the southwestern provinces asking them not to send any troops, on the grounds that since the problem would soon be settled, provincial troops should remain at their stations. This roused even further the wrath and jealousy of the provincial authorities. T'ang Chi-yao was the first to repudiate this telegram, and he allied himself with the southwestern provinces to fight against Tuan.

After the end of the restoration, Lu Jung-t'ing, Ch'en Ping-k'un, T'an Hao-ming, and others repeatedly sent telegrams to Acting President Feng, asking his opinion concerning the parliamentary problem. As soon as it became known that a provisional parliament was to be convened, these Southern governments unanimously objected.

Before Sun Yat-sen set up a government at Canton, he circulated a telegram seriously criticizing Tuan Ch'i-jui:

> It is unfortunate that the republic should suddenly have been usurped by the false Manchu emperor. You launched with much solemn ceremony a military expedition from Ma-chang to restore the republic and to recapture the capital. This provided the opportunity for the destruction of the usurper and for you to regain your power. I have noticed that China has alternated three times between

republicanism and monarchism; this indicates widespread uncertainty about right and wrong and about punishment and reward. Those ministers who supported Yüan Shih-k'ai as emperor and those who restored the Manchu emperor to the throne are guilty of criminal acts against the republican system. Last year the ringleaders of Yüan's monarchical movement were not executed, and since they were pardoned, other people who attempted to restore a monarchy under the Manchu emperor certainly had nothing to fear. ... You first requested that war be declared against Germany; then you had parliamentary members beaten in order to force the motion through the parliament. You were still not satisfied and dissolved the parliament. ... When President Li Yüan-hung had no choice but to order your dismissal, you were still unrepentant and angrily refused to be held responsible for any of the disorders. Having now gained a victory over the restoration, your merits may balance your faults, and this will doubtless be recognized by everyone under heaven. Nevertheless, the decree reappointing you as premier has neither been seconded nor cosigned by anyone and is therefore illegal. It is also uncertain whether the reappointment was actually issued by President Li. You claimed to be the leader of a righteous army fighting against the restoration; but how could you assume the title of premier? Your dismissal caused warfare, and it was through warfare that you restored yourself to power. Being alone responsible for all these sly tricks, you can hardly be considered a man of integrity. [10]

The Military Government Organized in Canton

Realizing that Tuan would turn a deaf ear to his remarks, Sun then took the navy south to Canton to lead the Constitution Protection Movement.

The navy and the Kuomintang had a long history of cooperation. The first restoration of the parliament was brought about by the navy through its declaration of independence. Ch'en Pi-kuang, the minister for the navy, had resigned immediately after the dissolution of the parliament and gone south. Sun Yat-sen, who arrived in Canton on July 20 aboard the warvessel *Hai-chi*, announced that he had brought the fleet to Canton because he wanted to establish a naval base there. His plan had the support of Governor Chu and of the Kwangtung members of the parliament. Ch'en Pi-kuang led his entire fleet on July 22 from Woosung to Canton, accompanied by Lin Pao-i, commander of the first fleet, and declared his intention of protecting the constitution. T'ang Shao-i, Wang Ching-wei, and Chang Ping-lin were also in Ch'en's company. Thus the Constitution Protection Forces were organized.

The fleet reached Huang-pu about ten miles from Canton, on August 5. Members of the parliament, coming in response to telegrams received from the Kwangtung provincial government and provincial assembly, also began to arrive. When over 250 of them had reached Canton, Sun Yat-sen decided to hold a special conference of the parliament at Canton on the twenty fifth to discuss the organization of a government. By August 30, rules had been drawn up concerning the organization of a Military Government, which was to have one grand marshal (*ta yüan-shuai*) and two marshals. On September 3 Sun Yat-sen was elected grand marshal, and Lu Jung-t'ing and T'ang Chi-yao marshals. Sun was inaugurated on the tenth, and men were nominated, to be approved and appointed by the grand marshal, as ministers of finance, foreign affairs, domestic affairs, war, navy, etc. Affairs were dominated by Lu Jung-t'ing and Ch'en Pi-kuang. The ministers were powerless, and several of them never actually took up their positions. Had Lu and Ch'en been well handled by Tuan Ch'i-jui, they would long before have joined him, for they had their own personal interests at heart.

The Break Between the Southern Provinces and Peking

Lu Jung-t'ing traveled from Canton to Peking in March 1917 for negotiations with the central government regarding the consolidation of the Liang-Kwang under his own influence. These negotiations led to two noteworthy agreements: (1) Ch'en Pi-kuang was to become tuchun of Kwangtung, and T'an Hao-ming tuchun of Kwangsi. Since Ch'en was then the tuchun of Kwangsi, and Lu tuchun of Kwangtung, while T'an had no position, Lu wanted to secure a title for himself, which would place him above Ch'en and T'an. (2) Hunan was to be governed by a native leader, and it was not to be invaded by the soldiers from Liang-Kwang, but the central government was not to change the tuchun of Hunan without very careful consideration. This was obviously meant to mark the division of Lu's sphere of influence and that of the Peiyang clique, since Hunan was the threshold of Liang-Kwang, and T'an Yen-k'ai, then tuchun of Hunan, was respected and trusted by Lu Jung-t'ing.

After Lu Jung-t'ing left Peking on April 10, Tuan announced that Lu was to be commissioner to oversee the affairs of Liang-Kwang [*Liang-kuang hsün-yüeh-shih*], while Ch'en was to be tuchun of Kwangtung, and T'an that of Kwangsi. After the dissolution of the parliament, Liang-Kwang had declared independence temporarily, partly because Li Lieh-chün and others had urged a Northern Expedition and Lu had to show some respect for these Kuomintang members, Lu also wished to demonstrate his own power before the Peiyang clique by indicating that Liang-Kwang would tolerate no invasion of Hunan.

If Tuan Ch'i-jui had not sent troops to Hunan and replaced the tuchun of that province after the end of the restoration, Lu Jung-t'ing would not have permitted the Military Government proclaimed by the Kuomintang to survive in Kwangtung. But Tuan, mistaking the demonstrations of Lu and Ch'en for genuine cooperation with the Kuomintang, ordered an army division from the North to Hunan in the last ten days of July. On August 6 he appointed Fu Liang-tso tuchun of Hunan because Fu was both a native of Hunan and a partisan of the Peiyang clique.

Since Tuan had broken his tacit agreement with Lu by invading Hunan and menacing the safety of Liang-Kwang, Lu had, for his own protection, no choice but to permit the rise of the Military Government and to prepare to give military aid to Hunan. When Liu Chien-fan, the commander of the garrison at Linling, declared his independence of southern Hunan from the central government, the troops of Kwangsi marched to Hunan to provide military aid. Although for the protection of the constitution the Military Government in South China had grown out of the parliamentary problem, the actual war for the protection of the constitution resulted from the seizure by the Peiyang military clique of the post of tuchun of Hunan.

THE STRIFE BETWEEN FENG AND TUAN IN THE NORTH

Tuan Ch'i-jui's policy toward Southwest China was to use Hunan as a basis for conquering Kwangsi and Kwangtung, and to use Szechwan as a springboard for controlling Yunnan and Kweichow. At the same time he took advantage of China's participation in the World War to secure from Japanese militarists a large loan—which he used to finance his preparations for a civil war.

At this time although the various provinces in Southwest China were trying to unite themselves under the banner of "Constitution Protection," there was actually no unification. T'ang Chi-yao and Lu Jung-t'ing were not comrades of Sun Yat-sen, and Szechwan was fighting against Yunnan and Kweichow. Moreover, since some of the military men of Hunan had already surrendered to the Peiyang group, the power of Southwest China was no match for that of the North.

But within the Peiyang clique, seeds of internal dissension had been scattered long ago. The secret struggle between Feng and Tuan became much more severe than that between Li and Tuan. The Peiyang militarists were not only unable to unify Southwest China but were unable to prevent their clique itself from splitting into two factions. This division precipitated the failure of military action in Szechwan and Hunan and the collapse of the Tuan Cabinet.

War in Hunan

After the appointment of Fu Liang-tso as tuchun of Hunan was announced on August 6, T'an Yen-k'ai, who was then the Hunan tuchun, could only accede; in the Hunan army the chief of the Second Division and the garrison commander of Linling were already under the control of the Peiyang clique. T'an even ordered the garrison commander to Peking to welcome the new tuchun. But while the commander was on his way to Peking, T'an appointed Liu Chien-fan as garrison commander of Linling and relocated other troops so as to make close connections with the Kwangsi army, which had been sent to the border of Hunan to build a foundation for future independence.

Before Fu Liang-tso started his trip to Hunan, he declared that he would neither take any soldiers nor change any army officers in that province. Nevertheless, shortly after his inauguration to the new office, the Northern Army, stationed at Yochow, was moving southward, and a new garrison commander of Linling was appointed. Liu Chien-fan accordingly on September 18 declared autonomy. At that moment the Kwangsi army also marched to the aid of Hunan.

The Northern Army sent to Hunan consisted of the Eighth Division under the control of Wang Ju-hsien and the Twentieth Division under the command of Fan Kuo-chang. Both Wang and Fan took orders from Feng Kuo-chang. At that time the Chihli and the Anhwei cliques had not yet been clearly formed and the cleavage between Feng (Chihli) and Tuan

(Anhwei) was not yet very wide. When Fan and Wang asked for military instructions from Tuan, he gave them much encouragement; but when they visited Feng, he seemed to disapprove the use of military force to solve the political problem and his attitude was clearly conveyed to his two subordinates.

The war between North and South China broke out on October 6 in southern Hunan. From October to November the war did not go well for the Southern Army. The arrival of the reinforcements from Kwangsi, however, restored their morale. Now the Northern Army lost one battle after another. Fu Liang-tso escaped from the capital city, Changsha, and Wang and Fan also followed suit, withdrawing their troops from southern Hunan.

War in Szechwan

In the area of Szechwan, Liu Ts'un-hou drove away Lo P'ei-chin in April. Tuan again urged Lo to reduce the number of the Szechwan army, but Lo, fearing that this might cause further war, secretly telegraphed Tuan suggesting redeploying Liu's soldiers. Tuan deliberately showed Lo's telegram to Liu in order to irritate him. A clash between the soldiers of Lo and Liu occurred on April 19. Taking this opportunity, Tuan on April 20 dismissed Lo from his position as tuchun and Liu Ts'un-hou from the commandership of the Second Division, and appointed Tai K'an as acting tuchun of Szechwan.

Szechwan and Kweichow troops were also at odds, and Tai K'an was killed during a sharp brief battle during one of these persistent local wars. When the Tuan government appointed Fu Liang-tso tuchun of Hunan, Wu Kuang-hsin was made commander in chief of the army in the upper valley of the Yangtze River and concurrently, a commissioner of investigation of Szechwan. Wu was ordered to command two regiments of troops from Yochow to Szechwan and was made the presumptive tuchun.

But Wu took a long time transferring a part of his troops to

Chungking. There the commander of the Fifth Division of the Szechwan army, Hsiung K'o-wu, who had secret connections with the Southwest and the Kweichow troops, disarmed Wu's Northern troops. Wu escaped by boat, losing all his ammunition and weapons. Chungking was occupied by Hsiung Ko-wu. Now Tuan's plan for controlling Szechwan, like his plan for Hunan, had failed.

The failure in Szechwan had been caused by the incompetence of Wu Kuang-hsin and the inclination of Hsiung K'o-wu toward the Southwest. Failure in Hunan grew out of reluctance to fight on the part of Wang Ju-hsien and Fan Kuo-chang. On November 14, Wang and Fan circulated telegrams asking that the war be stopped, as did also the four tuchuns of Chihli, Hupeh, Kiangsi, and Kiangsu.

Feng Dismisses Tuan

Then Tuan Ch'i-jui extended his resignation to President Feng, who made a polite gesture to retain him. When the joint telegram of the four tuchuns was circulated, Tuan began to realize that the requests for a peaceful solution and the withdrawal of troops by Wang and Fan were all instigated by President Feng. Tuan therefore extended his second resignation on the twentieth; it was accepted by the president. On the twenty-second a presidential order approved Tuan's resignation and appointed Wang Ta-hsi acting premier. When several parliamentary members of the Research Clique resigned, including Liang Ch'i-ch'ao, T'ang Hua-lung, Lin Ch'ang-min, and Fan Yüan-lien, Tuan's cabinet completely disintegrated. This was the first round of fighting between Feng and Tuan.

When Tuan left office, chagrined at his failure, he issued a secret telegram to his Peiyang Army, arousing its sympathy and support. He believed that the Peiyang clique was the only protector of the nation, without which there could be no China; he preferred to forget that he himself had incited the Association of Tuchuns to start a revolution in order to restore himself to power. He blamed Feng's clique for stirring up civil war, appearing to forget that he himself had taken advantage of foreign affairs in order to control the domestic situation. He accused the Southwest of starting all the trouble, ignoring the fact that he himself had been the instigator. He accused the Southwest of secret plots, bribery, and sowing dissension in order to break the organization of the Northerners. As a matter of fact, the split between Feng and Tuan was chiefly the work of Tuan's confidant, Hsü Shu-cheng.

According to *A Brief History of the Peiyang Military Clique* [*Pei-yang chün-fa hsiao-shih*]: "The split between Feng and Tuan came to light gradually after Feng went to Peking to become president and all Feng's associates were considered by Tuan as Feng's clique; at that time Hsü Shu-cheng, dominating state affairs, stirred up the unanimous hatred of Feng's following." Tuan blamed Wang Ju-hsien for betraying him. At the same time he still hoped to make the Peiyang clique the pillar of China. Unfortunately this pillar had long been rotting beyond repair.

Liang Ch'i-ch'ao's Disappointments

The failure was not only a bitter disappointment to Tuan, but even more to Liang Ch'i-ch'ao, who believed that a nation must maintain a central force, which he thought should be the Peiyang militarists. Liang had first tried to reform Yüan Shih-k'ai; then he had tried to reform Feng and Tuan. Now even the central force of the Peiyang clique had collapsed.

Liang hoped to make Tuan a national hero, but Tuan refused to be improved. With regard to the declaration of war against Germany, Liang had done some substantial diplomatic work toward enhancing the international position of China; Tuan focused his attentions on domestic troubles. Liang had promised the ministers of the Allied Powers in Peking to do something important for the World War; Tuan would not back him up. Liang tried to find hope for China through the Western Powers; Tuan, on the other hand, seemed with the help of Japan to be dragging

China to the brink of death. Liang could merely watch while Tuan was led by the Communications Clique to rely on Japan. After this bitter lesson, Liang's political life and his hopes came to an end. The Peiyang militarists, now completely influenced by the Communications Clique, could no longer be reached by Liang's research group.

Failure of Feng's Peace Policy and the Return of Tuan

Thereafter Feng Kuo-chang's peace attempts also failed and before long Tuan's power was restored. Tuan's resignation was not a real victory for Feng. The Tuan faction still had great potential political power. After the dismissal of Tuan, Feng announced the members of his new cabinet on December 1. The premier and minister of war was Wang Shih-chen, a good-natured man inclined to support the conciliatory policy toward the Southwest maintained by Feng's clique. But the tuchuns of the Tuan faction strongly objected. On December 3, the Association of Tuchuns held at Tientsin a conference sponsored by Ni Ssu-ch'ung. At this time Chang Tso-lin also joined Tuan and participated in the conference, which discussed the method for solving the situation in the Southwest by military force.

At first Feng did not pay much attention to the Tientsin conference. On December 7, he appointed T'an Yen-k'ai tuchun of Hunan, but T'an did not go to take up the position. This action by Feng was an indication of a solution of the Southwestern problem. Actually, by this time, Hunan was already under the control of the troops of the Southwest; the Peiyang militarists held only Yochow in the northern border of that province. Some important figures of the Southwest, like Ch'en Ch'un-hsüan, also favored peace. Feng therefore on December 25, formally announced his intention of ceasing hostilities, and for a time a peaceful atmosphere prevailed.

But Feng had other problems in getting along with Tuan's faction. Tuan, who had been the leading advocate of war against Germany, had kept in close touch with the Western and Eastern imperialists even after his resignation. Feng too had to get along with the imperialists; and accordingly, before he announced China's intention to participate in the war, he especially appointed Tuan Ch'i-jui on December 18 to be the commander in chief in charge of all forces to fight abroad.

Tuan, taking advantage of this new position, was able to float a loan from Japan for the expansion of his own military strength. When Tuan at this time was also assigned by the premier to the post of minister of war, the power of the Peking government again fell directly in his hands.

The leaders of Southwest China, now realizing that Feng was unable to maintain peace, refused to cooperate with his reconciliation policy. In the middle of January 1918 the independent provinces in South China launched a military expedition. On January 27 Yochow was taken by the troops of Kwangsi and Hunan, and the safety of Hupeh was threatened.

With Tuan's followers urging a solution of the Southwestern problem by force, Feng was in a dilemma. Unable to escape the pressure from Tuan and the Tuan faction, he subsequently had to order Ts'ao K'un and Chang Huai-chih to lead troops into Hupeh to give support to Tuan. Near the end of February, by Hsü Shu-cheng's invitation, Chang Tso-lin's Fengtien troops came to garrison Chihli, partly to aid Tuan and partly to threaten Feng. On March 19 the tuchuns of Tuan's following issued a threatening telegram. Yielding to Tuan's force, on March 23 the president made Tuan Ch'i-jui premier again.

Before Tuan became the premier, Yochow had been retaken by the Northern armies. Changsha was captured on April 2 by Ts'ao K'un's subordinate, Wu P'ei-fu, who was later to become a dominant figure of North China. On April 18 Wu P'ei-fu captured Heng Shan, farther south of the capital of Hunan. Now, to encourage the troops and to make a close alliance with the three tuchuns in the middle part of the Yangtze River, Premier Tuan personally went to Hupeh to reward his subordinates.

But when Wu P'ei-fu, whom Tuan regarded as an invincible general, reached Hengchow, his soldiers were worn out. His officers, to avoid a possible loss of his forces, advised him not to risk a further advance toward Kwangtung and Kweichow. But there were also personal reasons why General Wu did not continue fighting. He considered himself the great conqueror of Hunan, yet the position of tuchun of that province had been given to Chang Ching-yao; now because Wu would fight no more, his superior Ts'ao K'un returned to Tientsin.

In order to conciliate these military leaders, Tuan on June 20 offered the grand title of Supreme Commander over the four provinces Kwangtung, Kiangsi, Hunan, and Szechwan to Ts'ao K'un; and the position of associate commander in chief to Wu P'ei-fu. Tuan even promised Ts'ao K'un in strict confidence the future vice-presidency. Ts'ao, however, was not to be persuaded by these private promises, nor was either he or Wu to be pacified by the titles conferred upon them by Tuan. On August 21 the associate commander even led his officers to issue a circular telegram advocating the discontinuance of the civil war. Tuan's military policy now completely evaporated.

The An-fu Clique and Japanese Loans

Although Tuan failed in his military plans, he had borrowed a great deal of money from foreign nations during his last premiership and had created two formidable new forces: one, the so-called European War Participation Army; the other, the so-called New Parliament, which was controlled by the An-fu clique. During the half year of his premiership from March 23 to the middle of October 1918, Tuan borrowed $120,000,000 from Japan. [11]

There were other loans which were never announced. Since the brief war against the imperial restoration, when Tuan proclaimed himself premier, he had made close connections with the Japanese government, and from 1917 to 1918 he borrowed nearly two billion dollars from Japan.

Part of this huge amount of money, now called the Nishihara loan, was loaned from August 1917 to January 1918, and Liang Ch'i-ch'ao participated in the negotiations. For the purpose of buying armaments a specific loan was received in November 1917, with Liang participating in the negotiations, and a further loan in July 1918. Several loans were never announced to the public. The exact amounts involved in the whole Nishihara loan even now cannot be exactly determined, and different authors arrive at different figures. [12]

Part of this huge loan was used for the war with the Southwest. A large amount was spent for the training of an army for participation in the European War. Another small portion was wasted on the so-called New Parliament created by the warlords of the An-fu clique.

The New Army consisted of three divisions and four mixed brigades. Under the name of fighting against a common enemy in the European War, an agreement was made with Japan to have the New Army organized and trained by Japanese officers. The real purpose behind this army, however, was to use the new force to wipe out all military cliques, including the Chihli group, in China.

The An-fu Club was under the nominal leadership of Wang I-t'ang, although its real backbone was Hsü Shu-cheng. The Research Clique proposed the reorganization of the parliament and expected a large number of its members to be elected. But the result of the election revealed the domination by the An-fu militarists. When this New Parliament convened in the first part of August 1918, only about 20 members belonged to the Research Clique, while 330 belonged to the An-fu militarists and more than 100 belonged to the Communications Clique.

With the New Parliament and the New Army as his supporting forces, Tuan could not easily be overthrown. However, apprehension was growing in the minds of the people because of the foreign loans. This apprehension was first expressed by Chinese students in Japan, who on May 12 quit their schools and returned to China to organize a student union for the salvation of the nation. On May 21 students of Peking University and other colleges in the capital marched to the office building of the president petitioning the abrogation of the joint Sino-Japanese participation in the war, and especially the Japanese training of Chinese soldiers. After the students' parade, merchants and other citizens all over the nation began to understand that Tuan was selling out the country in order to stamp out his enemies in China. Popular meetings and circular telegrams were sent either asking for an end to the Civil War or attacking Tuan's action.

The old Communications Clique, under the leadership of Liang Shih-i, also attacked Tuan Ch'i-jui. After Yüan Shih-k'ai's attempt to restore the empire, Liang Shih-i was under a general order of arrest and Ts'ao Ju-lin became the new leader of the clique. When the order to arrest Liang Shih-i was later rescinded, Liang was active again, but his sphere of influence had been taken over by Ts'ao. Hsü Shu-cheng, who had never been on good terms with Liang, now joined Ts'ao in receiving all benefits from Tuan's improper loan negotiations. Henceforth Liang Shih-i was part of the anti-Tuan movement, associating himself with the warlords of President Feng's camp in advocating peace.

In September 1918 Hsü Shih-ch'ang was elected president by the New Parliament and inaugurated on October 10. [13] Tuan Ch'i-jui, realizing his own unpopularity, resigned his premiership, but retained his position as commander in chief of the army for participating in the European War. Nevertheless, the conflict between the Chihli and the Anhwei cliques continued unabated. Hsü Shu-cheng kept on expanding his War Participation Army until the great civil war between the two military cliques broke out in the fall of 1920.

REORGANIZATION OF THE MILITARY GOVERNMENT IN THE SOUTH

While Feng and Tuan were wrangling in the North, there was

similar trouble between political and military groups in the South. Since neither Lu Jung-t'ing nor T'ang Chi-yao cooperated sincerely with Sun Yat-sen, the Military Government was crippled from the start. Sun refused to recognize the Peking government as legal; Lu and T'ang merely denied Tuan as a legal premier. In the hope of an alliance with Feng, Lu and T'ang [during Feng's tenure of office until October 1918] gave full recognition to him as president.

Factions in the South

Not only did Lu and T'ang differ with Sun Yat-sen, but also the parliamentary members who went to South China were divided into moderately progressive and radically progressive factions. Since the Research Clique favored a thorough reorganization of the parliament, none of its parliamentary members had gone to the South. Those who went to Canton, mostly old Kuomintang members, had long since divided into factions: The Political Study Group, the Good Friends Association, and the Association of Friends of the People. The nature of the Political Study Group was similar to that of the Research Clique. The Research Clique's suggested reorganization of the parliament was seconded by the members of the Political Study Group. Since Tuan had secured moral support from the Research Clique, he ignored the Political Study Group; for this reason the parliamentary members of the group went to the South.

Their leader, Li Ken-yüan, a native of Yunnan, had long desired to support Ch'en Ch'un-hsüan as the puppet head of the Military Government, since Ch'en, a former superior of Lu Jung-t'ing, would provide an opening wedge in the plan to make use of the warlords of Yunnan and Kwangsi. Another leader of the Political Study Group was Ku Chung-hsiu. Ku, a native of Chihli, also planned to control Tuan's ambitions by cooperating with the Chihli warlords and with Feng.

Of the three political factions in the parliament known as the Extraordinary Parliament of South China, the Political Study Group represented the extreme right wing, while the Association of Friends of the People, including the basic members of Sun Yat-sen's China's Revolutionary Party, made up the extreme left wing. Although none of the three factions enjoyed a majority, the Good Friends Association, the moderate party, dominated three of its four major positions: the speakers and associate speakers in the two houses. Although the Political Study Group joined with the Yunnan and Kwangsi warlords, they could not defeat the ideas of the left wing without the support of the middle faction. If the middle faction cooperated with the left wing, they could dominate the parliament; but they had no backing from the militarists, and accordingly could not enforce their decisions.

Weakness of the Military Government

In such a political environment the Military Government existed from September 1917 to the early spring of 1918. Although Sun Yat-sen kept the Extraordinary Parliament under his control, he obtained no actual help from the militarists, except for the very small navy. It could properly be said that the Military Government had government without military force and the warlords had military force without government. Sun Yat-sen's hope to build up an army in addition to the navy, brought him much trouble with the Kwangsi military clique, which did not want Sun's Military Government to have any military power.

The frustration of his plans angered Sun Yat-sen and his struggle with the Kwangsi clique continued. Mo Ching-yü, who had underhand dealings with Tuan Ch'i-jui, became tuchun of Kwangtung. Some of Mo's forces, pretending that they were bandits, proceeded to kill Sun Yat-sen's several dozen bodyguards. This murder so infuriated Sun Yat-sen that on January 3, 1918, he ordered his naval vessel to bombard the office building of the tuchun. Mo, however, did not exchange fire. Then on February 26 the minister of the navy, Ch'eng Pi-kuang, was assassinated. Ch'eng had been favored by Sun Yat-sen and a number of the local gentry for the governorship of Kwangtung, and Lu Jung-t'ing and other Kwangsi militarists had ostensibly expressed their consent. But the contemplated appointment was interrupted by the assassination, which was almost like the loss of an arm to Sun.

The next step of the militarists was to get rid of Sun Yat-sen. In November 1917 Ch'en Ch'un-hsüan joined the peace movement from Shanghai, expressing the same desire for peace as had Lu Jung-t'ing and the Political Science Study Group. Sun Yat-sen himself had no objection to this campaign, but he strongly insisted upon the restoration of the constitution and a parliament in accordance with the constitution as the first essential for peace negotiations.

Sun had no intention of making a compromise with the Northern warlords. At that time the Political Study Group was making an alliance with the powerful members in the southwestern provinces, and was also very active in the Extraordinary Parliament. On January 20, 1918, appeared the Union for the Protection of the Constitution by All Independent Provinces in the Southwest. These six provinces included Szechwan under the domination of Hsiung K'o-wu, who had allied himself with Yunnan and Kweichow under the banner for constitutional protection. Hunan and Kwangsi also joined. Thus the six provinces in the Southwest were united; if there had been some method of linking the powerful provincial leaders with the Extraordinary Parliament, the unification would have been very formidable indeed.

The Rejection of Sun Yat-sen

Since the members of the Political Study Group in the Extraordinary Parliament were not many, they had to join hands with the middle faction, Good Friends Association, whose leaders, Wu Ching-lien and Ch'u P'u-ch'eng, were then the speakers of the house of representatives. With these two men the Political Study Group tried its best to cooperate closely. In April 1918 the opportunity was ripe for the reorganization of the Military Government, to cancel the grand marshalcy and replace it by a committee consisting of powerful, provincial authorities. Actually this was a change from the dictatorship by one grand marshal to that by a military clique, and a rejection of Sun Yat-sen.

Understanding its significance, Sun sent his resignation to the Extraordinary Parliament on the fourth of May. These words of Sun's telegram are noteworthy:

> Ever since the illegal dissolution of the parliament ... there has been no lawful government in China ... Attempts by Feng and Tuan to use the Peiyang military power to subdue the whole nation resulted in the provocation of the war between Szechwan and Hunan and the disunification of the whole country ... Accordingly, I have been in cooperation with the elders of the republic in Shanghai in sponsoring the Constitutional Protection Society. The Navy officers followed me to the South. When the Provincial Government of Kwangtung invited the parliamentary members to come from Peking to Canton for meetings, there emerged in Canton the Extraordinary Parliament, through which the rules of the organization of the Military Government were proclaimed on the first of August, 1917. Unworthy as I am, I was elected the grand marshal ... Thereafter the provinces Kwangtung, Kwangsi, Yunnan, Kweichow, Szechwan, and Hunan declared their intention of protecting the constitution. Unfortunately ... even under the banner of the protection of the constitution, the militarists would not obey the law or public opinion. Even though the Military Government has been established, many militarists who have been elected to responsible positions have not taken up their duties, nor do they pay much respect to the Extraordinary Parliament ... Recently the Extraordinary Parliament passed a resolution for the reorganization of the Military Government ... I therefore hand in my resignation and briefly recount for the public record my connection with the grand marshalcy.[14]

In sum, this telegram implies a warning to the parliamentary members not to be cheated by the warlords or fooled by the latters' ostensible interest in protection of the constitution.

In the reorganization of the Military Government, the grand marshal system was replaced by a seven-man committee. On May 20 the members of the Extraordinary Parliament elected Sun Yat-sen, T'ang Shao-i, Wu T'ing-fang, Ch'en Ch'un-hsüan, Lu Jung-t'ing, T'ang Chi-yao, and Lin Pao-i as the committee members of the Military Government. On August 21 Ch'en Ch'un-hsüan was elected executive chairman of the committee. Thus the Political Study Group scored a great success.

The choice of the committee members appears to be fair because Sun Yat-sen was not excluded from the reorganized Military Government; T'ang Shao-i and Wu T'ing-fang were Kwangtung leaders, while Lin Pao-i was the navy leader. But in reality the center, of gravity was entirely in the Kwangsi clique, because T'ang Chi-yao could not attend the meetings from Yunnan; nor could T'ang Shao-i and Sun Yat-sen do so from Shanghai; Ch'en Ch'un-hsüan became a figurehead. Therefore only the remaining members of the Kwangsi clique dominated the power of the Military Government, with the members of the Political Study Group as its henchmen.

In Shanghai Sun Yat-sen made preparations to reorganize his Revolutionary Party and at the same time wrote a book which he hoped would be influential in China. This was called *Sun Wen's Political Theory* [*Sun Wen hsüeh-shuo*]. Although Sun's activity in the Military Government had failed for the time being, the Kuomintang was hereby given a renewed vigor.

THE PEACE CONFERENCE BETWEEN NORTH AND SOUTH CHINA

A peace conference between the South and North convened in

February 1919. The reorganization of the Military Government in the South, and the election of Hsü Shih-ch'ang as president in the North, paved the way for these peace negotiations. Nevertheless, the election of Hsü Shih-ch'ang partly facilitated the peace talks and partly impeded the prospective peace. The position of President Hsü himself became a problem in the peace conference.

The harbinger of peace was Wu P'ei-fu, who on August 21 when Ch'en Ch'un-hsüan was elected chairman of the Military Government issued a circular telegram from Hengchow advocating the end of civil war. Nine days later, Ch'en Ch'un-hsüan replied and seconded Wu's motion.

At this time the New Parliament in North China was ready to elect a new president because Feng Kuo-chang was to complete his term on October 10. On the day after the reply was sent to Wu P'ei-fu, Ch'en Ch'un-hsüan dispatched another circular telegram in the name of the Military Government denying the right of the New Parliament to elect a president. Nevertheless, in spite of the objections of South China, the New Parliament convened in the North proceeded to elect Hsü Shih-ch'ang the new president.

On September 26 the army officers on both sides of the battle front of Hunan issued another telegram urging prompt restoration of peace, an action approved by the Military Government, but regarded as rebellious by Tuan's clique in the North. The latter, however, could do nothing against the army officers at the front, except continue its organization of the War Participation Army, with the hope that the insurgents could be dealt with in the future. (The war participation loan was signed formally on September 28.)

The Elections of President and Vice-President in the North

Since the New Parliament was controlled by the An-fu faction, how was it possible for Hsü Shih-ch'ang, a native of Chihli, to be elected president? And why was Tuan not elected? Because Tuan was favored neither by public opinion nor by the Communications Clique in the new parliament, many people suggested that both Feng and Tuan retire. Hsü Shih-ch'ang, one of the elders among the Peiyang warlords, had maintained a neutral attitude in the feud between Feng and Tuan. Moreover, he was gentle and amicable by nature and his election to the high position might help to solve the strife between Feng and Tuan as well as the war between the South and the North. Since a number of parliamentary members of the Communications Clique maintained such hope, Tuan's following thought that so long as Tuan held the War Participation Army in his hand as a weapon, the election of Hsü would not do him much harm. Tuan acknowledged the opinion of the Communications Clique. It seems clear that the election of Hsü as president by the An-fu faction was an effort to get rid of Feng, while the election of Hsü by the Communications Clique did show some intention of unifying China.

It was now time for the vice-president to be elected. On October 9 a meeting for the elections was held, but for several reasons it reached no conclusion. North China wished to keep this position for an important figure of South China as a bargaining point for the peace negotiations, but the Southerners were not primarily interested in the vice-presidency. The Military Government, which considered the election of Hsü illegal, declared that the president's office was vacant and that the Military Government in the South could temporarily exercise the authority of the president. After the inauguration of Hsü Shih-ch'ang as president, however, an impulse toward peace within and without China suddenly accelerated.

Foreigners Urge Peace in China

The international situation itself, especially after the end of the European War in November 1918, created pressure for peace in China. Woodrow Wilson cabled President Hsü his congratulations, bidding him influence the various leaders in the parliament to work for an early unification. President Wilson also ordered the American minister to give counsel to President Hsü, and the American consul general at Canton to persuade the Military Government to bring about unification and peace in China. The governments of the allied powers of England and France ordered their ministers to Peking to deliver strong protests against the fact that China had participated in the war in name only and that the Peking government had only delayed payment for the Boxer indemnity and used the money for selfish strife among various political factions. This protest dealt a severe blow to the Tuan clique.

When the Terauchi cabinet in Japan was dissolved and succeeded by that of Hara Takashi, the Military Government commissioned Chang Shih-chao to go to Japan and request the new premier to change the previous pro-Tuan policy. Because of Western disapproval of Japanese interference in China, Japan's formerly strong pro-Tuan policy became somewhat altered, and another blow was suffered by Tuan's clique.

Ch'ien Neng-hsün succeeded Tuan as premier and on November 23 sent a telegram directly to Ch'en Ch'un-hsüan to resolve the dilemma between the South and the North. On the same day, venerable political leaders, Hsiung Hsi-ling, Chang Chien, Ts'ai Yüan-p'ei, Wang Ch'ung-hui, and more than twenty others sent a telegram sponsoring an Association to Promote Peace. In response to this request, various groups expressed their desire for peace. President Hsü Shih-ch'ang, accordingly, issued an order for a truce. However, the peace conference which was to be held in Shanghai, with the delegation from the North headed by Chu Ch'i-ch'ien and that from the South by T'ang Shao-i, was not to open until February 1919.

The Peace Conference at Shanghai, 1919

The belated opening of the peace conference was caused by two knotty problems: one was that of a truce in Shensi, where independence had been declared in the early spring of 1918. The Northern government was attempting to have that area excluded from the zone of truce, but this plan was rejected by the Southern authorities. The other problem involved the disbanding of the War Participation Army, and prohibiting the use for military purposes of the money borrowed from Japan. Although the European War had been concluded, Tuan still continued to use this money to train his army. Furthermore, according to his agreement with Japan, a large number of Japanese officers were being used to train Chinese soldiers. The Southwest China authorities demanded that the Sino-Japanese Military Agreement and the War Participation Army be abolished and that no more borrowed funds be used by the Peking government; the latter did not comply with the demands. These two problems deferred the opening of the peace conference at Shanghai for a long time even though the representatives for both sides had long since arrived.

Later on, through the efforts of the tuchun of Kiangsu a compromise was reached by which the truce would include the area of Shensi. With the first problem solved, the peace meeting was opened formally on February 28. Immediately T'ang Shao-i moved that the military agreement with Japan be abolished, the War Participation Army be disbanded, and the loans be discontinued. In addition, he moved that all diplomatic documents concerning the military agreement with Japan should be sent to the peace conference for investigation; the motion was passed by the participants of the conference and accepted by Chu Ch'i-ch'en, the representative of the North. But when the two chief delegates of both parties sent a joint telegram to the Peking government asking it to accede to the agreement, Peking ignored the whole matter, although it did agree to send the four documents concerning the military alliance to the peace conference. As a further insult, this government even announced a new document, a prolongation of the military cooperation with Japan, signed by Hsü Shu-cheng on February 5 at a time when the peace conference was already in preparation.

This new document was a scheme by the Japanese to compel China to sign the forthcoming peace treaty in Paris. Concerning the Shantung problem, Japan had arrived at a secret understanding long ago with the allied powers, which allowed Japan to succeed to the rights and privileges of Germany in that province. But Tuan, whose only desire was to keep an iron hold on his military power, was ignorant of the trap set by Japan. The announcement by the Peking government of the new Sino-Japanese agreement showed that the requests of South China, agreed upon at the peace meeting, would not be accepted. Fearing criticism by the Southerners, the Peking government changed the name of the War Participation Army to the National Defense Army, utilizing the new name as a shield for the expansion of its military force. Needless to say, this new maneuver greatly enraged the Southern representative.

Just at this moment, the Southern representative received reports that Northern forces were attacking Shensi and that the military situation was very grave. T'ang Shao-i accordingly addressed a strong inquiry to the Northern representative, demanding a reply within forty-eight hours and stating that if there were no answer he would interpret that as an indication that the Peking government had no desire for peace.

The Northern representative wired the inquiry to the Peking government, which in turn refused to reply. T'ang Shao-i interpreted this as a clear indication that the Northern delegation lacked the power to represent the Peking government, and on March 2 a telegram was dispatched announcing the suspension of peace negotiations. Immediately afterward the Northern delegate tendered his resignation.

Final Breakdown of the Peace Conference

After this suspension it took more than a month for all circles to work out a mediation and compromise. Subsequently, the three tuchuns of the middle Yangtze Valley and the division commander Wu P'ei-fu in

Hengchow sent a telegram to the delegations of the South and the North asking for a real truce in Shensi in order once more to resume the negotiations. Along with this came a report from Shensi indicating that warfare had actually been stopped. Now the peace talks were resumed.

For the agenda, proposals introduced by the Southern delegation included cancellation of the military agreement with Japan, the abrogation of the office for national defense and its special troops, the liquidation of the War Participation Loan, the free exercise of authority by the parliament, the joint use by North and South of the war loans for reconstruction purposes, and the rehabilitation of Shensi and Hunan. On the agenda, at the suggestion of the Northern delegation, were rather vaguely stated measures concerning the reduction of the army in the whole nation, the separation of civil and military governments, local self-government, the development of the national economy, and rehabilitation loans.

The first three proposals made by the Southern delegation received support from the public, but had they been accepted, they would have affected the very life of the Tuan military clique which controlled the Northern participants at the conference. The parliamentary problem also proved a great stumbling block because the split between the North and South was supposed to be over the illegal dissolution of the parliament. Obviously, the Southern delegation must insist on the restoration of the Old Parliament despite the fact that public opinion was indifferent to the problem; but actually, not only the Tuan military clique but even Hsü Shih-ch'ang could not tolerate the restoration, since to do so would jeopardize his own position.

But far more acute than these surface difficulties were the political frictions involved in the allotment of lucrative and powerful positions to the various political factions in the Southern and Northern governments. These frictions, which of course were never publicly discussed, agitated the entire peace conference and prevented any kind of reconciliation.

Early in May the news of the European peace conference reached China. Now the results of the secret agreement signed by Tuan's government with Japan expressing China's "happy concurrence" with Japan's succession to Germany's rights in Shantung became all too clear. China's request for the return of that province received a complete rebuff. The consequent general indignation in China resulted in the famous May Fourth Movement of 1919, led by students in Peking. On this day some three thousand students paraded in Peking as a mass protest against the Shantung decision and the presence in Peking of three pro-Japanese traitors, Lu Tsung-yü, who arranged the war loans with Japan, Ts'ao Ju-ling, minister of communications, and Chang Tsung-hsiang, Chinese minister to Japan—all protégés of Tuan Ch'i-jui. Ts'ao's residence, where the three "traitors" happened to be, was set afire.

Students in other cities soon organized unions and further demonstrations to express their opinions on current affairs. The May Fourth parade marked the beginning of students' movements in modern China.

T'ang Shao-i, availing himself of the strong anti-Tuan atmosphere, suddenly introduced several demands in the agenda of the Peace Conference held on May 13. These demands included: (1) The Shanghai peace conference was to refuse to acknowledge Japan as the successor of German rights in Shantung as had been decided by the Paris peace conference; (2) All secret treaties between China and Japan should be declared null and void, and the treaty makers punished; (3) The War Participation Army, or the National Defense Army, or any other similar army was to be disbanded; and (4) All unpopular or notably corrupt tuchuns or governors were to be dismissed.

These items were presented without the knowledge of some members from the South (for among the Southern delegates, as among the Northern ones, there was little harmony or coordinated action) T'ang Shao-i himself was so pessimistic that there appeared to be no possibility at all of making any progress in the peace conference. After a short meeting the two delegations asked for dismissal from their respective governments.

The Peking government, however, wished to discuss the first of T'ang's items although it defiantly rejected the rest. Not only were the resignations of its delegation readily accepted but all delegates were ordered to leave Shanghai immediately for Peking in order to demonstrate absolute severance from the negotiations. Although the Military Government did not approve of the resignation of its delegates, and announced the determination of the South to continue with the peace attempt, there was really no hope of reopening the peace conference; the break this time was final.

Deterioration After the Conference, 1919-1920

After the breakdown of the peace conference the American minister to Peking invited the ministers of England, France, Japan, and Italy to give advice to both South and North China on June 5. President Hsü Shih-ch'ang undoubtedly favored peace, but he was powerless against the arrogance of Tuan's clique. Chu Ch'i-ch'ien was determined to have nothing to do with the peace negotiations. Even though he had the title of sole plenipotentiary for the Northern government, he was completely controlled by the clique and had no actual power to represent the government. Ch'en Neng-hsün's cabinet in the Peking government was also dissolved. Kung Hsin-chan was made acting premier, but the cabinet still remained under the control of the An-fu faction.

On June 24 Hsü Shu-cheng was appointed commissioner to plan for defense of the northwestern frontier, and concurrently was made commander in chief for defense of the northwestern frontier. The War Participation Army and the National Defense Army were then changed into the Frontier Defense Army. On July 24 the Office of War Participation Affairs was converted into the Office of Frontier Defense

Affairs. Tuan Ch'i-jui was appointed director of frontier affairs.

Wang I-t'ang was made chief representative for peace negotiations on August 12. Wang, speaker of the house of representatives of the so-called New Parliament in the North, also was the head of the An-fu Club and a henchman of Hsü Shu-cheng. Both the military government of South China and the Chihli military clique were violently opposed to this appointment. Wu P'ei-fu wired the Peking government of his disapproval of Wang, whose appointment as chief representative signified lack of sincerity in negotiating for peace. On September 5 the Military Government informed the Peking regime that Wang I-t'ang would not be accepted as the chief representative, and that another man must be appointed; the Peking government did not comply with the request. As a result, most of the representatives of the South and North absented themselves from the peace meeting.

From the autumn of 1919 to the autumn of the following year peace negotiations hung on by a thread. During this time the Peking government, taking advantage of the internal disagreements of the various factions in the Southwest, tried to negotiate directly with the Military Government, or to reach an independent compromise with this or that province in the Southwest. In addition it also utilized the lack of unity among the various Northern factions by attempting agreements with first one faction and then another. But all these attempts were futile. Finally the war between Chihli and Anhwei in the North was fomented, and the war to bar the return of the Cantonese troops to Canton also broke out in the South.

The primary cause of the failure of the peace conference between the North and the South was Tuan's overbearing military clique, which received so much support from Japan that it insisted on using military power to subdue all rivals. Another reason was Hsü Shih-ch'ang's unwillingness to lose his position as president. So long as the New Parliament existed, members of the Old Parliament, now in the South, could not recover power in the North.

Another fundamental block against the reunion of the South and the North was the inability of the two parties to work honestly. The "destruction" of the constitution by the Northern authorities was certainly wrong, and the protection of the constitution by the Southern authorities was not sincere. Militarists and politicians of the two parties merely fought for territory and personal rights. It was too much to hope, given the selfishness of the people involved, that the good of the country could be served.

THE OVERTHROW OF TUAN'S CLIQUE

Factions in both the South and the North tried to make alliances. A Kwangsi clique of the South openly essayed an alliance with the Chihli faction in the North; the Tuan clique also plotted to ally the force of Yunnan and Kwangtung to attack the Kwangsi clique. But none of these plots could be carried through. In the summer and autumn of 1920 Tuan's power was wiped out during the war between Chihli and Anhwei; and the Military Government was also dissolved as a result of the war over the return of the Cantonese troops to Canton.

The last stronghold of Tuan's power was the New Parliament under the control of the An-fu clique and the War Participation Army (now the Frontier Defense Army). As a result of pressure brought by Hsü, the government of Outer Mongolia on November 2, 1919, rescinded its previous declaration of autonomy and announced its willingness to be controlled temporarily by Hsü Shu-cheng. Hsü and his An-fu Club now became even more overbearing, and the acting premier, Kung Hsin-chan, who could not endure any more pressure from the group, resigned. The premiership was given on September 24, 1919, to Chin Yün-p'eng; the new cabinet remained under An-fu influence. Even the premier, who was concurrently minister of war, could not interfere at all with the Frontier

Defense Army. From September 1919 to the middle of May in the following year the premier tendered four resignations.

Hsü Shu-cheng's cheerful satisfaction with his predominant position in Outer Mongolia actually brought about his failure in Northern China. Heretofore Hsü's power had been not only in his War Participation Army but also in the warlord of Fengtien, Chang Tso-lin. Chang's power had been fostered by Hsü, who had used Chang to compel Feng Kuo-chang by asking the Fengtien troops to enter Shanhaikwan toward Peking; and there- after, the Fengtien army became strong. While Hsü was enjoying his power in Outer Mongolia, Chang Tso-lin began to nurture ill feeling because he considered the Mongolian frontier the sphere of influence of the Fengtien Army. As Hsü's satisfaction increased, the more jealous and displeased Chang became, and he gradually attempted to do away with Hsü's power. Furthermore, in the moves against Tuan Ch'i-jui, leaders of the Chihli group not only tried for an understanding with the Kwangsi clique, but also approached Chang Tso-lin in Fengtien province so as to form a large-scale alliance to overthrow Tuan.

Meanwhile, as a token of compromise with the South, the Military Government supplied $1,000,000 (one source says $600,000) for the army rations of Wu P'ei-fu, asking Wu to withdraw his troops to the North and give up the defense line in southern Hunan so that the Southern troops would be free to expel the Hunan governor, Chang Ching-yao. Although Chang had been appointed by the Peking government, the position of tuchun of Hunan had been long coveted by Wu Kuang-hsin, Tuan's relative. Tuan wished to put his relative in this position in order to threaten Ts'ao K'un, tuchun of Chihli. Discerning the peril, Ts'ao K'un organized an alliance of eight provinces including the tuchuns of Chihli, Kiangsu, Kiangsi, Hupeh, Honan (the five provinces of the Chihli faction), and the tuchuns of the three provinces in Manchuria under the sphere of the Fengtien clique. Thus the alliance of the Chihli and Fengtien factions was formed. Chin Yün-p'eng, anticipating a great change in the political situation, resigned from the premiership on the fourteenth of May.

General Wu P'ei-fu, who had withdrawn from Hengchow in March 1920, took his troops to Wuchang on May 31, where he received supplies and financial support from the tuchun of Hupeh. Thence Wu distributed his troops to garrison strategic areas in Honan and Chihli along the Peking-Hankow Railway. He had made a secret agreement with the Canton government long before, and let the territory withdrawn by his soldiers be taken over quickly by Southern troops. Within a short time Hunan was largely occupied by native forces under the control of the Canton government, except for those of Feng Yü-hsiang, a subordinate of General Wu. Feng still stayed at Changteh in western Hunan, to watch the troops of Wu Kuang-hsin stationed at the frontier, Hsin-ti, between Hunan and Hupeh.

Chang Tso-lin went from Fengtien to Peking to have an interview with President Hsü Shih-ch'ang on June 19. After two days, he paid Tuan Ch'i-jui a visit. On the twenty-second, he went to Paoting to see Ts'ao K'un under the pretense of offering to be a mediator for the two parties, although actually he went to join the anti-Tuan movement. President Hsü dismissed Hsü Shu-cheng on July 4 from his duties with the northwestern frontier and the Frontier Army. This army was ordered to be under the control of the minister of war. Chang Tso-lin returned to Fengtien on the seventh and was ready to mobilize his troops.

Tuan's Army Crushed

Tuan Ch'i-jui, much disturbed by President Hsü's order of the fourth which deprived Hsü Shu-cheng of military power, summoned a military conference in his office to reorganize the Frontier Defense Army into the National Pacification Army [*Ting-kuo-chün*], of which he was the commander in chief. This newly converted army was to be used to fight against the power of Ts'ao K'un and Wu P'ei-fu. Tuan then coerced the president into dismissing Ts'ao and Wu, saying, "For the maintenance of order and discipline of the government, I must conduct a punitive expedition against them." Hsü Shih-ch'ang permitted Ts'ao to stay in office, at least for the time being; but these summary dismissals initiated the war between the Chihli and the Anhwei cliques.

When the two parties were about to fight, public opinion of the whole nation was sympathetic with Wu P'ei-fu and was concerned with Wu's lot. Because Tuan's so-called National Pacification Army was trained by many Japanese, people believed that Tuan's military power should be much superior to that of Ts'ao K'un. On July 10 Ts'ao K'un sent a letter to the Legation Quarter listing all the evidence to prove that Japan was supporting Tuan. Since England, the United States, and other nations had long been displeased by Japan's action in China and were no longer occupied in a European war, Japan showed some apprehension with regard to international public opinion. Even though Japan still supported Tuan confidentially, on July 14 the Japanese minister declared that his nation did not support Tuan.

Meanwhile on July 12 Ts'ao K'un and Chang Tso-lin issued a joint telegram declaring their intention of fighting against Tuan, and the Fengtien army had already entered Shanhaikwan. On the fourteenth the actual fighting began. Within five days (July 14-18) Tuan's National Pacification Army was crushed at Tso-chow, Liu-li-ho, and other points along the Peking-Hankow Railway where the Fengtien troops also participated.

In self-punishment, Tuan Ch'i-jui asked the president to deprive him of all his government and military positions as well as his ranks. The president complied on July 28 with Tuan's request and, with the official degradation of Tuan as a warning, the three state ministers of the Anhwei clique fled. By August Tuan's faction was completely liquidated. Chin Yün-p'eng was called to reorganize the cabinet on August 9, and the war between the Chihli and the Anhwei cliques came to an end.

DISSOLUTION OF THE MILITARY GOVERNMENT IN SOUTH CHINA

While the war was going on in the North, the domestic dissension in the South among the members of the Military Government was accelerating. The Kwangsi militarists and the Political Study Group hoped to reconcile themselves with the Northern warlords; they had no intention of preserving the Old Parliament. Sun Yat-sen and his following, on the contrary, took the Old Parliament as the fundamental basis for a campaign for "protection of the constitution." Sun was disgusted with the Kwangsi military clique for its lack of sincerity and was displeased with the Political Study Group for its surrender to the warlords.

After the reorganization of the Military Government, the Political Study Group was the center of gravity in Southwestern politics. The unsuccessful job-seeking politicians of other factions tried to sow dissension in all groups.

Apart from the competition of political factions with each other, there was another war going on between Kwangtung and Kwangsi. "Kwangtung for the natives" was the slogan used in the attack on the Kwangsi clique. Although the latter did employ some Cantonese, those employed had to be willing to take orders from Kwangsi superiors. In June 1919 when the peace conference between South and North was broken off, a great storm arose over the contest for the governorship of Kwangtung, which the Cantonese wished to have filled by Wu T'ing-fang. The disapproval of the Kwangsi clique, however, resulted in the appointment of Yang Yung-t'ai, also a Cantonese, but an influential member of the Political Study Group.

Sun Yat-sen did not participate in the reorganized Military Government except by delegating someone on his behalf. On August 1919 he formally asked to resign his position. On October 4 T'ang Shao-i resigned his position as chief representative for peace negotiations. The Military Government was disintegrating.

The Political Study Group attempted to insure its power in the Military Government by allying other factions in the Old Parliament in the South as its supporters and relying on Li Ken-yüan, who commanded a large number of Yunnan troops in Kwangtung. Ever since the peace conference, the parliamentary members of the middle wing had been aware of the intention of the Political Study Group to associate itself with the politicians in the North; hence, this middle wing joined the left wing. The Political Study Group then lost its control over the parliament. Its protector Li Ken-yüan was also lost, because the Yunnan and Kwangsi factions were split and the parliament was moved from Kwangtung to Yunnan.

Parliamentary Troubles in Kwangtung

The Old Parliament in Canton at no time had enough members to make up a quorum; for this reason it was called the Extraordinary Parliament. In June 1918 it was planned that those parliamentary members who were not present one month after the convention would be dismissed and replaced by new candidates. Nevertheless, the dismissal of parliamentary members must be voted by more than half of the total numbers. Since the attendance of members in the parliament was less than half, the dismissal could not be legal either. Even so, the dismissal and replacement method was forced through, and by September 1918 a quorum was available and a formal parliament convened.

The constitution committee continued to investigate the unfinished draft of the constitution. During the peace negotiations between the South and the North in 1919 many parliamentary members had left Canton. When the members returned in November, the constitution committee resumed its work in November 1919.

This parliament, which had neither the confidence of the people nor a legal basis, would have had no authority to enforce any constitution that it might have passed. The members of the Political Study Group, fearing that a constitution produced under such conditions would bar the possibilities of a peaceful compromise between the South and the North, used various methods to impede the work of the constitution committee. They used the filibuster against the organization of the local government, the authority of the provincial governor, and other similar questions. Later on they refrained from attending the parliament, thus making the constitution committee unable to hold a legal meeting. On January 24, 1920, permanent suspension of the constitution committee was announced.

The Kwangsi military clique considered this Kwangtung parliament an obstacle against any compromise between the South and the North. On the pretence of financial difficulties, no maintenance fee was given to the parliamentary members, who therefore cherished ill feeling against the Kwangsi clique. When Yunnan and Kwangsi were at loggerheads in March 1920, the left-wing parliamentary members wished to make a living by working under the Yunnan militarists. Accordingly, the parliament was moved to that province.

The Move to Yunnan

Thereafter, Wu T'ing-fang also left Canton, and only three out of the seven executives of the Military Government remained. Sun Yat-sen, T'ang Shao-i, Wu T'ing-fang, and a majority of the parliamentary members formed a united front and declared that they would move the Military Government to Yunnan too.

The Political Study Group and the Kwangsi military clique tried in May to appoint substitutes to the Canton executive committee. Sun Yat-sen, T'ang Shao-i, and others declared that since the executives of the Military Government could not make a quorum, all the new ordinances of the Canton military government should be invalid.

At this time, Wu P'ei-fu had withdrawn his troops and the Hunan army had occupied Changsha. Tuan Ch'i-jui took this opportunity to make secret connections with T'ang Chi-yao of Yunnan and also to make a friendly show to Sun Yat-sen. For a quick overturn of the Kwangsi military power and a prompt seizure of Canton as a revolutionary base, Sun Yat-sen tried his best to associate with Tuan. The latter was not successful in his plan of alliance with the Yunnan authorities, but he reached a compromise with some Cantonese troops quartered in southern Fukien. Li Hou-chi, tuchun of Fukien, was under Tuan's influence and supplied Ch'en Hsiung-ming's Cantonese troops with rations to make them move back to Canton.

War Throughout South and North, 1920

These homesick soldiers started the war between Kwangtung and Kwangsi in August 1920. During the preceding three years the Kwangsi troops, who had accumulated a great deal of money in the rich province of Kwangtung, had greatly deteriorated in discipline and training. Consequently, they were rather quickly driven out of Kwangtung. Near the end of October the Military Government was automatically dissolved.

The war between the Chihli and the Anhwei factions in the North had broken out in July 1920; that between Kwangtung and Kwangsi troops occurred in August. Near the end of May, Hsiung K'o-wu of Szechwan had fought against T'ang Chi-yao of Yunnan. Later on, there was domestic dissension in the Szechwan army itself. The Yunnan army returned to its home province, waged war, and drove T'ang Chi-yao away. Liu Hsien-shih, tuchun of Kweichow, was also expelled by the commander in chief of the Kweichow army in November 1920. In short, in the latter part of 1920, not only was the Military Government dissolved, but also all the Southwestern provinces, which had been fighting under the name of Constitutional Protection, were split with dissensions.

In North China, after the collapse of the Anhwei clique, a contest developed between the Fengtien and the Chihli cliques; and the war between these two was much more severe than that between Chihli and Anhwei. Thereafter China entered a period of chaotic fighting among all warlords in both South and North China. The constitutional protection movement was replaced by another movement called Self-government in Provinces under a Federal Government [*Lien-sheng tzu-chih*]. That is to say, the hope for national unification was given up and was replaced by efforts to create a federal government through an association of independent provinces.

CHAPTER THIRTEEN A FEDERAL GOVERNMENT MOVEMENT AND MELEE AMONG THE WARLORDS

After the wars between the Anhwei and Chihli cliques in the North and the return of the Kwangtung troops to their native province in the South, both South and North China became arenas for competing warlords. Though neither South nor North China had the strength to unify the entire nation, some leaders hoped that through a loosely unified confederation the chaotic warfare of the warlords might be controlled.

But while the movement for a federal government was under way, dogged warfare was also being carried on. Some warlords favored federal government; others were much against it; a few others sincerely worked for the unification of the nation. Those who opposed the federal system believed that only their military power could unify the country, while those who supported it merely took it as a shield to justify their occupation of various territories. The term "federal government," no matter how often it was shouted, proved no match for the noise made by the warlords' artillery.

From 1921 to 1922 in addition to a number of small fights there were many major wars: in central China there was a war to rescue Hupeh during the summer and autumn of 1921; in the North, the first war between the Feng-tien and Chihli cliques; and in the South, a war between Sun and Ch'en. Both these latter wars occurred in the summer of 1922. By 1923 the Military Government in South China was re-established; and in North China, Ts'ao K'un had usurped the presidency. Likelihood of unification was far, far away.

After 1920, except for the left-wing Kuomintang, which was preparing for reorganization, the political factions lost all semblance of being political parties. Attaching themselves to powerful warlords in order to secure lucrative positions, individual sycophantic politicians spread rumors inciting further degrading struggles. Not until the spring of 1924, when the reorganization of the Kuomintang was completed, did any new hope appear in Chinese politics.

THE FEDERAL GOVERNMENT MOVEMENT

The Federalist Movement Before 1920

The movement for federal government, which did not become popular until after 1920, did not occur by accident. The vastness of China and the complexity within the provinces provided fertile soil for the seeds of a federal system. During the reform movement of 1898 the leaders of the Constitutional Party, as well as the Revolutionary Party, already cherished the idea. Liang Ch'i-ch'ao in 1900 wrote a treatise on Rousseau in which he concluded that if a large nation, imitating the Swiss federal system, should divide itself into a number of small autonomous states with a central federal government over all, then the nation would be strong and the people free. Liang was of the opinion that even each city within a province should be a single unit and have its own law based upon local custom but that a federal government should always be above the various local units.

In the Revolutionary Party paper the *People's Tribune* [*Min-pao*] an article suggested that the final goal of the Revolutionary Party was to establish a republican federal government similar to the republic of France or the federal government of the United States.

In 1911 the plan for federal government was made even clearer by the Shantung declaration of independence in which the provincial parliament made eight demands of the Manchu regime. Four of these were: (1) The constitution of the central government should clearly indicate that China was to be a federal government. (2) The government organization and local tax should be decided by this province without any interference from the government. (3) The regulations of the provincial assemblies should become the constitution of this province and should be made or amended by the local government. (4) The province should have freedom to train soldiers for self-protection.

The preamble to the regulations concerning the organization of the revolutionary provisional government clearly stated that "the system of the federal government of the United States of America should be the model of our nation in the future" and that the selection of representatives should be based on the provinces as units. Furthermore, the regulations of the provisional government organization should be passed by the provincial representatives, and the provisional president should be elected by them, with each province limited to one vote. The idea of a federal government appears to have been predominant even at the beginning of the revolution.

But after the establishment of the provisional government and for the sake of unification, the federal government system gave way to the concentration of power within a central government. When Yüan Shih-k'ai was the major power of China, all the provinces were under the control of the Peiyang military clique, the Kuomintang had been almost entirely destroyed, and the Progressive Party was unable to act. Progressive Party members then suddenly began to advocate self-government in all the provinces, and discussions of the federal government system by leading scholars like Chang Tung-sun and Chang Shih-chao appeared in influential magazines.

But the real purpose of those advocates of a federal government was to protest against the unrestricted power of Yüan Shih-k'ai. Using the federal system as a wedge, they tried to open up a field of activity for themselves as well as to stir up anti-Yüan sentiments. With the death of Yüan Shih-k'ai, the federal government movement promptly disintegrated—or appeared to do so. Federalist theories continued to be favored by some members of the Kuomintang.

In 1916 and 1917 Kuomintang members wanted a clear statement in the constitution that the governor of a province must be elected by the people; the Progressive Party, on the other hand, opposed popular elections of governors and objected to any statement in the constitution regarding the provincial system. Later on, the Association of Tuchuns, incited by Progressive Party members, announced their objection to any interference with the constitution on the grounds that the Kuomintang parliamentary members by advocating a federal system wanted to destroy national unification.

Revival of Federalism in the 1920's

Because the second dissolution of the parliament was followed by the War for the Protection of the Constitution and the feud between Feng and Tuan, people began seriously to question the possibility of concentration of power in the central government by force. Hsiung Hsi-ling, in particular, now began to campaign for a federal system as the only feasible system of government.

A new tide of discussion of the federal system, pro and con, appeared in periodicals. Li Chien-nung published two articles on the problem of China's unification in the *Pacific Magazine* [*T'ai-p'ing-yang tsa-chih*] Nos. 8-9. In the first article he pointed out that the lack of unification in China was the result of the abuse of power in the central government, and that the adoption of a federal government would serve to achieve unity. In the second article he maintained that the failure to distinguish civil from military rule was also a result of the concentration of power in the central government and that there was now only military rule and no civil authority. Having set out a thorough exposition of the advantages and disadvantages of a federal government system, Li hoped that the term "federal government" would no longer be distasteful to the people. Before and during the prolonged peace meetings, however, few people paid much attention to the federal system. After the peace meetings failed and the Military Government in the South was dissolved and full-scale war developed between the Anhwei and Chihli factions the federal government slogan once more became popular.

The purpose of this movement in the early 1920's for a federal government system was twofold. First, it permitted each province self-government and the power to make its own constitution and to manage its domestic affairs, with which neither the central nor other provincial governments could interfere. In this way it was expected that the Pan-Yunnan-ism and Pan-Kwangsi-ism could be barred. The other purpose was to permit a new constitution to be made by provincial representatives for the federal government, so that war between the South and the North for the protection of the constitution might be ended. Military power was to be concentrated in the central government in order to avoid the occupation of territory by warlords.

Unfortunately, only the members of the Progressive Party and some of the old Kuomintang members both understood and supported the movement. The military leaders of Hunan did campaign for a confederation, and they were seconded by the militarists of Szechwan, Yunnan, Kweichow, Kwangsi, and Kwangtung. These powerful militarists supported confederation because they enjoyed their independence and their control of territory. For this reason Sun Yat-sen and his close associates were fearful of the federal movement.

From the latter half of 1920 to 1924 the term "federal government" was often heard, but the only result was a short-lived provincial constitution made in Hunan. Unified federal government remained a dream.

The Constitution of Hunan, 1922

Since Hunan was the spearhead in the federal government

movement, its provincial constitution needs some discussion. The War for the Protection of the Constitution occurred first in that province, where the people, resenting the greed of Chang Ching-yao and the misbehavior of his troops, were roused to demand self-government. No sooner had Wu P'ei-fu withdrawn his troops than the Hunanese arose unanimously to expel Chang Ching-yao. After Chang's flight, they set up their flag of self-government and also proclaimed themselves free from any further involvement in political affrays between the South and the North. No permission was given to the soldiers of either side to pass through that province.

At that time, T'an Yen-k'ai, commander in chief of the Hunan army, was in charge of all political and military affairs of the province. On July 22, 1920, came his announcement of the proposed self-government for Hunan, immediately echoed and applauded by eminent Hunanese residing in Peking and Shanghai. But in November T'an was compelled by his own subordinates to leave the provincial capital. Chao Heng-t'i succeeded him as commander in chief and Lin Chih-yü, elected governor by the provincial assembly, formally declared the independence of Hunan as a self-governing province.

A constitution for Hunan was prepared by a committee of thirteen experts invited by the governor, who agreed not to interfere with the work. After the draft was completed, 150 delegates, elected by the people from each of the districts, formed a committee to examine and revise the draft constitution. After this, the text was announced to the public, and each item was to be voted upon by the citizens.

The procedure for making the constitution was strict, but the knowledge of the people at large was too limited for passing any judgment; the referendum was only a formality. After much needless harangue and unnecessary minor alterations by the committee, the document was voted upon in November by the citizens; it was proclaimed on January 1, 1922.

Two points in the constitution of Hunan are noteworthy. The first was a list of the rights of the province. Since it was expected that Hunan would be under a federal government, it was deemed necessary to make a clear demarcation of rights between the central and the provincial government. The second point was the extension of civil rights to both men and women. A governor was to be selected by popular vote of the citizens of the whole province, who in turn were to enjoy the right of initiative, referendum, and impeachment. These ideas were very advanced for China at that time, but the people at large could hardly appreciate them. The provincial assembly was given great power; and the provincial cabinet, which consisted of seven ministers, was responsible to the provincial assembly.

Influenced by Hunan, other provinces also tried to create their own constitutions, but none was ever put into practice because the warlords would not enforce the constitutions for fear that their actions would be restricted by such formal documents. Only one province, Hunan, was actually administered according to the provincial constitution, and this for only three years. Even this rare exception was a constitutional government in name only. When the nationalist revolutionary army entered Hunan in 1926, the constitutional government of Hunan ceased to function.

THE WAR FOR THE RESCUE OF HUPEH

The movement for self-government in Hunan purported to be a shield to keep this province independent of the political struggle between South and North. During the process of making their own constitution, why, then, did this province have to fight for the rescue of Hupeh? Since the causes are complicated and the war not only affected the two provinces of Hunan and Hupeh but also served to expand the power of General Wu P'ei-fu, they should be carefully explained.

Hupeh, a pivotal spot in the upper valley of the Yangtze, had fallen into the hands of Wang Chan-yüan, a Peiyang warlord who had quartered in that province as a division commander since 1913. He was promoted in 1916 to be tuchun of Hupeh, a position he held until 1921. After the war between the Anhwei and Chihli cliques, Wang was promoted to be inspecting commissioner of Hupeh and Hunan; actually he could not inspect the latter province. He was, moreover, a person of little talent who had accumulated wealth from the rich province and suppressed insurrections; other than this he accomplished nothing. He even neglected the provisioning and discipline of his troops, who mutinied in many cities. The people of Hupeh hated Wang intensely.

At the beginning of the movement for provincial constitutions, the people of Hupeh availed themselves of this opportunity to get rid of Wang under the slogans, "Self-government for Hupeh" and "Government by Natives." Since most of the soldiers in that province belonged to the National Defense Corps of the Peiyang clique, it would be impossible to expel Wang unless some aid came from the neighboring province of Hunan.

Anhwei and Chihli Factions in Hupeh

From the domestic condition of Hunan another cause of the Hupeh war may be adduced. After the expulsion of Chang Ching-yao and the beginning of preparations for the provincial constitution, the number of troops was beyond the ability of the provincial treasury to sustain. Furthermore, the various commanders were collecting taxes from the people within their jurisdiction and depriving the provincial treasury of any income. Since some areas were richer than others, the commanders of the poorer zones frequently demanded military rations from the provincial income. Self-government in this province served only as window dressing. The army officers spoke for self-government while at the same time they planned to expand their influence outside the province. If the natives of

Hupeh did not ask for help from the Hunanese, the latter would be unable to expand. Hunanese militarists, under the guise of helping their neighboring province, were enabled to satisfy their own selfish plans for aggression.

Moreover, Hupeh was a strategic area under the control of the great Chihli military clique, of which Wang Chan-yüan was an important member. He had rendered enormous assistance to Wu P'ei-fu in withdrawing Wu's troops from Hengchow and to the Chihli clique in its war with the Anhwei clique. Wu Kuang-hsin's arrest in Hupeh and the disarmament of Chang Ching-yao's troops were all handled by Wang. Consequently, the Anhwei military clique, hating Wang, was searching for an opportunity to overthrow him. The former Shensi tuchun, Ch'en Shu-fan, who had lost his position when the Anhwei clique lost power, also loathed the Chihli faction.

The warlords and the politicians of the Anhwei clique had opened a bank at Hankow to finance their political activities. Ch'en Shu-fan, who had amassed huge wealth from the opium tax in Shensi, also deposited his money in this bank. The Hunan government was so impoverished that there was no money to pay the soldiers, so it could not finance the expeditions for which the army officers were so eager. At this juncture, a Hunanese employed in the bank used his influence to get funds for his native province. When the war to succor Hupeh was in preparation, the Anhwei clique exploited the same argument in order to secure resources for destroying the power of the Chihli clique in Hupeh. Motivated by this common interest, the bank served as a supplier of military funds for the Hunan soldiers to go to the succor of Hupeh.

Szechwan province had also a close relationship with the war. Szechwan, formerly an affluent province, since the anti-monarchical war of 1916 had frequently been the point of contention between the Yunnan and Kweichow warlords. During the long struggle Szechwan fell into the hands of the native warlords. Later on, the province also declared itself

self-governing. Among the warlords in Szechwan—a motley group without adequate leadership or coherence—the ambitious ones harbored the idea of developing their power outside the province. Understanding the existence of such elements, the Hunan warmongers went to Szechwan to negotiate with the expansionists there. An agreement was made to fight cooperatively toward the Wuhan area; after this was captured, they planned to create here a central force.

Triumph of the Chihli Clique

After the Hunan militarists received financial support from the bank of the Anhwei clique and also learned that Wang Chan-yüan's troops were incompetent, they believed that Wuhan could be taken by one simple assault. Without even waiting to mobilize their allies in Szechwan, they plunged into a military expedition which served only to create an opportunity for Wu P'ei-fu to become inspecting commissioner of Hunan and Hupeh.

Warfare commenced in the middle of July 1921. The native leaders in Hupeh were Chiang Tso-pin, Kung Keng, Hsia Tou-yin, and others, who from Hunan proclaimed a provisional constitution for the self-government of Hupeh. Chiang was elected director of provincial affairs; Kung, commander of the Self-government Army; and Hsia, director of the vanguard of the Self-government Army. Hunan sent two army divisions to advance toward Hupeh and won one victory after another. In the early part of August they approached the vicinity of Wuchang. On August 7 Wang Chan-yüan resigned and shortly after fled from Wuchang.

The Peking government appointed Wu P'ei-fu to be the inspecting commissioner of Hunan and Hupeh on August 9; Hsiao Yao-nan was made tuchun of Hupeh, and Sun Ch'uan-fang commander in chief in the upper Yangtze Valley.

Wu P'ei-fu went southward from Loyang. Several warships were secretly ordered to sail upstream to the rear of the Hunan troops. On

August 27 Yochow was taken by Wu's troops. Facing attack from enemies in the front as well as in the rear, the Hunan army was routed, and on September 1 a truce was agreed upon.

The Szechwan warlords, unaware that the Hunan army could fight no longer, began to attack Ichang on September 6. Wu P'ei-fu, after subduing the Hunan army, concentrated on the Szechwan soldiers, who were unable to offer much resistance. On October 11 they withdrew from the boundary of Hupeh, and before long, a truce with them was also reached. These two truces concluded the brief warfare.

Results of the War

Let us now look at the results of the war. In Hupeh the greedy Wang Chan-yüan was replaced by the strong-handed Hsiao Yao-nan, a native of Hupeh and a subordinate of Wu P'ei-fu of the Chihli clique. "Hupeh for the Hupehnese" was a lost cause. The province of Szechwan had nothing to gain and little to lose.

The reward for the bank of the Anhwei clique was bankruptcy. The dream of the Hunan army officers for "outside expansion" vanished; they returned to their native province and each man occupied a few districts to enrich himself. Although in Hunan the provincial constitution was quickly passed, the people of that province had to face many hardships.

The humiliating truce with Wu P'ei-fu ceded Yochow, a gateway between Hunan and Hupeh, as a garrison district to Wu's force. Through his agent, Hsiao Yao-nan, Hunan was closely watched. The Hunan authorities hoped to cooperate with Kwangtung, but they were afraid that they might incur more trouble if soldiers from another province invaded their own territory.

Wu P'ei-fu had made a great contribution in defeating the Anhwei clique. Now he was made inspecting commissioner of Hupeh and Hunan; thereafter the territory along the Peking-Hankow Railway belonged to the sphere of influence of Ts'ao K'un and Wu P'ei-fu. "When a cat upsets a jar, the dogs get a good meal," can appropriately be used to describe the result of the Rescue Hupeh War. The people of the two provinces gained nothing; Wu P'ei-fu gained everything.

THE WAR BETWEEN FENGTIEN AND CHIHLI

The first Fengtien-Chihli war broke out in the summer of 1922, but the seeds had been scattered during the Anhwei-Chihli war two years before, when Chang Tso-lin sent a large force inside Shanhaikwan. Wu P'ei-fu, who was then the brains of the Chihli army, did not expect Chang to fight hard, but he did count on him not to give any assistance to Tuan. After Tuan's fiasco, Chang Tso-lin took to Fengtien all the ammunition and heavy weapons abandoned by Tuan's troops. The officers and soldiers of the Chihli army were so incensed that they were ready to intercept the Fengtien troops by force, but Wu P'ei-fu forbade such action.

Achieving a Balance of Power in North China

After the conclusion of the Anhwei-Chihli war, Ts'ao K'un, Chang Tso-lin, and Wu P'ei-fu attended the so-called Aftermath Conference in Peking. Wu P'ei-fu considered himself to have made the greatest contribution to the wars, and he had been highly praised by the press. In the eyes of Chang Tso-lin, however, Ts'ao K'un was the hero, while Ts'ao's subordinate, Wu P'ei-fu, was only a minor figure. It has been asserted that Chang did not allow Wu to sit in the conference on the grounds that a division commander was not qualified to have such honor, until Ts'ao intervened in Wu's behalf. This episode engendered a feud between Chang and Wu, the culmination of which was the Fengtien-Chihli war.

The problem in North China was the distribution or division of the spheres of influence between the Chihli and the Fengtien cliques. It involved (1) the control of the Peking government and (2) the division of territories in North China.

Concerning the first question, Chin Yün-p'eng, backed by the leaders of both Chihli and Fengtien, was again made premier. Chin had to maintain a balanced relation with both parties; he dared not have any bias. With regard to the territorial distribution, at first an agreement was made to maintain *the status quo*. Before the fall of Tuan Ch'i-jui, Chang Tso-lin had already obtained the title of inspecting commissioner of the Three Eastern Provinces; and Ts'ao K'un that of inspecting commissioner of Chihli, Shantung, and Honan. But Wu P'ei-fu had no actual territorial base. This situation could not exist for long.

The most difficult problem in the central government was finance. The Western and Japanese imperialists had formed a banking corporation to make investments in China on condition that there must be a unified government. Premier Chin Yün-p'eng, in order to borrow money from this corporation, consulted President Hsü Shih-ch'ang on the dissolution of the parliament, which was under the control of the An-fu faction. He announced that the parliamentary organization law and the election law proclaimed in 1912 would be taken as a basis to form another parliament.

But the South paid little attention to this announcement, and the Extraordinary Parliament under the guidance of Sun Yat-sen continued to work under the standard of Protection for the Constitution. Premier Chin's plan for unification and for floating a loan soon evaporated. Since he could not borrow money from foreign countries, he had to seek help from Chinese banks. These were mostly monopolized by the Communications Clique. Neither the finance minister, Chou Tzu-chi, nor the communication minister, Yeh Kung-cho, both influential members of the Communications Clique, was congenial with Premier Chin. Failing to secure financial help, the premier attempted to effect the dismissal of these two ministers; this action shook the Peking government to its foundations.

Chang Tso-lin had cooperated with the Chihli clique in fighting against Tuan because Hsü Shu-cheng was overrunning Mongolia, thus seriously threatening Chang's Pan-Three-Eastern-Provinces principle. Even after the disappearance of the Anhwei influence, Chang still did not control Mongolia. He was also ambitious to obtain the territory along the Yangtze River. In order to accomplish this, he tried to ally himself with Wang Chan-yüan in order to control Wu P'ei-fu.

The Tientsin Conference, 1921

Ts'ao and Wu hoped to expand their territory just as Chang did. Since the Yangtze had been largely under their control, the only place for their expansion was Shensi. On April 25, 1921, at the so-called Tientsin Conference, the participants were the three inspecting commissioners: Ts'ao K'un, Chang Tso-lin, Wang Chan-yüan, with Premier Chin Yün-p'eng. Their published purpose was to discuss the great problems concerning South and North China; and accordingly, on April 27 a telegram was issued objecting to the Extraordinary Parliament of Kwangtung and to the election of Sun Yat-sen as president of the Southern government. Actually, however, the aim of this conference was to work out the reorganization of the cabinet and the balance of power.

After the Tientsin Conference, the participants went together to Peking on May 2. On the fourteenth, Chin Yün-p'eng's cabinet was reorganized by the unanimous resignation of all the cabinet members. After the resignation Premier Chin was reinstated, and he reorganized the cabinet by dropping Chou Tzu-chi and Yeh Kung-cho and appointing Li Shih-wei as finance minister, and Chang Chih-t'an as communications minister. Being accused of a pro-Japanese inclination because he had negotiated a loan, Li did not take up his duties, which were carried out by the vice-minister, Feng Yü-hsiang, a subordinate of Wu P'ei-fu was eventually made tuchun of Shensi; and Chang Tso-lin was concurrently made development commissioner [*ching-lüeh-shih*] in Mongolia and Sinkiang, with authority over the governors of the Three Special Zones:

Jehol, Chahar, and Suiyuan. This was a new distribution of the territory between the Chihli and the Fengtien cliques in order to maintain a new balance of power. Wang Chan-yüan did not gain much except that he was honored as one of the Big Three.

After the Tientsin Conference, Wang Chan-yüan returned to Wuchang, where his troops started mutinies in several localities. In July the Rescue Hupeh War occurred, Wang lost his position, and his title as inspecting commissioner of Hunan and Hupeh was taken by Wu P'ei-fu. Thus Chang's plan of making an alliance with Wang for the control of Wu failed. Since Wu's reputation had increased, the distribution of power was still unbalanced.

Cliques Around Chang and Wu

In the central government, after the reorganization of the cabinet, the financial predicament was not improved. Chou Tzu-chi and Yeh Kung-cho, who had been maneuvered out by the premier and the Communications Clique, were seething with resentment and sought an opportunity to avenge the insult. Joining with Chang Tso-lin, they worked for the expansion of Chang's power and for Liang Shih-i to replace Chin as premier. On December 14, 1921, Chang Tso-lin came to Peking, and two days after, Premier Chin Yün-p'eng resigned. On the nineteenth, Ts'ao K'un was invited to Peking. Five days later, Liang Shih-i's cabinet was organized and Yeh Kung-cho's position as communications minister was restored. Yeh was the power behind the organization of the new cabinet. The new cabinet purported to have the consent of Ts'ao K'un; actually, it was entirely dominated by Chang Tso-lin, under whom the influential members were the leaders of the Communications Clique. Distribution of power in the central government also lost balance, and the war between Wu and Chang drew near.

After Wu P'ei-fu obtained the title of inspecting commissioner of Hunan and Hupeh, it was easy for the Communications Clique to form a coalition with Chang, who envied Wu's position. The Anhwei adherents were also active behind the scene. The Communications, the Anhwei, the Fengtien, and the Chihli factions were said to have made a secret alliance to paralyze Wu by cutting off the military funds without which he could not maintain his soldiers. Eight days after the establishment of Liang's cabinet on December 24, an order was issued to pardon many leaders of the Anhwei faction who had been under general arrest. All those pardoned were Wu P'ei-fu's enemies. When Liang organized the cabinet, he had promised Wu to raise three million dollars for his military funds, but after Liang became premier, he did not keep his promise.

The Disgrace of Liang Shih-i

It was during the Washington Conference that the Shangtung problem was under consideration. Liang Shih-i, hoping to get some money from Japan, cabled the Chinese delegation in America to yield some ground. This cable irritated the Chinese people very much. Wu P'ei-fu seized this opportunity to oppose Liang Shih-i on patriotic grounds. His telegram read as follows:

> There is no harm greater than selling the interest of the nation and no treachery worse than currying favor with foreigners ... The Shantung controversy has lasted several years, and has been discussed by several cabinets in China ... The Kiaochow-Tsinan Railway is the key point of the Shantung controversy in which the Chinese delegation argued for months in the Washington conference ...
>
> The Chinese people tried to raise funds so that the railway could be bought without borrowing money from a foreign power ... The Japanese minister to China insisted that China must take a loan from Japan ... Liang Shih-i did not care about the harm involved, but directly promised the Japanese minister to borrow money from

Japan... Liang did not consult the minister of foreign affairs... but... instructed the Chinese delegates in Washington to obey his own order. That meant that the railway would still be managed by the Japanese, and China would have to undertake to accept loans of many millions of dollars. All that the previous cabinets did not dare to do is now done by Liang Shih-i... who gave up our rights over the railway. Why should he favor the foreigners and be so unconcerned about his fatherland? ...I am urgently cabling to our delegates in Washington, hoping that they will firmly maintain the original agreement for settling the Shantung problem. All our fellow countrymen will support them.[1]

After Wu released this telegram to the press, Liang realized his mistake. On January 7 [1922] he dispatched a telegram defending himself on the ground that he was continuing the policy of borrowing money from Japan which had been laid down by the preceding cabinet. Wu P'ei-fu replied by castigating Liang's telegram and openly calling him a traitor to the country. Wu's last telegram attacking the Liang cabinet received the approbation of Feng Yü-hsiang, tuchun of Shensi, and also of the tuchuns of Kiangsi, Kiangsu, Hupeh, Shantung, Shensi, Honan and Anhwei.

Chang Tso-lin, who did not wish to have his handpicked cabinet over turned by Wu P'ei-fu, sent a telegram to the central government whitewashing Liang's action. But regardless of this attempt, it was a fact that Liang did cable the Chinese delegation in Washington to yield ground; Wu had definite evidence to vindicate his charge. Furthermore, the Japanese minister in Peking even announced that his request had been accepted by the Peking government.

A reply from a number of the Chinese delegates in Washington also referred to the fact that Liang actually agreed to borrow money from Japan and to arrange for a joint management of the railway by the two nations. In addition, shortly after Liang became premier, he appointed

Ts'ao Ju-lin, a notorious traitor, as mayor of the Peking municipal government. On the nineteenth the tuchuns and governors of six provinces, headed by Wu P'ei-fu, urged the central government to dismiss Liang and encourage the people to ostracize the Liang cabinet. The following day, more than forty associations, including the so-called Association of Foreign Affairs. Union of All Circles, and Associations of All Provincial Governments, dispatched a joint telegram listing ten major crimes committed by Liang Shih-i. This joint telegram was obviously designed to reinforce Wu's anti-Liang campaign. Liang asked sick leave to get away from Peking; that sick leave was renewed many times. And war broke out again.

The Shooting War

This new war started in January 1922 and lasted until May. At first the Fengtien warlord was very stubborn and the Chihli clique was relatively quiet. On March 10 Wu P'ei-fu dispatched another telegram to assert that he objected only to Liang, not to Liang's cabinet. At the last moment, when arrangements were made for open battle, Wu's tone became strong and aggressive once more.

The interval between the mild and strong tones in this quarrel saw a play of politics by both sides. Chang Tso-lin tried to make an alliance with the distant foe, Sun Yat-sen, in order to fight against an enemy near at hand. He sent delegates to Canton in February. At the same time Sun also sent Wu Chao-shu to Fengtien to make an alliance to fight against the Chihli clique. Chang also attempted to restore the power of Chang Hsün, who had essayed the restoration of the Manchu emperor to the throne in 1917. In the belief that Chekiang and Shantung belonged to the sphere of influence of the Anhwei clique, Chang decided that if he cooperated with this clique, Kiangsu could be watched by his friendly force in Chekiang. Chang also reached an agreement with the military governor of Honan. Wu's nominal superior, Ts'ao K'un, and his brother were reluctant to fight with their relative, Chang Tso-lin, and were therefore neutral. After these arrangements had been made, Wu P'ei-fu was well-nigh surrounded; and hence Chang's tone became considerably stronger, while Wu P'ei-fu, whose troops were scattered in Shensi, Hupeh, and elsewhere, could not but adopt a milder tone in order to gain time for troop concentration.

In Kwangtung, Sun Yat-sen and Ch'en Hsiung-ming were having a secret struggle which impeded Sun's plans for a Kuomintang Northern Expedition, and Chang Hsün could not be persuaded to be active again. The tuchun of Anhwei only wished to keep his province in good order; and the leader of the Anhwei clique, Tuan Ch'i-jui, took no interest in the new wrangle. Now it was Wu P'ei-fu's turn to take the upper hand.

From the middle of April both sides were mustering troops. On the nineteenth, Fengtien soldiers were sent to China proper. Feng Yü-hsiang and Ts'ao K'un dispatched telegrams on the twenty-second objecting to this action; three days later Wu P'ei-fu headed a joint telegram announcing ten significant accusations against Chang Tso-lin. On April 29, soldiers on the two sides began to shoot at each other in the vicinity of Peking; the Fengtien army was shortly defeated.

President Hsü Shih-ch'ang on May 5 ordered the Fengtien troops to leave Shanhaikwan. The instigators, Liang Shih-i and Yeh Kung-cho, were deprived of their positions and ranks and were to be punished by the court. On the tenth, another order deprived Chang Tso-lin of all his duties pending future punishment. But Chang Tso-lin, after losing his ranks and his dominating position in the central government, was still the actual ruler of the Three Eastern Provinces. Now he declared his independence and rejected the order of the president.

Since the Fengtien-Chihli war started with Liang's cabinet, after Chang Tso-lin was defeated, Liang's cabinet was doomed. It seemed safe, however, for Hsü Shih-ch'ang to continue as president. Unexpectedly, on May 14 Sun Ch'uan-fang issued a demand for the restoration of the constitution of 1913, the restoration of Li Yüan-hung to the presidency, and the summoning of the Old Parliament [dissolved in 1917]. Unification was not thereby achieved; but Hsü Shih-ch'ang had to resign on June 2, 1922.

THE HOSTILITY BETWEEN SUN AND CH'EN IN THE SOUTH

The outbreak of hostility between Dr. Sun Yat-sen and General Ch'en Hsiung-ming coincided with the first Fengtien-Chihli war in the North, but its commencement can be traced back to 1920.

The Recession of Sun's Influence

When the warlords of the Kwangsi military clique withdrew from Kwangtung in October, the Military Government disintegrated and the Cantonese Army under Ch'en Hsiung-ming returned from Fukien to Canton. When Sun Yat-sen, Wu T'ing-fang, and T'ang Shao-i had restored the Military Government, they announced their hope that if the authorities of North China would discuss problems with them, the peace conference could be resumed. The highly besieged Extraordinary Parliament was still convening in Canton, with a total membership of more than 220. The sphere of influence of the Military Government was, however, limited to Kwangtung. Kwangsi province had then joined the Chihli clique; Hunan had declared itself independent; while Szechwan, Kweichow, and Yunnan had little connection with the Canton government. Of the seven former execurives, only three were left. Among these three, T'ang Shao-i, who differed with Sun Yat-sen, did not perform any government duties. Sun Yat-sen and Wu T'ing-fang were the two real executives.

Harassed by the problem created by the diplomatic corps, which had cut off the Southern government's supply of funds from customs duties,

Sun Yat-sen suggested the election of a president through whom a new government could be formed. His suggestion was accepted by a majority of th members of the Extraordinary Parliament. The constitution of 1912 was to be continued, and therefore it was necessary for the Old Parliament to elect a president and organize a formal government.

Sun and Chen Disagree Over Reorganization

Unfortunately, however, Ch'en Hsiung-ming was now inclined toward the federal government system. Many of Ch'en's subordinates and part of the parliamentary members disapproved of the idea of electing a new president and formally organizing a new government. Moreover, only a little more than 200 parliamentary members remained in Canton—far too few for a quorum. Ch'en's group favored consolidating the self-government of Kwangtung first and then operating under a federation with other self-governing provinces.

But Sun Yat-sen could not concur, and after much argument, Ch'en was forced to yield. On April 7, 1921, the 200-odd members of the Extraordinary Parliament convened and decided on an outline for the organization of the government of China. According to Article 2 of the outline, a president was to be elected; Sun Yat-sen received 213 votes. On the tenth the Extraordinary Parliament informed the nation that Sun Yat-sen had been inaugurated president on the fifth of May.

Immediately afterward Sun issued two declarations to the people at home and abroad. In his domestic declarations he stated:

> The parliament represents the opinion of the people. Its members entrusted me with the duty of stopping the disorders and of working for a better government. Since this great responsibility falls upon me, how could I dare to decline it? ... Now I wish to iron out the trouble between the central and local governments permanently and I realize that the only way is to let the people of the several

provinces establish autonomy, make their own constitutions, and elect their own governors. The central government distributed a number of rights to the provinces and the latter again have distributed a number of rights to districts. Respecting the divergent local practices of districts, an independent republic can still become reunited under the principle of self-government. It is unnecessary to resort to war.[2]

From this declaration one may see that Sun Yat-sen did try to appease those who favored the federal government system. The difference was that Sun would like to have the district as a unit of self-government; he disapproved of the use of a province as a unit, since a provincial unit could easily be dominated by a warlord.

After being inaugurated as president, Sun Yat-sen immediately appointed Wu T'ing-fang minister of foreign affairs and concurrently minister of finance, Ch'en Hsiung-ming minister of war and minister of domestic affairs, Hsü Chien minister of justice, T'ang Ting-kuang minister of the navy, and Ma Chün-wu secretary-general. Ch'en Hsiung-ming accepted Sun's appointment, but in his heart he did not approve Sun's actions.

Sun's Northern Expedition Checked by Ch'en

At that time the Kwangsi military clique was still waiting for a chance to reoccupy the territory in Kwangtung. They found their opportunity when the Peking government, hoping to overturn Sun's government, allied with the Kwangsi clique for a joint attack on Kwangtung. Sun and Ch'en, despite their differences, had to cooperate in coping with the Kwangsi enemy. In June 1921 the war between Kwangtung and Kwangsi resumed. On June 21 Wuchow, a gateway to Kwangsi, was taken. The troops of Kwangtung advanced gradually until the end of July, when the Kwangsi enemy was liquidated.

The break between Ch'en and Sun followed immediately. After the conquest of Kwangsi, Sun Yat-sen decided to carry on a Northern Expedition from Kweilin to Hunan. The troops under the command of Ch'en Hsiung-ming were at Nanning, Sun Yat-sen, knowing that Ch'en was unwilling to join the expedition, went to Nanning to make a compromise with him, saying "If my Northern Expedition is successful, I will not return to Kwangtung and Kwangsi; if it is a failure, I will lack face to return to the two provinces, and I will trust you to govern them. I hope you will not block my Northern Expedition, and I request that you will give me supplies of arms and rations."

Ch'en Hsiung-ming did not agree with Sun's plan. Nevertheless, Sun organized a headquarters at Kweilin, capital of Kwangsi, and appointed Chu P'ei-te commander in chief of the Yunnan army, P'eng Ch'eng-wan commander in chief of the Kiangsi army, and Ku Cheng-lun commander in chief of the Kweichow army. He had also a number of Cantonese troops under the command of Hsü Ch'ung-chih and Li Fu-lin. Li Lieh-chün was made chief of staff and Hu Han-min chief of civil officers. The plan was to enter Hunan in the spring of 1922.

After Ch'en Hsiung-ming's return from Nanning to Canton, he set about his plan for the reorganization of Kwangtung and Kwangsi. Ch'en held the titles of minister of war, commander in chief of the Kwangtung Army, and governor of Kwangtung. He had full control of the provincial finances and could be confident of the support of the provincial assembly or parliament. He was enthusiastic in drafting the provincial constitution, but continued cool to the Northern Expedition.

The only funds for the Northern Expedition which Sun Yat-sen relied on were two million dollars' worth of bank notes which he had ordered Liao Chung-k'ai to draw from the Kwangtung Provincial Bank on the eve of the expedition. For future supply, he entrusted the chief of staff of the Cantonese Army with the responsibility of raising funds from the people. In the spring of 1922 the news of the Northern Expedition was spread all over the nation, and the vanguard had even advanced to the border of Hunan. Eventually, however, they failed in the attempt to enter Hunan, because, as Sun later reported, Ch'en Hsiung-ming instructed the Hunan authorities to create as many hindrances as possible so that Sun's force could not advance further. Ch'en Hsiung-ming neither supplied Sun with any military funds or arms, nor the Yunnan and Kweichow troops with rations, in spite of repeated pleas from Sun; he continued to block the advance of Sun's expeditionary force and partially cut off his return route to Canton. When the man whom Sun entrusted with the responsibility of securing funds was assassinated at the Canton railway station on March 21, 1922, there was no further hope for Sun to obtain supplies from the rear.

On March 26 Sun Yat-sen ordered his forces to begin a secret march from Kweilin to Kwangtung. Ch'en Hsiung-ming was unaware of the new move until Sun's forces reached Wuchow. At that time, Ch'en's main forces were still mostly in Nanning. Knowing that he could not resist Sun's forces, he tendered Sun his resignation.

When Sun Yat-sen reached Wuchow on April 16, he summoned Ch'en for an interview. Ch'en dared not go. Sun Yat-sen accordingly issued on the nineteenth an order which accepted Ch'en's resignation as commander in chief of the Kwangtung Army and governor of the province, but permitting him to remain as minister of war. Wu T'ing-fang replaced him as Kwangtung governor, and his post as head of the Kwangtung Army was abolished, this army now being placed under the direct control of Sun's headquarters. On the evening of April 20, Ch'en left Canton for Hweichow with all his trusted subordinates and soldiers, who prepared for positional warfare at Hu-men and other points.

Chiang K'ai-shek, then only a military advisor of the Second Division— the Cantonese troops in the Northern Expedition—advocated an immediate attack at Hweichow in order to annihilate Ch'en Hsiung-ming's forces before the Northern Expedition. But on the grounds that

Ch'en had not yet rebelled against him openly and because he hoped to keep the Cantonese troops under Ch'en's control, Sun Yat-sen ignored this advice. Moreover, Sun had a previous understanding with Fengtien to attack the Chihli forces jointly. If he waited until the annihilation of Ch'en's forces before he launched the Northern Expedition, he was afraid that he might lose the advantage of the time element.

Ch'en Betrays Sun in Canton, 1922

Sun continued to believe that Ch'en was merely being uncooperative and that dismissal from his Kwangtung post would be sufficient rebuke. Sun continued his plans for the Northern Expedition and moved his headquarters to Shaochow. On May 6, the day after the Fengtien Army was defeated, Sun Yat-sen formally launched his expedition.

In the meantime Sun continued his correspondence with Ch'en Hsiung-ming, explaining that so long as Ch'en placed no hindrance upon his expedition, he would trust him as before. Ch'en expressed a desire to retain the title of minister of war, and promised to aid in the expedition, after a brief rest in Hweichow. But when the expeditionary force was fighting in Kiangsi, more than fifty battalions of Ch'en's force rushed to Canton. Receiving this bad news, Sun tried to persuade the insurgents to continue the expedition; his order was defied. Instead, they requested that Ch'en Hsiung-ming be returned as commander in chief of the Kwangtung Army and governor of Kwangtung. Sun Yat-sen intended to refuse the request bluntly; but on account of the hard righting at the front, he tried to placate the insurgents.

Sun ordered Ch'en Hsiung-ming on May 27 to take general charge of all military affairs of Kwangtung and Kwangsi. Ch'en replied by telegram saying that "he would do his best to carry out, his new duties" would order the insurgents to return to their original stations, and would persuade these soldiers, pledging his reputation and life, not to take illegal action again. On the other hand, the insurgents were still stationed at Canton demanding payment. The citizens of the city were frightened. Sun had to return to Canton on June 1 to take care of the situation personally; the headquarters at Shaochow were left to the care of Hu Han-min.

The Northern Expedition Army captured Kanchow, Kiangsi, on June 13. Here a confidential telegram was discovered which indicated that Ch'en Hsiung-ming was communicating with the Kiangsi provincial commander, Ch'en Kuang-yüan. This was strong evidence that Ch'en Hsiung-ming was trying to block the progress of the Northern Expedition. If the Northern Expedition Army suffered a defeat, Ch'en Hsiung-ming would start a war in the rear; but since it fought victoriously, Ch'en dared not take any careless action. On the fifteenth Sun Yat-sen decided to continue the Northern Expedition.

Unexpectedly, on the same day, mutinous soldiers surrounded the president's office at Canton, and Sun Yat-sen was in great danger. He escaped, however, to a gunboat. From June 16 on he had only a few gunboats facing the attack of Ch'en Hsiung-ming's soldiers, which lasted more than fifty days. At first he expected that the Northern Expedition Army would fight back to Canton to annihilate Ch'en's troops. But by the beginning of August he began to realize that the way for his troops to return to Canton had been blocked by Ch'en. On August 9 he managed to flee from Canton.

Why Sun Failed in Canton

On the surface, the feud between Sun and Ch'en in the South was an entirely different matter from the Fengtien-Chihli war in the North; but at bottom the two incidents were closely related. Ch'en Hsiung-ming worked in collusion with the Chihli clique and Sun Yat-sen with the Fengtien clique. After the Fengtien clique was defeated by the Chihli group, Sun Yat-sen's Northern Expedition had little hope of success. Furthermore, Sun Yat-sen's alliance with the Fengtien against the Chihli clique was unpopular among the people, who could not understand that Sun's relationship with the Fengtien was a temporary cooperation in the hope that the more evil and powerful Chihli clique could be defeated first. The people disapproved more of Chang Tso-lin than they did of Wu P'ei-fu. Moreover they had serious doubts that the motley Northern Expedition forces would ever be able to defeat Wu.

On the other hand, the plan to restore the old constitution of 1912 by the Chihli clique was well received. Hope for peace and unification made the Chinese people expect Sun Yat-sen to relinquish the banner of war. The people assumed that the office of the president would be abolished and the war between the South and the North would cease.

When Sun Yat-sen deprived Ch'en of some of his posts, the people who were sympathetic with Ch'en said that Ch'en's uncooperativeness toward the Northern Expedition was for the purpose of protecting the territory under his jurisdiction from being involved in warfare. Ch'en responded this way, they said, in order to consolidate the domestic affairs of the province. Sun Yat-sen was criticized for having been too harsh in his treatment of Ch'en. When Hsü Shih-ch'ang resigned, when the old constitution was restored, and when the president's office at Canton was surrounded and attacked, many people thought that the war for the protection of the old constitution was also won. Sun Yat-sen was requested to resign simultaneously with Hsü Shih-ch'ang. All intellectual circles expressed by telegram their support of unification and tried to persuade Sun Yat-sen to resign from the presidency. Even famous scholars like Ts'ai Yüan-p'ei responded in the same manner. The people were desperate for peace.

After Sun Yat-sen left Canton for Shanghai, he made a report to his Kuomintang comrades, the concluding part of which reads:

> For thirty years I have led my comrades in the fight for the republic, and I have been in and out of mortal danger and of failure

and success innumerable times. But no failure has ever been so sad as this recent one. My previous failures were caused by my enemies. But this time, while my enemies have been defeated, the one who rises and replaces my enemy is Ch'en Hsiung-ming, who has been my protégé for more than ten years. Furthermore, he is so malignant and wicked-hearted that what my real enemies dare not do he has done. It is not only a misfortune for the Republic, but also an indication of a decline in moral integrity. [3]

As a matter of fact, Ch'en's action was in accord with the general desire of the people for peace. Sun's failure, which he attributed to Ch'en Hsiung-ming's rebellion against him, was actually caused by the people themselves, who could not understand Sun's ideology.

THE OLD CONSTITUTION AND THE FEDERAL GOVERNMENT MOVEMENT

The so-called "legitimate" or "orthodox" constitution, which compared as to validity with the "legitimate" chronology of Chinese history or the "orthodox" school of philosophy, had long been used merely as a weapon or a placard by the revolutionists. It served the fight against the Peiyang warlords and then supported a trade by which more than a hundred members of the parliament were able to make a living. The members elected in 1913 had a legal term of three years (senators, six years). In 1922 these same members asked to be allowed to restore the parliament of 1913. During these long years, the term of President Yüan Shih-k'ai had been completed by Li Yüan-hung and Feng Kuo-chang. Feng had filled out his term and three years more had elapsed, while the parliamentary members and the revolutionists still requested that Li Yüan-hung should resume the presidency. Yet at that time, cunning politicians and overbearing militarists acted so solemn that an objective observer would have been highly amused at the comedy. The populace, ever anxious for peace, was made to believe that the dispute between the South and the North was really caused by the problem of the orthodox constitution. As soon as the orthodox constitution was restored, the unification and peace of the nation would, they supposed, automatically follow.

Forces Favoring the Old Parliament

The restoration of the "orthodox" constitution of 1912 was suggested by Sun Ch'uan-fang, but the idea had been in the air for a long time. Wu P'ei-fu had never liked Hsü Shih-ch'ang, and when Wu was stationed at Hengchow, he frequently referred to Hsü Shih-ch'ang as *Mr*. Hsü in his telegrams, refusing to address him as *President* Hsü. Wu had no friendly regard for the Old Parliament either. After Tuan Ch'i-jui was overthrown in the autumn of 1920, Wu suggested the convention of the national people's assembly to attempt to solve the dispute between the North and the South; he did not suggest the restoration of the orthodox constitution. The national people's assembly proposed by Wu did not draw any attention from other militarists, and Wu could not solo any longer. In 1921 after the conclusion of the Rescue-Hupeh War, Wu hinted to Chang Shao-tseng, tuchun of Jehol, that he should advocate the opening of the national people's assembly on October 10. Only a few tuchuns of the Chihli clique closely associated with Wu followed the line; other militarists were indifferent. Because of frequent newspaper references to this plan, however, it became increasingly popular.

At this time in the North, Liang Shih-i's cabinet was established and the Fengtien-Chihli war was imminent. On the eve of the war there were two rumors. One concerned the Fengtien clique, which tried to ally itself with Sun Yat-sen and the Anhwei clique to defeat Wu P'ei-fu. After their success, it was agreed that the Extraordinary Parliament should be transferred back from Canton to Peking and that Sun Yat-sen or Tuan

Ch'i-jui should be elected president, while the actual power would be in the hands of the Fengtien warlords. For this reason the Fengtien clique wished to make use of the 1912 constitution.

The other rumor concerned the Chihli clique, which already controlled a large territory and was in league with Ch'en Hsiung-ming; their hope was to unify the nation, if there were no impediments from Chang Tso-lin and Sun Yat-sen. The Chihli clique also wished to restore the Old Parliament and to make Li Yüan-hung resume the presidency, as a counterattack against Sun Yat-sen's constitutional movement. This clique also wished the Old Parliament to make a constitution in order to curb the federal government movement.

At the beginning of April 1922 the members of the Old Parliament in Peking opened daily meetings and announced to the public the resumption of their functions. Their action was supported by Chang Shao-tseng, tuchun of Jehol, who suggested that the Old Parliament should function freely and that the fundamental reconstruction problems should be discussed cooperatively by all provinces. Chang's telegram also said that the idea was approved by Wu P'ei-fu, Ts'ao K'un, and Chang Tso-lin. But the real controversy between the Fengtien and Chihli cliques was whether or not Liang Shih-i was a traitor. In their opinion this problem could be solved nowhere except on the battlefield. Therefore no one responded to Chang's telegram.

The Old Parliament Restored in Peking, 1922

After the Fengtien clique was defeated, Wu P'ei-fu dispatched a telegram on May 14, 1922 consulting all provincial authorities about the restoration of the Old Parliament. On the following day Sun Ch'uan-fang led his subordinates in sending a circular telegram in which he said: "A short cut to the reunification of the nation is the restoration of the orthodox constitution." He urged that Li Yüan-hung be reinaugurated as president, the Old Parliament of 1917 be reconvened, and a constitution be drafted so that a vice-president could be elected according to the new election law. "Now if the orthodox constitution is restored," he added, "there will be no reason for the Southern government to continue in existence."

At that time Sun Ch'uan-fang was but a commander in chief of the armies in the upper Yangtze Valley. His troops were quartered in the north of Hupeh and neither his position nor his reputation could bear much attention from the public. Sun Ch'uan-feng's telegram, conveying the ideas of Ts'ao K'un, was intended to confuse the public. On May 19 Ts'ao and Wu consulted the tuchuns of the Chihli clique by telegram as if they had no predetermined opinion. But on May 24 a number of members of the Old Parliament of 1917 were opening a preparatory meeting at Tientsin and announcing that they were having conversations "according to law."

On May 28 Sun Ch'uan-fang advised the two presidents of the Southern and Northern governments to abdicate simultaneously. On the same day Ts'ao and Wu, too, assented to the restoration of the Old Parliament. On June 1 more than 150 members of the Old Parliament, at a meeting at Tientsin, made a public declaration to the effect that they were performing their duties and had decided to abolish the old Southern and Northern governments and to organize a new legal government.

The next day Hsü Shih-ch'ang resigned. Ts'ao and Wu headed a list of signatures of tuchuns and governors of ten provinces requesting Li Yüan-hung to resume the presidency. The time from the day when Sun Ch'uan-fang made his first suggestion to Hsü's abdication amounted to only half a month. The change could not have had such a prompt effect had not Ts'ao and Wu made their plans long beforehand.

Ts'ao K'un had long desired to become president. When Hsü Shih-ch'ang was elected to that position, Ts'ao K'un campaigned for the vice-presidency without success, and then he hated Hsü Shih-ch'ang and Liang Shih-i.

For a long time Wu P'ei-fu tried to snatch the banner of Sun Yat-sen as the protector of the constitution. A number of members of the parliament who desired to keep their well-paid positions had planned with Chang Shao-tseng to restore the orthodox constitution in order to carry out the idea of Ts'ao and Wu. Thus Sun Ch'uan-fang's suggestion was quickly accepted and put into effect.

The reaction to a restoration of the orthodox constitution varied. Li Yüan-hung's reaction, for example, was that of a naive man who could not discern the plots of Ts'ao and Wu. A great scholar, Chang Ping-lin, wrote a confidential letter to Li advising him to live as a hermit for at least three months in order to watch the changes of the time. This advice was meant to tell Li that he should not be fooled by Ts'ao and Wu. Unfortunately, Li could not withstand the persuasion of his henchmen, who would have liked Li to become president again in order to secure profitable positions. Li did not take up the presidency immediately, but first issued a long telegram in which he set out two conditions, "abolishing the tuchuns and reducing the number of soldiers," as preface to his resumption of the presidency. These two conditions were exactly what the people desired. The tuchuns of the Ts'ao and Wu clique were so anxious to have Li accede to their request that they did not care what conditions he made. On June 11 Li announced that he would first go to Peking to become acting president of the country in order to maintain peace. Thus he fell again into the trap.

Sun Challenges the Chihli Restoration

As to Sun Yat-sen's reaction, he was not so foolish as Li Yüan-hung. He recognized the plot of the Chihli clique. While Li Yüan-hung advocated the abolition of the tuchuns and the reduction of troops, Sun Yat-sen declared:

> We should first punish the ringleaders who have brought a

> cataclysm upon the nation, and secondly, we should protect the safety of the parliament.... Soldiers should be converted into laborers and their weapons should be replaced with tools.... As a token of sincerity for the protection of the constitution, one half of the troops under the command of the Chihli generals should be converted to laborers by the government; this conversion should be a condition of the truce. The remaining half should be retained for the time being and reorganized with other forces of the whole nation. If this request is accepted by the Chihli generals, this president [Sun Yat-sen] would order the whole nation to stop the war, to restore peace, and to plan reconstruction jointly.[4]

If the Chihli militarists refused to reduce their own military force by half in order to evince sincere respect for the orthodox constitution, their plot would be uncovered. Obviously, the Chihli clique could not meet Sun's conditions. Furthermore, Ch'en Hsiung-ming, who had made a conspiracy with the Chihli clique, attacked Sun Yat-sen on June 16, to Wu's great pleasure.

Sun Yat-sen still maintained his stand even after his flight from Canton to Shanghai. On August 15, 1922, he issued a declaration reaffirming his "plan of soldiers as workers" [*kung-ping chi-hua*]; but since he had lost his headquarters in Canton, the Chihli clique ignored him.

Restoration of the Old Parliament in the South

The third reaction was that of the members of the Old Parliament. Theoretically they should have had no objection to the restoration of the orthodox constitution. But since 1917 the parliament had disintegrated. The Old Parliament as convened in Canton and called the Extraordinary Parliament was only one-half of the original legislative body. In 1919 many vacancies were filled up by "extraordinary" methods. After the dissolution of the Military Government in 1920, less than half of the members of the Extraordinary Parliament still maintained their political standing. Some members of this parliament, a minority, had largely been recruited in 1919 to fight for the protection of the constitution, and hence they were called "the 1919 members."

The movement for the restoration of the Old Parliament was carried out by the Wang Chia-hsiang faction, which did not go to Canton, and the Wu Ching-lien faction, which had withdrawn from Canton. These two factions made secret connections with the Chihli warlords to work for the restoration of the parliament as it existed before the dissolution in 1917. The restoration of this 1917 parliament was planned as a device to destroy the claims of the 1919 parliament.

Conceiving that their jobs would be lost soon, the members of the 1919 parliament dispatched circular telegrams on June 3, 1922, advocating the continuation of the 1919 parliament and denying the legality of the other. But the 1917 parliament gradually made up a quorum, and on August 1 meetings were opened.

Other Reactions to the Restoration

As to the Fengtien clique with regard to the orthodox constitution, Chang Tso-lin was then defeated and he had little voice in this problem. However, he still had the Three Eastern Provinces under his control. He was indifferent to any other issue. On June 3, having declared the Three Eastern Provinces autonomous, he called a military conference in which the policy of neutrality was decided. He then began to train his troops for a second war.

As for the Anhwei clique, after the fall of Tuan Ch'i-jui, it controlled only one province, Chekiang. The tuchun of Chekiang, Lu Yung-hsiang, was one of the objectors to the restoration of the orthodox constitution, as was also the garrison commander of Shanghai, Ho Feng-lin. When Li Yüan-hung went to Peking, Lu and Ho declared by telegram that they recognized him only "as president *de facto*, not as president *de jure*." Since Li Yüan-hung suggested the abolition of tuchuns and the reduction of the number of soldiers, on June 16 Lu took the initiative by giving up his official title as tuchun of Chekiang; his subordinates elected him a director of Chekiang military affairs. This was tantamount to a declaration of independence, and thereafter Chekiang was basically self-governing.

The attitude of the autonomous provinces in the Southwest was at first vague. Ch'en Hsiung-ming of Kwangtung was in open revolt against Sun Yat-sen. Others, like Hunan, Szechwan, Kweichow, which had all declared themselves autonomous, were silent for fear that their independence would suffer. When the restoration was to become a *fait accompli*, they promoted the federal movement for self-protection. They maintained that parliament should make a federal constitution, but that each province should have the right to make its own constitution. Since Ts'ao and Wu had the Old Parliament under their control, they did not mind what suggestions other governors made. The only result was much talk in the newspapers, which served to make a federal government system popular in China.

The Federalist Movement

Meanwhile, in Shanghai a union of eight organizations, consisting mainly of school teachers and merchants, advocated a conference at Shanghai to discuss national affairs. This conference, which actually opened on March 15, 1922, announced that each province was to make its own constitution and all provinces were to assemble together to make a constitution for the Republic of China. A "constitution-drafting committee" was even organized for this purpose.

In Peking a new periodical, *Effort Weekly* [*Nu-li chou-k'an*], published by a number of scholars, approved of the restoration and the making of the constitution by the Old Parliament as a matter of exigency, but lent no support to the movement for the orthodox constitution. They advised Li Yüan-hung to admit himself as a president *de facto* and the Old Parliament as a parliament *de facto*, and advocated a cessation of political arguments. Most important of all, they advocated the adoption of the federal government system to save the nation from partitioning by the warlords. These ideas represented the healthy opinion of an active intellectual group. The two popular sentiments, the restoration of the orthodox constitution and the federal government movement, were developing simultaneously. But both Sun Yat-sen and Wu P'ei-fu objected to the federal system.

Watching these current opinions, President Li Yüan-hung issued on July 1 a rescript saying: "Local self-government is fundamental for a constitutional nation .... Now the parliament has decided to convene on a certain date; in the future constitutions, the rights between the central and local governments must be carefully demarcated.... The hope for the unification of the nation lies in the federal constitution."[5]

This rescript was intended to comply with the demand from those who favored federal government. After the opening of the parliament, the committee appointed to work out a text for a revised constitution decided by a majority vote on August 19 that the rights of the provinces would be briefly mentioned in general terms, and those of the central government would be listed in detail. On August 26 the said committee passed two other resolutions: (1) Each province could have its own constitution so long as it did not conflict with the federal constitution. (2) The general principles of provincial constitutions should be briefly mentioned in the federal constitution.

Unfortunately for the federal government system, Ts'ao K'un had been dreaming of becoming president for a long time and Wu P'ei-fu had been longing to unify China by military power alone. Li Yüan-hung and the Old Parliament were merely their temporary toys or instruments. Before long the Military Government was re-established at Canton and

Ts'ao K'un actually bribed his way into the presidency.

THE RE-ESTABLISHMENT OF THE CANTON MILITARY GOVERNMENT, 1923

After the restoration of the orthodox constitution, Ts'ao K'un and Wu P'ei-fu were satisfied; especially Ts'ao K'un, who had thought that his chance to become president would not arrive. He did not anticipate that before his ambition was satisfied, the Military Government at Canton would be established.

Sun Yat-sen reached Shanghai on August 14, 1922; Ch'en Hsiung-ming returned to Canton on the following day, and before long Ch'en made himself commander in chief of the Kwangtung Army, acting as if he were king of that province. He did not, however, maintain that kingship long before he was driven away to be king of Hweichow.

Defeated by Ch'en Hsiung-ming, Sun Yat-sen's Northern Expedition Army was divided into two parts. One, under the command of Hsü Ch'ung-chih and Li Fu-lin, withdrew to the frontier at Fukien; the other, consisting mainly of Chu P'ei-te's Yunnan Army, retreated from the perimeter of Hunan to Kweilin, Kwangsi. Hsü Ch'ung-chih had made some connections with a garrison commander, Wang Yung-ch'üan, in Fukien; Wang was a close friend of the provincial tuchun, Li Hou-chi. Both Wang and Li were members of the Peiyang military clique. After the failure of Tuan Ch'i-jui and the rapid rise of Ts'ao and Wu to power, Li was prone to adhere to the camp of Ts'ao and Wu in order to protect his own position. Wang, on the other hand, intended to seize Li's position as tuchun of Fukien; and accordingly, Wang and Hsü made joint plans to drive Li away.

Sun Reorganizes to Defeat Ch'en, 1922

In Shanghai Sun Yat-sen was also working hard to restore his territory in Kwangtung; he still maintained the same relations with the Fengtien and Anhwei militarists and even showed good feelings toward Wu P'ei-fu. The Anhwei clique was anxious to invade Fukien and Kiangsu. While a clandestine understanding was reached between Hsü Ch'ung-chih and Wang Yung-ch'üan, Tuan Ch'i-jui urged them to take the same action in order to cooperate with Sun. In October Wang and Hsü advanced from different directions on Foochow, which was taken on October 12 by Li Fu-lin's army; Li Hou-chi fled. The military affairs of the provincial government were turned over to Wang Yung-ch'üan, while civil affairs were entrusted to Lin Shen, a member of the Kuomintang. This marked the beginning of cooperation between the Kuomintang and the Anhwei clique.

At this time the Fengtien group sent a delegate to advise Sun Yat-sen to give up his plan of restoring Canton and to order Hsü Ch'ung-chih's troops from Fukien and the Yunnan soldiers from Kweilin to advance from Kwangsi and Hunan toward the Wuhan cities. Meanwhile, the Fengtien soldiers would be responsible for assaulting Peking from the north. Because Sun Yat-sen now hated Ch'en Hsiung-ming bitterly, he replied that it was necessary for him to consolidate his base in Canton before he could essay the Northern Expedition. He therefore reorganized the soldiers in Fukien as the East Route Army to fight against the rebel Ch'en Hsiung-ming, and appointed Hsü Ch'ung-chih as its commander in chief. Hsü appointed Chiang Kai-shek as his chief of staff.

When Ch'en Hsiung-ming learned that Hsü Ch'ung-chih was active in Fukien, he was much disturbed for fear Hsü might follow his own footsteps and fight back from Fukien to Canton. As a preventive measure, he put a heavy garrison along the barrier between Kwangtung and Fukien.

But now, though the military clash in Fukien had not yet taken place, trouble had already begun in Kwangsi. Sun Yat-sen, after making connections with Hsü and Wang to take Fukien, sent Tsou Lu to Hong

Kong to make arrangements for the troops of Yunnan and Kweichow stationed at Kwangsi to march eastward from Wuchow, Kwangsi, to attack Ch'en Hsiung-ming. The commander of the Cantonese troops in the garrison of Wuchow had promised cooperation with the Yunnan and Kweichow troops when they reached that city. Military action started in the middle of December, and Wuchow was taken with ease. On January 15, 1923, Ch'en was further pressed and had to withdraw to Hweichow, where he announced his retirement.

Sun Returns to Canton, 1923

Sun Yat-sen in Shanghai was delighted to receive this welcome news, but still realized he would have another round to fight with the warlords. On the one hand, Sun had to deal with the big warlords in the North; and on the other he had to tackle numerous small warlords in Kwangtung. Besides Ch'en Hsiung-ming, there were other warlords of the Yunnan and Kwangsi armies. Though these now professed to welcome Sun's return to Canton, actually each of them intended to occupy some territory for his own enrichment. The warlord who caused Sun immediate trouble was Shen Hung-ying of Kiangsi, who had been offered a position as garrison commander of Kweilin by the Peking government.

Wu P'ei-fu, believing that Shen would be a good man to take Kwangtung, lost no time in urging the Peking government to appoint Shen as the director of military affairs in Kwangtung. But after accepting such bribery from Wu, Shen Hung-ying realized the weakness of his own military power and refused to start an uprising when he first arrived at Canton. At this time Ch'en Hsiung-ming, hoping to sow seeds of dissension among the various warlords, spread rumors that when troops of other provinces came to Canton, the sovereignty of Kwangtung province would be gone. Promptly Shen Hung-ying seized the opportunity afforded by this rumor to stir up sentiment in the Yunnan Army. He said that the native troops were consolidating to liquidate first the Yunnan troops and then the Kwangsi soldiers.

The commander of the Yunnan troops, Yang Hsi-min, convinced of the truth of this rumor, invited Hu Han-min, who was the governor of Kwangtung appointed by Sun Yat-sen, and others to a conference in the office of Yang Hsi-min's subordinate. During this conference Shen Hung-ying planned to arrest all the participants. The plot was carelessly executed, resulting in the arrest of only one participant. From that time on, the Yunnan and Kwangsi troops perceived Shen's ambitions and kept a vigilant eye on him.

At the beginning of February 1923 the Kwangtung troops, led by Hsü Ch'ung-chih, left Fukien for Canton. Under such circumstances, Shen Hung-ying had no way to carry out his plan of occupying that province. On February 6 he moved his headquarters to the suburb of Canton where he also dispatched telegrams indicating that Sun Yat-sen was welcome to return to his former headquarters. On February 15 Sun left Shanghai. Reaching Canton via Hong Kong on the twenty-first, he sent to Tuan Ch'i-jui, Chang Tso-lin, and others a telegram emphasizing that the lords of the Chihli clique were silent toward his plan for turning soldiers into laborers, that Wu P'ei-fu was trying to unify China by military power, and that one-half of the military force in Kwangtung would be reduced so as to set an example for other militarists to follow. That was the reason for his return to Canton. He added that rehabilitation and reconstruction could not begin until after a reduction of the number of soldiers throughout the whole nation.

The implication here was obviously a warning to Ts'ao K'un and Wu P'ei-fu. But how could the warlords of Kwangtung allow Sun to cut off their soldiers? Furthermore, Ch'en Hsiung-ming at Hweichow was waiting for a chance to fight back, and Shen Hung-ying was still ready to take action.

Sun's Military Government Reorganized at Canton, 1923

When Sun Yat-sen made this declaration, he was at the same time organizing a Military Government, on the grounds that before the military reduction, it was necessary to have a supreme overall organization to handle the various complicated military units. On February 24 he used his new title, Grand Marshal, to assign the various army commanders to stay where they were. No one was permitted to move at will from one place to another.

On March 2 Sun's Military Government was organized; it included a ministry of domestic affairs headed by T'an Yen-k'ai, a ministry of foreign affairs headed by Wu Chao-shu, a ministry of finance headed by Liao Chung-k'ai, a ministry of reconstruction, and other offices such as chief of staff, secretariat, office of auditing. It is important to note that the organization of the Military Government under the grand marshal was the prototype of the future nationalist government.

Upon hearing of the reappearance of the grand marshal in the South, Ts'ao K'un and Wu P'ei-fu daily urged the Peking government to appoint Sun Ch'uan-fang tuchun of Fukien, and Shen Hung-ying tuchun of Kwangtung in order to control Sun Yat-sen. Chang Shao-tseng at once led all his cabinet members to resign in a body as a protest against the military action which Ts'ao and Wu tried to take. On March 20, 1923, the appointments were nevertheless made by Chang's cabinet, exactly as Ts'ao and Wu demanded. On March 25 Shen Hung-ying declined the appointment of the Peking government and announced that he would obey the order of the grand marshal to transfer his troops to the West River for garrison and set up his headquarters at Chao-ch'ing. Nevertheless, on April 10 Shen concentrated his troops at Shao-kuan, where a secret military conference was held. Two days afterward, Shen took the position given him by the Peking government as commander of Kwangtung military affairs. He dispatched a circular telegram asking Sun Yat-sen to leave Kwangtung. Sun Yat-sen had taken preventive measures and immediately ordered all his generals to fight against Shen. The latter was crushed by the middle of May and the grand marshal's Military

Government was made secure.

Shortly after the end of the anti-Shen campaign, Ch'en Hsiung-ming's troops started a war in the zone of the East River of Kwangtung. It took a long time for Sun Yat-sen to subdue this formidable foe, and while this war was still going on, Ts'ao K'un made history in Peking.

TS'AO K'UN'S USURPATION OF THE PRESIDENCY, 1923

The military power of Ts'ao K'un was entirely in the hands of Wu P'ei-fu. Wu was not imbued with that covetousness so characteristic of other Peiyang warlords. Appearing to be an honest man, he was admired by many people. Since Ts'ao's force was based on Wu's support, Ts'ao also enjoyed some popularity.

Ts'ao and Wu, however, did not always agree in their policies. Wu did not want to support Ts'ao for the presidency until China was unified by means of the orthodox constitution. On the other hand, Ts'ao had only one purpose: to obtain the presidency, whether South China was unified or not. Their henchmen, accordingly, had also divergent factions: the active factions at Tientsin and Paoting were anxious to make Ts'ao president as soon as possible; the conservative faction in Loyang followed closely Wu P'ei-fu's policy. Before Chang Shao-tseng as a premier organized the cabinet, the faction in Loyang was the stronger. After the organization of Chang's cabinet, Ts'ao's followers overran the area of Tientsin and Paoting.

But at that time Wu P'ei-fu's reputation was at its height, and the politicians in Tientsin and Paoting dared not hurt his feelings. Nonetheless, they spread rumors that a particular "someone" was going to be prime minister. Wu P'ei-fu strongly rebuked them, saying that, for the sake of a unified republic of China, he had invited Li Yüan-hung to resume the presidency. He added that it was regrettable for politicians and militarists to work for their private ends when the nation was in chaos.

The Able Men Cabinet

After Li Yüan-hung resumed the presidency, he appointed Yen Hui-ch'ing acting provisional premier to organize a cabinet. At the beginning of August the parliament was convened and then T'ang Shao-i was nominated for the premiership, T'ang understood that the central government was dominated by the Chihli clique. He therefore declined the offer, but sent one of his confidants to participate in the cabinet. Consequently the minister of education, Wang Ch'ung-hui, was made concurrently acting premier. On September 19, 1922, the newly organized cabinet included Premier Wang Chung-hui, Finance Minister Lo Wen-kan, Foreign Affairs Minister Ku Wei-chün [Wellington V. K. Koo] and Justice Minister Hsü Chien. The first three ministers on the list just mentioned were proponents of government by men of intellect and proved ability, and this cabinet accordingly was called the "Able Men cabinet". The ministers of domestic affairs and communications were Wu P'ei-fu's confidants, and for this reason Wu's followers were satisfied with the new cabinet and were ready to support it. According to Chou Lu's *Draft History of the Kuomintang in China*, Premier Wang Ch'ung-hui intended to make Wu accept Sun Yat-sen's Three Principles of the People, an intention much resented by the followers of Ts'ao K'un.

The organization of Wang's cabinet was only temporary, for it was not approved by the parliament. Naturally the members were unhappy with the Able Men cabinet and did all they could to cause trouble. In the first part of October the premier as well as his cabinet members had to tender repeated resignations. On November 18 Wu Ching-lien, the speaker of the house of representatives, accused the finance minister of taking a bribe in signing a treaty with Austria. He personally brought a letter to the president urging the latter to issue an order for the arrest of the finance minister. On the following day the president was criticized for having acted illegally; on the twentieth, Wu P'ei-fu sent a telegram to the president charging him with the illegal arrest of the finance minister. On the twenty-third, Ts'ao K'un dispatched telegrams attacking the finance minister, Lo Wen-kan, and requested the organization of a special court to examine the bribery case thoroughly. This request was vociferously supported by Ts'ao's followers.

Wu P'ei-fu and his faction in Loyang were determined to maintain the Able Men cabinet. Ts'ao K'un tried to curry the favor of the parliament and was equally determined to get rid of the Able Men cabinet. Wu's and Ts'ao's factions began to wrangle openly. Fearing that the affray might weaken the power of the Chihli military clique, Wu yielded ground by declaring on the twenty-fourth his support of President Li, his obedience to Ts'ao, and his abandonment of Lo's bribery case.

On November 25, 1922, Wang's cabinet was dissolved. It took a long time to find a new premier who could meet the approval of the two factions; by the middle of December when Chang Shao-tseng was finally accepted by Ts'ao's faction and by the parliament as premier, Wu's faction was refraining itself from meddling in political affairs. Thereafter Ts'ao's factions in Tientsin and Paoting were very active in securing the presidency for their leader.

Parliamentary Quarrels and Ts'ao's Intrigues

Apart from the internal struggle within the Chihli clique, the parliament itself also had much trouble. At the beginning of the restoration of the parliament, a group of parliamentary members suggested that the parliament should concentrate its energy on making a constitution. Another group of members advocated the solution of the presidential problem first to see whether the new president was legal or not; if illegal, the parliament should consider the present government as provisional and elect a new president. This advocacy of a new election was to pave the way for their political plot.

In the middle of October 1922, the question was introduced in the parliament: how the term of the president should be counted and when the term should be completed. After the establishment of Chang Shao-tseng's cabinet, many members of the parliament had received financial allowances from Ts'ao's faction. Immediately the beneficiaries were told to elect Ts'ao president. A few tuchuns of the Chihli clique feared that premature action might do the clique harm; consequently on January 8, 1923, they advised Ts'ao to take cautious action. This telegram might have been privately suggested by Wu P'ei-fu.

The members of Chang Shao-tseng's cabinet were mostly "stooges" of Ts'ao K'un. The premier himself was avaricious and fond of prestige. After taking up the premiership he tried to keep on good terms with the parliamentary members and the politicians of Ts'ao's faction, as well as with the press. He declared that his cabinet aimed at peace and unification and that he planned to call a conference consisting of provincial representatives to discuss such problems as unification, disarmament, and financial reorganization.

But this proposal for a provincial representative conference was strongly criticized by both Ts'ao and Wu. Wu was afraid that such a conference might change the political system into a federal government; Ts'ao feared that the discussion of the presidential problems might turn in favor of Sun Yat-sen. Because of this vociferous disapproval, Premier Chang gave up his avowed aims.

Before long Ch'en Hsiung-ming in Kwangtung was driven away by the troops of Yunnan and Kwangsi. Shen Hung-ying had entered Canton and Sun Ch'uan-fang also marched to the frontier of Fukien. Observing this development, Ts'ao and Wu agreed to make use of the military power of Shen and Sun to subdue the Southeast. Premier Chang was pressed to appoint Shen and Sun as tuchuns of Kwangtung and Fukien respectively. Fearing that Sun Yat-sen might become president of South China, Ts'ao and Wu urged Premier Chang to make the two appointments, which were considered by the premier as an act tantamount to the declaration of war against the South. He therefore resigned with his whole cabinet.

Premier Chang himself, however, was still reluctant to give up his position. A few days after his resignation he shamelessly continued to issue the orders that were demanded by Ts'ao and Wu. But through Ts'ao's followers the entire cabinet storm had become public knowledge. Their plan was to discredit Chang first and make President Li unable to organize a new cabinet, so that the central government would be chaotic, disturbances would appear among soldiers and policemen, and thus President Li would also be compelled to resign. This covert plan was not perceived by many members of the parliament. Premier Chang also had a number of supporters in the parliament and the two groups had many bitter fights with each other.

Intrigue for the Presidency

After Li Yüan-hung resumed his presidency, he declared in a telegram that he would wait for the parliament to discuss and decide the legal problem regarding his own position. When the parliament convened, opinion concerning the length of his term varied greatly. Those who were enthusiastic to complete the constitution wished to prolong President Li's term until the proclamation of the new constitution. The followers of Ts'ao K'un preferred on the contrary to shorten Li's term so that a new presidential election would have to take place earlier, and to their own advantage. During April and May those who relied on President Li for their livelihood fought to prolong Li's term at least until September 1925. Stimulated by this intention, Ts'ao's followers found it impossible longer to tolerate the president. At the beginning of May they insisted that the term of President Li was limited to 160 days, a term already exceeded, and that he should resign automatically, his position and functions to be performed by the cabinet for the time being until a president was elected.

President Li, aware that he could not remain much longer, urged the two houses to prepare for a new election. The faction in the parliament enthusiastic for a constitution was frightened by Li's suggestion, lest its work should be interrupted again. They made August 31, 1923, the time limit for the completion of the constitution and set September 30 for the presidential election and the proclamation of the constitution.

But many members of the parliament cared only for their own interests and were so frequently absent that it was difficult to make up a quorum. Zealous supporters of the constitution tried to amend the laws governing the meetings for the discussion of the draft constitution. They reduced the number of participants for making a quorum and at the same time passed a new regulation to give $20 to those who were present for the constitutional discussion and to set up a fine of $20 on those who were absent. When the leaders of the two houses, accompanied by a number of other members, went to see President Li to ask him to raise funds for the designated purpose, he instantly summoned the premier, the finance minister, and other financial authorities. An allotment of $170,000 per month was assigned for the drafting of the constitution, to be taken from the revenue of the customs duties for a period of four months.

Upon learning this news, Ts'ao K'un and his adherents in Tientsin and Paoting interpreted this action of the president as an attempt to win the favor of members of the parliament in order to win the presidential election. They immediately caused trouble on the pretext that President Li did not consult the cabinet for allotment of the money, an action opposed to the spirit of the responsible cabinet system. All cabinet members were compelled to resign on June 6, 1923, and the Chang cabinet failed. Premier Chang himself was said to be unwilling to resign but he was persuaded by Ts'ao's liegemen that after President Li was driven out, he would again be made premier.

Li Driven Out by Ts'ao, 1923

On June 7 the army inspector, Feng Yü-hsiang, and the garrison commander of Peking, Wang Huai-ch'ing, led more than 500 soldiers and policemen to the office of the president, demanding an interview concerning their military rations, on the grounds that since there was no one responsible for the cabinet, they had to ask the help of the president instead. Li promised that they would be paid two days before the spring festival—still twelve days ahead. On June 8 a large group of rascals and beggars claiming to be a Citizens' Corps paraded outside T'ien-an Gate. Influenced by student parades, they carried placards and flags on which was written, "Down with President Li." They paraded to the private house of the president, surrounding it and making much noise. The president called the police chief and the garrison commander to suppress them, but his request was ignored and the troublemakers did not disperse until midnight. On the ninth the policemen of Peking went on strike on the grounds that they had not been paid for a long time and were too hungry to perform their duties. Thereafter, the president was daily annoyed by the so-called Citizens' Corps, and the soldiers and policemen demanding their pay. But Li still remained. Observing the situation, Army Inspector Feng Yü-hsiang and the garrison commander, Wang Huai-ch'ing, tendered their resignations to the president, indicating that they would not be responsible for the maintenance of order and safety in the capital.

The president returned the two resignations, but Feng and Wang refused to withdraw them. Then Li asked Ku Wei-chün and Yen Hui-ch'ing to organize a new cabinet. Both Ku and Yen, who understood the plot of Ts'ao K'un, whom they dared not offend, declined the offer. The president also sent telegrams to Ts'ao K'un and Wu P'ei-fu asking for their help; naturally Ts'ao ignored President Li's solicitation, while Wu, who had formerly declared that he would support the president, now also ignored him. At that time only one minister, the minister of agriculture and commerce, who was outraged at the vicious behavior of Ts'ao's clique, was ready to assist Li to the end.

On June 13 Li determined to leave Peking for Tientsin. Before his departure he prepared several orders: (1) He approved the resignation of Premier Chang. (2) He approved the resignation of all cabinet members except Li Ken-yüan. (3) He appointed a new minister of war. (4) He abolished such titles as army inspector and tuchun. All these orders were cosigned by Li Ken-yüan. After the president's signature the orders were to be given out for publication. This was a step to battle the Chihli clique. But at that time even the office for proclaiming orders was controlled by Ts'ao's faction, and the orders were withheld. Li actually left Peking at two o'clock in the afternoon of June 13.

Before Li was coerced into leaving the capital, all stationery and stamps of the president's office were carried by his family to the French Hospital in the Legation Quarter for safekeeping. Discovering the disappearance of these indispensable items, one of Ts'ao's followers immediately sent a telegram to the Chihli governor, Wang Ch'eng-pin, to detain the president. Wang ordered his police chief and a number of policemen to intercept the president at the railroad station at Yang-ts'ui, about fifteen miles from Tientsin. As soon as Li's train reached the station, he was asked the where-abouts of the presidential stationery and stamps. Li did not give them the exact information until he was threatened and his train was not permitted to leave the station. After the presidential stamps and the other material had been recovered from the Legation Quarter, Governor Wang compelled Li to sign three telegrams—one to the two houses of parliament, one to the cabinet, and a third to the people of the whole nation. The main idea of the telegrams was to say that for some reason he had to leave the capital, that he asked leave of the parliament to resign, and that he asked the cabinet to perform his functions as president. Governor Wang threatened that if the telegrams were not signed, Li would never leave the station.

Reaction Against Ts'ao

Since the action of Ts'ao's followers was so impudent, it is hard to understand why they did not put Ts'ao K'un simply and directly into the presidency, and why they should instead take so much trouble and spend so much money to bribe the members of the parliament to elect Ts'ao president. On June 14 the cabinet announced that it was taking over the duties of the president. On the sixteenth the speaker, Wu China-lien, persuaded many unprincipled members of the parliament to pass a resolution that all orders issued by Li Yüan-hung from Tientsin after the thirteenth would be ineffective. After Li reached Tientsin, he was still issuing orders with Li Ken-yüan as cosignatory to embarrass the Chihli clique. Feng Yü-hsiang and Wang Huai-ch'ing also announced the resumption of their duties. Ts'ao K'un sent a telegram from Paoting ordering Feng and Wang to maintain order in Peking. Ts'ao even went so far as to state that "parliament is the foundation of law of the nation; it should be respected and protected."

Of the parliament members some with integrity left Peking for Tientsin and tried to save the situation. Public opinion was now sharply opposed to Ts'ao K'un and his henchmen. The politicians of the entire Chihli clique busily traveled around to form a league with other circles in order to carry on a war against Ts'ao's clique, but since they themselves had divergent opinions, their efforts were not very effective.

Ts'ao Buys the Presidency, 1923

Afraid that the departure of a part of the parliament to the South might affect the quorum for the presidential election, Ts'ao's followers found two methods to keep more members from going away and to persuade those who had left Peking to return. Noticing that most of the remaining members were those avid to complete the constitution, they invited them to continue to work on it. Understanding that most of the members had no objection to receiving money, they offered $5,000 to each member to remain or return, but most important of all, to elect Ts'ao K'un as president. Even those of known integrity were tempted by the generous offer. By October 5 more than five hundred members had valued the money more than integrity, and for this reason they were labeled the "piggish" [*chu-tzu*] members. Thus Ts'ao K'un's plot to usurp the presidency was carried out.

The success of Ts'ao K'un's plot marked the decline of Wu P'ei-fu's reputation and power. Before the occurrence of Finance Minister Lo's case, many people thought that Wu P'ei-fu was an outstanding member of the Peiyang warlords. After that much publicized case, Wu, for the purpose of preserving the power of the Chihli clique, followed along with all the distasteful actions of Ts'ao K'un's faction as if he had forgotten that Ts'ao's power entirely relied on him, and that his own potential power was built on the sympathy and support of public opinion. Because he obeyed Ts'ao absolutely, he destroyed this sympathy and support; he expressly relied on his military power to disturb South China and to subdue the Fengtien clique in Manchuria. The people at large now considered him only a henchman of Ts'ao K'un.

A few days before the presidential election the five hundred or more parliament members began to feel ashamed. To redeem themselves, they rushed the constitution, which had been in the making for more than ten years, to completion. Within two or three days it had passed second and third readings. On October 10, 1923, Ts'ao K'un was inaugurated as president, and on the same day Speaker Wu China-lien proclaimed the constitution. The contents of the new document showed favor toward a federal government, but it was in reality only a means to cover the guilt of the parliament. It looked as though the parliament had committed suicide. There were no more people who wished to stand up for the protection for the constitution. Nor was there any more momentum in the movement for federal government. Hereafter the only new hope was the Kuomintang.

CHAPTER FOURTEEN REORGANIZATION OF THE KUOMINTANG AND THE END OF THE PEIYANG WARLORDS

In January 1924, three months after the election by which Ts'ao' K'un bribed his way into the presidency, the Chinese Kuomintang held its first national congress at Canton; the party was reorganized and a new era of Chinese political history was ushered in. Thereafter political arguments revolved, not around the constitution, but around the party. Efforts now were concentrated on the "legitimate party" rather than the "legitimate constitution." However, during the first two years of the reorganization, the party did not gain much strength and the big warlords were still powerful.

Important political changes occurred, nevertheless, from the spring of 1924 to the summer of 1926. The Kuomintang created its own army and suppressed the uprising of the Canton Merchants' Association, which was operating under the protection of foreign imperialists. In North China the warlords of Kiangsu and Chekiang were battling, and the second war between the Fengtien and Chihli cliques also took place during the autumn and winter of 1924. Feng Yü-hsiang's revolt against Wu P'ei-fu precipitated the fall of Wu and Ts'ao, and also the organization of the Executive Government in Peking by the Peiyang warlords—their last real attempt at control of the government.

Anticipating the failure of this Executive Government, the Kuomintang decided not to cooperate with it but to consolidate its bases in Kwangtung and Kwangsi. In the autumn of 1925 the warlords in the North were engaged in another fracas which lasted until the summer of 1926, when the Peking Executive Government was overthrown. While the Northerners were fighting, the Kuomintang had completed its internal reorganization and was ready to demonstrate its real power in a final struggle against the Peiyang warlords.

CHINESE SOCIAL THOUGHT BEFORE THE KUOMINTANG REORGANIZATION

In order to understand the significance of the party reorganization in 1924, it is necessary to have first a clear view of the turning tides of social thought. Before 1911 Chinese social thought was concentrated on the racial problem between the Chinese and the Manchu. Although the T'ung-meng Hui had long made known the Three Principles of the People, a majority of its members still maintained a narrow nationalism or racialism. After the overthrow of the Manchu dynasty, the people at large, confident of peace, prosperity, and comfort, believed that the golden age had begun. The political parties meanwhile argued the relative merits of a strong presidential system versus a responsible cabinet system, and the bicameral versus the unicameral system. In short, their interest was limited to political systems. Despite their low standard of living, the people did not feel overwhelmed by imperialist pressures upon China. What they were concerned about most was whether the monarchy should be restored or not. From 1912 to 1916 political theories and activities had little to do with actual social conditions.

Language Reform and the Russian Revolution

In 1915 a farsighted newspaperman, Huang Yüan-yung, began to realize that political discussions should start with the simplification of the Chinese language. Unless this were done, most of the people could not take part in discussion of modern social ideas.

After the failure of the monarchical attempt in 1916 and the beginning of the Constitution Protection Movement in the following years, the Chinese intelligentsia received two great stimuli from China and abroad. That from China was the literary revolution sponsored by the magazine *New Youth* [*Hsin-ch'ing-nien*], published in 1917 and 1918; the other was the Russian Revolution. The national literary revolution seemed to have little relation to the reorganization of the Kuomintang—Sun Yat-sen preferring to retain the classical Chinese style. Nevertheless, the simplified *pai-hua*, or spoken-language style of writing, at least gave the Kuomintang a new and effective means for propaganda.

Before 1911 the official party periodicals, especially Chang Ping-lin's essays, could hardly be understood even by college students. Today the text of the "Three Principles of the People" [*San-min chu-i*], written in *pai-hua* style, can be understood by even junior-high-school graduates. Emancipation from the restriction of classical style promoted the emancipation of the thinking of the people. Thus the literary revolution preceded and influenced a new cultural movement, an invigorated and enriched Chinese thinking world. Now it was possible for almost everyone to buy newspapers and other periodicals—a phenomenon unknown in China before the literary revolution.

The socialist revolution in Russia almost coincided with the Chinese literary revolution. The overthrow of one of the strongest despotisms by Bolshevism, followed by the defeat of powerful emperor William II in Germany by the Socialist Party, shook the whole world. These events naturally awakened Chinese thinking circles, and the literary movement already existing in China assisted in this awakening. Formerly, the Chinese intelligentsia regarded Sun Yat-sen's principle of people's livelihood, a form of Western socialism, as merely a Utopian idea. But now Russia had shown that this idea was workable, and sympathy for Sun Yat-sen began to grow. Even the conservatives tried to use socialism as a weapon in the fight against the warlords.

Those who promoted China's new cultural movement disagreed among themselves. Some advocated socialism as the only salvation of China; others thought Chinese society had not yet developed to the stage where socialism could be practiced. The supporters of the *New Youth* magazine were also divided into two groups: Hu Shih and others issued new periodicals, the *Weekly Review* in Peking and the *Pacific Monthly* in Shanghai, and published articles arguing against the radical ideas of Ch'en Tu-hsiu and Li Ta-chao. Ch'en and Li tried their best to propagate their new political ideas, while Hu Shih suggested that the people make a thorough study of various problems but talk little about political theories or "isms." These vehement arguments heralded a great change in Chinese social thinking. From 1919 to 1923 numerous new magazines appeared; some were political, issued by the Kuomintang and the Communist Party, others were academic, and still others were semipopular.

Student Action

During this period discussions of social problems were not the only means of expression. The most striking action was the May Fourth Movement of 1919. This demonstration and parade of several thousand students in Peking against the government's weak foreign policy in the Paris peace conference developed into student and merchant strikes, which spread like wildfire from Peking to Shanghai, and on through the entire nation. The peace conference between the South and the North was thereby broken up. The immediate outcome of this great student demonstration was the removal of the three pro-Japanese traitors, Ts'ao, Lu, and Chang, but it also had a far-reaching general influence.

The background of the May Fourth Movement was a protest against the warlords' policy of selling out the interests of the nation as well as against the making of unequal treaties. In other words, it was a prelude to antimilitarism and antiimperialism. Starting from this movement, students' unions were organized in leading cities of all the provinces, and the National Students' Union was also organized. The latter organization proved to be even more effective and more active than the powerful Kuomintang. Later on, under the strong pressure of the warlords, propaganda and recruiting activities of the Kuomintang and the Communist Party in China were largely carried out by the student unions.

Early Communism and Workers' Movements

As early as 1912 there had been a political party which tried to promote socialism, but it did not attract much attention. Active socialist organization came into existence after the new cultural movement, through the stimulation of the Russian Revolution. China had been badly pressed by militarists and imperialists, who absorbed all the people's money. School funds, which were badly needed, had been used up by militarists for civil war. Poverty-stricken students could not continue their studies. There were not enough factories to give them work, and it was very difficult for them to find jobs in factories owned by foreign imperialists in China. Radical leaders of the new cultural movement tried to adopt Russian Communism and to arouse class consciousness in the Chinese people. The poorer Chinese were agitated to unite together to fight against the warlords and the imperialists. Such propaganda paved the way for the growth of Chinese Communism.

China's Youth Organization for Socialism was organized in 1919, and the Secretariat of the Laborers' Union in 1920. The Chinese Communist Party was formally established in 1921, when it held its first national congress in Shanghai.

A series of disruptive strikes occurred in the period between 1920 and 1923. The railroad workers of the Canton-Hankow line went on strike on January 1, 1921; K'ai-p'ing coal miners went on strike on March 2; on June 20 the mechanics of the Peking-Suiyuan Railway left their jobs; the Canton-Hankow Railway workers went out on October 12. But these were not all. On January 12 the Chinese seamen went on strike in Hong Kong, and similar actions were taken by the Hanyang steel and iron workers on July 22, by the Shanghai silk mill workers on August 5, and by the K'ai- luan miners on October 23. Because the students participated in the K'ai- luan miners' strike, the famous T'ang-shan University was dissolved on November 18 by the government. On February 7, 1923, Wu P'ei-fu's soldiers suppressed the strikers of the Peking-Hankow Railroad and killed a number of workers. Two days later students in Peking organized a great demonstration and parade to show their sympathy with the workers' strike.

Did this whole chain of strikes show that China's workers were really awakened? Most of these strikes were directly agitated and led by Communist students. Their purpose was to stimulate the class consciousness of the workers, to cultivate their rebellious spirit, and to organize them in the fight against warlords and imperialists.

Soviet Russia and the Intellectuals

Another new phenomenon was the friendly and sympathetic attitude of the Chinese intelligentsia toward Soviet Russia. Before the arrival of the Ignatius Yourin [or Yurin] mission to Peking in August 1920, a manifesto from the Moscow government, proclaimed by Leo Karakhan, assistant commissar for foreign affairs for Soviet Russia, denounced all unequal treaties signed by Czarist Russia and China. This was, of course, a diplomatic move by Soviet Russia toward expansion in the Far East. But the Chinese intellectuals, regarding the Soviet government as a great improvement over the Czarist regime, were delighted with the manifesto as an expression of good will.

The Chinese warlord government, under the control of the Western imperialists, dared not support a denunciation of imperialism from Russia. After spending several months in Peking, Yourin was unable to score any diplomatic success; but during his sojourn, he did build up relations with some professors and students of Peking University.

On August 12, 1922, the representative of Soviet Russia, Adolf Joffe, came to Peking, where the New Tide Society and thirteen other organizations honored him with a great welcoming party—an unusual procedure for Chinese people's organizations. This extraordinary social event demonstrated the good will of the Chinese intellectual class toward Russia. The Chinese warlords' government could not prevent such an action; and the diplomatic corps of the imperialists was envious of this reception for the Soviet representative.

The national organization of students indicated the desire of Chinese social thinkers to organize and unify the people. The influence of Marxist principles and the development of the Communist Party paved the way for the Kuomintang policy of accepting Communist members and allying itself with Soviet Russia. "Down with Warlords" and "Down with Imperialism" became the slogans of the day. Such was the background in which the reorganization of the Kuomintang was accomplished.

THE PROCESS OF THE KUOMINTANG REORGANIZATION

The reorganization of the Kuomintang was divided into three stages: (1) the definite adoption of the name of the party in 1919, (2) the preparation for the acceptance of Communist members and the alliance with Russia in 1923, and (3) the fulfillment of this policy in 1924.

The Underground Kuomintang

After Yüan Shih-k'ai dissolved the Kuomintang in 1913, it was reorganized in Tokyo in the following year under the name, Chinese Revolutionary Party [*Chung-hua Ko-ming Tang*], with the members of the old Kuomintang left out. The Chinese Revolutionary Party was an underground organization; for the purpose of registering in foreign countries, some branches still used the old name *Kuomintang*. After the death of Yüan Shih-k'ai in 1916, the party continued to exist and was active in the parliament. The two names, *Kuomintang* and *Chung-hua Ko-ming Tang* were used concurrently. The unification and the formal adoption of the party name, *Chung-kuo Kuo-min-tang*, was decided on October 10, 1919, by its headquarters at Shanghai.

From 1918 to 1919 when Sun Yat-sen was compelled to retire to Shanghai, he tried to reorganize his party and write books to change the thinking of the people. During this period his works, *Sun Wen's Political Theory* [*Sun Wen hsüeh-shuo*] and his *Industrialization Plan* [*Shih-yeh chi-hua*] were combined under the title *Plans for the National Reconstruction* [*Chien-kuo fang-lüeh*]. He stressed the need for psychological change and material rehabilitation. The views Sun Yat-sen sets out in these works help explain the basis of revised rules of operation in his newly organized party.

In the first stage the reorganized Kuomintang had not yet much contact with the people at large. Politics were controlled by Hsü Shih-ch'ang in the North and by Lu Jung-t'ing in the South, neither of whom could tolerate any open activity of the party. Therefore, the revision of the party rules of October 1919 applied only to its overseas members. Sun had not yet announced any mandatory political platform.

In 1920 Sun received some substantial financial aid from his overseas members which he used to order the Cantonese troops under the command of Ch'en Hsiung-ming to return to Canton and seize the whole territory of Kwangtung province. By that time some public attention was being paid to the party's affairs. Nevertheless, when in the summer of 1922 Ch'en Hsiung-ming revolted against Sun Yat-sen, most people supposed the incident to be a struggle for political power between the two men and did not perceive that this was Ch'en's revolt against the party. Because the activity of the Kuomintang had been kept confidential so long, few outsiders knew the position and relationship of the two persons within the party.

The Kuomintang and Communism

After Sun Yat-sen fled from Canton to Shanghai, the Kuomintang began to enter its second stage. Sun Yat-sen considered that it was necessary for one party to monopolize the government during the revolutionary period, and for party members to obey their leader absolutely. For these reasons, in his work *Revolutionary Strategy* [*Ko-ming fang-lüeh*], Sun divided his revolution into three stages, military conquest, political tutelage, and constitutional government. When he reorganized the Chinese Revolutionary Party, he emphasized the idea of the monopoly of the government by one party and the obedience of members to their party leader [*tsung-li*]. This conception was further reinforced by the effectiveness of the Bolshevist Revolution in Russia.

Party dictatorship in Russia meant that Russian Bolshevists were obedient to the command of their party leader, Lenin. Chinese Kuomintang members, however, could not be commanded by Sun Yat-sen. Even Ch'en Hsiung-ming revolted against him. Sun Yat-sen was so discouraged that he had to reconsider the organization and revolutionary method of his own party.

By this time the Chinese Communist party had been established and had joined the Third International. Being harassed by imperialism in Europe, Soviet Russia was seeking friends in the East. According to Wang Ching-wei's *Political Report*, Sun Yat-sen sent a telegram to Soviet Russia from Shanghai in 1918, congratulating her and encouraging the leaders to continue their struggle, an action which was said to have cheered Lenin considerably. Thereafter he tried his best to cooperate with the Kuomintang. According to Wang Ching-wei, among the Comintern delegates a man called Maring went in 1921 to see Sun Yat-sen in his headquarters at Kwangsi. Sun's reaction was described to Liao Chung-k'ai in Canton by telegram; he said that he had been surprised at hearing of the practice of Communism in Russia, where economic conditions were not prepared for Communism, until Maring informed him that Russia was practicing the New Economic Policy which Sun regarded as the same as his own Industrial Plan. He added that he was much excited. This interview marked the beginning of Sun's hope for an alliance with Soviet Russia.

On the day before Sun Yat-sen had fled to Shanghai, on August 13, 1922, the Soviet envoy Joffe reached Peking. The two men corresponded and came close to an agreement. In Sun Yat-sen's letter dated August 30, 1922, to Chiang Kai-shek, he said that he "had correspondence with Joffe and invited the latter to Shanghai." In another letter to Chiang dated November 21, Sun said that the problem was complicated and troublesome, for Joffe requested the admission of the Chinese Communists to the Kuomintang. By this time some Chinese Communists, like Li Ta-chao, had already joined the Kuomintang.

Reorganization and Russian Example

During the period of negotiations between Sun Yat-sen and Joffe, the reorganization of the Chinese Kuomintang was decided upon. On September 4, 1922, a meeting of fifty party representatives from all provinces was held in Shanghai; the consensus was in favor of the reorganization of the party. A reorganization committee drafted the reorganization plan, which was carefully re-examined on November 15 by another plenary meeting of the representatives. Hu Han-min and Wang Ching-wei were elected to draft a declaration, which was revised and approved by Sun Yat-sen on December 16.

The manifesto proclaiming the reorganization of the Kuomintang of China, enacted on January 1, 1923, announced that after changing the name from the Chinese Revolutionary Party to the Chinese Kuomintang, its concrete political platforms would be made known to the nation; the Three People's Principles were newly defined and interpreted in a broad sense. The principle of nationalism, in the minds of the members of the T'ung-meng Hui, had been limited to the overthrow of the Manchu. The Three People's Principles were consequently regarded chiefly in terms of "two people's principles" emphasizing "peoples' self-determination" and nationalism. But before 1923 the connotation of the principle of nationalism had not been clearly defined.

In the Kuomintang manifesto of 1923 the definition of the principle of nationalism [*min-tsu chu-i*] is given in a negative sense as the elimination of unequalities among all races or nations, and in a positive sense as unification of all races within China and national equality in the world. Even though such slogans as "Down with imperialism" and "Abolish unequal treaties" were not put forward, the revision of treaties to enhance the Chinese international position to the level of freedom and equality became the party platform. The definition of the principle of people's rights [*min-ch'uan chu-i*] was also expanded from the "establishment of a republic" to "democracy with referendum" [*chih-chieh min-ch'uan*]. The principle of people's livelihood [*min-sheng chu-i*] had its meaning extended from "equal distribution of land" to the "control of capital."

The party reorganization of this time, though it had undergone a change, was still not as strict as the organization of the Soviet Communist Party. Sifting of old members and recruitment of new members was not yet thoroughly carried out. Although some Communists had joined the Kuomintang, there was not yet open acceptance of Communist members. The policy of making an alliance with Soviet Russia was under discussion but was not yet completed.

After the manifesto of January 1, 1923, Sun Yat-sen and Joffe made a joint declaration on the twenty-sixth. According to Wang Ching-wei's *Political Report*, Sun Yat-sen ordered Liao Chung-k'ai to accompany Joffe to Japan, where they spent one month in Atami discussing political and economic conditions, the Russian attitude toward the oppressed peoples in the East, and reasons why Russia wished to join hands with China. Returning from Tokyo to Canton, Liao assisted Sun Yat-sen in making an alliance with Soviet Russia. At that time, although many comrades were dubious of the wisdom of such a policy, relations between Sun Yat-sen and Soviet Russia, through Liao, were daily drawn closer.

Sun Yat-sen sent Chiang Kai-shek to Russia in the summer of 1923. When Chiang reached Moscow, Lenin was already seriously ill; but Chiang had conversations with Trotsky and other leaders. After a thorough field investigation of the Soviet military system, the organization of the Red Army, and the strict discipline of the Communist Party, Chiang returned to China charged with new momentum to reorganize the party and to train the party army. The party leader, Sun Yat-sen, was more determined than before to join hands with Russia. Soviet Russia, to support the Kuomintang, commissioned Michael Borodin to Canton, where he met with Sun Yat-sen.

A provisional Central Executive Committee consisting of nine members was formed and Borodin invited to be its advisor. Members were carefully recruited in Canton, and party offices were established in cities, towns, and other smaller divisions. The economic conditions of farmers, workers, and the bourgeois class were investigated. A unified propaganda office was set up and the party members were forbidden to express any opinions about the party before outsiders. Special schools or classes were opened to train party workers.

The First National Party Congress, 1924

A national congress, with 165 participants, was held at Canton, on January 20, 1924. Each province sent six delegates, three of whom were appointed by the party leader, Dr. Sun, and the other three elected by the local members.

Sun's inauguration speech to the congress reviewed party history:

> Formerly, because China was in great turmoil, and the people were ignorant of modern political ideas, I advocated "the ruling of the nation by one party." Now in retrospect, I realize that my plan was premature. The nation is still in great confusion and the social structure is still full of corruptions; therefore the responsibility of the

> Kuomintang is, first, the reconstruction of the nation; it is too early as yet to discuss in detail the administration of the nation.
>
> The initial goal of the revolution was the overthrow of the Manchu dynasty and its emperor. But after the Manchu dynasty was overthrown, numerous small emperors emerged. Therefore party rule in China cannot as yet be like party rule in England and America.... We must do more work to rebuild the nation....
>
> ...During the last thirteen years we have gained various kinds of political experience and discovered all sorts of methods .... The calling of many comrades from provinces to this congress was to offer an account of these methods to you for your adoption.... These new methods have been obtained through a careful, comparative study of the revolutionary methods used in the most advanced revolutionary nations as well as in the less advanced revolutionary nations .... I invite you all to make a study of them....
>
> There are two guiding principles in the reorganization of the Kuomintang: to reorganize the party so that it will become a powerful political organ with concrete platforms; and to use the power of the political party to reconstruct the nation. [1]

Sun meant by announcing adoption of a new revolutionary method that the party would be placed above the nation in order to rebuild the nation.

After this speech Sun Yat-sen formed a presidium consisting of five persons, including Hu Han-min, Wang Ching-wei, Lin Shen, and Li Ta-chao. The declared platform of the First National Congress of the Kuomintang was to be examined by the congress before its publication. The congress lasted ten days and was adjourned on January 30. During its session the Soviet ambassador Karakhan sent a congratulatory telegram. While the congress was discussing a pertinent reply, the news of Lenin's death was received. It was then decided to send to Moscow a telegram expressing grief. The meeting was extended for three days and the policy of alliance with Russia was clearly stated.

ORGANIZATION OF THE KUOMINTANG, 1924

NATIONAL PARTY CONGRESS

CENTRAL EXECUTIVE COMMITTEE CENTRAL SUPERVISORY COMMITTEE

CENTRAL PARTY HEADQUARTERS [*Tang-pu*]

PROVINCIAL TANG-PU SPECIAL DISTRICT TANG-PU

SPECIAL MUNICIPAL TANG-PU SPECIAL TANG-PU

HSIEN TANG-PU DISTRICT TANG-PU

COUNTY PARTY HEADQUARTERS [*Ch'ü tang-pu*]

BRANCH PARTY HEADQUARTERS [*Ch'u fen-pu*]

During the sessions of the congress someone suggested that the Kuomintang should not accept as members applicants who still retained membership in another party. The Communist member, Li Ta-chao, replied that Communist members of the Third International who joined the Kuomintang must obey the Kuomintang's principles and rules: that they should participate in the nationalist revolution, should entertain no intention of converting the Kuomintang members to Communism, and should join the Kuomintang as individuals, not as a group bent on infiltrating the Kuomintang.

During the ten-day conference many important resolutions were passed including those on the party rules and the text of the public declaration of policy. This text is divided into three large sections. Part I deals with the current situation in China; Part Ⅱ deals with the Three Principles of the People; and Part Ⅲ sets out the party's domestic and foreign policies. During the congress twenty-four members of the Central Executive Committee were elected as well as seventeen alternates and five members for the Central Supervisory Committee with five alternates.

This completed the reorganization of the Kuomintang. The accompanying chart of party organization shows the order of relationships within the party, all power converging in the National Party Congress.

The National Party Congress was recognized as the highest and most powerful organ of the whole party, with the branch party office as the smallest unit. The various levels from the provincial to the district party organizations also each had its own congress, of representatives and each had its executive committee.

After the conclusion of the First National Congress all party units were organized according to the new regulations and propaganda work was launched. Propaganda for the party's views had previously been circulated by means of lectures or published articles by individuals; now a systematic, large-scale propaganda machine was put into action.

Kuomintang propaganda promoted the views expressed both in the Kuomintang Manifesto of 1923 and the Declaration by the First National Congress of the Kuomintang in January 1924. Since the 1923 Manifesto forecast the views which were more fully developed in the 1924 Declaration it is useful to examine the two documents together.

THE KUOMINTANG MANIFESTO, 1923[2]

To understand the character of the Chinese revolution and the reason for its success requires at least a summary view of China's past and the complex of circumstances which has evolved with time. In the far past a single tribe formed a state, and with the passage of time various and variously associated tribes formed racial units. As larger numbers of these units were brought into association, the boundaries of the state expanded. That the rights of the people are the foundation of the state is an idea deeply lodged in the minds of the people; and for more than four thousand years few tyrants have escaped retribution visited upon them by the people. That the people's livelihood and not the wealth of the few should be the primary concern of the ruler of the state and that he should concern himself to prevent or correct unequal distribution of property is a theory proved valid in experience. Those who strive for good government are obliged to devote wholehearted effort to the labor of curbing the rich and powerful and preventing the seizure by the rich and powerful of property belonging to others. A benevolent state policy assures a distribution of property which reduces any marked difference between the rich and poor. That China has survived has been the result of the recurrent practice of these policies during our long history.

Whenever among our peoples equality has been denied and those administering the state have failed to insure the rights of the people and neglected equitable distribution of land, rebellions, wars, and revolutions have occurred. In natural course these revolutions have destroyed dynasties and given rise to new dynasties, since we have lacked reliable methods for assuring continuous peace and security.

More reliable methods comprised in the ideas of nationalism, democracy, and socialism have brought about revolutionary changes in modern Europe and in America, and these ideas have now spread to eastern Asia. In the process of development in other parts of the world nationalism, democracy, and socialism have been tested and perfected through hard experience and long discussion, and we now have the advantage of this experience and discussion among other nations. Since no nation can separate itself from the general trend of the world, we must now exert our own energy as a nation to share in the new world era ushered in by the revolutionary changes in the rest of the world.

Sun Wen, the leader of this party, has appraised the domestic situation in China, has watched the tide of the world, and has selected out of the experience of the whole world the most successful methods of procedure and incorporated them in his *Three Principles of the People*. These principles are to serve as the basic principles of our nation, with his Five Power Constitution as the basis of state administration. Since our government will be a democratic government, the nation will be established on a rock-solid foundation .... As our methods are new methods, so the object of our revolution is also different from that of the revolutions which have occurred in the past. The revolutions which have overthrown the dynasties, though begun by the people, have usually ended in the triumph of a new dictator and in no advantage for the people. Unlike revolutions in the past a modern revolution is directed by a leader who fights for the people .... The revolutionary effort is begun by the people and completed by the people. In carrying on this effort the Revolutionary Party as it developed from the Hsing-Chung Hui to the T'ung-meng Hui had already gathered members active not only in all the provinces but also overseas.

After the overthrow of the Manchu dynasty and the establishment of the Republic of China, many people thought that the period of destruction had ended, that reconstruction should begin at once, and that a constitutional government should be established immediately. In an effort to accomplish these ends a political party was requisite and the Kuomintang was organized. The failure of the Revolution of 1913 and the subsequent major crises compelled us to reorganize as the Chinese Revolutionary Party. Gathering many adherents, the party devoted its whole energy to crushing the traitor and all monarchists. With the crushing of the monarchists, revolutionary effort appeared to have accomplished its purpose. The attempts of the militarists to abrogate the constitution and the subsequent years of unremitting warfare destructive of all national security forced us to recognize that the basic principles of the revolution were not yet thoroughly established among the people and that it was incumbent upon us to continue our efforts to establish and protect these principles. To complete the great task of national reconstruction in cooperation with the whole Chinese people we have therefore reorganized the Kuomintang in order that our hopes for the peace and security of China may be fulfilled.

We have changed our party name and we have modified our rules but the principles we serve are the principles we have held from the beginning. Throughout the past thirty years, from the founding of the Hsing-Chung Hui to the present, our party has devoted all its efforts to the welfare of the whole nation. Not all of our efforts to serve the welfare of the people have thus far succeeded, but wherever we have been successful that success is evidence of the validity of our basic principles. Up to 1912 our party strove to establish a Republic founded upon these principles; after 1912 our party has served as the guardian of the Republic. The enemies of the Republic, from those who attempted to restore the monarchy on to those who tampered with the legitimate constitution, have indeed been powerful enemies; but the ultimate defeat of these reactionary forces has been the inevitable result of two continuing factors: the needs of the people and the tide of the times. Even so, the stubbornness of reactionaries and the indifference of those who claim to be spectators or neutrals have retarded national reconstruction, and the Three Principles of the People and the Five Power Constitution have yet to be established in wholly effective operation.

To establish the Three Principles of the People and the Five Power Constitution is our primary concern.... Our only choice is to continue our work day and night, to labor unremittingly.... Accordingly we present a carefully considered plan for carrying on the work of national reconstruction and an account of our present policy, developed with scrupulous regard for the Three Principles and the Five Power Constitution.

To implement their policies the Manchu despots did not rely upon the people of China, but depended on foreign assistance, and as a result concluded unequal treaties with other nations at the expense of the rights of our own people. Even with the overthrow of the Manchu dynasty our nation continues to function as a colony for foreign powers. In accordance with the principle of nationalism our party will continue to work for removal of all inequalities of status between our nation and foreign powers and we shall continue to work also for the integration of all the peoples of our country as a single Chinese nation. With respect to the principle of the self-determination of peoples which has received increasing acceptance since the conclusion of the European War, we accept this principle as favorable to the development of all the peoples within the nation and we shall also work for recognized equality of status among the other races of the world. To achieve this goal we must enforce universal education as a means to improvement of the cultural level of the whole nation. We must also employ every effort to accomplish revision of the treaties in order to restore our nation to a position of freedom and equality within the international family.

In accordance with the principle of democracy our party cannot approve of the present parliamentary system since elections based on class distinctions offer ready opportunities for abuse of power by the privileged few. To establish a genuine democracy we advocate a system of universal suffrage and the abolition of elections based on distinctions of class and property. Through either public assembly or universal ballot the people should exercise the rights of initiative, recall, and referendum. The people must also be assured of absolute freedom of speech, of assembly, of association, publication, residence, and religion.

With regard to the principle of the people's livelihood we recognize that unequal distribution of property, the cause and source of disputes, is still the defect of the European and American economic systems. China's extreme poverty can be relieved by active development of the country's natural resources. Although through development of the nation's natural resources the whole people can prosper, we shall still not escape conflicts within the nation so long as there is unequal distribution of property. From the experience of Europe and America we can learn the need for maintaining balance between social and economic development, and we must work for an adequate solution of all social and economic problems.

In the solution of these problems the state must codify an adequate land law, including laws for the use and taxation of landholdings. A designated period of time must be declared, beyond which no landholdings in excess of a specified legal limit may be retained. A value on individual landholdings must be set and reported to the state and on the basis of this declared value the state shall levy taxes or purchase such lands as excede the legal limit for individual holdings.

Railways, mines, forests, irrigation works, and other capital holdings for industry and commerce properly belong to the whole people and are to be governed and managed by the state. All workers in these major industrial and commercial enterprises shall also participate in their management.

On the basis of a new census of population and of arable land the production and consumption of food shall be regulated by law to ensure equal and sufficient distribution of food to the whole people.

To assure the economic security of the nation all fiscal matters shall be re-examined, the currency issues controlled, the customs duties reappraised, and the national debt readjusted.

To improve working conditions, and gradually to bring about equality of status between employer and employee, workers' protection laws shall be enacted.

Equality of opportunity shall be maintained for both men and women and equality of opportunity for the development of talent shall be fostered.

Toward the gradual development of equal status as between landlord and tenant, measures shall be undertaken to ameliorate farming conditions and enrich the life of rural communities.

These points here set forth comprise our essential aims. Other national problems are to be studied by special committees established under the rules of the party and the subsequent recommendations of these committees shall be presented for consideration by the governing elite [*sic*] and by the whole people.

This is the declared policy of the Kuomintang, January 1, 1923.

The much lengthier document issued at the end of January 1924 provides a summary of the vicissitudes of the Republic and an expanded account of party views and policies.

DECLARATION BY THE FIRST NATIONAL CONGRESS OF THE KUOMINTANG, 1924[3]

Report on the State of the Nation

The revolution in China has been in process since 1895, reached its crest in 1900, and in 1911 swept away the monarchy. Revolution does not come suddenly. Inequality of status and opportunity has oppressed and depressed the peoples of China since the Manchus first occupied China. When restrictions on maritime trade were lifted, China was further overwhelmed, as under raging tides, by the military pressures and economic pressures from foreign imperialists, which deprived China of independence and submerged her to the status of a semicolony. The Manchu government not only lacked means of stemming foreign aggression but, as if further to assist the foreign powers, it increasingly surrendered the powers of government to eunuchs and court favorites. Following our leader Sun Yat-sen, who realized that for the reconstruction of China the Manchus must first be overthrown, the members of our party rose courageously, fighting as the vanguard of the people to hurl down the corrupt Manchu government. The fall of the Manchu in 1911 accomplished only one stage in the whole process of revolution for the reconstruction of China. In the enthusiasm over the fall of the dynasty it appeared that the despotism of one race over other peoples had been wholly abolished and that an equal union of all races had immediately ensued, that the monarchy was disposed of and the nation securely established as a republic, and that old handicraft industries would be immediately transformed to machine production supported by large capital investments.

The actual social and political conditions of the early days of the Republic were not so far advanced as our first enthusiasm led us to believe, but our hopes in those days still represent the direction in which we must work in order to free China from semicolonial status and establish her as an independent nation respected among the major nations of the world.

In liberating the Chinese people from enslavement by the Manchus the revolution appeared to be already successful but the Republic soon suffered from other pressures which forced temporary compromises with dictators and counterrevolutionaries. The several links between the counterrevolutionaries and the foreign imperialists contributed to the pressures which held back the process of revolution. Though Yüan Shih-k'ai, representative of the despotism of the counterrevolutionaries, was not himself very powerful, the Revolutionary Party constrained itself from attacking him directly in the hope, thereby, of avoiding a prolonged civil war. The party was also handicapped in these years by members who lacked discipline and lacked adequate understanding of the party's function and purpose. Had we at that time possessed a thoroughly disciplined party, we could most certainly have outwitted the plots of Yüan Shih-k'ai and prevented his exploitation of members of the party. As it was, during those years the Revolutionary Party yielded power to this man who, as leader of the Peiyang warlords, intrigued with foreign powers and with militarists and politicians who depended on his favors. It goes without saying that the outcome of these compromises was disastrous for the Republic.

Even after the death of Yüan Shih-k'ai the efforts of the revolutionists met repeated failure. The warlords have now become so arrogant and so unprincipled that like knives and swords hacking cattle and fish they hack the people to pieces. No political democracy worth mentioning has as yet existed; the warlords conspire with foreign imperialists; and the so-called republican governments, controlled by the warlords, abuse the authority of government to serve the pleasure of foreign powers. In return, the foreign powers, by lending the warlords funds to finance unremitting civil war in China, obtain special privileges and secure their spheres of influence. Furthermore, by indirectly supporting China's civil wars, the foreign powers secure the services of the warlords in conflicts among foreign powers who themselves have competing spheres of interest in China.

The continuing civil wars not only hinder the development of Chinese industry but fill the Chinese market with foreign goods. Chinese industrial goods cannot compete with foreign goods even in the domestic market. Foreign capitalists control our economic as well as our political life.

Because of our failure thus far to complete the process of revolution, the middle class has undergone many vicissitudes and has become impoverished. Small businessmen have become bankrupt and handicraft workers have become vagrants, soldiers, or bandits. Having no capital with which to work their land, farmers have been forced to sell their best fields at a loss. The cost of living increases daily, rents grow more exorbitant, and the misery of the whole people is everywhere visible.

Since 1911 the national situation, politically and economically, has deteriorated year by year and day by day. The accelerating lawlessness of the warlords and the encroachments by foreign powers have not only reduced China to a semicolony but visited upon the people of China the tortures of hell. With the nation in the throes of death, farsighted people have no choice but to find means of instilling new life in the whole people.

How shall we proceed to discover and establish this new life? Many political parties and many individuals, both Chinese and foreigners residing in China, all offer their own suggestions.

The Constitutionalists, for example, assert that only the lack of a constitution prevents unification and causes chaos. They do not recognize that a constitution can be effective only when it is actively supported by the whole people' a constitution as words on paper cannot defend the rights of the people from the arrogance of the warlords. Furthermore, since 1912 China has had the text of a constitution, but this has not deterred the monarchists, the warlords, or corrupt career politicians from exploiting the text of the constitution as an excuse for visiting further injury upon the people. Ts'ao K'un, for example, recently bribed his way into the presidency, using the text of a so-called constitution to gloss over his usurpation. From experience we must now recognize that the whole people must be prepared to defend the constitution before a constitution can be effective. An unorganized people cannot make a constitution. Furthermore no constitution can be effective until we have first driven out the foreign imperialists and destroyed the warlords.

As for the Federalists, they argue that the present chaos has been created by overconcentration of power in the central government. Concluding that we must allot the power of the central government to the provinces, they argue that with limited power the central government can do no evil. But the Federalists have not sufficiently reflected upon the fact that although the Peking government was not bestowed by law on the big warlords, these warlords control it and utilize it to expand their own military power. Instead of proposing to destroy the military power of the great warlords, the Federalists have been encouraging the small warlords in the provinces to flout the authority of a central government. In practice China has been divided and every self-seeking small warlord not only occupies a province from which he can compete for status with the great warlords of Peking but is also a supporter of this *status quo* which serves his personal interests. Can this be called self-government? Genuine democracy is a prime requisite, but no single province can maintain true freedom and independence so long as the whole nation is not yet free and independent.

As for the Peace Conventioners, they suppose a civil war of which they are desperately weary can be stopped by a conference. But war in China is waged by feuding warlords who are concerned only for personal advantage and wholly indifferent to the welfare of the nation. Competing personal interests among individual warlords make both reconciliation and reunion impossible.

As for business executives, they assume that if China were ruled by capitalists rather than by militarists and politicians the nation could live in peace. These businessmen argue that people hate militarists and career politicians because such men do not represent the people's interests. Would the capitalists represent the people's interests? Militarists and our career politicians notoriously rely upon foreign support. Can the capitalists be independent of foreign capital? We have no basic objection to businessmen in government. We urge, however, that all the people organize a government to represent all interests and not solely the interests of commerce and industry. The government must be independent, must not ask help from special interests, and must represent the principles and interests common to the whole people.

Our Kuomintang has long believed that China's only resource for new life is the nationalist revolution and enforcement of the Three Principles of the People. This present survey of the state of the nation helps us understand that the nationalist revolution is inevitable and imminent. We are therefore proceeding to an explanation of our principles and a declaration of our political platform to the people of the whole nation.

The Principles of the Kuomintang

Sun Yat-sen's doctrine of the Three Principles of the People is accepted as the political doctrine of the Kuomintang. As the only means of saving the people of China, the nationalist revolution must proceed to implement the Three Principles of the People. The recent thorough reorganization of party structure and the discipline established for party members are intended to encourage every member to devote all his energy to the fight for establishment and enforcement of the Three Principles.

Of these three principles the principle of nationalism [*min-tsu chu-i*] supports two aims: the liberation of China by the Chinese people; and establishment of equal rights for all the races living in China.

In support of the first aim of nationalism the Kuomintang proposes to secure the recognition of the freedom and independence of China among the nations of the world. Although before 1911 the Manchus dominated all the other races in China, the foreign imperialists also dominated the Manchus. The nationalist revolution was aimed both at destroying the Manchus and putting a stop to the aggressions by foreign powers who were slicing the empire of China like a melon. Since 1912 Manchu domination has been disposed of, but we have not yet driven off the foreign imperialists. Although their former military encroachments are now relinquished in favor of economic oppression, so long as such oppression exists China has neither freedom nor independence. Because Chinese militarists conspire with the imperialists and Chinese capitalists share the profits, the Chinese people are robbed daily of both political and economic independence.

Members of the Kuomintang must exert utmost effort in the fight to emancipate the Chinese people. In this fight they rely on the intelligentsia, on the farmers, and on the merchants for defense and support, because all classes are suffering from imperialist aggression, which the nationalist revolution has set out to destroy. Nationalism is the defense of industry because only release from the economic pressure of foreign powers can make it possible for China to develop as an industrial nation. Nationalism is the support of the industrial workers because only in a nationalist China can they escape exploitation by militarists and by native and foreign capitalists on whom they now depend and who squeeze and choke them and grudge them a living.

In the eyes of the masses the fight for the emancipation of the Chinese people is an anti-imperialist movement. Nationalism is a powerful weapon against imperialism. When imperialsm has been beaten down, the people can then enlarge their activities and unify themselves to accomplish the other aims of the revolution. We must assist and encourage the organization of the proletariat to help our people recognize their own powers and abilities. Only a firm alliance between the Kuomintang and the common people can realize China's hope for freedom and independence.

In support of the second aim of nationalism, equality of the Chinese with all the other races living in China, the Kuomintang will work for alliances and organized discussion of problems which concern us all. The Kuomintang solemnly declares that the party will recognize the right of self-determination for all the peoples in China and that following the defeat of the imperialists and the warlords and the establishment of a free and united Republic of China, every people in China shall be allowed freedom of decision in joining the Republic.

Of the Three Principles of the People, the principle of democracy [*min-ch'uan chu-i*] is recognized by the Kuomintang as supporting not only many indirect rights but also the specific rights of election, initiative, referendum, and recall. The exercise of these rights is described in Sun's Five Power Constitution, which provides for the separation of powers: namely the legislative, judicial, administrative, examining, and supervisory powers. This system of government avoids the defects of other modern parliamentary governments and also corrects the weaknesses of the traditional Chinese civil service examination system.

In contrast to most modern democratic governments in which power is monopolized by capitalists who oppress the common people, Kuomintang democracy means government shared by the common people. Kuomintang democracy is, however, different from any system which claims to bestow rights on everyone; Kuomintang democracy must meet the needs of the Chinese revolution and therefore it must be understood that the rights enjoyed by recognized citizens of the Republic are not allowed to enemies of the Republic. Upright individuals and recognized organizations will be permitted freedom and the rights enjoined by the constitution, but those who betray the nation, those who give their loyalty to the imperialists or to the warlords, will be permitted neither freedom nor rights.

As to the third of the Principles of the People, the principle of livelihood for the people [*min-sheng chu-i*] comprises two major aims: equalization of landholdings and regulation of capital. To achieve economic equilibrium we must no longer permit to a minority among our people a monopoly in land ownership. The state must regulate the ownership, use, and purchase of land as well as tax levies on land. Such regulations implement the principle of equality in property rights.

To prevent private capitalism from controlling the people's livelihood, the state will manage and control all banks, railroads, and ship lines, and all other large-scale enterprises. With the regulation of landholdings and the regulation of capital we establish socialism on a secure foundation.

Our farmers will understand us when we assert that agriculture is the basic source of China's wealth; and at the same time, of all classes in the nation, farmers have endured the greatest hardships. Under the Kuomintang the state will grant land to all landless and tenant farmers and also issue tools to work the land. Moreover, the state will repair irrigation works, instruct farmers in the rotation of crops, and assist farmers in the cultivation of new lands. By establishing and managing banks for farmers, the state will assist those who lack capital and have now been enslaved by enforced loans at exorbitant rates of interest. Ultimately farmers will enjoy the good life they deserve.

Chinese laborers without security and protection may be assured that it is the express policy of the Kuomintang to protect workers and to find employment for those who are out of work. Since poverty-stricken farmers and laborers exist everywhere in China and share in the common misery, they understand the need of liberation from oppression and should be able to understand the need to drive out the imperialists. Since the success of the nationalist revolution depends on cooperation from farmers and laborers, the Kuomintang must actively assist farmers' and workers' movements and also subsidize such efforts. We must also work untiringly to persuade farmers and workers to become members of the Kuomintang, making clear to them that since the Kuomintang is fighting against the imperialists and the warlords and all privileged classes, the nationalist revolution is also a revolution to emancipate farmers and laborers. Farmers and laborers participating in the work of the Kuomintang will be working for their own best interests.

We are here presenting a definitive interpretation of the Three People's Principles. To maintain the effectiveness of the party as now reorganized, party members will receive education and training under strict discipline to enable them to propagate the party doctrine, rouse the masses of the people, and qualify as experts in revolution and political organization. To maintain our effectiveness we must also develop an active propaganda to draw all the people of the nation into the revolutionary movement, to assist us in seizing political power and vanquishing the enemies of the people. When political power is in our hands and a new government established, the Kuomintang will continue to function as the nerve center of the state, controlling political power to check any subsequent counterrevolutionary effort and to guard against any conspiracy by foreign powers to oppress our victorious people. We must attack and remove whatever hinders the enforcement of Kuomintang principles. Only an efficiently organized and aggressive party can adequately protect an aroused people and properly fulfill its duty to the people of the whole nation.

The Kuomintang Political Platform

A. *Foreign policy*

1. All unequal treaties are to be abolished: foreigners' leased territories, consular jurisdiction, foreigners' management of customs duties, all political power exercised by foreigners in China at the cost of Chinese sovereignty. New treaties are to be concluded based on recognition of China as an equal and sovereign nation.

2. Any nation voluntarily surrendering special rights and abrogating all treaties which violate Chinese sovereignty will be accorded status as "most favored nation."

3. Any and all treaties harmful to China's interests will be reexamined and revised under the guiding principle of removing any commitments injurious to the sovereignty of any of the signatory powers.

4. All China's obligations for foreign loans, insofar as they are not harmful to Chinese government and industry, will be honored and repaid.

5. The Boxer indemnity shall be entirely appropriated as a fund for education.

6. The Chinese people will not undertake responsibility for repayment of such foreign loans as were contracted for by an irresponsible government, such as the Peking government, to maintain the power of the warlords through bribed elections and other misappropriations, loans not contracted for the purpose of serving the welfare of the people.

7. All professional trade organizations, such as banking firms and commercial houses, and social organizations such as institutions of learning will be invited to send representatives to a conference for the discussion of the repayment of foreign loans and methods of repayment, thereby to put an end to the semicolonial status of China largely occasioned by the acceptance of such loans.

B. *Domestic policy*

1. Maintaining an equal division of powers between the central

government and local governments is to be interpreted as assumption by the central government of power in all matters affecting the whole nation and retention of power by local governments in matters which vary with respect to specific localities. Concentration of power in the central government shall not be emphasized and the power of local governments shall not be excessively stressed. Although the people of each province shall prepare the constitution for that province and elect the governor of that province, no provision in a provincial constitution shall enjoin principles or procedures contrary to the purport of the national constitution. The governor of a single province administers the government of the province as the elected officer of the people for that province but also receives and honors all orders from the central government for the administration of affairs of national scope.

2. The *hsien* [district] is the local unit of self-government and the people of each *hsien* shall have the right of direct election and dismissal of *hsien* officers and the rights of initiative and referendum.

3. The *hsien* government shall receive the local land taxes and rents, the products from public lands and charges for the use of mountains, rivers, mineral resources, and water power and shall use these revenues in the administration of local affairs, for the support of needy and otherwise unprotected children and of the poor, for the provision of relief in famine, and for the financing of public sanitation. If the funds accessible to the *hsien* are insufficient to support proper development of natural resources and the inauguration and support of major industrial and commercial enterprises, the national government shall provide subsidies and also share in surplus profits. From the total income of each *hsien* not less than ten per cent and not more than fifty per cent of the revenues shall be remitted to the national government.

4. Universal suffrage shall be the established practice and election based on property qualifications shall be abolished.

5. All examination systems shall be revised and defects corrected.

6. The people shall be assured complete freedom of assembly, association, speech, publication, residence, and personal and religious beliefs.

7. The employment of mercenary troops shall gradually be discontinued and replaced by a system of military conscription. Concurrently the economic and legal status of soldiers and officers in the lower ranks shall be ameliorated; the qualifications for officers in the armed forces shall be strictly regulated and also the procedures for promotion and demotion.

8. The land tax and other taxes shall be fixed by law and other charges such as likin shall be strictly forbidden.

9. The census of population and arable land shall be rechecked and the production and consumption of food regulated to improve the distribution of food throughout the nation.

10. The state shall devote attention to the improvement of rural communities and enact measures to assist the farming population.

11. Laws shall be enacted and enforced to improve the welfare and working conditions of laborers and to assist and protect labor unions.

12. The principle of legal, economic, educational, and social equality for both men and women shall be explicitly recognized and political suffrage for women encouraged.

13. State-supported education shall be provided for all children, the school system reorganized, funds for education increased, and measures instituted to protect these funds from assignment to other purposes.

14. The state shall proclaim a land law governing land use and land tax....

15. Any commercial or industrial enterprise such as tends to monopoly and such as cannot be administered by a single individual, including such enterprises as railroads and navigation lines, shall be managed and operated by the national government.

The items listed above represent the considered conclusions of this party as to the minimum essentials in a political platform adequate to serve China in the present national emergency.

THE REORGANIZED KUOMINTANG IN KWANGTUNG: THE STRUGGLES OF THE FIRST YEAR

The reorganized Kuomintang encountered during its first year of operation a series of crises in Kwangtung. Nevertheless in this period of convulsive struggles the party succeeded in its efforts to establish an organized Nationalist Army.

In 1923-1924 the authority of the Military Government under Sun Yat-sen did not extend beyond the city of Canton. Outside the city, throughout the East River zone, Ch'en Hsiung-ming and other warlords were firmly ensconced with an army of approximately 30, 000 men. Southern Kwangtung was occupied by another warlord with approximately the same number of troops. The warlords along the East River and the warlord in the southern section of the province were active and vociferous enemies of the Military Government.

Presumably committed to the flag of the grand marshal, Sun Yat-sen, Yunnan troops served under the command of Yang Hsi-min, Kwangsi troops under Liu Chen-huan, Hunan troops under T'an Yen-k'ai, Kwangtung troops under Hsü Ch'ung-chih, Honan troops under Fan Chung-hsiu. There were also many other units under various commanders. If all these generals and soldiers had taken orders from Sun Yat-sen, the enemies along the East River and in the southern part of the province could have been conquered easily. But unhappily for Sun, some of the generals supposedly under his command were his covert enemies.

Weakness of Sun's Military Position

The strongest army units were commanded by Yang Hsi-min and Liu

Chen-huan, who had driven away Ch'en Hsiung-ming and supported Sun Yat-sen on his return to Canton. But for this very reason these two arrogant men would not accept orders from the grand marshal. Thus on the eve of the reorganization of the Kuomintang, the Military Government had very little power. Because Sun Yat-sen clearly understood the situation, members of the Central Executive Committee elected to head the reorganized Kuomintang included several important military leaders, such as T'an Yen-k'ai and Yang Hsi-min. Their inclusion, however, did not help strengthen the authority of the party over the militarists.

Yang Hsi-min and Lin Chen-huan came to Canton mainly to make money. They stubbornly ignored all party decisions. At that time the Hunan troops under T'an Yen-k'ai could hardly survive in Kwangtung, having "no food for the hungry, no clothes for the cold, no medicine for the sick, and no burial for the dead." Since the financial income of Kwangtung was almost entirely in the hands of Yang and Liu, their Kwangsi troops were well-fed and satisfied.

Sun Yat-sen could bear this situation no longer. At a military conference before the army officers of Yang and Liu he stated:

> Officers of the Yunnan and Kwangsi troops: You have driven away Ch'en Hsiung-ming, for which I am very grateful. At that time I was in Shanghai and without any effective military power. I had no intention to return to Canton. I wished to devote all my energy to writing books expressing my political ideas to my elders and brothers in Kwangtung. Then you sent your delegates to Shanghai asking me to return to Canton immediately and swearing that you would genuinely support me, obey my orders, and enforce my principles, for which I am also very grateful. Because of your promises I decided to return.
>
> But you now carry my flag only to devastate my own province. I am a member of the Revolutionary Party; I do not shrink from

sacrifices. If it were beneficial to the nation, my fellow elders and brothers would not flinch, no matter how acute the necessary suffering. But you occupy yourselves in devastating my home province; you are conferring no benefit on the nation. I can cooperate with you no longer. I must leave you. My only wish is to return to my home town of Hsiang-shan. [4]

After listening to this angry and bitter speech, Yang, Liu, and other generals, pretending to be deeply stirred, replied: "Why should our grand marshal be so angry? Whatever you wish us to do, we will hereafter absolutely obey you."

Sun Yat-sen then moved the passage of a resolution to unify the financial administration; the motion carried, unanimously. But the resolution could not be enforced. Each army still monopolized the financial resources within the area under its garrison, and each army officer collected his own taxes. In September 1923 Sun Yat-sen appointed Liao Chung-k'ai finance minister of the Military Government, finance commissioner of the Kwangtung provincial government, and concurrently chief superintendent of military rations, hoping thereby to accomplish unified control.

Liao Chung-k'ai issued an inauguration telegram stating that if all army officers were unselfish and were willing to let the Military Government concentrate its financial resources, these resources should be adequate to support all troops. So long as each army unit still permitted its arrogant officers and soldiers to do what they liked and allowed greedy officials to embezzle, the soldiers were unable to fight, officers could do no work, and the people were becoming more and more impoverished. The army officers' reply was presented in highly polished diplomatic language which sounded very attractive but granted nothing.

Liao Chung-k'ai was so dismayed that he resigned and returned all financial authority to the grand marshal. Hereafter, Liao concentrated his energy on party affairs in the central party organization, and was also the party representative in the Whampoa Military Academy in which he directed the political training of the army cadets. Such was the military and financial condition of the Military Government.

Imperialists and Canton Merchants Against Sun

The merchants of Canton also cherished ill feeling toward the Military Government. After 1916 the province of Kwangtung had almost continually been under the heel of troops from other provinces. Kwangtung was a relatively rich province, but after prolonged military devastation the merchants were by now weary and impatient. Ch'en Hsiung-ming had used the slogan "Canton for the Cantonese" to reject troops from other provinces. Sun Yat-sen, on the contrary, had to rely on the power of the Yunnan and Kwangsi troops to uphold the Military Government in order to carry out his revolutionary tasks. But the merchants could understand only that Sun Yat-sen was using other provincial troops to contest political power with Ch'en Hsiung-ming, and in so doing was making the merchants suffer tremendously.

For this reason merchants gave only the mildest kind of support to the Military Government. When the merchants learned of the decision of the Kuomintang to admit Communists as members and to make an alliance with Russia, they believed the disaster of Communism was near at hand. Although the reorganized Kuomintang did not oppose a private-property system, it did support farmers' and workers' movements, and its propaganda particularly favored the farmers and workers. This stand considerably decreased what little sympathy the merchants had still retained for the Military Government.

Another great enemy of the Military Government was the wealthy imperial colony, the Hong Kong government, which never had harbored any friendly feelings toward the revolutionary regime. Moreover, Great Britain and Soviet Russia—representing European and Asian imperialism respectively—now were irreconcilable foes. As soon as Borodin arrived at Canton, the Hong Kong government was disturbed, aware that cooperation of the Kuomintang with Soviet Russia for the purpose of putting down imperialism meant that their first target would probably be Hong Kong. As a preventive measure the British began to agitate among the dissenting Cantonese merchants to support Ch'en Hsiung-ming and other warlords in order to overturn the Canton government. Hong Kong then became a headquarters for all anti-revolutionary forces.

To sum up, there were enemies within and without the Military Government of Kwangtung. On the inside there were arrogant officers and soldiers and disobedient warlords; on the outside, shortsighted merchants, supplied with powerful money by imperialists, who also furnished weapons and clandestine plans. Pressure coming from all directions made it impossible for the revolutionary forces to remain in Canton.

The Whampoa Military Academy

In spite of these difficulties, the reorganized Kuomintang managed to establish one of its most important assets, the Whampoa Military Academy. His scores of years in revolution and in organizing the Revolutionary Party had not secured for Sun Yat-sen a genuine Revolutionary Army. He used his party members to persuade the mercenary troops or to infiltrate the troops to spread propaganda among the soldiers. But one abortive revolutionary uprising after another only produced numerous small warlords. For instance, the entire Kwangtung Army under Ch'en Hsiung-ming, having sworn its allegiance to the party, had been supported by almost the entire energy of Sun Yat-sen with the hope that Ch'en's troops could be regarded as the party army.[5] But it was this party army which had surrounded and attacked the office building of the Military Government.

At last realizing that the old-fashioned troops were undependable,

Sun Yat-sen made plans to train army officers who could understand his principles. In the summer of 1923, as has already been mentioned, he sent Chiang Kai-shek to Russia to study the organization and training of the Red Army. At the time of the Kuomintang's reorganization, Chiang, back from Moscow, was appointed by Sun to prepare an army officers' college for the Kuomintang. The school, located at the old site of the Navy Academy at Whampoa, was named the Whampoa Military Academy. The academy was opened in May 1924 and Chiang was made its president.

In a speech at the inauguration, Sun Yat-sen said:

> We have not thus far had a secure base from which to defend the Republic because our revolution has had only the support of the revolutionary party without the assistance of a revolutionary army. Because we have lacked a revolutionary army, the warlords have dominated the Republic and impeded the progress of the revolution. Our aim in opening this academy is to create the revolutionary task anew from this day and students of this academy... will be the bones and trunk of the forthcoming Revolutionary Army. [6]

For the Whampoa Military Academy, students were selected on the strict basis of their comprehensive understanding of the principles and spirit of the Kuomintang; they had to be young, strong, and enthusiastic about the gigantic task. The academy stressed morale and technical training.

The organization of the army cadets became the model of the future party army. In the academy there was a party representative, with power equal and parallel to that of the president, under whom there were organizations of smaller party divisions. This system was later introduced to all levels of the army. There was a party representative in the headquarters of each army division as well as in the office of every company. The Central Executive Committee issued two instructions to the party army academy and the party army:

1. All orders in the military academy and in the troops must be cosigned by the party representative and enforced by the president or the appropriate army officers. The party decisions in the army should also be enforced according to the same procedure.

2. Only those rules and orders for the military academy and for the troops which have been cosigned by the party representative will be fully effective.

This system was designed to make the academy and the troops direct instruments of the party. Obviously, it was patterned after the organization of the Red Army in Soviet Russia, although a counterpart can also be found in the army supervisory system in medieval China.

But all did not go well with the academy. According to Chiang Kai-shek's report on the Whampoa Military Academy in May 1924, there were scarcely more than 460 students, the weapons were insufficient, and funds precarious, because all the financial income of Kwangtung was controlled by the Yunnan and Kwangsi army. Consequently, it was almost impossible to do anything. The students found it difficult to study efficiently, and the academy as a whole could hardly maintain itself. Chiang goes on to say, "A number of our difficulties have been created by antirevolutionary troops, who recognize the purpose of this military academy and are very jealous of its success. They know that after the establishment of the party army, we will undoubtedly oppose them and they will no longer be able to extort money from the people. They therefore try to destroy us by every means."[7]

Yet in spite of all these impediments, the foundation for the Revolutionary Army was finally well established. The resentful Yunnan and Kwangsi troops did not long survive.

Sun Launches the Northern Expedition, 1924

Within a few months after the foundation of the Whampoa Military

Academy, it should have been clear that it was impossible both to create a party army and to build up enough strength for the Northern Expedition. Nevertheless, in September 1924 Sun Yat-sen launched the expedition from Shao-kuan. This was not mere foolhardiness. The premature attempt was necessitated by circumstances.

In the first place, the war of the Northern warlords between the provinces of Kiangsu and Chekiang broke out on September 1. War between Fengtien and Chihli was once more also imminent. Since Ts'ao K'un had usurped the presidency, all the other military cliques within the nation had formed a great anti-Chihli union. Tuan Ch'i-jui of the Anhwei clique, Chang Tso-lin of the Fengtien clique, and others now made an alliance with Sun Yat-sen. Even though these warlords were incompatible with the Kuomintang, they had the common objective of overthrowing Ts'ao K'un and Wu P'ei-fu. After military action began in Kiangsu and Chekiang, Sun Yat-sen could not watch idly. This was the immediate situation motivating his hasty Northern Expedition. Secondly, the environment around Canton was extremely bad. Sun Yat-sen wished to open a new field and to find a new way of life.

These intentions can be seen from his declaration to the Cantonese people concerning his Northern Expedition. In the concluding paragraph he says:

> I have troubled many of my fellow elders and brothers in my native province by commanding several armies to fight here and there and by asking all sorts of supplies.... The price of commodities is exorbitant and maintaining a livelihood for the people is increasingly difficult. The responsibility of revolution should be borne by the people of the whole nation; instead, a majority of responsibility has been taken by the people of Kwangtung. That is enough to make Cantonese people feel unjustly treated. In addition, arrogant soldiers and unruly officers have frequently neglected military discipline and

played havoc with the people. Greedy officials and dirty politicians, under the name of raising military funds, are profitably supporting themselves. The life of the people, their freedom and property, has no protection. Communications and means of transportation have been frequently severed .... The people of Kwangtung have been suffering and have been dismayed with revolutionary government; the merchants in particular are deeply disturbed. They should know, however, that revolutionary principle is one thing, while revolutionary process is another .... The present embarrassing condition in Kwangtung is caused by imperfect methods during the revolutionary process; it has nothing to do with revolutionary principles. Those who are dissatisfied with the present situation, who slander the revolutionary principle and oppose the revolutionary government, must for the protection of their principles subdue their antirevolutionary efforts....

Now the Revolutionary Party makes every effort to modify its process in order to improve cooperation with its people. We solemnly declare that (1) within a very short time all army units will be sent on the Northern Expedition; (2) the people of Canton will be given the right of self-government and the municipal government will be recognized within a few days; ... (3) numerous heavy taxes will be abolished and a new tax rate fixed by the newly elected officials.

These three decisions will be enforced resolutely by the revolutionary government. We wish the people of Kwangtung to understand the method and process of revolution. The revolutionary government is willing to follow the wishes of the people in order to make improvements. It is hoped that the people of this province will wholeheartedly support the revolutionary government and united in valiance defy the enemy of the government and its people in order to put the revolutionary principles into effect at the earliest possible moment.... The Republic of China will be truly benefited by your support.[8]

Sun Yat-sen understood that the Canton merchants had suffered from the covetousness and lawlessness of officers and soldiers and harbored ill feeling against the revolutionary government. He therefore wished to avail himself of the occasion of the Northern Expedition to order all troops to leave the province so that the revolutionary government could reorganize the finances of the province and win the sympathy and cooperation of the people.

On September 13 Sun Yat-sen issued a public declaration of his intention to fight against Ts'ao K'un. He gave the seal of the grand marshal to Hu Han-min, delegating him to perform the grand marshal's duties. Then, in company with T'an Yen-k'ai, Sun went to Shao-kuan.

The troops ordered to leave the province comprised only the Hunan army under T'an Yen-k'ai, the Yunnan troops under Chu P'ei-te, and the Honan troops under Fan Chung-hsiu. The other Yunnan and Kwangsi troops, those of Yang Hsi-min and Liu Chen-huan, rejected Sun's order to march and retained their hold on the territory in the vicinity of Canton. Yang and Liu had become even more reactionary and more antirevolutionary than before. In Chiang Kai-shek's *Military Report* he said that the Northern Expedition of 1924 was to help the government to see more clearly whose army was obedient and whose army was rebellious. All those who denied the transfer were, by government order, regarded as enemy troops, which must be disbanded. As for the Northern Expedition, obviously no achievement could be expected under such conditions.

The Merchants' Association Incident, 1924

The strikes by the Canton Merchants' Association occurred at the time when the revolutionary government was launching its Northern Expedition. Connected with this merchants' plot were Ch'en Hsiung-ming and the Yunnan and Kwangsi troops. The action began in the latter part of May 1924, a few months before the Northern Expedition marched. The municipal government of Canton announced a new law governing property and streets in the city: the streets would be widened, straightened, and rebuilt; and the stores along both sides would have to pay a special tax for the reconstruction. A conference representing all the Canton merchants promptly decided to go on general strike, and a sort of militia was organized by the Merchants' Association to prevent any military pressure from the government. The government had to rescind the law, and this general strike was called off. The militia, however, continued and the Merchants' Association worked out a detailed set of regulations for joint offensives.

Then on August 1 the president of the Merchants' Association, Ch'en Lien-po, who was a comprador for the Hongkong and Shanghai Banking Corporation [*Hui-feng yin-hang*] managed to acquire from the Military Government a license to buy guns. Within four days after receiving the license, he bought more than 9000 guns which had been carried to Canton by a Danish ship.

Upon receiving this news Sun Yat-sen knew that Ch'en Lien-po had intrigued with Ch'en Hsiung-ming. These guns must have been purchased long before, loaded aboard ship, and held ready to enter port; otherwise the whole procedure of licensing, purchasing, and unloading could not have been accomplished within four days. Sun Yat-sen ordered his subordinates to detain all these guns at the Whampoa Military Academy. The number of weapons was found to be much greater than that provided for by the license. It was an obvious case of smuggling. The Merchants' Association objected to the confiscation of the guns by the government. Accordingly a general strike by the Merchants' Association was again instituted.

The British consul general openly interfered in this case. On August 27 a communiqué similar to an ultimatum was sent to the ministry of foreign affairs of the Military Government saying that the British had learned that Chinese troops were about to attack the Merchants' Association, and that if it were true, the British admiral would order his navy to attack the Chinese government troops. Sun Yat-sen filed a protest against such a plan with the MacDonald cabinet of Great Britain.

In view of this hazardous situation the revolutionary government was prone to compromise with the Merchants' Association. A few generals of the Yunnan army, Fan Shih-sheng and others, who had connections with the Merchants' Association, offered their services as mediators in the capacity of neutrals. They suggested signing an agreement with the Merchants' Association guaranteeing that the government would return to it all the guns and in return the Association would give the government half a million dollars; but this arrangement could not be negotiated. Later on, Sun Yat-sen permitted the militia and the Merchants' Association to buy guns directly from his headquarters, so that the total number of the guns could not fall into the hands of a few ambitious merchants. But the merchants' representatives stubbornly insisted that all guns should be given to them to be redistributed to their members.

Early in October the government tendered another compromise by giving 5000 guns to the Merchants' Association to be redistributed, for which the latter were to pay $200,000 to the government. In addition, the government was to collect one month's house rent from the whole city. The Merchants' Association consented to such arrangements, and all stores were readied for business. On the tenth of October 5000 guns, including rifles and pistols, were shipped from Whampoa to the Merchants' Association.

On this same date, the Chinese national holiday, many students, workers, and farmers paraded in celebration of the foundation of the Chinese Republic. The paraders had a skirmish with the Merchants' Association. The merchants opened fire on the unarmed crowds, killing and wounding a number of paraders. On the following day the Merchants'

Association distributed handbills accusing the government of giving them less than half the guns which they had purchased and demanding that, unless all guns were given back to them, their stores would not be opened. About half of the stores in the city remained closed.

The headquarters of the Merchants' Association again pasted public notices on the walls ordering its militia to patrol the streets and to punish severely any lawless persons who should dare disturb the peace. At the same time the stores which had opened for trade were compelled repeatedly to go on strike. Rumors were spread that Ch'en Hsiung-ming's troops were coming to attack Canton within a day or so from the East River. Some militia along the zone of the West River, stirred up to cooperate with the Merchants' Association, cut off the railway communication between Canton and Shao-kuan.

Soon after October 11, Sun, who was then in Shao-kuan, asked Chiang Kai-shek to transfer all weapons quickly from Whampoa to Shao-kuan. The first installment of weapons from Russia had also been received at the beginning of October and was deposited at the Military Academy. Many army officers asked to divide the weapons themselves. Sun also advised Chiang to give up Canton for Shao-kuan, using it as a base for training troops.[9] Some leaders in Canton, owing to the untrustworthiness of Kwangsi troops, also favored withdrawal from Canton, with all officers, troops, and equipment, to Shao-ch'ing on the West River.

But finally it was decided that the Canton base should not be given up hastily. All troops which could be mobilized by the government, such as the Cantonese troops under Hsü Ch'ung-chih, the Fukien troops under Li Fu-lin, the garrison troops under Wu T'ieh-ch'eng, and the student cadets of the Whampoa Military Academy, were mustered to take military action on the night of October 14. The following day the militia of the Merchants' Association was surrounded by the government troops and disarmed.

This was the first participation of the Whampoa cadets in military action. The weapons gathered from the militia of the Merchants' Association were used to form a battalion of military instructors. At that time the Yunnan troops were still attempting to destroy the Whampoa Military Academy in order to secure the weapons stored there. Very seriously Chiang Kai-shek told them: "If you really have the ability, come and attack Whampoa; otherwise it is better for you to say nothing."[10] The Whampoa Military Academy force was now a formidable one; the foundation of the Nationalist Revolutionary Army was firmly laid.

THE FALL OF TS'AO K'UN AND WU P'EI-FU

While the Merchants' Association incident was going on in Canton, the war between Kiangsu and Chekiang and the second Fengtien-Chihli war were in process. On October 23, 1924, not long after the solution by force of the Merchants' Association incident, Feng Yü-hsiang in the North rebelled against his superior, Wu P'ei-fu.

Unpopularity of Ts'ao as President

Ts'ao K'un's power was built entirely on Wu P'ei-fu's power, which in turn depended on the support and sympathy of a large part of public opinion. After Wu had driven out President Li Yüan-hung and consented to the election by bribery of Ts'ao K'un as president, Wu lost the support of public opinion. Ts'ao K'un nevertheless acknowledged his debt to Wu; Ts'ao declared to his friends, "Without Wu P'ei-fu I could never have reached my present position." He appointed Wu P'ei-fu high inspecting commissioner of Chihli, Shantung, and Honan, with headquarters in Loyang, and he consulted Wu before making decisions on any affair, large or small.

Wu P'ei-fu was content with his own power, for he had consolidated the military strength of the Chihli clique, taking over the flag of orthodox constitution from the hands of Sun Yat-sen, and had made Ts'ao K'un president according to the orthodox constitution. Considering himself unconquerable, he set out to unify China by force, intending to defeat Sun Yat-sen in the South, and Chang Tso-lin in the Northeast. His plan for subduing the South was to use Sun Ch'uan-fang to invade Fukien and thence advance to Kwangtung, where Ch'en Hsiung-ming would cooperate with him from the inside. Wu also tried to use his influence in Kiangsu, Anhwei, Kiangsi, and Fukien to conquer Chekiang. To deal with the Northeast, Wu was making large-scale preparations to command personally the military expedition to Manchuria.

Only a few politicians of the Tientsin and Paoting faction, who had worked hard for the election, were dissatisfied with Ts'ao K'un's dependence on Wu P'ei-fu. There were many jokes concerning the competition of politicians for the premiership. The speaker of the house of representatives, Wu Ching-lien, desired very much to become the first premier. But President Ts'ao K'un made Kao Ling-wei acting premier. Wu Ching-lien saw to it that the house approved only Sun Pao-ch'i as the premier. In July 1924, Ku Wei-chün became acting premier, and in September Yen Hui-ch'ing was the premier. The premiership changed hands many times during the tenure of President Ts'ao K'un. Wu P'ei-fu ignored cabinet and parliament.

The enemies of Ts'ao and Wu were meanwhile very active. Sun Yat-sen had issued a telegram to the whole nation on October 9, 1923, declaring his determination to fight against Ts'ao, and inviting Tuan Ch'i-jui, Chang Tso-lin, and others to take simultaneous military action against the president. On the tenth, when Ts'ao K'un was inaugurated in Peking, citizens of Shanghai, Hangchow, and other cities held great anti-Ts'ao parades. Lu Yung-hsiang, head of Chekiang, declared in a telegram on October 12 that he would sever all communications with the Peking government. On the following day, an Association of All Provincial Representatives led by Wang Ching-wei declared its decision to fight against Ts'ao. The parliament members who had not participated in the election briberies and the politicians still loyal to ex-president Li Yüan-hung gathered in Shanghai, intending to organize a new government at Hangchow and to use Lu Yung-hsiang as the central figure of this movement against the Chihli clique.

But this scheme was abortive, because Li's politicians still campaigned for Li, while the Kuomintang members opposed him. The merchants of Kiangsu and Chekiang, though anti-Ts'ao, feared a prolonged war. Observing the feelings of the people, Lu Yung-hsiang dared not undertake open battle against Ts'ao and Wu. Furthermore, in Kwangtung the feud between Sun and Ch'en was not yet resolved.

Outbreak of the Kiang-Che War

In the winter of 1923 a war between Kiangsu and Chekiang was inevitable because of the controversy over the territory of Sung-Hu [Sungkiang and Shanghai]. Originally Sung-Hu was under the jurisdiction of Kiangsu. When Lu Yung-hsiang had been promoted from garrison commander of Sung-Hu to tuchun of Chekiang, he had appointed his subordinate as garrison commander of Sung-Hu, bringing this area within the jurisdiction of Chekiang instead of Kiangsu. The authorities of Kiangsu had tried a few times to recover their sovereignty, but Lu Yung-hsiang stubbornly refused. When Ch'i Hsi-yüan became the new tuchun of Kiangsu, he continued the efforts to recover Sung-Hu. Both Lu Yung-hsiang and Ch'i Hsi-yüan were members of the Peiyang clique, but one belonged to the Anhwei and the other to the Chihli faction. Thus the Sung-Hu problem engendered a war between Kiangsu and Chekiang [the Kiang-Che war].

The police chief of the Sung-Hu district was assassinated on November 10, 1923. The authorities of Chekiang and Kiangsu each appointed a successor. Finally the one appointed by Chekiang managed to seize the post and retain it. The tuchun of Kiangsu, Ch'i Hsi-yüan, decided to attack Chekiang; but since the Fukien problem was not yet solved, Wu P'ei-fu disapproved of Ch'i's military action. Ch'i was compelled to sign a peace agreement with Chekiang to appease the gentry and the people of the two provinces, but both sides were still preparing for war.

In Fukien the internal problem was complicated. Ever since Sun Ch'uan-fang had been appointed tuchun of that province in March 1923, he had tried his best to put the province in order. With the help of Chou Yin-jen he had driven Wang Yung-ch'üan away from Foochow and expelled Tsang Chih-p'ing from the south of the province. Chou Yin-jen was then made lieutenant commander of Fukien (April 1924). In May the Peking government, planning to use Sun Ch'uan-fang to take Kwangtung, made him commander of frontier affairs of Fukien and Kwangtung; Chou Yin-jen was made tuchun of Fukien. Since Sun Ch'uan-fang was unable to control Kwangtung and his title was merely a brevet, he joined hands with Ch'i Hsi-yüan to work on Chekiang. Both of them suggested to Ts'ao K'un and Wu P'ei-fu that military action be taken.

Because Ts'ao and Wu hated Lu Yung-hsiang and because Fukien was now well under control, they accepted the suggestion of Sun and Ch'i. They planned a joint attack by four provinces, Kiangsu, Anhwei, Kiangsi, and Fukien.

Since Sun Ch'uan-fang and Chou Yin-jen had gained control of Fukien, Lu knew that his position was vulnerable. Consequently, when Tsang Chih-p'ing was expelled from southern Fukien and led his troops to Chekiang through the border of Kiangsi, Lu Yung-hsiang reorganized and incorporated Tsang's force into his own. Ts'ao and Wu blamed him for reorganizing the insurgent troops, but he did not yield any ground. Wu P'ei-fu ordered the governor of Honan to persuade Lu to disband Tsang's troops. Lu replied that Tseng's hundred thousand men belonged to the nation for the safety of Chekiang as well as for maintaining peace in the whole nation. On August 25 Sun Ch'uan-fang commanded his troops from

Foochow to the border of Chekiang. At the beginning of September the troops of Kiangsu and Chekiang engaged in full-scale war, starting along the railroad between Shanghai and Nanking.

A triple alliance of Chekiang, Kwangtung, and Fengtien provided that when Lu redeployed his troops from one point to another in Chekiang, the authorities of Kwangtung and Fengtien should also send soldiers to his aid. Sun Yat-sen had made plans to send soldiers to the North, at least enough to limit the movement of enemy troops in Kiangsi. Soldiers from Fengtien entering China proper could prevent any rescue force directed by Ts'ao and Wu from moving south to Kiangsu. Then the joint attack on Chekiang, supposedly by four provinces, would be actually reduced to two provinces, Kiangsu and Fukien. Against them Lu Yung-hsiang could make a stand.

As soon as the Kiang-Che war started, Kwangtung and Fengtien took coordinated action. On September 9, Sun Yat-sen issued a declaration saying that he would mobilize his force for the Northern Expedition within a few days. Shortly after, he personally went to Shao-kuan to prepare for the attack against Kiangsi, but as mentioned above, he could not make much headway.

In Fengtien the opinion of the old and new factions was at first divided: the old, represented by Chang Tso-hsiang, preferred to wait until the Kiang-Che war was over before taking any action; the new faction headed by Chang Hsüeh-liang, son of Chang Tso-lin, and Yang Yü-t'ing maintained that the Chihli clique, having to deal with the war in the Southeast, had no more forces to defend the North; therefore the Fengtien troops should avail themselves of this golden opportunity to attack Chihli. After careful consideration, it was decided to send troops through Shanhaikwan.

At the inception of the Kiang-Che war, Chang Tso-lin repeatedly sent telegrams to Ts'ao K'un counseling him not to rely too much on Wu P'ei-fu and not to start a war inadvertently. On September 4 when warfare between Kiang-Che troops had begun, Chang Tso-lin, in response to Lu Yung-hsiang's action, sent another telegram blaming Wu P'ei-fu. On September 15, 1924, Chang, as commander in chief, actually advanced his troops, dividing them into six routes. At the same time he dispatched to Ts'ao a telegram similar to an ultimatum saying: "This year many natural catastrophes have occurred and there are hungry people everywhere. I have advised against the military expedition to Chekiang, and you have written that you would maintain peace. Yet while that ink is not yet dry, the order for war has been sent, your troops have proceeded to the border of Fengtien, detained all locomotives and severed railway communication.... In recent years you have been Wu P'ei-fu's puppet and have incurred the people's resentment .... I originally intended to commission another envoy to consult with you, but since the interruption of train communication, it is impossible to reach Peking. For this reason I have to use airplanes to present you our regards, and our weapons are ready, awaiting your final reply.... "

On September 12, Wu P'ei-fu went from Loyang to Peking. Ts'ao K'um appointed Wu commander-in-chief and Feng Yü-hsiang as the commander of the third army, to fight shoulder to shoulder with the first and second armies, in a war on Chang Tso-lin. The second great war between Fengtien and Chihli formally began on September 18, 1924.

At first Lu Yung-hsiang won several battles in the war between Kiangsu and Chekiang. Then, in the middle of September, Sun Ch'uan-fang's troops advanced from Fukien to Chekiang and occupied the city of Ch'ü-chou. Being threatened from the rear and again suspecting that some of his own troops within the metropolitan area of Hangchow in Chekiang had made clandestine connections with Sun Ch'uan-fang, Lu Yung-hsiang led his troops from Hangchow, under the pretense of commanding the battle near Shanghai; actually he was not ready to give up Chekiang.

The Peking government on September 20 appointed Sun Ch'uan-fang tuchun of Chekiang, and concurrently high inspecting commissioner. In the first part of October Lu Yung-hsiang's troops were completely routed, and on October 12, resigning his duties, Lu went to Japan. The Kiang-Che war ended in defeat for the anti-Chihli faction.

Split in the Chihli Clique

But in the North the great war between Fengtien and Chihli [the Feng-Chih war] was still going on, now complicated by the rebellion of Feng Yü-hsiang against Ts'ao and Wu. Heretofore, Ts'ao and Wu had always taken Feng Yü-hsiang as their confidant. His revolt against Wu P'ei-fu was totally unexpected. Wu had believed that the organization of the Chihli military clique was solid and was unaware that there was any chance for a split.

After the first Feng-Chih war, Feng Yü-hsiang had been given the position of tuchun of Honan, while Wu P'ei-fu himself resided at Loyang. Wu considered Feng his subordinate and expected abject obedience. He even withdrew Feng's appointment as tuchun, with the promise of a position as high inspecting commissioner of the three special zones of Jehol, Chahar and Suiyuan; but Feng was given only a brevet title of high inspector of the army. Feng, however, now had soldiers even though he had no territory. When Feng asked permission to rescue Kiangsu, with the hope of securing territory in the Southeast, Wu refused him, offering instead the promise of the high inspectorship of the Three Eastern Provinces in return for assistance in the assault on Manchuria. This completed the break between Wu and Feng.

Because of Wu P'ei-fu's dictatorial pride, many of his other direct subordinates were also disgruntled. While Wu was preparing the military expedition to Manchuria, Wang Ch'eng-pin, Hu Ching-i, Sun Yo and others, along with the anti-Chihli clique, who had secretly agreed with Feng to get rid of Wu, were also seriously preparing for military action. When the order to fight against Chang Tso-lin was issued, Wu, unaware of the plots against him, made Feng commander of the Third Division, taking charge of the military affairs in Jehol. Wu himself took personal charge of the First Route Army to advance to Shanhaikwan. The distribution of arms and rations, strictly controlled by Wu himself, provided generous allotments to the First Route Army and little for Feng's troops. The unequal distribution of military rations antagonized Feng and his subordinates. When the mobilization orders were issued, Feng's troops made a very slow start. Wu was now somewhat suspicious of Feng's loyalty. Wu ordered Wang Ch'eng-pin to Jehol to perform the duties of the commander on Feng's behalf, but Wu did not know that Wang had already also joined the plot against him.

Feng Takes Peking

Finally Feng reached the front. He sent a telegram to Peking angrily requesting more rations. On October 9 a severe battle was being fought near Shanhaikwan; Feng again sent a telegram to Ts'ao K'un and other generals of the Chihli clique, omitting the name of Wu P'ei-fu. Feng berated them as warmongering politicians responsible for the misery of the people; and he said strongly that they must resign before there could be any hope for pacification of national affairs.

Ts'ao was surprised at this telegram and Wu likewise was disturbed; but there was not much they could do. On October 13 Feng's vanguard made a compromise with the Fengtien troops. On the nineteenth Feng secretly ordered his troops to turn and make a rapid march on Peking. Since the garrison commander of Peking, Sun Yo, had made an agreement with Feng long before, at 2 A. M. on October 23 Feng's troops occupied all important points in Peking and surrounded the president's house. On the same day Feng Yü-hsiang, Hu Ching-i, Sun Yo, and others, as well as their division commanders and colonels, dispatched a joint announcement to the whole nation urging suspension of the war. This telegram fell like a thunderbolt upon Ts'ao K'un and Wu P'ei fu.

On the following day President Ts'ao K'un was compelled to issue four orders: (1) to stop fighting at the front; (2) to cancel the titles "commander in chief of the army against rebels" etc.; (3) to deprive Wu P'ei-fu of all his assignments; and (4) to appoint Wu P'ei-fu director of land cultivation in distant Chinghai. Meanwhile Wu P'ei-fu was assigning part of his troops to defend his interests in Fengtien and sending other detachments to fight against Feng in Peking.

Feng and his collaborators organized their own Nationalist Army [*kuomin chün*] of three divisions, for which Feng was the commander in chief and concurrently, the First Division commander. Hu Ching-i and Sun Yo were associate commanders in chief, and at the same time they were the commanders of the Second and Third divisions, respectively. Wu was now on the horns of a real dilemma; he commanded his remaining troops to go by sea from the Tai-ku bar southward on November 3. The war came to an end, for the time being.

While Wu and Feng were fighting, Hsiao Yao-nan and Ch'i Hsi-yüan, along with Sun Ch'uan-fang, intended to assist Wu. They declared war against Feng; but the railroad communication between Peking and Hankow had been cut off by Yen Hsi-shan. In Shantung the tuchun declared neutrality and barred the railroad between Tientsin and Pukow. Both Yen and the Shantung tuchun, on bad terms with Wu P'ei-fu, were close to Tuan Ch'i-jui. Because of these hindrances, the troops of Hsiao, Ch'i, and Sun Ch'uan-fang could not come to the relief of Peking.

At first Ts'ao K'un, thinking that Feng's insurgent force could be defeated by Wu, returned to Peking from the front still hoping to hold on to the presidency. But Feng and others organized a cabinet on October 25 and an order was issued on October 21 under the name of Ts'ao K'un permitting Yen Hui-ch'ing's cabinet to resign and appointing Huang Fu premier. Ts'ao announced his resignation on November 2, and Premier Huang was made acting head of the government.

THE PROVISIONAL EXECUTIVE GOVERNMENT AND THE KUOMINTANG

Huang Fu's regent cabinet was intended to serve as a transitional organization. Huang's cabinet lasted until November 24. Then the so-called Provisional Executive Government was formed.

After Ts'ao K'un had been driven away, it was generally agreed to give up the orthodox constitution and to make a new one; but little agreement was possible on the process for making the new constitution. The Kuomintang members in the North maintained that there was no need of a president and recommended that a federal government committee system should be established. At first Feng Yü-hsiang also supported this idea. Some people even assumed that the chief members of such a committee should be Sun Yat-sen, Tuan Ch'i-jui, Chang Tso-lin, and Feng Yü-hsiang and a few other dignitaries, because the downfall of Ts'ao and Wu had been achieved through their combined efforts. But this was either merely a rumor or a sounding board. Tuan Ch'i-jui did not approve of the committee system, although he was not in a position to voice any open objection. Chang Tso-lin did not express any opinion except to hint that he was inclined to make use of Tuan. The politicians and militarists of the An-fu clique tried to restore themselves to power again by assisting Tuan to take the highest position in the government. Tactfully and cleverly Tuan tried to prevent the creation of the committee system.

At this time the Kuomintang had decided to ally itself with Soviet Russia. Feng Yü-hsiang also had communications with the members of the Soviet embassy in Peking. Since Soviet Russia's government was a committee form, the politicians who had their own reasons for opposing the committee system easily utilized the people's fear of communism by asserting that those who favored the committee system also were sympathetic to communism. The imperialistic Legation Quarter, wary of Soviet Russia's influence, also made the same observation. Feng Yü-hsiang was so frightened that he dared not mention the committee system any more.

The attitude of the tuchuns of the provinces along the Yangtze Valley also had some effect on the organization of the new government. Although Ts'ao and Wu had been beaten and the power of the Chihli clique in the North had been destroyed, the forces of their Chihli faction in the Yangtze Valley were still formidable. When Feng first started his own revolution, Ch'i Hsi-yüan, Sun Ch'uan-fang, Hsiao Yao-nan, and others, as already mentioned, had expressed their staunch support of Ts'ao and Wu. Now Ch'i, Sun Ch'uan-fang, Hsiao, and others feared they would lose their territory. But public opinion was against prolonging the war. Should they make a compromise with or surrender to the opposite side?

Tuan Returns as Chief Executive

During the twenty days after the resignation of Ts'ao K'un, the several tuchuns along the Yangtze Valley were hesitant. They knew that Tuan Ch'i-jui did not have sufficient power of his own, but he was a senior member in the military circles. In addition, he was the leader of the Peiyang clique. To surrender to Tuan would not be a great shame and would not be objected to by Wu P'ei-fu either. Since Tuan had no real strength, he might be glad to accept their surrender. Then, through Tuan's mediation, the pressure from Feng and Chang might be alleviated. For this reason they showed respect toward Tuan Ch'i-jui but adopted a resistant attitude toward the newly founded regent cabinet. A joint telegram signed by Ch'i Hsi-yüan, Hsiao Yao-nan and many others was issued on November 10, to the effect that they supported Tuan. On the thirteenth Ch'i Hsi-yüan called a joint defense conference at Nanking, consisting of the military authorities of the eight provinces and the navy leaders. The result was another joint telegram signed by eight leading participants declaring that they would not accept any new orders from Peking, since the functions of a central government in Peking had been suspended.

On November 11 Chang Tso-lin and Feng Yü-hsiang traveled to Tientsin to persuade Tuan Ch'i-jui to come out of retirement. In their conference no decision was reached about the title Tuan should have as head of the Peking government. The joint telegram of Ch'i Hsi-yüan and others issued on the thirteenth, which defied all orders from Peking, made further evident to them the need for Tuan to deal with the military powers along the Yangtze Valley. Accordingly, on the fifteenth, Chang, Feng, and others dispatched a joint telegram expressing their determination to welcome Tuan as chief executive of the provisional government. Their use of the term "chief executive" indicated the discontinuation of the title "president." It also showed that the government was not to be a committee system. This is the background for the adoption of the name "Executive Government." Tuan Ch'i-jui did not, however, immediately accept the offered title.

After Wu P'ei-fu sailed southward with his remaining force, he at first intended to go ashore in Shantung, but was barred by the local garrison. On November 15 he sailed from Shanghai to Nanking, where he had a conference with Ch'i Hsi-yüan. Thereafter he sailed to Hankow. On the seventeenth, he used the name of Ch'i Hsi-yüan to head a list of more than twenty generals and admirals of ten provinces to dispatch a telegram suggesting the organization at Wuchang of a military government for the protection of the constitution.

Although Ch'i Hsi-yüan and others did not actually agree with this proposition, they were not in a position to oppose it. Nevertheless, on November 19 the governor of Kiangsu rebuffed the suggestion of a military government at Hankow. At the same time Ch'i Hsi-yüan, Sun Ch'uan-fang, and seven others issued a request for the return of Tuan

Ch'i-jui at the earliest possible date. For Tuan, now, the opportunity' was ripe. On the twenty-first he accepted the new title. Three days later he was inaugurated as chief executive. His first action in this new office was a proclamation of six articles for the organization of the government and the list of his cabinet members.

According to the articles governing the provisional government, the chief executive had control of military and civil affairs. Assisted by a cabinet consisting of the heads of various ministries, his actual power was a combination of the powers of the former president and the premier. In practice his authority was unlimited and he enjoyed much more freedom than the former president.

Unfortunately for Tuan Ch'i-jui, he lacked the power to make full use of this clever setup. He was dominated and plagued by his supporters, who had the military power in their hands. The Kuomintang members could have no confidence in him at all.

Right and Left Wings in the Kuomintang

The Kuomintang had at that time a great potential power in the North, built almost entirely on young students and professors. With the exception of Feng Yü-hsiang, the warlords were too shortsighted to see the increasing power of this organization. Some of them knew of the activities of Kuomintang members in the North, but regarded these activities as merely the antics of simple-minded students or radicals. Sun Yat-sen, with his highsounding words, was seen as an empty threat, and no warlord bothered about or wished for any cooperation with him. Nevertheless, because of the historical alliance against the Chihli clique, these warlords could not ignore him entirely. Consequently, Feng Yü-hsiang, Tuan Ch'i-jui, and Chang Tso-lin, among others, sent Sun a gracious invitation to come to the North.

Within the Kuomintang the attitude toward Sun Yat-sen's acceptance of this invitation was at first divided. The left wing and the communist faction objected to the trip lest Sun should make a compromise with the warlords. The right wing and the conservative members, anxious to secure political power, favored a compromise with the Northern warlords.

The Imperialists' Reaction to Sun Yat-sen

Sun Yat-sen decided to leave Canton for Peking on November 4, 1924. His main purpose, which was completely overlooked by the two parties, was to make close contact with, and thereby spread his ideas to, the populace in the North. Under the name of *Tsung-li* [Chief Director] of the Kuomintang of China, he declared his opinions on November 10. After explaining that the aim of the nationalist revolution was to eradicate the warlords permanently and to abolish all unequal treaties, he advocated the calling of a national people's assembly, preceded by a preparatory conference.

Sun Yat-sen arrived at Shanghai on November 17. Here, summoning all local newspapermen for a press conference, he said: "My trip to the North has a twofold purpose: first, to call a national people's assembly to fight against warlords; second, to strike a blow against the imperialists by abolishing the unequal treaties." And he added, "The responsibility which I am undertaking is very dangerous, but I am not afraid of it if only all of our people can understand my aims."[11]

After the reorganization of the Kuomintang systematic and well-organized propaganda had been carried on against imperialism. In Peking, Shanghai, and other leading cities there were organizations of what was called "a great alliance against imperialism." The air of anti-imperialism was stirring everywhere. Sun Yat-sen's talk in Shanghai had served to incite fear and jealousy in diplomatic circles; a leading English language newspaper hinted that it was questionable whether the grand marshal, loaded with political duties, ought to live in Shanghai. This sentence was a hint to the authorities of the International Settlement to interfere with his residence there. With reference to this move, Sun Yat-sen told a Japanese correspondent, "Although now there is much foreign sentiment in Shanghai, the city is still in Chinese territory, and I am a Chinese host, whereas the foreigners residing in Shanghai are guests. The host in his own territory can certainly do whatever he likes; his guests cannot interfere."

Sun Yat-sen left Shanghai on November 22 for Japan. Thence he came across to Tientsin, arriving on December 4. Here the French consul refused to permit him to pass or to stop over in the French concession. This incident indicated once more the suspicion and hatred of Sun among the imperialists.

Tuan Ch'i-jui, who had seen Sun Yat-sen's declaration, announced on November 21 that he would call an "aftermath conference" [*shan-hou hui-i*] within one month and a national people's representative assembly within three months. In reality this plan was a petty attempt to conciliate Sun Yat-sen and to confuse the people. His aims were far removed from Sun Yat-sen's.

Tuan entered Peking on the same day that Sun left Shanghai, and when Sun reached Tientsin, Tuan established his Executive Government and drafted the rules concerning the aftermath conference. These were passed by the cabinet on December 2. Although the enactment awaited a consultation with Sun Yat-sen, Tuan had made up his mind to enforce them regardless of Sun's approval or disapproval.

The Peking imperialist diplomatic corps, which had nurtured ill feeling toward Sun Yat-sen, now played a double game—to coddle the Executive Government and at the same time to put pressure on it. During the time of Huang Fu's regent premiership, Huang, on account of the urgent need for foreign help, had extended to the diplomatic corps on November 14 a banquet invitation, which was unexpectedly declined. After Tuan Ch'i-jui's accession to the position of chief executive of the provisional government, the diplomatic representatives of all nations, through the suggestion of the Japanese minister, went to the executive office to extend their congratulations as an informal recognition of Tuan's government. A communication signed by the ministers of Holland, the United States, Belgium, Great Britain, France, and Italy was delivered to the ministry of foreign affairs on December 9, recognizing the Provisional Executive Government under the condition that it should respect all existing treaties. When the problem of the unequal treaties was discussed, Sun Yat-sen was criticized for having had unfavorable relations with foreign powers. The Executive Government decided to reject Sun Yat-sen's methods in order to gain a more favorable position for dealing with foreign nations.

According to Wang Ching-wei's *Political Report*, Chang Tso-lin, after an interview with Sun Yat-sen in Tientsin, told Wang: "Formerly I thought that Mr. Sun was a very stubborn person, but today I found him to be a perfectly mild gentleman: the only trouble is that the foreign ministers in Peking do not like him. This is probably caused by Mr. Sun's alliance with Russia. I wonder whether you can persuade him to give up his policy of allying himself with Russia? If so, then I can guarantee that all the foreign ministers will be friendly to him."[12] This remark was made when Chang and others were negotiating with the diplomatic corps for the recognition of the provisional government under the condition that it would respect the unequal treaties.

Sun Breaks with the Government Over Imperialism

Sun Yat-sen was very angry when he heard the news of the acceptance of the ultimatum from the diplomatic corps, nor did he agree with the rules for the aftermath conference which were drafted by the Executive Government. Although Sun had suggested a preparatory conference before the national people's assembly, his plan for representatives at the conference included: personnel from modern industrial organizations; merchants' associations; education associations;

representatives of universities; students' unions of all provinces; labor unions; farmers' unions; all anti-Ts'ao and anti-Wu army divisions; and political parties.

On the contrary, the conference planned by the Executive Government was organized by elements of (1) those who had made great contributions to the nation; (2) the high army leaders who were instrumental in fighting against the bribery election and checking the civil war; (3) civil and military authorities of all provinces and special zones such as Mongolia and Tibet; and (4) those who enjoyed special reputations, profound learning, and experience and who would be invited or appointed by the provisional government, the number not exceeding thirty.

If the members of the first three elements could not participate in the conference personally, plenipotentiary representatives were to be dispatched on their behalf. In these two very different lists may be seen the widely divergent attitudes of the two men—Sun and Tuan. Sun Yat-sen represented the Kuomintang, which had then a strict organization and whose potential power had already penetrated into all walks of life. If Sun's organization were followed, the "aftermath conference" would have been easily controlled by the Kuomintang. On the other side, it becomes more and more evident that the existence of the Executive Government was built on the militarists and had little relation with civilian organizations.

On December 24 the Executive Government, disregarding Sun Yat-sen's stubborn objections, enacted its rules for the "aftermath conference." On the thirtieth, according to the rules, telegrams were sent to all circles concerned, asking that the conference be called at Peking before February 1, 1925. The Kuomintang voiced strong objections to this arrangement.

On December 31 Sun Yat-sen moved, on his sickbed, to Peking. He was given an impressive public welcome at the capital and even Tuan Ch'i-jui pretended to show him deep respect. The extreme right wing of the Kuomintang, fearing a split between Sun and Tuan, tried their best to cement the relation and urge Sun to yield some ground. As a consequence Sun Yat-sen on January 17 issued two somewhat modified statements as a condition of Kuomintang participation: (1) the conference should include participants from modern industrial organizations, merchants' associations, educational associations, universities, students' unions, farmer and labor unions; and (2) the final decision on military and financial problem should be reserved for the national people's assembly.

The Executive Government held a special conference, on January 21, to discuss Sun Yat-sen's modifications. A reply was given on the twenty-ninth promising to invite the chairmen of all provincial assemblies, educational associations, the chiefs of merchants' associations, the provincial farmers' associations, as well as the general merchants' associations of such leading cities as Shanghai, Tientsin, and Hankow as special representatives to the conference. These special representatives, invited or appointed by the chief executive according to Article 6 of the original rules, were, however, permitted only to make reports or express opinions.

The Death of Sun, 1925

Sun Yat-sen was by then gravely ill. Because his Kuomintang members anticipated the impossibility of cooperation with the Executive Government, the party decided, on the thirtieth, to ignore the conference. But a few members of the extreme right wing, anxious to grasp some political power, still participated in the conference in spite of the party decision, denouncing the others as radicals trying to use the grave illness of Sun Yat-sen as a means to break the cooperation between Sun and Tuan.

The "aftermath conference" was formally opened on February 1, 1925. On the second the Kuomintang announced to all civilian organizations of the whole nation that "the Central Executive Committee of this party, obeying the will of its party leaders, has decided to withdraw approval of the 'aftermath conference.'" On the tenth the committee issued a telegram advocating the organization of the national people's assembly by the people themselves, and reaffirming their desire that the aftermath conference should mainly comprise people's organizations through which the national people's assembly might be produced. It added that the Kuomintang hereafter would object to all actions by the Executive Government.

Sun Yat-sen died on March 12, 1925. He was accorded a huge funeral in Peking. To see the body of Sun Yat-sen the populace of the capital, led by the Kuomintang members, thronged to the palace from which, heretofore, they had been barred. Sun's political ideas, though not yet realized, were effectively spread by means of organized propaganda during the period of the funeral ceremonies.

Interim for the Executive Government

The Executive Government's aftermath conference held its first formal meeting on February 13 and adjourned on April 21. It passed three sets of regulations concerning (1) the organization of the national people's representatives assembly, (2) a committee on military affairs, and (3) a committee on financial affairs. All these regulations were enacted by the Executive Government on April 24. But none of these regulations were more than paper. They were an effort to placate the people, but the Kuomintang objected to them, and the warlords of course ignored them.

Nevertheless, the Executive Government continued to enact rules to justify its existence. On May 1 the Executive Government proclaimed a number of rules concerning the preparation for the national assembly. On the third it issued regulations dealing with a draft committee which was to prepare a constitution for approval by the national people's representative assembly. On July 1 it issued a further order fixing the date for the election of the candidates for the national people's representative assembly. The primary election period was set for August 16-31, 1925, and the final period for September 1-20.

The constitutional draft committee actually held its inauguration meeting at Peking on August 3, 1925, electing Lin Ch'ang-min as its chairman. A draft constitution was even passed by the committee on December 12 and sent to the Executive Government. Unfortunately for the committee, this draft constitution was never to be discussed in the national people's representative assembly. The coalition front of the warlords in North China collapsed before the time established for the election of members for the assembly. War was ready to break out and no one after that took any interest in the meaningless election.

The second Kiang-Che war was started by the Fengtien Army in the first part of October 1925. In November the Fengtien Army was involved in an internal conflict—General Kuo Sung-ling revolted against Chang Tso-lin. The chairman of the national constitution draft committee, Lin Ch'ang-min, was at the military camp of General Kuo while his committee members were still discussing the document. Kuo's revolt was a plot of the Executive Government against Chang. The life of the Executive Government was now definitely near its end, even without the objections of the Kuomintang. Since Chang Tso-lin and Feng Yü-hsiang were the government's two pillars, when Chang became its enemy, Feng was unable to support it much longer.

THE GREAT WARLORDS' MELEE IN THE NORTH

The fate of the Executive Government was controlled by the warlords. The allegiance to Tuan of the lords along the Yangtze Valley was a measure of exigency, as was well understood by Tuan himself. He relied chiefly on Chang Tso-lin's Fengtien Army and on Feng Yü-hsiang's personal Nationalist Army. The latter, a new force, was not a very powerful one. The Fengtien Army, which possessed the affluent territory of the Three Eastern Provinces, naturally had a stronger position and influence than Feng's Nationalist Army. In addition Tuan Ch'i-jui's former subordinates, such as Lu Yung-hsiang and Wu Kuang-hsin, had long since transferred their allegiance to Chang Tso-lin, and a number of politicians of the An-fu clique had also turned to Chang's camp. Tuan came to depend more on Chang's Fengtien Army than on Feng's Nationalist Army.

The underhand struggle between the Fengtien Army and Feng's Nationalist Army had already begun at the foundation of the Executive Government. Huang Fu's regent cabinet was under Feng's influence. The members of the Fengtien clique were mostly absent from the cabinet, because it was very unsatisfactory to Chang Tso-lin. Feng's Nationalist Army defeated Wu P'ei-fu in the vicinity of Tientsin and took the city on November 3, 1924, before the arrival of the Fengtien Army. The Fengtien Army, commanded by Wu Kuang-hsin, occupied T'ang-ku on the following day. Fearing that the Fengtien soldiers and Feng's Nationalist Army might fight against each other, the citizens of Tientsin requested that Tuan Ch'i-jui stop the advance of Wu Kuang-hsin's force to Tientsin. Tuan's order went unheeded and Wu ordered his forces to continue their march to Tientsin and even advanced to the railway between Tientsin and Pukow.

At Tientsin the tuchun of Chihli, Wang Ch'eng-pin, disarmed and reorganized the remaining force of Wu P'ei-fu into the Twenty-third Division. Wang had taken the same steps with Feng when the latter revolted against his superior, but Wang was not listed in the joint telegram requesting suspension of warfare. Feng permitted Wang to reorganize the new division army as a way of bringing Wang under his flag. On November 11 Wang was compelled by Li Ching-lin of the Fengtien clique to resign from his position as the tuchun of Chihli. Li's force reached Tientsin and disarmed the Twenty-third Division on the twelfth. Wang was forced to take shelter in the British concession at Tientsin. Remnants of Wu P'ei-fu's forces reorganized by Feng Yü-hsiang were also disarmed by Wu Kuang-hsin's Fengtien troops. Li Ching-lin made himself "commander for peace" in Chihli upon the alleged request of several citizens' organizations of Tientsin. Feng's influence in Tientsin was swept away completely by the Fengtien troops.

Feng Yü-hsiang's influence on the regent cabinet was demonstrated only once. On November 7 the regent premier ordered the dismissal of the Honan tuchun and governor and their replacement by Feng's comrades, Hu Ching-i and Sun Yo. Thus Feng built up a base in the middle stretch of the Peking-Hankow Railway.

Not yet inaugurated as Chief Executive, Tuan could not take sides between Feng and Chang. On November 22 Tuan went from Tientsin to Peking accompanied by Feng Yü-hsiang, at which time the latter tendered his resignation, saying that he intended to travel abroad. On Tuan's inauguration day Feng dispatched a nation-wide telegram announcing his voluntary severance from political and military life, and as a private citizen issued an invitation to Wu P'ei-fu to join him on his travels.

Tuan read Feng's mind very well and tried his best to placate him and show him that he was impartial. But Chang Tso-lin was determined to extend his power along the Tientsin-Pukow Railway to the Yangtze Valley, and that determination could not be altered. Furthermore, the former head of Chekiang province, Lu Yung-hsiang, was anxious to avenge himself against Ch'i Hsi-yüan. Even Tuan himself would have liked, for self-protection, to restore the territory to his former subordinates. After he became the chief executive, he approved the Fengtien Army influence over the zone along the Tientsin-Pukow Railway. To show favor to Feng Yü-hsiang, he recognized the province of Honan, along the middle stretch of the Peking-Hankow Railway and the area in the Northwest, as under the control of Feng's Nationalist Army.

On December 2 Chang Tso-lin left Peking for Tientsin. Part of his troops were marching southward from Shantung. On the seventh he called not only Lu Yung-hsiang, who had been appointed tuchun of Chihli, but also the generals of the Fengtien Army and Wu Kuang-hsin, who was a representative of the central government, to discuss problems of the provinces in the middle Yangtze Valley. A decision was made to request Tuan to dismiss Ch'i Hsi-yüan and to authorize the Fengtien Army to continue its southward march.

On December 11 the Executive Government, dismissing Ch'i Hsi-yüan from his position as tuchun of Kiangsu, appointed Lu Yung-hsiang as pacification commissioner of Kiangsu and Anhwei. Lu's post as tuchun of Chihli was filled by Li Ching-lin. On January 17, 1925, Chang Tsung-ch'ang was made commander of bandit suppression in Kiangsu, Anhwei, and Shantung. Chang's Fengtien troops had early followed Lu Yung-hsiang southward and had penetrated far into the territory of Kiangsu. Thus the Fengtien Army now occupied the zone along the Tientsin-Pukow Railway. The occupation by Feng's Nationalist Army of the central and northern part of the Peking-Hankow Railway had also become an accomplished fact. On November 5 Sun Yo took Paoting, about a hundred miles south of Peking. On the twelfth Hu Ching-i extended his garrison district from a section along the Peking-Hankow railway into the province of Honan. The Executive Government on December 6 formally appointed Hu Ching-i tuchun of Honan. On January 4, 1925, the Executive Government appointed Feng Yü-hsiang commander of frontier affairs in the Northwest and Li Ming-chung acting tuchun of Suiyuan. Sun Yo was also appointed commander of bandit suppression in Honan, Shensi, and Kansu. As a result of these appointments the province of Honan and the area in Northwest China were now also under the control of Feng's Nationalist Army.

During the first half of 1925 both the Fengtien Army and Feng's Nationalist Army expanded their respective areas of influence. In the

Southeast there was a struggle between Ch'i Hsi-yüan and Lu Yung-hsiang and in Honan a struggle between Hu Ching-i and Han Yü-k'un. The Fengtien troops and Feng's Nationalists had not yet come to open conflict. In the latter half of 1925, the struggle between the Fengtien and Chekiang cliques was extended to that between Fengtien and Feng's Nationalists in the Northeast. War between the Fengtien troops and Feng's Nationalists in North China resulted in a coalition of the Fengtien and the Chihli cliques to overwhelm Feng's Nationalist Army. The subsequent war involved virtually all warlords. The Executive Government completely disintegrated during the fight.

The Struggle Between Ch'i and Lu

Lu Yung-hsiang was eager to avenge his losses and insults; the Fengtien Army was determined to enlarge itself. Accordingly Ch'i Hsi-yüan was dismissed on December 11 and Lu Yung-hsiang was appointed pacification commissioner of Kiangsu and Anhwei. After the announcement of this appointment, many telegrams from the people of Kiangsu were published in the newspapers opposing Lu's transference to the South because they were well aware that a war would follow. But the people were powerless. Ch'i Hsi-yüan announced that he would obey the order of the central government. His subordinates, who had communications with his enemy, were out of his control. On December 14 his duties as tuchun of Kiangsu were transferred temporarily to the provincial governor, while he himself went to Shanghai.

Lu Yung-hsiang and Chang Tsung-ch'ang led Fengtien troops along the Tientsin-Pukow Railway to Nanking on January 7. Lu intended not only to drive Ch'i away, but also to conquer Chekiang. One of his former division commanders, who had been defeated, took shelter in Shanghai and the division was incorporated in Sun Ch'uan-fang's force. Lu surreptitiously assisted his former division commander, hoping that the latter would instigate his old soldiers to attack Chekiang from Shanghai and Sungkiang. But before Lu himself reached Nanking, his advance troops had already been defeated by Sun Ch'uan-fang. His plot for taking Chekiang was foiled.

After Ch'i left Chekiang, the Fengtien Army moved southward. Sun Ch'uan-fang, having lost a satellite force with Ch'i's departure, was exposed to a direct attack by the Fengtien Army. But the day after Lu Yung-hsiang reached Nanking, Ch'i Hsi-yüan declared himself allied with Sun Ch'uan-fang and ordered his former subordinates to disarm the garrisons of Sungkiang and Shanghai. Ch'i declared himself commander in chief of the First Route Army of the Chekiang and Shanghai allies and Sun Ch'uan-fang, commander in chief of the Second Route Army. They issued a joint declaration against the southward movement of the Fengtien Army.

Learning of the Shanghai incident, Lu Yung-hsiang organized the so-called Pacification Army in Nanking, and appointed the division commander of the Fengtien Army, Chang Tsung-ch'ang, to be commander in chief to attack Shanghai. The Shanghai Merchants' Association, fearing that their city might become a battlefield for the Fengtien and Chekiang armies, moved that Shanghai should be a nonmilitary zone, that the arsenal be moved elsewhere. Sun Ch'uan-fang agreed with the conditions set out by the Merchants' Association, because, lacking sufficient preparation, he feared that he was no match for the Fengtien Army. Tuan Ch'i-jui also approved the move of the Merchants' Association lest the rapidly expanding war should prove difficult to conclude. On January 14 he ordered the abrogation of the post of garrison commander of Shanghai and Sungkiang, the closing of the arsenal, and the demilitarization of Shanghai.

To please Sun Ch'uan-fang, Tuan on January 16 appointed Lu Yung-hsiang tuchun of Kiangsu and at the same time appointed Sun himself tuchun of Chekiang, and Chou Yin-jen tuchun of Fukien. Tuan intended to show that, although he had dismissed Ch'i Hsi-yüan, there was no danger of an invasion of the territory of Chekiang and Fukien. On the following day he commissioned the minister of war, Wu Kuang-hsin, to go southward, ostensibly to investigate Ch'i and to discuss with Lu a pertinent settlement of the Shanghai incident; the actual purpose was to prevent Sun from assisting Ch'i. As a result of this commission, Sun for the time being adopted a watchful attitude but avoided taking any immediate action.

Chang Tsung-ch'ang, with a strong Fengtien Army at his disposal, forced his way along the Nanking-Shanghai Railroad and won one battle after another. Ch'i's force had to retreat from Soochow to Shanghai on January 28 and Ch'i himself fled to Japan. On the next day more than ten thousand Fengtien troops under Chang Tsung-ch'ang reached Shanghai and disarmed all of Ch'i Hsi-yüan's soldiers. Thus the war between Ch'i and Lu ended.

The war minister, Wu Kuang-hsin, was successful in concluding the second peace treaty between Chekiang and Kiangsu on February 3. It was signed at Shanghai by Sun Ch'uan-fang and Chang Tsung-ch'ang, after which the troops on both sides withdrew from Shanghai. Chang Tsung-ch'ang ordered his troops to move farther south to Hsuchow on March 19. The war clouds in the Southeast were temporarily dispersed. The Fengtien Army, however, was still dissatisfied about the disposal of Shanghai.

The Struggle Between Han and Hu in Honan

Hu Ching-i ordered the Second Division of Feng's Nationalist Army to Honan, where remnants of Wu P'ei-fu's forces were still offering resistance. Tuan Ch'i-jui, wary lest Wu should revive his power, secretly ordered the Shensi tuchun, Liu Chen-hua, to lead troops into Loyang. Promptly Lu assigned his division commander, Han Yü-k'un, to march eastward. Wu P'ei-fu was forced to flee from Loyang to Hankow on December 1 and eventually to Yochow in Hunan. Wu's remaining forces in Honan were completely blotted out.

But Hu and Han were at loggerheads. Tuan's dispatch of the Shensi Army to Honan was apparently a move against Feng's Nationalist Army, reducing the latter's controlling position in that province. Nevertheless Tuan could not avoid giving the post of the tuchun of Honan to Hu Ching-i, and accordingly Tuan formally authorized Hu to take that post on December 11.

Proud of his contribution to the expulsion of Wu P'ei-fu from Honan, Han Yü-k'un determined that unless he was made tuchun of Honan, he would never return to Shensi. As a result, Tuan tried to pacify him with the deputy commandership of bandit suppression in Honan, Shensi, and Kansu, a post already assigned to Sun Yo. But neither Han nor Hu was satisfied with this double play. In the middle of February Feng Yü-hsiang tried to arbitrate the feud between Hu and Han, but Han, feeling himself at a disadvantage, refused to be reconciled. On February 21, Tuan's Executive Government commissioned Sun Yo with a large force to inspect the troops in Honan. Sun was the Third Division commander of Feng's Nationalist Army. He belonged to the same faction as Hu Ching-i, and although he was ostensibly sent as a mediator, he was actually delegated to control Han and to put a damper on his political ambitions.

The Shensi tuchun, Liu Chen-hua, also harried at this time by the defense commissioner of Shensi, Wu Hsin-tien, went from Shensi to Loyang on February 25 under the pretense of arranging an amicable settlement between Hu and Han, but actually to assist Han in his fight against Hu. In this manner arbitration conferences and battle action were carried on simultaneously. At the beginning of March the arbitrators themselves became major belligerents. The result was that Liu Chen-hua and Han Yü-k'un were defeated and the latter committed suicide. The defense commissioner, Wu Hsin-tien, then became tuchun of Shensi. Hu Ching-i died on April 10. One of his chief subordinates had been recommended by him and confirmed by the Executive Government as his successor. Honan definitely now belonged to the sphere of influence of Feng's Nationalist Army.

The war described above was only a local war waged between Feng's Nationalist Army and its rival, indirectly connected with the Fengtien Army. After this incident, however, the Feng Nationalists and the Fengtien armies drew closer to a frontal war.

The Struggle Between the Fengtien and Chekiang Cliques

The war between Fengtien and Chekiang did not take place until mid-October, but the long fuse had been lighted by the fighting between Ch'i and Lu during the spring. After Chang Tsung-ch'ang was frustrated in his attempt to control the lower valley of the Yangtze River and had shipped his troops to Hsuchow, he tried to seize the territory of Shantung. Chang Tso-lin also aimed at controlling the lower Yangtze Valley and Shantung province. There was danger in the middle stretch of the Tientsin-Pukow Railway of a war with other troops favorable to Chang. Chang Tso-lin therefore requested the Executive Government to transfer the Shantung tuchun to another post and to appoint Chang Tsung-ch'ang successor to Shantung. Tuan, not daring to disobey Chang's request, transferred the former Shantung tuchun to the same position in Anhwei. Thus the Fengtien clique obtained a springboard to develop its power toward the lower Yangtze Valley.

Chang Tso-lin was not yet satisfied. He noted that the territory surrounding Peking was occupied by Feng's Nationalist Army and that Tuan was not yet completely free from Feng's control. In mid-May he ordered a large number of Fengtien troops from his home bases in Manchuria to the vicinity of Peking to compel Feng's Nationalist Army to withdraw. As a result, Feng's Nationalists were forced to yield their barracks around Peking to the newcomers. Tuan lived thus under pressure of the two military cliques, trying his best to please both sides, but satisfying neither.

The Shanghai Massacre

On May 30 occurred the Shanghai incident—the shooting of a number of unarmed people by the municipal government of the foreign settlements. The initiating cause was the killing, by management orders, of several striking laborers at a Japanese cotton mill. This had considerably angered the students' and laborers' unions, whose members called for students and factory workers to go on parade and make public speeches. The policemen of the municipal government arrested many students. At the request of the mob for their release, the municipal government ordered the policemen to fire at the mob. On May 31 the city was in turmoil as a result of a general strike.

Chang Tso-lin ordered his son, Chang Hsüeh-liang, to avail himself of this opportunity to dispatch 2000 Fengtien troops to Shanghai. They arrived on June 13, marching in the name of order and peace. This military action broke the Kiang-Che truce, which had provided that no Chinese soldiers should again be quartered in Shanghai.

The May 30 incident was prolonged for many days without reaching any solution. Chang Hsüeh-liang led his men back north on June 21 but he was replaced by one of his subordinates, who led a much larger force to Shanghai. The governor of Kiangsu declared martial law in Shanghai and Sungkiang and appointed one of the newly arrived generals to implement martial law. In this way the Sung-Hu area became the sphere of influence of the Fengtien army clique. Sun Ch'uan-fang, greatly alarmed, speeded his own preparations for a major clash. In the middle of July the clouds of the Kiang-Che war daily grew more ominous.

The Feng-Che War

At that time Chang's harassment of Tuan had caused a serious breach between the two men. After a fruitless attempt to bring about peace between the two, Lu Yung-hsiang resigned his post of tuchun of Kiangsu.

Executive Tuan, in compliance with Chang Tso-lin's demand, appointed on August 29 Yang Yü-t'ing tuchun of Kiangsu, and another Fengtien general as tuchun of Anhwei. At the same time the chief executive had to keep abreast of his appeasement policy toward Feng Yü-hsiang by appointing him commander of frontier affairs in the Northwest and tuchun of Kansu; Sun Yo was made tuchun of Shensi. The appointment of Yang Yü-t'ing, a leading general of the Fengtien military clique, was instrumental in spreading Fengtien influence in Southeast China. Chekiang was seriously threatened.

But much to everyone's surprise, Yang so effectively asserted a policy of peaceful occupation that even his enemy withdrew the reinforcements sent as a garrison against an attack from Sungkiang. It looked as though now all would be quiet at the front. However, Yang's peaceful pose proved to be only a scheme to gain time to complete his own military preparations. Perceiving this, Sun Ch'uan-fang took quick action to outflank his enemy. Under the camouflage of military inspection on the Double Ten holiday [October 10], Sun secretly mobilized his force. On the fifteenth, proclaiming himself commander in chief of the allied army of the five provinces of Chekiang, Fukien, Anhwei, Kiangsi, and Kiangsu, he ordered his forces to advance on the enemy by five different routes.

Yang Yü-t'ing, aware that he would be unable to resist the five-pronged attack, ordered his subordinates to retreat from Shanghai. Two days later, on October 16, Shanghai was occupied by Sun's allied army. Sun now dispatched a telegram charging the Fengtien Army with violating the truce agreement by having soldiers stationed at Shanghai and disturbing the order and peace of the locality. This telegram was responded to and supported by army officers in Hupeh, Anhwei and Kiangsi. They even requested that Wu P'ei-fu be invited to come out from retirement to conduct the war together with Sun Ch'uan-fang.

This quick action had its beginnings at the time Yang Yü-t'ing and others were appointed to their new posts and the militarists of the Chihli clique in the Yangtze Valley were allying themselves to fight against the Fengtien clique for protection of their own territories. So, as soon as Sun Ch'uan-fang mentioned battling the Fengtien enemy, echoes immediately resounded.

Operating in a new territory unfamiliar to Yang Yü-t'ing and with a defense line too long and too far away from a supply line and from reinforcements from the North, the Fengtien Army retreated without any attempt to take up the challenge. On October 18 Yang left Nanking to go north, accompanied by the governor of Kiangsu. The Fengtien troops now were concentrated at Hsuchow near the border between Kiangsu and Shantung, where connections were made with the reinforcements under the leadership of Chang Tsung-ch'ang.

Wu P'ei-fu arrived at Hankow on October 21. There he announced that he had accepted the recommendation and encouragement of the military authorities of the fourteen provinces and would assume the post of the commander in chief of the allied army to fight against "the bandits." At Hankow he set up headquarters with the intention of sending troops by way of Honan to join Sun Ch'uan-fang's force at Hsuchow. But the Honan governor, who sympathized with Feng Yü-hsiang's Nationalist Army, would not allow Wu's troops to pass through his territory. Nor was Sun Ch'uanfang happy to become Wu's subordinate. Thereupon Sun, in order to demonstrate his power, on the one hand made every effort to show respect to Wu, and on the other openly declined Wu's military assistance. On November 7 the Fengtien troops were forced to withdraw farther from Hsuchow.

Sun, now contented with the turn of events, had no intention of advancing beyond his present strategic position. On November 20 he announced his intention to return to Hangchow, the provincial capital of Chekiang, via Nanking. Before his journey Sun called a military conference. Participation in this conference by the governor of Honan indicated that Sun was working in cooperation with Feng's Nationalists. Sun also agreed to permit the Honan Army to attack Shantung in the west, while his own troops would undertake the frontal attack from the railroad. But in fact his plan was to allow the Honan troops to challenge the Fengtien Army in Shantung in order to prevent any renewed attack southward by Fengtien soldiers.

The Feng-Che war in the Southeast was now concluded. The five provinces, Kiangsu, Anhwei, Kiangsi, Fukien, and Chekiang, were entirely controlled by Sun Ch'uan-fang. Sun thereupon became the most powerful leader of the Chihli military clique and Wu P'ei-fu's position was greatly weakened.

The Struggle Between the Fengtien and the Feng Nationalist Cliques

Prior to the outbreak of the Che-Feng war in the Southeast, Feng's Nationalist Army had been frequently oppressed by the Fengtien Army. Nominally, Honan was under the control of the Nationalist Army; actually it could not govern the whole Peking-Hankow Railway because the northern part of the line was in the province of Chihli, whose governor, Li Ching-lin, was a member of the Fengtien clique. The Honan governor had for some time controlled the two cities Paoting and Taiming in the southern part of Chihli, but these two cities were abandoned by the Feng Nationalists in order to rescue Honan. The northern part of the Peking-Hankow Railway then fell to the Fengtien clique. The First Division of the Nationalist Army, which was quartered in the vicinity of Peking, was forced by Fengtien troops to move elsewhere. This was a great humiliation to Feng Yü-hsiang. When Sun Ch'uan-fang launched the expedition against the Fengtien Army, Chang Tso-lin, anticipating that the Nationalist Army would take this chance to avenge itself, delegated envoys to placate Feng Yü-hsiang, and at the same time took vigilant preventive measures against any threat from Feng. Feng also returned the courtesy by sending envoys to visit Chang and to assure him of the maintenance of order and peace in the North, while he at the same time made undercover arrangements for an eventual war.

As soon as the Fengtien Army lost Hsuchow, the Feng Nationalists in Honan started military action toward the western part of Shantung. They advanced toward Taiming and Paoting along the Peking-Hankow Railway. The Fengtien Army in the vicinity of the capital surrounded the capital, which had been under Feng's garrison, on three sides. Major war between the Fengtien and Feng Nationalist cliques was near at hand.

Tuan Ch'i-jui still tried his best to bring the two parties together. In mid-November messengers from the two parties were busily discussing at Tientsin an amicable settlement of their differences. Feng demanded that the Fengtien troops withdraw completely from the northern part of the Peking-Hankow Railway in the province of Chihli. Tuan was ordered on November 13 to place the whole railway under the control of Feng Yü-hsiang's subordinate, and the Tientsin-Pukow Railway under Chang Tso-lin's subordinate, Li Ching-lin, then governor of Chihli. But Governor Li was dissatisfied with this order, made at the cost of the territory under his jurisdiction. Even so, the grave situation forced him reluctantly to abandon Paoting. On November 18 the Second Division of Feng's Nationalists moved to Paoting, where part of the outgoing troops still remained, and a conflict between the incoming and outgoing soldiers occurred. War between Feng and Chang was now drawing nearer.

Suddenly Kuo Sung-ling's revolt occurred in Fengtien on November 23, 1925. Kuo, a deputy division commander of the new faction in the Fengtien military clique, was a favorite of Chang Hsüeh-liang. The crack Fengtien troops, nominally in the hands of Chang, were actually controlled by Kuo Sung-ling—a good reason for envy on the part of other generals. During the second Feng-Chih war, Kuo, in conflict with another general, intended to lead his soldiers to his home bases in Fengtien. He was stopped by Chang Hsüeh-liang only through much persuasion. While other Fengtien generals, such as Chang Tsung-ch'ang,

Yang Yü-t'ing, and Li Ching-lin, were each assigned a province, Kuo obtained nothing. He was not even successful in asking for Jehol, because Yang Yü-t'ing, with whom he was incompatible, did not wish him to have it. Kuo was disappointed and outraged. Even among the generals Kuo could get along only with Li Ching-lin.

Feng Yü-hsiang, aware that his own power could not defeat the Fengtien military clique, tried his best to sow dissension among the generals in order to subdue his formidable foe. For this reason Kuo Sung-ling became Feng's comrade. Between Feng and Kuo there was a secret agreement providing that (1) Kuo Sung-ling would request Chang Tso-lin to retire and set up Chang Hsüeh-liang as a puppet; (2) when Kuo revolted and fought against Chang Tso-lin, the Nationalist Army would carefully watch Li Ching-lin so that Kuo need have no anxiety about an attack from the rear; and (3) if Li Ching-lin took joint action or remained neutral, he would be given after the revolution the province of Jehol as a reward.

Feng Yü-hsiang was very anxious to secure a sea outlet near Tientsin, but he was aware of the objection of Li Ching-lin, who would not give up his position in Tientsin. Feng therefore made use of Kuo's power to overcome Chang and Li. After the signing of the secret agreement, both Feng and Kuo asked for Li's cooperation. When Li inquired about the assignment of the territory of Chihli, Feng gave him only a vague reply. But since Kuo and Feng had reached an agreement and in addition had strong power in their hands, Li dared not express any objection. To make it appear that he had no antagonism toward Kuo, he even sent a telegram requesting Chang Tso-lin to retire. He was determined, however, that he would not give up the territory in Chihli.

On November 22, Kuo Sung-ling requested Chang Tso-lin's retirement. During the following few days his troops were marching from Luanchow in northeastern Chihli toward Fengtien. At this time he arrested a number of enemy generals and officers and killed general

Chiang Teng-hsüan.

Learning of this *coup d'état*, Chang Tso-lin and his son offered strong resistance. But Kuo's almost invulnerable forces marched rapidly on. Now the military head of Jehol rushed with his troops to the rescue of Fengtien. Feng Yü-hsiang quickly availed himself of this opportunity to order one of his subordinates, Sung Che-yüan, to occupy Jehol. With support from Sung, Kuo now advanced even more confidently. In the middle of December, Mukden was threatened. It looked as though the headquarters of the Fengtien military clique would soon be taken.

But interference by Japanese soldiers changed the whole situation. The Japanese would not allow Kuo's insurgent army to proceed in the vicinity of the Japanese-controlled Southern Manchuria Railroad. The insurgents had to make a long detour through icy roads to Mukden. The Japanese troops also offered a great deal of direct assistance to Chang Tso-lin. On December 23 a decisive battle was fought not far from Chang's headquarters. The insurgents were crushed. Kuo Sung-ling and his wife were arrested and subsequently executed. The position of Chang Tso-lin and his son was secure again.

In North China Li Ching-lin's persistence in keeping his Chihli territory annoyed Feng's Nationalists. From December 1, the Nationalists were assaulting Li Ching-lin with their full strength. Li Ching-lin was knocked out on the twenty-third, the day after Kuo's crushing defeat. Li took shelter in a foreign concession at Tientsin, and the majority of his troops were either disarmed by the Nationalists or in flight to Shantung. Tientsin now became a possession of the Nationalist Army. Though it had failed in achieving its aim of utilizing Kuo Sung-ling to get rid of Chang Tso-lin it was successful in obtaining the entire Chihli province. However, this victory was only temporary.

The Feng-Chih Alliance Against Feng's Nationalist Army

The combat between the Fengtien clique and the Nationalists in the

Northwest derived from the Feng-Che war in the Southeast. Sun Ch'uan-fang was then the leader of the Chihli military clique. After he had taken Hsuchow, however, he was no longer interested in any further territorial expansion. He returned to headquarters at Hangchow where he tried his best to put in order the political and military affairs of the five provinces under his jurisdiction, Kiangsu, Chekiang, Fukien, Anhwei and Kiangsi. He was indifferent to the former leader of the Chihli clique, Wu P'ei-fu, and let the latter remain at Hankow almost completely isolated.

Wu attempted to go north, but he could not pass Honan; he also wished to go east, but he was not welcomed by Sun Ch'uan-fang. Even Wu's direct subordinate, Hsiao Yao-nan, was not very cooperative. But when Kuo Sung-ling mutinied against Chang Tso-lin in the Northeast and a large part of the Nationalist Army had to be concentrated in the Chihli area to fight against the Fengtien clique, a loophole in Honan opened for Wu P'ei-fu.

Wu now quickly re-emerged from obscurity, proclaiming himself commander in chief of the allied armies against the "bandits." By "bandits" he had once meant Chang Tso-lin; but now, since he planned to ally himself with Chang, he used the term to refer to Kuo Sung-ling and Feng Yü-hsiang. Chang Tso-lin, who was then in an extremely dangerous position, was very agreeable to an alliance, particularly between the Fengtien and Chihli cliques, for the purpose of the subjugation of Feng's Nationalist Army.

As mentioned before, a part of the Nationalist Army had launched an expedition from Honan to Shantung before the Kuo Sung-ling incident, had taken several important cities, and was even ready to conquer the provincial capital, Tsinan. But these Nationalist troops were largely of Honan soldiers who had formerly belonged to Wu P'ei-fu. For this reason, Wu ordered a Honan leader, Chin Yün-e, to Shantung to entice his fellow soldiers to change sides. As a result, a few regiments joined the standard of Wu P'ei-fu's envoy, Feng's plan to attack the Shantung capital was foiled, and the army subsequently retreated from the few large cities which they had occupied.

With a few regiments that had recently joined him, Wu's envoy, Chin Yün-e, made a secret alliance with Chang Tsung-ch'ang in the middle of December—Chang Tsung-ch'ang then being greatly in need of help because of the fierce and unpredictable war with Kuo Sung-ling. In the latter part of the month, Li Ching-lin was defeated and the province of Shantung was opened for invasion by the Nationalist Army. Since Chin was ordered by Wu P'ei-fu to come to Shantung, Chang Tsung-ch'ang tried his best to bring Chang Tso-lin and Wu P'ei-fu together. On January 5, 1926, Chang Tso-lin telegraphed Wu P'ei-fu, forgiving him for his erstwhile enmity. The alliance between the Fengtien and the Chihli cliques against Feng's Nationalists was completed.

Li Ching-lin, after being defeated by the Nationalist Army, fled from a foreign concession at Tientsin southward to Tsinan. There he reorganized the remnants of his former troops who had escaped to Shantung. Li allied himself with Chang Tsung-ch'ang, under the title Chihli-Shantung Allied Army, to attack Chihli.

In the Three Eastern Provinces the scattered troops of Kuo Sung-ling near Shanhaikwan were reorganized by Wei I-shan into the Fourth Division of the Nationalist Army. This new division declared its continued support of Feng.

Under the name of suppressing Wei I-shan's troops, Chang Tso-lin announced, on January 11, 1926, his military expedition toward the interior of Shanhaikwan. On January 19, Wu P'ei-fu called a military conference at Hankow and decided to attack Honan. Four days afterward, when Chin Yün-e signed an alliance in Shantung with Chang Tsung-ch'ang and Li Ching-lin, Chang Tsung-ch'ang supplied Chin with military funds to attack Honan. Thus the territory in the Peking-Tientsin area and the two provinces of Chihli and Honan under the control of the Nationalist Army were being surrounded, from three sides, by the allied forces of the

Fengtien and Chihli cliques.

After taking Tientsin, Feng Yü-hsiang asked the Executive Government to appoint Sun Yo as tuchun of Chihli. This appointment caused disagreement among other Nationalist generals. Since on account of Kuo Sung-ling's fiasco Feng Yü-hsiang anticipated that Chang Tso-lin would avenge himself against Kuo's ally, and that Wu P'ei-fu, Chang Tsung-ch'ang and others would try to take Honan, on January 1, 1926, Feng tendered his resignation. Relinquishing all his duties, Feng declared that he planned to go abroad as soon as his resignation was accepted. He added that hereafter he would decline to receive any telegrams concerning political matters. Furthermore, he announced that the title "Nationalist Army" should not be used again.

Three days after his New Year's Day telegram he transferred his duties to his subordinate, Chang Chih-chiang, to suggest that he was now a man without any official capacity. He prepared to travel from Kulun, Outer Mongolia, through Russia to Europe. His territory in the Northwest was divided into five parts: the vicinity of Peking, Chahar and north of Kalgan, Suiyuan, Jehol, and Kansu were to be taken care of by Liu Chung-lin, Chang Chih-chiang, Li Ming-chung, Sung Che-yüan, and Liu Yü-fen respectively. He asked the Executive Government to make these appointments.

On January 9 it was officially announced by the chief executive that Feng Yü-hsiang had relinquished all his duties in order to investigate industry in Europe and America. Chang Chih-chiang was appointed to succeed Feng as commander of frontier defense in the Northwest and concurrently as tuchun of Chahar. Other military leaders of various territorial zones were also appointed, according to Feng's plan, as a defense measure.

But his defense plans were applicable only to the area in the Northwest; he had no way to defend the vicinity around Peking nor the two provinces, Chihli and Honan. In the latter part of January, Wu P'ei-fu had sent five regiments to Honan from the south. Coinciding with Wu's expedition, Chin Yün-e's troops were also attacking Honan from Shantung and had occupied Kaifeng on either February 27 or 28. The Nationalists retreated to the city of Shihkiachwang, where they were intercepted by General Yen Hsishan's troops from Shansi. While this was being done, Yen sent a telegram to Feng Yü-hsiang telling him that the interception was merely to prevent Fan Chung-hsiu's soldiers from invading Shansi. At the same time he informed Wu P'ei-fu that he was cooperating with him. Confronted by these coordinated attacks, the Nationalist Army in Honan was completely defeated. Now Wu P'ei-fu lost no time in ordering one of his generals to attack Tungkwan at the border of Shensi.

On the northeastern side the Fengtien troops had occupied Shanhaikwan on January 19. The Fengtien-Chihli allies under Chang Tsung-ch'ang and Li Ching-lin also took action at the same time with expeditions in Honan. When Kaifeng was taken, Li Ching-lin's troops were pressing the suburb of Tientsin from the south. Lu Chung-lin led a strong force from Peking to combat Li. After taking Chengchow in Honan, Wu P'ei-fu ordered Chin Yün-e's forces to advance along three separate routes. Chin's advance troops occupied Shihkiachwang on March 18, an event which threw Peking into a state of panic. Some senior retired military leaders like Wang Shih-chen promptly offered themselves as mediators for peace. Leaders of the Nationalist Army supported Wang Shih-chen's peace movement, and at the same time withdrew troops from the front lines along Tsinpu, and from the Ching-Feng railroads toward Peking. Tientsin, abandoned, was occupied on March 23 by Li Ching-lin's force. Chang Hsüeh-liang, and Chang Tsung-ch'ang subsequently reached Tientsin.

Lu Chung-lin, Chang Chih-chiang, and others still intended to defend Peking as a bargaining point for reaching a compromise with Wu P'ei-fu. Wu, however, could not trust them. The attempt by Tuan Ch'i-jui's henchmen to ally with the Fengtien clique in an uprising inside Peking was discovered by Lu Chung-lin. On April 9 Feng's Nationalists surrounded the chief executive's office building, announcing a series of "crimes" allegedly committed by Tuan Ch'i-jui, who then took shelter in the Legation Quarter. At the same time the former president, Ts'ao K'un, was set free. Although the Feng Nationalists invited Wu P'ei-fu to come to Peking immediately to take over all state affairs, he was not moved by the invitation. Peking was then besieged from the three sides. The Nationalist Army, withdrawing on April 15 to the northwest, put up a strong defense at Nankow, about thirty miles west of the capital. After Wu P'ei-fu had harried Nankow for several months with no success, the Fengtien Army joined the attack with heavy artillery. Then war came to a rapid conclusion.

The End of the Executive Government

In the first half of 1925, the Executive Government was under pressure from both Feng and Chang. Nevertheless Tuan could not bear to give up his position as chief executive. After the Fengtien troops were forced to withdraw from the Southeast and after Kuo Sung-ling's revolt, the pressure from the Fengtien clique was removed. But at the same time in losing Chang's support Tuan lost his main defense against other factions.

In Peking the Kuomintang members stirred up troubles in schools. But Tuan Ch'i-jui paid no attention to unarmed partisans, hoping that the man with military power, Feng Yü-hsiang, would protect him. On November 26, three days after Kuo Sung-ling's revolt, a few of Tuan's confidants were arrested by the garrison commander of Peking, who was Feng Yü-hsiang's henchman. All important politicians of the An-fu clique, who were close to Chang Tso-lin, now took shelter in the Legation Quarter. Then another special conference called by Tuan decided to send Huang Fu, the former premier-regent, to Kalgan to welcome Feng Yü-hsiang back to Peking. Huang reported that Feng still favored the existence of the Executive Government, whereupon Tuan immediately decided to revise the government structure into a responsible cabinet government in order to appease the Kuomintang members.

On December 20, Hsü Shih-ying was announced as premier of the cabinet, which included several Kuomintang members. However, both Hsü and the Kuomintang adherents refused the honor. Finally the minister of war, Chia Te-yao, who was Feng's adherent, was made premier. But when in April 1926 Feng Yü-hsiang's Nationalist Army was completely routed, there was no alternative left for Tuan except retirement.

Nevertheless, Tuan's partisans of the An-fu clique still made a desperate effort to prolong his political life. They begged that Chang Tso-lin forgive Tuan and they incubated an uprising within Peking. This plot, discovered in advance by the Nationalist Army, resulted in the besieging of the Executive Government offices and the disarming of Tuan's bodyguards on April 9. Tuan and his An-fu clique members, fleeing to the Legation Quarter, fully expected that the Fengtien clique would reinstate Tuan after the Nationalist Army was driven away from Peking. Tuan announced a *coup d'état* by the Nationalist Army on the ninth, but did not mention his retirement. Ten days later he sent delegates to welcome Chang Hsüeh-liang in Tientsin, but Chang ignored the delegation. Tuan finally realized that his luck had been reversed. On April 20, Tuan was permitted to pass the defense line of the Chih-Lu allies on his way from Peking to Tientsin, and on the same day the newly appointed premier also resigned. A deputy premier, Hu Wei-te, was hurriedly appointed as premier-regent to take care of the provisional administration after the fall of the Executive Government.

Now came a period of argument between Chang Tso-lin and Wu P'ei-fu as to the form of the new government. Wu P'ei-fu wished to restore Ts'ao K'un to the presidency and to make Ts'ao's former premier, Yen

Hui-ch'ing, the premier-regent. Wu's plan was flatly rejected by Chang Tso-lin. At the end of June, Yen Hui-ch'ing was eventually permitted to take up the post but immediately resigned by appointing the minister of the navy, Tu Hsi-kuei, to serve concurrently as the premier-regent. Peking had only the empty form of a premier-regent cabinet—to watch after the old palace and the government buildings. In 1927 Chang Tso-lin made himself grand marshal of the Peking government.

THE CONSOLIDATION OF KUOMINTANG FORCES

The Cadets Secure Kwangtung

During the dogged fighting of the warlords in North China, the Kuomintang was again in the process of reorganization. After Sun Yat-sen had left Canton for Peking, Ch'en Hsiung-ming had taken this opportunity to recover his territories in the province of Kwangtung. After having learned of Sun Yat-sen's illness, an item of news which delighted him, he made an agreement with the Yunnan and Kwangsi troops, quartered in the suburbs of Canton. These were to coordinate attacks inside the city with the movements of his troops advancing toward the city. He also sent delegates to Peking to establish relations with Tuan Ch'i-jui's close advisers and to persuade the chief executive to annihilate the Communist government in Canton. As early as January and February 1925 Ch'en Hsiung-ming's troops were waging full-scale war to retake Canton.

Fortunately for the Kuomintang, the graduates of the first and second classes of the Whampoa Military Academy numbered more than 1100, there was a battalion of new and fresh cadets, and the Army of Kwangtung had been given training by Whampoa graduates. Taking the offensive by three routes against Ch'en's forces, the troops led by the cadets were victorious. The central and left routes, however, composed of the Yunnan and Kwangsi troops, were inactive because of the agreement previously made with Ch'en Hsiung-ming. Nevertheless, the cadets proved to be such effective commanders that within two months Ch'en Hsiung-ming's troops were driven out of Chaochow and Swatow.

When this cadet-supported Eastern Expedition Army took Hsingning, several confidential telegrams between the Yunnan Army and Ch'en Hsiung-ming's were discovered. Also found were documents recording the private trip of the Kwangsi military leader Liu Chen-huan to Yunnan to persuade T'ang Chi-yao to send troops from Kwangsi to attack Kwangtung. Further uncovered evidence showed that Yang Hsi-min, who resided in Hong Kong, had worked to consolidate support from the imperialists and also to instigate merchants to petition the Peking Executive Government to appoint Yang military leader of Kwangtung.

The commander of the Hunan Army, T'an Yen-k'ai, and Chu P'ei-te, Commander of part of the Yunnan Army, dispatched delegates to discuss with Chiang Kai-shek and Hsü Ch'ung-chih procedures for exterminating Yang Hsi-min and Liu Chen-huan. Liao Chung-k'ai and Wang Ching-wei also participated in this conference. Finally, military action was taken on June 13 in the vicinity of Canton. Within six hours more than twenty thousand Yunnan and Kwangsi troops under the command of Yang and Liu were completely disbanded.

After the liquidation of the Yang and Liu forces, there were still some motley troops whose loyalty to the Revolutionary Government was dubious. In the months of August and September this problem was also tackled. Because one of the army officers among these troops was a direct subordinate of Hsü Ch'ung-chih, Hsü was also obliged to leave Canton.

The formidable foe of the Revolutionary Government was still Ch'en Hsiung-ming, who had the advantage of strong defense topography in Hweichow and the zone of the East River. Near the end of September the second Eastern Expedition was decided upon.

At the start of this expedition it was discovered that the Szechwan troops under Hsiung K'o-wu, quartering in Kwangtung, had had communications with the enemy. Hsiung was detained and all his Szechwan fighters were dismissed. Hsiung K'o-wu, who had had his name listed in the Kuomintang, was an elected member of the Central Executive Committee. His Szechwan troops had once entered Hunan, and when driven back by the local garrison, had been admitted to Kwangtung to seek for food.

After discharging these ungrateful troops, the Eastern Expedition marched on October 1 and fought its way through to lay siege to the city of Hweichow on the twelfth. After severe fighting the city was won, and in the first part of November the enemies in the zone of the East River were cleaned up. Other small and unreliable units were also wiped out. In the spring of 1926 the domestic situation in Kwangtung was secure.

The Kuomintang Consolidates Kwangsi

The province of Kwangsi was however still problematic. After Sun Yat-sen had returned to Canton and re-established the Military Government, the complicated and dangerous situation in Kwangtung prevented him from concerning himself with Kwangsi. The old warlord of the Kwangsi military clique, Lu Jung-t'ing, secretly returned to Kweilin. President Ts'ao K'un appointed Lu commander of military affairs in Kwangsi on January 30, 1924. Since Lu's former troops had been scattered, he now mustered a number of officers and soldiers from Kwangsi. Unfortunately for him, most of these officers desired to be autonomous within a small territory and were reluctant to accept orders from Lu.

At that time a relatively strong force in Kwangsi consisted of two factions: one was under the command of Shen Hung-ying, a former enemy of Sun Yat-sen; the other under Li Tsung-jen and Huang Shao-hsiung, who had been close to Sun. Neither of the two factions wished to have Lu Jung-t'ing rule over Kwangsi again.

The Peking government, however, still hoped to bring Shen Hung-ying and Lu Jung-t'ing together. In the middle of May 1924 Shen Hung-ying had been appointed by the Executive Government commander of frontier affairs of Kwangtung and Kwangsi. Hoping to monopolize Kwangsi, Shen Hung-ying had defied the amicable arrangement made for him by the Peking government and laid seige to Kweilin, where Lu Jung-t'ing was badly harassed. Lu then asked to have Hunan troops under the command of a native of Kwangsi assist in the defense of Kweilin.

While Shen Hung-ying and Lu Jung-t'ing were at a stalemate at Kweilin, Sun Yat-sen had ordered Li Tsung-jen and Huang Shao-hsiung to attack the strategic city of Nanning. Learning this news, Shen and Lu hurriedly signed a truce; but Li and Huang took Nanning on June 26. On July 16 Li Tsung-jen, demanding that Lu Jung-t'ing resign, proclaimed himself "commander in chief of the allied armies of Kwangtung and Kwangsi against the 'bandits.'"

In the first part of August, Li Tsung-jen's troops headed northward and occupied the large city of Liuchow. Shen Hung-ying now changed sides and joined the onslaught at Kweilin. The city fell to Li Tsung-jen on August 24, and Lu Jung-t'ing was driven away. Before long his resignation was published.

The three leaders, Li Tsung-jen, Huang Shao-hsiung, and Shen Hung-ying, held a conference. Sun Yat-sen had appointed the Kwangsi army leader quartering at Kwangtung, Liu Chen-huan, to be governor of Kwangsi. Shen, Li, and others as a countermeasure elected Li Tsung-jen as commander of rehabilitation of Kwangsi, and Huang Shao-hsiung as associate commander and governor. In the last part of November Huang Shao-hsiung was summoned by the Canton military government to a conference with Hu Hanmin, who was in charge of the grand marshal duties while Sun Yat-sen was on his way to the North. Hu agreed with Huang to establish a "pacification office for the entire province of

Kwangsi," of which Li Tsung-jen was to be the director and Huang Shao-hsiung associate director.

Shen Hung-ying's purpose in allying himself with Li and Huang in expelling Lu Jung-t'ing was fundamentally to win domination over Kwangsi. Now Li and Huang, with assistance from the Canton government, had full power to govern Kwangsi. Immediately Shen broke his relationship with Li and Huang and resorted to war again. With the assistance of part of the Kwangtung troops under the command of Li Chi-ch'en, a native of Kwangsi, Li and Huang defeated Shen Hung-ying's forces in the middle of February 1925. The entire province of Kwangsi was then unified.

As soon as Shen Hung-ying was defeated, another formidable enemy, T'ang Chi-yao of Yunnan, appeared in Kwangsi. For many years T'ang had dreamed of extending the power of Yunnan province. Now frustrated in Szechwan and Yunnan, he hoped to fulfill his dreams in Kwangtung and Kwangsi. Since Sun Yat-sen was ill in Peking and T'ang had enlisted Yang Hsi-min and Liu Chen-huan on his side within the Kwangtung force, he invaded Kwangsi by seizing the opportunity provided by Li Tsung-jen's war against Shen Hung-ying. On February 23 T'ang occupied the strategic city of Nanning, whence he divided his troops into two routes to continue the advance.

Because T'ang Chi-yao had indicated his support of Sun Yat-sen's Northern Expedition plans in the fall of 1924, Sun Yat-sen had honored T'ang with the deputy marshalship. When T'ang received the news that Sun Yat- sen had died in Peking, he proclaimed in Yunnan on March 17, 1925, his assumption of duties as deputy marshal, and almost openly asserted his desire to be the lord of Southwest China.

The Canton Military Government immediately declared war against T'ang by sending the Yunnan troops stationed at Kwangtung, under command of Fan Shih-sheng, to Kwangsi to join the assault led by Li and Huang. After much fierce combat the progress of T'ang's troops was checked. On May 12, however, T'ang as deputy marshal appointed Liu Chen-huan commander and governor of Kwangsi. Liu even tried to take up the post. Finally, in mid-July, Liu Chen-huan's soldiers in the suburb of Canton were crushed and T'ang Chi-yao's troops were forced to withdraw from Nanning to Yunnan. Kwangsi was actually unified. By the spring of 1926 the bases at Kwangtung and Kwangsi were completely consolidated.

The Formation of the Nationalist Government

After the reorganization of the Kuomintang of China in January 1924 and the convention of the First National Congress, a decision was made to organize a Nationalist Government in place of the Military Government. The decision, belatedly carried through on July 1, 1925, was delayed by the numerous unprincipled generals and soldiers like Yang Hsi-min and Liu Chen-huan in Kwangtung, who might still be brought under temporary control by the military government system and the title of grand marshal, a post still held in 1924 by Sun Yat-sen. Therefore, the military government structure and the title grand marshal were kept until Sun Yat-sen's death. Shortly after Sun's death the leaders in Canton held several meetings discussing the abolition of the title in order to avoid its usurpation by some ambitious militarist such as T'ang Chi-yao.

At the beginning of June the members of the Central Executive Committee at Canton decided that the reorganization of China must start with reorganization at Canton, and the reorganization of Canton must begin with the reorganization of military affairs. The outlined order of procedure stressed (1) military unification, (2) civil administration unification, (3) financial unification and independent control of military necessities, and (4) political training of the armies by the party members. A declaration of the reorganization of the Nationalist Government was proclaimed on June 25. The Nationalist Government was formed on July 1.

The government thus established was a committee system. Among the sixteen committee members in charge of political affairs were Wang Ching-wei, Hu Han-min, Sun Ko, Hsü Ch'ung-chih, Wu Chao-shu, Hsü Chien, Chang Chi, T'an Yen-k'ai, Tai Chi-t'ao and Lin Shen. Wang Ching-wei was elected the chairman, Hsü Ch'ung-chih minister of war, Hu Han-min minister of communication, and Liao Chung-k'ai minister of finance. The Kwangtung provincial government was also reorganized on July 3 according to the law enacted by the Nationalist Government dealing with local governments.

Military Reorganization

The work for military unification was accomplished by a committee of military affairs under the central government. Under this committee, all former names or titles of local units were canceled; all armed forces were simply called "the National Revolutionary Army" (*Kuo-min ko-ming chün*). At first, the revolutionary forces were divided into five armies: the First Army consisted of the party troops newly trained by the graduates of the Whampoa Academy and some Cantonese troops whose loyalty was indisputable; the Second Army comprised the Hunan soldiers under T'an Yen-k'ai; the Third Army comprised the Yunnan troops under Chu P'ei-te; the Fourth Army was made up of the reorganized Cantonese troops in Fukien; and the Fifth Army comprised the Fukien troops under Li Fu-lin. The Sixth Army, which was added later, consisted of troops organized under Ch'eng Ch'ien to attack Hupeh. The Seventh Army was made up of the Kwangsi troops after the unification of Kwangtung and Kwangsi. Hsü Ch'ung-chih, resigning from the post of commander in chief of the Kwang-tung Army on August 1, gave his military authority to the military committee of the Nationalist Government.

Civil Administration

The next task was the unification of finance and civil administration.

Separation of these two branches of government had come about through the monopoly of revenues by warlords in each locality. Now that the warlords had been removed, it was comparatively easy to solve financial and administrative problems.

The Nationalist Government organized a committee in February 1926 for the unification of the two provinces Kwangtung and Kwangsi—militarily, politically, and financially. On March 15 the political committee passed a unification act which included three items: (1) The Kwangsi provincial government was to take orders from the Nationalist Government in dealing with political affairs of the whole province. (2) All Kwangsi troops were to be reorganized into the Nationalist Revolutionary Army. (3) The finances of the two Kwang provinces must be directed and supervised by the Nationalist Government. The Kwangsi provincial government was formally organized on June 1 according to this act. Huang Shao-hsiung was made provincial chairman, and Li Tsung-jen head of the Seventh Army. Thus the political unification of the two Kwangs was also completed according to schedule.

The Settlement of Party Dissension

After the unification of the two Kwangs in the spring of 1926, the Nationalist Government was almost ready to mobilize its forces for the Northern Expedition. In January, Chiang Kai-shek made his second military report to the Second National Party Congress, saying:

> The Nationalist Revolutionary Army is entirely under the control of the government and it can be mobilized by a single order. The number of soldiers is 85,000. There is a definite budget for military expenditures and the life of soldiers has also been improved. We have also 6000 army cadets; the number is equivalent to an army division. If we use further energy to reorganize and consolidate the strength of our party, it will not be difficult for us to unify China.

This report certainly did not exaggerate the situation or the possibilities. Nonetheless, open conflict between the Communist Kuomintang members and the non-Communist Kuomintang members was already vehement. Party dissension had to be controlled before a large-scale military undertaking could go forward.

At the time of the reorganization of the Kuomintang, many old party members had been doubtful about the admission of Communist members. Shortly after the reorganization, the senior members, Chang Chi and others of the Central Supervisory Committee, moved on June 18, 1924, to impeach the Communist members and pointed out their several plots against the Kuomintang. Sun Yat-sen, who was then still alive, could control all factions and even the Communist members still dared not to be too recalcitrant. After Sun Yat-sen's death the Communist sparks became a roaring blaze; and the fear of non-Communist members increased accordingly.

In August 1925, Liao Chung-k'ai was assassinated. He had incurred the hatred of unemployed reactionary militarists; the assassination also involved the anti-Communist elements. On account of this imbroglio, Hu Han-min was compelled to go to Russia. Henceforward, wrangling was aggravated. The important members of the right wing lost ground and left Canton for Peking.

In November the right-wing members of the Central Executive Committee, assembled at Peking, held the fourth Central Executive Committee meeting before the coffin of Sun Yat-sen in the Western Hills (Hsi Shan). Here they passed a resolution to abolish the political committee, to dismiss the Communist members from the Kuomintang, to cancel the employmen of Borodin as the adviser of the Nationalist Government, and to revise the election laws for the Second National Party Congress.

The authorities in Canton declared the resolution of the Western Hills Conference null and void because its members could not make a legal quorum. Another fourth Central Executive Committee, meeting at Canton, decided to convene the Second National Party Congress on January 1, 1926, when the congress would decide the punishment of the members who had called the Western Hills Conference. From now on the Western Hills faction set up a separate party organization at Shanghai, though it lacked military power.

After the separate establishment of the Western Hills group, the open wrangling in Canton did not cease. Not only were the old members of the Western Hills group dissatisfied with the Communists' activities, but even a large number of young party members did not approve their actions. These young members organized a Society for the Study of Sun Yat-sen's Principles [*Sun Wen Chu-i hsüeh hui*] as a counterweight to a Communist Youth Corps [*Kung-chan chu-i ching-nien t'uan*]. In the Whampoa Military Academy the Communist elements formed the Young Army Men's Association [*Ch'ing-nien chün-jen lien-ho hui*] to compete with the newly formed Sun Yat-sen group.

In the midst of such complicated circumstances the famous incident of the ship *Chung-shan* occurred on March 20, 1926. The truth of this case has not yet been officially determined. One statement indicates that the Communist faction and its sympathizers, observing that Chiang Kai-shek's influence in the army was daily increasing, attempted to kidnap Chiang and take him away on the *Chung-shan*. But Chiang refused to tell the inside story of the case, saying that not until after his death would it be fully revealed.

Since even the chairman of the National Government, Wang Ching-wei, was not consulted by Chiang in settling the case, Wang resigned. Wang's published excuse, illness, gave rise to the suspicion by outsiders that Wang himself might have been involved. Chiang Kai-shek arrested Li Chih-lung, the head of the navy bureau and captain of the S. S. *Chung-shan*. Chiang also deprived the Communist representatives at all levels of the First Army of their duties and dismissed many Russian advisers in military organizations. All these advisers were immediately sent back to Russia.

It looked as though the policy of alliance with Russia was near the breaking point. But both sides, the Kuomintang and the Communists, deemed it too early to break the relationship. Furthermore, Chiang Kai-shek dissolved the Society for the Study of Sun Yat-sen's Principles, as well as the Young Army Men's Association, and even put some pressure on the right-wing faction. In this way the breach of the two parties was temporarily cemented.

On May 15, 1926, the Central Executive Committee opened a plenary conference. Four resolutions for the readjustment of party affairs were passed. In the first resolution the important points were: (1) to improve the relation between the Kuomintang and the Communist Party; (2) to rectify those actions and the words of the members of the two parties which are detrimental to their cooperation; (3) to protect the unitary authority of the party principles and the regulations of the Kuomintang; and (4) to define the position and significance of the Communist members in the Kuomintang.

To realize these basic points and remove the confusions within the party, a joint conference of the Kuomintang and the Communist Party was called. Its significant outcome was the change of policy from "admitting Communists" [*jung-kung*] to "allying with the Communists" [*lien-kung*]. After this measure of reconciliation, the internal party confusion subsided for a time.

THE END OF THE PEIYANG WARLORDS

The North in 1926

When the Kuomintang commenced the Northern Expedition, the Chihli military clique under the leadership of Wu P'ei-fu possessed Hupeh and Honan and controlled the whole Peking-Hankow Railway. The junior leader of the Chihli military clique, Sun Ch'uan-fang, had bases at Nanking and governed five provinces: Kiangsu, Chekiang, Fukien, Anhwei, and Kiangsi. Although he esteemed Wu P'ei-fu, he refused to act as Wu's subordinate; his military power was undoubtedly larger than that of Wu.

The Fengtien military clique, after expelling Feng Yü-hsiang's Nationalist Army from Peking, occupied the territory along the railway from Peking to Fengtien and the northern part of the Tientsin-Pukow Railway. The tuchun of Shantung was still Chang Tsung-ch'ang; his subordinate was made tuchun of Chihli to replace Li Ching-lin, who was disliked by Chang Tso-lin. Sun Ch'uan-fang promised that he would not invade the territory in the North; Chang Tso-lin and Chang Tsung-ch'ang also assured Sun that they would not infringe upon his sphere of influence in the South. The two erstwhile enemies seemed to have given up their grudges and to have resumed an amiable neighborliness. All three of these great military forces, under Wu P'ei-fu, Sun Ch'uan-fang and Chang Tso-lin, were absolutely incompatible with the Kuomintang.

Feng Yü-hsiang's Nationalist Army was now distressed in the Northwest and Feng himself had gone to Russia. His troops, commanded by his subordinates Chang Chih-chiang and others, were at a stalemate with the Fengtien-Chihli allied armies facing them at Nankow, about thirty miles north of Peking. They also were making no further headway against Liu Chen-hua in the contest for Sian. Although this Nationalist Army of Feng's was friendly to the Kuomintang, it was not yet the party's army. On the eve of the Kuomintang's Northern Expedition, Feng Yü-hsiang decided to join the Kuomintang formally; he knew that it would be difficult for him otherwise to protect his forces, which were then isolated and hard pressed in the Northwest. In August 1926 Feng delegated one of his chief subordinates to Canton to report to the Nationalist Government that Feng had led his Nationalist Army to join the

Kuomintang en masse. Upon hearing this, the Canton government acted instantly, making Feng a member of the Central Executive Committee of the Nationalist Government.

There was in the North another warlord, Yen Hsi-shan, who had been the warlord of Shansi for many years. Closely associated with Tuan Ch'i-jui, he might be considered an adherent of the old Peiyang military clique. But he was a very astute and clever politician. After the division of the Peiyang military clique, he steered his ship wherever there was favorable wind; his own position as lord of Shansi province was not affected and Shansi did not suffer from military disaster. Prior to the Kuomintang's Northern Expedition, while the Feng Nationalists were desperately fighting against the Fengtien-Chihli Allied Army, Yen Hsi-shan accelerated the pressure on Feng's Nationalist Army. Since he was not a friend of Feng's Nationalists, he might not be expected to befriend the Nationalist Revolutionary Army from Kwangtung. He seemed ready to cooperate, nonetheless, but his habitual flexible policy made the allies unable to trust him.

This was the alignment of the warlords in the North in 1926. As to Hunan, under the flag of autonomy, this province was and had been repeatedly at the disposal of Wu P'ei-fu. In the spring of 1926 its governor, Chao Heng-t'i, was forced to resign and was replaced by his insurgent general, T'ang Sheng-chih. T'ang, while he was still stationed in the southern part of Hunan, had already made secret connections with the revolutionary forces in Canton. Now as governor he tried to capture the military power from other generals in the province. One of these oppressed generals, Yeh K'ai-hsin, left to work under Wu P'ei-fu. He asked that a strong force be sent from the Chihli military clique to Hunan. Unable to resist this attack, T'ang withdrew to Hengyang in the south central part of the province and asked to join the Kuomintang in Canton and to reorganize his troops within the Nationalist Revolutionary Army structure. The Nationalist Government, complying with his request, reorganized his troops as the Eighth Nationalist Revolutionary Army. A strong Kwangsi force was sent to Hunan to assist T'ang. This action provided an excellent opportunity to initiate the Northern Expedition from Kwangtung.

Chiang's Northern Expedition

On June 6, 1926, the military committee of the Nationalist Government appointed Chiang Kai-shek commander in chief of the Nationalist Revolutionary Army. Chiang took up duty on June 9 with an elaborate flagraising ceremony; and his troops were mobilized on that very day. On June 27 Chiang went out from Canton to his headquarters at the front.

The first step in Chiang's military plan was to make a compromise with Sun Ch'uan-fang for a while and to ignore Chang Tso-lin in order to concentrate power to dispose of Wu P'ei-fu. Wu was then in personal command at Nankow. When this strong post was taken on August 14, the Nationalist Revolutionary Army had penetrated deeply into Hunan and had even occupied Yochow, an important city on the border between Hunan and Hupeh. Wu P'ei-fu hurried to the South, where he again commanded the war against the revolutionists, but lost one battle after another. Near the end of August the Nationalist Revolutionary Army swiftly advanced to Wuchang, the captial of Hupeh. Although this city did not fall until October 10, the two adjacent cities, Hanyang and Hankow had already surrendered. The whole of Hupeh province was very soon in the possession of the Revolutionary Army.

Wu P'ei-fu was not yet completely beaten, but his time was near. The Nationalist Revolutionary Army judged that there was no more need to maintain a reconciliatory policy with Sun Ch'uan-fang. Sun himself also predicted that the time was not far away for a showdown with the Revolutionists.

The war against Sun Ch'uan-fang was fought by an encircling

movement using the First Nationalist Revolutionary Army from western Kiangsi and another army from southern Fukien. A stubborn battle was engaged near Nanchang, the capital of Kiangsi, which was finally captured the first part of November. Sun Ch'uan-fang then moved his headquarters from the front to Nanking. In March, 1927, the National Revolutionary Army, pressing Nanking, soon occupied it without much difficulty. The territory south of the Yangtze River was securely held by the Revolutionists.

The two big warlords of the Chihli military clique were near the end of their tether. Their life was prolonged, however, because the Kuomintang continued to have internal dissensions. Nanking and Hankow became the capitals of two governments: those of the right and left wings of the Kuomintang respectively. Wu P'ei-fu and Sun Ch'uan-fang, utilizing this break in the Kuomintang, allied themselves with the Fengtien military clique for a last stand.

While the Kuomintang authorities of Nanking and Hankow were at odds, both nevertheless continued the Northern Expedition. Feng Yü-hsiang's Nationalist Army also joined the expedition from the Northwest and crossed the boundary from Shensi to Honan and Chihli. Watching the direction of the wind, Yen Hsi-shan, who had ordered his troops in April to believe the "Three Principles of the People," quickly became a friend of the Nationalist Revolutionary Army. Wu P'ei-fu commanded his remaining forces to flee to western Honan, leaving the Fengtien Army to test the prowess of the Revolutionary Army. In the first part of June the Fengtien forces suffered a severe defeat. Honan was then occupied by the Nationalist Revolutionary Army from Hankow. About the same time the Revolutionary Army sent from Nanking also occupied the traditionally strategic city of Hsuchow. Sun Ch'uan-fang's territory was completely lost and he himself and his troops became merely an appendage of the Fengtien military clique.

In the first part of August the military leaders of Nanking and

Hankow shook hands again. When Chiang Kai-shek declared the relinquishment of his military duties as commander in chief, Sun Ch'uan-fang seized this opportunity to recover his territory. He reorganized his remnants with a strong force from the Fengtien Army to make a secret and desperate attack on Nanking. Near the end of August Nanking was in grave peril. Ultimately, however, the attackers were thoroughly and mercilessly crushed on the battlefield of Lung-t'an. Sun Ch'uan-fang again retreated to Shantung and eventually to obscurity.

The narrow escape from military disaster for the Revolutionists, however, indicated the great need for Chiang's military leadership. In the spring of 1928 Chiang was asked to resume the post of commander in chief of the Nationalist Revolutionary Army. He continued the Northern Expedition in April. The troops of Yen Hsi-shan and Feng Yü-hsiang also mobilized their forces toward the final goal, Peking. Near the end of April the Nationalist Revolutionary Army occupied the Shantung capital, Tsinan.

Chang Tso-lin returned to Fengtien from Peking on June 3. The next day while his train was passing the junction between the Peking-Fengtien Railway and the Japanese-controlled Southern Manchurian Railway at Huang-ku-t'un, a mine exploded and the train was blown up. Chang was fatally wounded and died after a few days. His successor as leader of the Fengtien military clique, Chang Hsüeh-liang, soon changed his allegiance to the Nationalist Revolutionary Army. He declared his adoption of the flag of the Nationalist Government on December 31, 1928. This ended the war between the Kuomintang and the Peiyang warlords.

NOTES

Since most of the data provided in the following notes have been supplied by the present translators and editors, it has seemed advisable to omit the usual notation [Ed.], which would otherwise appear at the end of nearly every note in the following pages. Rather, we have appended the abbreviation [L. Cn.], indicating notes by Li Chien-nung which have been transferred from his original text.

CHAPTER ONE

1. Sixteen years later Hugh H. Linsay was on a secret mission along the China coast. He demanded, *inter alia*, free trade and equality of treatment. He observed China's military weakness and suggested English use of force. A study by C. Y. Hsü of this neglected mission is available in *Harvard Journal of Asiatic Studies*, Vol. 17 (1954).

2. Liu Yen says in his *Ti-kuo chu-i ya-po Chung-kuo shih* [*History of Imperialists' Oppression of China*] that Elliot sent a messenger to negotiate peace at Canton, but that Lin Tse-hsü did not respond; this seems to be untrue. We have consulted the memorials and letters of Lin Tse-hsü and found no reference to this matter. Everything Lin did in Canton, no matter how trifling, was always faithfully reported to the throne. If Elliot did send a messenger to negotiate peace, Lin would have recorded it. [L. Cn.]

3. See *I-wu shih-mo* (T. K.) 17: 13-17, 25-28; 20: 31; 21: 11, 12b, 13; and 22: 11-15.

4. Ch'i-shan's duties were carefully defined by Emperor Tao-kuang's endorsements on his memorials. See *I-wu shih-mo* (T. K.) 13: 40-41.

5. *Ch'ing shih-lu, Hsüan-tsung*, 345. 18.

6. *Ibid.*, 351. 34b.

7. Liang-Kiang or the two Kiang—Kiangnan and Kiangsi provinces—comprises modern Kiangsu, Anhwei, and Kiangsi.

8. For a detailed account of the inside story, see *Chang Hsi and the Treaty of Nanking*, 1842, prepared by Teng Ssu-yü.

9. Cf. Teng and Fairbank, *China's Response to the West*, 19.

10. *Ibid.*, 24-27.

CHAPTER TWO

1. The T'ai-p'ing T'ien-kuo was formally inaugurated on January 11, 1851, at Chin-t'ien in Kwangsi, although orders for a general mobilization of God-Worshippers for the "rebellion" had been issued in June 1850. See Lo Erh-kang, *T'ai-p'ing T'ien-kuo shih k'ao-cheng-chi* [A Collection of Critical Essays Concerning the History of the Taiping Rebellion] Shanghai, 1948, pp. 1-5.

2. See year entries in *Ch'ing shih-lu*.

3. *Ch'ing shih-lu, Hsüan-tsung*, 418. 21.

4. *Tseng Wen-cheng kung tsou-kao*, 1. 22 (dated March 21, 1853).

5. *Chung-wang Li Hsiu-ch'eng tzu-chuan*, 42-44.

6. *Ibid.*, 46-47.

7. *T'ai-p'ing T'ien-kuo*, 1. 67-68.

8. *T'ai-p'ing T'ien-kuo yeh-shih*, 12. 1.

9. *Liang-ssu-ma* was an ancient official title mentioned in the *Chou-li* for the leader whose chariot maneuvers were supported by twenty-five soldiers.

10. *T'ien-ch'ao t'ien-mou chih-tu*, 7.

11. *Ibid.*, 1-2.

12. *T'ai-p'ing T'ien-kuo*, 1. 161.

13. *Tseng Wen-cheng kung shu-chia*, 1. 34-35.

14. *Ibid.*, 2. 17.

15. Wang Ting-an, *Ch'iu-chüeh-chai ti-tzu chi*, 4. 13.

16. *Ibid.*, 4. 17.

17. *Ch'ing shih-lu, Hsüan-tsung*, 147. 24; 153. 6-7.

18. *Chung-wang Li Hsiu-ch'eng tzu-chuan*, 85, 152, 160.

19. *Ibid.*, 126-27.

20. *Wuhan* is a common abbreviation for Wuchang and Hankow.

21. The "big four" of modern Hunan were Tseng Kuo-fan, Tso Tsung-t'ang, P'eng Yü-lin, and Hu Lin-i, all of whom came into prominence during the period of the Taiping rebellion.

22. *Chung-wang Li Hsiu-ch'eng tzu-chuan*, 65.

23. *Ibid.*, 152.

24. H. F. MacNair, *Modern Chinese History, Selected Readings*, 348.

25. *Ibid.*, 350-51.

26. *I-wu shih-mo, Hsien-feng*, 88. 34.

27. See S. Y. Teng, *The Nien-fei and Their Guerrilla Warfare*, 4, 15-16.

28. These conversations are recorded in *Tseng wen-cheng-kung ta-shih-chi* [Accounts of Major Affairs Concerning Tseng Kuo-fan, Ch. 4, pp. 15-16]. [L. Cn. and Ed.]

CHAPTER THREE

1. According to unofficial or private accounts, some of the emperor's eunuchs induced him to go out of the palace in disguise and soon after this excursion he was found to have contracted the venereal disease which resulted in his death. This rumor was strongly denied by Yün Yü-ting, who said he succumbed to smallpox. Hsüeh Fu-ch'eng also believed that the eunuchs induced him to go beyond the proprieties. Possibly smallpox is a euphemism. When the emperor died in 1875, he was only nineteen years old. [L. Cn.]

2. See Yün's *Ch'ung-ling ch'uan-hsin-lu*, p. 457.

3. The Yüan-ming Yüan, the imperial pleasure park of former Manchu rulers, had been laid waste in 1860 by soldiers of the Anglo-French alliance. Its destruction was ordered by Lord Elgin as a deliberate act of reprisal. The well-known description of the Yüan-ming Yüan written by the Jesuit Father Attiret in 1743 details the more than two hundred smaller palaces of cedar wood and the central palace, like a great city, of gray brick with glazed tile roofs in red, yellow, blue, and violet. Park areas with waterfalls and fountains were said to have been reminiscent of Versailles.

4. Li Hung-chang's correspondence [*P'eng-liao han-kao*], 3. 16-17 and 19.

5. *Ibid.*, 19b.

6. See Liang's biography of Li Hung-chang, p. 41.

7. Cf. *China's Response to the West*, 99-102.

8. Li Hung-chang's correspondence, 17. 14b.

9. Cf. *China's Response to the West*, 76-77.

10. *I-wu shih-mo* (1867), 47. 15-16.

11. Cf. *China's Response to the West*, 108-110.

12. Kuo Sung-tao, *Yang-chih sbu-wu wen-chi*, 11. 3-11.

13. Li Hung-chang's correspondence, 17. 12-14.

14. *Tso Wen-hsiang kung tsou-i*, 61. 10b-11.

15. Wei Kung-tao, *K'an-ting Hsin-chiang-chi* (1899 ed.) 3. 9-10.

16. *Ibid.*, 67. 11, 16-17.

17. *Chang Wen-hsiang kung ch'üan-chi*, 2. 6.

18. Li Hung-chang, *I-hsiü han-kao*, 11. 26.

19. *Tso Wen-hsiang kung ch'üan-chi*, 76. 14-15.

20. "Annam has since ancient times been a vassal of China" was roughly translated "Elle a été tributaire de la Chine," instead of "Elle est depuis longtemps…." Therefore the French minister mistakenly assumed

that China was now relinquishing her sovereignty over Annam. See Henri Cordier, *Histoire des relations de la Chine avec les puissances occidentales*, I, 278; and Shao Hsün-cheng, *Chung-fa chan-cheng* [The Sino-French War], I, 55 and V, 102-103.

21. Gordon's farewell words are collected in the *Correspondence of the Tsungli Yamen* [*I-hsü han-kao*, 11. 25-28] in the *Complete Works of Li Hun-chang*, and his farewell words bring into focus China's essential weaknesses. [L. Cn.]

22. *Ch'ing shih-lu, Te-tsung*, 215. 4.

23. Li Hung-chang's correspondence, 20. 60.

24. *Ibid.*, 20. 63.

25. *Yoshida sho in zen shu*, I. 349, 350-51 (1940 ed.).

26. The passage from Sato Shinen's *Kodo hisaku* is quoted from Liu Shu-ya's essays on the invasion of China by Japan in the *Tu-li p'ing-lun* [19 (Sept. 1932), 11-12, and 20 (Oct. 1932), 9-12. See also *Sato Shinen bugaku shu*, I, 192 (1932 ed.)]. [L. Cn. and Ed.]

27. The rulers of the Liuchiu [Ryukyu] Islands for centuries sent tribute to both China and Japan. [L. Cn.]

28. Nago Ariga's chapter on "Diplomacy" in *Japan by the Japanese*, Alfred Stead, ed. London: 1904, 161-63.

29. *I-wu shih-mo* (T. C.) 93. 27. and T. F. Tsiang, "Sino-Japanese Diplomatic Relations, 1870-1894," *The Chinese Social and Political Science Review*, Vol. 17 (1933-34) 4-26.

30. These cables can be found in the "telegram" [*tien-kao*] section of Li Hung-chang's collected writings [15. 26-27. 31. 32]. [L. Cn. and Ed.]

31. Li Hung-chang, *Tien-kao* [Telegram correspondence], 15. 34.

32. *Ibid.*, 32b-33.

33. *Chung-Tung chan-chi pen-mo* [A Complete Account of the War Between China and Japan], 5. 23.

CHAPTER FOUR

1. In *Chung-shan ch'üan-shu*, 1. 15 (Shanghai: 1928 ed.).

2. See Chang Po-chen, *Nan-hal K'ang hsien-sheng chuan* [Biography of K'ang Yu-wei], 2.

3. *Ibid.*, Ch. 2.

4. See Wu Chih-hui, *Wo I-chiang Chung-shan hsien-sheng* [Let Me Also Talk About Sun Yat-sen] in *Chung-shan chüan-shu*, 4. 148 (Shanghai: 1928). [L. Cn. and Ed.]

5. Wu Chih-hui's essay in *Chung-shan ch'üan-shu*, 4. 198.

6. *Nan-hai hsien-sheng ssu-shang shu-chi*, 15. 148.

7. *Ibid.*, 17.

8. Many Chinese books were burned at the command of the emperor in 213 B. C. Several decades later a few elderly scholars who had learned the classics by heart recited versions which were set down in the modern characters used during the Han dynasty (202 B. C. -A. D. 220). Still later, old copies of the classics written in archaic characters became available, said to have been discovered between the double walls of an old building and in old tombs. Those who believed in the authenticity of the texts written in the Han dynasty script charged that the texts in the archaic script were forgeries; and those who trusted the texts in archaic script charged that the texts of the Modern Text School were erroneous both because they had been set down only from personal memory and because they contained fewer chapters than the "ancient text." This chronic academic war between the Modern Text School and the Ancient Text School continued, reaching maximum intensity in the eighteenth and nineteenth centuries.

9. Liang Ch'i-ch'ao, *Yin-ping shih ho-chi, wen-chi*, 3. 98-99.

10. With regard to K'ang Yu-wei's opinions as a scholar see Liang Ch'i-ch'ao's *Ch'ing-tai hsüeh-shu k'ai-lun*, 56-58 in *Yin-ping shih*

ho-chi, *tuan-chi*, 10.

11. *Weng Wen-kung kung jih-chi*, 34. 53, 60 (Wu-hsü: 1898). Cf. Yün Yü- ting, *Ch'ung-ling ch'üan-hsin lu*, 461.

12. *Nan-hai hsien-sheng wu-shang shu-chi*, 18.

13. The six officials included both Manchu and Chinese. See *Ch'ung-ling ch'uan-hsin-lu*, 461-62.

14. *Ch'ung-ling ch'uan-hsin-lu*, 462.

15. A detailed record of T'an Ssu-t'ung's persuasion of Yüan Shih-k'ai is set down in Liang Ch'i-ch'ao's biography of T'an Ssu-t'ung and in Yüan Shih-k'ai's "Wu-hsü Diary" in *Chung-kuo chin-pai-nien shih tzu-liao*, Ⅱ. 495-500. The two sources tell much the same story, but Yüan's diary in-clines to whitewash Yüan and Jung-lu and also suggests that T'an was abrupt and blunt, not mincing his words or his opinions.

16. See the account in *Ch'ing-shih chi-shih pen-mo* [Topical Reports of Ch'ing History], 66. 4.

17. *Wu-hsü pien-fa*, 1. 476.

18. In *I-chiao ts'ung-pien*, 1. 11.

19. See Yeh Te-hui's letter to P'i Hsi-jui, *I-chiao ts'ung-pien*, 6.

20. In *Yin-ping shih ho-chi*, 1. 3.

CHAPTER FIVE

1. *I-chiao ts'ung-pien*, 6. 20-21.

2. The Eight Diagrams (*pa kua*) are of very ancient origin and are exhaustively treated in the *Book of Changes*. The names of the diagrams are *ch'ien*, heaven; *k'un*, earth; *k'an*, water; *li*, fire; *tui*, moisture; *sun*, wind; *chen*, thunder; and *ken*, hill. These symbols have a major function in divination and fortune-telling in China. When the eight symbols are multiplied by eight, they make the sixty-four diagrams. Such changes were regarded as demonstrating that nature is not static but dynamic.

3. In Tso Shun-sheng, *Chung-kuo chin-pai-nien-shih tzu-liao ch'u-pien*, 544.

4. Huang Hung-shou, *Ch'ing-shih chi-shih pen-mo*, 67. 3.

5. See Ch'ou-ming's note at the end of *Keng-tzu kuo-pien-chi* [An Account of the Incident of 1900] in Tso Shun-sheng, *Chung-kuo chien-pai-nien-shih tzu-liao ch'u-pien*, 577. [L. Cn. and Ed.]

6. *Chung-kuo chin-pai-nien-shih tzu-liao ch'u-pien*, 552-53.

7. For an account of the enthronement of Kuang-hsü see *Ch'ing-shih chi-shih pen-mo*, published by the Wen-ming shu-chü [Ch. 56]. [L. Cn.]

8. *Chung-kuo chin-pai-nien-shih tzu-liao ch'u-pien*, 550-51.

9. *Ibid.*, 466-67.

10. *Ibid.*, 464-65.

11. *Ch'ung-ling ch'uan-hsin-lu*, 467-70.

12. According to *Ch'ing shih-lu*, *Kuang-hsü*, the declaration of war was made on June 20, not June 21, when an imperial decree proclaimed that "a state of hostilities between China and the foreign nations had existed" (Ch. 464, p. 12).

13. *Ch'ung-ling ch'uan-hsin-lu*, 470-71.

14. *Ibid.*, 553-54.

15. *I-ho t'uan*, 1. 72.

16. See Feng Tzu-yu's *Chung-hua Min-kuo k'ai-kuo-chien ko-ming shih* [A History of the Revolution before the Establishment of the Republic], I. 57-61.

17. *Chung-shan ch'üan-shu*, 1. 22.

18. Cf. Ralph L. Powell, *The Rise of Chinese Military Power*, 69, 71, 83, 102.

19. Instituted in 1861, the office of *pei-yang ta-ch'en*, with residence at Tientsin, involved control of coast defenses and trade for the three ports of Tientsin, Chefoo, and Newchwang. The superintendent

also handled foreign relations, the adoption of Western techniques, and the training of a modern navy and army. This superintendency was usually a concurrent post of the Chihli governor-generalship. Li Hung-chang held both positions through a very long tenure.

20. For a more detailed study see Ralph L. Powell, *The Rise of Chinese Military Power*, 1895-1912.

CHAPTER SIX

1. *Yin-ping shih ho-chi*, *wen-chi*, 1. 38-39.
2. Chou Jung, *Ko-ming-chün in Man-i hua-hsia shih-mo*, 7. 30.
3. Sun's autobiography in *Chung-shan ch'üan-shu*, 1. 23.
4. *Chung-kuo chin-pai-nien shih tzu-liao*, 575.
5. *Tung-hua hsü-lu*, 169. 7.
6. Cf. *Jung-an ti-tzu chi*, 3. 18.

CHAPTER SEVEN

1. *Chung-shan ch'üan-shu*, 1. 24.
2. Feng Tzu-yu, *Ko-ming i-shih*, Ⅲ. 209.
3. *Chung-shan ch'üan-shu*, 1. 19.
4. "Miscellaneous Writings," *ibid.*, 4. 1-2.
5. *Yin-ping shih ho-chi*, *wen-chi*, 7. 49.
6. See Liang's "Further Discussion of the Gain and Loss from Racial Revolution and Political Revolution" in *Yin-ping shih ho-chi, wen-chi*, 7. 43.
7. See the *Min-pao*, No. 2. [L. Cn.]
8. *Yin-ping shih ho-chi, wen-chi*, 7. 34.
9. The National Assembly, or the Provisional Assembly, was set up by a decree of September 1907 having the rights, privileges, and attributes of a parliament. The assembly was unicameral, but contained

the elements of two chambers: the representatives of specific privileged classes as the basis for a future upper house; and the representatives of the Provincial Assemblies. It was to be the foundation or forerunner of a parliament, but it was discontinued in 1912. See Pan Wei-tung, *The Chinese Constitution* (Washington: 1946), 5, 6, and 9.

10. *Shun-t'ien shih-pao*, editorial, November 12, 1906.

11. *Jung-an ti-tzu chi*, 3. 12.

12. *Ibid.*, 4. 14.

13. *Yin-ping shih ho-chi, wen-chi*, 7. 28-29.

14. Feng Tzu-yu, *Chung-kuo ko-ming yün-tung erk-shih liu-nien chu-ckih-shih*, Shanghai: Commercial Press, 1949, p. 137.

15. Ito's explanation on this occasion was published in No. 3 of the *People's Tribune* along with a sharp criticism by the editor, Wang Ching-wei. [L. Ch.]

16. According to the account by Sun Yat-sen, Huang Hsing did not participate in the uprising at Hokow because he was detained by the Annam government. According to the statement by Feng Tzu-yu, however, Huang Hsing personally led the soldiers in the fight. At that time Sun Yat-sen was not in Annam and his memory may be at fault; therefore Feng's statement is followed here. [L. Cn.]

17. *Chung-shan ch'üan-shu*, 1. 25.

CHAPTER EIGHT

1. Yün Yü-ting, *Ch'ung-ling ch'uan-hsin lu*, 486-87.
2. *Jung-an ti-tzu chi*, 4. 28.
3. *Tung-fang tsa-chih*, Vol. 7, No. 11 (Nov., 1910) 163.
4. *Ch'ung-ling ch'uan-hsin lu*, 483.
5. *Tung-fang tsa-chih*, Vol. 7, No. 2 (Feb. 1910) 32.
6. *Chung-shan ch'üan-shu*, 1. 29.

CHAPTER NINE

1. *Chung-shan ch'üan-shu*, 1. 31.

2. Yang Sung, Jung Meng-yüan, *et al.*, *Chung-kuo chin-pai-nien-shih tzu-liao hsüan-chi*, 652-53.

3. There are two versions of the assassination of Wu Lu-chen, neither of which can be verified. According to the account in the newspaper *Min-li*, Liang-pi ordered the assassination. Other current sources indicate that Yüan, realizing that his own position was endangered because of Wu, himself ordered the death sentence, [L. Cn.]

4. *Chung-shan ch'üan-shu*, 2. 4-5.

5. See *Sun Wen hsüeh-shuo in Chung-shan ch'üan-shu*, 4. 391.

6. Tsou Lu, *Chung-kuo kuo-min-tang shih-kao*, 918.

7. *Shun-t'ien shih-pao*, January 1, 1912.

8. *Tsung-li ch'üan-shu*, IX, *Wen-tien* (Taipeh: Chung-yang men-wu kung-yin-she, 1954), p. 58.

9. See the last chapter of *Sun Wen hsüeh-shuo*.

10. *Shun-t'ien shih-pao*, January 1, 1912.

11. *Tung-fang tsa-chih*, Vol. 8, No. 10 (April 1912) 17.

12. *Min-kuo shih-chou chi-shih pen-mo*, 42-43.

13. Tsou Lu, *Chung-kuo kuo-min-tang shih-kao*, 933.

14. *Tung-fang tsa-chih*, Vol. 8, No. 10 (April 1912) 17.

CHAPTER TEN

1. The provisional parliament consisted of members appointed by provincial governors or elected by the people to deal with legislative, financial, and diplomatic matters and to serve as counselors to the president. The 42 representatives formally convened at Nanking January 28, 1912. After the organization of the formal parliament, it was divided

into two houses: the senate or upper house (*ts'an-i-yüan*) and a house of representatives (*chung-i yüan*).

2. See Huang Yüan-yung, *Yüan-sheng i-chu*. [L. Cn.]

3. Tso Shun-sheng, *Chung-kuo chin-pai-nien-shih tzu-liao hsü-pien*, 523-7.

4. *Yüan-sheng i-chu*, 2. 101 (Shanghai: 1938).

5. *Ibid.*, 2. 114-115; 105.

CHAPTER ELEVEN

1. Pai Chiao "Yüan Shih-k'ai yü Chung-hua min-kuo," *Jen-wen*, Vol. 13, No. 1 (Jan. 1916) 4-6. For further details on Yüan's interview with G. E. Morrison see *Far Eastern Review*, 12 (1915) 105.

2. *Yin-ping shih ho-chi*, *tuan-chi*, 9. 100-102.

3. See *Tokyo Mai-nichi Shimbun*, June 17, 1915, quoted in *Chia-yin* magazine. [L. Cn.]

4. *Tung-fang tsa-chih*, Vol. 13, No. 1 (Jan. 1916) 4-6.

5. *Yün-nan cheng-pao*, "Yüan Shih-k'ai wei-ts'ao min-i."

6. *Ying-ping shih ho-chi, tuan-chi*, 9. 99.

7. *Chia-yin* (1916), correspondence section, 1-2.

8. *Kuo-t'i chan-cheng kung-li tan* [An Account of the War for the National Polity, with Personal Experiences] in Liang's *Tun-pi chi, Yin-ping shih ho-chi*, *tuan-chi,* 9. 145-46.

9. *Ts'ai Sung-p'o hsien-sheng i-chi* (Li Chien-nung, comp. Shaoyang, Hunan: 1943) 4. 16 (movable type edition). Ts'ai Ao's letter, to Liang Ch'i-ch'ao, is dated January 5, 1916.

10. *Tung-fang tsa-chih*, Vol. 13, No. 4 (April 1916) 6-7.

11. *Yin-ping shih ho-chi, tuan-chi*, 9. 34.

12. *Tung-fang tsa-chih*, Vol. 13, No. 6 (June 1916) 6.

13. *Ta Chung-hua*, Ⅱ. 10 (October 1916) 3.

14. Cf. *Tung-fang tsa-chih*, Vol. 13, No. 7 (July 1916) 6.

15. *Yin-ping shih ho-chi, tuan-chi*, 9. 108-109.

16. *Ts'ai Sung-p'o hsien-sheng i-chi*, 4. 25.

CHAPTER TWELVE

1. *Tung-fang tsa-chih*, Vol. 13, No. 7 (July 1916) 6.

2. *Ibid.*, Vol. 13, No. 10 (Oct. 1916) 9-10. Also, Kao Lao, *Ti-chih yün-tung shih-mo chi*, 9-10.

3. Yang Yu-ch'iung, *Chin-tai Chung-kuo li-fa shih* (Shanghai: 1936), p. 249.

4. *Tung-fang tsa-chih*, Vol. 13, No. 8 (August 1916) 3.

5. The four groups within the Kuomintang were the *Ko-lü* [Temporary Resident Group], the *Ping-ch'en chu-lo-pu* [Political Club of 1916], the *Tao-yüan-pai* and the *Cheng-hsüeh-hui* [Political Study Group]. Chang Chi and Wang Cheng-t'ing were members of the Ko-lü, which itself was divided into three branches, one of which was headed by Chang Chi. In the Political Club of 1916, Lin Shen and Chü Cheng represented the Revolutionary Party. The Tao-yüan-pai had among its leaders members of the old Progressive Party such as Sun Hung-i and Ting Shih-i. The Political Study Group was organized by Ku Chung-hsiu. [L. Cn.]

6. The central government order with reference to the titles *tuchun* and *sheng-chang* appears to imply a reaffirmed distinction between military and civil authority; this distinction, thoroughly blurred in the careers of several of the tutus, was soon blurred again in the careers of subsequent tuchuns.

7. *Tsung-li ch'üan-shu*, II, *wen-tien*, 423.

8. These decrees composed by K'ang Yu-wei were later discovered by a newspaper correspondent who had them published in the Peking Times [*Pei-ching Shih-pao*]. [L. Cn.]

9. *Tung-fang tsa-chih*, Vol. 14, No. 8 (August 1917) 206.

10. *San-shui Liang Yen-sun hsien-sheng nien-p'u*, Ⅱ, 183 (second printing, 1946).

11. Of the ＄120,000,000 borrowed from Japan, ＄20,000,000 was borrowed for building telegraph lines (April 30, 1918); ＄10,000,000 for building the railway from Kirin to Huitang (June 8); and ＄30,000,000 for developing gold mines and forestry in Kirin and Heilungkiang (August 2); ＄20,000,000 for building four railways in Manchuria and Mongolia (September 28); ＄20,000,000 for building railways in Shantung (September 28); and ＄20,000,000 for China's participation in the European War (September 28). [L. Cn.]

12. "The militaristic government of General Terauchi engineered the Nishihara loans to the Chinese government of Premier Tuan and his An-fu clique as a leverage for further economic and political gains.... The series of loans aggregating 145 million yen were arranged between September 28, 1917, and September 28, 1918, by a certain Nishihara under instructions from the military and without knowledge of the foreign office." Chitosubi Yanaga, *Japan Since Perry* (McGraw-Hill, 1949), 363-364.

13. Yüan Shih-k'ai became president in October 1913 for a legal tenure of five years. After Yüan's death Li Yüan-hung succeeded him as president. After Li's resignation, Vice-President Feng succeeded him until October 1918, when the five-year legal tenure was filled, and he was succeeded by Hsü Shih-ch'ang, who had been elected in September 1918.

14. *San-shui Liang Yen-sun hsien-sheng nien-p'u*, Ⅱ, 183 (second printing, 1946).

CHAPTER THIRTEEN

1. *Tsung-li ch'üan-shu*, VI, hsüan-yen, 52.
2. *Chung-shan ts'ung-shu*, Ⅳ. 29 (Shanghai, 1927).
3. *Tsung-li ch'üan-shu* Ⅳ. 60.

4. *Chung-shan ch'üan-shu*, 4. 12.

5. *Chung-shan ts'ung-shu*, Ⅲ. 133-4.

CHAPTER FOURTEEN

1. *Sun Chung-shan ch'üan-chi, hsü-chi*, Ⅱ. 7.

2. *Chang* Ch'i-yün, *T'ang-shih k'ai-yao*, Ⅰ. 257-59.

3. *Ibid.*, I. 266-68.

4. *Sun Chung-shan ch'üan-chi, hsü-chi*, Ⅲ. 223.

5. The soldiers of Ch'en Hsiung-ming's Kwangtung Army had originally been transferred by Sun Yat-sen from the Kwangsi military base and assigned to Ch'en as their commander. [L. Cn.]

6. *T'ang-shih k'ai-yao*, Ⅰ. 350-51.

7. *Chiang Chieh-shih ti ko-ming kung-tso* (Wen Ti, comp. Shanghai: T'ai-p'ing-yang shu-tien, 1928) Vol. 2, A (reports) p. 12.

8. *Sun Chung-shan ch'üan-chi, hsü-chi*, Ⅲ. 265.

9. See Sun Yat-sen's autograph correspondence. [L. Cn.]

10. See Chiang Kai-shek's *Military Report*. [L. Cn.]

11. Interview given on November 24. See *Chung-shan ts'ung-shu* (Shanghai: Ta Chung-hua Book Co., 1927) III. 265.

12. Cf. *Tsung-li ch'üan-shu*, correspondence, Part 8, p. 1112, 1141.

SELECTED BIBLIOGRAPHY

BACKGROUND READING

Cheng Tien-hsi, *China Moulded by Confucius: The Chinese Way in Western Light*. London: Stevens & Sons, 1946.

Creel, H. G., *Chinese Thought from Confucius to Mao Tse-tung*. Chicago: University of Chicago Press, 1953.

——*Confucius: The Man and the Myth*. New York: The John Day Company, Inc., 1949.

Cressey, George B., *Land of the 500 Million*. New York: McGraw-Hill Book Company, Inc., 1955.

Eberhard, Wolfram, *A History of China*. London: Routledge and Kegan Paul, Ltd., 1950.

Fairbank, John King, *The United States and China*. Cambridge: Harvard University Press, 1948.

Fitzgerald, Charles P., *China: A Short Cultural History*, 3d ed. London: Cresset, 1950.

Fung Yu-lan, *A History of Chinese Philosophy*. Translated by Derk Bodde. Princeton: Princeton University Press, 1953.

Gallagher, Louis J., S. J. (transl.), *China in the Sixteenth Century: The Journal of Matthew Ricci, 1583-1610*. New York: Random House, Inc., 1953.

Goodrich, L. Carrington, *A Short History of the Chinese People*. New York: Harper & Brothers, 1943.

Hu Shih, *The Chinese Renaissance*. Chicago: University of Chicago Press, 1934.

Kao, George (ed.), *Chinese Wit and Humor*. New York: Coward-

McCann, Inc., 1946.

Latourette, Kenneth Scott, *The Chinese, Their History and Culture*, 3d ed. New York: The Macmillan Company, 1946.

Lattimore, Owen and Eleanor, *The Making of Modern China: A Short History*. New York: W. W. Norton & Company, Inc., 1944.

MacNair, Harley F. (ed.), *China*. Berkeley: University of California Press, 1942.

Michael, Franz, *The Origin of Manchu Rule in China*. Baltimore: The Johns Hopkins Press, 1942.

Needham, Joseph, *Science and Civilization in China*. Vol. 1. London: Cambridge University Press, 1954.

Reischauer, Edwin O., *Wanted: An Asian Policy*. New York: Alfred A. Knopf, Inc., 1955.

Steiger, G. Nye, *A History of the Far East*. Boston: Ginn & Company, 1936.

Wang Chi-chen (transl.), *Traditional Chinese Tales and Contemporary Chinese Tales*. New York: Columbia University Press, 1944.

Williams, Edward Thomas, *China Yesterday and Today*. New York: Thomas Y. Crowell Company, 1923.

Winfield, Gerald F., *China*. New York: William Sloane Associates, 1948.

Wittfogel, Karl A., and Feng Chia-sheng, *History of Chinese Society: Liao (907-1125)*. Philadelphia: The American Philosophical Association, 1949.

Wright, Arthur F. (ed.), *Studies in Chinese Thought*. Chicago: University of Chicago Press, 1953.

BIBLIOGRAPHIES ON MODERN CHINA

Chan Wing-tsit, *An Outline and a Bibliography of Chinese Philosophy*, revised edition. Hanover, N. H.: Dartmouth College, 1955.

Chang Ch'ün, *Min-kuo hsüeh-shu lun-wen so-yin* [An index to articles in learned periodicals published since 1912]. Taipei: China Cultural Publication Commission, 1954.

Chao Kuo-chün, *Selected Works in English for a Topical Study of Modern China*. Cambridge: Harvard University, Regional Studies Program on East Asia, 1952.

Chao Kuo-chün, *Source Materials from Communist China*. Cambridge: Center for International Studies, Massachusetts Institute of Technology, and Russian Research Center, Harvard University, 1952. Hectographic ed.

Cordier, Henri, *Bibliotheca Sinica: Dictionnaire bibliographique des ouvrages relatifs à l'Empire chinois*, 2d ed., 4 vols. Paris, 1904-08. Supplement, 1 vol., Paris, 1924. There is an *Author Index to the Bibliotheca Sinica*, prepared by the East Asiatic Library, Columbia University, 1954.

Davidson, M., *List of Published Translations from Chinese into English, French, and German*. Part I. Washington: American Council of Learned Societies, 1952.

Detailed Catalogue of the Blue Books [parliamentary papers] *on China*, 1820- 1907. Dairen, 1943.

Fairbank, John King, and Masataka Banno, *Japanese Studies of Modern China*. Tokyo: Charles E. Tuttle Company, 1955.

Fairbank, John King, and Liu Kwang-ching (comp.), *Bibliographical Guide to Modern China: Works and Documents in Chinese*. Draft compiled for the Regional Studies Program on China. Section I. Cambridge: Harvard University, 1947. Mimeographic.

The Far Eastern Quarterly. Annual Bibliography.

Franke, Herbert, *Sinologie*. Berne: A. Franke, 1953.

Goodrich, L. C., and H. C. Feen, *A Syllabus of the History of Chinese Civilization and Culture*, 5th ed. New York: China Society of

America, 1950.

Mote, Frederick, *Japanese Sponsored Governments in China*, 1937-1945. Stanford: Stanford University Press, 1954.

Papers on China, Vols. 1-9. Duplicated for private distribution by the East Asia Program of the Committee on Regional Studies, Cambridge: Harvard University, 1947-1955. Each paper is followed by a bibliography of Western and Chinese sources.

Suan, L. King, *A Survey of Material from Communist China in the Library of Congress and A Pilot Study on Chinese Communist Statements on the United States*. Washington: Library of Congress, 1951.

Sun, I-tu, Jen, *Bibliography of Chinese Social History: A Selected and Critical List of Chinese Periodical Sources*. New Haven: Yale University Press, 1952.

Teng Ssu-yü, and Knight Biggerstaff, *An Annotated Bibliography of Selected Chinese Reference Works*. Cambridge: Harvard University Press, 1950.

Teng Ssu-yü, and John K. Fairbank, *Research Guide for China's Response to the West: A Documentary Survey, 1839-1923*. Cambridge: Harvard University Press, 1954.

Yang Lien-sheng, *Topics in Chinese History*. Cambridge: Harvard University Press, 1950.

Walker, Richard L., *Western Language Periodicals on China*. New Haven: Yale University Press, 1949.

Wilbur, C. Martin, *Chinese Sources on the History of the Chinese Communist Movement*. Reproduced for private distribution by the East Asian Institute of Columbia University, 1950.

Wilbur, C. Martin (ed.) and Ichiro Shirato (comp.), *Japanese Sources on the History of the Chinese Communist Movement*. Reproduced for private distribution by the East Asian Institute of Columbia University, 1953.

SELECTED REFERENCE WORKS

Brunnert, H. S. and V. V. Hagelstrom, *Present-Day Political Organization of China*. Shanghai, 1912.

Cheng Ho-sheng, *Chin-shih Chung-hsi shih-jih tui-chao piao* [A Comparative Daily Calendar of Chinese and Western Dates from 1516 to 1941]. Shanghai, 1936. See Teng and Biggerstaff, p. 269.

Hashikawa, Tokio, *Chung-kuo wen-hua-chieh jen-wu tsung-chien* [A General Directory of Chinese Intellectual Personages]. Peking, 1940. See Teng and Biggerstaff, p. 241.

Hummel, Arthur W. (ed.), *Eminent Chinese of the Ch'ing Period*. 2 vols. Washington: Government Printing Office, 1943.

Mayers, William Frederick, *The Chinese Reader's Manual*. Shanghai, 1874, and later reprints.

Perleberg, Max, *Who's Who in Modern China*. Hong Kong: Ye Old Printerie, 1954.

Ting V. K., Wong Wen-hao, and others, *Chung-hua min-kuo hsin ti-t'u* [A New Atlas of the Chinese Republic]. Shanghai, 1934. See Teng and Biggerstaff, p. 223.

GOVERNMENT AND POLITICS

Backhouse, Edmund, and J. O. P. Bland, *Annals and Memoirs of the Court of Peking from the 16th to the 20th Century*. Boston, 1914.

Bland, J. O. P., and E. Backhouse, *China Under the Empress Dowager, Being the History of the Life and Times of Tzu Hsi*. London, 1910.

Buck, Pearl S., *Imperial Woman: Story of the Last Empress of China*. New York: The John Day Company, Inc., 1955.

Cameron, Meribeth E., and others, *China, Japan and the Powers*.

New York: The Ronald Press Company, 1952.

Chang Ch'i-yün, and others, *Chung-kuo cheng-chih ssu-hsiang yü chih-tu shih lun-chi* [Essays on the History of Chinese Political Thought and Systems]. 3 vols. Taipei: China Cultural Publication Commission, 1954.

Chang Ch'i-yün, *Chung-hua min-kuo ch'uang-li shih* [History of the Founding of the Chinese Republic]. Taipei: China Cultural Publication Commission, 1953.

Chen, Stephen, and Robert Payne, *Sun Yat-sen: A Portrait*. New York: The John Day Company, Inc., 1946.

Ch'ien Tuan-sheng, *The Government and Politics of China*. Cambridge: Harvard University Press, 1950.

Fairbank, John K., and Teng Ssu-yü, "On the Transmission of Ch'ing Documents," "On the Types and Uses of Ch'ing Documents." *Harvard Journal of Asiatic Studies*, Vol. 4 (1939) 12-46; and Vol. 5 (1940) 1-71.

Han Yü-shan, "The Chinese Civil Service, Yesterday and Today." *Pacific Historical Review*, Vol. 15 (1947) 158-170.

Headland, Isaac Taylor, *Court LiJe in China: The Capital, Its Officials and People*. New York, 1909.

Ho, Alfred Kuo-liang, "The Grand Council in the Ch'ing Dynasty." *Far Eastern Quarterly*, Vol. 7 (1948) 239-251.

Hsiao Kung-ch'üan, *Chung-kuo cheng-chih ssu-hsiang shih* [A History of Chinese Political Thought]. 2 vols. Shanghai: Commercial Press, 1946.

Hsieh Pao-chao, *The Government of China, 1644-1911*. Baltimore: The Johns Hopkins Press, 1925.

Hsü, Leonard Shih-lien, *Sun Yat-sen: His Political and Social Ideals*. Los Angeles: University of Southern California Press, 1933.

Jansen, Marius B., *The Japanese and Sun Yat-sen*. Cambridge: Harvard University Press, 1954.

Johnston, R. F., *Twilight in the Forbidden City*. London: Victor Gollancz, Ltd., 1934.

Kent, P. H. B., *The Passing of the Manchus*. London: E. Arnold, 1912.

Linebarger, Paul, *The China of Chiang K'ai-shek: A Political Study*. Boston: World Peace Foundation, 1941.

——*Government in Republican China*. New York: McGraw-Hill Book Company, Inc., 1938.

——*The Political Doctrines of Sun Yat-sen: An Exposition of the San Min Chu I*. Baltimore: The Johns Hopkins Press, 1937.

Linebarger, Paul, Djang Chu, and Ardath W. Burks, *Far Eastern Governments and Politics: China and Japan*, 2d ed. Princeton: D. Van Nostrand Company, Inc., 1956.

Lo Chia-lun, *Liu-shih-nien lai chih Chung-kuo Kuo-min-tang yü Chung-kuo* [The Kuomintang and China in the Last Sixty Years]. Taipei: Committee on Kuomintang History, 1954.

MacFarquhar, Roderick L., "The Whampoa Military Academy." *Papers on China*, Vol. 9. Cambridge: Harvard University Press, 1955.

MacNair, Harley F., *Modern Chinese History: Selected Readings*. Shanghai: 1923.

Meng, Ssu-ming, *The Tsung-li Yamen*. Ph. D. dissertation. Harvard University, 1949.

Pan Wei-tung, *The Chinese Constitution*. Washington: Institute of Chinese Culture, 1946.

Sharmon, Lyon, *Sun Yat-sen, His Life and Its Meaning: A Critical Biography*. New York: The John Day Company, Inc., 1934.

Pritchard, Earl H., "Political Ferment in China, 1911-1951." *Annals of the American Academy of Political and Social Science*, Vol. 277 (1951) 67-75.

Tong, Hollington K., *Chiang Kai-shek, Soldier and Statesman*. 2 vols. Shanghai: China Publishing Company, 1937. The authorized

biography.
Tsao, V. Y., *The Constitutional Structure of Modern China*. Melbourne: Melbourne University Press, 1948.
Walker, Richard L., "The Control System of the Chinese Government." *Far Eastern Quarterly*, Vol. 7 (1947) 2-21.
Wang Kan-yu, *The Local Government of China: A Study of the Administrative Nature of Local Units*. Chungking: China Institute of Pacific Relations, 1945.
Wright, Mary C., *The T'ung-chih Restoration*. Ph. D. dissertation. Radcliffe College, 1950.
Wu Hsiang-hsiang, *Wan-Ch'ing kung-t'ing chi-shih* [A Veritable Record of the Late Ch'ing Court]. Taiwan: Cheng-chung shu-chü, 1952.
Yano Jin'ichi, *Kindai Shina shi* [Modern Chinese History]. Kōbundō, 1926.

THE TAIPING AND OTHER REBELLIONS

Boardman, Eugene P., *Christian Influence upon the Ideology of the T'ai. p'ing Rebellion, 1851-1864*. Madison: University of Wisconsin Press, 1952. There is a good bibliography at the end of this book.
Chiang Siang-tseh, *The Nien Rebellion*. Seattle: University of Washington Press, 1954.
Fang Wen-lan and others (ed.), *Nien-chün* [a collection of source material on the Nien Army]. 6 vols. Shanghai: Shen-chou kuo-kuang she, 1953.
Hail, W. J., *Tseng Kuo-fan and the Tai Ping Rebellion*. New Haven: Yale University Press, 1927.
Hanson, Lawrence and Elizabeth, *Chinese Gordon: The Story of a Hero*. New York: Funk & Wagnalls Company, 1954.
Hsiang Ta and others, *T'ai-p'ing T'ien kuo* [A collection of source material on the T'ai-p'ing Rebellion]. 8 vols. Shanghai: Shen-chou

kuo-kuang she, 1952.

Hsiao I-shan, *Tseng Kuo-fan* [a biography of Tseng Kuo-fan]. Chungking: Shen-li ch'u-pan she, 1944.

Li Hsiu-ch'eng, *Chung-wang Li Hsiu-ch'eng tsu-chuan yüan-kao chien-ch'eng* [The Autobiography of the Loyal Prince, Li Hsiu-ch'eng, edited by Lo Erhkang and based on the original manuscript]. Peking: K'ai-ming shu-chu, 1951.

Ling Shan-ch'ing, *T'ai P'ing T'ien-kuo yeh-shih*. Shanghai, Wen-ming shu-chu, 1923.

Meadows, T. T., *The Chinese and Their Rebellions*. London, 1856. Reprinted by Stanford University Press, 1953.

Pai Shou-i (ed.), *Hui-min ch'i-i* [A collection of source material on the Mohammedan Revolution]. 4 vols. Shanghai: Shen-chou kuo-kuang she, 1952.

Shih, Vincent Y. C., "The Ideology of the Taiping T'ien-kuo." *Sinologica*, Vol. 3 (1951) 1-15.

Shih, Vincent Y. C., "Interpretation of the Taiping T'ien-kuo by Non-Communist Chinese Writers." *Far Eastern Quarterly*, Vol. 10 (1951) 248-257.

T'ai-p'ing t'ien-kuo ch'i-i Pai-nien chi-nien chan lan hui (ed.), *T'ai-p'ing t'ien-kuo ko-ming wen-wu t'u-lu* [Album of an Exhibition of Materials of the T'ai P'ing Rebellion]. Shanghai, 1952-53.

Taylor, George, "The Taiping Rebellion, Its Economic Background and Social Theory." *Chinese Social and Political Science Review*, Vol. 16 (1933) 545-614.

Teng Ssu-yü, *New Light on the History of the Taiping Rebellion*. Cambridge: Harvard University Press, 1950.

——*The Nien-fei and Their Guerrilla Warfare, 1851-1868*. To be published by the University of Chicago Press.

T'ien ch'ao t'ien-mou chih-tu [The Land System of the Celestial Dynasty]. Hsiao I-shan, *T'ai-p'ing T'ien-kuo Ts'ung-shu* edition.

Wu, James T. K., "The Impact of the T'ai-p'ing Rebellion upon the Manchu Fiscal System." *Pacific Historical Review*, Vol. 19 (1950) 265-275.

Yap, P. M., "The Mental Illness of Hung Hsiu-ch'üan, Leader of the Taiping Rebellion." *Far Eastern Quarterly*, Vol. 13 (1954) 287-304.

WESTERN IMPACT ON CHINA

Bales, W. L., *Tso Tsung-t'ang, Soldier and Statesman of Old China*. Shanghai, 1937.

Chang Chung-li and others, *Guide to the Materials of Seven Leading Officials of Nineteenth Century China*. Seattle: University of Washington Press, 1955.

Ch'en, Gideon, *Lin Tse-hsü, Pioneer Promoter of the Adoption of Maritime Defense in China*. Peiping, 1935.

——*Tso Tsung-t'ang, Pioneer Promoter of the Modern Dockyard and the Woolen Mill in China*. Peiping, 1938.

Cheng Lin, *The Chinese Railways: A Historical Survey*. Shanghai, 1935. China Today Series No. 5.

Chiang Kai-shek, *China's Destiny and Chinese Economy Theory*. New York: Roy Publishers, 1947.

Chiang Monlin, *Tides from the West: A Chinese Autobiography*. New Haven: Yale University Press, 1947.

Clyde, Paul Hibbert, *The Far East: A History of the Impact of the West on Eastern Asia*, 2d ed., New York: Prentice-Hall, Inc., 1952.

De Francis, John, *Nationalism and Language Reform in China*. Princeton: Princeton University Press, 1950.

Hughes, E. R., *The Invasion of China by the Western World*. London: The Macmillan Company, Ltd., 1937.

La Fargue, Thomas E., "Chinese Educational Commission to the United States." *Far Eastern Quarterly*, Vol. 1 (1941) 59-71.

Latourette, K. S., *A History of Christian Missions in China*. New York: The Macmillan Company, Ltd., 1929.

Murphey, Rhodes, *Shanghai, Key to Modern China*. Cambridge: Harvard University Press, 1953.

Peake, C. H., "Some Aspects of the Introduction of Modern Science into China." *Isis*, Vol. 63 (1934) 173-219.

Rowbotham, Arnold H., *Missionary and Mandarin: The Jesuits at the Court of China*. Berkeley: University of California Press, 1942.

Sun, E-tu Zen, *Chinese Railways and British Interests, 1898-1911*. New York: Columbia University Press, 1954.

Teng Ssu-yü and John K. Fairbank, *China's Response to the West: A Documentary Survey, 1839-1942 and Research Guide*. Cambridge: Harvard University Press, 1954.

Tsien, Tsuen-hsuin, "Western Impact on China Through Translation." *Far Eastern Quarterly*, Vol. 13 (1954) 305-327.

Wright, Stanley F., *Hart and the Chinese Customs*. Belfast: Wm. Mullan and Son, 1950.

INTERNATIONAL RELATIONS

A. GENERAL WORKS

Biggerstaff, Knight, *The Far East and the United States*. Ithaca: Cornell University Press, 1944.

China Treaties, Conventions, etc. Between China and Foreign States. Published by order of the Inspector General of Customs. Shanghai, 1917. The documents date from 1689 to 1915. Text is in Chinese, English, and French.

Clyde, Paul Hibbert, *The United States Policy Toward China*. Durham: Duke University Press, 1940.

Dulles, Foster Rhea, *China and America: The Story of Their Relations Since 1784*. Princeton: Princeton University Press, 1947.

Hsia Ching-lin, *Studies in Chinese Diplomatic History*. Shanghai, 1933.

Keeton, George W., *China, the Far East, and the Future*. London: Stevens & Sons, 1949.

Levi, Werner, *Modern China's Foreign Policy*. Minneapolis: University of Minnesota Press, 1953.

Morse, H. B., *The International Relations of the Chinese Empire*. 3 vols. Shanghai, 1910-1918.

Morse, H. B. and Harley F. MacNair, *Far Eastern International Relations*. Boston: Houghton Mifflin Company, 1931.

MacNair, Harley F., and Donald F. Lach, *Modern Far Eastern International Relations*, 2d ed. Princeton: D. Van Nostrand Company, Inc., 1955.

Quigley, H. S., and G. H. Blakeslee, *The Far East: An International Survey*. Boston: World Peace Foundation, 1938; New York, 1939.

Vinacke, Harold M., *A History of the Far East in Modern Times*. Revised ed. New York: Appleton-Century-Crofts, Inc., 1956.

Whyte, Sir Frederick, *China and Foreign Powers*. New York: Oxford University Press, 1927.

Yano Jin'ichi, *Kinsei Shina gaikōshi* [History of Modern Chinese Foreign Relations]. 3d printing. Kōbundō, 1938.

B. WORKS DEALING WITH THE OPIUM WAR

Ch'i Ssu-ho and others (ed.), *Ya-pien chan-cheng* [Collected Source Materials on the Opium War]. 6 vols. Shanghai: Shen-chou kuo-kuang she, 1954.

Collis, Maurice, *Foreign Mud; Being an Account of the Opium Imbroglio at Canton in the 1830's and the Anglo-Chinese War that Followed*. New York: Alfred A. Knopf, Inc., 1947.

Costin, W. C., *Great Britain and China, 1833-1860*. New York: Oxford University Press, 1937.

Fairbank, John K., "Chinese Diplomacy and the Treaty of Nanking, 1842." *Journal of Modern History*, Vol. 12 (1940) 1-29.

——"Tributary Trade and China's Relations with the West." *Far Eastern Quarterly*, Vol. 1 (1942) 129-149.

——*Trade and Diplomacy on the China Coast: The Opening of the Treaty Ports, 1842-1854*. 2 vols. Cambridge: Harvard University Press, 1953.

Fairbank, John K., and Teng, S. Y., *On the Ch'ing Tributary System*. Cambridge: Harvard-Yenching Institute, 1941.

Fox, Grace, *British Admirals and Chinese Pirates, 1832-1869*. London: Kegan Paul, 1940.

Greenberg, Michael, *British Trade and the Opening of China, 1800-1842*. London: Cambridge University Press, 1951.

Hsü Ti-shan (ed.), *Ta-chung chi, ya-p'ien chan-cheng ch'ien Chung-Ying chiao-she shih-liao* [Historical materials concerning Sino-British relations before the Opium War]. Shanghai, 1931. English caption inside back cover: "A Collection of Letter Writings, Appeals and Ordinances."

Kuo, P. C., *A Critical Study of the First Anglo-Chinese War, with Documents*. Shanghai, 1935.

Morse, H. B., *The Chronicles of the East India Company Trading to China, 1635-1834*. 4 vols. New York: Oxford University Press, 1926, and Vol. 5 (for the years 1742-1774) 1929.

Owen, D. E., *British Opium Policy in India and China*. New Haven: Yale University Press, 1934.

Pelcovits, Nathan A., *Old China Hands and the Foreign Office*. London: The King's Crown Press, 1948.

Pritchard, Earl H., *Anglo-Chinese Relations During the Seventeenth and Eighteenth Centuries*. Urbana: University of Illinois Press, 1929.

——*The Crucial Years of Anglo-Chinese Relations, 1750-1800*. Pullman: Research Studies of the State College of Washington, 1936.

——"The Kotow in the Macartney Embassy to China in 1793." *Far Eastern Quarterly*, Vol. 2 (1943) 163-203.

Teng Ssu-yü, *Chang Hsi and the Treaty of Nanking, 1842*. Chicago: University of Chicago Press, 1944. Bibliographical notes, pp. 122-137.

C. FROM THE SECOND WAR WITH CHINA TO THE 1890's

Biggerstaff, K., "The Official Chinese Attitude Toward the Burlingame mission." *American Historical Review*, Vol. 41 (July 1936) pp. 682-707. "A translation of Anson Burlingame's instructions from the Chinese Foreign Office." *Far Eastern Quarterly*, Vol. 1 (1942) 277-279. "The Ch'ung-hou mission to France 1870-1871." *Nankai Social and Economic Quarterly, October 1935*. "The First Chinese Mission of Investigation sent to Europe." *Pacific Historical Review*, Vol. 5 (1937).

Bonner-Smith, D., and W. R. Lumby, *The Second China War, 1856-1860*. London: The Navy Records Society, 1954.

Cordier, Henri, *Histoire des relations de la Chine avec les puissances occidentales, 1860-1900*. 3 vols. Paris: Alcan, 1901-02.

Huang Yen-yü, "Viceroy Yeh Ming-ch'en and the Canton Episode (1856-1861)." *Harvard Journal of Asiatic Studies*, Vol. 6 (1941) 37-127.

Kiernan, . E. V. G., *British Diplomacy in China, 1880-1885*. London: Cambridge University Press, 1939.

Liu Hsiung-hsiang, *Ch'ing-chi shih-nien lien-O cheng-ts'e* [A Decade of Pro-Russian Policy in the Late Ch'ing Dynasty]. Chungking, 1943.

Lu Ch'in-ch'ih, "Ying-Fa lien-chün chan-chü Kuang-chou shih-mo" [The AngloFrench Occupation of Canton in 1857]. *Shih-hsüeh nien-pao*, Vol. 2 (1938) 265-304.

McCordock, R. Stanley, *British Far Eastern Policy, 1894-1900*. New York: Columbia University Press, 1931.

Swisher, Earl, *China's Management of the American Barbarians: A Study of Sino-American Relations, 1841-1861*. Far Eastern Association Monograph No. 2. New York: Far Eastern Publications, Yale University, 1953.

Torr, Dora, *Marx on China: Articles from the New York Daily*

Tribune, 1853-1860. London: Lawrence & Wishart, 1951.

Townsend, Mary E., and Cyrus H. Peake, *European Colonial Expansion Since 1871*. Philadelphia: J. B. Lippincott Company, 1941.

Tsiang, T. F., "Sino-Japanese Diplomatic Relations, 1870-1894." *Chinese Social and Political Science Review*, Vol. 17 (1933) 1-106.

Wang, S. T., *The Margary Affair and the Chefoo Convention*. New York: Oxford University Press, 1939.

Wang Yün-sheng (ed.), *Liu-shih nien-lai Chrung-kuo yü Jih-pen* [China and Japan During the Past Sixty Years (1856-1916)]. 6 vols. Tientsin, 1932-1933.

D. THE BOXER UPRISING AND THE OPEN DOOR

Campbell, Charles S., *Special Business Interests and the Open Door Policy*. New Haven: Yale University Press, 1951.

Chien Po-tsan and others (eds.), *I-ho-t'uan* [A collection of source material on the Boxer movement]. 4 vols. Shanghai: Shen-chou kuo-kuang she, 1951.

——*Wu-hsü piea-fa* [Collected source materials on the reform movement of 1898]. 4 vols. Shanghai: Shen-chou kuo-kuang she, 1953.

Dennett, Tyler, *Americans in Eastern Asia*. New York: Barnes and Noble, 1941.

Ho Ping-ti, "Ying-kuo yü men-hu k'ai-fang cheng-tse chih ch'i-yüan" [England and the Origin of the Open Door Policy]. *Shih-hsüeh nien-pao*, Vol. 2 (1938) 321-340.

Langer, W. L., *The Diplomacy of Imperialism, 1890-1902*. 2 vols. New York: Alfred A. Knopf, Inc., 1935.

Sheeks, Robert B., "A Re-examination of the I-ho-ch'uan and Its Role in the Boxer Movement." *Papers on China*, Vol. 1, Harvard University, 1947.

Steiger, G. N., *China and the Occident: The Origin and Development of the Boxer Movement*. New Haven: Yale University Press, 1927.

Tan, Chester C., *The Boxer Catastrophe*. New York: Columbia

University Press, 1955. Bibliography, pp. 245-263.
Varg, Paul A., *Open Door Diplomat: The Life of W. W. Rochhill*. Illinois Studies in the Social Sciences, Vol. 33, No. 4. Urbana: The University of Illinois Press, 1952.
Vevier, Charles, "The Open Door: An Idea in Action, 1906-1913." *Pacific Historical Review*, Vol. 23 (1955) 49-62.
E. TWENTIETH-CENTURY RELATIONS
Bisson, T. A., *Japan in China*. New York: The Macmillan Company, 1938.
Borg, Dorothy, *American Policy and the Chinese Revolution, 1925-1928*. New York: Institute of Pacific Relations, 1947.
Chang Chung-fu, *Chung-hua min-kuo wai-chiao shih* [History of the Foreign Relations of the Republic of China]. Peiping, 1936.
Fifield, Russell H., *Woodrow Wilson and the Far East: The Diplomacy of the Shantung Question*. New York: Thomas Y. Crowell Company, 1952.
Fishel, Wesley R., *The End of Extraterritoriality in China*. Berkeley: The University of California Press, 1952.
Friters, Gerard, *Outer Mongolia and Its International Position*. Baltimore: The Johns Hopkins Press, 1950.
Jones, F. C., *Manchuria Since 1931*. London: Royal Institute of International Affairs, 1949.
Latourette, Kenneth Scott, *The American Record in the Far East, 1945-1951*. New York: The Macmillan Company, 1952.
Lattimore, Owen, *Nationalism and Revolution in Mongolia*. New York: Oxford University Press, 1955.
Li Tien-yi, *Woodrow Wilson's China Policy, 1913-1917*. Lawrence: University of Kansas Press, 1952.
Pavlovsky, Michel N., *Chinese and Russian Relations*. New York: Philosophical Library, Inc., 1949.
Pollard, Robert T., *China's Foreign Relations, 1917-1931*. New York:

The Macmillan Company, 1933.

Reid, John Gilbert, *The Manchu Abdication and the Powers, 1907-1912*. Berkeley: University of California Press, 1935.

Seaver, George, *Francis Younghusband, Explorer and Mystic*. London: John Murray, 1952.

Shen Tsung-lien and Liu Shen-chi, *Tibet and Tibetans*. Stanford: Stanford University Press, 1953.

Smith, Sara R., *The Manchuria Crises, 1931-1932*. New York: Columbia University Press, 1948.

Stuart, John Leighton, *Fifty Years in China: The Memoirs of John Leighton Stuart, Missionary and Ambassador*. New York: Random House, Inc., 1954.

Tseng Yu-hao, *The Termination of Unequal Treaties in International Law*. Shanghai, 1943.

United States Relations with China, with Special Reference to the Period 1944-1949. Washington: The Department of State, 1949.

Vevier, Charles, *The United States and China, 1906-1913: A Study of Finance and Diplomacy*. New Brunswick: Rutgers University Press, 1955.

Whiting, Allen S., *Soviet Policies in China, 1917-1924*. New York: Columbia University Press, 1954.

Wu, K. Aitchen, *China and the Soviet Union*. New York: The John Day Company, Inc., 1950.

REFORM AND REVOLUTION

Cameron, M. E., *The Reform Movement in China, 1898-1912*. Stanford: Stanford University Press, 1931.

Chapman, H. Owen, *The Chinese Revolution, 1926-27*. London: Constable and Co., Ltd., 1928.

Fitzgerald, Charles Patrick, *Revolution in China*. London: Cresset

Press, 1952.

Ho Ping-ti, "Wang T'ung-ho and the One Hundred Days of Reform." *Far Eastern Quarterly*. Vol. 10 (1951) 125-135.

Holcombe, A. N., *The Chinese Revolution*. Cambridge: Harvard University Press, 1930.

——*The Spirit of the Chinese Revolution*. New York: Alfred A. Knopf, Inc., 1931.

Isaacs, Harold Robert, *The Tragedy of the Chinese Revolution*. London, 1938. Revised ed. Stanford: Stanford University Press, 1951.

Levenson, Joseph R., *Liang Ch'i-ch'ao and the Mind of Modern China*. Cambridge: Harvard University Press, 1953.

Liang Ch'i-ch'ao, *Wu-hsü cheng-pien chi* [The Coup d'Etat of 1898]. In *Yin-ping shih ho-chi*.

MacNair, H. F., *China in Revolution*. Chicago: University of Chicago Press, 1931.

North, Robert C., *Moscow and Chinese Communists*. Stanford: Stanford University Press, 1953.

Roy, Manabendra Nath, *My Experience in China*. Calcutta: Renaissance, 1945.

——*Revolution and Counter-revolution in China*. Trans. from the German, ed. of 1931. Calcutta, 1946.

Snow, Edgar, *Red Star over China*. New York: Random House, Inc., 1944.

Strong, Anna Louise, *China's Millions: The Revolutionary Struggles from 1927 to 1935*. New York: Knight Publishing Company, 1935.

T'ang Leang-li, *The Inner History of the Chinese Revolution*. London: G. Routledge and Sons, 1930.

Townsend, P., *China Phoenix: The Revolution in China*. London: Kegan Paul, 1955.

Tsui Shu-chin, "The Influence of the Canton-Moscow Entente upon Sun Yat- sen's Political Philosophy." *Chinese Social and Political Science*

Review, Vol. 18 (1934) Nos. 1, 2, 3.
Utley, Freda, *The China Story*. Chicago: Henry Regnery Company, 1951.

CIVIL WAR AND WARLORDS

Chang Chün-mai [Carsun Chang], *Kuo-nei chan-cheng liu-chiang* [Six Lectures on the Civil War]. Shanghai, 1924.
Ch'ien Tuan-sheng, "The Role of the Military in the Chinese Government." *Pacific Affairs*, Vol. 21 (1948) 239-251.
Michael, Franz H., "Chinese Military Tradition." *Far Eastern Survey*, Vol. 15 (1946) 65-69, 84-87.
Okano Masujiro (ed.), *Go Hai-fu* [Wu P'ei-fu]. Banseikaku, 1939.
Powell, Ralph L., *The Rise of Chinese Military Power, 1895-1912*. Princeton: Princeton University Press, 1955.
Teng Chih-ch'eng, "Hu-kuo chün chi shih" [An Account of Military Opposition from Yunnan in 1915-16]. *Shih-hsüeh nien-pao*, Vol. 2 (1935) 1-22.
Weisshart, Herbert, "Feng Yühsiang: His Rise as a Militarist and His Training Programs." *Papers on China*, Vol. 6. Cambridge: Harvard University Press, 1952.

SOCIO-ECONOMIC CONDITIONS

Buck, J. L., *Land Utilization in China*. 3 vols. Chicago: University of Chicago Press, 1937.
Chan Wing-tsit, *Religious Trends in Modern China*. New York: Columbia University Press, 1953.
Chang Chung-li, *The Chinese Gentry: Studies on Their Role in Nineteenth-Century Chinese Society*. Seattle: University of Washington Press, 1955.

Chiang Wen-han, *The Chinese Student Movement*. New York: King's Crown Press, 1948.

Escarra, Jean, *China Then and Now*. Peiping: H. Vetch, 1940.

Fei Hsiao-tung, *China's Gentry: Essays in Rural-Urban Relations*. Chicago: University of Chicago Press, 1953.

Fried, Morton Herbert, *Fabric of a Chinese Society*. New York: Frederick A. Praeger, 1952.

Hsü, Francis L. K., *Americans and Chinese: Two Ways of Life*. New York: Henry Schuman, Inc., Publishers, 1953.

——*Religion, Science and Human Crises: A Study of China in Transition and Its Implications for the West*. London: Routledge and Sons and Kegan Paul, 1952.

Kirby, E. Stuart, *Introduction to the Economic History of China*. New York: The Macmillan Company, 1953.

Levy, Marion J., Jr., *The Family Revolution in Modern China*. Cambridge: Harvard University Press, 1949.

Peake, C. H., *Nationalism and Education in Modern China*. New York: Columbia University Press, 1932.

Shih Kuo-heng, *China Enters the Machine Age*. Cambridge: Harvard University Press, 1944.

Stanley, Charles J., "Chinese Finance from 1852 to 1908." *Papers on China*, Vol. 3. Cambridge: Harvard University Press, 1949.

Tamagna, Frank M., *Banking and Finance in China*. New York: Institute of Pacific Relations Inquiry Series, 1942.

Tawney, R. H., *Land and Labor in China*. London: G. Allen and Unwin, 1932.

Wales, Nym, *The Chinese Labor Movement*. New York: The John Day Company, 1945.

Yang Lien-sheng, *Money and Credit in China: A Short History*. Cambridge: Harvard University Press, 1952.

FURTHER READING IN THE RECENT HISTORY OF CHINA

Brandt, Conrad, and others, *A Documentary History of Chinese Communism*. Cambridge: Harvard University Press, 1952.

Casseville, Henry, *De Chiang Kal Shek à Mao Tse Tung*. Paris: Chas. Lavauzelle, 1950.

Chassin, Lionel Max, *L'Ascension de Mao Tse-tung*. Paris: Payot, 1953.

Ch'in Hsiao-i, *Tsung-t'ung yen-lun hsüan-chi* [Selections of President Chiang Kai-shek's lectures]. 4 vols. Taipei: China Cultural Publication Commission, 1955.

Hsia Yen-te, *Chung-kuo chin-pai-nien ching-chi ssu-hsiang* [Chinese Economic Thought in the Past Hundred Years]. Shanghai: The Commercial Press, 1938.

Hutheesing, Gunottam, *The Great Peace: An Asian's Candid Report on Red China*. New York: Harper & Brothers, 1953.

Johnson, Hewlett, *China's New Creative Age*. New York: International Publishers, 1953.

Mao Tse-tung, *New Democracy*. New York: New Century Publishers, 1945.

——*Selected Works of Mao Tse-tung*. London: Lawrence & Wishart, 1954.

Rosinger, Lawrence K., *China's Wartime Politics, 1937-1944*. Princeton: Princeton University Press, 1944.

Rostow, W. W., *The Prospects for Communist China*. Cambridge: The Massachusetts Institute of Technology, 1954.

Schwartz, Benjamin, *Chinese Communism and the Rise of Mao*. Cambridge: Harvard University Press, 1951.

Shabad, Theodore, *China's Changing Map: A Geography of the*

Chinese People's Republic. New York: Frederick A. Praeger, 1955.

Snow, Edgar, *The Battle for Asia*. New York: Random House, Inc, 1941.

Tang, Peter S. H., *Communist China Today*. New York: Frederick A. Praeger, 1955.

Thomas, S. B., *Government and Administration in Communist China*. New York: Institute for Pacific Relations, 1953.

Walker, Richard K., *China Under Communism*. New Haven: Yale University Press, 1955.

A FEW CHINESE SOURCES

Chang Ch'i. yün, *Chung-hua min-kuo shih-kang* [An Outline of the History of the Chinese Republic]. 3 vols. Taipei: China Cultural Publication Commission, 1953.

Chao Erh-sun and others, *Ch'ing-shih kao* [Draft History of the Ch'ing Dynasty]. 543 *chüan*. Peiping, 1928.

Ch'en Kung-lu, *Chung-kuo chin-tai shih* [History of Modern China]. Shanghai, 1935.

Ch'en Tu-hsiu (ed.), *Hsin ch'ing-nien, "La Jeunesse."* Shanghai and Peiping, 1915-21.

Chiang T'ing-fu, *Chin-tai Chung-kuo wai-chiao-shih tzu-liao chi-yao* [Selected Documents on Modern Chinese Diplomatic History]. 2 vols. Shanghai, 1931 and 1934.

Ch'ing shih-lu. See *Ta Ch'ing li-chao shih-lu*.

Ch'ou-pan i-wu shih-mo [A Complete Account of the Management of Barbarian Affairs]. Peiping, 1930.

Chu Shou-p'eng, *Tung-hua hsü-lu* [Tung-hua Documents, continued]. Shanghai, 1909.

Fan Wen-lan, *Chung-kuo chin-tai shih* [Modern Chinese History]. Yenan: Hsin-hua shu-chu, 1947.

Hsiao I-shan, *Ch'ing-tai shih* [History of the Ch'ing Dynasty]. Taipei:

China Cultural Publication Commission, 1952.
I-wu shih-mo. See *Ch'ou pan i-wu shih-mo*.
Ku Chieh-kang, *Tang-tai Chung-kuo shih-hsüeh* [Modern Chinese Historiography]. Shanghai: Sheng-li ch'u-pan kung-ssu, 1947.
Kuo-wen chou-pao [Kuowen Weekly Illustrated]. Published by the Kuo-wen chou-pao she, Shanghai and Tientsin, 1924-1937.
Kuo T'ing-i, *Chin-tai Chung-kuo shih* [Modern Chinese History]. Shanghai, 1940.
Li Shou-kung, *Chung-kuo tsui-chin ssu-shih-nien shih* [Chinese History of the Most Recent Forty Years (*ca*. 1912-1952)]. Taipei: Chung-hua Book Company, 1954.
Li Ting-i, *Chung-kuo chin-tai shih* [A History of Modern China]. Taipei: Chung-hua Book Company, 1953.
Ta-Ch'ing Li-chao shihlu [True Records of the Various Reigns of the Ch'ing Dynasty]. Tokyo, 1937.
T'ang Tsu-p'ei, *Min-kuo ming-jen hsiao-chuan* [Biographical Sketches of Noted Personages of the Republic]. Hong Kong, 1953.
Tso Shun-sheng, *Chung-kuo chin-pai-shih tzu-liao* [Material for Chinese History of the Last Hundred Years]. Shanghai, 1926; and *Hsü-pien* [Supplement], Shanghai, 1933. 2 vols.
Tung-fang tsa-chih. [The Eastern Miscellany]. Shanghai: The Commercial Press, 1904 to 1940's.
Wang Yen-wei and others (eds.), *Ch'ing-chi wai-chiao shih-liao* [Historical Material on Foreign Relations in the Later Part of the Ch'ing Dynasty]. 112 *ts'e*. Peiping, 1932-1933.
Yang Sung and Teng Li-ch'ün (original eds.); Jung Meng-yüan (new ed.), *Chung-kuo chin-tai-shih tzu-liao hsüan-chi* [Selected Source Materials on the Modern History of China]. Peking, 1954.
Yün Yü-ting, *Chung-ling chuan-hsin lu* [The True Story of the Emperor Kuang-hsü]. In Tso Shun-sheng, *Chung-kuo chin-pai-nien shih tzu-liao*.